B
U
P

MyBook http://mybook.egeaonline.it

Type your username and password or register by clicking on **Create a new account**.

Username

Password

In MyBook you can access the accompanying resources (both text and multimedia), the **BookRoom**, the **EasyBook** app and your purchased books.

CODE

> 047226CLML

Type the code in the **Activation Code** field.

MY PURCHASED BOOKS

ENTER YOUR CODE Activation code

The code must be typed only the first time you access **MyBook** and cannot be used thereafter.

CORPORATE AND INVESTMENT BANKING

A Hands-On Approach

Stefano Caselli
Gimede Gigante
Andrea Tortoroglio

Foreword by
Massimo Della Ragione

Typesetting: Corpo4 Team, Milan
Cover: Cristina Bernasconi, Milan

EGEA S.p.A.
Via Salasco, 5 - 20136 Milano
Tel. 02/5836.5751 – Fax 02/5836.5753
egea.edizioni@unibocconi.it – www.egeaeditore.it

First edition: May 2021

ISBN Domestic Edition	978-88-99902-76-6
ISBN International Edition	978-88-31322-15-7
ISBN Digital International Edition	978-88-31322-40-9
ISBN Digital Domestic Edition	978-88-238-8267-6

Table of Contents

Foreword

When Stefano, our Professor Caselli, asked me to work on the preface of this book, I accepted with a lot of curiosity and enthusiasm.

Curiosity has naturally arisen as there is no book on the market which describes with discipline and accuracy the state of the art of Corporate and Investment Banking (or CIB). We have masterpieces in corporate finance, in capital markets, in corporate evaluation but we do not have a book which provides the reader with a fully comprehensive guide to CIB as a whole.

Enthusiasm has grown through the reading of the manuscript. It is a book which accepts the challenges intimately associated with the nature of the corporate investment business. CIB is not a static topic. On the contrary, it is a topic that requires a constant and continuous update; it is a business that changes and evolves year in year out. As a result, this book can be viewed as the first step of a long journey of thoughts, experiences and evolutions.

This book is a unique combination of academic analysis supported by cases and real professional experiences. Through the academic dissertations combined with the key takeaways of the various cases, the reader has the possibility to think about a number of challenges which are affecting the global CIB market these days.

When I started my career in the early '90s, the global market was almost equally split between American and European banks. After the Global Financial Crisis, the global market has dramatically consolidated and now the US banks are controlling 70-80% of the total global market. This consolidation drives most of the discussions on whether the European banking model (mainly loan-centric) is the right answer to the economic challenges EU is facing or it is better to develop an EU capital markets to allow European banks to shift their business mix toward a more securities-driven, US-style model.

The impact of technology is extremely important. Global Sales and Trading, Asset management, Equity capital market, Custody and Transaction banking are business immensely affected by the technology available now and more importantly in the future. A personal experience is, in my mind, self-explanatory. Last year I worked on a convertible issuance of an Italian Fintech: the whole transaction has been originated, structured, priced, distributed, allocated and finally traded remotely; no physical interaction with neither the issuer nor the investors. There is no doubt that technology will represent a more and more important part of the Corporate and Investment Banking business.

Growth is a must for each institution. Only one third of the growth initiatives of corporates generate real value creation. The remaining two thirds either do not generate value for shareholders, or are unsuccessful. To pursue growth with discipline and vision, corporates need the support of a strong Corporate and Investment Banking system.

The low interest rate environment will remain as it is for a number of years. On one side, the cost of capital will remain below historical average, but, on the other side, I strongly believe that the focus of investors, entrepreneurs and corporate will be laser-focused on how to boost Ebitda of their initiatives and, as a result, the managerial skills will be paramount to a successful implementation of the-long term strategy. Corporate and Investment bankers will need more sophisticated skills to support their own clients.

I wish to all students a joyful reading of the book with the conviction that it will be the first of a series of chapters of a journey for the years to come.

Massimo Della Ragione

Introduction

by Stefano Caselli, Gimede Gigante, Andrea Tortoroglio

A new book on the relationship between banks and corporates is a challenge that must be accepted: we need to revert the narrative on banks and provide a proper perspective on what they can do for the economy overall. Corporate and Investment Banking (CIB) is in fact the banking activity that most affects the growth of companies and their ability to be more robust and competitive. In the financial world, the key variable for development is technology, enabling the use of information to the benefit of customers. The availability of data and the ability to read them on a large scale makes it possible to overcome segmentations and artificial classifications, which have been part of the history of banking strategies, and move towards a precise offer tailored to the real profile of each individual customer. For the corporate market, the tailor-made design of products involves a more complex choice, which entails the replacement of credit services open to the whole range of financial operations: from debt capital markets, equity capital markets, private equity and restructuring to M&A deals. In this sense, the role of banks is crucial because only banks have knowledge and authority to push and guide managers and entrepreneurs to choices that are not easy, such as to open up their capital and use the markets for funding; acting as an advisor, an investor, or a financial sponsor. All these decisions are decisive for their growth.

The debate around the need for a European CIB system is much more relevant and impactful, as it involves the European community and European stakeholders at large. The question does not merely regard the financial industry per se and the Banking Union, but it must embrace the larger political debate about the strategy Europe has to pursue. The risk the EU is facing appears crystal clear: the European financial industry could become a huge lending system wherein the role of banks would come under pressure. On the one hand, more value-added CIB services are delivered by non-EU players; on the other, fintech companies generate a lot of competition with a significant disruptive power, or at least generate a disruptive effect on margins. Is this acceptable? Alternatively, shall we suggest more proactive and concrete actions not against someone, but in favour of a more diversified eco-system where the European voice matters? Is it too late to promote concrete actions to stimulate the emergence of a competitive European CIB industry? It is not, but actions have to be focused and they have to be identified through bottom-up and top-down recommendations and suggestions related to the architecture of the Banking Union.

In setting new positioning goals and benchmarks, the challenges are not only regulatory, but political as well. The European banking system must be steered into a support role as a facilitator of business development and overall economic growth, well aware that while this system survived the sub-prime bubble, all its energy has necessarily been spent resolving the crises regarding sovereign debt and then Non-Performing Loans (NPLs). In the US, meanwhile, the banking system has had time to recoup, increasing in size and generating innovation, in pace with the capital markets. What is more, Chinese banks are gradually acquiring expertise, gaining agility at an international level, and above all, growing in size like their US counterparts. Therefore, the risk is clear: the European economic system could be crushed between the US and China, due in part to the lack of an equally strong banking system.

The challenges that need to be tackled quickly on the European playing field are growth and M&As and the business model of banks.

The issue of the growth and size of European banks must be top priority for a genuine Banking Union, beyond shared supervision and the three pillars in general. The European banking system has experienced consolidation processes within member states, first in the 1990s and later in the 2000s. Nevertheless, progress, which seems to be at a standstill, must begin again with intensity and determination. Only growth can facilitate the rise of more sophisticated business areas, such as capital markets, M&A, corporate finance, and private equity.

A comparison with the American market, as we provide throughout the entire paper, is very constructive, as the two systems are similar in size and underlying GNP, but in some ways, the contrast is discouraging. The top three American banks ranked by total assets (Bank of America, JP Morgan, and Wells Fargo) represent 30% of the market, while Europe's top three asset holders (HSBC, BNP Paribas, and Crédit Agricole) cover little more than 12% of the market. All the data reported in this paper speak volumes: the US banking system is far more concentrated and profitable. US banks have what it takes to be global players, to sit at the table on the biggest deals, and to leverage the economies of scale necessary to innovate and meet the needs of their broad customer base, from corporate to retail. In light of this, an aggregation approach is more crucial than ever before in Europe, and must be reactivated aggressively with domestic M&As and even more importantly, cross-border deals.

In addition to size, the business model of banks is another penalizing aspect of the European banking system. The most revealing statistic in this regard can be found in the breakdown of the funding of American and European institutions. In the US, 70% of funding for companies consists of securities, while in Europe the same percentage is covered by bank loans. This substantial difference makes European companies less capitalized and less competitive from the market's perspective. Moreover, from a lender's standpoint, this means that European banks appear to be very dependent on the lending business and as such are exposed to the (mostly external) volatility of interest rates. Vice versa, the dependence of US banks on the securities market protects them from reliance on interest margins. However, the question of the business model does not imply that a radical transformation of European banks is either obligatory or even desirable. Instead, there needs to be a shared (European!)

commitment among banks to progressively transition toward a complete range of investment banking activities. This should be endorsed, once again, on the political, supervisory, and regulatory fronts, while engaging shareholders as well. All this is not only for the good of the profit and loss accounts of banks, but more importantly for the sake of the financial growth – and real growth – of businesses.

To provide a deep, exhaustive and hands-on analysis of the CIB industry, this book is organized in two different parts. The first is devoted to gaining an understanding of the pillars of the CIB industry within the overall setting of universal banking. The content of banks' balance sheets, a very detailed deep-dive into the regulatory framework and capital adequacy criteria, and the fixing of the taxonomy of the CIB industries are the key contents of the first part, always supported by a continuous link to updated facts and figures on the CIB sector using the League Tables and the other market sources. The second part is devoted to deal-making and every chapter is covers a specific deal/industry which characterises CIB activity, having in mind the three categories of customers relevant for CIB activity, i.e. corporates, FIGs, and governmental institutions. Two chapters address the role of debt capital markets and syndicated loans, covering the debt side of funding for customers, through the technicalities of syndication as the key feature for debt raising. On the equity side, three different chapters tackle the topic. The first one is devoted to ECM for primary offering, mainly with IPOs, while the second addresses ECM for secondary offering, i.e. for already-listed corporates and FIGs. Last, the third chapter involves private equity activity, where the role of the CIB is mostly to be a financial sponsor enabling the deal or an advisor for the customer. The M&A very large business arena is examined covering all the phases of origination and execution, while a separate chapter tackles the perspective of risk management within M&A transactions. The topic of restructuring ends the deals analysis, highlighting its special nature, much more than other deals, as a crossroads of legal issues and of financial technicalities.

The common denominator, which distinguishes the cutting edge DNA of this book, is to be hands-on, as is written in the title. What is the true meaning of being hands-on? First, it is to give a unique perspective on deal making, highlighting the very concrete and real steps of origination and execution using both the language of practitioners and the tools supporting the deal flow of every business (such as Bloomberg screen-shots, agreements and NDAs, covenants and formulas, among others). Second, it means involving in the chapters, with the different roles of co-authors and of first-class business case writers and testimonials, many protagonists of the CIB world. Their fabulous task is to give a different view – from the CEO perspective to the business perspective – underlying the key features of each deal, giving the right balance between the different forces, which make a deal real and possible. The third aspect is to provide a solid and rigorous academic framework, whereas the challenge is to balance very different angles: cases, examples, definitions and rules, theoretical contributions, data. This is quite important to allow the readers to maximize their use and to bridge the business world with an effective learning experience. The audience for this book is very diversified. Master of Sciences students, MBA and Executive MBA students, as well as practitioners belonging to several industries:

bankers and analysts, advisors and business lawyers as well as regulators, and also consultants and the business communities related to a specific deal (i.e., M&A or restructuring or private equity). What is important to stress is that this book aims to be an open project: CIB never sleeps and always evolves. It is not possible to fix the state-of-the-art for years; it is necessary to update continuously knowledge, contents, cases, and best practices. This is the ambition of this first edition, which is the outcome of intense teamwork in recent months in the backstage of the book.

Acknowledgments

As a team, Stefano, Gimede, and Andrea, thank all the contributors to the success of the book: it has been a privilege and a pleasure to work with all of you. A special thank you to the Department of Finance of Bocconi University, to the colleagues and to the students of the Bachelors and Masters programs at Bocconi, and to Massimo Della Ragione, who wrote the preface and provided a lot of inspiration.

Stefano: In particular, I would like to express my gratitude and thanks to the many colleagues and friends I have been interacting with and who gave me inspiration, contents, and challenges. To better understand all the angles of investment banking, it must be considered as a long journey, where you cannot stop and say you get it, because finance is always evolving. It is a long list and it is an honour to mention them: Andrea Beltratti, Marina Brogi, Leonardo Etro, Stefano Gatti, Eugenio Morpurgo, Francesco Perilli, Fabio Sattin, Davide Serra, Andrea Sironi, and Andrea Vismara. Moreover, a special thank you goes to prestigious initiatives at Bocconi, which gave me a stronger view on the investment banking perspective. First of all is the Algebris Chair in Long-Term Investment and Absolute Return, which I have the privilege to hold, with a strong sense of gratitude to Davide Serra. Moreover, there is the Equita Lab on Capital Markets at the Baffi-Carefin Research Center, where capital markets and investment banking industry are continuously analysed and supported as a key tool to promote growth.

Gimede: I would like to thank all the people who have inspired, fostered, and nurtured my growth over my years at Bocconi University, giving me a chance to take part in this amazing publishing challenge with Stefano and Andrea. I would like to start by thanking Stefano Gatti for being among the first, together with Stefano Caselli, who trusted me to take an academic path at Bocconi and for always mentoring me by sharing technical and methodological knowledge about teaching and research processes. A sincere thanks goes to Andrea Sironi for the attentiveness he has always given me and the interest he took in following my first steps in the finance department at Bocconi. I would therefore like to thank all my colleagues in the same department and in particular, although in different ways, Laura Zanetti and Cesare Conti, with whom I share the exciting experience of managing CLEF and the Master of Finance, respectively; Carlo Favero and Fulvio Ortu, my department directors, and Giancarlo Forestieri, Stefano Zorzoli and Lucia Spotorno, who over the years have allowed me to deepen my knowledge about banks and financial intermediaries.

Thankful appreciation goes both professionally and personally to all those who over the years have enriched my knowledge on the topics covered in the book and that of the students through their valuable contributions, and in particular Marco Alverà, Marcella Caradonna, Giuseppe Caputo, Stefano Caspani, Andrea Conso, Michele Conte, Maria Elena Gasparroni, Leona Hu, Maria Teresa Iardella, Elisabetta Magistretti, Stefano Manghi, Guido Mecozzi, Alessandro Migliavacca, Riccardo Mulone, Giorgio Ronchi, Stefano Sardo and Giorgio Tinacci. Thanks to Andrea Cerri, Vittoria Ciferri, Andrea Locatelli, Rodolfo Pambianco and Giulia Zanetello for the valuable work of proofreading the various chapters and for having effectively contributed with suggestions, adjustments and support in the deepening of some topics dealt with in Chapters 9, 10 and 11. Thanks to Baptiste Gilliot for the excellent bibliographic research and support work, as a research assistant, in writing and critical proofreading of the drafts of Chapters 9, 10, and 12. Thanks to Maria Teresa Iardella and the entire Mediobanca team for the extensive support of data and bibliographic material in the drafting of Chapters 9, 10, 11, and 12. Thanks to Matteo Arpe for his heartfelt friendship and willingness to share with me and the students his great knowledge on banking, finance, and economics in general, for me one of the most brilliant intellects I have ever met. A warm thanks to Andrea Agnelli for his mentoring and leadership skills, that are so inspiring to me and the students who have had the opportunity and the privilege to listen to him during his classes. Many thanks to my colleague and friend Massimo Della Ragione for his professional and academic activity, who has taught me a lot in the field of investment banking, but also for having always maintained an attentive and caring approach with me, which has helped me to grow in all these years. A big thanks to all the students I have met so far in these years at Bocconi, because if teaching has always been my greatest passion, they have always been the strongest torch keeping this fire burning. Last but not least, a grateful tribute to co-author Stefano Caselli who not only granted me the privilege of taking part in this publishing project but also for having literally taken me by the hand in a path of growth that began when I was a university student of his at Bocconi, followed by the privilege of having been supported by him as my supervisor for my degree dissertation at Bocconi and lastly for being my manager and reference at Bocconi for many of the initiatives I am now involved in at the University; he is responsible for many of the achievements I accomplished and for this I will always be grateful to him. Stefano is not only a first-class professional guide to be followed and from whom to draw inspiration in an effort to improve and learn something new, but from a personal point of view he is a person whose values and principles help those around him to be better.

Andrea: I am particularly grateful to my co-author and friend Stefano Caselli, with whom I co-teach the Investment Banking course at Bocconi University: he gave me the opportunity to write this book with him and Gimede, providing invaluable guidance, input, and constant support. My chapters could not have been completed without the efforts and precious contributions of the authors of the case studies, extraordinary top-notch professionals in investment banking industry, who provided all their expertise and practical guidance: Giulio Baratta, Pietro Bianculli, Chiara

Campagner, Antonio De Luca, Luca Falco, Paolo Garzarelli, Carolina Marazzini, Riccardo Mulone, Jean Pierre Mustier, Vittorio Ogliengo, Francesco Papa, and Aldo Sioli. Moreover, many thanks to their investment banks: BNP Paribas, Deutsche Bank, Goldman Sachs, UBS, and UniCredit. I also want to express gratitude to the following friends, colleagues, and practitioners, whom I mention with honour: Marco Branchini, Giorgio Luca Bruno, Carlo Cimbri, Michele Cohen, Roberto Coletta, Francesco Correale, Luca De Meo, Claudio Detti, Francesco Falcone, Giancarlo Forestieri, Angela Gamba, Patrizio Leoni, Alessandro Massimelli, Bernardo Mingrone, Francesco Nicolini, Roberto Parazzini, Lars Schickentanz, Lucia Spotorno, Andrea Viganò, and Stefano Zorzoli. A special thank you also to Anna Sassu Tortoroglio, Paola Tortoroglio, Riccardo Alessio, Vittorio Gola, Francesco Ronsisvalle, Stefano Salvi, and Teresa and Paolo Vergani. Lastly, a special thought to my father Ezio.

Some special persons are unique for all of us. The most important thank you – this is Stefano speaking – is for my wife Anna, my daughter Elisa, and my son Lorenzo. When I started studying investment banking our family was not there, and now Elisa and Lorenzo are adults. Without their support this journey would not have been possible at all. The most important thank you – this is Gimede speaking – is for my wife Carlotta and my two daughters Giulia and Ginevra; their love meant that I have never lacked their support and encouragement. The most important thank you – this is Andrea speaking – is to my wife Carolina and my daughter Camilla, for their love, support, encouragement, and sacrifice during the weekends that usually would have been dedicated to them.

About the authors

Stefano Caselli is Vice Rector for International Affairs at Bocconi University, where he is a Full Professor of Banking and Finance at the Department of Finance and Algebris Chair in "Long-Term Investment and Absolute return." He is also a member of the management board of SDA Bocconi School of Management. For the international activity of Bocconi, he covers several roles within the most important academic networks: he is a member of the Steering Committee of CIVICA, the University of Social Sciences (www.civica.eu); he is a member of the management board of CEMS, the Global Alliance in Management Education (www.cems.org); he is the Chair for the EMEA Region of PIM, Partnership in International Management (www.pimnetwork.org); he is the Executive Secretary of the External Advisory Board of the School of Transnational Governance at EUI, the European University Institute in Florence. His research activities focus on the relationship between banking and the industrial system, addressing issues of both banking credit risk management and of corporate finance and capital structure. He is the author of numerous books and articles on the subject. His works have been published in Journal of Financial Intermediation, Journal of Banking and Finance, European Financial Management, Journal of Financial Services Research, and Journal of Applied Corporate Finance and Economia & Management, among others. He acts as a columnist and opinion maker for "L'Economia del Corriere della Sera," as well radio and television programs, and is a member of the advisory board of "Rivista di Politica Economica." His course on Private Equity and Venture Capital is available on Coursera at https://www.coursera.org/learn/private-equity and has reached 100,000 participants. He has got a long experience as an independent director in several boards of corporations and financial institutions as well as an advisor of investment committees (among them: at present Generali Real Estate, Credito Valtellinese as Vice Chairman, Fondazione Cassa di Risparmio di Padova e Rovigo, Istituto Diocesano di Sostentamento del Clero della Diocesi di Milano; in the past, Santander Consumer Bank, ICF Group S.p.A., EPS Equita PEP SPAC S.p.A., SIAS S.p.A., Manutencoop S.p.A. and MP Venture SGR. He is a research fellow at BAFFI-CAREFIN (the research centre for financial innovation of Bocconi University), where he is in charge of the Investment Banking and Structured Finance Unit and he supervises the project on Capital Markets with Equita Group. He is also a member of the advisory board of Confindustria (2018-2020).

Gimede Gigante is a Lecturer at the Finance Department of Bocconi University where since 2019 he has served as Academic Director of the Bocconi Summer School. The Deputy Director of the Master of Science in Finance, he is also Deputy Director of the Bachelor's Degree Program in Economics and Finance at Bocconi University. He earned a business degree from Bocconi University, a PhD in Banking & Finance from the University of Rome II, and the ITP qualification (International Teachers' Program) from SDA Bocconi. He has held visiting positions at the Finance Department of Columbia Business School, and at the Salomon Brothers Center (Stern School of Business, NYU). A Certified Public Accountant and professional auditor, his main areas of research are international finance, financial markets, corporate finance, investment banking, and private equity. He has published a variety of papers on banking areas and acts as a consultant to several financial and non-financial institutions. He is the Winner of the Award for Excellence in Teaching in 2015 and in 2016. From 2020 he is a Harvard Business Review advisory council member and from 2021 he is board member of Assofintech.

Andrea Tortoroglio is a Director at Deutsche Bank Wealth Management, serving as Head of Institutional Clients in the Italian UHNWI team. With more than fifteen years of professional experience in the banking industry, he advises on, structures and originates sophisticated investment solutions, structured lending deals, and derivatives. Previously, he worked at UniCredit Group for twelve years in private banking and wealth management, developing synergies with the Investment Banking division on the more complex deals of wealth management. He started his career at KPMG in the Milan financial services practice and subsequently at Eni S.p.A. as an analyst in the corporate structure and transactions team. Since 2006 he has been an academic fellow at Bocconi University in the Department of Finance, where he teaches Financial Markets and Institutions (undergraduate) and Investment Banking (graduate). As contributor, he has collaborated with some finance publications and handbooks. Andrea holds an MSc in Business Administration with a major in Corporate Finance from Bocconi University and he is a registered Financial Advisor (*Albo Unico dei Consulenti Finanziari*).

About the authors of the case studies

As of November 2020

Giulio Baratta joined BNPP in 2005 and is currently responsible for Corporate DCM in EMEA. In his responsibility, Giulio is in charge of corporate relationships and coordinates the activity of the European-based teams originating Capital Markets business with the clients of the bank. Prior to that, Giulio was responsible for the DCM business with Italian and CEEMEA clients. Earlier, he worked at Citi in the Corporate and Investment Banking division, and JP Morgan. Giulio earned a Degree in Business Administration with a Major in Corporate Finance and Capital Markets from Bocconi University, Milan.

Pietro Bianculli started his career in 1994 at JPMorgan in the Securities Lending team. In 1996 he moved to BNP Paribas and acted as government bond trader between Milan and Paris. In 2002 he was hired by UniCredit as Senior SSA trader. In 2004 he moved to Bond syndicate team. In 2020 he was appointed Head of SSA and FIG Bond Syndicate.

Chiara Campagner is Associate - DCM FIG Italy at Deutsche Bank since 2017, working in the DCM and credit solutions origination team for Italian financial institutions. After graduating in Economics from Cattolica University in Milan, Chiara joined Deutsche Bank's graduate programme in 2016.

Antonio De Luca holds 15+ years' experience in Investment Banking. After graduating from Bocconi University in 2004, he started his career at Banca IMI in the corporate finance division. In 2007 he joined UniCredit equity capital markets team, where he currently acts as managing director with focus on Italian small/mid cap companies.

Luca Falco holds 30+ years' experience in Investment Banking. After graduating from Bocconi University, Luca joined Banque Paribas Capital Market where he spent 12 years between London and Milan. In 2001 he joined UniCredit where he headed Corporate Trading and Bond Syndicate before moving to Debt Capital Market. Since March 2020, he is the Head of Global Syndicate and Capital Markets at UniCredit, heading a team of 170+ professionals in seven locations worldwide.

Paolo Garzarelli is a 20+ years' professional in the equity capital markets business. After graduating with honours in Economics at Bocconi University, he joined the Corporate Finance Execution Group at Salomon Smith Barney (now Citigroup) in 1999. After a full time Masters in Finance at London Business School he joined the ECM desk at UniCredit, where he now heads the Italian ECM team and oversees its international effort.

Carolina Marazzini has 20 years' experience in the debt capital markets business. She graduated with honours in Economics from Bocconi University, Milan. She started her career in 2002 at UBM in the Debt Capital Markets team. In 2016, she was appointed Head of Debt Origination Italy in UniCredit Group. Since 2019 she is also the Deputy Co-Head of Debt Origination at UniCredit with international responsibilities.

Riccardo Mulone is Country Head of UBS Group in Italy, Head of UBS Europe SE, Succursale Italia and Head of UBS Investment Bank in Italy. With almost 25 years of experience across different sectors, products and countries, Riccardo has led the origination and execution of 100+ transactions worth about €150bn cumulative value. Riccardo started his career in 1996 in Arthur Andersen in Milan. In 1999, he moved to the M&A team at UBS Investment Bank (London), becoming Managing Director in 2009 and Head of UBS Investment Banking Italy in 2011. Riccardo holds a degree cum-laude in Business Administration from the University of Catania and he is a chartered accountant (Dottore Commercialista).

Jean Pierre Mustier started his career in Société Générale, working primarily within the Corporate & Investment Banking division. Jean Pierre held numerous senior positions in various markets and financing activities. In 2015, he became a London based partner of Tikehau Capital, an investment management group, with specific focus and responsibility for Tikehau's international expansion; he also advised many financial institutions and completed large amounts of fundraising for various social enterprises and non-profit institutions, also as trustee. He was appointed Chief Executive Officer of UniCredit in July 2016. On July 1, 2019, Jean Pierre became President of the European Banking Federation (EBF).

Vittorio Ogliengo was appointed in March 2018 Executive Chairman BNP Paribas Corporate and Institutional Banking Italy and Deputy General Manager BNL Spa. He joined BNPP Group from Unicredit where he was Head of Corporate and Investment Banking since 2013, after holding several managerial positions between 2005 and 2013. Vittorio began his career in 1983 as an auditor and held several roles in Corporate Banking, Corporate Finance and Investment Banking at Citibank from 1985 to 1988. He then joined the Fiat Group and became Assistant International Treasurer of Fiat Spa and afterwards Head of the Finance Department and General Manager of Fiat Deutschland. In 1994 he joined Barilla, where he was appointed CFO and CEO of Barilla Holding. Vittorio graduated in Economics from the University of Turin.

Francesco Papa is a Managing Director of Goldman Sachs responsible for Equity Capital Markets activities in Italy and Switzerland with c. 15 years of investment banking experience in London and Milan. He holds a degree in Business Administration from the University of Firenze.

Aldo Sioli is Managing Director – Head of DCM FIG Italy. At Deutsche Bank since September 2009, he is responsible for the debt new issue and the strategic credit solutions business for Italian banks and insurance companies. Previously at Merrill Lynch & Co. within the New Product Development Structuring Group. Aldo holds an MBA from IESE Business School and a PLD degree from Harvard Business School.

About the contributors

Giulia Negri is a Fellow of Corporate Finance at the Bocconi School of Management and Fellow at the Baffi Carefin Research Center at Bocconi University. She teaches Executive level and Executive MBA-level courses. She has been the Project Manager for "Bocconi StartupDay" and she has conducted several financial consulting projects for small and medium-sized companies. She graduated *summa cum laude* from Bocconi University and earned her PhD from the University of St. Gallen.

Kim Salvadori is an Executive Director at Goldman Sachs. She is part of the Leveraged Finance team and is responsible for the origination, structuring, and execution of leveraged loan and high-yield bond offerings for European issuers within the sub-investment grade space. She received her BSc in Business and Management and her MSc in Finance from Bocconi University.

Marta Zava is an Academic Fellow at the Department of Finance at Bocconi University, Milan, and a Ph.D. Candidate in Economics at GSEFM – Goethe-Universität, Frankfurt am Main. Previously, she worked as Supervision Analyst at the European Central Bank, holistically covering Banking Supervision topics.

Matteo Scalfi started his career at Deutsche Bank London at the Structured Solutions desk, joining the 2013 summer internship program. He subsequently moved to the Equity Sales & Trading division, covering the Southern European institutional client base from both London and Milan. Currently, Matteo works at Deutsche Bank Wealth Management, focusing on the Italian UHNW client base. He is a Bocconi Academic Fellow for the Financial Markets & Institutions course. Matteo holds an MSc in Finance from Bocconi University and an MSc in Business Administration from Erasmus University (Double Degree Program), and a BSc in Economics and Finance from Bocconi University.

Maria Teresa Iardella is the Managing Director – Head of Debt Division & Co-Head of the Abs Team at Mediobanca S.p.A., with the responsibility for all debt products of the Bank (including origination, execution, and syndication), reporting to the Head of CIB. She is a Member of the CIB Executive Committee, the Credit Risk Committee, and the ALM Committee, and Chairman at Messier Maris et Associes US, and a Board Member at Selmabipiemme Leasing S.p.A. and Valore D.

Luigi Caprotti is the Head of Financial Planning and Analysis, as well as member of the Board of Executives, for the Italian division of one of the largest FMCGs worldwide, leader in the beverage industry. He earned his undergraduate degree in Management at Bocconi University and later graduated from the same University in both the Master of Science in International Management and the CEMS MIM (Master in International Management).

Baptiste Gilliot is a Principles of International Finance Teaching and Research Assistant at Bocconi University, where he graduated in Economics and Finance.

1 The Fundamentals of Banks

by Stefano Caselli and Marta Zava

1.1 Banks and banking today

The role that banks perform in modern economic systems is very complex: on the one hand, firms and individuals make use of most of the services, while on the other, banks play an essential role in the control of money and credit. Nevertheless, banks are often seen in a negative fashion: following the 2007 financial crisis, the criticisms increased and several heated clashes took place – especially outside the field – leading to political controversy. The underlying reasons are numerous. In fact, several banks failed or found themselves in awful circumstances, involving the public sector in the rescue process. Furthermore, the credit pumped into the economy was reduced, sometimes generating recessive effects. Also, the market felt the signs of difficulty and the losses also affected investors' savings.

The renewed interest in the activities undertaken by banks and financial intermediaries and the rules to be followed is helpful and represents a chance to newly discuss the function, strategies, governance models, and services offered by financial institutions. However, the debate is often messy and ideological. The banks we will describe here are very different from the ones that we knew a decade ago. Nowadays, a bank offers a wide range of services, operates in different markets, builds and sells new products, and aims at very different clients. Furthermore, activities belonging to the banking function are also performed by entities that we would not have considered banks in the past, whose key interests reside in other sectors, such as commercial distribution (like Amazon), or technological services (like Google, Facebook and Apple).

Notwithstanding the rapid changes to which a bank is subject, the primary functions of a bank are to accept deposits and to grant loans and advances. To do so, banks must be authorized by the bodies with supervisory functions. Let us delve into these basic aspects.

As mentioned, to be a bank, an entity has to perform two main functions: generate debt and give credit – i.e. intermediate financial resources. Therefore, banks are financial intermediaries, although not all financial intermediaries are banks. For instance, those who are specialized in lending, without incurring debt with respect to the depositors (i.e. taking deposits), are defined as credit intermediaries, as is the case with financial leasing companies and factoring companies.

An intermediary offers a service to at least two subjects. In our case, the subjects differ based on their financial position: on the one side we have those who have a financial surplus, on the other those who have a financial deficit. The **financial balance** can be defined as the difference between income (of an individual, a firm, or a country), consumption, and fixed investments. In other terms, all the income that is not intended to be spent constitutes the financial balance. If income is above consumption and fixed investments, the balance is positive and the entity is in financial surplus. To the contrary, if income is not enough to cover consumption and fixed investments, then the balance is negative and the entity has a deficit, and thus will need to go into debt.

There are two main solutions to satisfy the needs of these two types of entities: the direct and the indirect way. The former, the **direct way**, is what occurs in financial markets when the entity with a deficit goes into debt directly from the entity with a surplus. The latter, the **indirect way**, foresees the involvement of a third subject (the financial intermediary) who collects the savings of the entity with aim surplus and employs these resources by lending them to the entity with a deficit (**Figure 1.1**).

Intuitively, if the exchange occurs without an intermediary, and thus through a financial market, the two entities gain an advantage, as happens when we buy a used car or a house;: when the transaction is executed directly by the seller we do not need to pay agency costs. Therefore, why do we rely on banks if they are less convenient than financial markets? In general terms, we can affirm that financial markets are only theoretically preferable to banks, and this happens only if markets are perfectly efficient. The issue is that financial markets are affected by **three types of inefficiencies**.

The first inefficiency lies in the fact that transactions in efficient markets should not be subject to any kind of **transaction costs**. This situation almost never occurs, and there are at least the following four costs:

a) cost of searching for the counterparty;
b) cost of defining and stipulating a contract to safeguard the funds provider;
c) cost of assessment of the creditworthiness of the funds taker;
d) cost of monitoring the relationship.

Net of these costs, which would be rather high for people who are inexperienced in economic, financial, and legal matters, the intermediation carried out by the bank becomes more convenient than direct transactions in financial markets.

Figure 1.1 The function of financial intermediaries and markets

The second imperfection in markets is linked to **information costs**. In most marketplaces, the parties to an exchange have different information related to the object of the transaction, regardless of whether it is the quality of the food that we buy daily or the car that we more rarely purchase. This difference is defined as **information asymmetry**, and constitutes a new element of inefficiency, since it leads us to formulate prices which potentially differ from the correct value of goods. More precisely, we are unable to define the quality of a good while knowing that several different levels of quality exist, and therefore we are induced to accept an average price that is higher than the value of mediocre goods, and at the same time, lower than the value of excellent goods. The consequence is that sellers of excellent goods will abandon the exchange, leaving the market to mediocre goods sellers. This is defined as **market failure.**

If we apply information asymmetries to the financial market, we will end up with a situation in which funds providers (i.e. the ones with a financial surplus) are unable to estimate the creditworthiness of funds takers. Therefore, all the funds seekers will obtain an average rate, regardless of their quality. This results in a market failure, since all the high-quality funds seekers will not accept paying the same cost of those who have lower quality, and thus they will leave the market. The failure generates credit rationing, inefficient financial allocation, and incorrect risk assessment. Therefore, the existence of a bank specialized in recognizing the creditworthiness of individuals and firms will allow for reductions in costs and related asymmetries.

Markets also suffer from a third imperfection, linked to **risks**. The existence of several degrees of risk aversion within market agents represents an element of inefficiency which discourages direct exchanges in financial markets. When investing financial savings, the investor faces numerous risks, among which are the following:

a) credit risk, the risk related to the return of principal and interest at the set schedule and quantity;
b) liquidity risk;
c) market risk;
d) operational risk.

If investors operated directly on the financial markets, they would face these risks. Through financial intermediaries, though, they can transfer a consistent portion of the risks to others.

Notwithstanding the intrinsic differences between market inefficiencies and the independent development of underlying theories, they all bring us to the same conclusion: banks exist and potentially prosper because the market alternative could be costlier and riskier.

The development of banks has produced another factor that is crucial to understanding their usefulness: the **monetary function**. To transfer financial balances to their clients, banks offer liabilities which have a unique characteristic: they are debts that the banks agrees to pay without notice to its creditors, at their nominal value (in some cases, also with interest). Thus, the bank is a very peculiar enterprise, which resembles the Issuing Institutions that historically have been used by sovereigns to finance their debts.

In other terms, we have a central bank that issues legal tender and commercial banks that issue bank money. As recently recalled, "the value of bank money largely depends on the value of bank assets. The money produced by banks – together with a wide range of instruments for its use – is the means of central payment and an important instrument of accumulation and conservation of value through time" (Mottura, 2018). This means that commercial banks promise to pay back their monetary debt, which becomes a necessary instrument for economic exchange, but they will be able to fulfil the promise only if their operations remain liquid and solvent. If this situation is not maintained, the banks (and potentially the entire banking system) enter a crisis which in turn destabilizes the real economy.

During the financial crisis that started in 2007-2008, we witnessed several cases of bank defaults; an unexpected event, in particular for systems which were used for decades to ensure absolute stability and protection of savers. Some investors unexpectedly learned they had lost their savings (not really monetary savings, as we are going to explain).

Where did the money end up? The bank transformed the money collected through liabilities on one side of its balance sheet into credit on the other side, which for a firm means transforming a bond into a share. The loan or bond, while representing money owed to the bank, is considered an asset whose value should reflect the repayment risk; the higher the risk, the lower the financial value of the asset. The loan provides new value to the bank through the form of interest, a small part of which is paid on deposits as a reward for their trust in the bank. The remainder is profit for the bank and its shareholders and partners.

For this reason, banks are historically considered "special" even with respect to other financial intermediaries, and over time it was thought that their activities should be governed with the primary objective of ensuring that bank assets can always cover bank liabilities. Regulation is a crucial element to understanding bank behavior, and we will dedicate the second chapter to it.

We will now focus on the functions that make a bank peculiar, namely the monetary function, the credit function, and the financial function.

1.2 The functions of a bank

1.2.1 Money, the monetary function and the payment system

It is commonly thought that the creation of bank money is the outstanding feature that characterizes banks. Money plays several functions, but often the focus falls on the payment function. In each economic transaction, two actions occur: the exchange, which could be the purchase of a good or service, and the payment. Often the exchange and the payment occur at the same moment, but in some cases the payment is postponed and the need for an organized payment system able to manage the debit-credit relationship arises.

The payment system is constituted by instruments, banking processes, and interbank fund transfer systems that ensure and ease the circulation of money. As specified by the European Central Bank itself, payment systems are the "hydraulic network that enables money to flow in the economy." Basically, they facilitate firms, the public administration, and consumers in mutual funds transfers. The payment system has been historically characterized by the following elements:

a) Coexistence of two types of money: that directly issued by the central bank, which ensures payments due to its legal form, and commercial bank money, which is accepted due to the trust that economic operators have in the issuing institution;
b) The centrality and predominant position of commercial banks;
c) The interbank payment circuit, based on a national and international network built by the banks within the system;
d) The role of central banks as lenders of last resort in the case of illiquidity of one or more financial institutions.

Banks, among their peculiarities, can issue payment instruments. In the balance sheet, these are indicated as "payables to customers." There are several forms of collection that allow banks to obtain the financial resources necessary to grant loans and make investments. The payables can be current accounts, free deposits, time deposits, or repurchase agreements, among which current accounts are the most liquid, and thus they are the ones that most resemble money. Lastly, banks are not limited to the issue of payment instruments, but they participate in the construction and enable the functioning of the payment system.

Currently, money transfer services are changing. Once a monopoly of the banking system, they now represent a disputed business area between players coming from other sectors and start-ups. The spread of mobile devices such as smartphones and tablets has sharply increased mobile commerce. In 2019, e-commerce sales accounted for 365 billion US dollars in the United States.[1] There are various possibilities to make purchases on mobile devices or apps, and e-commerce leaders such as eBay and Amazon offer apps and websites for online shopping. Mobile devices can also be used in physical shops as a method of payment, using near-field communication (NFC) technologies. Firms operating in this area are Payment Processing Companies, among which the forerunner (and thus the most important case) is PayPal; however, we can list Due, Stripe, Flagship Merchant Services, Payline Data, Revolut, and Square, among others.

[1] https://www.statista.com/statistics/272391/us-retail-e-commerce-sales-forecast/

1.2.2 Credit and credit function

The credit function is intuitive: the bank receives financial resources from the depositors, and uses these resources (or part of them) to finance economic projects or temporary financial needs. In other terms, the bank balances its own liabilities, stemmed from money collection, through the emission of loans, which are recorded among the assets.

For instance, if a firm is willing to build a new plant, it needs to pay for the construction now, which will generate a profit in the coming years. The money spent today could come from the firm's liquidity or from other sources, such as a bank. Basically, it is an exchange of money today for money tomorrow. If banks did not exist, the firm looking for financing to support an investment project would need to raise money from a large number of single savers. Thus, the market would have to be very efficient, otherwise the firm would not be able to sustain the high costs, and probably would not be able to obtain all the necessary resources.

The credit function is performed through *deadline transformation*. As we mentioned, money collection takes place through deposits that are reimbursable upon the depositor's request. These resources are transformed into a credit whose deadlines have to be in line with the borrower's goals (which could also be long-term). Since depositors act in a heterogeneous fashion, a part of the funds collected can be used to finance long-term activities, such as mortgages.

In the Seventies and Eighties, Hyman P. Minsky focused attention on the division of funding into three types. The first one, defined as "covering financing," is the safest: the firm counts on its cash flows to reimburse the loans it takes out. In order for the process to work, firms should have limited loans and sound profits.

The second one, "speculative financing," is riskier: firms count on their cash flows to pay the debt back, but since cash flows are not enough to repay the principal, the debt has to be periodically renewed. The technical form for this kind of financing is *bullet*: a loan in which the whole principal is due at the end of the loan period. A bullet loan can be a mortgage, a bond, a note, or any other type of credit. The process should be manageable as long as the economy is running smoothly, but a recession could cause difficulties.

The third one, "hyper-speculative financing," is the riskiest. Cash flows cannot cover the principal or the interest; firms bet only on the fact that the underlying asset will increase in value enough to cover the debt. When this does not occur, not only could firms – or debtors in general – face difficulties in paying back their debts, but the bank could also be unable to pay its depositors. Bank money might not be returned at its nominal value. The "Minsky moment" is the financial market crash following a long period of prosperity and investment gains which leads to an overall lower perception of risk in the market. The bullish period induces investing with borrowed money instead of owned capital, and thus investments with leverage, exposing investors to a potential liquidity crisis, which could start with a modest price decrease. Losses on speculative activities lead lenders to ask for the repayment of loans. When loans become irrecoverable due to the insolvency of the debtor, the financial institution incurs credit risk and has to reclassify its loans as non-performing (NPL), decreasing their value in the balance sheet. A full discussion of credit risk is offered in Chapter 2.

1.2.3 Financial investments, securitization, and the evolution of the role of banking in markets

The third function which characterizes banks is the financial one. This refers to managing a portfolio analogous to that of a common financial investor. Among all banking activities, it is the least peculiar, but in recent times it has distinguished itself as the most impactful in terms of evolution and strategic model.

The reasons underlying the transformation are linked to the process of financing the economy and to role covered by banks. Nowadays, banks are necessary as underwriters of bonds issued by public and private entities, and they transform them through securitization. As a result, banks now became an essential player integrated in the market, where they play a crucial role.

At the same time, underwriting a high amount of bonds exposes banks to insolvency risk, with the possibility of financial contagion in the event that debtors decrease or lose their credibility. The financial function is strictly associated, on the one hand, with the opportunity of gains if prices rise, and on the other hand, with market risk, if prices decline.

The situation described resembles what happened in several phases of the crisis, first with the crash of securitized loans value, and then with the loss in value of sovereign bonds issued by countries with considerable financial imbalances. Securitization played an important role in the process of generating the financial crisis, pushing families to incur excessive debt, and at the same time contributing to the fast and intense transmission of that debt in the financial system and the real economy at the global level.

Securitization significantly modified the strategic model of banks, which went from "originate-to-hold" to "originate-to-distribute." The first model is present when lenders grant loans with the intention of holding them until their maturity, instead of selling them to other financial institutions or investors. On the other hand, the second model is observed when lenders grant loans with the intention of selling them to other entities or investors, instead of holding them until their maturity. The banks which opted for the second model, reduced the incentive to reassess the value and risk of the underlying securities. Specifically, the performance of banks' obligations encouraged excessive financial leverage (a fundamental element of the crisis). Furthermore, the securitization process had the consequence of increasing opportunities for regulatory arbitrage aimed at reducing the absorption of capital by credit risk by transferring the mortgage credit exposure from the banking book to the trading book.

An analysis of the financial function shows that banks are developing their traditional role, with further integration in the financial markets.

We will now focus on the bank from an accounting perspective, namely on the balance sheet and the income statement.

1.3 The financials of banks

1.3.1 Understanding the financials of banks

A bank balance sheet is a key way to draw conclusions regarding a bank's business and the resources used to be able to finance its activities.

Figure 1.2 displays the key areas of a bank's balance sheet. It has three main areas of focus. The first one is represented by **cash and cash equivalents**. Cash is usually held as deposits and banks often hold cash on behalf of other banks. A bank must hold some cash to maintain its solvency, namely to be able to meet withdrawal requests from depositors and pay its bills. Cash equivalents are short-term investments that can either be used as cash or can be quickly converted to cash without a loss of value, such as treasuries and government agency bills, on which a bank earns a yield, and commercial paper. Due to their short-term nature, cash equivalents are basically immune from interest rate risk. Moreover, deposits in other commercial banks are treated as cash. Such deposits may bring no income directly but are maintained to establish a line of credit for present or possible future requirements.

Secondly, **financial assets held for trading** are usually short-term assets, a debt or equity investment purchased with the intention of short-term gain. They consist of items such as interest-bearing deposits purchased from other financial institutions, repurchase agreements, mortgage-backed securities, etc. Financial assets held for trading generate interest and trading income for the bank and are also used for liquidity purposes. Most of the securities are highly liquid, have low default risk, and can be traded in secondary markets. They provide financial institutions with liquid-

Figure 1.2 Key areas of the Balance Sheet of a Bank

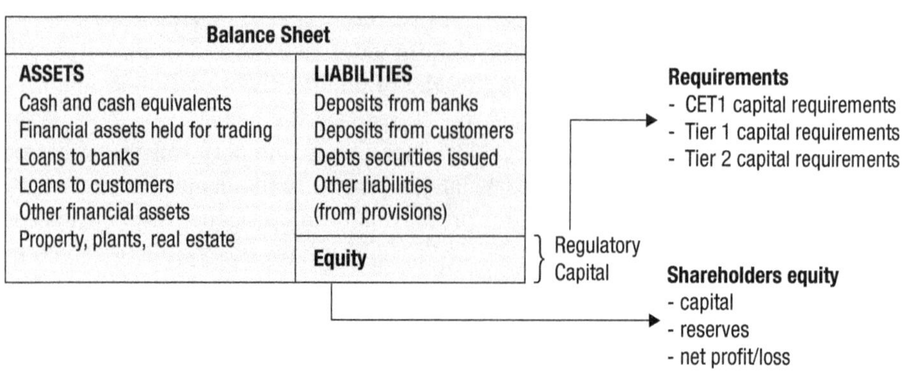

ity. It must be taken into account that commercial and investment banks are exposed to high levels of liquidity risk, i.e. the risk that arises when a financial institution's liability holders demand cash for a financial claim they hold with the financial institution. Therefore, significant amounts of cash and financial assets held for trading are necessary to meet liquidity demands. From a pure accounting perspective, the assets are reported at fair value, and unrealized gains and/or losses are included as earnings. Over time, their value changes, but the adjustment is recorded only in earnings.

The third key area of focus is **loans**, which often represent the largest asset on a bank's balance sheet, and are the basis of the "traditional" banking model, as we will have the opportunity to see. For instance, this section includes commercial and industrial (C&I) loans, residential and commercial real estate loans, consumer loans (i.e. credit cards, auto loans), as well as loans to other banks. While commercial loans are relatively more important for larger banks, consumer loans, small business loans, and residential mortgages are more important for small banks. But, a number of long-term and temporary influences have brought changes to banks' loan portfolios. For instance, the growth of the commercial paper market, and of the public bond market, which have become competitive and alternate funding sources, has decreased the volume of loans to major corporations. Consequently, banks are often left with a pool of increasingly smaller and riskier borrowers in the commercial and industrial loan market. It goes without saying that credit risk plays a crucial role. Another important factor has been the securitization of loans into asset-backed securities which can in turn be sold to investors. This allows banks to earn origination fees and/or servicing fees on the securitized loans while also freeing up capital to grant more loans.

On the liability side, commercial banks usually have two sources of funds, other than equity: deposits and borrowed or other liability funds.

Deposits are traditionally the largest budget item for banks. They consist of both transaction accounts, i.e. non-interest-bearing demand deposits and interest-bearing checking accounts, and retail or household savings and time deposits. The second category can be distinguished into smaller accounts (usually less than \$100,000), which include small non-transaction amounts and represented 76.7% of deposits in the U.S. in 2016, and larger accounts, which are primarily negotiable certificates of deposit – i.e. deposit claims with promised interest rates and fixed maturities – that represented approximately 7.7% of total deposits in the U.S. in 2016. Thus, deposits are expected to be withdrawn and pay out interest payments, generating an economic outflow in the near future.

Non-deposit liabilities consist of a broad array of instruments, such as purchases of bank reserves on the interbank market, repurchase agreements, and the issuance of bonds and notes.

Overall, the liability structure of banks' balance sheets tends to reflect a shorter maturity structure than that of their asset portfolio. Moreover, relatively more liquid instruments such as deposits and interbank borrowings are used to fund relatively less liquid assets such as loans. Thus, maturity mismatch risk and liquidity risk are key exposure concerns for bank managers.

The last major section is **equity**, also referred to as **bank capital**. Bank capital is represented by funds that are raised by either selling new equity in the bank, or that come from retained earnings (profits) the bank earns from its assets net of liabilities. Therefore, it consists of common and preferred stock, surplus or additional paid-in capital, and retained earnings. Capital is subject to capital requirements, which are set out by the Basel Committee for Banking Supervision and consist of the amount of equity a financial institution must have in relation to its assets. Capital requirements follow specific rules which we will examine fully in the next chapter. Because of the relatively low cost of deposit funding, banks tend to hold equity close to the minimum levels set by the regulator.

Off-balance sheet (OBS) activities deserve mention because they are becoming increasingly important. They include issuing various types of guarantees (such as letters of credit), often involving a strong insurance underwriting element, future commitments to lend, and derivative transactions (futures, forwards, options, and swaps). Academically speaking, **off-balance sheet assets** are defined as items which, when a contingent event occurs, move onto the asset side of the balance sheet, or lead to the realization of an income item in the income statement. Conversely, **off-balance sheet liabilities** are defined as items which, when a contingent event occurs, move onto the liability side of the balance sheet or produce an expense item in the income statement. By undertaking OBS activities, banks hope to earn additional fee income to complement declining margins or spreads on their traditional lending business. However, OBS activities can involve risks that add to the overall insolvency exposure of a financial intermediary.

Figure 1.3 displays the key areas of the income statement or profit and loss account of a bank. The sources of income can be grouped into net interest income, net fees and commissions income, and net trading income.

Net interest income is composed of the total interest earned from the bank's loans and investments and cash positions minus the expenses incurred (i.e. interest paid out to depositors). For commercial banks, the earnings the bank obtains through the lending activity represent an essential part of the interest income. Depending on several factors, such as the type of assets and liabilities that are held as well as the use of fixed rates or variable rates, banks can be more or less sensitive to changes in interest rates. Intuitively, banks owning variable-rate assets and liabilities will be more sensitive to changes in interest rates than those with fixed-rate assets and liabilities. Interest income is recorded on an accrual basis. Net interest income is an important tool in assessing the bank's ability to generate profits and control interest rate risk.

Net fees and commissions income flows from the products and services offered by the financial intermediary, and thus from both on- and off- balance sheet activities. For instance, it includes bank account and service fees, trust income, loan and

Figure 1.3 Key areas of the Income Statement of a Bank

Income Statement
Net interest (and dividends) income Net fees and commissions income Net trading income
Operating income Operating costs (administrative expenses, payrolls, etc.) Amortisation and depreciation
Operating profit (or loss) Write down loans and provisions
Net operating profit (or loss) Other margins and provisions
Profit before tax Taxes
Net profit

mortgage fees, brokerage fees, asset management services income, and advisory services income. In the current low-interest rate environment, this type of income is gaining importance relative to net interest income. Moreover, in the Corporate and Investment Banking environment, in which the lending activity is not core, fees and commissions are generated by most of the activities performed by the financial intermediaries, which we will consider Chapter 3. Therefore, they are the main source of revenues.

Lastly, **net trading income** represents income from trading activities. It is composed of gains (or losses) on financial instruments held for trading, such as trading securities and derivatives, gains (or losses) from fair value hedging, and gains (or losses) from instruments designated at fair value.

The sum of the various sources of income (interest, fees and commissions, and trading) is referred to as **operating income**, or total revenue. Operating costs, amortization, and write-downs of loans and provisions are subtracted from it. **Provisions for loan losses** are a non-cash, tax-deductible expense. They are the allocation from the current period to the allowance for loan losses listed on the balance sheet. This item represents the bank management's prediction of loans at risk of default for the current period. While the loan remains on the balance sheet, the expected losses from any bad loans affect net income and equity on the income statement and balance sheet, respectively. Lastly, income taxes are paid and extraordinary items and adjustments made.

The **net profit**, or loss, is then added to the balance sheet on the equity side. In the case of a profit, it corresponds to an increase in equity and a corresponding increase in asset value. Vice versa, in the case of a loss, the bank incurs a decrease in both equity and asset value.

1.3.2 Deriving the business model from the financials

By looking at the balance sheet and income statement of banks, it is possible to get a glimpse of the business model they follow. Specifically, it is useful to focus on balance structure and profit and loss ratios. Broadly speaking, from an accounting perspective, entities can be classified as investment banks, universal banks, and retail lenders.

Investment Banks are financial intermediaries that perform several services, focusing on large and complex financial transactions. Services will be described more in detail in Chapter 3, but investment banks are usually involved in underwriting, they act as an intermediary between issuers and investing entities, they facilitate corporate finance activities, and they act as advisors. Therefore, having fees, commissions and trading activities as their main income sources, investment banks display a low share of net interest income. Moreover, investment banks are primarily wholesale funded, since their activities are mostly focused on wholesale, and they are only partially involved in lending related businesses.

For instance, the traditional big American players (i.e. Goldman Sachs, Morgan Stanley) are pure Investment Banks. The case of Goldman Sachs will be commented on in **Box 1.1**. Due to the nature of investment banking activities, the following peculiar characteristics are evident:

- high levels of trading portfolio and fees income vs. net operating income ratio;
- low levels of retail lending;
- low levels of customer funding vs. total financing;
- low levels of net interest income vs. net operating income ratio.

Box 1.1 Goldman Sachs Group, Inc.

The Goldman Sachs Group, Inc. is a leading global investment banking, securities and investment management firm that provides a wide range of financial services to a substantial and diversified client base that includes corporations, financial institutions, governments, and individuals. Founded in 1869, the firm is headquartered in New York and maintains offices in all major financial centers around the world.

Goldman Sachs is a pure investment bank, engaging in activities such as providing advice and services to help organizations with mergers and acquisitions, financing, and other transactions. It offers asset management services and investment products, as well as private wealth management and direct private investing. In 2019, it was second largest fee collector in the world, second only to JP Morgan, for a total value of $6,109 million. Its collected fees stem mainly from M&A activities (42%), followed by equity (26%), bonds (24%), and loans (9%).

By delving into the bank's financial statements, and specifically into its balance sheet, we can note that the most important asset is represented by trading assets, which together with securities borrowed and purchased under agreements to resell, represent approximately 60% of the bank's assets. As usually happens, cash and equivalents are kept at the minimum necessary levels. Unlike traditional banks, loans account for a bare 11% of total assets, displaying very low levels of retail lending. Symmetrically, considering liabilities, only a small part of the bank's funding stems from customers (namely deposits). For a comparison, you might look at the BNP Paribas' financial

THE GOLDMAN SACHS GROUP, INC. AND SUBSIDIARIES

Consolidated Balance Sheets

$ in millions	As of December 2019	2018
Assets		
Cash and cash equivalents	**$133,546**	$130,547
Collateralized agreements:		
Securities purchased under agreements to resell (includes **$85,691** and $139,220 at fair value)	**85,691**	139,258
Securities borrowed (includes **$26,279** and $23,142 at fair value)	**136,071**	135,285
Customer and other receivables (includes **$53** and $160 at fair value)	**74,605**	72,455
Trading assets (at fair value and includes **$66,605** and $47,371 pledged as collateral)	**355,332**	280,195
Investments (includes **$57,827** and $45,579 at fair value, and **$10,968** and $7,710 pledged as collateral)	**63,937**	47,224
Loans (includes **$14,386** and $13,416 at fair value)	**108,904**	97,837
Other assets	**34,882**	28,995
Total assets	**$992,968**	$931,796
Liabilities and shareholders' equity		
Deposits (includes **$17,765** and $21,060 at fair value)	**$190,019**	$158,257
Collateralized financings:		
Securities sold under agreements to repurchase (at fair value)	**117,756**	78,723
Securities loaned (includes **$714** and $3,241 at fair value)	**14,985**	11,808
Other secured financings (includes **$18,071** and $20,904 at fair value)	**19,277**	21,433
Customer and other payables	**174,817**	180,235
Trading liabilities (at fair value)	**108,835**	108,897
Unsecured short-term borrowings (includes **$26,007** and $16,963 at fair value)	**48,287**	40,502
Unsecured long-term borrowings (includes **$43,661** and $46,584 at fair value)	**207,076**	224,149
Other liabilities (includes **$150** and $132 at fair value)	**21,651**	17,607
Total liabilities	**902,703**	841,611
Commitments, contingencies and guarantees		
Shareholders' equity		
Preferred stock; aggregate liquidation preference of **$11,203** and $11,203	**11,203**	11,203
Common stock; **896,782,650** and 891,356,284 shares issued, and **347,343,184** and 367,741,973 shares outstanding	**9**	9
Share-based awards	**3,195**	2,845
Nonvoting common stock; no shares issued and outstanding	**–**	–
Additional paid-in capital	**54,883**	54,005
Retained earnings	**106,465**	100,100
Accumulated other comprehensive income/(loss)	**(1,484)**	693
Stock held in treasury, at cost; **549,439,468** and 523,614,313 shares	**(84,006)**	(78,670)
Total shareholders' equity	**90,265**	90,185
Total liabilities and shareholders' equity	**$992,968**	$931,796

THE GOLDMAN SACHS GROUP, INC. AND SUBSIDIARIES

Consolidated Statements of Earnings

in millions, except per share amounts	Year Ended December 2019	2018	2017
Revenues			
Investment banking	**$ 6,798**	$ 7,430	$ 7,076
Investment management	**6,189**	6,590	5,867
Commissions and fees	**2,988**	3,199	3,051
Market making	**10,157**	9,724	7,853
Other principal transactions	**6,052**	5,906	5,951
Total non-interest revenues	**32,184**	32,849	29,798
Interest income	**21,738**	19,679	13,113
Interest expense	**17,376**	15,912	10,181
Net interest income	**4,362**	3,767	2,932
Total net revenues	**36,546**	36,616	32,730
Provision for credit losses	**1,065**	674	657
Operating expenses			
Compensation and benefits	**12,353**	12,328	11,653
Brokerage, clearing, exchange and distribution fees	**3,252**	3,200	2,876
Market development	**739**	740	588
Communications and technology	**1,167**	1,023	897
Depreciation and amortization	**1,704**	1,328	1,152
Occupancy	**1,029**	809	733
Professional fees	**1,316**	1,214	1,165
Other expenses	**3,338**	2,819	1,877
Total operating expenses	**24,898**	23,461	20,941
Pre-tax earnings	**10,583**	12,481	11,132
Provision for taxes	**2,117**	2,022	6,846
Net earnings	**8,466**	10,459	4,286
Preferred stock dividends	**569**	599	601
Net earnings applicable to common shareholders	**$ 7,897**	$ 9,860	$ 3,685
Earnings per common share			
Basic	**$ 21.18**	$ 25.53	$ 9.12
Diluted	**$ 21.03**	$ 25.27	$ 9.01
Average common shares			
Basic	**371.6**	385.4	401.6
Diluted	**375.5**	390.2	409.1

statements (in the next box), in which customer deposits account for approximately 40% of assets, which is considered an intermediate level. In the case of retail lenders, the ratio is definitely higher. By taking another glance at the liabilities' side, it becomes clear that Goldman Sachs is mostly financed by unsecured short and long-term borrowings, collateralized financing (securities), and trading liabilities.
Looking at the income statement, or statement of earnings, the high level of assets held for trading translate into high revenue streams from market making activities and the other principal transactions, which constitute the trading income. Furthermore, the investment banking and investment management revenues are remarkable. Thus, we confirm that the levels of trading portfolio and fee income are high with respect to net operating income. Lastly, as expected from the low magnitude of lending activity, net interest income is in an opposite situation. The relevant level of interest income is also offset by the substantial interest expenses, thus having a very low level compared to net operating income.

Source: https://www.goldmansachs.com/investor-relations/financials/current/annual-reports/2019-annual-report/annual-report-2019.pdf

The concept of **Universal Bank**, which evolution is described in **Box 1.2**, is defined as a system in which financial intermediaries perform both "traditional" banking activities and typical Corporate and Investment Banking functions. From a historical perspective, following the crisis of the 1930s, the model was severely criticized and revised in light of a normative current which was more inclined towards the principle of separation of the two activities. It was only after the 1990s that the regulator showed a renewed interest in the integration approach, favoring the development of the universal model in Europe (1993) and in the United States (1999).

Box 1.2 The evolution of Universal Banks

In the United States, universal banks were forbidden for most of the Twentieth Century. Following the Wall Street Crash of 1929, the heavy involvement of banks in the stock market and the wide variety of financial activities they performed were considered as the triggering causes of the crisis. The mixing of commercial and investment banking activities was considered too risky and speculative. Therefore, in 1933, the Congress introduced an act to separate investment and commercial banking activities: the Glass-Steagall Act (GSA).
A regulatory firewall was set up between the two types of activities, and banks were given a year to choose between specializing in commercial or investment banking. A commercial bank's total income stemming from securities was set at 10% maximum, but an exception allowed commercial banks to underwrite government-issued bonds. The barrier was created with the aim of preventing the banks' use of deposits in the case of a failed underwriting operation. Furthermore, the act was seen as an incentive to fund commerce: banks were encouraged to use their funds for lending rather than investing those funds in equity markets. The act was considered very controversial in the financial industry.
An extension of the Glass-Steagall Act was introduced in 1956, focused on the separation between insurance and banking. It is called the Bank Holding Company Act and it prohibits banks from underwriting insurance, while it still allows the sale of insurance and insurance products.
The limitations imposed on the banking sector were considered controversial. It was argued that such restrictions could have an adverse effect by denying the possibility to diversify, making the industry de facto riskier. The Glass-Steagall Act – as well as the Bank Holding Company Act – was

superseded in 1999 by the Gramm-Leach-Bliley Act, which reintroduced the possibility of affiliations between commercial banks, investment banks, and insurance providers.
In Europe the approach to universal banks has always been more relaxed, making them a common bank type in Europe, where some of the most notable universal banks, such as Deutsche Bank, ING Bank, and BNP Paribas, reside. Financial liberalization was linked to the implementation of European Union legislation, mainly composed of directives that had to be introduced into national legislation with an element of discretion. The European legislation aimed at unifying the level playing field among European financial institutions and introducing a single model of banking charters. The European banking system, shaped according to national legislation, transformed itself according to the newly introduced rules. It opted for the creation of larger and more diversified universal banks, reached through cross-border and cross-industry merger and acquisition operations. Over the period 1990-1999, a total of 1,459 transactions occurred, of which 56% involved within-border/within-industry deals, 20% within-border/cross-industry deals, 17% cross-border/within-industry deals, and 6% cross-border/cross-industry deals. The current form of the European banking sector took shape in that period.

Source: https://www.ecb.europa.eu/pub/pdf/other/transformationeuropeanfinancialsystemen.pdf

Universal banks are involved in lending activities and non-lending business such as insurance and non-lending fees, and in commission business such as asset management, securities-related fees, and trading activities. Furthermore, some universal banks are conglomerates or banc-assurances (i.e. partnership between a bank and an insurance company that is aimed at offering insurance products or insurance benefits to the bank's customers, in which bank staff and tellers become the point of sale and point of contact for the customer); thus both wholesale and customer funding is important. They have the following features:

- intermediate levels of customer funding vs. total funding;
- intermediate levels of trading portfolio;
- intermediate levels of net interest income vs. net operating income ratio.

European mixed banks (i.e. Deutsche Bank, UBS, Credit Suisse, ING Bank) and traditional big American players (i.e. JP Morgan Chase, Bank of America Merrill Lynch, Wells Fargo) belong to this category: we will further examine the case of BNP Paribas in **Box 1.3**.

Box 1.3 **BNP Paribas S.A.**

BNP Paribas S.A. is a French universal banking group. It is the world's 8th largest bank by total assets, and currently operates in 71 countries. It is a well-diversified bank offering virtually every financial service and is equipped with a strong culture of risk control. During the global financial meltdown that began in 2007, BNP Paribas was one of the very few large banks to post profits without interruption.
As mentioned, BNP Paribas engages in a vast variety of financial services. Its retail banking networks serve more than 30 million customers in its three domestic markets (France, Belgium, and Italy) alone, while being present also in the United States (as Bank of the West) and in emerging

BALANCE SHEET AT 31 DECEMBER 2019

In millions of euros	Notes	31 December 2019	31 December 2018
ASSETS			
Cash and balances at central banks		155,135	185,119
Financial instruments at fair value through profit or loss			
Securities	5.a	131,935	121,954
Loans and repurchase agreements	5.a	196,927	183,716
Derivative financial instruments	5.a	247,287	232,895
Derivatives used for hedging purposes	5.b	12,452	9,810
Financial assets at fair value through equity			
Debt securities	5.c	50,403	53,838
Equity securities	5.c	2,266	2,151
Financial assets at amortised cost			
Loans and advances to credit institutions	5.e	21,692	19,556
Loans and advances to customers	5.e	805,777	765,871
Debt securities	5.e	108,454	75,073
Remeasurement adjustment on interest-rate risk hedged portfolios		4,303	2,787
Financial investments of insurance activities	5.i	257,818	232,308
Current and deferred tax assets	5.k	6,813	7,220
Accrued income and other assets	5.l	113,535	103,346
Equity-method investments	5.m	5,952	5,772
Property, plant and equipment and investment property	5.n	32,295	26,652
Intangible assets	5.n	3,852	3,783
Goodwill	5.o	7,817	8,487
Non-current assets held for sale	8.c		498
TOTAL ASSETS		2,164,713	2,040,836
LIABILITIES			
Deposits from central banks		2,985	1,354
Financial instruments at fair value through profit or loss			
Securities	5.a	65,490	75,189
Deposits and repurchase agreements	5.a	215,093	204,039
Issued debt securities	5.a	63,758	54,908
Derivative financial instruments	5.a	237,885	225,804
Derivatives used for hedging purposes		14,116	11,677
Financial liabilities at amortised cost			
Deposits from credit institutions	5.g	84,566	78,915
Deposits from customers	5.g	834,667	796,548
Debt securities	5.h	157,578	151,451
Subordinated debt	5.h	20,003	17,627
Remeasurement adjustment on interest-rate risk hedged portfolios		3,989	2,470
Current and deferred tax liabilities	5.k	3,566	2,255
Accrued expenses and other liabilities	5.l	102,749	89,562
Technical reserves and other insurance liabilities	5.j	236,937	213,691
Provisions for contingencies and charges	5.p	9,486	9,620
TOTAL LIABILITIES		2,052,868	1,935,110
EQUITY			
Share capital, additional paid-in capital and retained earnings		*97,135*	*93,431*
Net income for the period attributable to shareholders		*8,173*	*7,526*
Total capital, retained earnings and net income for the period attributable to shareholders		**105,308**	**100,957**
Changes in assets and liabilities recognised directly in equity		2,145	510
Shareholders' equity		107,453	101,467
Minority interests	8.d	4,392	4,259
TOTAL EQUITY		111,845	105,726
TOTAL LIABILITIES AND EQUITY		2,164,713	2,040,836

countries. As an investment bank and international financial services provider for corporate and institutional clients, it is present across Europe, the Americas, and Asia. BNP Paribas is especially engaged in fixed income operations, equity and derivatives, commodity derivatives, M&A and IPO advisory and support, structured finance operations and banking services such as international cash management. Lastly, it is involved in some insurance activity.

As a result, the balance sheet and income statement appear balanced across business areas. Starting from the lending activity, the volume of loans to customers is particularly substantial, consisting of almost 40% of total assets. In fact, as previously said, lending is a considerable part of BNP Paribas' business, and the high volumes of loans are reflected in the high interest revenue streams in the profit and loss accounts. They are the top source of revenues. This is no surprise, since BNP Paribas has been the largest collector of loan fees over the past 10 years, only occasionally being

PROFIT AND LOSS ACCOUNT FOR THE YEAR ENDED 31 DECEMBER 2019

In millions of euros	Notes	Year to 31 Dec. 2019	Year to 31 Dec. 2018
Interest income	3.a	37,327	35,723
Interest expense	3.a	(16,200)	(14,661)
Commission income	3.b	13,265	12,925
Commission expense	3.b	(3,900)	(3,718)
Net gain on financial instruments at fair value through profit or loss	3.c	7,111	5,808
Net gain on financial instruments at fair value through equity	3.d	350	315
Net gain on derecognised financial assets at amortised cost		3	(5)
Net income from insurance activities	3.e	4,437	4,064
Income from other activities	3.f	13,502	12,324
Expense on other activities	3.f	(11,298)	(10,259)
REVENUES		44,597	42,516
Salary and employee benefit expense	7.a	(17,553)	(16,617)
Other operating expenses	3.g	(11,339)	(12,290)
Depreciation, amortisation and impairment of property, plant and equipment and intangible assets	5.n	(2,445)	(1,676)
GROSS OPERATING INCOME		13,260	11,933
Cost of risk	3.h	(3,203)	(2,764)
OPERATING INCOME		10,057	9,169
Share of earnings of equity-method entities	5.m	586	628
Net gain on non-current assets		1,569	358
Goodwill	5.o	(818)	53
PRE-TAX INCOME		11,394	10,208
Corporate income tax	3.i	(2,811)	(2,203)
NET INCOME		8,583	8,005
Net income attributable to minority interests		410	479
NET INCOME ATTRIBUTABLE TO EQUITY HOLDERS		8,173	7,526
Basic earnings per share	8.a	6.21	5.73
Diluted earnings per share	8.a	6.21	5.73

the second largest (in 2008, 2012, and 2017). Symmetrically, the relevant lending activity is reflected in the liability side, in which deposits from customers account for 40% of total liabilities.

Moving forward, in considering the trading portfolio, we notice that financial assets held for trading play a quite significant role, consisting of approximately 27% of total assets, and are balanced by their counterpart in liabilities. The gains they generate are fundamental to cover the liquidity needs of the whole bank.

Lastly, insurance also plays a role among BNP Paribas' activities. Accounting for approximately 12% of total assets, financial investments of insurance activities generate 10% of gross revenues, thus being among the most important side activities.

To conclude, by looking at the profit and loss account, as expected, the top source of revenues is net interest income (€21 billion), due to the important component of lending operations in BNP Paribas' business structure. It is followed by commission income (€10 billion) and lastly by trading income (€7 billion) (recorded as net gains on financial instruments). Therefore, revenues are well distributed across the several business areas.

Source: https://invest.bnpparibas.com/sites/default/files/documents/cf_audites_eng_31.12.2019.pdf

The choice of a system composed of universal banks has several advantages. Offering services able to satisfy a broad spectrum of clients' financial necessities, the universal bank normally manages to acquire a wider range of information at lower costs and can benefit from economies of scale. But, the multiplicity of activities could negatively influence the stability of the financial institution, increase conflicts of interest with clients, and without doubt, require more investment in supervisory activities.

Retail lenders, as their very same name states, are focused on lending to the retail sector. Popular retail lending products include personal loans, line of credit accounts, and credit cards, but in many cases they have a strong focus on residential real estate lending. Moreover, retail lenders are mostly funded by their retail clients through deposits, with a moderate reliance on wholesale funding. Lending is the most traditional banking activity, despite the fact that lenders must have well-established origination procedures which allow them to appropriately manage risk across their credit portfolio and also to highly customize the origination and underwriting in order to ensure they are taking on appropriate levels of risk. In some cases, retail lenders offer their clients other related services and products, thus leading to a significant fee and commission business. However, the majority of those fees can be associated with lending-related charges to clients. Therefore, they show the following characteristics:

- high levels of retail lending;
- high levels of customer funding vs. total funding;
- high levels of net interest income vs. net operating income ratio;
- low levels of trading portfolio.

Later on, we will explain how Corporate and Investment Banking is related to investment banks and universal banks more than to retail banks. Lending is among the activities of Corporate and Investment Banking, but it is to be considered as a source of support for the other CIB business areas rather than a core activity. These aspects will be analyzed in Chapter 3.

An interesting concept that must be mentioned is that of the **private bank**, often referred to as wealth management (which, to be more precise, is the broader category to which private banking services belong). Private banking consists of offering personalized wealth management services to high-net-worth individuals (HNWIs). In general, these include advisory services related to vehicles for real estate planning, hereditary succession planning, or for the purchase of financial assets and the use of hedging derivatives against large blocks of share packages. Traditionally, high-net-worth individuals may need a higher service level, product offer, and sales staff with respect to other clients. Parallel to the recent increase of wealthy investors, the demand for sophisticated financial solutions and skills has increased worldwide.

1.4 Corporate and Investment Banking: A definition

Following a short introduction to the definition of Corporate and Investment Banking, this chapter will provide an analysis of the strategic models of CIB, focusing on the following three main approaches: the global model, the international model, and the local model.

1.4.1 The fundamentals of Corporate and Investment Banking

In recent years, the changes in the economic and legislative landscape and the growing complexity of globalization and liberalization have influenced and modified the management and financial structure of the banking model. Besides the "traditional" model of the commercial bank, focused on the activities of collecting and investing savings, which are the foundation of an economic model based on interest margins, the Corporate and Investment Banking (CIB) world grew in importance, orienting itself towards offering services to *corporate clients* and operating in capital markets (*investment banking*) where fees are collected.

Notwithstanding the renewed importance of Corporate and Investment Banking functions, a single, global definition of the term does not yet exist; for this reason, the classic vision of investment banking is counter posed to the emerging perspectives representing the evolution of the new market.

As a consequence of Corporate and Investment Banking activities, the role of banks is changing, and does its most characteristic function, that of providing credit. *Lending* is no longer a *core* activity, but a supporting element, integrated into the planning of *advisory services*, financial consultancy, and more structured processes and services. It follows that, in a broader vision, Corporate and Investment Banking could be defined as a structured and organized financial services system, planned, implemented, and managed by financial intermediaries and directed towards enterprises, financial institutions (the so-called FIG, i.e. Financial Institutions Group) and public entities. The breakdown of Corporate and Investment Banking activities and business will be addressed in Chapter 3, where we will determine both the taxonomy and the contents. However, it is important to stress from the beginning that Corporate and Investment Banking is a business which around the world is characterized by some distinctive overall features, which represent its fundamental DNA: a strong orientation to designing and implementing very customized solutions, a strong sense of advisory underlying the support for customers' decision-making processes, a tension towards innovative solutions, an inclination to cross-selling to support customers' decisions throughout their life-cycle, the concept of scale and size. When we explore the understanding of business in chapter 3, the reasons underlying all of these statements will become evident.

1.4.2 The evolution of Corporate and Investment Banking

The lack of a shared definition and the objective challenge in building the framework that delineates Corporate and Investment Banking activities is often attributable to the strong influence of the underlying financial and cultural system. For instance, in the United States CIBs are frequently recognized as investment banks, an incomplete (and obsolete) term which was influenced by the predominance of a market model centered on the subscription and negotiation of financial instruments on capital markets. To the contrary, in the United Kingdom, CIBs were historically influenced by *merchant banking activities*, and therefore it is common to refer to CIBs as *merchant banks*. Lastly, in Europe and Japan, countries where universal banks are most common, the generic term "bank" is often used as a synonym of CIB. Regardless of the numerous and different terminologies, the determinants at the basis of Corporate and Investment Banking are widespread and shared. They are the following:

- Prevalence of consulting and advisory activities;
- Strong and continuous interaction with customers' financial choices;
- Medium-large operations with respect to a commercial bank;
- A strong international perspective;
- A client portfolio composed of enterprises (SMEs and large companies), financial institutions, and governing bodies (i.e. FIG).

It is important to stress that despite the evolution and new challenges, such as disruption due to technology and big data, the crisis resulting from Covid-19, the asymmetric evolution of countries towards the globe?, privatization or nationalization in various countries, the needs of customers remain, even in different forms. Moreover, the CIB business can be a stand-alone activity or it can be inserted within the spectrum of universal banking activities. For this reason, we have to consider the business of banks as a puzzle in which three large business are feasible: Corporate and Investment Banking, Retail Banking, and Private Banking. For each business, the purpose is to match products with customers. Each bank must make a strategic choice as to whether it makes sense to manage the three together (universal bank strategy) or to focus on one of the three, as many small/regional banks do by operating only in the retail banking sector and doing some private banking. The strategic decision is obviously driven by the legacy of the bank, the skills required, the valuation of synergies, and the expected profitability. What is clear is that the three businesses represent three different worlds.

1.4.3 Strategic models of the Corporate and Investment Banking system

The strategic model is the foundation of the Corporate and Investment Banking system and defines the reference framework in which the medium to long-term activities of financial intermediaries can be found. The models delineate the strategic placement of the players in the sector, and are analyzed, structured, and implemented according the following three main elements of the C-P-M model:

- **Customers:** evaluation of the depth of the customer portfolio, resulting in the classification of customers according to their type (public or private entities, corporate or not) and size (small, medium, large);
- **Products:** analysis of the breadth of services offered with reference to the seven areas of business of CIB;
- **Markets:** investigation of the geographic areas and industrial sectors covered.

The strategic borders of each market player's activities are often delineated by a mix of endogenous factors, essentially referring to long-term management plans, and exogenous factors, i.e. reflection on the economic environment. The impact linked to the interaction with the surrounding economic environment is often due to the following factors:

- the historical and cultural background of the country of reference (i.e. South America for Spanish banks, North Africa for French banks, Commonwealth regions for British banks, etc.);
- legislative principles and regulations;
- size of the most important clients;
- size of the reference country;
- availability of financial resources;
- trends and political dynamics of the reference country.

At this point, on the basis of the concepts introduced, empirical evidence suggests the existence of the following three strategic models of Corporate and Investment Banking:

- Global model;
- International model;
- Local or domestic model.

The intermediaries that adopt the **global model** follow a global strategy on all the C-P-M elements, offering a wide and complete range of CIB services to clients from (ideally) every country in the world. Actually, since the very definition of an integrated system of business areas is clearly complex, efficiently offering every service for every client at global level could be deemed as impossible. Therefore, the client portfolio is often limited to large corporations and public entities and coordinated through a global network structured in headquarters (HQs), legal entities, branches, and country managers.

On the one hand, this model surely takes advantage of numerous benefits deriving from the strong global network, the presence of economies of scale, the ability to sustain conspicuous investments in R&D, and diversification. However, besides the benefits, some clear limits emerge from the administrative complexity linked to relations with medium-size clients, the definition of an optimal organizational structure, conflicts of interest, and lastly, an efficient control system.

The global approach is adopted by heterogeneous groups of financial intermediaries with intrinsically different cultural and historical profiles. Apart from the traditional big American players (i.e. JP Morgan, Goldman Sachs, Bank of America Merrill Lynch, Morgan Stanley), the global approach is also being followed by historical Japanese banks (i.e. Nomura and Mitsubishi), European mixed banks (i.e. Deutsche Bank, UBS, Credit Suisse), and big international conglomerates (i.e. Citigroup), together with new emerging Chinese players.

The **international model** follows a similar approach to the one just described, thus showing global features along the three C-P-M lines. The only difference between the two models regards the market profile, which is confined to specific geographic areas. In brief, the model offers a complete range of CIB services to all the clients with their operational headquarters in a determined country or regional cluster (i.e. Europe, Asia, Latin America, etc.). In this way, administrative complexity is sharply reduced, allowing for the expansion of the client portfolio to medium-size corporations and public entities.

The international strategic approach offers benefits similar to the global model, which essentially refer to network breadth, economies of scale, the ability to sustain higher R&D expenses, and diversification; these are associated with the benefits deriving from a more focused strategy that allows the financial intermediary to develop deeper knowledge of the countries served.

The disadvantages linked to the complexity of structuring an optimal and efficient organizational structure and to conflict of interest risk are still present, and are paired with the lower competences of players in managing global deals, if compared to their counterparts following the global approach. Furthermore, it is clear that the broader client portfolio makes the coordination of large and medium-sized firms' needs more difficult.

There exists no clear *fil rouge* among players that opt for an international strategy. Besides big European banking groups (i.e. BNP Paribas, RBS, ABN Amro, Unicredit, Santander, Barclays Capital), we also find historic American credit institutions (i.e. Wachovia, Wells Fargo), Asian financial intermediaries (i.e. Bank of China, CITIC, HSBC), Australian and South American financial intermediaries (i.e. Banco ITAU, Samba Financial Group, Macquarie Group).

The last strategic approach is represented by the **local model**, in which financial intermediary activities are limited to a single country or regional cluster, and thus are undoubtedly more limited with respect to the global and international strategies. Notwithstanding the greater focus of the geographic scope, players applying this model can still display global elements across the C-P-M areas; for instance, there are (infrequent) cases in which the offer range of CIB services is addressed to all the potential clients within the geographic scope. The lack of access to economies of scale could be an obstacle to the development of a complete product portfolio, but at the same time, the fewer administrative complexities ease the consolidation of the relationship with medium-sized clients.

From the client's perspective, the model's limited geographic scope is a disadvantage when its activities are performed on a global scale, thus requiring global and international professional competences in managing the deal. For this reason, intermediaries that adopt a local strategic approach are characterized by a portfolio of medium-sized clients, as they do not have an organizational structure suitable to satisfy the needs of larger clients.

The benefits and limits of the local model are clear. On the one side, players can rely on stronger and more complete knowledge of the country and can be able to easily consolidate relationships with corporate clients and medium-sized FIGs present in the area. On the other side, the disadvantages are attributable to the lack of economies of scale and of a global network, to weak knowledge regarding global and international deals, and to low brand recognition and reputation outside of the geographic scope.

This approach is often used by European universal banks and financial boutiques (i.e. Calyon Crédit Agricole, Intesa San Paolo, Mediobanca, Commerzbank, Dresdner Kleinworth, Societé General, Fortis, Rothschild, Lazard, ING, etc.), and in some Japanese credit institutions (i.e. Sumitomo, Mitzhuo).

In conclusion, the three strategic profiles described above are structurally and temporally stable. Nevertheless, a strong dynamism and variability has been noticed over time in the approaches adopted by single players, with continuous evolution from local to global and international models, which have often resulted in substantial investments in growth processes and M&A operations that have reshaped the dynamics of the sector.

Questions and answers

1. *What are the main types of inefficiencies affecting financial markets? Provide a brief description.*
   Inefficiencies linked to transaction costs, to information asymmetries, and to risks. Section 1.1 can serve as reference for their description.

2. *Provide a brief introduction to the main functions of a bank.*
   Monetary function, credit function, financial function. Refer to section 1.2 to define them.

3. *Briefly describe the key areas of a bank's balance sheet.*
   Section 1.3 and Figure 1.2 should be used as reference.

4. *Provide a definition of off-balance sheet (OBS) activities, stating their pros and cons.*
   Off-balance sheet assets are defined as activities which, when a contingent event occurs, move onto the asset side of the balance sheet or an income item is real-

ized in the income statement. Conversely, off-balance sheet liabilities are defined as activities which, when a contingent event occurs, move onto the liability side of the balance sheet or an expense item is realized in the income statement. By undertaking OBS activities, banks hope to earn additional fee income to complement declining margins or spreads on their traditional lending business. However, OBS activities can involve risks that add to the overall insolvency exposure of a financial intermediary.

5. *Briefly describe the key areas of a bank's income statement.*
   Section 1.3 and Figure 1.3 should be used as reference.

6. *Identify for each key business model the key characteristics of their financials.*
   Investment bank:
   - high levels of trading portfolio and fees income vs net operating income ratio;
   - low levels of retail lending;
   - low levels of customer funding vs total financing;
   - low levels of net interest income vs net operating income ratio.

   Universal bank:
   - intermediate levels of customer funding vs total financing;
   - intermediate levels of trading portfolio;
   - intermediate levels of net interest income vs net operating income ratio.

   Retail lender:
   - high levels of retail lending;
   - high levels of customer funding vs total financing;
   - high levels of net interest income vs net operating income ratio;
   - low levels of trading portfolio.

7. *A financial intermediary presents the financial statement displayed below. Identify the business model followed by the bank and compute the main financial ratios.*

Balance Sheet

ASSETS		LIABILITIES	
Cash and cash equivalents	500	Deposits from banks	1500
Financial assets held for trading	1500	Deposits from customers	4000
Loans to banks	1000	Debt securities issued	1000
Loans to customers	5000	Other liabilities (from provisions)	2000
Other financial assets	1000	EQUITY	1500
Property, plants, real estate	1000		

Income Statement

Net interest (and dividends) income	65
Net fees and commissions income	20
Net trading income	15
Operating income	100
Operating costs (administrative expenses, payrolls, etc.)	40
Amortisation and depreciation	20
Operating profit (or loss)	40
Write down loans and provisions	7
Net operating profit (or loss)	33
Other margins and provisions	18
Profit before tax	15
Taxes	5
Net Profit	10

Retail lender. Ratios:

- Trading portfolio and fees income on net operating income: 35%;
- Customer funding on total financing: 73%;
- Net interest income on net operating income: 65%.

8. *A financial intermediary presents the financial statement displayed below. Identify the business model followed by the bank and compute the main financial ratios.*

Balance Sheet

ASSETS		LIABILITIES	
Cash and cash equivalents	500	Deposits from banks	1800
Financial assets held for trading	5000	Deposits from customers	500
Loans to banks	1500	Debt securities issued	4700
Loans to customers	400	Other liabilities (from provisions)	2000
Other financial assets	1600	EQUITY	1000
Property, plants, real estate	1000		

Income Statement

Net interest (and dividends) income	15
Net fees and commissions income	45
Net trading income	40
Operating income	100
Operating costs (administrative expenses, payrolls, etc.)	30
Amortisation and depreciation	15
Operating profit (or loss)	55
Write down loans and provisions	5
Net operating profit (or loss)	50
Other margins and provisions	24
Profit before tax	26
Taxes	6
Net Profit	20

Investment Bank. Ratios:

- Trading portfolio and fee income to net operating income: 85%;
- Customer funding to total financing: 22%;
- Net interest income to net operating income: 15%.

9. *Compute the following ratios on Goldman Sachs and BNP Paribas financials, and verify that the characteristics of their respective models are respected:*
   - *Trading portfolio and fee income to net operating income;*
   - *Customer funding to total financing;*
   - *Net interest income to net operating income.*

   The characteristics are respected.

10. *What are the three directives of the C-P-M model?*
    - Clients: evaluation of the depth of the customer portfolio, resulting in the classification of customers according to their type (public or private entities, corporate or not) and size (small, medium, large);
    - Products: analysis of the breadth of services offered with reference to the seven areas of business of CIB;
    - Markets: investigation of the geographical areas and industrial sectors covered.

11. *What are the three main strategic models of Corporate and Investment Banking? Provide a brief description.*
   Global model, international model, local or domestic model. Refer to section 1.4.2 as reference for the description.

12. *Associate each key strategic model with a few examples.*
   - Global approach: the traditional big American players (i.e. JP Morgan, Goldman Sachs, Bank of America Merrill Lynch, Morgan Stanley), historical Japanese banks (i.e. Nomura and Mitsubishi), European mixed banks (i.e. Deutsche Bank, UBS, Credit Suisse), and big international conglomerates (i.e. Citigroup);
   - International approach: big European banking groups (i.e. BNP Paribas, RBS, ABN Amro, Unicredit, Santander, Barclays Capital), historical American credit institutes (i.e. Bank Wachovia, Wells Fargo), Asian financial intermediaries (i.e. Bank of China, CITIC, HSBC), Australian and South American financial intermediaries (i.e. Banco ITAU, Samba Financial Group, Macquarie Group);
   - Local model: European universal banks and financial boutiques (i.e. Calyon Crédit Agricole, Intesa San Paolo, Mediobanca, Commerzbank, Dresdner Kleinworth, Societé General, Fortis, Rotschild, Lazard, ING, etc.), and some Japanese credit institutes (i.e. Sumitomo, Mitzhuo).

2 The Regulation of the Banking System and of Capital Adequacy

by Stefano Caselli and Marta Zava

2.1 Banking supervision

The objective of this chapter is to examine the framework of financial regulation and understand the various techniques for estimating capital requirements. The chapter starts by explaining the arguments in favour and against banking supervision and its approach, to then illustrate the several levels of the financial regulatory framework. Furthermore, it examines capital adequacy requirements, their function, and their estimation methods and supervisory procedures.

2.1.1 Why does banking supervision exist?

First of all, not all economists believe that banking supervision is necessary. A line of thought, attributable to Eugene F. Fama, assumes that the mix of activities of banking institutions, in both the short and long-term, will be driven by market forces. Therefore, the attempt to calibrate the best mix of banking portfolios through a regulatory framework is considered useless and harmful. Fama believes that banks are not regulated because they are special per se, but they become special because they are regulated. Thus, banks suffer a competitive disadvantage (due to all the costs sustained to fulfil legislative and regulatory requirements) with respect to other markets players, which are less regulated. This school of thought believes that without any type of structural regulation the market will be able to find the best possible allocation of resources and institutions mix. Further, the disadvantage attributable to regulation is converted into banking regulatory costs, which ultimately fall on clients.

To provide an example, we could state that the market cannot accept a firm, for instance a pharmaceutical firm, producing poisonous or lethal substances. Sooner or later it will be expelled. However, before the expulsion, the system will have to suffer severe damage (or externalities). For this reason, regulation and supervision of behaviour in potentially "dangerous" markets are important. The banking sector, since it trades money and other financial activities, is among these.

Since the Eighties, the literature that more had influence on banking regulation than any other has been intermediation theory, with a particular focus on transaction costs, uncertainty, and information asymmetries. It is based on the idea that markets can suffer imperfections that offer banks and other financial intermediaries the possibility to operate more efficiently. Thus, regulation should be conceived in such a way as to manage inefficiencies and reach an optimal market allocation.

In the meantime, imperfections could affect banking activity and should be regulated to reach equilibrium. Specifically, asymmetrical information theory provides many tools not only to explain the existence and crucial role of banks in the financial markets and the general economy, but also to interpret financial fluctuations and their recurrent deterioration into severe financial crises.

In the most recent crisis, the asymmetric information approach is divided into a few basic explanations with radically different political implications. The crucial differences are rooted in a different understanding of the evolution of the banking sector in the Eighties and in particular the crucial role played by securitization. To simplify the analysis, we focus on two opposing approaches: those of Frederic S. Mishkin (the *originate-to-distribute* hypothesis) and Gary Gorton (the *shadow banking* hypothesis, 2009).

The former hypothesis, *originate-to-distribute*, indicates a correction of the most significant deficiencies in the new banking model, repairing the distortions generated by investment banking, securitization, and shadow banking activities. Opinions diverge with regard to the most efficient and urgent measures to be adopted. In general, actions should be addressed towards the efficient repression of shadow banking and securitization, and all operations, thus including off-balance sheet operations, should be registered in the financial reports.

The latter hypothesis, *shadow banking*, is based on the observation that, over the past few years, a shadow banking system has greatly expanded; a system made up of financial intermediaries which facilitate the provision of credit in the entire global financial system, but whose members are not subject to regulatory supervision. Shadow banking also refers to all the unregulated activities performed by supervised entities. For instance, speculative funds, unlisted derivatives and other unlisted instruments are unregulated intermediaries, while credit default swaps (CDS) belong to the unregulated activities performed by supervised institutions. According to the supporters of the *originate-to-distribute* approach, they represent a degeneration of the traditional banking system and thus should be repressed. On the other hand, those who support the *shadow banking* approach believe that institutions that operate in this fashion should be controlled and regulated. To understand this crucial step, the recent evolution of the banking system should be seen from a long-term perspective with the idea that if we do not learn from history we are condemned to repeat the errors of the past.

The majority of economists agree on the fact that unregulated firms best serve the economy and costumers if markets are competitive. But in the majority of countries the banking sector is regulated. An underlying reason could be that banks produce money. To protect our money, banks should not be authorized to take hefty risks that could cause their failure. However, today the central bank controls money issuance. If people are worried about the failure of a bank, they would transfer their funds to another bank. Naturally, the failure of a bank is expensive for some people, but the failure of a firm comparable in size would have similar effects.

Another possible reason lies in preserving the trust of the public in the banking system. If people do not have trust in the system, everyone could try to withdraw money at the same time. In this case, a bank will fail because of the losses due to the fast sale of assets necessary to fulfil its liquidity needs. However, this argument has several flaws: first of all, on very few occasions have we witnessed runs on banks which were not insolvent.

A third reason is that deposit insurance is required by law or by custom in the most of the countries. If depositors are protected from losses, they have very few reasons to be worried.

This last reason solves a few issues, but allows some banks to incur greater risks. The cost of that risk is sustained, first of all, by well-managed banks, which have to save the depositors of failing banks through insurance premiums or valuations, and subsequently by taxpayers once insurance funds are exhausted and the government has to cover the cost. Nevertheless, it is not necessary or desirable for those who regulate or supervise banks to limit their activities. The logical conclusion is that banks must keep a sufficient amount of capital at their disposal, so that only stockholders will have to sustain the cost of losses and the mistakes committed by their managers.

2.1.2 The style of banking supervision

As we mentioned, the objectives of supervision mainly involve the stability and efficiency of the banking system. Yet these two objectives could be in conflict with each other. If the aim is to obtain efficiency though a more competitive banking services market, all the implications stemming from competitiveness have to be accepted, among which is a higher turnover of institutions, since some of them will not be able to sustain the economic pressure. It means accepting bank failures. However, this would run counter to the objective of stability and the guarantee on banking liabilities (money).

We find ourselves faced with a dilemma: if we aim for stability the system must have very few banks (ideally only one, which could not fail). If we aim for efficiency, we should grant access to whoever would like to enter the system and we should avoid saving inefficient institutions. In the latter case, the issue of protecting savings arises, which at least in Italy, is a constitutional principle (article 47).

In the past decades, the supervisory authorities have preferred to pursue the stability objective. For this reason, European banks had to face obligations and prohibitions aimed at reducing the intensity of competition. In the second half of the Eighties, the regulatory model became more sensitive to the efficiency objective, opening the market to banking institutions from several other countries. To maintain an adequate level of stability, the supervisory style changed radically: it shifted from structural interventions (such as entry barriers, restrictions on movement of branches and legal entities, restrictions on mergers and acquisitions, etc.) to so-called prudential interventions, aimed at strengthening the structure of banks' balance sheets, mainly through capital interventions.

For this purpose, to avoid the introduction of national rules in a system seeking a global approach, the Basel Committee on Banking Supervision (BCBS) was introduced. Its mandate was to propose uniform rules, applying at least to banks with activities in more than one country, inspired by the principle of *levelling the playing field* and oriented towards reaching capital adequacy with respect to the risks undertook by each bank. Given an increase in risk, and thus of the consequent potential losses, the capital must be adjusted. The criticism that this set of rules is too expensive for banks and their shareholders is addressed with the assumption that costumers are not able to assess the safety and soundness of banking institutions. Prudential regulation is necessary due to the imperfect information held by costumers and the agency issues connected to the nature of the activities performed by financial institutions. Apart from any potential systemic distortions, there are well-founded reasons to prudentially regulate a financial institution when: the institution performs a fiduciary role, costumers are not able to assess the safety and soundness of the institutions at the moment of the purchase or deal, or a potential request for a refund from an insurance fund or a compensation system exists (since the costs of an individual institution's risky behaviour could weigh on the whole society through the need for public intervention).

The principle of prudential supervision is persuasive but based on an assumption that is difficult to apply: that banks and their regulators are potentially able to estimate risks and losses, and thus to determine the adequate level of regulatory capital. This is a very complex process for to several reasons, among which are the following: risks are heavily interrelated and subject to rapid changes, future loss estimates may not be precise (or they may be only from a probabilistic perspective), and the ability of capital to cover all the losses depends on the actual capacity of the items considered in the balance sheet by the supervisory authorities. Lastly, when extraordinary events occur, risk estimation models could be fragile.

The crisis highlighted issues both in the previous regulation and in the behaviour of banks, such as the following:

a) Low levels of capital: many of the banks asking for public intervention had pre-crisis capital ratios above the minimum threshold;
b) High pro-cyclicality, which intensified the crisis, especially with regards to the credit process;
c) High interconnection between large financial institutions, which increased the risk of contagion;
d) High rate of debt (or leverage ratio) of banks;
e) Low pre-crisis attention to liquidity risk, from both the banks' managers and the supervisory authorities.

To strengthen the prudential system, after the crisis the authorities introduced a new set of rules, including: increased capital requirements in both qualitative and quantitative terms, introduction of a maximum leverage ratio, new liquidity requirements, higher capital ratios related to market risk and counterparty risk, the countercyclical capital buffer, and higher capital requirements for systemic banks (the ones at higher risk of contagion).

However, regulation also intervened through the imposition of rules aimed at introducing structural elements and strengthening banks' internal audit and risk culture, to avoid decisions that are excessively speculative and hyper-speculative (as Minsky believes). The sum of this kind of rules is defined as internal governance, because they strengthen control within financial institutions.

2.2 The financial regulatory framework

The financial regulatory framework refers to the set of authorities and institutions which regulate and supervise the financial system. In Europe, three levels are to be considered (the international framework, the European Union framework, and the national framework), while in other countries, for instance in the U.S. or in India, only the international framework and the national framework are considered, respectively the Fed and the Reserve Bank of India (RBI). For the purpose of the chapter, we will focus on the European architecture.

All financial frameworks should cover both the macroprudential and the microprudential perspective. Both aim at financial stability, but the macroprudential perspective focuses its attention on the stability of the financial system as a whole and its links with the macroeconomy, while the microprudential perspective focuses on the safety and soundness of individual banking institutions. The tasks are complementary, but they must not be performed by one single actor to avoid conflicts of interest and conflicts in their execution due to their inherent differences. In fact, in addition to the distinct focus, the macroprudential perspective focuses on long-run objectives adopting a top-down approach and stressing correlation across institutions, while the microprudential perspective targets short-run objectives using a bottom-up approach and not considering correlation across institutions.

2.2.1 How is the financial regulatory framework structured?

The financial regulatory framework is split according to two dimensions: the type of regulation (macroprudential and microprudential) and the level (international, supranational, and national). The case of Europe is displayed in **Figure 2.1**. Starting from the international framework, the institution in charge of the macroprudential side is the Financial Stability Board (FSB), while the one responsible for the microprudential tasks is the Basel Committee on Banking Supervision (BCBS). Together they form the **Bank for International Settlements (BIS)**.

On the macroprudential side, the **Financial Stability Board (FSB)** is an international body that promotes international financial stability, monitoring and making recommendations about the global financial system. It was established in April 2009 as the successor to the Financial Stability Forum (FSF), and it is composed

Figure 2.1 **Financial Regulatory Framework in Europe**

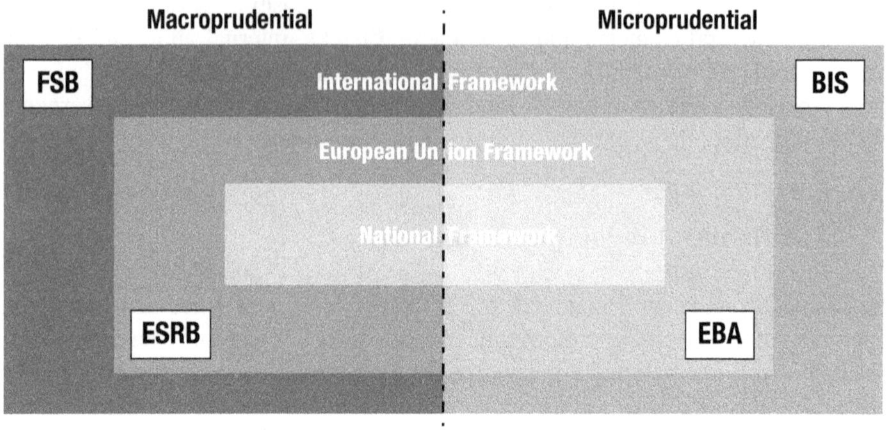

of 68 members, comprising 24 countries and other institutions such as the BIS, the ECB, the IMF, and the European Commission. The FSB assesses the vulnerabilities affecting the global financial system and identifies the necessary actions to address them, promotes coordination and information exchange among the authorities within the financial regulatory framework, pushes for the implementation of agreed commitments, standards and policy recommendations, and monitors and provides advice on best practices in meeting regulatory standards. It must be pointed out that the FSB's decisions are not legally binding, and therefore the organization has to operate through moral suasion and peer pressure.

On the microprudential side, the **Basel Committee on Banking Supervision (BCBS)** is the primary global standard setter for the prudential regulation of banks and provides a forum for cooperation on banking supervisory matters. It was established at the end of 1974 to solve the problems arising with the internationalization of banking activities, namely duplications and gaps in regulation and supervision. Since its creation, the Basel Committee has expanded its membership from the G10 to 28 different jurisdictions. Its main activities involve the exchange of information on developments in the banking sector and financial markets – aimed at identifying current or emerging risks for the global financial system, the sharing of supervisory issues, approaches, and techniques to promote common understanding, the establishment and promotion of global standards for the regulation and supervision of banks, and the recognition of regulatory and supervisory gaps – aimed at overcoming them. Similarly to the FSB, the BCBS also does not have legal force, but it relies on its members' commitments. Its main publications are the following:

- **The Concordat** (1975): sets out principles for sharing supervisory responsibilities for international banks between the different authorities involved;

- **Basel Core Principles for effective banking supervision** (1997): after several revisions, the document now includes 29 principles, covering supervisory powers, the need for early intervention and timely supervisory actions, supervisory expectations of banks, and compliance with supervisory standards;
- **Basel Capital Accords**: set of recommendations for regulations in the banking industry. Their purpose is to ensure that financial institutions have enough capital to meet obligations and absorb unexpected losses.

The Basel Capital Accords have evolved extensively over time, resulting in Basel I (1992), Basel II (2007), Basel III (2013), and Basel IV (2017). In Europe, Basel III was translated into Regulation 575/2013, better known as the Capital Requirements Regulation (CRR), Directive 2013/36/EU, better known as the Capital Requirements Directive (CRD IV), and the Binding Technical Standards.

With reference to the European Union framework, the two relevant authorities are the European Systemic Risk Board (ESRB) and the European Banking Authority (EBA). The **European Systemic Risk Board (ESRB)** is responsible for the macroprudential oversight of the EU financial system and the prevention and mitigation of systemic risk. It was established in 2010, following the recommendations of the Larosière report, and it is composed of the National Macroprudential Authorities of the 28 Member States, 2 observers (Norway and Iceland), and the European Institutions (ECB, EC, EBA, etc.). Its main functions are to identify systemic risks and classify them according to their priority, issue warnings and recommendations addressed to the EU as a whole, the European Commission, the Member States or the supervisory authorities (not directly to the credit institutions), and monitor the actions taken in response to warnings and recommendations. It issues warnings and recommendations to face potential systemic risks, which are not binding, but are governed by the rule of "comply or explain."

The **European Banking Authority (EBA)** is an independent European Union authority which works to ensure effective and consistent prudential regulation and supervision across the European banking sector. It was established on January 1, 2011 and took over all existing responsibilities and duties of the Committee of European Banking Supervisors. Its main decision-making body is the Board of Supervisors, composed of representatives of the 28 national supervisory authorities. The EBA contributes to the creation of a single set of harmonized prudential rules for financial institutions throughout the European Union (the Single Rulebook) and promotes the convergence of supervisory practices to ensure a harmonized application of prudential rules (the Single Handbook). Furthermore, it assesses risks and vulnerabilities in the European banking sector through regular risk assessment reports and the pan-European stress test, conducted once every two years. Lastly, the EBA can produce a number of regulatory and non-regulatory documents. Regulatory documents are essentially the Binding Technical Standards (BTS), which comprise the Regulation Technical Standards (RTS) and the Implementing Technical Standards (ITS). Non-regulatory documents are every guideline, recommendation, Q&A, and ad-hoc or regular report.

2.2.2 Banking Union

The Banking Union refers to the project of shifting banking-sector policy instruments from the national to the European level. It is the third step of the formation of the European Union, after free movement and the single currency, and before the fiscal union. As the financial crisis evolved into the euro area debt crisis, it became clear that deeper integration of the banking system was needed for the euro area countries. Non-euro countries can participate upon request and subject to a comprehensive assessment of their institutions.

The main objectives are to break the bank-sovereign vicious circle (correlation between sovereign risk and bank risk), to ensure that banks are robust and able to withstand any future financial crises, to prevent situations where taxpayers' money is used to save failing banks, to reduce market fragmentation by harmonizing financial sector rules, and to strengthen financial stability in the euro area and the European Union as a whole.

The three Banking Union Pillars are the Single Supervisory Mechanism (SSM), aimed at having a uniform approach to banking supervision, the Single Resolution Mechanism (SRM), to have uniform rules for banking resolution, and the European Deposit Insurance Scheme (EDIS), to offer uniform insurance coverage for retail depositors.

The **Single Supervisory Mechanism (SSM)** is an EU-level system for prudential supervision of credit institutions, whose purpose is to ensure enhanced supervision of the European banking sector. Its main objectives are to supervise credit institutions' compliance with prudential requirements, detect weaknesses at an early stage, and ensure action is taken to correct those weaknesses, in order to prevent the situation from developing into a threat to overall financial stability. It is composed of the European Central Bank (ECB) and the National Supervisory Authorities (NCA) of the participating EU member states. The SSM entered into force in 2014 with Regulation (EU) No 1024/2013.

The **Single Resolution Mechanism (SRM)** is an EU-level system for resolution of credit institutions, which aims at ensuring an orderly resolution of failing banks with minimal costs to taxpayers and to the real economy. Its main objectives are to strengthen confidence in the banking sector, prevent bank runs and contagion, minimize the negative relationship between banks and sovereigns, and eliminate fragmentation in the internal market for financial services. The SRM is structured into the Single Resolution Board (SRB) and the Single Resolution Fund (SRF). The former is an EU-level resolution authority, which operates as the main decision-making body in the SRM, while the latter is a fund established at the supranational level and financed by the banking sector. It is to be used for resolving failing banks, after other options, such as the bail-in tool, have been exhausted. The SRM entered into force in 2016 following Regulation (EU) No 806/2014.

The **European Deposit and Insurance Scheme (EDIS)**, as the name says, is a deposit insurance scheme for bank deposits, aimed at providing a stronger and more uniform degree of insurance coverage. Its main objectives are to unify depositor protection across the European Union, prevent panic withdrawals (or bank runs) in cases in which a bank becomes unviable, and contribute to overall financial stability in the single market. The EDIS would apply to deposits below €100,000 of all banks in the banking union. When one of these banks is placed into insolvency or in resolution and it is necessary to pay out deposits or to finance their transfer to another bank, the EDIS will intervene. In November 2015, the Commission adopted a proposal to set up an EDIS. However, no final agreement has been reached yet because there is no consensus among the states.

2.2.3 The SSM explained

The SSM is one of the largest banking supervisory authorities in the world. Currently 115 banking groups (Significant Institutions – SIs) in 19 countries are under direct ECB supervision (almost 82% of euro-area banking assets).[1] Around 2,874 smaller institutions (Less Significant Institutions - LSIs) are directly supervised by the National Competent Authorities (NCAs), with the ECB being responsible for the system at large.[2] The banking assets under direct and indirect ECB supervision amount to more than 23 trillion Euros (about 2.1 times euro-area GDP).[3]

A credit institution is considered significant if any one of the following conditions is met: the total value of its assets exceeds €30 billion or 20% of national GDP (unless the total value of its assets is below €5 billion); it is one of the three most significant credit institutions established in a Member State; it is a recipient of direct assistance from the European Stability Mechanism; or the total value of its assets exceeds €5 billion and the ratio of its cross-border assets/liabilities in more than one other participating Member State to its total assets/liabilities is above 20%. Regardless of the fulfilment of these criteria, the SSM may declare an institution significant to ensure the consistent application of high-quality supervisory standards.

As mentioned, the Single Supervisory Mechanism (SSM) combines the European Central Bank (ECB) and the National Supervisory Authorities (NCA) of the participating EU member states. Therefore, duties are shared among institutions. Some, defined as common procedures, are performed jointly by the two institutions: authorizations, acquisitions of qualifying holdings, and withdrawal of authorizations fall in this category. Moreover, the ECB is responsible for the overall functioning of the SSM, the direct supervision of Significant Institutions (SI), and the indirect supervision of Less Significant Institutions (LSI). The NCAs are responsible for the direct supervision of Less Significant institutions (LSI) and collaboration on the supervision of Significant Institutions (SI).

The tasks performed in direct banking supervision are to conduct superviso-

[1] As at March 2019
[2] As at March 2019
[3] As at end of 2017

ry reviews, on-site inspections and investigations, ensure compliance with EU prudential rules, authorize the opening of branches, and ensure proper corporate governance. As mentioned, direct supervision related to SIs is performed by the ECB, while direct supervision related to LSIs is performed by NCAs. The tasks related to indirect supervision are different for SIs and LSIs. In regard to SIs, the NCAs are involved through participation on the Joint Supervisory Teams (JST), On Site Inspections (OSI), and the Supervisory Board of the ECB, which takes the final decisions. When performing the indirect supervision of LSIs, on the other hand, the ECB issues guides and instructions for the supervision of the LSI, monitors the supervision carried out by the NCA, may request any information of the NCA, and may decide to directly supervise any bank in the SSM area.

Moreover, supervision is divided into on-going supervision and on-site supervision. On-going supervision is conducted by the JSTs, which include staff from both NCAs and the ECB. Its main duties are to analyse the reporting information, hold regular and ad hoc meetings, and conduct on-going risk analyses. It results in the SREP (Supervisory Revision and Evaluation Process), which concludes with the prescription of ad hoc supervisory measures for each institution. On the other hand, on-site supervision is conducted by a Head of Mission (HOM) and the team members appointed by the ECB in consultation with the NCAs. The need for an OSI, as well as its scope, is determined by the JST in the context of the SREP. The report is then sent to the JST, based on which the JST is responsible for preparing recommendations.

The SSM is structured as in **Figure 2.2**.

The **Supervisory Board** discusses, plans and carries out the ECB's supervisory tasks. It proposes draft decisions to the Governing Council under the "non-objection procedure". The **Governing Council** is the highest authority of the ECB. It makes decisions on monetary policy and is ultimately responsible for the supervisory function. The **Mediation Panel** ensures a separation between monetary policy and the supervisory tasks. It resolves differences of views regarding an objection by the Governing Council to a draft decision of the Supervisory Board. The **Administrative Board of Review** produces internal administrative reviews of the ECB's supervisory decisions, ensuring that such decisions are compliant with rules and procedures. Administrative reviews may be requested by any person or legal entity directly affected by an ECB supervisory decision.

The SSM has several decision-making procedures in place, but the most-known and commonly used is the "non-objection procedure," outlined in **Figure 2.2**. The Supervisory Board submits a draft decision to the Governing Council. If the latter does not object to a proposed draft decision within a set period of time that may not exceed ten working days, the decision is deemed to be adopted. It may adopt or object to draft decisions but not change them. The Mediation Panel, as mentioned above, is meant to resolve differences of views expressed by the NCAs when objecting to a proposal in the context of the Governing Council.

We will now focus on the aspects related to the regulatory capital requirements that apply to financial institutions.

Figure 2.2 **Structure and decision-making bodies within the SSM: the non-objection procedure**

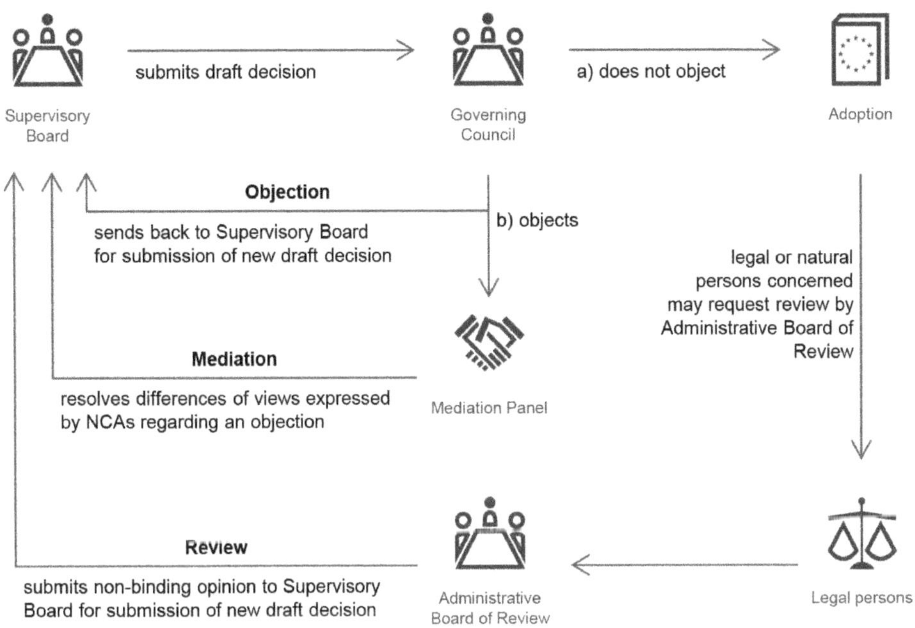

Source: ECB Banking Supervision

2.3 Regulatory capital requirements

2.3.1 Functions

The aim of regulatory capital requirements is to ensure that banks hold sufficient capital to meet their current and expected liabilities. But, the ultimate goal of banking supervision, and therefore of prudential capital requirements, is to strengthen the stability of a resilient and well-functioning banking sector which can fulfil its service-providing function to the economy.

From a microprudential perspective, capital requirements, also called own funds requirements, are set to ensure that financial institutions do not rely excessively on high-risk investments, or more in general, investments that substantially increase the risk of default. Moreover, a financial institution should have enough capital to cover its operational expenses and withdrawals. Thus, capital requirements ensure that banks stay solvent and avoid default, and in the meanwhile they ensure that depositors have access to funds.

From a macroprudential perspective, banks cannot be considered as "an island" but are interconnected: a shock to one can affect many. Furthermore, capital requirements can provide a means to compare and evaluate the soundness of institutions, and set industry standards.

Among the main drawbacks, it must be mentioned that higher capital requirements may reduce risk-taking activity by banks, and therefore the ability to invest and compete in the financial sector. Furthermore, the availability of funds and loans for customers could be lower. Lastly, costs for banks, that reflect on clients, for instance in borrowing costs, can easily rise.

Capital requirements for banks focus on Risk-weighted Assets (RWA), and are the sum of a bank's assets, weighted by risk. We will examine the computation of RWA in the second part of this chapter. Based on the RWA, the capital ratios are computed. Total capital requirements are defined on the basis of the minimum capital adequacy ratio (CAR) to be respected, and are subject to the other capital ratios to be met (e.g. CET1, Tier 2, etc.). The topic is tackled in the next sections of the book.

2.3.2 Capital Adequacy Ratio (CAR)

The Capital Adequacy Ratio (CAR) helps make sure banks have sufficient capital to protect depositors' money, since a bank that has a good CAR has enough capital to absorb potential losses, and thus incurs less risk of becoming insolvent. Following the 2008 financial crisis, CAR requirements became stricter.

The Basel Committee defines the CAR as follows:

$$CAR = \frac{regulatory\ capital}{RWA}$$

Capital Adequacy Ratio

The Capital Adequacy Ratio measures a bank's capital in relation to its risk-weighted assets. The Basel Committee separates capital into Tier 1 capital and Tier 2 capital, based on its function and quality.

Tier 1 capital is the core capital held in reserve. It can be considered a proxy for a bank's financial health. Tier 1 capital is also defined as going-concern capital, since it is permanently and easily available to cushion losses suffered by a bank without impacting business operations. It is composed of both Common Equity Tier 1 (CET1) capital and Additional Tier 1 (AT1) capital. Common Equity Tier 1 capital (CET1) is the highest quality of regulatory capital, as it absorbs losses immediately when they occur. Additional Tier 1 capital (AT1) also provides loss absorption on a going-concern basis, although AT1 instruments do not meet all the criteria for CET1. Tier 1 capital consists of equity capital, ordinary share capital, intangible assets, and audited revenue reserves.

Tier 2 capital is gone-concern capital. That is, when a bank fails, Tier 2 instruments must absorb losses before depositors and general creditors do. It is used to absorb losses if a bank loses all its Tier 1 capital. Tier 2 is composed of unaudited retained earnings, unaudited reserves, and general loss reserves. As can be inferred, it has lower quality, it is less liquid, and thus more difficult to measure. For the cited reasons, it is also known as supplementary capital.

Risk-weighted assets (RWA) are the sum of a bank's assets, weighted by risk. We will examine the computation of RWA in the second part of this chapter.

The CAR level is set by the Basel Committee. Under Basel III, the minimum mandatory ratios for each type of capital are defined as in **Table 2.1**:

Table 2.1 Tier 1 and Tier 2 capital composition

Tier 1 (going concern)	Common Equity Tier 1 (CET1)	Sum of common shares (equivalent for non-joint stock companies*) and stock surplus, retained earnings, other comprehensive income, qualifying minority interest and regulatory adjustments	CET1 >4.5%
	Additional Tier 1 (AT1)	Sum of capital instruments meeting the criteria for AT1 and related surplus, additional qualifying minority interest and regulatory adjustments	CET1 + AT1 >6%
Tier 2 (gone concern)		Sum of capital instruments meeting the criteria for Tier 2 and related surplus, additional qualifying minority interest, qualifying loan loss provisions and regulatory adjustments	CET1 + AT1 + Tier 2 >8

* The standard requires instruments issued by non-joint stock companies to meet a set of criteria to be deemed equivalent to common shares and included in CET1.

Source: Definition of capital under Basel III – Executive Summary (BCBS, 2019)

Lastly, the Basel Committee imposed the express requirement that all capital instruments must be able to fully absorb losses at the so-called point of non-viability (PoNV) before taxpayers are exposed to loss. The PoNV condition requires all AT1 and Tier 2 instruments to be capable of being converted into common equity or written off. The trigger for the conversion/write-off is the earlier of either a decision of the relevant authority that the conversion/write-off is necessary, given that the bank is assessed to be non-viable, or a decision to inject public funds to prevent the bank's failure. This may happen based on either the authority's statutory powers or the contractual features of the capital instruments.

2.3.3 Basel: The three pillars

The three pillars prescribed by the Basel Committee can be summarized as follows.

Pillar I outlines the capital adequacy requirements, or minimum capital requirements. Under Basel I, it used to take into account only credit risk. Following the introduction of Basel II, it also started considering market risk and operational risk.

Box 2.1 ICAAP

The internal capital adequacy assessment process (ICAAP) is central in making banks more resilient and avoiding adverse situations. It is performed by the banks themselves, to ensure that they possess adequate capital resources in the long term to cover all of its material risks. Under the European legislation, the ICAAP, in accordance with the provisions in art. 73 of the CRV IV, must be prudent and conservative. ICAAP requirements state that the institution is expected to have in place sound, effective and comprehensive strategies and processes to assess and maintain capital that it considers adequate to cover the nature and level of the risks to which it is or might be exposed.
To better understand the ICAAP, we will walk through seven principles for the ICAAP set out in the ECB guide. The principles also concern the ILAAP (the internal liquidity adequacy assessment process), which we will not discuss. The first principle states that the management body is responsible for sound governance of the ICAAP. The Board and senior management team are expected to discuss and challenge the reports, and to produce and sign a statement of capital adequacy. The second principle defines the ICAAP as an integral part of the overall management framework. From this perspective, the internal processes and arrangements are expected to ensure that quantitative analysis of risks, as reflected in the ICAAP, is integrated into all material business activities and decisions. Furthermore, the links between the ICAAP and the risk appetite framework, or the recovery plan, should be clear and consistent.
Principle 3 states that the ICAAP provides a fundamental contribution to the continuity of the institution by ensuring its capital adequacy from different perspectives, i.e. the economic and the normative perspectives. The normative perspective is the banks' ability to fulfil its capital-related quantitative regulatory and supervisory requirements, and to cope with other external financial constraints, on an on-going basis. Otherwise, the economic capital is aimed at ensuring that risks are adequately covered by internal capital, and at supporting its strategy on an on-going basis.
Moving forward, principle 4 states that all material risks are identified and taken into account in the ICAAP, principle 5 states that internal capital is of high quality and clearly defined, and principle 6 that ICAAP risk quantification methodologies are adequate, consistent, and independently validated. Lastly, principle 7 specifies that regular stress testing is aimed at ensuring capital and liquidity adequacy in adverse circumstances.

Lastly, Basel III sets capital requirements for liquidity risk as well. In the second part of this chapter we will focus on the computation of minimum capital requirements.

Pillar II is the supervisory review. Its aim is to address all the risks for which the supervisor feels that the capital requirements outlined in Pillar I are not sufficient. It is based on the assessment of a bank's internal capital adequacy. Under Pillar II, financial institutions are obliged to conduct periodic internal capital adequacy assessments, defined as the ICAAP process. The intensity and extent of the process should be proportionate to the bank's risk profile. Furthermore, in the context of the ICAAP, a strategy to keep sufficient levels of regulatory capital ratios should be outlined. (**Box 2.1**)

Pillar II also includes the Supervisory Review and Evaluation (SREP) process through which supervisors review and evaluate a banks' ability to monitor its compliance with the regulatory capital ratios, and the strategies that a bank follows to fulfil its specific capital requirements. (**Box 2.2**)

Box 2.2 The SSM SREP

The SSM SREP represents an example of the SREP processes (**Figure 2.3**) implemented worldwide. The SREP gives supervisors a harmonised set of tools to examine a bank's risk profile from four different perspectives, called elements: business model, governance, capital, and liquidity. It is aimed at assessing the way in which a bank deals with its risks and where a bank stands in terms of capital and liquidity requirements, as well as its adequacy in term of internal arrangements and risk controls.

Figure 2.3 The SSM SREP

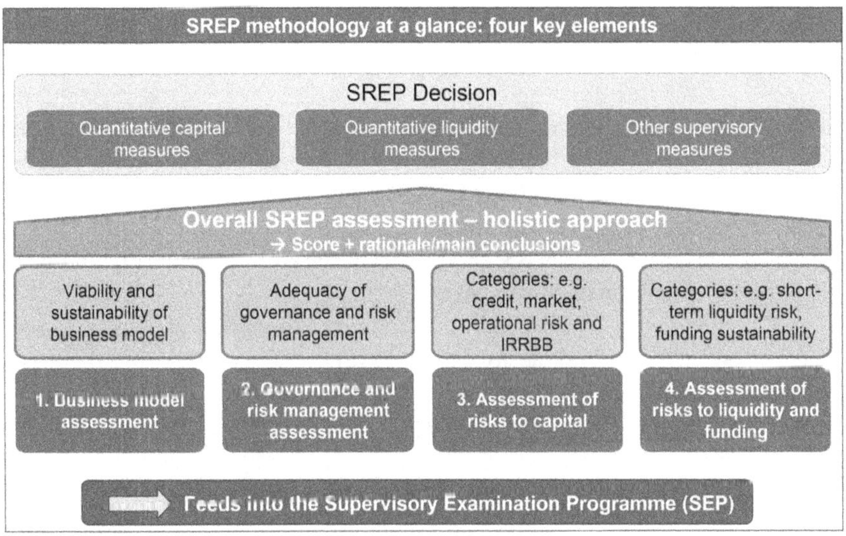

Source: ECB Banking Supervision

The first element, business model, assesses the sustainability and profitability of a bank's activities and business lines. The second element, governance and risk management, analyses the bank's organisational structure by monitoring its management bodies and checking whether risks are being managed properly. The third element, risks to capital, is performed on a risk specific basis, including credit risk, market risk, operational risk, and interest rate risk in the banking book (IRRBB) under normal and stressed conditions. The results feed into a preliminary determination of capital requirements. The fourth element, risks to liquidity and funding, focuses on short-term funding, long-term funding, and the institution's internal identified risks in normal and stressed scenarios. These assessments feed into a preliminary determination of a liquidity requirement to cover the risks and an assessment of liquidity adequacy.

For each element, the evaluation is conducted through a dedicated risk assessment system (RAS). The RAS is fed with data stemming from regular reporting, such as common reporting (COREP) and financial reporting (FINREP), qualitative information, and ad-hoc information obtained by JSTs on an on-going basis. For each of the four elements, the approach con-

sists of a quantitative perspective (risk level) and a qualitative perspective (risk control), each composed of three phases (data gathering, automated anchoring score, and supervisory judgement).
The key feature of SREP is that it is an on-going, quantitative and qualitative, forward-looking and proportionate assessment. To ensure a standardized approach, it applies constraint judgment through anchor points and SREP methodology. Moreover, each step is documented and justified to ensure accountability. The SREP applies a holistic approach, which takes into account all risks and mitigants, looks at the four elements together, and it is flexible enough to allow for all material aspects to be included. Lastly, the SREP is characterized by accountability: since it results in supervisory actions, high quality supervision is necessary.
The SREP has three main outcomes: a holistic, forward-looking assessment of the overall viability of the institution; issuance of decisions requiring banks to implement supervisory measures such as meeting their capital/liquidity requirement; and an input on the determination of the minimum level of supervisory engagement for a specific institution as part of the next Supervisory Examination Programme (SEP).

Lastly, Pillar II also gives indications on the capital structure (which we will examine in the next section), prescribing that regulatory capital should be kept above the minimum levels defined by Pillar I. Supervisors should ensure that banks maintain a capital level higher than the minimum. In cases where capital could potentially fall below the minimum level, supervisors must seek to intervene in the daily decision-making process in order to prevent this from happening.

Pillar III is market discipline. It is aimed at complementing the first and second pillar and it outlines a discipline for banks to follow when disclosing their capital structure, Tier 1 and Tier 2 requirements, and processes to assess the capital adequacy. Market discipline is ensured by making it mandatory to disclose relevant market information, in order to ensure that users of financial information receive the relevant information to make informed trading decisions and ensure market discipline.

2.3.4 Capital stack

Under European legislation, Common Equity Tier 1 (CET1), Additional Tier 1 (AT1), Tier 2 (T2), the Pillar II Requirement (P2R), the Combined Buffer Requirements (CBR) and the Pillar II Guidance (P2G) all form the capital stack, as displayed in **Figure 2.4**.

Pillar 1, the minimum capital requirement, comprises Common Equity Tier 1 (CET1), Additional Tier 1 (AT1), and Tier 2 (T2) capital, which we discussed amply above. Pillar II requirements are bank-specific and are defined according to the supervisory review process. Pillar I and Pillar II capital form the total SREP capital requirements (TSCR).

On top of TSCR, banks have to meet the Combined Buffer Requirements (CBR), in an amount sufficient for the so-called Maximum Distributable Amount (MDA) threshold to be reached. If a bank's total capital falls below the MDA threshold, supervisors will automatically restrict earnings distribution. Every institution is re-

Figure 2.4 Capital stack

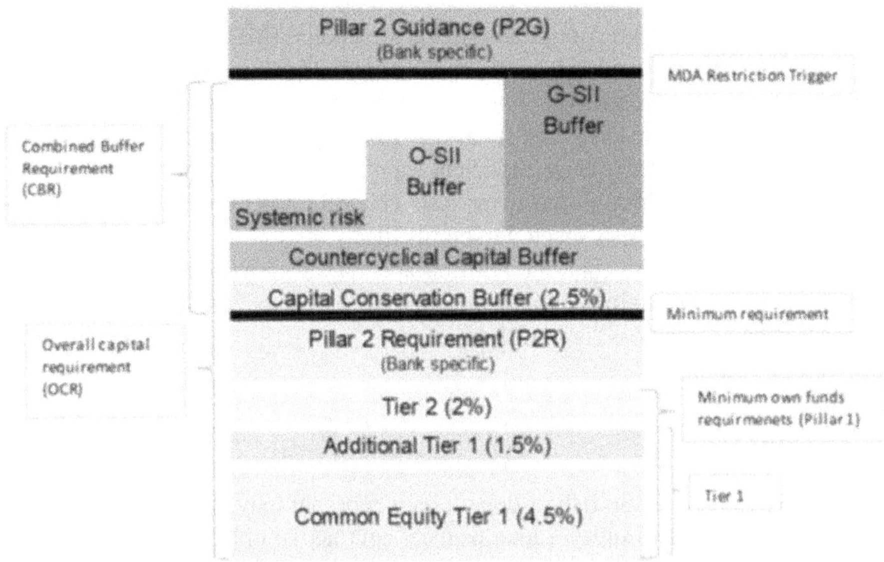

Source: The new Capital Stack confirmed (KPMG, 2019)

quired to hold 2.5% of its total exposures as a Capital Conservation Buffer (CCoB), with the objective, as its name says, of conserving a banks' capital. When a bank breaches the buffer, automatic safeguards apply to limit the amount of dividends and bonus payments it can pay out.

On top of this, the capital stack foresees the Countercyclical Capital Buffer (CCyB), which takes into account the macroeconomic financial environment in which the bank operates. It is aimed at protecting the banking sector from periods of excess aggregate credit growth, associated with the build-up of system wide-risk. When the economy shows an upward trend, the CCyB is supported by the build-up phase of the credit cycle, while when the cycle is inverted, and thus when the economy is in a downturn, the CCyB helps reduce the risk that the supply of credit will be constrained by the regulatory capital requirements, which could undermine the performance of the real economy and result in additional credit losses in the banking sector.

In addition, the system risk buffers are applied. For each bank, the higher among the following three buffers applies: Systemic Risk Buffer (SRB), Other Systemically Important Institutions Buffer (O-SII), or Global Systemically Important Institutions Buffer (G-SII). The Systemic Risk Buffer (SRB) addresses the systemic risks of a long-term, non-cyclical nature which are not covered by the CRR, while the Global and Other Systemically Important Institutions Buffer (O-SII and G-SII) address the potential negative effects that the institution may have on the international or domestic financial system.

The requirements described so far, i.e. Pillar I, Pillar II, and the Combined Buffer Requirements, make up the Overall Capital Requirements (OCR) and are binding for institutions. As we mentioned, if a bank's total capital falls below the threshold set by the OCR, the Maximum Distributable Amount (MDA) threshold, then the bank cannot distribute dividends to its shareholders. However, on top of the OCR, the capital stack foresees a further non-binding block, defined by the Pillar II Guidance (P2G). It is bank-specific and its aim is to reach the adequate level of capital to be maintained in order to have sufficient capital as a buffer to withstand stressed situations, as assessed through the stress test. The P2G was introduced in 2016, and whether binding or not, it is expected to be fulfilled.

This Chapter will now continue with an accurate description of the main risks affecting financial institutions and how capital requirements, and thus risk-weighted assets, are calculated across risk categories.

2.4 Credit risk

Credit risk is defined as the risk of default on a debt that may rise as a consequence of a borrower's failure to repay a loan or meet contractual obligations. It is affected by numerous factors of both an idiosyncratic nature (i.e. relative to the debtor) and a systemic nature (i.e. relative to the industry and to macroeconomic conditions).

With reference to the latter, it must be noted that banks, when operating in the expansion phase, occasionally underestimate their risk exposure, loosening selection criteria and reducing the reserves held against future losses. When the cycle is inverted, clients' profitability decreases and creditworthiness deteriorates, making bad debt arise. This phenomenon is often paired with a decrease in the assets' market value, thus reducing the clients' wealth held by banks. The banks' exposure to credit risk increases, requiring higher reserves and a higher level of protection in terms of capital, at the very same moment in which it is more expensive and less available on the market.

In an economic phase of generalized hustle and uncertainty with respect to the next cyclical evolution, even operators with potentially profitable projects could find difficulties in being granted credit. The opposite happens in expansion phases, when intermediaries are more prone to grant credit and borrowers are less creditworthy.

The cyclical effect of credit policies and the actual impact on creditors depends on the relevance of asymmetric information or, in other terms, on the capacity of lenders to accurately estimate risk. Smaller firms, for instance, which are generally characterised by low capitalization and high opaqueness, are impacted by the restrictions on credit much more than larger firms, which have easier access to capital markets.

To compensate for the cyclical implications on the lending function and on the bank's equilibrium in general, it is essential to focus attention on the most foreseeable variables related to the borrowers. The credit market is typically characterized by two informative issues. The first one is *moral hazard*, defined as the risk that one of the two parties was not in good faith when entering the contract, or provided misleading information on its assets, liabilities, or credit capacity. Moreover, moral hazard could also include the case in which one of the two parties has an incentive to assume unusual risks to obtain some kind of profit before the end of the contract. The second issue is *adverse selection*, described as the difficulty in selecting and distinguishing creditworthy firms from riskier firms. Adverse selection in the field of financial intermediaries is an ex-ante problem: due to the many lending requests made by firms, banks' need to select to whom to grant credit.

To minimize risk, it is necessary to design complex, but inevitably incomplete, contracts. Banks must mitigate risk, in order to protect themselves from insolvency issues and to guarantee a more efficient allocation of funds. Credit risk valuation performs a crucial role in the industry: traditionally, banks have used a number of methods to assess the creditworthiness of counterparties, such as credit scoring, ratings, and assessments within credit committees. But now, to improve the quality of the available information, it is necessary to invest in technological solutions and develop valuation models of possible future losses. Therefore, banks have to process quantitative, qualitative, and behavioural trends information, i.e. information that identifies the historical behaviour of borrowers with respect to banks.

Risk-weighted assets related to credit risk can be computed following either the Standardized Approach or the Internal Ratings-Based Approach.

2.4.1 Credit risk: Standardized approach (SA)

The standardized approach is suitable for banks with a smaller volume of operations and a simpler control structure. It is applied by the majority of Less Significant Institutions (LSIs), although is not usually implemented for bigger institutions, such as Significant Institutions. It involves the use of credit ratings from external credit assessment institutions for the evaluation of the creditworthiness of a bank's debtor.

The standardized approach was first introduced by the BCBS Accord of 1988 as a risk-sensitive requirement of capital. It established the requirement of own funds as 8% of the "risk-weighted assets." In order to estimate risk-weighted assets, the following four buckets, with their respective risk weights, were defined: exposure to cash, central banks, and sovereign (0%); exposure to banks (20%); mortgages with maximum loan-to-value ratio (LTV) of 80% (50%), other assets (100%). Exposure is calculated on both on- and off-balance sheet assets. On-balance sheet assets are considered at their accounting value, while off-balance sheet items are considered at their nominal value scaled by a credit conversion factor.

Starting from the basic approach we have just described, Basel II (2008) introduced a more risk-sensitive approach. The risk weight for exposure belonging to each asset class is calibrated as defined in **Tables 2.2, 2.3, 2.4.**

With respect to Table 2.4, calibration for exposure to sovereign, it is important to point out that, at national discretion, a lower risk weight may be applied to banks'

Table 2.2 Calibration for exposure to banks (Basel II)

Credit Assessment of Banks	AAA to AA-	A+ to A-	BBB+ to BBB-	BB+ to B-	Below B-	Unrated
Risk weight under Option 2	20%	50%	50%	100%	150%	50%

Source: The Standardised Approach to Credit Risk (BIS, 2001).

Table 2.3 Calibration for exposure to corporate (Basel II)

Credit Assessment	AAA to AA-	A+ to A-	BBB+ to BB-	Below BB-	Unrated
Risk weight	20%	50%	100%	150%	100%

Source: The Standardised Approach to Credit Risk (BIS, 2001).

Table 2.4 Calibration for sovereign exposure (Basel II)

Credit Assessment	AAA to AA-	A+ to A-	BBB+ to BBB-	BB+ to B-	Below B-	Unrated
Risk weight	0%	20%	50%	100%	150%	100%

Source: The Standardised Approach to Credit Risk (BIS, 2001).

exposure to their sovereign of incorporation denominated in domestic currency and funded in that currency.

Moreover, Basel II reduced the risk weight for retail exposures. The retail exposures bucket is introduced and assigned a risk weight of 75% (exposure to individuals or small businesses), if some requirements such as diversification (maximum exposure must be less than 0.2% of the portfolio) and low-value (less that € 1 million) are respected. Mortgages with a maximum LTV of 80% are assigned a risk weight of 35%.

Further, the concept of high-risk exposures, for which the risk weight is equal to 150%, is introduced. These include investments in venture capital firms, investments in alternative investments funds (art. 4.1.a 2011/61/EU Directive), investments in private equity, speculative real estate financing (loans for the purpose of acquisition or development or construction on land in relation to real estate property, or of and in relation to such property, with the intention of reselling for profit).

Under European regulations, credit quality steps are used instead of ratings. They are issued or endorsed by external credit assessment institutions (ECAI), and are mapped as described in Commission Implementing Regulation EU 2016/1799 (mapping) reported in **Table 2.5**.

Table 2.5 Mapping credit rating vs. credit quality step

Credit assessment	Credit quality step
AAA	1
AA	1
A	2
BBB	3
BB	4
B	5
CCC	6
CC	6
R	6
SD/	6

Source: Authors' elaboration based on data from CEBS.

Other European specificities are related to sovereign exposures and exposures to small and medium enterprises. When the former is considered, art. 114 CRR distinguishes between two cases: exposures to central governments and central banks not belong to Member States, and exposures to Member States' central governments. The former should be assigned a risk weight according to **Table 2.6** below, which corresponds to the credit assessment of the ECAI in accordance with art. 136 CRR. A credit assessment by a nominated ECAI should be available. Conversely, exposures to Member States' central governments and central banks denominated and funded in the domestic currency of that central government and central bank shall be assigned a risk weight of 0%.

Lastly, under the European Regulation (article 501 CRR) exposures to SME are to be multiplied by the factor of 0.7619. Exposures in default are to be excluded. The factor has been denominated a supporting factor, and it raised concerns in the industry. They were addressed by the EBA in the "EBA Report on SME and SME supporting factor" stating that: "the EBA notes that the SME Supporting Factor appears to have been introduced by legislators as a precautionary measure in order to

Table 2.6 Calibration for non-Member States' sovereign exposures (art. 114 CRR)

Credit quality step	1	2	3	4	5	6
Risk weight	0%	20%	50%	100%	100%	150%

Source: Authors' elaboration based on data from CEBS.

not jeopardise lending to the SME sector, and thereby does not aim to be solely a prudential measure."

At both the European and American level, the reliance on credit ratings has been heavily criticized. In the United States, it reached the point that Dodd-Frank prohibits approving new regulations based on ratings. In the meantime, the European legislation tried to avoid "over-reliance on ratings" by reducing the weight of ratings in banking regulation through the due diligence requirements, also known as the non-mechanistic approach. Described in the European Commission's document "Implementing the Final Basel III Reforms in the EU," it states that "banks must perform due diligence to ensure that they have an adequate understanding, at origination and thereafter on a regular basis (at least annually), of the risk profile and characteristics of their counterparties. In cases where ratings are used, due diligence is necessary to assess the risk of the exposure for risk management purposes and whether the risk weight applied is appropriate and prudent" and "banks should have in place effective internal policies, processes, systems and controls to ensure that the appropriate risk weights are assigned to counterparties. Banks must be able to demonstrate to their supervisors that their due diligence analyses are appropriate. As part of their supervisory review, supervisors should ensure that banks have appropriately performed their due diligence analyses, and should take supervisory measures where these have not been done".

2.4.2 Credit risk: Internal ratings-based approach (IRB)

The internal ratings-based approach (IRB) is suitable for banks engaged in more complex operations, with more developed risk management systems. It is the preferred approach of the Significant Institutions across the Euro area. It focuses on the frequency of bank insolvencies arising from credit losses. The amount of losses which will be exceeded is estimated by means of a stochastic credit portfolio model, with a small and pre-defined probability, reflecting bank insolvency.

As in the standardized approach (SA), the objective of the internal ratings-based approach (IRB) is to quantify risk-weighted assets. The formula for risk-weighted assets (RWA) does not change, as reported below:

$$RWA = RW \times EAD$$

As previously mentioned, exposure at default (EAD) is an estimate of the amount outstanding in case the borrower defaults. The difference between the two approaches lies on how risk weights are computed. In the internal ratings-based approach, risk weights (RW) account for both expected losses (EL) and unexpected losses (UL). The formula is stated in Article 153(1) of the CRR, and is reported below:

$$RW = \underbrace{\left(\underbrace{LGD \times N\left(\frac{1}{\sqrt{1-R}} \times G(PD) + \sqrt{\frac{R}{1-R}} \times G(0.999)\right)}_{\text{Maximum loss (confidence level 99.9\%)}} - \underbrace{LGD \times PD}_{\text{EL}}\right)}_{\text{Unexpected loss}} \times \underbrace{\frac{1+(M-2.5)\times b}{1-1.5\times b}}_{\text{Adjustment (M)}} \times \overset{\text{Conversion to RWA}}{12.5} \times \underbrace{1.06}_{\text{Scaling factor}}$$

Let us break the formula down.

- N(x) is the cumulative distribution function for a standard normal random variable (i.e. the probability that a normal random variable with mean zero and variance of one is less than or equal to x);
- G(Z) denotes the inverse cumulative distribution function for a standard normal random variable (i.e. the value x such that N(x) = z), where Z denotes the set confidence interval;
- PD, the probability of default, is the proportion of debtors that might default over a one-year horizon;
- LGD, the loss given default rate, denotes the percentage of exposure the bank might lose in case the borrower defaults;
- R denotes the correlation coefficient and is defined as:

$$R = 0.12 \times \frac{1-e^{-50\times PD}}{1-e^{-50}} + 0.24 \times \left(1 - \frac{1-e^{-50\times PD}}{1-e^{-50}}\right)$$

- b is the maturity adjustment factor, which is defined as:

$$b = (0.11852 - 0.05478 \times \ln(PD))^2$$

Expected and unexpected losses

As mentioned, the most interesting concepts are expected and unexpected losses, graphically depicted in **Figure 2.5**.

The curve of probability density describes the likelihood of losses of a certain magnitude. It should be noted that small losses occur more frequently than large losses. The white area denotes the Value-at-Risk (VaR), composed of provisions, revenues (aimed at covering EL), and capital (aimed at covering UL). Under Basel II, the threshold for the VaR is set to maintain a supervisory fixed confidence level. If EL is covered by provisions and revenues, and UL is covered by capital, then the likelihood that the bank will remain solvent within one year is equal to the confidence level. At the same time, the likelihood that a bank will not be able to meet its own credit obligations through its provisions, revenues, and capital (i.e. that losses will exceed EL and UL), equals the hatched area under the right hand side of the curve.

Figure 2.5 Covering expected and unexpected losses

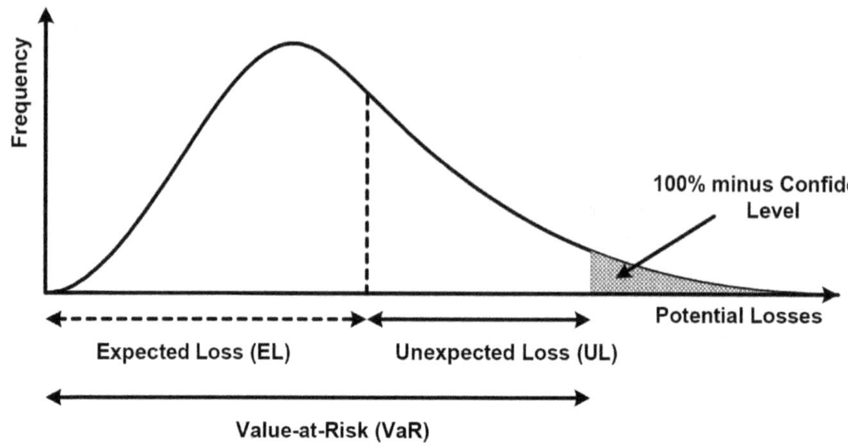

Source: An Explanatory Note on the Basel II IRB Risk Weight Functions (BIS, 2005).

According to *An Explanatory Note on the Basel II IRB Risk Weight Functions* (BCBS, 2005):

> "A bank can forecast the average level of credit losses it can reasonably expect to experience. These losses are referred to as **Expected Losses (EL)**. Financial institutions view Expected Losses as a cost component of doing business, and manage them by a number of means, including through the pricing of credit exposures and through provisioning."

The expected loss is computed as following:

$$EL = PD \times EAD \times LGD$$

That is, the expected loss (EL) is the proportion of debtors that might default within 1 year (PD), multiplied by the loss given default rate (LGD) and multiplied by the outstanding exposure at default (EAD). As stated in the definition, expected losses (EL) are covered by provisions and revenues.

Unexpected losses (UL) are to be considered, too. Again according to *An Explanatory Note on the Basel II IRB Risk Weight Functions* (BCBS, 2005):

> "One of the functions of bank capital is to provide a buffer to protect a bank's debt holders against peak losses that exceed expected levels. Peak losses do not occur every year, but when they occur, they can potentially be very large. Losses above expected levels are usually referred to as **Unexpected Losses (UL)** – institutions know they will occur now and then, but they cannot know in advance their timing or severity. Capital

is needed to cover the risks of such peak losses, and therefore it has a loss-absorbing function."

Unexpected losses (UL) are covered by capital requirements, which are computed as the difference between Value-at-Risk (VaR) and expected losses (EL) and are composed of both Tier 1 and Tier 2 capital.

Under Basel II, the confidence level is fixed at 99.9% – i.e. an institution is expected to incur losses which exceed its expected and unexpected loss level once in a thousand years. This seems rather high, however it was chosen to protect against estimation errors, that inevitably arise from banks' internal PD, LGD, and EAD estimations, as well as from other uncertainties related to the model. Also, Tier 1 does not have the loss absorbing capacity of Tier 2.

The hatched area accounts for the case in which the bank would lose its entire credit portfolio in a given year; as said, a highly unlikely event. Banks have an incentive to minimize the capital they hold, in order to direct economic resources to profitable investments. Therefore, holding capital against the hatched part would be highly economically inefficient.

In order to make the IRB framework applicable to a wider range of countries and institutions, the model should be **portfolio invariant**, i.e. the capital required for any given loan should only depend on the risk of that loan and must not depend on the portfolio it is added to. In the context of regulatory capital allocation, portfolio invariant allocation schemes are also called ratings-based.

Internal ratings-based models are of the following two types: IRB foundation (F-IRB) and IRB advanced (A-IRB). In the former, the **IRB foundation (F-IRB) approach**, only the probability of default (PD) is obtained by the entity, while loss given default (LGD) and exposure at default (EAD) are computed applying regulatory factors. In the latter, the **IRB advanced (A-IRB) approach**, all three factors are computed by the entity. It must be noted that A-IRB is not allowed for some portfolios.

Probability of Default (PD)

As mentioned in advance, at the portfolio level the probability of default is the proportion of debtors that might default (i.e. be unable to meet their debt obligations in full or on time) over a one-year horizon. At the loan level, the risk of default is derived by analysing the obligor's capacity to repay the debt in accordance with the contractual terms, and the probability of default is an estimate of the likelihood that the default event will occur.

Under Basel II, a default event on a debt obligation is said to have occurred either if it is unlikely that the obligor will be able to repay its debt to the bank without giving up any pledged collateral, or if the obligor is more than 90 days past due on a material credit obligation. As mentioned, under Basel II, the confidence level is fixed at 99.9% – i.e. an institution is expected to incur losses which exceed its expected and unexpected loss level once in a thousand years. Critics argue that the probability of a bank failure is significantly higher than the official 0.1%, but it must be considered that the high requirement is set in order to take into account potential estimation errors that could occur in the model, together with various uncertainties.

It is easily inferable that the PD of an obligor does not only depend on the risk characteristics of that particular obligor, but also on the economic environment and the degree to which it affects the obligor. Thus, the information available to estimate the probability of default is of both a macroeconomic and individual nature. Based on these factors, we can derive two estimations for the probability of default: the unstressed and the stressed PD. The former is calculated considering the current macroeconomic conditions and the debtors' individual features, while the latter is estimated taking into account stressed macroeconomic conditions, and as for the previous one, the debtors' individual features.

In practice, however, the probability of default should be based on the historical experience of the entity and it should be a conservative estimate of the long-term average of the PD of each exposure category. The estimate is defined as **through the cycle (TDC)** – i.e. it contemplates a complete cycle. Thus, the minimum observation period accounts for five years. In theory, the PD could also be computed as a point in time (PIT). However, the alternative is not permitted by the legislation, since it would make it easy to manipulate results.

Moreover, the importance of computing the PD through the cycle was highlighted in the economic crisis, when the excess of cyclicality risk measurements was identified as one of the causes of the instability of the metrics of financial institutions, revealing the importance of anticipation in risk management. The probability of default varies according to the cycle: it is greater during recessions and lower in boom periods. Therefore, contemplating a complete economic cycle and making the proper cycle adjustments are necessary steps to produce a reliable measure.

According to the new legislation set out in Basel IV, which will enter into force in January 2022, the PD floor (minimum PD level) for corporate exposures passed from 0.03% as set in Basel II, to 0.05%. Further changes in the minimum parameter values are outlined in **Table 2.9**.

Loss Given Default (LGD)

Under the F-IRB approach, loss given default (LGD) is computed according to the regulatory factors stated in Article 161 of the CRR, and summarised in **Table 2.7**.

Under the A-IRB approach, loss given default (LGD) is provided by the supervised entity. When producing its own estimates, the bank should consider a minimum observation period of 5 years initially, which will be increased until reaching a period of 7 years. The final LGD should reflect **downturn conditions** – i.e. an unfavourable economic conjuncture.

Changes to the IRB approach introduced by the Basel III reforms (Basel IV)
The Basel III reforms will be enforced as of January 2022

The main changes introduced by the Basel III reforms to the IRB approach are due to the need to address the lack of robustness in modelling certain asset classes and enhance comparability among banks. They are related to the following areas:

- Removal of the option to use the advanced IRB approach for certain asset classes, as shown in Table 2.8;
- For asset classes where the advanced IRB approach remains available, adoption of input floors for internal estimates of PD and LGD to ensure a minimum level of conservatism in model parameters, as indicated in Table 2.9;
- Provide greater specification of parameter estimation practices.

Table 2.7 **LGD value per exposure type as in Art. 161 CRR**

Exposure type	LGD value
Senior exposures without eligible collateral	45%
Subordinated exposure without eligible collateral	75%
Covered bonds eligible for the treatment set out in Article 129(4) or (5)	(may be assigned) 11,25%
Senior purchased corporate receivables exposures*	45%
Subordinated purchased corporate receivables exposures*	100%
Dilution risk of purchased corporate receivables	75%

* exposures where an institution is not able to estimate PDs or the institution's PD estimates do not meet the requirements set out in Section 6

Source: Authors' elaboration based on data from https://eba.europa.eu/regulation-and-policy/single-rulebook/interactive-single-rulebook/1598

Table 2.8 **Revised scope of approaches available under Basel III**

Portfolio/exposure	Basel II: available approaches	Basel III: available approaches
Large and mid-sized corporates (consolidated revenues > €500m)	A-IRB, F-IRB, SA	F-IRB, SA
Banks and other financial institutions	A-IRB, F-IRB, SA	F-IRB, SA
Equities	Various IRB approaches	SA
Specialised lending*	A-IRB, F-IRB, slotting, SA	A-IRB, F-IRB, slotting, SA

* With respect to specialised lending, banks would be permitted to continue using the advanced and foundation IRB approaches. The Committee will review the slotting approach for specialised lending in due course.

Source: High-level summary of Basel III reforms (BIS, 2017)

Table 2.9 Input floors under Basel IV

	Probability of default (PD)	Loss-given-default (LGD)		Exposure at default (EAD)
		Unsecured	Secured	
Corporate	5 bp	25%	Varying by collateral type: • 0% financial • 10% receivables • 10% commercial or residential real estate • 15% other physical	EAD subject to a floor that is the sum of (i) the on-balance sheet exposures; and (ii) 50% of the off-balance sheet exposure using the applicable Credit Conversion Factor (CCF) in the standardised approach
Retail classes:				
Mortgages	5 bp	N/A	5%	
QRRE transactors	5 bp	50%	N/A	
QRRE revolvers	10 bp	50%	N/A	
Other retail	5 bp	30%	Varying by collateral type: • 0% financial • 10% receivables • 10% commercial or residential real estate • 15% other physical	

Source: High-level summary of Basel III reforms (BIS, 2017)

2.5 Market risk

Market risk is defined as the risk of losses arising from movements in market prices. It is based on both the sensitivity of the financial institution's earnings or the economic value of its capital to adverse changes in interest rates, foreign exchanges rates, commodity prices, or equity prices; and the ability of management to identify, measure, monitor, and control exposure to market risk given the institution's size, complexity, and risk profile.

Market risk comprises risks of different natures, which are treated differently from a supervisory perspective. The most significant are risk arising from interest rate related instruments and equities in the trading books. Interest rate risk is the potential for losses in on- or off-balance sheet positions from adverse changes in interest rates. In the case of debt instruments, it is necessary to calculate the incremental risk change (IRC) for default and migration risk and a comprehensive risk measure (CRM) for the correlation trading portfolio. Debt, but also Equity, can be affected by general interest rate risk (i.e. risk of losses created by variation of risk free rate) and specific interest rate risk (i.e. losses caused by changes in the creditworthiness of a single issuer). However, it must be pointed out that, in the case of equity instruments, the distinction is less clear.

Furthermore, market risk includes credit spread risk and equity risk. The former, credit spread risk, is defined as the risk arising from the reduction in market value of a financial instrument due to changes in the credit quality of the debtor or counterparty. This risk is driven by a change in the price (or yield) of a fixed-income instrument, for instance, as a result of a credit rating downgrade. The latter, equity risk, is the potential for losses in on- and off-balance sheet positions arising from adverse changes in equity prices.

Moreover, market risk includes foreign exchange risk, commodity risk and settlement risk, which affect both the trading and the banking books. Foreign exchange risk is the risk that the value of on- or off-balance sheet positions will be adversely affected by movements in exchange rates. For instance, positions denominated in foreign currency may decline in value when the domestic currency appreciates. Foreign exchange risk can also arise in the banking book where a bank has loans in any currency other than the bank's reporting currency. Commodity risk is the risk that on- or off-balance sheet positions will be adversely affected by movements in commodity prices, i.e. the risk of losses owing to positions in commodities and trading in commodity-related financial instruments. Commodity categories include energy, metals, and agricultural products. Furthermore, settlement risk is defined as the risk of incurring losses due to failure to settle transactions in debt instruments. Lastly, concentration risk is related only to the trading book, and it relates to the concentration and correlation factors in market transactions which are not captured by credit concentration risk.

To estimate the levels of market risk that they face, banks implement two categories of risk measures: portfolio-specific, which target the unique characteristics of certain instruments or portfolios, and comprehensive measurement methods, which are used to calculate risk exposures across all financial instruments in their on- and off-balance sheet positions. Among the specific measures, we list volatility, duration, and beta. Volatility is the degree to which the price of an asset goes up or down over a given period of time. High volatility implies high risk, but also high returns. Duration, the primary function of maturity, is defined as the degree to which the price of an asset goes up or down over a given period of time. Lastly, beta is the measure of whether individual stocks are more or less risky than the average stock. Less risky betas assume values which are less than 1, while riskier betas are above 1.

Among the comprehensive measurement methods, Value-at-Risk (VaR) provides an estimate of the most that a portfolio is expected to lose over a given time period (usually, one day) in all but, for example, 1% of the time (i.e. 99% confidence level). It can be calculated with several methods, such as the following: variance and covariance method; Montecarlo simulation method; and historical simulation method. VaR is particularly useful since it allows for the comparison of risk in different businesses, such as fixed income and equity, and also provides a means to aggregate and net a variety of positions within the same portfolio, in order to reflect correlations between different assets.

Following the financial crisis, it became clear that VaR is not an adequate measure for risk. It has several limitations. For instance, VaR assumes a normal distribution of market data, but in times of stress, the assumption of a normal distribution is misleading. Therefore, tail risk, the risk of extreme losses beyond the confidence level selected, is not captured. Such losses are very unlikely to occur, but their incidence would place an extreme strain on a bank's capital. Moreover, the VaR framework is unable to adequately capture credit risk in trading exposures. As a result, when banks were affected by large trading losses driven by a deterioration in credit quality in 2007–08, their capital buffers were inadequate. Furthermore, the VaR framework makes the assumption that individual banks can exit or hedge their trading book exposures over a 10-day period without affecting market prices. However, at times of severe market stress, such as illiquidity in the market during a systematic crisis, liquidation may not be possible or only available at very high cost via fire sales. This risk is called the market illiquidity risk, and VaR fails to capture it.

A more general issue was an embedded feature of the regulatory framework for market risk, that is, the generous recognition of the risk-reducing effects of hedging and diversification. This derived from the fact that the framework was calibrated on the basis of estimates of correlations based on historical data under 'normal' market conditions. During a time of severe market stress, such as that experienced in 2007–08, hedging benefits that were assumed to hold under normal conditions disappeared, leaving banks exposed to a severe underestimation of their potential losses. A final limitation that should be kept in mind is related to usage of the historical simulation method to compute VaR. The historical simulation method, for instance, looks at the last two years of price fluctuations and then applies the historical changes in price levels to the current market prices of assets in today's trading book. As part of the calculation, banks usually assume each year to be 250 trading days (the estimation is made by excluding weekends and national holidays). If a bank uses a confidence level of 99% (which is the required level when calculating VaR for regulatory purposes), then it must also use the fifth worst day of trading from the past two years to inform its VaR estimate. The fall experienced on the fifth worst day is applied to all the exposures in the trading book. Once calculated, the bank can be 99% confident of not losing more than that amount on the next day. VaR can be applied to all financial instruments with sufficient price histories.

2.5.1 The supervisory framework

The supervision of market risk, and therefore regulatory capital requirements, evolved to address the limits described above. The first Basel regulations introduced two approaches to compute the market risk related to risk-weighted assets: the standardized approach and the internal model-based approach. As for credit risk, the standardized approach required assigning each asset to a bucket with a predefined weight, while the internal model approach allowed banks to use their own risk models, including VaR, conditional on regulatory approval. The supervisor's assessment of the bank's internal risk model is then reflected by a multiplier for which the supervisor multiplies the VaR to compute the regulatory capital.

As mentioned, following the financial crisis it became clear that VaR, as it was computed, was not an adequate measure for risk. The need for additional measures became urgent, and thus an interim regulation (Basel 2.5) was enacted in order to introduce higher regulatory requirements for market risk aimed at avoiding regulatory arbitrage. In addition to VaR, several other new measures were introduced, among which we can list sVaR, incremental risk charge, comprehensive risk measure, standardised specific risk charges, and risks not in VaR. The sVaR indicator, unlike VaR, does not use data from the most recent reference period. Instead, it considers data from a reference period that must always include a period of high market stress data against today's portfolio. The incremental risk charge (IRC) seeks to capture default and credit migration risk, i.e. the risk that the credit quality of a portfolio of assets will materially deteriorate. A bank's IRC is designed to capture risks stemming from market and issuer-specific concentrations, credit quality and liquidity horizons, and recognises the impact of correlations between default and migration events among issuers. Examples of products covered by IRC are corporate bonds, which involve credit risk as well as market risk, and credit default swaps (CDS). The IRC adds a longer horizon than VaR (1 year instead of 10 days) and a higher confidence level (99.9% instead of 99%). It also covers credit risk type issues (like default and migration). In addition, the IRC also introduces the concept of liquidity horizons.

Moreover, the comprehensive risk measure (CRM) is a measure of risk stemming from securitised products. It covers default and migration risk, as does the IRC, as well as other risks, such as multiple defaults, credit spread volatility, basis risks, volatility of implied correlations, and recovery rate. It adds a longer horizon than VaR (1 year instead of 10 days) and a higher confidence level (99.9% instead of 99%). In the meantime, Standardised specific risk charges (SSRC) are applied to any debt or equity position that has not received a modelled specific risk charge (that is VaR, CRM, or IRC) or a non-modelled securitisation charge. SSRC charges for corporate bonds, for example, are derived as a percentage of the bonds' market value, with the appropriate percentage level being a function of product type, time to maturity, and credit rating. Lastly, the Risks Not in VaR (RNIV) charge is intended to ensure that capital is held to meet all risks that are not (or not adequately) captured by a bank's VaR and SVaR models. RNIV might also have to be used when, for a new instrument, there is insufficient back data to develop a two- to three-year time series.

An alternative to VaR is represented by the Expected Shortfall (ES) method. Expected shortfall is also known as "conditional VaR" or expected tail loss, and is a way of estimating losses that attempts to make up for VaR's inability to handle tail risk well. ES determines the average of the expected losses that occur beyond the confidence level selected. For regulatory purposes, the confidence level ES uses is 97.5%.

Basel III introduced additional requirements. For instance, in order to avoid regulatory arbitrage, "positions held with trading intents are those held intentionally for short-term resale and/or with the intent of benefiting from short-term price movements or to lock in arbitrage profits" can be inserted in the trading book. The portfolio must be actively managed and should be free of covenants on their tradability. Furthermore, most illiquid categories, such as open equity stakes in hedge funds, private equity investments, positions in a securitization warehouse, and real estate holdings, are excluded from trading books. Moreover, the capital requirements to apply to trading books instruments include a charge for market risk, reflecting price movements in equity and debt positions, and a specific risk charge, related to the credit quality of the issuer of the debt or equity instrument. Banks can determine the capital requirements by using either a standardized measurement method (SMS) or Internal Models approach (IMA).

2.6 Operational risk

Operational risk is defined as the risk of loss resulting from inadequate or failed internal processes, people, and systems or from external events. Losses stemming from processes, could be, for example, collateral management failures, vendor disputes, or shortcomings in the loan approval process, while examples of losses deriving from people are incompetency, ignorance of established policies or procedures, and staffing shortages. In addition, losses deriving from systems are, for example, model errors, cyberattacks, financial accounting system errors, while losses stemming from external events can reflect events such as earthquakes and other natural catastrophes, power outages, and terrorism.

Operational risk includes legal risk, compliance risk, conduct risk, model risk of models not related to other SREP categories, and information technology risk, but it excludes reputational and strategic risk. However, reputational risk is assessed in this category since they are highly interrelated.

Operational losses are classified in the following seven categories: internal fraud, external fraud, employment practices and workplace safety, clients' products and business practices, damage to physical assets, business disruption and system failures, and execution, delivery, and process management.

This is a complex risk of non-financial nature, whose importance has been often underestimated. However, operational risk is related to all other risk types and can only be contained at the root, since additional capital will not be effective against potential contagion and systemic risk. Operational risk management requires banks to consider how an operational risk event (for example, the mismarking of a trading position), the effect or impact of the event (a financial loss) and its cause (a keying error) are different, and understand how they relate to one another. Moreover, it must be pointed out that the nature of operational risk is per se controversial since operational risk is: inherent in virtually all of a bank's products, activities, business lines, processes, systems, and locations; heavily influenced by human behaviour, which is uncertain, at best; a potential loss from a single operational risk event can dwarf those arising from other risks; and lastly it is difficult to measure, in part due to the very small number of large losses experienced by an individual bank. Thus, the supervision methodology, which focuses exclusively on losses, could have several limitations.

2.6.1 The supervisory framework

The capital requirements for operational risk are listed in articles 312 to 324 of the CRR. Three different approaches could be used to compute the capital requirements, however their combined use is limited.

The first and simplest approach is the **Basic Approach (BIA)**, which works by default. It is not intended for internationally active banks or banks with significant exposure to operational risk. The BIA consists of two components: a bank's gross income, and an income-based proxy for its exposure to operational risk alpha (α), a fixed factor set by the BCBS based on its estimate of the industry-wide level of required capital relative to the industry-wide level of gross income.

The formula for calculating a bank's capital charge under the BIA is as follows:

$$K_{BIA} = [\Sigma(GI_{1,\dots,n} x \propto)]/n$$

where:
K_{BIA} = the capital charge under the BIA;
GI = annual gross income, where positive, over the previous three years;
n = number of the previous three years for which gross income is positive;
$\propto = 15\%$.

The **Traditional Standardised Approach (TSA)** foresees that the institution divides the activities into the following business lines: corporate finance, trading and sales, retail brokerage, commercial banking, retail banking, payment and settlement, agency services, and asset management. It uses gross income and a set of prescribed factors (β) to determine a bank's capital charge for operational risk. The TSA, however, can be applied only upon the fulfilment of certain qualifying criteria, and must be agreed on with the supervisor. A bank applying the TSA must calculate its gross income in each of the eight standard Basel II business lines, described above. As a proxy for the scale of business operations, gross income is intended to reflect the scale of operational risk exposure in a given business line. Basel II prescribes β for each business line as a proxy for the industry-wide relationship between the operational risk loss experience in a given business line and the aggregate level of gross income for that business line. Moreover, the institution should perform an operational risk internal assessment, which should be well-documented, integrated into the risk management process, and involve a system of reporting to senior management. The bank also has the duty of notifying the supervisory institution upon completion of the assessment and if any additional risk of an operational nature arises.

The formula for calculating a bank's capital charge under the TSA is as follows:

$$K_{TSA} = \left\{ \sum_{years1-3} max\left[\sum(GI_{1-8} x \beta_{1-8}),0\right] \right\}/3$$

where:
K_{TSA} = the capital charge under the TSA;

GI_{1-8} = annual gross income in a given year for each of the eight business lines;
β_{1-8} = a fixed percentage set by the Basel Committee, ranging from 12% to 18%.

Lastly, the most complex approach is the **Advanced Measurement Approach (AMA)**. Use of the AMA is subject to supervisory approval and relies on both quantitative standards and qualitative standards. From the quantitative perspective, internal data, external data, scenario analyses, and business environment and internal control factors are collected by type of event and business line. Through a statistical model, the frequency and severity of distributions are computed and the loss distribution simulated. Therefore, expected losses, unexpected losses, and losses not covered by capital are computed.

From a qualitative perspective, an operational risk measurement system should be integrated into day-to-day risk management, the risk management function should be independent, operational risk exposures and loss experience and related corrective actions should be reported, internal/external auditors and internal validation processes should be reviewed, and data flows and processes should be transparent and accessible.

In 2015-2016, BCBS conducted a review of banks' operational risk models and concluded that AMA is complex and lacks comparability, and that despite an increase in the number and severity of operational risk events, the capital requirements remained stable or declined. Following the review, in December 2017, the Basel Committee published a revised operational risk capital framework that will replace the AMA, BIA, and TSA with a single, risk-sensitive (but non-model-based) standardised approach for determining a bank's operational risk capital requirements.

Therefore, the new formula that will replace the previous approaches will be the following:

$$operational\ risk\ capital = BIC \times ILM$$

The Business Indicator Component, BIC, is the sum of three components (the interest, leases and dividends component, the services component, and the financial component) multiplied by a set of marginal coefficients based on 3 buckets.

The Internal Loss Multiplier, ILM, is a function of the BIC and the Loss Component (LC), where the latter is equal to 15 times a bank's average historic losses over the preceding 10 years. The ILM increases as the ratio of (LC/BIC) increases, although at a decreasing rate, specifically as follows.

$$ILM = ln\ [exp(1) - 1 + (LC/BIC)^{0.8}]$$

At national discretion, supervisors can elect to set ILM equal to one for all banks in their jurisdiction. The new approach to operational risk will be implemented as of January 2022.

2.7 Liquidity risk

Liquidity is the ability to fund increases in assets and meet obligations as they come due. It is crucial to the on-going viability of any banking organization. Ideally, a bank would like to invest at the highest yields and fund this investment at the lowest possible cost. This might mean borrowing very short-term (for example, by taking deposits) and lending at a higher yield for a longer term (for example, mortgages). Borrowing short and lending long, however, can create a funding mismatch, which might mean that a bank does not have sufficient liquidity to meet commitments as they come due.

Basel III introduced new liquidity requirements.

The **Liquidity Coverage Ratio (LCR)** requires banks to have sufficient high quality assets to withstand a 30-day stressed funding scenario specified by the supervisor. It focuses on a short-term perspective: the 30-day period allows banks to have a cushion of high quality liquid assets in the event of a run on banks during a financial crisis. The 30-day requirement also provides central banks and governments time to step in and implement corrective measures to stabilize the financial system.

$$LCR = \frac{High\ quality\ liquid\ asset\ amount\ (HQLA)}{Total\ net\ cash\ flow\ amount}$$

High-quality liquid assets include only those with a high potential to be converted easily and quickly into cash. The three categories of liquid assets with decreasing levels of quality are level 1, level 2A, and level 2B. Under Basel III, level 1 assets are not discounted when calculating the LCR, while level 2A and level 2B assets have a 15% and 50% discount, respectively. For instance, central bank reserves and securities guaranteed by specific sovereign entities are considered level 1 liquid assets, while level 2A could be corporate debt securities and marketable sovereign securities that satisfy specific requirements. Level 2B consists of residential mortgage-backed securities, corporate debt, and equity that have specific features.

The LCR was implemented and measured in 2011, but the full 100% minimum was not enforced until 2015, and it applies to Significant Institutions.

The **Net Stable Funding Ratio (NSFR)** is a long-term structural ratio designed to address liquidity mismatches. It covers the entire balance sheet and provides incentives for banks to use stable sources of funding, requiring banks to maintain a stable funding profile in relation to their off-balance sheet assets and activities. The NSFR is defined as the ratio between the amount of stable funding available and the amount of stable funding required. The NSFR is expressed as a ratio that must equal or exceed 100%.

$$\frac{Total\ Available\ Stable\ Funding\ (ASF)}{Total\ Required\ Stable\ Funding\ (ARF)} \geq 100\%$$

Total Available Stable Funding, or ASF, is the portion of a banks' capital and liabilities that will remain with the institution for more than one year. Total Required Stable Funding (ARF), is the amount of stable funding that a bank is required to hold given the liquidity characteristics and residual maturities of its assets and the contingent liquidity risk arising from its off-balance sheet exposures. The NSFR became a minimum standard applicable to all internationally active banks on a consolidated basis on 1 January 2018. Financial institutions must meet the NSFR requirement on an on-going basis and report on a quarterly basis.

Other relevant banking supervision topics which we would like to deepen are the Stress Tests (**Box 2.3**) and TLAC and MREL (**Box 2.4**).

Box 2.3 **Stress Tests**

The concept underlying stress tests is intuitive: a stress test is a simulation of a bank's reactions to several specific scenarios of economic downturn. Its aim is to identify a bank's vulnerabilities and understand how to treat them. The test consists of both quantitative and qualitative measures. In purely quantitative terms, the goal is to assess whether a bank has sufficient funds to survive and protect itself in the case severe losses occur. It focuses on some key areas, such as credit risk, market risk, and liquidity risk. Simulations are conducted on the balance sheet of the financial institution, and are performed by the bank itself, and then confirmed by the supervisors.

As mentioned, the bank is tested against several unfavourable scenarios. Initially, however, the base scenario is formulated in order to have a forecast of events without shocks. The other scenarios, called adverse scenarios, are meant to test the institution's performance in the case of a net worsening of the real economy. Scenarios vary at each stress test, but the most common involve a sharp decline of national GDP, a difficult situation in the real estate market, or a sudden increase in the unemployment rate. In Europe, the features of the scenarios are chosen by the European Systemic Risk Board (ESRB).

Banks that undergo stress tests are required to publish their results. These results are then released to the public to show how the bank would handle a major economic crisis or a financial disaster. Regulations require companies that do not pass stress tests to cut their dividend pay-outs and share buybacks to preserve or build up their capital reserves. Banks that came close to failing and risk not being able to make further distributions in the future pass on a conditional basis; which implies having to resubmit a plan of action.

Box 2.4 **TLAC and MREL**

Following the 2008 financial crisis, the need to have an orderly resolution in case of failure by making debt/equity holders absorb losses, therefore enabling a "bail-in," instead of using public funds with the so-called "bail-out" option, arose. Specifically, the requirements were deemed particularly relevant in the case of globally systemically important banks (G-SIBs), perceived as "too big to fail." The FSB addressed this need in 2015 through the publication of the **Total Loss-Absorbing Capacity (TLAC) standards**. The TLAC requires G-SIBs to have financial instruments available during resolution to absorb losses and enable them to be recapitalised to continue performing their critical functions while the resolution process is ongoing. The TLAC requirement is applied to the resolution entity, the entity to which resolution measures are applied based on a G-SIB's resolution plan, and its subsidiaries, called a resolution group.

The TLAC requirements are the following:

$$\frac{TLAC\ instruments}{RWA} \geq X \text{ and } \frac{TLAC\ instruments}{Leverage\ exposure\ measure} \geq Y$$

where:

- X=16% and Y=6% in January 2019 (Phase 1)
- X=18% and Y=6.75% in January 2022 (Phase 2)

The TLAC requirements can be met by the minimum regulatory capital requirements (own funds) plus an additional layer of debt that is earmarked for conversion into capital to absorb losses and recapitalise the bank.

Following the same spirit, at the European level, the Bank Recovery and Resolution Directive (BRRD) set out a framework for all European banks and investment firms, to satisfy a **Minimum Requirement for Own Funds and Eligible Liabilities (MREL)**. Its aim is to enable financial institutions to absorb losses and restore their capital position, allowing them to continuously perform their critical economic functions during and after a crisis. The MREL was introduced via the 2014 BRRD/SRMR package, and has been in force since January 2016. Nonetheless, several changes were made to the MREL framework, with its latest version being published in May 2020.
Differently from the TLAC requirements, MREL requirements are defined bank-by-bank by the European resolution authorities (namely the Single Resolution Board [SRB] and the National Resolution Authorities [NRAs]), taking account of whether a bank would be liquidated or resolved if it were to fail. Ideally, they are designed as a percentage of total liabilities and own funds. The instruments eligible to fulfil the MREL requirements were broader with respect to the ones required to meet TLAC requirements, but new standards were defined under the BRRD2/SRMR2, published in May 2020. Thus, starting from 2020, the MREL decisions implementing the new framework are now taken based on the MREL Policy under the Banking Package in the 2020 resolution planning cycle, and are going to be communicated to banks in 2021. Each decision foresees setting two binding MREL targets for each bank: an intermediate one to be met in 2022, and the full one to be met in 2024.

Questions and answers

1. *What were the key issues for the financial system which emerged during the crisis?*
   a) Low levels of capital: many of the banks asking for public intervention had pre-crisis capital ratios above the minimum threshold;
   b) High pro-cyclicality, which intensified the crisis, especially with regards to the credit process;
   c) High interconnection between large financial institutions, which increased the risk of contagion;
   d) High grade of debt (or leverage ratio) of banks;
   e) Low pre-crisis attention to liquidity risk, both on the part of bank managers and of the supervisory authorities.

2. *Provide a brief description of the Financial Regulatory Framework structure.*
   Section 2.1.1. and Figure 2.1. should be used as reference.

3. *What is the Banking Union? What are its three pillars?*
Refer to Section 2.1.1.

4. *How is the Capital Adequacy Ratio defined?*
The Capital Adequacy Ratio (CAR) helps make sure banks have enough capital to protect depositors' money, since a bank that has a good CAR has enough capital to absorb potential losses, thus it incurs less risk of becoming insolvent.
The Basel Committee defines the capital adequacy ratio (CAR) as follows:

$$CAR = \frac{regulatory\ capital}{RWA}$$

5. *What are the differences between Tier 1 and Tier 2 capital? What are their minimum mandatory ratios?*
The Basel Committee separates capital into Tier 1 capital and Tier 2 capital, based on its function and quality.
Tier 1 capital is the core capital held in reserve. It can be considered a proxy for a bank's financial health. Tier 1 capital is also defined as going-concern capital, since it is permanently and easily available to cushion losses suffered by a bank without impacting business operations. It is composed of both Common Equity Tier 1 (CET1) capital and Additional Tier 1 (AT1) capital. Common Equity Tier 1 capital (CET1) is the highest quality of regulatory capital, as it absorbs losses immediately when they occur. Additional Tier 1 capital (AT1) also provides loss absorption on a going-concern basis, although AT1 instruments do not meet all the criteria for CET1. Tier 1 capital consists of equity capital, ordinary share capital, intangible assets, and audited revenue reserves.
Tier 2 capital is gone-concern capital. That is, when a bank fails, Tier 2 instruments must absorb losses before depositors and general creditors do. It is used to absorb losses if a bank loses all its Tier 1 capital. Tier 2 is composed of unaudited retained earnings, unaudited reserves and general loss reserves. As can be inferred, it has lower quality, is less liquid, and thus more difficult to measure. For the cited reasons, it is also known as supplementary capital.
Minimum mandatory ratios: CET1 > 4.5%; CET1+AT1>6%; CET1 +AT1+Tier2>8%.

6. *How is the Capital Stack composed?*
Refer to Section 2.3.4 and Figure 4.

7. *Briefly explain the key components of the formula for Risk Weighted Assets under the Internal Ratings-based approach for credit risk.*
Section 2.4.2 should be used as reference.

8. *Provide an explanation of the concepts of Probability of Default and Loss Given Default.*
Section 2.4.2 can serve as reference.

9. *Explain the concept of Value-at-Risk and what measures were introduced by Basel 2.5 to complement it. Also mention an alternative to VaR.*
Value-at-Risk (VaR) provides an estimate of the most that a portfolio is expected to lose over a given time period (usually, one day), in all but, say, 1% of the time (i.e. 99% confidence level). It can be calculated with several methods, such as the following: variance and covariance method; Montecarlo simulation method; and historical simulation method. VaR is particularly useful since it allows for a comparison of risk in different businesses, such as fixed income and equity, and also provides a means to aggregate and net a variety of positions within the same portfolio, in order to reflect correlations between different assets.
Following the financial crisis, it became clear that VaR, as it was computed, was not an adequate measure for risk. The need for additional measures became urgent, and thus an interim regulation (Basel 2.5) was issued in order to introduce higher regulatory requirements for market risk aimed at avoiding regulatory arbitrage. In addition to VaR, several other new measures were introduced, among which we can list sVaR, incremental risk charge, comprehensive risk measure, standardised specific risk charges, and risks not in VaR. An alternative to VaR is represented by the Expected Shortfall (ES) method. Expected shortfall, also known as "conditional VaR" or expected tail loss, is a way of estimating losses that tries to make up for VaR's inability to handle tail risk well. ES finds the average of the expected losses that occur beyond the confidence level selected.

10. *Provide a brief description of the Liquidity Coverage Ratio and the Net Stable Funding Ratio.*
The Liquidity Coverage Ratio (LCR) requires banks to have sufficient high quality assets to withstand a 30-day stressed funding scenario specified by the supervisor. It focuses on a short-term perspective: the 30-day period allows banks to have a cushion of high quality liquid assets in the event of a run on banks during a financial crisis. The 30-day requirement also provides central banks and governments time to step in and implement corrective measures to stabilize the financial system. The high-quality liquid assets include only those with a high potential to be converted easily and quickly into cash.

$$LCR = \frac{High\ quality\ liquid\ asset\ amount\ (HQLA)}{Total\ net\ cash\ flow\ amount}$$

The Net Stable Funding Ratio (NSFR) is a long-term structural ratio designed to address liquidity mismatches. It covers the entire balance sheet and provides incentives for banks to use stable sources of funding, requiring banks to maintain a stable funding profile in relation to their off-balance sheet assets and activities. The NSFR is defined as the ratio between the amount of stable funding available and the amount of stable funding required. The NSFR is expressed as a ratio that must equal or exceed 100%. The Total Available Stable Funding, ASF, is the portion of a banks' capital and liabilities that will remain with the institution for more than one year. The Total Required Stable Funding (ARF), is the amount of stable funding required to be held given the liquidity characteristics and residual maturities of assets and the contingent liquidity risk arising from off-balance sheet exposures.

$$\frac{Total\ Available\ Stable\ Funding\ (ASF)}{Total\ Required\ Stable\ Funding\ (ARF)} \times 100\%$$

3 Introduction to Corporate and Investment Banking

by Stefano Caselli and Marta Zava

3.1 The business areas of Corporate and Investment Banking

The objective of the chapter is to delve into the analysis of the context of the evolution and the main activities and business areas of Corporate and Investment Banking. Following the description of the activities, the chapter will concentrate on the League Tables analysis over the decade from 2009 to 2019. To offer a framework for Corporate and Investment Banking activities, we can identify seven main areas, categorized by type of products and services offered, technical and professional competencies required, risks and exposure of the financial intermediary in single operations, form of remuneration, and lastly, the type of clients' needs. Thus, we identify the following business areas (**Figure 3.1**):

- Capital Markets;
- Corporate Finance;
- Private Equity (or Merchant Banking);
- Structured Finance;
- Asset Management (or Wealth Management);
- Risk Management (or Corporate Risk Management);
- Corporate Lending.

With reference to this last activity, we must consider that lending activities are not a business area per se, but are to be deemed as support functions for other business areas.

Each of the sections below is devoted to studying each of the cited business areas,

Figure 3.1 The 6+1 CIB system

focusing on the types of products and services offered, the main features of the productive processes, the role of the financial intermediary, and the professional profile required. Every business has its own characteristics, its own products and services, and its own profit model. This last aspect is important, and a lot of attention is required to continuously understand where the sources of profit stand (and where they come from) as well as the impact (or lack thereof) on the regulatory capital. While operating costs come from the organizational design, synergies, and human capital and are allocated on the business according to certain criteria, revenues and the cost of regulatory capital are strictly related to each business. The difference between the revenues and the cost of regulatory capital represents the gross profit a single deal or the entire business unit generates, which we identify as the EVA generated.

3.2 Capital markets

The main business area in Corporate and Investment Banking is represented by capital markets. In this business segment, the financial intermediary offers structured support to corporate clients to satisfy their financial needs by means of issuance and trading of financial instruments in capital markets. The purpose of capital markets is clearly to finance customers. But going into detail, it is possible to distinguish the following two main market segments, i.e. two ways to finance customers, often suited to two different types of businesses:

- **Primary market:** the system of support and advisory activities oriented towards the placement of newly-issued financial instruments (both on the stock exchange with IPOs and in the private market by private placement);
- **Secondary market:** brokering operations and negotiation of financial instruments already circulating in the market.

In the **primary market**, financial intermediary activities are mainly aimed at collecting funds to finance public and private clients through the issuance of new financial instruments such as shares or bonds. In the case in which shares are issued, we can distinguish between clients admitted to regulated capital markets trading for the first time, who will have an initial public offering (IPO), and clients already listed on the stock exchange, who issue additional shares to collect new financial resources. In this sense, operations with customers in primary market are "liability side," as they have to issue securities to raise financial resources.

With reference to the role of the financial intermediary, we now define the following four phases of the process.

Origination: this is the phase before the actual issuing of financial instruments and it is characterized by promotional activity with regard to investors and the preliminary technical analysis to plan a successful operation. The objective is to delineate the best strategy in terms of timing, market target, potential investors, price, etc.

Advisory and arranging: this identifies the system of financial activities performed to define the economic profile of the operation, through the evaluation of the financial feasibility, methods, and the issuance pricing of stock. The function requires high professional expertise in fiscal and legal matters to optimize the design of the operation. The last activity performed in this phase is *syndication*, in which a pool of intermediaries is selected to place the shares in the market segments defined jointly with the advisor and the issuer.

Underwriting: this refers to the phase of underwriting the newly-issued instruments, which will be owned by the intermediary until the public placement takes place. From an investment bank's perspective, the possible exposure to issuance risk is part of the range of guarantees offered in the initial underwriting deal. An *underwriting commitment* occurs when the intermediaries buy the entire issuance at the predefined price established with the issuer, facing both the risk of not selling the whole stock at the offering and of selling at a lower price with respect to the issuing entity. Alternatively, *in underwriting with assumption of guarantee*, the financial intermediary guarantees the underwriting of unsold stock, but it does not bear the price risk. Lastly, under the *best effort commitment*, the financial intermediary plays only a mediation role, which consists of selling the shares to investors, but does not offer any guarantee service, avoiding both unsold risk and price risk. Clearly, as the guarantees offered change, the remuneration levels requested by the investment bank also vary: the higher the coverage, the higher the commission fees and the operation cost for the issuer. By considering a deal of value of 1,000 and fees equal to 3%, in which the bank underwrites 30%, with a capital gain of 20%, the impact on a bank's financial statement is displayed below. The assets are increased by the value of the underwritten stock (300), while equity increases by 24 due to regulatory capital requirements (8%). Capital gains are computed on the underwritten part (300x20%), resulting in 60, while fees are to be computed on the whole amount issued (1000x3%). Therefore, profit is the sum of capital gains and fees. Cost of capital is driven by the 8% regulatory capital impact and the 15% cost of equity, multiplied by the underwritten amount. Therefore, the actual EVA is 86.4.

Exercise 1 Underwriting

assets	liabilities
300	
	equity
	24

P&L	
interest margin	
capital gain	
	60
fees	
	30
total	
	90

EVA	
Profit	
	90
cost of capital	
	3.6
total	
	86.4

- **Placement and selling:** this represents the last phase of the IPO placement process. We can distinguish two main types of placement by means of the investors to whom they are directed. In the *public placement* hypothesis, financial instruments are placed to a wide public of savers, individuals who have the right to access to the sale. Alternatively, in *private banking*, the sale is oriented only towards a restricted group of institutional investors (i.e. insurance companies, investment companies, pension funds, etc.), who are equipped with the technical and professional expertise to evaluate the risk-reward of the stock, and the economic burden of facing losses in the future. In general, the last placement approach is used to issue shares of companies which have recently been funded, that are especially risky, and mostly unknown to the general public.
  By considering a deal of value 1,000 and fees equal to 2.5%, the impact of placement and selling on a bank's financial statements is shown below. The gain stems exclusively from fees, leaving the balance sheet unaltered and increasing profits. Regulatory capital is left unchanged.

Exercise 2 **Placement and Selling**

assets	**liabilities**
	equity
	0

P&L	
interest margin	
capital gain	
fees	*25*
total	**25**

EVA	
profit	*25*
cost of capital	
total	**25**

The four phases, taken together, offer an overall perspective of the functions that capital markets cover. But, it often happens that the relationship between the issuing company and the financial intermediary is confined to only some of the above-mentioned areas. For instance, if the client has already selected the potential investors with whom to place the shares, it could ask for support only with regard to the advisory function on the technical aspects of the stock title, or for guarantees in the underwriting phase, etc.

Lastly, it must be mentioned that the mediation activity conducted by the financial intermediary does not alter the requisites relating to the supervisory capital, apart from the case in which it exits an underwriting agreement in which the investment bank agrees to partially or completely cover the issuance.

With reference to the **secondary market**, the capital markets business area offers assistance to clients in their investment activities in the capital markets through the negotiation of circulating securities. More in detail, the financial intermediary executes the buy and sell orders in every market circuit and gathers the necessary information to optimize the trade decisions of clients, protecting their financial balance. In this sense, operations with customers in the secondary market are "asset side," as they have to sell some securities they own on their balance sheet to raise financial resources.

Trading activities could be classified in the following two main categories based on the role and risks undertaken by the financial intermediaries.

Brokerage: the broker covers the role of facilitating the matching of supply and demand, and is remunerated by fees. Specifically, the broker searches for potential investors and negotiates financial instruments on behalf of clients. The mediation activity is fundamental for the broker, thus it is reasonable to conclude that its financial position is independent and immune from the risks involved in single trade operations. By considering a deal of value 1,000 and fees equal to 4%, the impact of brokerage on a bank's financial statements is displayed below. The gain stems exclusively from fees, leaving the balance sheet unaltered and increasing profits. Since equity is unchanged, regulatory capital does not change.

Exercise 3 Brokerage

assets	liabilities
	equity
	0

P&L	
interest margin	
capital gain	
fees	
	40
total	
	40

FVA	
profit	
	40
cost of capital	
total	
	40

Dealing: contrary to the broker, the dealer is the direct counterparty in the trading of clients' securities, overcoming the need to find a counterparty. From a financial approach, the dealer has its own portfolio of financial assets and a minimum level of capital to buy the amount of securities that the client wants to sell at any time. In this context, the dealer's role is to safeguard the liquidity of the market, minimizing the fluctuations in prices. Assuming a deal of value 1,000, with fees equal to 3.5%, a success hypothesis of 90% and capital gains of 30%, and considering that the securities are on the books (therefore they have an impact on the regulatory capital), the financial statements change as shown below. The bank buys 100 in securities, for which it has to set aside 8 in regulatory capital (equity side of the balance sheet). According to the success hypothesis and the capital gains percentage, capital gains in absolute value are equal to 270 (1000 x 90% x 30%). Fees are computed on the total deal value. And the cost of capital consists of 15% of equity.

Exercise 4 Dealing

assets	liabilities
100	
	equity
	8

P&L	
interest margin	
capital gain	*270*
fees	*35*
total	**305**

EVA	
profit	*305*
cost of capital	*1.2*
total	**303.8**

The two markets, primary and secondary, can be divided into three sub-segments, identified on the basis of the securities traded: stock market, bond market, and derivatives market (i.e. futures, options, warrants). The distinction is driven by the fact that each security class involves different risks, profits, and complexities than the others, and thus specific professional competencies and modus operandi should be developed for each category. For this reason, in the capital markets division it is common to identify sub-segments aimed at the management of the three securities classes. Furthermore, to satisfy the increasing need for personalized service, these areas are again divided into dedicated teams of specialists, built ad hoc to efficiently combine product volumes, sectors, and markets.

The presence of the bank in the dealing activity has a powerful consequence, i.e. the bank has the expertise, people, and IT system to be active in the capital market to trade securities. The outcome is to leverage this asset both by offering services to the customers and by generating profit for the bank itself. On the customers' side, the services that can be offered are market making and specialist support. On the bank's side, the activity implemented to generate profit is proprietary trading, or simply "prop trading."

Market Making: this covers the role of guaranteeing the negotiability of one or more financial instruments quoted on the stock market, continuously providing information on purchasing and selling prices (i.e. "bid" and "ask"), with the objective of ensuring a high level of liquidity and market volume. In many stock exchanges, the presence of market makers is crucial to ensure visibility and liquidity. The continuity element separates the role of the market maker from that of the dealer: the latter can decide to suspend the buy and sell proposals. Considering a deal value of 1,000 and fees equal to 5%, we can see how profit stems solely from fees.

Exercise 5 Market Making

assets	liabilities
	equity
	0

P&L	
interest margin	
capital gain	
Fees	*5*
total	**5**

EVA	
profit	*5*
cost of capital	
total	**5**

Specialist: as the market maker, the specialist covers the role of guaranteeing the negotiability of one or more financial instruments quoted on the stock market, continuously providing information on purchasing and selling prices (i.e. "bid" and "ask"), with the objective of ensuring a high level of liquidity and market volume. But the obligation of the specialist is stronger than in the previous case, as the specialist has the obligation to execute any proposals coming from the market, matching the bid price and the ask price. In many stock exchanges the presence of the specialist is not only crucial to ensure visibility and liquidity, but it is actually mandatory. The impact on the profit model is significant, as the bank could have securities on its asset side and regulatory capital usage. Again considering a deal value of 10,00 and fees equal to 5% as in the previous case, if nobody is going to match the specialist's prices, the outcome is the same as that of a market maker; while if somebody is going to sell 1,000 at the price offered by the specialist, the specialist has to buy this stake and the consequence is regulatory capital calculated on 1,000 and a capital gain or loss when the bank decides to sell the stake itself. The profit model would be the same as that of a dealer. The outcome is also the same if somebody is going to buy 1,000 from the bank. In this case, the bank has to buy 1,000 from the market, has to calculate the regulatory capital, and has to sell the stake to the buyer, facing a capital gain or loss.

Proprietary trading. The availability of trading desks to support dealing and to offer market making or specialist services to customers creates the overall know-how allowing to enhance investment decisions for the bank itself. Proprietary trading means that the bank buys and sells securities without having a link or an obligation with customers, but simply to pursue its own profit. For the profit model, the consequence is to have capital gains (or losses) and use of regulatory capital. The trading of securities can provide significant support for profits, but it can also expose the bank to obvious conflicts of interests. The first is related to the use of information, as the bank could have confidential and sensitive info and data coming from customer relationship, exploiting them to create profits. However, insider trading and con-

Box 3.1 The Volcker Rule

The Volcker Rule refers to section 619 of the Dodd-Frank Wall Street Reform Act of 2010. It generally prohibits banking entities from engaging in proprietary trading or investing in or sponsoring hedge funds or private equity funds.

As part of the Dodd-Frank Act, it was developed in the context of the post-crisis reforms, in order to protect customers' savings from speculative investments made by banks. Specifically, its aim is to prevent banks that receive federal and taxpayer backing in the form of deposit insurance and other support from engaging in risky trading activities. It was proposed by economist and former Fed Chair Paul Volcker, after whom the rule is named.

The Volcker Rule limits investments in derivatives and hedge funds up to 3% of tier 1 capital and limits the ownership stake of hedge funds or of private equity funds to 3%.

First, as we have already mentioned, banks are extremely limited in engaging in proprietary trading, which comprises the trading of securities, derivatives, commodities, futures, and options for on own account. Trading is allowed when it is within the limits of their own risk, as are other activities such as market making, underwriting, and hedging. For instance, a bank can hedge interest rate risk. Moreover, a bank can act as an agent, broker, or custodian for their customers, i.e. trade on behalf of their customers with the customers' approval. Very strenuous compliance requirements are placed on all proprietary trading activities, particularly on the ones exempted from the Volcker Rule. Requirements include internal controls and extensive documentation.

Second, banks are extremely limited in owning interests in covered funds, generally defined as hedge funds and private equity funds. However, banks may continue to offer hedge funds and private equity funds services allowing their customers to generate profits, except in cases where the activity would generate material conflicts of interest or instability within the bank or the financial system in general. As might be inferred, the rule was also seen also as a first step towards restoring the distinction between commercial and investment banking.

The regulations were developed by five federal financial regulatory agencies, including the Federal Reserve Board, the Commodity Futures Trading Commission, the Federal Deposit Insurance Corporation, the Office of the Comptroller of the Currency, and the Securities and Exchange Commission, which currently continue to supervise their application.

The Volcker Rule was not exempt from criticism. In 2014, the US Chamber of Commerce claimed that its costs outweighed the benefits. In 2017, the International Monetary Fund (IMF) stated that regulations aimed at preventing speculation are hard to enforce, and that the Volcker Rule could unintentionally decrease liquidity in the bond market.

On 25 June 2020, the five federal financial regulatory agencies finalized a rule modifying the prohibitions established in the Volcker Rule. The restrictions stemming from the Volcker Rule will be loosened, allowing banks to more easily make large investments in covered funds. Moreover, prudential capital requirements related to derivatives trading activities will be diminished. The loosening of the requirements will take effect as of 1 October 2020 and are expected to free up billions of dollars in the US banking industry.

flict of interest rules around the world act against this misbehaviour, and Chinese wall systems are set up by the banks themselves to prevent any risks that could damage their reputation on the market. The second is not related to information but to the use of financial resources. To let banks trade by themselves means that deposits (if the bank has them) provide cash to be traded. This concept is simple, but the magnitude is important, because deposits represent savings and it could be very risky, not only as a signal, to give banks the option to use savings to trade securities and thus put savings at risk. US regulations tried to mitigate this problem after the 2007-2008 crisis by introducing the "Volcker Rule," which created a limit for prop trading based on a certain proportion of deposits.

3.3 Corporate Finance

Corporate Finance defines the system of activities used to manage and optimize the financial structures of corporate clients. In this case, the financial intermediary is often an advisor, offering consulting services able to support and satisfy the different needs of corporate clients. Under the perspective of the company, the operations often have an extraordinary nature and a high strategic value. Thus, they influence: decisions relative to the growing process, mergers, and acquisitions (mergers and acquisitions); expansion in international markets, recovery and restructuring plans (restructuring, turnaround); and privatization activities (privatization). By now, the central role of the corporate finance business area should be clear. It stands side by side with every pivotal managerial decision, the company's strategic placement, and the long-term vision.

The corporate finance function is organized around the following three main areas:

- mergers and acquisitions;
- restructuring;
- advisory.

The activity of **mergers and acquisitions (M&A)** offers financial and advisory services dedicated to the supporting the client in strategic decisions regarding corporate governance or interventions on the financial structure. In general, M&A has the feature of being a cyclical business (i.e. subject to many fluctuations), highly influenced by the competitive dynamics of various economic sectors and macroeconomic market trends. Furthermore, it is characterized by numerous types of operations, among which the followings must be pointed out:

- **Acquisitions and disposals:** operations that transfer the ownership of a company to one or more purchasing companies. If the acquisition is agreed upon among the parties, the acquisition is referred to as "*friendly*"; on the contrary, all operations with which the buyer obtains the target company against the target's will are called "*hostile.*" Regarding execution methods, the ownership can be transferred as an asset purchase or a stock purchase. According to the type and features of the transaction, the role of the financial intermediary can be more or less broad and include processes of capital valuation, identification of potential buyers in the market (in the case of a friendly acquisition), definition of the optimal financial structure, and active participation in the negotiation and corporate financing.

- **Mergers:** transactions through which two or more companies merge to form a new entity. If the result of the merger is that the two companies involved cease to exist from a legal perspective and found a new and independent company, we talk of *perfect fusion*. Contrarily, *mergers by incorporation* occur when one company absorbs its counterparty, which ceases to exist. In mergers, the role the financial intermediary resembles the one in acquisitions (i.e. it involves consultancy and advisory services, and professional and technical competencies in fiscal, accounting, and legal matters).
- **Spin-off:** operation that establishes a new company through the unbundling of another company, which transfers the whole activities system or a single business line, keeping an important directive role in term of competencies and activities performed. Deeper in detail, the unbundled company, upfront of the transfer of activities and know-how, gets newly-issued stock of the spun-off company. The trade of assets between counterparties significantly alters both the strategic and structural order.
- **Break-up:** the process through which a company's capital is divided and attributed to other contracting (already existing or newly set up) companies. In the operation, the broken-up company's shareholders are compensated with new shares of the companies benefitting from the transfer. Under a technical profile, the break-up process can be total or partial. In the former case, the split company ceases its activities and the shareholders become *pro quota* owners in the other contracting companies. On the contrary, in the latter case, the target company continues to exist but its capital is reduced proportionally to the contribution made by the other companies involved in the operation. Similarly, stockholders, besides maintaining ownership of the split company, are compensated with new stock of the benefitted companies. Moreover, in the definition of the new corporate governance aspects, the share placement is *proportional* when the shareholders of the split companies are compensated with a number of shares corresponding to the proportion of capital of the initial company, or *not proportional* in the opposite case.
- **Joint venture:** a contract in which two or more companies formulate an agreement for financial collaboration aimed at accomplishing a goal or executing a common project. With respect to the cited operation, a joint venture is a contract which does not originate a new legal entity separate from the contracting companies. The companies continue to exist in a separate form, but cooperate on the realization of a shared industrial or commercial goal, strategically deploying the resources brought to the venture (for instance, know-how and capital) and sharing the investment risk through a fair apportionment of potential profits and losses.
- **Carve-out:** this is a special type of spin-off, frequently used in corporate reorganization processes. When this operation takes place, the company puts one of its

branches at the disposal of a new special purpose vehicle created specifically to go public through an IPO. The objective is to collect financial resources in capital markets while maintaining the control and management of the new enterprise; in fact, usually only a part of the vehicle's shares are offered to investors, while the majority share package is kept by the parent company. New resources could be allocated to several goals, left to the vehicle as part of its capital, or channelled to the parent company through the payment of dividends, share buybacks, or intragroup financing.

The concept of restructuring is wide and complex. First of all, it could refer to the voluntary choices a firm undertakes when it wants to improve its strategic placement with respect to the competitive context. On the other hand, it could identify turnaround processes, which are activated in circumstances of economic or financial distress to restore the usual operating conditions. In the latter case, the restructuring methods and the advisory role could change based on the following factors:

- the stage of distress;
- the nature of the intervention.

With reference to the former, we can distinguish between legal restructurings, when the instruments offered by law are used, and non-legal procedures, managed by means of agreements between interested entities. According to the stage of distress, the advisor will play a different role, which involves different tasks and responsibilities.

The reconstructing processes can be distinguished on the basis of the operation's nature and be focused on asset restructuring or liability restructuring. In the former case, the advisor performs the task of planning interventions able to rationalize and optimize assets and to generate, in the short term, enough liquidity to set the company free from the debt that inhibits regular operations. The process can involve single balance sheet items, or entire divisions, or product and market portfolios, to pursue the goal of focusing the company's activities on the core business, thus delineating a new strategic placement in the sector.

Liability restructuring interventions have the goal of restoring the balance of the financial structure of the company facing a crisis. The role of the financial intermediary changes. After having formulated the recovery plan, the financial intermediary needs to both convince the company's creditors to participate in the restructuring process (asking for deadline consolidation, partial bank loan forgiveness, interest rate renegotiation, etc.), and rebalance the total financing costs taking the company's income skills into consideration.

Lastly, in the function of corporate finance we also find the pure financial consultancy activities. In general, the advisory activity can be useful for restructuring and mergers and acquisitions, or it can play an independent role and be sold to the client as a stand-alone service. In the latter case, for instance, we can think of consultancy in capital budgeting matters, the preparation of the medium-long term business plan, or the sectorial strategic analyses aimed at offering a wider perspective on competitive market trends, besides providing support for M&A operations.

With reference to the role and competencies of the advisor, consultancy activities perform the task of taking care of the different needs of clients by satisfying more or less complex demands. Thus various technical, economic, and legal competencies are required on the following matters: financial structuring, tax planning, corporate and investment project evaluation, international law, etc.

Considering both mergers and acquisitions and restructuring deals, the impact on a bank's financial statement is similar. Let us consider a deal of value 1,000 and fees equal to 4.5%. Strictly speaking, the gains stem solely from fees, as shown below.

Exercise 6 Mergers & Acquisitions

assets	liabilities
	equity
	0

P&L	
interest margin	
capital gain	
fees	*45*
total	**45**

EVA	
profit	*45*
cost of capital	
total	**45**

However, as mentioned previously, all corporate finance deals involve some cross-selling favouring other areas of the bank, to some extent. Thus, the profit and loss account of the capital markets area, corporate lending, and private equity would also be affected.

3.4 Private Equity

Private Equity activities belong, in general, to forms of corporate financing. Unlike from traditional lending activities, where the financial intermediary represents the company's creditor, in private equity operations (or merchant banking) financing is made in terms of equity and is intended to create a financial partnership with the corporate client. It is clear that the new role of the financial intermediary is going to be associated with a different economic profile. The traditional remuneration of credit activity, the interest margin, is substituted by capital gains. The key point is that capital gains are the difference between the transfer price and the cost of the initial investment.

The private equity function could be managed directly by the financial intermediary or through the creation a closed-end fund. The two formulas have different economic and regulatory impacts. In the former model, private equity activities are regulated by banking directives on capital gains and are subject to the regulatory requirements of supervisory capital. In the latter model, the financial intermediary can choose whether to manage and/or invest in the closed-end fund and thus opt for a remuneration system focused on fees payment for management services, and/or a structure similar to the case described previously. To clarify, in this section, private equity is used as a synonym for financial intermediaries.

The concept of private equity is generic per se, and could encompass operations of different kinds, types of remuneration, and risk levels. It is possible to identify two main criteria to classify private equity firms, based on the following features:

- the volume of private equity participation;
- the investment phase in the corporate life cycle.

The first classification groups private equity into two different categories according to whether the investment is directed at obtaining a minority or majority stake. Based on the share package volumes, private equity will have different types of influence on the strategic direction of the company. In the case of minority holdings, investments are of a financial nature, often characterized by limited influence on management. To the contrary, the purchase of a majority stake has an industrial nature, and as a consequence private equity has a strong influence on the management and strategic direction of companies in the medium-long term.

The second set of classification criteria emphasizes the differences in investment policies and strategic investments in the private equity business based on the company life cycle. We have the following areas:

- **Seed financing:** financing to companies in the seed phase, the initial one. This is the moment when founders create and develop a new business idea, and production activities have not started yet. In this stage, technologies, products, and the strategic model are in an embryonic and experimental phase.
- **Early-growth financing:** financing to recently-established companies in which, contrary to seed financing, production activities have started. The uncertainty level is still very high since the commercial power of the new product or service has not been validated in the target market yet.
- **Expansion financing:** financing to growing companies which have successfully passed the phases of development and start-up. In general, we are talking about companies expanding with several development opportunities, often oriented towards an IPO at the moment in which the private equity firm disinvests. For this reason, it is often called *bridge financing*.
- **Replacement financing:** financing to mature and consolidated companies with a stable sales level. In this case, private equity's role is to reorganize the corporate structure through the direct purchase of the share package or by favouring extraordinary finance operations such as *leveraged* or *management buy-outs*.
- **Distressed (or vulture) financing:** financing to companies facing a crisis. The

operations are very risky due to the high probability of default. The goal of private equity is to provide professional competencies and financial resources for the purpose of company restructuring.

It must be pointed out that private equity activity may involve both direct and indirect investment. In the first case, the bank is exposed directly to the risks and the gains, and the investment is recorded as an asset. Considering a deal of value 1,000, and expected capital gains of 25%, the bank's financial statements will be impacted as shown below. The regulatory capital to be set aside corresponds to the 8% of assets, and 15% constitutes the cost of capital. Therefore, the actual profit is equal to the capital gains of 250 minus the cost of capital, thus 238.

Exercise 7 Private Equity – Direct Investment

assets	**liabilities**
1000	
	equity
	80

P&L	
interest margin	
capital gain	*250*
fees	
total	**250**

EVA	
profit	*250*
cost of capital	*12*
total	**238**

Direct private equity is a bit uncommon because of its high impact on regulatory capital. Even though this decision is strategic, it can be said that direct private equity is mostly related to "political decisions" such as the need to have a direct stake as a "trophy asset" or due to the need for restructuring or even saving from bankruptcy a company which is crucial for a certain economic environment.

The bank can also be involved in indirect investments through an asset management company. This the most common way to deal with private equity and does not necessarily mean having ownership of the asset management company. In many cases, the role of the Corporate and Investment Bank is to be the financial sponsor of either asset management companies or specific deals. However, let us consider an operation of value 1,000, for which the expected carried interest is equal to 45% of the fund value. The bank invests 2% of the AMC, with an expected yield of 30%. Thus, the asset side increases by 20 and consequently the regulatory capital, corresponding to equity, increases by 8% (1.6). Capital gains flow from the 2% AMC investment, while fees are 45% of the whole deal value. The cost of capital is 15% of the regulatory capital.

Exercise 8 Private Equity – Indirect Investment

assets	liabilities
20	
	equity
	1.6

P&L	
interest margin	
capital gain	*6*
fees	*450*
total	**456**

EVA	
profit	*456*
cost of capital	*0.24*
total	**455.76**

We need to clarify that the concept of private equity is intended broadly and also includes venture capital, i.e. firms specialized in investments in companies in the start-up or growing phase, and with high growth potential.

In conclusion, private equity activities are often comparable to corporate finance operations, but the crucial difference, with respect to merger and acquisition activities, is based on the fact that the target company's equity share is not purchased by another firm, but by the same private equity firm.

3.5 Structured finance

Structured finance (also called "leveraged finance") identifies all the operations managed by Special Purpose Vehicles (SPV) and characterised by assets or investment projects able to generate cash flows, often contractually linked to the reimbursement of the debt incurred to finance the operation. Since they can autonomously satisfy their debt obligations, structured finance activities are often denominated as asset-based deals or self-financing deals.

Going into more detail, in extraordinary finance projects the financial intermediary can intervene in different forms in each project phase through origination, advisory and consulting, fundraising, and direct investment financing activities. Apart from the last of these, the services are among the sources of active commissions for the intermediary and do not alter the supervisory capital.

In practice, it is possible to identify the following three categories of operations, differentiated by the respective asset types:

- **Securitization:** when the base activities of the project are real estate, loans, commercial credit, or other company assets;
- **Project Financing:** related to large projects or infrastructure investments (i.e. highways, bridges, hospitals, etc.) which require a significant financial effort, that is difficult for a single company to bear;

- **Leveraged buy-out (LBO):** when the asset in the operation is the same company that has been purchased. This type of deal can also be included in the area of private equity and of M&A.

Box 3.2 The special feature of securitization

As mentioned in Chapter 1 in the section describing the financial functions of banks, securitization significantly changed the strategic model of banks, which went from "originate-to-hold" to "originate-to-distribute." **Securitization** is an operation by which a company's assets (usually characterized by low liquidity) are transformed into liquid financial securities placed and traded on securities markets. It involves the creation of bonds whose principal and interest payments derive from the cash flows generated by tranches of assets. Financial institutions and firms use securitization to anticipate the value of a cash flow generating activity. Usually, the activity is of financial nature, such as loans, commercial loans, or leasing. In most cases, the originator anticipates a regular cash flow. Creating a portfolio of financial assets, cash flows can be used to pay the bonds' principal and interest payments. When assets are securitized, the originator receives the cash flows in a single lump-sum instead of having them distributed over time. There are two main types of securitization: mortgage-backed securities (MBS) and asset-backed securities (ABS). Securitization operations require the collaboration of several specialised players that intervene in the process, divided into the following phases:

a. A special purpose vehicle (SPV) is created, and owns the underlying assets;
b. The originator or the holder of the assets (existing or prospective) sell them to the SPV;
c. The SPV, with the help of an investment bank, issues the bonds which are in turn distributed to the investors;
d. The SPV pays the originator with the proceedings coming from the sale of the bonds.

The players involved are exposed to risks and gains to different extents. Commercial banks, investment banks, financial companies and service companies, as well as rating agencies, can be involved. The advantages and disadvantages of securitization are widely treated in the economic and financial literature. Among the main advantages, we can identify the possibility of calibrating the risk/revenue profile of the originated portfolio. Furthermore, the process allows for the creation of a secondary liquid market for mortgages and other debts, which in turn increases the capital available to grant new loans. Moreover, it contributes to the reduction of credit costs through the reduction of financial costs, offering lenders the possibility to collect funds on capital markets at lower interest rates. Furthermore, securitization reassigns risk by transferring to investors the credit risk associated with the securitised assets, instead of leaving it completely to the originating institutions.

Disadvantages mainly regard asymmetric information, which occurs when securitization introduces incentives to reduce credit monitoring under both a financial and a legal perspective, which could help identify the critical issue related to the financing process and to the responsibilities in the distribution of revenues and wealth.

The securitization process has recently undergone a revision at the European level, specifically with regard to the capital market union. The objectives were the following:

1. to restart markets in a more sustainable fashion, in order to make simple, transparent and standard (STS) securitization an efficient financing channel for the economy;
2. to allow institutional investors and banks to carry out efficient and effective transfers of risk;
3. to allow securitization to work as an effective financing mechanism for banks and some non-banking players;
4. to protect investors and manage systemic risk, avoiding the creation of faulty "originate-to-distribute" models.

To accomplish the goals indicated above, more simple, transparent and standard (STS) securitizations were designed, characterized by the following features:

i. simplicity criteria: including normative and regulatory recommendations aimed at making underlying assets homogeneous (no mixed-asset portfolios);
ii. transparency criteria: operations must respect transparency and informational obligations, such as the submission of loan level data;
iii. standardization criteria: underlying exposures should be transferred to the SPV under a strong legal perspective.

Let us consider a deal of value 1,000, with an arrangement fee for the structuring of the operation equal to 3.5% and an SPV management fee equal to 4.5%. Moreover, the bank invests 10 in the SPV, and the dividend yield is 2%.
Therefore, the asset increases by the purchased amount (10) and consequently the regulatory capital, recorded in equity, increases by 0.8. Capital gains stem from the dividend yield on the purchased part (thus, 0.2), while fees are applied to the whole operation ([3.5+4.5]% x 1000). As in the previous exercises, the cost of capital is computed as 15% of regulatory capital.

Exercise 9 **Securitization**

assets	liabilities
10	
	equity
	0.8

P&L	
interest margin	
capital gain	*0.2*
fees	*80*
total	**80.2**

EVA	
profit	*80.2*
cost of capital	*0.12*
total	**80.14**

Box 3.3 **Exploring project financing**

Project financing is a fast-growing area of structured finance related to major infrastructure and other large projects, which has gained more and more importance in recent years. It is entirely related to the project's ability to repay the debt contracted and remunerate investors consistent with their expectations, excluding the soundness and creditworthiness of the parties involved and the debt collateral from the evaluation. Project financing identifies a new investment project, distinguished from the sponsor's activities and completely independent from an organizational, managerial, and financial perspective: a new ad hoc project company is set up.
From the investor's point of view, the capital reimbursement and the interest payments are subordinated to the project's ability to generate positive cash flows over time; thus, investors cannot exercise rights on the sponsor's capital in the case the investment underperforms. Cash flows generated by the project must be sufficient to cover payments for operating costs, then to service the debt in terms of capital repayment and interest, and only afterwards can dividends be paid to sponsors.
In the case of default, the sponsor's financial liability is limited to the risk capital contributed to the project (collateral is usually provided by the sponsors to the lenders). It must be pointed out that the risks related to the project are allocated between all parties involved in the transaction, with the aim of assigning each of them to the parties best able to control and manage them.

Let us assume a deal of value 1,000, for which the bank invests 5% in the SPV's equity with a dividend yield of 7%, and requests an arrangement fee for the structuring of the operation equal to 5%; the impact on a bank's financial statements is displayed below. The 5% invested in the SPV is accounted for under assets. Since the regulatory capital is 8%, the equity increase is 4. Capital gains flow from the dividend yield multiplied by the purchased SPV equity (thus, 50 x 7%). Lastly, fees are computed on the entire amount of the operation. As usual, the cost of capital is 15% of the increase in equity. Moreover, project financing operations usually generate cross-selling to manage the liabilities of the SPV. Thus, the bank will issue bonds (capital market area) and collect loans (corporate lending area).

Exercise 10 Project Financing

assets	liabilities
50	
	equity
	4

P&L	
interest margin	
capital gain	*3.5*
fees	*50*
total	**53.5**

EVA	
profit	*53.5*
cost of capital	*0.6*
total	**52.9**

Lastly, a **leveraged buy-out (LBO)** is a specific M&A operation, by means of which a target company is acquired through the use of third-party capital, i.e. debt. The resulting company will have a higher debt ratio after the operation with respect to the ratio before the acquisition; therefore, only low-debt companies with high and stable cash flows are qualified as potential LBO targets. By considering a deal of value 1,000, for which the arrangement fee that the bank requests for the structuring and execution of the deal is 5%, the bank's financial statements are impacted as shown below. The gain stems exclusively from fees, leaving the balance sheet unaltered and increasing profits. As no capital is involved, regulatory capital also does not change.

Exercise 11 Leveraged Buy-Out

assets	liabilities
	equity
	0

P&L	
interest margin	
capital gain	
fees	*50*
total	**50**

EVA	
profit	*50*
cost of capital	
total	**50**

It must be considered that LBO operations usually cross-sell the SPV financing, often through loans.

Thus, the corporate lending area will obtain the syndication fee, and if the bank lends, it will earn the lending interest margin.

3.6 Asset management

Asset management is a system of activities dedicated to managing customer's assets. Its function is to maximize investor benefits by making their capital grow through a set of professional competencies and services aimed at allocating and protecting the invested resources.

Under the managerial profile, asset management activities are often integrated into the CIB division dedicated to high-net worth individuals (HNWI) capital management. In some cases, the organizational structure can contemplate a specialized team for each type of investment, such as the following:

- **financial asset management:** securities investment activities;
- **management of other assets:** investment activities in assets different from securities, for instance real estate or art.

The activities could be managed directly by the financial intermediary or indirectly by a company specialized in asset management and are compensated by the payment of commissions for the services rendered to investors. The division is often involved in managing conspicuous amounts of liquidity, a feature that makes it especially interesting in the eyes of large institutions with considerable financial resources (i.e. pension funds, foundations, insurance companies, etc.).

The activities require high professional competencies and technical market knowledge, delineating the role of the asset manager, who has to perform the following tasks:

- identifying and evaluating the capital investment opportunities;
- developing specific knowledge, applicable to several investment modalities and markets (i.e. real estate, private equity, etc.);
- acquiring broad legal and fiscal competencies (e.g. related to holdings and trust management);
- offering insurance know-how;
- knowing in detail the features and peculiarities of the country in which it operates.

By considering a hypothetical 3% management fee, and a managed assets value of 1,000, the activity impacts a financial institution's balance sheet as shown below.

Exercise 12 Asset Management

assets	liabilities
	equity
	0

P&L	
interest margin	
capital gain	
fees	
	30
total	
	30

EVA	
profit	
	30
cost of capital	
total	
	30

3.7 Risk management

In a Corporate and Investment Bank, the risk management division offers services aimed at managing risk with the goal of protecting the corporate clients' activities from losses due to unforeseen events and of optimizing the efficiency of managerial and production processes.

The concept of risk is broad, but it could be easily limited to one of the following categories:

- financial risks;
- industrial risks or pure risks.

Financial risk represents the potential impact of certain events on corporate liquidity, and is linked to cash flow balance. Therefore, the risk is associated with the concept of volatility, i.e. the element of variability in investments which could lead to unexpected losses or profits. The main financial risks are the following:

- **exchange risk:** a drop in exchange rates could cause a loss in value related to the assets denominated in foreign currency, while an increase in exchange rates could represent a gain in value (in domestic currency) of the same assets.
- **interest rate risk:** interest rate fluctuations expose the investors in financial instruments to the risk of suffering capital losses. In practice, interest rate risk also occurs when, regardless the issuer's respect of contractual duties, the investor records an actual cost or a missed gain.
- **insolvency risk:** the creditor faces the risk of not being able to sell a financial instrument at its real price for several reasons, among which we can find the lack of a reference market or of interested buyers.

As previously described, the occurrence of financial risks could result in unexpected losses or gains, thus it is described as a symmetric risk. To the contrary, industrial risks are asymmetric risks, since they can only result in losses to be faced by the company. Let us consider the natural risks category. The occurrence of an unexpected and dreadful event, such as a fire, an earthquake, or a volcanic eruption, can only seriously damage a company's assets.

Risk management activities are often paired with consulting services aimed at evaluating and classifying risks and potential damages from unforeseen events. Thus, the advisory function and the preliminary analysis of risks are a fundamental step on which to build the subsequent coverage operations. After the definition of the economic environment in which the company operates, in this phase it is first of all necessary to identify, analyse, and evaluate corporate risks, and consequently to build a specific control and management scheme for potentially damaging events.

Among the modalities of covering for risks of a financial nature, the intermediary could offer an internal matching service through the definition of a structure of assets and liabilities able to immunize the risk faced by the company (i.e. duration matching). Alternatively, ad hoc financial products have been created to reduce volatility exposure (i.e. futures, options, derivatives). For instance, the distribution of derivatives with a 3% fee applying to 50% of volume, and the construction of derivatives on the other 50% of volume with a 4% arrangement fee and a 10% expected yield, would lead to the following impact on a bank's financial statements. Considering a deal of value 1,000, 500 are accounted for as assets in the banks' balance sheet. Consequently, the regulatory capital on the equity side increases by 40 (8% x 500). Capital gains are driven by the expected yield, and thus are equal to 50 (10% x 500). Fees are computed on one side as the 4% arrangement fee applying to half of the deal amount, and the 3% fee applying to the distributed part.

Exercise 13 Building and distribution of financial products

assets	**liabilities**
500	
	equity
	40

P&L	
interest margin	
capital gain	*50*
fees	*70*
total	**120**

EVA	
profit	*120*
cost of capital	*6*
total	**114**

In the case of pure risks, the asymmetric profile requires obtaining dedicated coverage through specific insurance products (i.e. insurance policies). By offering insurance, the bank's gains stem solely from fees. Considering a deal of value 1,000 and a 2% origination fee, the impact on a bank's financial statements is shown below. Under a normative perspective, the financial intermediary is free to structure and sell its clients the instruments dedicated to financial risk coverage, while it can only distribute and place insurance policies.

Exercise 14 Insurance offering

assets	liabilities
	equity
	0

P&L	
interest margin	
capital gain	
fees	*20*
total	**20**

EVA	
profit	*20*
cost of capital	
total	**20**

3.8 Corporate lending

Corporate lending activities have always been considered the core activity of traditional banking, which have generated the largest portion of its profits from interest margin. Actually, in Corporate and Investment Banking, the role of credit services changes, passing from being the core activity to being a source of support for the other six business areas previously described (capital markets, corporate finance, private equity, structured finance, asset management, and risk management). Yet they are not to be considered as less important. Bank financing is often paired with other CIB activities, especially when conspicuous capital investments, which are not usually available to the company, are required. For this reason, it can be concluded that the corporate lending function is a source of profit both directly through interest margins, and indirectly through commissions, since it is auxiliary to performing other banking services.

Under a regulatory perspective, credit activities have an impact on the supervisory capital level, and thus on the prudential requirements set by the Basel Council.

Execution and management of lending activities vary based on the size and burden of CIB operations. The financial intermediary can choose to proceed through the *stand-alone* approach and bear the risk originated from the whole operation, or in more complex cases, it can opt for a *syndication strategy*, selecting and structuring a pool of investors with whom to share the losses and profits deriving from the investment.

On the basis of the lending features, duration, and purpose of use, it is possible to identify the following product categories:

- export and trade finance;
- short-term commercial loans (related to current assets);
- mortgage loans;
- leasing;
- hybrid instruments and mezzanine financing.

The corporate lending function can be based on more or less complex organizational structures, and can involve the set-up of specialised clusters according to the precise combination of market, client, and product (i.e. financing dedicated to the naval sector, energy sector, transport sector, etc.).

In its most basic form, lending produces revenues from interest margin and management fees. Let us consider a loan of value 1,000, which represents an asset for the financial institution. The bank is asked to set apart 8% of the asset as regulatory capital, which is recorded as equity. By assuming an interest margin of 0.5% and management fees equal to 1.5%, profit equals 20. However, the cost of capital, computed as 15% of regulatory capital, is equal to 12. Thus, the resulting EVA is 8.

Exercise 15 Lending

assets	**liabilities**
1000	
	equity
	80

P&L	
interest margin	*5*
capital gain	
fees	*15*
total	**20**

EVA	
profit	*20*
cost of capital	*12*
total	**8**

3.9 Analysing League Tables (2009-2019) worldwide

The Investment Banking League Tables, produced by Refinitiv and published by the Financial Times, list investment banks ranking them by fee revenues or deal sizes, based on a determined period (usually one year). They report the deals done by the banks, including mergers and acquisition, underwriting deals, and advisory services. In addition, to the overall league tables, the rankings are divided by business, namely: M&A, equity (ECM), loans, and bonds (DCM). Apart from the dollar value of deal transactions, the league tables can also list the market share value held by each bank in a given period. Fees and number or size of deals are considered a proxy for the performance of the financial institution. In fact, investment bank league tables assist investors involved in merger transactions in choosing firms based on performance (as in how many deals a firm has completed), fees owned as a result of a deal, and a transaction's terms and price. Rankings are made at a global level (reported as follows) and at a regional level (displayed in the next section), but any other level and sub-category can also be considered if necessary. While regional deal transactions collect lower fees (but might increase the overall number of deals made by a financial institution), global investment banks are more apt to collect higher transaction fees in cross-border deals as bankers are required to be in multiple locations working with international regulations, which increases the complexity of the task and can lengthen the deal completion period.

The ranking is considered a proxy for the banks' value, but recently league tables have started having an increasingly prominent role, becoming the most used tool to

Figure 3.2 League Tables – overall

Top 10 Banks	Fees ($m)	Changes in Fees vs. Prev Period*	% of Fees collected by product 2019			
			M&A	Equity	Bonds	Loans
JP Morgan	7,363.60	-4.16%	28	21	29	23
Goldman Sachs & Co	6,109.62	-6.95%	47	24	20	8
Bofa Securities Inc	5,784.78	+8.51%	23	17	33	27
Morgan Stanley	5,295.48	-1.94%	37	27	27	9
Citi	4,728.38	-1.47%	27	19	35	19
Credit Suisse	3,288.19	-7.78%	25	20	31	24
Barclays	3,282.46	+1.16%	29	13	37	22
Deutsche Bank	2,345.18	-7.39%	24	12	42	22
Wells Fargo & Co	2,188.77	+0.96%	12	10	44	34
RBC Capital Markets	2,006.60	--	22	16	37	25
Total	**106,114.21**	**+0.80%**	**30**	**17**	**32**	**21**

Data from Jan 1 2019 - Dec 31 2019 and Jan 1 2018 - Dec 31 2018

Data as of Mar 30 2020

Source: Refinitiv, an LSEG business.

Figure 3.3 League Tables – M&A

Top 10 Banks	Fees ($m)	Changes in Fees vs. Prev Period*	% of Fees collected by product 2019: Europe	Asia Pacific (ex Central Asia)	Japan	Africa/ Middle East/ Central Asia	Americas
Goldman Sachs & Co	2,900.21	-1.32%	20	7	2	3	67
JP Morgan	2,052.33	-13.88%	16	6	2	4	71
Morgan Stanley	1,943.86	-11.82%	18	8	7	2	65
Bofa Securities Inc	1,340.43	+12.28%	24	5	4	3	66
Citi	1,285.97	-14.21%	29	12	1	3	56
Lazard	997.90	-24.75%	40	3	1	2	55
Barclays	936.34	-3.01%	23	4	1	4	69
Evercore Partners	855.91	+15.09%	14	5	6	0	74
Credit Suisse	834.98	-29.02%	24	10	3	1	63
Rothschild & Co	775.13	-28.77%	71	7	0	6	15
Total	**31,872.36**	**-7.54%**	**28**	**9**	**5**	**2**	**55**

Data from Jan 1 2019 - Dec 31 2019 and Jan 1 2018 - Dec 31 2018

Data as of Mar 30 2020

Source: Refinitiv, an LSEG business.

Figure 3.4 League Tables – Equity

Top 10 Banks	Fees ($m)	Changes in Fees vs. Prev Period*	% of Fees collected by product 2019: Follow On	Convertible	IPO
JP Morgan	1,522.88	-0.86%	52	15	34
Goldman Sachs & Co	1,495.20	-3.23%	52	15	33
Morgan Stanley	1,434.38	-8.04%	55	10	34
Bofa Securities Inc	979.03	+6.05%	49	18	33
Citi	885.30	-2.65%	54	14	32
Credit Suisse	642.63	-10.83%	40	18	42
UBS	505.12	-4.30%	62	7	31
Barclays	431.24	+14.28%	45	24	31
Jefferies LLC	367.57	-7.42%	59	9	32
CITIC	346.97	--	33	13	54
Total	**18,252.04**	**-4.51%**	**51**	**11**	**34**

Data from Jan 1 2019 - Dec 31 2019 and Jan 1 2018 - Dec 31 2018

Data as of Mar 30 2020

Source: Refinitiv, an LSEG business.

Figure 3.5 League Tables – Bonds

Top 10 Banks	Fees ($m)	Changes in Fees vs. Prev Period*	% of Fees collected by product 2019: Invest. Grade	High Yield	Asset Backed	Mortgage Backed	Other
JP Morgan	2,110.78	+20.44%	48	29	6	5	11
Bofa Securities Inc	1,917.64	+21.81%	58	23	5	6	8
Citi	1,674.83	+18.13%	50	25	8	6	11
Morgan Stanley	1,434.83	+33.13%	50	30	4	7	8
Goldman Sachs & Co	1,203.92	-4.74%	44	36	6	5	9
Barclays	1,203.58	+8.58%	46	29	10	4	11
Credit Suisse	1,015.42	+7.40%	33	43	11	9	4
Deutsche Bank	989.85	+20.32%	39	39	9	3	11
Wells Fargo & Co	969.78	+13.55%	53	22	10	10	6
HSBC Holdings PLC	928.19	-3.40%	59	22	2	1	16
Total	**33,804.46**	**+21.79%**	**55**	**20**	**5**	**3**	**18**

Data from Jan 1 2019 - Dec 31 2019 and Jan 1 2018 - Dec 31 2018 Data as of Mar 30 2020

Source: Refinitiv, an LSEG business.

Figure 3.6 League Tables – Loans

Top 10 Banks	Fees ($m)	Changes in Fees vs. Prev Period*	% of Fees collected by product 2019: Highly Leveraged	Leveraged	U/D	Near Invest. Grade	Invest. Grade
JP Morgan	1,677.61	-16.59%	24	34	2	0	40
Bofa Securities Inc	1,547.67	-5.63%	29	28	2	0	42
Mitsubishi UFJ Financial Group	927.04	+3.85%	2	13	32	4	48
Citi	882.28	-9.31%	15	28	7	0	51
Mizuho Financial Group	866.70	+5.60%	2	7	48	5	38
Credit Suisse	795.16	+9.96%	61	30	3	1	5
Wells Fargo & Co	751.36	-12.39%	18	38	1	0	43
Barclays	711.30	-10.37%	38	31	2	0	29
Sumitomo Mitsui Finl Grp Inc	706.29	+0.05%	1	11	48	6	33
HSBC Holdings PLC	692.05	--	7	26	21	5	40
Total	**22,185.35**	**-7.27%**	**21**	**25**	**19**	**2**	**33**

Data from Jan 1 2019 - Dec 31 2019 and Jan 1 2018 - Dec 31 2018 Data as of Mar 30 2020

Source: Refinitiv, an LSEG business.

evaluate the reputation and the prestige that investment banks have. Moreover, the rank assigned is widely seen as a significant driver of future income or of the amount of fees an investment bank is able to charge as compensation for underwriting and advisory services. The increased importance of league tables has pushed banks to compete for the best rank, starting the phenomenon called "league table competition." Research on the effects of the phenomenon on bank performances is still ongoing.

3.10 A European focus[1] on League Tables

For many years now, the European investment banking market has been shrinking and European investment banks have been losing market share to their US peers. Every year since 2014, JPM has generated more investment banking revenues across Europe than anyone else, according to data compiled by Dealogic.

While deleveraging has been a common goal among both European and US banks, it was achieved by opposite means. On one side of the Atlantic, European banks have been scaling down their operations in order to become smaller, but more profitable. On the other side, their US peers have instead grown in size, mainly thanks to new capital injections. As a result, these banks have been able to gain market share and leadership positions across all deals types. Consistent with this trend, according to data on fees compiled by Dealogic across all rank-eligible deals in its database, US banks' share of the European investment banking revenue pool has also multiplied over time. Moreover, the gap between European and US banks has narrowed in the last decade, almost by half. US banks, which shared less than one-third of investment banking revenues in Europe in 2010 now account for almost 40%. Most importantly, all their gains have come almost exclusively at the expense of European banks.

To better understand where these gains come from and to identify areas where the progress of US banks has been more noticeable, we take a closer look at the evolution of the relative positioning in the league tables for different types of deals of European and US banks and the total fee revenues of the deals (**Tables 3.1-3.12**).

Table 3.1 League Tables Ranking evolution (position) – 2009-19

Advisors	2009	2010	2011	2012	2013	2014	2015	2016	2017	2018	2019
Goldman Sachs & Co	9	8	2	4	3	1	2	1	2	1	1
Bank of America Merrill Lynch	13	11	13	13	9	5	3	5	4	6	2

[1] "Investment Banking in Europe: where we are and where are we going. Implications for firms, financial institutions, and regulators," rapporto di ricerca Università Bocconi - Equita Group, Milano, 2020.

Advisors	2009	2010	2011	2012	2013	2014	2015	2016	2017	2018	2019
JP Morgan	2	2	5	3	2	3	1	3	1	2	3
Barclays	6	6	4	2	6	6	6	7	7	7	4
BNP Paribas SA	5	3	3	5	5	7	7	10	5	8	5
Citi	4	12	7	7	7	8	10	8	3	3	6
Morgan Stanley	7	4	12	9	4	4	4	2	8	4	7
Deutsche Bank	1	1	1	1	1	2	5	6	6	5	8
HSBC Holdings PLC	8	7	6	6	8	9	9	4	9	9	9
Credit Agricole CIB	14	14	10	12	13	12	16	12	12	16	10
UBS	10	10	11	11	15	13	14	11	14	15	11
Credit Suisse	3	5	8	8	11	10	12	9	10	11	12
Société Générale	12	9	9	10	10	11	15	14	11	10	13
UniCredit	15	17	15	14	12	16	18	16	16	17	14
Rothschild & Co	17	16	16	18	17	15	11	13	13	12	15
Natixis	21	18	17	16	16	17	21	18	17	22	16
ING	18	24	18	19	20	23	22	21	19	26	17
Commerzbank AG	20	22	21	23	18	21	24	19	21	25	18
Lazard	16	15	20	20	19	14	8	15	15	13	19
Jefferies LLC	50	57	71	70	47	56	46	62	44	45	20
Evercore Partners	39	39	61	65	52	63	34	55	52	14	21
NatWest Markets	11	13	14	15	14	19	20	22	20	24	22
Santander Corp & Invest Bkg	19	23	22	22	23	20	23	25	22	19	23
TD Securities Inc	36	52	64	47	51	50	47	50	41	41	24
RBC Capital Markets	25	21	24	24	24	26	27	35	23	20	25

Table 3.2 **League Table per business area – 2009 (data in thousands $)**

Rank	Advisors	M&A	Equity	Bonds	Loans	Total fees
1	Deutsche Bank	174,399	16,040	162,511	23,445	376,394
2	JP Morgan	120,334	47,937	162,434	13,615	344,320
3	Credit Suisse	159,243	20,005	114,906	7,380	301,534
4	Citi	160,293	10,296	100,278	15,329	286,195
5	BNP Paribas SA	40,355	10,353	175,973	44,703	271,385
6	Barclays	47,394	1,835	197,902	18,691	265,822
7	Morgan Stanley	166,699	22,704	71,467	868	261,737
8	HSBC Holdings PLC	48,381	9,188	176,848	15,134	249,551

Rank	Advisors	M&A	Equity	Bonds	Loans	Total fees
9	Goldman Sachs & Co	144,792	29,582	71,681	721	246,776
10	UBS	154,110	16,980	62,290	9,816	243,196
11	NatWest Markets	19,425	3,142	143,387	33,000	198,954
12	Société Générale	28,377	5,952	118,556	28,565	181,450
13	Bank of America Merrill Lynch	64,143	15,625	68,210	2,881	150,859
14	Credit Agricole CIB	9,079	8,494	89,338	29,095	136,006
15	UniCredit	14,485	4,365	80,744	10,792	110,386
16	Lazard	104,903	–	–	–	104,903
17	Rothschild & Co	101,802	–	–	–	101,802
18	ING	29,408	1,121	34,285	17,713	82,527
19	Santander Corp & Invest Bkg	27,574	581	26,955	12,163	67,272
20	Commerzbank AG	5,093	2,026	39,108	19,959	66,137
21	Natixis	350		50,573	8,353	59,277
22	BBVA	28,084	148	20,959	9,866	59,057
23	Banca IMI (Intesa Sanpaolo)	20,473	2,732	19,105	4,287	46,597
24	Mediobanca	35,668	5,796	3,470	1,227	46,161
25	RBC Capital Markets	16,629	71	26,702	413	43,314
26	Landesbank Baden-Wurttember	515	164	38,526	4,271	43,475
27	KPMG	40,008	–	–	–	40,008
28	DZ Bank	–	–	37,109	947	38,056
29	Lloyds Bank	–	58	27,515	9,115	36,688
30	Nomura	15,144	461	15,859	136	31,601

Table 3.3 League Table per business area – 2010 (data in thousands $)

Rank	Advisors	M&A	Equity	Bands	Loans	Total fees
1	Deutsche Bank	127,958	13,386	159,420	25,882	326,646
2	JP Morgan	130,133	13,303	122,092	23,414	288,942
3	BNP Paribas SA	85,372	4,034	122,660	45,826	257,892
4	Morgan Stanley	158,869	13,480	53,565	4,679	230,592
5	Credit Suisse	102,384	7,987	111,465	5,153	226,990
6	Barclays	55,617	4,451	142,655	22,690	225,413
7	HSBC Holdings PLC	66,846	4,432	125,008	21,463	217,748
8	Goldman Sachs & Co	123,301	16,944	64,157	5,655	210,057
9	Société Générale	54,831	4,905	77,805	37,985	175,527
10	UBS	76,272	9,672	78,740	3,690	168,373

Rank	Advisors	M&A	Equity	Bands	Loans	Total fees
11	Bank of America Merrill Lynch	75,607	10,798	68,091	12,987	167,483
12	Citi	75,643	6,438	64,275	20,136	166,490
13	NatWest Markets	23,927	1,845	94,360	34,902	155,033
14	Credit Agricole CIB	18,813	3,140	66,465	33,930	122,349
15	Lazard	117,351	34	–	–	117,385
16	Rothschild & Co	112,790	–	–	–	112,790
17	UniCredit	8,634	3,347	71,038	16,532	99,551
18	Natixis	12,331	217	50,160	16,598	79,306
19	Nomura	49,914	1,597	23,872	3,044	78,427
20	Banca IMI (intesa Sanpaolo)	31,154	976	16,976	12,078	61,185
21	RBC Capital Markets	23,217	1,715	30,254	2,255	57,441
22	Commerzbank AG	5,210	3,122	26,645	19,455	54,432
23	Santander Corp & Invest Bkg	9,166	2,135	27,793	11,291	50,384
24	ING	3,161	3,286	20,787	21,765	48,999
25	Lloyds Bank	–	47	28,132	15,009	43,188
26	DZ Bank	–	143	37,219	961	38,323
27	BBVA	6,919	559	17,964	12,711	38,152
28	PJT Partners Inc	34,396	–	–	–	34,396
29	VTB Capital	23,929	1,181	8,351	197	33,657
30	KPMG	29,090	–	–	–	29,090

Table 3.4 League Table per business area – 2011 (data in thousands $)

Rank	Advisors	M&A	Equity	Bonds	Loans	Total fees
1	Deutsche Bank	140,851	14,320	169,248	33,869	358,288
2	Goldman Sachs & Co	205,185	16,809	66,523	5,822	294,339
3	BNP Paribas SA	90,414	4,213	131,165	58,713	284,505
4	Barclays	104,295	3,981	133,177	28,364	269,817
5	JP Morgan	114,665	8,067	112,878	25,453	261,063
6	HSBC Holdings PLC	72,597	3,404	131,109	39,634	246,743
7	Citi	104,648	6,514	84,863	28,016	224,041
8	Credit Suisse	122,887	10,247	80,104	7,827	221,065
9	Société Générale	89,293	2,296	72,412	46,794	210,795
10	Credit Agricole CIB	72,044	1,548	71,111	48,435	193,138
11	UBS	96,868	7,093	31,043	7,204	192,207
12	Morgan Stanley	108,242	11,678	51,586	6,363	177,868

Rank	Advisors	M&A	Equity	Bonds	Loans	Total fees
13	Bank of America Merrill Lynch	82,032	9,408	67,492	15,552	174,484
14	NatWest Markets	40,872	985	89,713	41,785	173,354
15	UniCredit	35,487	3,666	55,505	26,513	121,171
16	Rothschild & Co	103,341	9	–	–	103,350
17	Natixis	13,693	23	57,836	29,254	100,807
18	ING	33,511	2,352	22,742	30,070	88,675
19	Nomura	57,866	2,621	24,488	984	85,959
20	Lazard	79,411	–	–	–	79,411
21	Commerzbank AG	4,140	1,131	29,761	30,403	65,435
22	Santander Corp & Invest Bkg	10,543	654	32,491	13,276	56,965
23	Banca IMI (Intesa Sanpaolo)	31,166	1,113	13,035	6,481	51,794
24	RBC Capital Markets	8,154	550	33,837	3,172	45,712
25	BBVA	9,701	–	25,720	10,093	45,514
26	Lloyds Bank	92	–	23,120	17,480	40,692
27	DZ Bank	–	6	37,334	3,167	40,508
28	Nordea	13,854	243	13,953	12,307	40,357
29	Ernst & Young LLP	31,150	–	–	–	31,150
30	Landesbank Baden-Wurttember	–	102	24,253	5,475	29,830

Table 3.5 League Table per business area – 2012 (data in thousands $)

Rank	Advisors	M&A	Equity	Bonds	Loans	Total fees
1	Deutsche Bank	140,851	11,473	153,059	153,059	458,440
2	Barclays	104,295	3,501	145,239	145,239	398,274
3	JP Morgan	114,665	11,296	134,595	134,595	395,151
4	Goldman Sachs & Co	205,185	15,311	81,194	81,194	382,883
5	BNP Paribas SA	90,414	4,001	119,884	119,884	334,183
6	HSBC Holdings PLC	72,597	3,144	128,346	128,346	332,434
7	Citi	104,648	5,666	92,779	92,779	295,871
8	Credit Suisse	122,887	8,433	80,357	80,357	292,034
9	Morgan Stanley	108,242	10,460	66,973	66,973	252,648
10	Société Générale	89,293	4,106	78,699	78,699	250,797
11	UBS	96,868	8,010	70,664	70,664	246,206
12	Credit Agricole CIB	72,044	680	80,366	80,366	233,455
13	Bank of America Merrill Lynch	82,032	7,294	61,351	61,351	212,027
14	UniCredit	35,487	1,340	85,560	85,560	207,948

Rank	Advisors	M&A	Equity	Bonds	Loans	Total fees
15	NatWest Markets	40,872	655	82,410	82,410	206,348
16	Natixis	13,693	–	62,916	62,916	139,526
17	Nomura	57,866	1,889	29,166	29,166	118,088
18	Rothschild & Co	103,341	–	–	–	103,341
19	ING	33,511	351	22,882	22,882	79,626
20	Lazard	79,411	–	–	–	79,411
21	DZ Bank	–	399	38,700	38,700	77,799
22	Santander Corp & Invest Bkg	10,543	673	33,273	33,273	77,763
23	Commerzbank AG	4,140	1,324	33,311	33,311	72,086
24	RBC Capital Markets	8,154	288	29,891	29,891	68,224
25	Banca IMI (Intesa Sanpaolo)	31,166	930	15,318	15,318	62,732
26	BBVA	9,701	347	23,223	23,223	56,493
27	Lloyds Bank	92	–	25,759	25,759	51,609
28	Danske Bank	3,307	39	22,484	22,484	48,313
29	VTB Capital	12,780	366	17,484	17,484	48,114
30	Landesbank Baden-Wurttember	–	465	22,935	22,935	46,335

Table 3.6 **League Table per business area – 2013 (data in thousands $)**

Rank	Advisors	M&A	Equity	Bands	Loans	Total fees
1	Deutsche Bank	98,824	19,310	155,245	33,143	306,521
2	JP Morgan	106,797	18,330	131,394	20,221	276,742
3	Goldman Sachs & Co	136,196	24,804	102,291	7,833	271,124
4	Morgan Stanley	125,968	18,546	80,918	8,852	234,285
5	BNP Paribas SA	50,398	4,922	130,508	45,355	231,183
6	Barclays	54,774	5,818	127,387	17,027	205,007
7	Citi	71,153	10,396	89,947	22,898	194,394
8	HSBC Holdings PLC	25,268	3,285	129,814	26,673	185,040
9	Bank of America Merrill Lynch	69,809	19,408	61,584	15,483	166,285
10	Société Generale	24,090	4,927	91,482	30,175	150,673
11	Credit Suisse	38,725	7,931	83,771	7,318	137,745
12	UniCredit	15,350	4,080	80,144	28,345	127,920
13	Credit Agricole CIB	10,285	3,687	79,991	24,167	118,130
14	NatWest Markets	5,776	1,832	75,944	25,992	109,544
15	UBS	47,319	17,103	37,577	6,645	108,645
16	Natixis	10,631	181	50,341	16,833	77,987

Rank	Advisors	M&A	Equity	Bands	Loans	Total fees
17	Rothschild & Co	70,913	–	–	–	70,913
18	Commerzbank AG	3,192	1,313	33,626	26,867	64,997
19	Lazard	62,028	152			62,181
20	ING	18,659	2,166	18,956	21,452	61,232
21	Nomura	18,804	1,944	28,575	3,692	53,016
22	Banca IMI (Intesa Sanpaolo)	17,310	947	25,009	7,286	50,552
23	Santander Corp & Invest Bkg	8,723	1,120	27,390	11,275	48,507
24	RBC Capital Markets	1,721	1,769	34,661	5,332	43,482
25	VTB Capital	20,268	808	17,334	127	38,536
26	BBVA	3,387	–	23,993	10,383	37,764
27	Ernst & Young LLP	31,896	–	–	–	31,896
28	Landesbank Baden-Wurttember	–	12	24,804	6,282	31,098
29	Cooperatieve Rabobank UA	14,382	869	8,068	7,622	30,941
30	SEB	11,513	1,834	9,962	7,085	30,394

Table 3.7 League Table per business area – 2014 (data in thousands $)

Rank	Advisors	M&A	Equity	Bands	Loans	Total fees
1	Goldman Sachs & Co	293,460	24,457	89,241	9,262	416,419
2	Deutsche Bank	171,718	21,263	165,479	53,357	411,817
3	JP Morgan	201,452	26,269	120,151	31,672	379,545
4	Morgan Stanley	235,579	18,580	70,980	10,533	335,673
5	Bank of America Merrill Lynch	212,130	21,274	69,980	21,635	325,019
6	Barclays	140,294	9,041	146,293	27,641	323,269
7	BNP Paribas SA	133,573	6,121	121,632	55,622	316,948
8	Citi	157,890	13,910	105,828	38,764	316,392
9	HSBC Holdings PLC	59,316	5,984	144,978	34,503	244,781
10	Credit Suisse	122,303	11,149	90,210	12,708	236,369
11	Société Générale	77,169	7,389	95,893	36,577	217,028
12	Credit Agricole CIB	85,691	2,119	81,689	40,119	209,617
13	UBS	104,800	22,328	41,358	5,471	173,957
14	Lazard	171,413				171,413
15	Rothschild & Co	153,827				153,827
16	UniCredit	9,331	3,149	84,663	31,291	128,434
17	Natixis	37,095	1,373	60,864	24,212	123,543
18	Perella Weinberg Partners LP	112,479				112,479

Rank	Advisors	M&A	Equity	Bands	Loans	Total fees
19	NatWest Markets	2,733	1,547	72,866	29,905	107,051
20	Santander Corp & Invest Bkg	20,098	2,308	33,998	19,059	75,464
21	Commerzbank AG	455	2,728	39,835	30,792	73,809
22	Nordea	15,631	2,300	37,036	14,808	69,775
23	ING	9,102	2,989	18,936	33,158	64,184
24	Zaoui & Co	63,495	–	–	–	63,495
25	Nomura	16,432	1,963	35,179	6,022	59,596
26	RBC Capital Markets	16,135	1,457	34,385	3,797	55,774
27	Banca IMI (Intesa Sanpaolo)	8,499	2,570	27,665	8,196	46,931
28	SEB	19,524	1,588	11,562	9,675	42,349
29	BBVA	10,614	1,650	21,126	8,151	41,541
30	Lloyds Bank	–	–	26,416	14,895	41,311

Table 3.8 League Table per business area – 2015 (data in thousands $)

Rank	Advisors	M&A	Equity	Bonds	Loans	Total fees
1	JP Morgan	371,474	22,690	96,129	31,398	521,691
2	Goldman Sachs & Co	396,150	22,837	66,413	13,893	499,292
3	Bank of America Merrill Lynch	314,651	22,117	74,850	23,948	435,566
4	Morgan Stanley	330,322	18,982	61,349	14,488	425,140
5	Deutsche Bank	242,060	16,575	103,074	37,761	399,470
6	Barclays	166,828	8,172	127,605	35,946	338,550
7	BNP Paribas SA	151,742	7,190	97,502	56,017	312,451
8	Lazard	298,113	–	1,200	–	299,313
9	HSBC Holdings PLC	36,988	5,124	133,528	45,794	221,434
10	Citi	70,575	11,628	91,413	28,767	202,383
11	Rothschild & Co	198,272	–	–	–	198,272
12	Credit Suisse	110,821	8,482	66,679	9,770	195,751
13	Robey Warshaw LLP	192,313	–	–	–	192,313
14	UBS	75,922	21,572	53,842	3,711	155,047
15	Société Générale	39,109	7,151	74,123	33,512	153,895
16	Credit Agricole CIB	25,292	2,155	73,819	34,126	135,393
17	Industrial & Comm Bank China	127,585	–	206	1,431	129,221
18	UniCredit	21,234	3,036	61,702	34,042	120,013
19	Centerview Partners LLC	119,319	–	–	–	119,319
20	NatWest Markets	147	1,032	44,063	25,693	70,935

Rank	Advisors	M&A	Equity	Bonds	Loans	Total fees
21	Natixis	4,582	1,346	43,605	17,638	67,170
22	ING	8,967	1,721	18,680	37,381	66,750
23	Santander Corp & Invest Bkg	4,112	2,487	28,048	23,726	58,372
24	Commerzbank AG	403	2,391	34,397	19,679	56,870
25	Nomura	17,591	1,946	33,476	1,443	54,456
26	Banca IMI (Intesa Sanpaolo)	19,040	1,707	15,454	14,442	50,644
27	RBC Capital Markets	9,963	1,023	27,185	5,110	43,280
28	Mediobanca	27,461	2337	4,929	3,312	38,239
29	Mitsubishi UFJ Financial Group	2,727	–	8,272	20,052	31,052
30	Lloyds Bank	–	–	21,617	9,402	31,019

Table 3.9 League Table per business area – 2016 (data in thousands $)

Rank	Advisors	M&A	Equity	Bands	Loans	Total fees
1	Goldman Sachs & Co	229,563	24,804	83,442	16,574	354,383
2	Morgan Stanley	206,750	18,546	53,936	12,368	291,605
3	JP Morgan	107,803	18,330	101,988	37,242	265,363
4	HSBC Holdings PLC	66,986	3,285	138,258	32,117	240,647
5	Bank of America Merrill Lynch	129,444	19,408	69,029	16,425	234,306
6	Deutsche Bank	63,889	19,310	96,624	29,974	209,796
7	Barclays	46,765	5,818	124,708	25,048	202,340
8	Citi	76,592	10,306	90,000	17,144	200,732
9	Credit Suisse	125,555	7,931	35,020	17,248	185,754
10	BNP Paribas SA	37,005	4,922	99,843	41,238	183,008
11	UBS	113,257	17,103	38,074	4,406	172,840
12	Credit Agricole CIB	37,953	3,687	77,986	27,156	146,782
13	Rothschild & Co	137,062	–	–	–	137,062
14	Société Générale	26,873	4,927	70,458	24,285	126,542
15	Lazard	115,362	152	–	–	115,514
16	UniCredit	13,750	4,080	61,298	33,471	112,600
17	CITIC	61,169	–	597	4,040	65,807
18	Natixis	10,731	181	39,531	14,811	65,254
19	Commerzbank AG	4,961	1,313	35,086	20,642	62,002
20	Mizuho Financial Group	40,950	–	10,000	7,679	58,630
21	ING	4,403	2,166	21,283	28,517	56,369
22	NatWest Markets	152	1,832	43,892	9,505	55,382

Rank	Advisors	M&A	Equity	Bands	Loans	Total fees
23	Industrial & Comm Bank China	51,624		522	2,123	54,269
24	Macquarie Group	53,087	116	600	118	53,920
25	Santander Corp & Invest Bkg	8,300	1,120	30,723	13,301	53,444
26	Alantra Partners SA	48,724	50	–	–	48,774
27	VTB Capital	24,426	808	22,301	40	47,574
28	China International Capital Co	46,063	–	159	–	46,222
29	China Construction Bank	43,988	–	2	854	44,844
30	Nomura	14,267	1,944	25,856	2,608	44,675

Table 3.10 League Table per business area – 2017 (data in thousands $)

Rank	Advisors	M&A	Equity	Bonds	Loans	Total fees
1	JP Morgan	124,902	21,531	116,216	31,013	293,662
2	Goldman Sachs & Co	158,739	16,107	91,399	13,490	279,736
3	Citi	128,449	15,516	111,573	14,443	269,981
4	Bank of America Merrill Lynch	144,184	12,423	79,023	31,751	267,381
5	BNP Paribas SA	89,705	8,913	108,922	38,440	245,980
6	Deutsche Bank	91,627	12,513	102,407	36,958	243,505
7	Barclays	52,323	8,770	128,190	30,289	219,572
8	Morgan Stanley	135,419	16,829	54,619	5,141	212,008
9	HSBC Holdings PLC	20,557	4,942	123,755	40,824	190,078
10	Credit Suisse	97,073	9,376	58,259	12,378	177,086
11	Société Générale	45,966	7,743	86,712	32,293	172,714
12	Credit Agricole CIB	48,392	3,197	74,830	32,212	158,630
13	Rothschild & Co	140,874	–	–	–	140,874
14	UBS	59,821	13,646	53,689	5,103	132,258
15	Lazard	113,878	–	–	–	113,878
16	UniCredit	2,863	2,870	73,303	28,969	108,005
17	Natixis	23,682	2,694	35,341	20,315	82,032
18	Nomura	21,971	–	32,917	10,593	65,482
19	ING	3,700	1,559	28,920	28,702	62,881
20	NatWest Markets	740	336	49,897	11,278	62,251
21	CommerzbankAG	385	2,524	36,499	22,074	61,481
22	Santander Corp & Invest Bkg	5,489	2,549	38,950	12,525	59,514
23	RBC Capital Markets	22,117	1,818	26,993	3,958	54,886
24	Mediobanca	40,781	2,932	6,146	3,439	53,298

Rank	Advisors	M&A	Equity	Bonds	Loans	Total fees
25	Nordea	15,378	2,169	19,151	4,365	41,061
26	BBVA	5,752	1,934	17,317	10,553	35,557
27	Banca IMI (Intesa Sanpaolo)	2,674	2,290	22,576	7,853	35,392
28	Mizuho Financial Group	238	–	17,311	14,464	32,014
29	Landesbank Baden-Wurttemberg	–	–	25,974	5,583	31,557
30	Alantra Partners SA	31,166	–	–	–	31,166

Table 3.11 **League Table per business area – 2018 (data in thousands $)**

Rank	Advisors	M&A	Equity	Bonds	Loans	Total fees
1	Goldman Sachs & Co	372,217	13,282	84,036	15,107	484,642
2	JP Morgan	275,109	14,528	118,495	38,792	446,924
3	Citi	256,672	8,084	103,258	28,950	396,964
4	Morgan Stanley	311,752	8,765	56,693	3,752	380,961
5	Deutsche Bank	143,544	7,271	92,135	30,247	273,197
6	Bank of America Merrill Lynch	156,873	6,365	78,372	19,082	260,692
7	Barclays	118,569	5,163	117,645	16,697	258,074
8	BNP Paribas SA	78,782	3,854	97,564	53,404	233,604
9	HSBC Holdings PLC	26,137	3,366	136,471	25,271	191,246
10	Société Générale	66,740	4,487	84,620	34,972	190,820
11	Credit Suisse	100,078	6,836	64,111	8,973	179,998
12	Rothschild & Co	169,908	–	–	–	169,908
13	Lazard	165,090	–	–	–	165,090
14	Evercore Partners	163,005	201	–	–	163,206
15	UBS	103,319	7,733	46,462	5,039	162,552
16	Credit Agricole CIB	21,175	1,661	71,399	43,776	138,011
17	UniCredit	7,251	2,245	69,119	37,356	115,971
18	Nomura	83,164	–	26,515	2,126	111,804
19	Santander Corp & Invest Bkg	51,731	1,036	36,403	20,940	110,110
20	RBC Capital Markets	32,072	965	41,912	11,047	85,996
21	Mediobanca	74,538	990	4,746	2,222	82,496
22	Natixis	9,844	451	44,075	24,981	79,350
23	Robey Warshaw LLP	79,037	–	–		79,037
24	NatWest Markets	3,238	121	55,684	11,021	70,065
25	Commerzbank AG	585	1,309	45,131	22,606	69,632
26	ING	2,440	852	32,219	31,597	67,107
27	PJT Partners Inc	64,194	–	–	–	64,194
28	Wells Fargo & Co	51,445	184	9,335	2,715	63,679

Rank	Advisors	M&A	Equity	Bonds	Loans	Total fees
29	KPMG	59,587	–	–	–	59,587
30	Nordea	26,980	1,282	15,621	8,900	52,783

Table 3.12 **League Table per business area – 2019 (data in thousands $)**

Rank	Advisors	M&A	Equity	Bonds	Loans	Total fees
1	Goldman Sachs & Co	180,197	7,620	60,285	13,494	261,595
2	Bank of America Merrill Lynch	148,441	4,731	69,150	25,214	247,536
3	JP Morgan	111,816	9,820	87,062	15,488	224,187
4	Barclays	102,273	3,233	93,139	11,806	210,451
5	BNP Paribas SA	76,097	3,187	86,658	34,037	199,978
6	Citi	94,939	5,711	82,686	16,428	199,764
7	Morgan Stanley	110,111	9,346	45,306	5,252	170,015
8	Deutsche Bank	66,774	1,276	75,364	21,445	164,860
9	HSBC Holdings PLC	23,769	2,059	92,960	13,312	132,100
10	Credit Agricole CIB	10,140	1,276	68,827	32,070	112,314
11	UBS	72,587	4,304	28,781	3,594	109,266
12	Credit Suisse	61,463	3,885	34,607	6,842	106,798
13	Société Générale	2,623	1,879	70,724	19,270	94,496
14	UniCredit	2,138	1,166	55,315	21,631	80,250
15	Rothschild & Co	73,678	–	–	–	73,678
16	Natixis	2,992	605	33,898	13,985	51,480
17	ING	8,433	604	25,415	15,160	49,613
18	Commerzbank AG	68	149	32,519	16,511	49,248
19	Lazard	48,603	–	–	–	48,603
20	Jefferies LLC	44,784	2360	942	336	48,423
21	Evercore Partners	47,384	175	–	–	47,559
22	NatWest Markets	149	7	41,556	5,515	47,227
23	Santander Corp & Invest Bkg	473	152	29,896	9,809	40,330
24	TD Securities Inc	12,150	50	25,566	820	38,586
25	RBC Capital Markets	4,542	1,153	25,907	2,652	34,253
26	Nordea	13,493	924	13,624	4,841	32,882
27	Nomura	7,896	119	23,238	1,044	32,297
28	Canson Capital Partners I Ltd	30,100	–	–	–	30,100
29	Danske Bank	9,836	282	15,857	2,742	28,717
30	SEB	10,849	951	12,947	3,107	27,854

For deals related to both bond and loan markets (DCM deals), we observe a slow but continuous decline in the share of proceeds corresponding to European banks, mostly in favour of US banks. The market share of European banks has dropped from 67.5% in 2008 to 54.1% for bonds, and from 77.2% in 2009 to 62.8% for loans. Consistent with this trend, we see an expanding presence over time of US banks at the top of the corresponding league tables, especially among the highest-ranked banks.

The weakness of European investment banks relative to their US peers clearly emerges for Equity (ECM) deals, too. While European and US banks share the proceeds of ECM deals almost evenly, US banks consistently outrank European banks at the top of the corresponding league tables. No European bank has made it to the top three positions of the league table since 2014, and none has even broken into the top five in 2019. This suggests that a few US banks are able to seize the larger and more remunerative ECM deals for themselves.

The same holds for M&A deals. The aggregate rank value shares corresponding to European and US banks are roughly comparable, with US banks taking the lead only in recent years. Still, US banks consistently outrank European banks at the top of the corresponding league tables. No European bank has made it to the top three positions of the league table since 2012 and the top four positions have been consistently occupied by US banks since 2014. Again, this suggests that a few US banks are able to seize a conspicuous part of the M&A market share for themselves, possibly by partaking in all high-profile deals in Europe.

Overall, this evidence suggests a polarization of European investment banking across all markets. On the one hand, a few large US banks compete aggressively and play a prominent role in the market for large and more remunerative deals, especially in ECMs and M&As, at the expense of their subscale European peers. On the other hand, European banks are left to compete among themselves for smaller, less remunerative deals.

3.11 How have US investment banks come to dominate European investment banking?[2]

US investment banks are strong globally and have major competitive advantages compared with their European peers. This gap stems from three different factors: the diverse sizes and characteristics of their domestic markets, their exposure to dissimilar macroeconomic conditions, and the different regulatory requirements with which they need to comply.

Above all, US investment banks enjoy a high level of concentration and a very

[2] "Investment Banking in Europe: where we are and where are we going. Implications for firms, financial institutions, and regulators.", rapporto di ricerca Università Bocconi – Equita Group, Milano 2020.

large domestic market. Financial markets are notably less deep in the Eurozone than in the US or the UK in a number of regards. Data from New Financial suggest that the US market is almost twice as deep as the UK, which is the deepest in Europe. The depth of capital markets in continental Europe is about one-third or less of the depth of the US market. Lack of harmonization in regulations across Europe limits capital flows, investment and extension of credit, all of which ultimately curbs the potential for greater, broader, and more stable GDP growth across the whole Eurozone.

In addition, US and European banks are exposed to different domestic macro-economic conditions. In particular, the longest period of economic growth in history in the US and rising short-term rates in that country have boosted the profitability of banks in the US over the last decade. As a result, US banks have grown in size, while European banks have slimmed down as weak economic growth, ultra-low interest rates and strict capital requirements have further reduced the resources at their disposal. Unlike in the US, where coming out of the crisis banks quickly raised capital and shed risk, the 2012 sovereign debt crisis put new pressure on European banks. Borrowing has slowed down, as has the economy, leading central banks to cut interest rates below zero, leaving banks struggling to squeeze out profit on loans. As a result, European banks have not been able to rely as much on retail businesses to prop up the investment banking side due to negative Eurozone interest rates and intense competition for customers in a less concentrated banking sector. In response to all of this, banks are cutting back on jobs and large parts of their trading operations.

Furthermore, European banks' capital allocation has proved poor compared to their US peers. A recent study by Société Générale shows that while US banks do not have operating divisions generating ROE lower than 10%, European banks keep a consistent proportion of capital allocated to businesses with disappointing returns. (For instance, Equity and FICC trading consume a substantial amount of capital and make low-to-mid single-digit ROEs compared to IBD businesses, such as M&A, ECM, and DCM, that make decent double-digit ROEs.) One explanation could be that managing the volatility of investment banking revenues is tougher for European banks given their cost inflexibility. In fact, the same study by Société Générale suggests that the cost/income ratio of European banks is generally more volatile than that of their US peers. As a result, European banks rely more than their US peers on flow trading businesses, which are difficult to maintain for banks lacking sufficient scale.

While investment banking is seeing its historical profit centres eroded by regulations, US and European institutions are held to different requirements in several respects. We identify three areas where inconsistent regulation has allegedly led to a competitive advantage for US banks: capital buffers, remuneration policies and MiFID II.

First, in the US, large banks have a high minimum supplementary leverage ratio requirement of 5%. As a result, European banks generally have weaker capital ratios than their US peers. More capital allows banks to take advantage of growth opportunities and build economies of scale. This limits European banks' ability to take on risk where appropriate and to absorb shocks when they arise. Consistent with this argument, stronger capital positions for US banks may have helped them win market share at the expense of European banks.

Second, according to CRD IV regulations in force in Europe since 2014, European banks have to defer a minimum of 40% of variable compensation of material risk-takers over at least three to five years, while there is no such restriction for US banks. Moreover, CRD IV regulations impose a bonus cap at no more than 100% of base salary. While the purpose of these provisions is to disincentivize inappropriate short-term risk-taking, the downside is that they drive European banks to augment fixed base salaries as a proportion of total compensation. As a result, banks' ability to cut costs at times when revenues are under pressure is reduced, and so is their flexibility in managing their cost/income ratios. Moreover, banks in Europe are relatively more vulnerable to large severance costs due to onerous redundancy regulations. More flexibility allows US banks to better manage their employees, resulting in a stronger talent pool and greater ability to manage capital market businesses at times of extreme volatility.

After the collapse of Lehman Brothers and Bear Stearns and the global financial crisis, the business models of the world's largest investment banks needed to change. In the US, legislation emerged to prohibit investment banks from proprietary trading and forcing them to keep more capital on hand. These regulations shrunk trading profits and created a need to cut costs, spurring investment banks to spin off unprofitable divisions or eliminate them entirely. While more recently the rules against proprietary trading have been loosened, the restrictions have still changed how investment banks operate.

In Europe, a package of financial industry reform legislation (MiFID II) came into effect in January 2018. MiFID II was instituted to regulate financial markets, with the goal of making European financial markets more transparent and strengthening investor protection. Among its broad and far-reaching consequences, we highlight its direct impact on the primary and secondary market activities of investment banks. In terms of primary markets, MiFID II dents the investment banking business by imposing additional technological and regulatory costs on banks. In particular, certain provisions (regarding order record keeping, allocation justification, and transaction reporting) expose banks' capital market operations to higher costs and technological challenges. In an increasingly competitive market, with declining fees, these additional costs test the ability of European banks to compete effectively with their US rivals.

Yet, MiFID II's more disruptive impact is on secondary markets, where it bans in- vestment banks from bundling research with trade execution, compelling them to price and sell their research as a separate product. This has driven asset managers (i.e. the buy-side) to seek out the cheapest trades with the best execution, often in block sizes. As a result, brokers' (sell-side) revenues and research spending is squeezed, especially for smaller houses focusing on the mid-sized capitalization market. As trading, research and investing in small-caps have become uneconomical, the market for research has started to concentrate and shrink. The headcount for equity research at twelve major investment banks went down by 16% between 2013 and 2019 (dropping 5% since 2018 alone). Accordingly, on the Stoxx Europe 600 Index and the Stoxx European Small-Cap Index, the number of ratings of companies has dropped by 9% and 12% respectively, according to data compiled by Bloomberg.

Questions and answers

1. *What roles can a financial intermediary perform with relation to the primary and secondary capital markets? Provide a short description of each of them.*
   - Primary market: origination, advisory and arranging, underwriting, placement and selling;
   - Secondary market: brokerage, dealing, market making.

   Refer to Section 3.1 Capital Markets for their definition.

2. *Describe the types of activities a bank can perform with relation to the underwriting phase. Then, show the impact on a bank's financial statement (below) of a deal with value 1000 and fees equal to 4%, in which the bank underwrites 55%, with a capital gain of 20%.*

assets	**liabilities**
	equity

P&L	
interest margin	
capital gain	
fees	
total	

EVA	
profit	
cost of capital	
total	

Underwriting refers to the phase of underwriting of the newly-issued instruments, which will be owned by the intermediary until the public placement takes place. From an investment bank's perspective, the possible exposure to issuance risk is part of the range of guarantees offered in the initial underwriting deal. An *underwriting commitment* occurs when the intermediary buys the entire issuance at the predefined price established with the issuer, facing both the risk of not selling the whole stock at the offering and of selling at a lower price with respect to the issuing entity. Alternatively, in *underwriting with assumption of guarantee*, the financial intermediary guarantees the underwriting of unsold stock, but does not carry the price risk. Lastly, under the *best effort commitment*, the financial intermediary plays only a mediation role, which consists of selling the shares to investors, but does not offer any guarantee, avoiding both unsold risk and price risk. Clearly, as the guarantees offered change, the remuneration levels requested by the investment bank also vary: the higher the coverage, the higher the commission fees and the transaction cost for the issuer.

assets	**liabilities**
550	
	equity
	44

P&L	
interest margin	
capital gain	*110*
fees	*40*
total	***150***

EVA	
profit	*150*
cost of capital	*6.6*
total	***143.4***

3. *Provide a brief description of the three main types of trading activities a financial intermediary can offer to its clients.*
   Brokerage, dealing, market making.

   - **Brokerage:** the broker plays the role of facilitating the matching of demand and supply, and is remunerated by fees. Specifically, the broker searches for potential investors and negotiates financial instruments on behalf of clients. The mediation activity is fundamental for the broker, thus it is reasonable to conclude that its financial position is independent and immune from the risks involved in single trade operations.
   - **Dealing:** contrary to the broker, the dealer is the direct counterparty in the trade of clients' securities, overcoming the need to find a counterparty. From a financial approach, the dealer has its own portfolio of financial assets and a minimum level of capital to buy at any time the amount of securities that the client wants to sell. In this context, the dealer's role is to safeguard the liquidity of the market, minimizing price fluctuations.
   - **Market Making**: this covers the role of guaranteeing the negotiability of one or more financial instruments listed on the stock market, providing continuous information on purchasing and selling prices, with the objective of ensuring a high liquidity level and market volume. The continuity element separates the role of the market maker from that of the dealer: the latter can decide to suspend the proposals to buy and sell.

4. *A financial institution is performing a dealing activity in the secondary market. Assuming a deal of value 1000, with fees equal to 4%, success hypothesis of 80%, and capital gains of 35%, and considering that the securities are in the books, how does the bank's financial statement (below) change?*

assets	liabilities
	equity

P&L	
interest margin	
capital gain	
fees	
total	

EVA	
profit	
cost of capital	
total	

assets	liabilities
100	
	equity
	8

P&L	
interest margin	
capital gain	*280*
fees	*40*
total	**320**

EVA	
profit	*320*
cost of capital	*1.2*
total	***318.8***

5. *Describe the most important types of M&A activities.*

- **Acquisitions and disposals:** operations that transfer the ownership of a company to one or more purchasing companies. If the acquisition is favourably agreed among the parties, the acquisition is referred to as "*friendly*"; on the contrary, all operations in which the buyer obtains the target company against its will are called "*hostile*." Regarding execution methods, ownership can be transferred as an asset purchase or a stock purchase. According to the type and features of the transaction, the role of the financial intermediary could be more or less broad and include processes of capital valuation, identification of potential buyers in the market (in the case of a friendly acquisition), definition of the optimal financial structure, and active participation in the negotiation and in corporate financing.
- **Mergers:** transactions through which two or more companies merge to form a new entity. If from the merger the two companies involved cease to exist from a legal perspective and found a new and independent company, we talk of *perfect fusion*. To the contrary, *mergers by incorporation* occur when one company absorbs its counterparty, which ceases to exist. In mergers, the role the financial intermediary plays resembles the one in acquisitions (i.e. it involves consultancy and advisory services, and professional and technical competencies in fiscal, accounting, and legal matters).

- **Spin-off:** operation that creates a new company through the unbundling of another company, which transfers the whole activity system or a single business line, keeping an important directive role in term of competencies and activities performed. Deeper in detail, the unbundled company, upfront of the transfer of activities and know-how, gets newly-issued stock of the spun-off company. The trade of assets between counterparties significantly alters both the strategic and the structural order.
- **Break-up:** the process through which a company's capital is divided and attributed to other contracting companies (whether already existing or newly set up). In the operation, the broke-up company's shareholders are compensated with new shares of the companies benefitting from the transfer. From a technical standpoint, the break-up process could be total or partial. In the former, the split company ceases its activities and the shareholders become *pro quota* owners in the other contracting companies. In the latter case, on the contrary, the target company continues to exist but its capital is reduced proportionally to the contribution made by the other companies involved in the operation. Similarly, stockholders, besides keeping the ownership of the split company, are compensated with new stock of the benefited companies. Moreover, in the definition of the new corporate governance aspects, the share placement is *proportional* when the shareholders of the split companies are compensated with a number of shares corresponding to the proportion of capital of the initial company, or *not proportional* in the opposite case.
- **Joint venture:** a contract in which two or more companies formulate an agreement on financial collaboration aimed at accomplishing a goal or executing a common project. With respect to the operation mentioned above, a joint venture is a contract which does not originate a new legal entity separated from the contracting companies. The companies continue to exist in a separate form, but cooperate on the pursuit of a shared objective of an industrial or commercial nature, strategically deploying the resources brought to the venture (for instance, know-how and capital) and sharing the investment risk through a fair apportionment of potential profits and losses.
- **Carve-out:** a special type of spin-off, frequently used in corporate reorganization processes. When this operation takes place, the company puts one of its branches at the disposal of a new special purpose vehicle created specifically to go public through an IPO. The objective is to collect financial resources in capital markets while keeping the control and direction of the new business; usually only a part of the vehicle's shares are offered to investors, while the majority share package is kept by the parent company. New resources could be allocated to several goals, could be left to the vehicle as part of its capital, or could be transferred to the mother company through the payment of dividends, share buybacks, or intragroup financing.

6. *Provide an explanation of the classification of investment policies and strategic investments in the private equity business based on the company life cycle.*

- **Seed financing:** financing to companies in the initial, seed phase. This is the moment when the founders create and develop a new business idea, and production activities are not started yet. In this stage, technologies, products, and the strategic model are in an embryonic and experimental phase.
- **Early-growth financing:** financing to recently-constituted companies in which, contrary to the case of seed financing, production activities have started. The uncertainty level is still very high since the commercial power of the new product or service has not been confirmed in the target market yet.
- **Expansion financing:** financing to growing companies which have successfully passed the phases of development and start-up. In general, we are talking about expanding companies with several development opportunities, often oriented towards an IPO at the moment in which the private equity disinvests. For this reason, it is often called *bridge financing.*
- **Replacement financing:** financing to mature and consolidated companies with a stable sales level. In this case, private equity's role is to restructure the corporate structure of the model through the direct purchase of the share package or by favouring extraordinary finance operations such as *leveraged* or *management buy-outs.*
- **Distressed (o vulture) financing:** financing to companies facing a crisis. The operations are very risky due to the high probability of default. Private equity's goal is to provide professional competencies and financial resources aimed at company restructuring.

7. *What is securitization? After having provided a brief explanation, consider a deal with value 1000, an arrangement fee for the structuring of the operation equal to 3%, and an SPV management fee equal to 5%. The bank invests 20 in the SPV, and the divided yield is 2%. Show how the financial statements are affected.*

assets	**liabilities**
	equity

P&L
interest margin
capital gain
fees
total

EVA
profit
cost of capital
total

Securitization is an operation by which a company's assets (usually characterized by low liquidity) are transformed into liquid financial securities placed and traded on securities markets. It is the creation of bonds whose principal and interest payments derive from the cash flows generated from tranches of assets. Financial institutions and firms use securitization to anticipate the value of a cash flow generating asset. Usually the asset is of financial nature, such as loans, commercial loans, or leasing. In most cases, the originator anticipates a regular cash flow. Creating a portfolio of financial assets, cash flows can be used to pay the bonds' principal and interested payments. When assets are securitised, the originator receives the cash flows in a unique lump-sum instead of having them distributed over time. There are two main types of securitization: mortgage-backed securities (MBS) and asset-backed securities (ABS).

assets	**liabilities**
20	
	equity
	1.6

P&L	
interest margin	
capital gain	*0.4*
fees	*80*
total	***80.4***

EVA	
profit	*80.4*
cost of capital	*0.24*
total	***80.16***

8. *How is financial risk defined and what are its main types?*
   Financial risk represents the potential impact of some events on corporate liquidity, and is linked to cash flow balance. Therefore, the risk is associated at the concept of volatility, i.e. the element of variability in investments which could lead to unexpected losses or profits. The main financial risks are the following:

   - Exchange risk: a drop in exchange rates could cause a loss in value related to the assets denominated in foreign currency, while an increase in exchange rates could represent a gain in value (in domestic currency) of the same assets.
   - Interest rate risk: interest rate fluctuations expose the investors in financial instruments to the risk of suffering capital losses. In practice, interest rate risk occurs also when, regardless the issuer's compliance with contractual obligations, the investor records an actual cost or a missed gain.
   - Insolvency risk: the creditor faces the risk of not being able to sell a financial instrument at its real price for several reasons, among which we can find the lack of a reference market or of interested buyers.

   As previously described, the occurrence of financial risks could result in unexpected losses or gains, and thus is described as a symmetric risk.

9. *What are the Investment Banking League Tables and what is their role?*
   The Investment Banking League Tables, produced by Refinitiv and published by the Financial Times, list investment banks ranking them by fee revenues or deal sizes, based on a set period (usually one year). They report the deals managed by the banks, including mergers and acquisition, underwriting deals, and advisory

services. League Tables can be considered a proxy for the prestige a financial institution holds in the industry. In addition to the overall league table, the rankings are divided by business segment, namely: M&A, equity (ECM), loans, and bonds (DCM). Apart from the dollar value of deal transactions, league tables can list also the market share value held by each bank in a given period. Fees and number or size of deals are considered a proxy for the performance of the financial institution. Investment bank league tables assist investors involved in merger transactions in choosing firms based on performance (as in how many deals a firm has completed), fees owed as a result of a deal, and a transaction's terms and price.

10. *In recent years, why have US banks started to dominate the European market?* Refer to the paragraph "How have US investment banks come to dominate European investment banking?"

4 Debt Capital Markets: Bond Offerings

by Andrea Tortoroglio

4.1 Introduction

In chapters 6 and 7, we will analyse all equity offerings, both primary and secondary, providing a complete overview on all the kinds of products, technicalities, and processes; the reader will realize that a bond offering is not so different from an equity offering. The players involved are the same: an issuer, the investors, and the syndicate in between, led by a global coordinator. The process is also pretty much the same, although there is a crucial difference from the equity offering, the pricing. In a bond offering, on average bonds are much easier to price relative to equity and therefore the fees applied to this kind of deal are also much lower than those of an IPO. One of the reasons why bonds are easier to price compared to stocks is related to credit ratings, which are opinions on the credit risk of a prospective debtor (a firm or a government), predicting their ability to pay back the debt, and an implicit forecast of the likelihood of the debtor defaulting, expressed by independent and reputed agencies (e.g. Standard and Poors, Fitch, Moody's). Obviously, the presence of ratings considerably facilitates the job of the investment bank(s) in pricing bonds. In addition, a bond offering has a less time-consuming process, as it can be completed in a range of time between approximately two and six weeks. Another factor to consider is volume: In 2019, EMEA issuers raised an aggregate of USD 53.6bn through 179 listings,[1] and the European IPO market raised EUR 22bn (global IPO activities raised USD 199bn),[2] whereas EMEA DCM volume totalled USD 2.20tr in 2019 (a total of USD 7.148tr worth of bonds were sold to investors globally via 22,188 deals).[3] Hence, it is normal that the fees applied are much lower, due to this remarkable difference in volume issued. Finally, bonds are usually placed through a "best

[1] Source: ECM Highlights: Full Year 2019, Dealogic, https://dealogic.com/insight/ecm-highlights-full-year-2019/. On 5 December 2019, state-owned giant Saudi Aramco priced the largest initial public offering in history, raising a total of $26.5bn and thus beating Alibaba's record $25.0bn listing in September 2014. Priced at the top of its indicative price range, the Saudi Kingdom sold a 1.5% stake in the company, making ARAMCO the most valuable quoted company in the world (as of December 2019) with a market cap of $1.71tr.

[2] Source: IPO Watch Europe Annual Review 2019, PWC, https://www.pwc.co.uk/ipowatch

[3] Source: DCM Highlights: Full Year 2019, Dealogic, https://dealogic.com/insight/dcm-highlights-full-year-2019/

effort" syndicate, without any kind of underwriting commitment (i.e. the issuer pays less fees).

The Debt Capital Market (DCM) team of an investment bank is organized to serve corporate, institutional and government clients, providing them debt origination, structuring, syndication and issuance, and loan portfolio products, ensuring clients a comprehensive range of solutions. The origination team works directly with issuers, including corporations, banks, and sovereign governments that seek funding. An investment bank advises these clients on debt financing strategies, from a simple bank loan to multi-billion-dollar capital raising across asset classes. This chapter is organised as follows. Section 4.2 presents an overview of bond offerings, with a complete description of products, players, and the process. Section 4.3 and the subsequent sections are dedicated to case studies, covering the three different main kinds of issuers: Financial Institutions Groups (Assicurazioni Generali, by Deutsche Bank), Governments (Italian BTP Dec 2030 by UniCredit), and Corporates (Snam Rete Gas by UniCredit and BP by BNP Paribas). Thanks to these real examples, we also have the chance to get some insights from top bankers regarding important current deals.

4.2 Bond Offerings: Definitions and DCM vocabulary

Before analysing the type of products and the process related to a bond offering, it is important to provide an exhaustive and complete explanation of the key elements of a **Bond**, that is, an interest-bearing security that obligates the issuer to pay the bondholder a periodic sum of money (usually at determined time intervals except for a zero-coupon bond) and to repay the principal amount at the maturity.

- **Issuers:** these may be **Corporates**, **Financial Institutions** (FIG) or **SSA**: Sovereign (e.g. the Republic of Italy, Germany, etc.), Supranational (e.g. European Investment Bank) and Agency (e.g. Municipal, City, State, Province).
- **The Guarantor**: usually the parent company of the group when the issuer is a subsidiary.
- **Credit Rating**: there are four categories, as follows:
  1. **Investment Grade – IG** (>BBB-, Baa3).
  2. **High Yield – HY** (<BBB-, Baa3). In credit agency jargon, also defined as Speculative Grade or Junk.
  3. **Cross-Over – XO** (one IG rating and one HY). A situation in which a bond is speculative grade but very close to investment grade or vice versa. It often refers to a split rating in which one credit rating agency gives the bond an investment grade rating and another gives it a junk rating. Generally speaking, regulators require bonds to receive investment grade ratings from two different agencies. Thus, crossover credit is often not strong enough to allow some IG-only institutional investors to invest in them.

4. **Not Rated – NR** Bonds with issuers that have not received a credit rating from one or more of the major credit rating agencies. A bond may be not rated for many reasons, including simply not wishing to pay the fee to the credit rating agency. This kind of bond is not necessarily risky, but it cannot be investment grade.

Usually, over 90% of the volume of the Eurobond market carries at least one rating from a major agency. The rating of the issue might deviate from rating of the issuer (e.g. lower in hybrid bonds vs higher in covered ones). The worse the rating, the higher the final coupon (the issuer is riskier) and the higher the fee paid to the investment bank(s) appointed as bookrunner(s), because it is more difficult to place.

- **Maturity Date/Tenor**: the 5, 7 and 10-year tenors remain the most sought-after tenors by investors on the EUR fixed rate market as the best to adapt to their portfolios requirements. However, any maturity is generally achievable between 1y-30y. Floating rate notes typically have shorter maturities (e.g. 2-4 years). A bond that matures in one year is much more predictable and thus less risky than a bond that matures in 20 years. Therefore, generally the longer the time to maturity, the higher the risk, the higher the reoffer yield and the coupon. A **Perpetual** bond, which is also known as a perpetual or just **perp**, is a bond with no maturity date. Therefore, it may be treated as equity, not as debt. Issuers pay coupons on perpetual bonds forever, and they do not have to redeem the principal. Most perpetual bonds issued nowadays are deeply subordinated bonds issued by banks. The bonds are counted as Tier 1 capital and help banks fulfil their capital requirements. Most of these bonds are callable, but the first call date is never less than five years from the date of issue, a call protection period.
- **Redemption Type: Bullet** (at maturity), **Amortizing** (along the life of the bond in several tranches, e.g. 20% of annual reimbursement until maturity).
- **Issue Size**: the minimal amount required to ensure liquidity is EUR 300mn, while it is possible that larger sizes (> EUR 1bn) are achievable also through multi-tranche and/or multi-currency issues.
- **Coupon: ZCB** (zero-coupon bond) vs **Fixed** vs **Floating** (based on the Euribor as the benchmark for EUR bonds). The coupon is expressed as a percentage of the par value.
- **Price**: after the issue, a bond's price fluctuates throughout its life in response to a number of factors, resulting in premium/discount trading.
- **Face value/Par value**: amount that the issuer must reimburse at maturity. It is also the reference to compute the coupon amount.
- **Investors**: typically, the investors are funds, asset managers, banks, private banks, insurance companies, pension funds, official institutions, central banks, and retail customers (if a retail tranche is present in the issuance).

It is also important to know and master the terms commonly used in the DCM world, along with the typical acronyms. A small DCM vocabulary follows:

- **New Issue Premium**: the **NIP** is the spread that an issuer will overpay (or underpay, if negative) in the offering of a new bond vs the fair value of the bonds outstanding (if any).
- **Initial Price Thought**: the **IPT** is the initial Reoffer Spread with which a new bond is announced to the market. It is generally expressed as range (90-95 bps) or area (90 bps area).
- **Guidance**: the revised Reoffer Spread announced to the market during the bookbuilding process of a new bond. It is generally expressed as a range in the form of (i) 80-85 bps or (ii) 82 bps +/- **WPIR** (Will Price In Range).
- **Reoffer Spread**: the final Spread vs the Reference rate which is used to price the bond. It is expressed as a precise number (e.g. 90 bps).
- **Fair Value**: the **FV** is the Reoffer Spread of a new bond determined on the basis of the secondary levels of already issued bonds of (i) the company itself or (ii) comparable issuers with similar characteristics to the one considered (in terms of rating/industry).
- **Interest Rate Swap**: an **IRS** is a derivatives contract between two counterparties involving the exchange of a fixed interest rate leg for a floating rate leg on a given notional amount and for a given maturity. Banks and financial institutions make extensive use of the IRS to manage their interest rate exposure in the short and medium term.
- **Mid Swap**: the **MS** represents an average of all the rates of IRS fixed legs with identical maturities traded on the market. MS is used as a reference rate to price EUR fixed notes.
- **YTM**: Yield to Maturity.
- **PP**: Private Placement – a bond issue through investors reverse inquiries.
- **LM**: Liability Management.
- **NC5**: Non-Callable before 5 years. This refers to a perpetual bond and means that the bond cannot be reimbursed by the issuer before 5 years. The number refers to the minimum duration, so it is possible to have other maturities as NC3, NC7, NC10, etc.
- **NG**: No-Grow, used in relation to issuance size, indicating that the announced amount will not be increased.
- **Books are subject**: this message sets the deadline for accepting new orders. After the books go subject, no further orders can be accepted.
- **iSpd**: the Interpolated Spread or I-spread or ISPRD of a bond is the difference between its yield to maturity and the linearly interpolated yield for the same maturity on an appropriate reference yield curve.
- **B&D**: Billing & Delivery. One of the investment banks of the syndicate acts as the B&D agent, being responsible for collecting money from investors at pricing and delivering the money to the issuer (and collecting the fees on behalf of other bookrunners) at closing.

4.2.1 Player and product types

When we talk about Debt Capital Market, we should consider that the main players involved in the process are the Issuers, the Investment Banks, and obviously the Investors. **Figure 4.1** shows a coincidental selection of the three kinds of players just mentioned, with a summary of the product types. As you can see, an important financial institution may at the same time hold the position of investment bank involved in the deal (through its DCM team) and issuer. In this section we analyse the main segments and product types for each of three kinds of issuers, providing a brief description.

1) SSA

SSA institutions almost exclusively issue senior unsecured bonds to meet their financing needs.

- **Sovereign**: the group of sovereigns consists of governments, both Republics and Kingdoms, that in order to finance the State Balance act through their Debt Management Offices (DMSs), within the State Treasury. DMOs act on the open market only through a group of selected financial institutions, awarded with the primary dealer role. For this kind of issuer, there are three bond placements options:

Figure 4.1 Main player selection and product types

Issuers (selection)

CORPORATES BP Pirelli Volkswagen Pfizer Snam Apple TIM Renault Eni Nestlé

FINANCIAL INSTITUTIONS GROUP Intesa Sanpaolo Deutsche Bank UniCredit UnipolSai Assicurazioni Generali Wells Fargo Crédit Agricole

SSA European Investment Bank World Bank ESM Repubblica Italiana KFW United States Treasury

Products Type

SSA: Syndicated issues / Auctions / Private Placements

FIG: Covered bonds / Senior unsecured bonds / Subordinated bonds

Corporates: Senior unsecured bonds (Rated / Unrated) / Hybrid bonds / High Yield bonds / Private Placements

Investment Banks (selection)

Goldman Sachs Deutsche Bank BNP Paribas UBS UniCredit JP Morgan Citi Mediobanca Barclays Morgan Stanley Bank of America Credit Suisse HSBC

Investors (selection)

T.Rowe Price BlackRock DWS Generali Pictet Asset Management Amundi Allianz Global Investors Aviva Investors Eurizon Abu Dhabi Investment Authority Anima Pimco Norway's Government Pension Fund Schroders Goldman Sachs Asset Management Algebris

1) **syndication** – a public bond issue led by a group of joint lead managers, 2) **auction** – a bond issue placed through the Sovereigns' primary dealer, and 3) **private placement** – a bond issue through investors reverse inquires.

- **Supranational**: agencies per se, except that in terms of ownership and mission, these have been expanded from one national identity to several nations (i.e. European Investment Bank – EIB, European Stability Mechanism – ESM, The World Bank). Creditworthiness of supranational institutions is underpinned by three factors: (i) preferred creditor status, an implicit agreement between borrower and lender that such institution will enjoy priority over other creditors, (ii) quality of shareholders and their very high proven commitment of support, although in most cases no direct guarantees are given, and (iii) regulatory environment ensures financial stability and/or supportive mechanisms for their debt obligations. In this case as well, syndication, auction (only ESM utilizes this method as a funding tool) and private placement are used to place the bond.
- **Agency/Sub-Sovereign**: national agencies like KFW (Germany) or ICO (Spain), regional governments and municipalities like the State of Berlin, the Generalitat Valenciana, or the City of Paris. In order to be qualified as an agency, an entity has to fulfil one or more of the following criteria: (i) it is fully or partly publicly owned, (ii) it enjoys an explicit or implicit government guarantee or some other form of support, (iii) it has a public policy mission, (i.e. CADES), and (iv) it is established under public sector law and operates either under public sector law. In this specific segment, the bond placement options are syndication and private placement.

2) Financial Institutions Group (FIG)

In the first chapters, we analysed the liability structure of banks' balance sheets and the capital requirements that follow specific rules which are set out by the Basel Committee for Banking Supervision. After the financial crisis of 2008/2009, international regulators decided that banks should have their own capital buffers to absorb any potential losses. These buffers would act as a shield against risks, in order to protect taxpayers, who largely contributed to the bail-out of banks during that financial crisis. Subsequently, the Financial Stability Board (an international regulator established in April 2009 as the successor to the Financial Stability Forum), created a ratio: the **TLAC** (Total Loss-Absorbing Capacity), that defines the capacity of a bank to absorb financial losses in the event of a crisis. The TLAC standard was designed so that failing global systemically important banks (the so-called G-SIBs[4]) will have sufficient loss-absorbing and recapitalisation capacity for authorities to implement an orderly resolution. This buffer, that comprises capital and similar instruments, would

[4] The 2019 list of G-SIBs is composed of 30 banks. The FSB releases the updated list annually, usually in November. The list is available on this page: https://www.fsb.org/wp-content/uploads/R221119.pdf

represent 16% of their total risk-weighted assets (RWA), that is higher than the minimum capital adequacy ratio under Basel III (8%). In 2022, this capital buffer will be raised to 18%.

As part of the post-crisis regulatory overhaul, Europe also decided to adopt its own legal framework: the Bank Recovery and Resolution Directive (**BRRD**), which has been in effect since January 2015. One of the pillars for dealing with failing banks is the so-called "bail-in tool," which was implemented in each EU member state in 2016. According to this tool, debt instruments can be converted into equity, or the principal amount can be reduced partially or in full. This scheme applies to all liabilities that are not exempt, such as covered deposits and covered bonds. In order to ensure that banks have sufficient debt outstanding that is not exempt from a senior bail-in, the EU introduced another measure for absorbing losses: the **MREL** (Minimum Ratio of Eligible Liabilities). While there are some important differences between TLAC and MREL, the conceptual ideas are the same. It still needs to be fine-tuned and the regulator is seeking to harmonise measures across Europe (differences exist between Germany, France, and Italy). These mechanisms serve as a protection: the cushions are made up of core equity capital (CET1), hybrid capital instruments (i.e. Additional Tier1 or AT1/CoCos), other subordinated bonds (Tier2) and finally, certain senior debt securities which are structurally junior compared with liabilities (the new so-called Senior Non Preferred). Thanks to this scheme, losses will be borne according to the rank of seniority of these notes, so the riskiest note will be the first to absorb the losses. If a bank faces serious difficulty (to avoid bankruptcy and favour business continuity), its capital will be impacted initially. The next stage is that coupons will not be paid on the AT1. Finally, losses will be taken according to a ranking structure, depending on the amount of losses to be allocated (see **Figure 4.2**).

Starting from the lowest degree of subordination (thus the safest kind of bond from the point of view of an investor), a bank can issue the following types of bonds:

- **Covered Bonds**: bonds backed by a segregated cover pool (i.e. a package of loans/mortgages), usually with benchmark size (i.e. EUR 750mn – 1bn), fixed or floating rate, bullet format, higher rating compared to the senior level, placed on a public or private basis, listed on a regulated market.
- **Senior Unsecured**: plain vanilla bonds, usually with benchmark size, fixed or floating rate, bullet format (or one call), rating usually in line with long-term issuer credit standing, placed on a public or private basis, and listed on a regulated market. France took the lead with the TLAC/MREL solution by implementing the Sapin 2 law, that was published in the JO (official journal of the French Republic) on 10 December 2016.[5] It authorises French banks to issue new bonds representing debt that can absorb losses, if necessary. They are also known as **Senior Non**

[5] In Italy, the new category of Senior Non-Preferred debt was introduced by means of the 2018 Italian Budget Law.

Figure 4.2 Bank liabilities structure

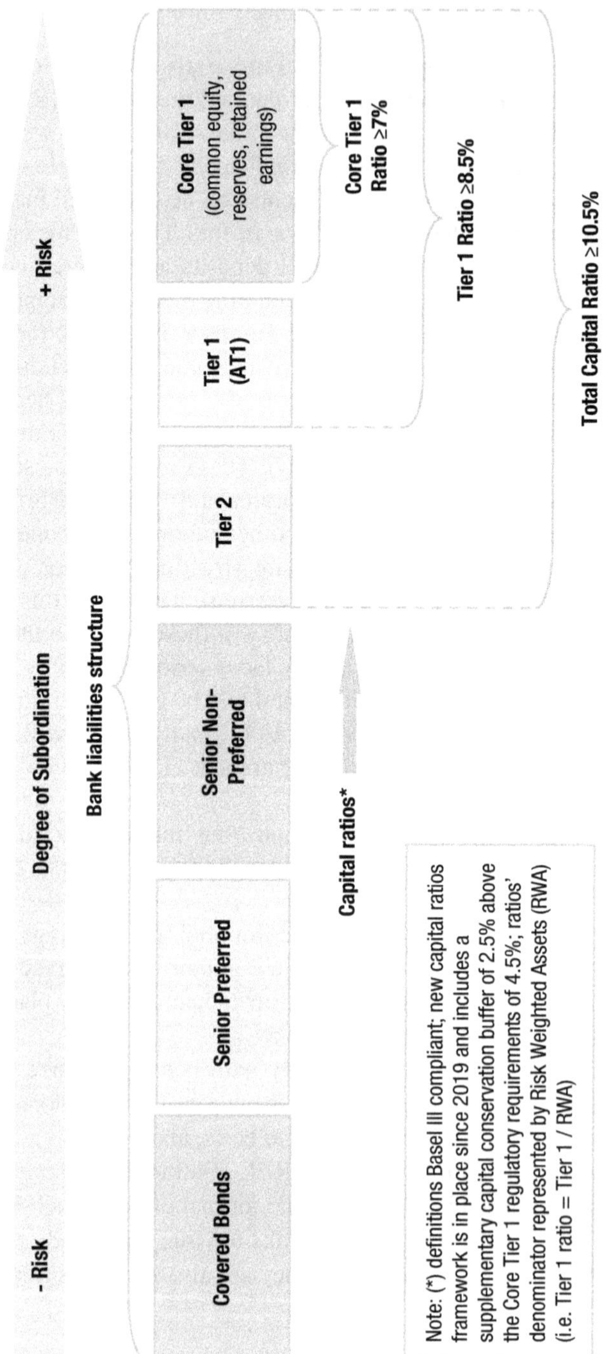

Preferred. These bonds have the status of senior debt but are nevertheless more risky than **Senior Preferred** notes, the second kind of bond we find in the senior unsecured segment. They are considered as "junior" senior debt, because in the event of default, priority for repayment is given to traditional senior debt. These notes do not replace senior debt, but simply introduce an additional layer in the hierarchy of creditors. Note that, in general, all senior unsecured bonds can be bailed in if necessary. The above-mentioned scheme just makes sure that the subordinated ones are affected first. If the respective volume is not sufficient, debt that ranks higher can also be bailed in. Senior bonds that are labelled as "preferred" can also be bailed in if necessary. They just rank senior to non-preferred ones. To be eligible for TLAC/MREL ratios, Senior Non Preferred bonds must have a residual maturity of one year.

There are still differences among countries in Europe, but the current trend is to converge towards a common approach in issuing this kind of bond.

- **Tier 2**: securities usually with benchmark size, fixed or floating rate, callable format, coupon payment flexibility (optional/cumulative), subordinated reimbursement, loss absorption, no incentive to redeem, notch-down rating vs senior, placed on a public or private basis, listed on a regulated market.
- **Additional Tier 1**: securities that incorporate equity features, perpetual maturity and callable format, benchmark size, fixed or floating rate, coupon payment flexibility (optional/mandatory/non-cumulative) subordinated reimbursement, loss absorption, no incentive to redeem, placed on a public or private basis, notch-down rating vs senior.

Insurance companies belong to the FIG segment, too; the types of bonds an insurance company can issue (starting from the lowest degree of subordination as previously shown) are:

- **Senior Unsecured**: plain vanilla bonds, usually with benchmark size, fixed or floating rate, bullet format, rating usually in line with long-term issuer credit standing, placed on a public or private basis, listed on a regulated market.
- **Tier 3**: subordinated securities, newly introduced under Solvency II (S2) as the lowest regulatory quality capital, are typically issued in bullet format with a fixed coupon structure. Minimum maturity requirement is 5 years. Interest payments are mandatorily deferrable at a lowest regulatory solvency level (so called MCR, Minimum Capital Requirement under S2).
- **Tier 2**: securities usually with benchmark size, dated or undated, usually with fixed or resettable coupons, callable format (sometimes also bullets), limited coupon payment flexibility (optional/mandatory/cumulative/dividend pushers), subordinated reimbursement, no principal loss absorption, with limited incentives to redeem, notch-down rating vs senior, placed on a public or private basis, listed on a regulated market.

- **"Restricted" Tier 1 (RT1)**: securities that incorporate equity features, perpetual maturity with no step-up in coupon and callable format (first call date being a minimum of 10 years after issuance), benchmark size, fixed or floating rate, coupon payment flexibility (optional/mandatory/non-cumulative), subordinated reimbursement, loss absorption, no incentive to redeem, placed on a public or private basis, notch-down rating vs senior. A typical RT1 instrument is written down (or converted to equity) when pre-specified trigger events occur (e.g. a breach of the issuer's Minimum Capital Requirement).

Figure 4.3 shows the insurance capital structure description.

3) Corporates

The corporate bonds segment comprises issuers of all other industries, except those of FIG and SSA described above.

- **Rated Investment Grade**: plain vanilla bonds (multi-tranche available) mainly issued by investment grade corporates, usually with min. EUR 300mn size, fixed or floating rate, bullet format, rating usually in line with long-term issuer credit standing, placed on a public or private basis, listed on regulated or unregulated markets. This category has traditionally represented most corporate debt capital market transactions in Europe (in Italy in particular).
- **Rated High Yield**: higher yielding bonds issued by weaker corporate credits (sub-investment grade – BB+ and lower) usually with min. EUR 150mn size, fixed or floating rate, bullet or callable format, placed on a private or public basis, "pari passu" or subordinated ranking respect to other liabilities, listed on regulated or unregulated markets. Traditionally in Europe high-yield debt has mainly been used in leveraged buyout transactions, but in recent years the share of high yield bonds issued by corporate issuers has been increasing.
- **Unrated**: plain vanilla bonds issued by unrated companies usually with min. EUR 250mn size, fixed or floating rate, bullet format, placed on a public or private basis, listed on regulated or unregulated markets. This is an increasingly common format of issuance in Europe. Pricing-wise, it comes at a premium vs comparable rated issues.
- **Hybrid**: these bonds sit between conventional debt and equity (they incorporate equity features), seeking to combine the main advantages of both. Hybrid bonds rank usually between senior debt and ordinary shares, at the level of subordinated debt or preference shares. Characteristics: perpetual maturity and callable format, benchmark size (min. EUR 250/300mn), fixed or floating rate, coupon payment flexibility (optional/mandatory/non-cumulative), subordinated reimbursement, placed on a public or private basis, notch-down rating vs senior.

Figure 4.3 Insurance capital structure

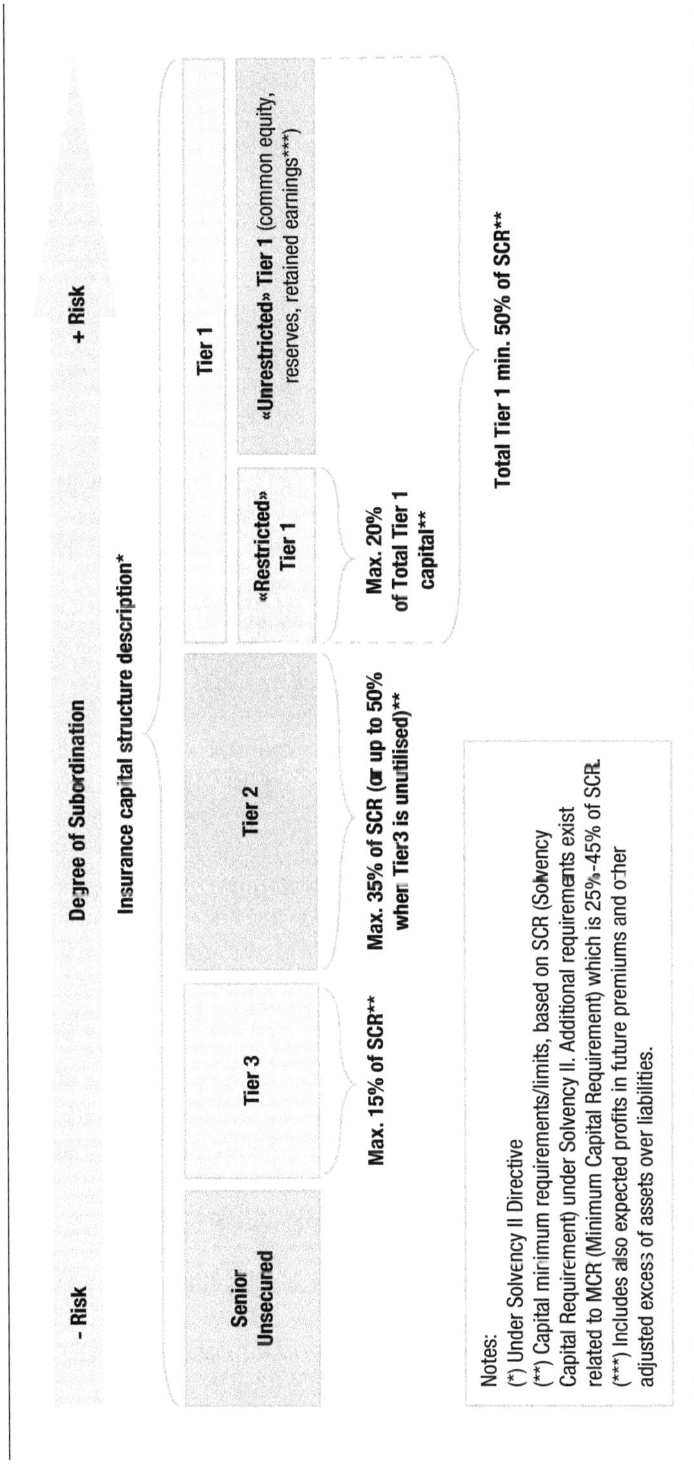

4.2.2 The process: Actors, workflow, and book building

The main actors involved in the placement of a new bond are (see **Figure 4.4**):

1. **Issuer** ("Client"): an institution that seeks to issue the new security.
2. **Bookrunners** ("Banks"/"Dealers"): usually five or six Investment Banks that support the issuer in approaching the primary market in all the steps required (from documentation through settlement as described afterwards). In other words, the Bookrunners perform the function of linking an issuer with a large set of investors in order to market, price, and distribute a new debt security. For each bank, the following divisions are involved:
   a) **Debt Capital Markets Origination** (DCM): the team represents the Investment Bank in the relationship with the issuer. Its key role is both advising clients throughout the transaction and coordinating the whole process within the other functions of the investment bank. Among other activities, DCM's goal is to maintain a constant dialogue with issuers, to identify and market ideas, and to establish a trusted relationship with the issuers' Group CFOs, Treasurers, Heads of Funding, and the Investor Relations teams.
   DCM is also responsible for the coordination of all the internal and external steps required before the pricing of the notes, including the drafting and finalisation of the documentation under the new issue process.
   b) **Syndicate**: Syndicate is constantly in contact with DCM and with the Sales Force. In this way, they are able to understand both the issuer's needs and investors' views. The desk provides DCM with indicative new issue levels and market colour for issuers. The Syndicate team closely monitors the secondary market (where investors trade existing securities) as an important reference to assess the fair value of a new transaction in the primary market (where securities are created – the focus of this analysis). During the execution of the deal, the desk manages the sale process and performs the pricing of the primary transaction.
   c) **Sales**: the "Sales Force," usually split by regions, provides the public contact with investors in the context of both primary and secondary markets. It is important to stress that before publicly announcing the new issue, no one within Sales would be aware of the transaction given the strict Chinese walls between the private side (DCM and Syndicate) and the public one. After the announcement, Sales are responsible for marketing the new notes to investors, collecting orders and feedback on pricing and determining with investors the relative value of the new issue.
3. **Fixed Income Investors**: Primarily institutional entities that want to participate in the new issue by buying a portion (or in some cases the full amount) of the bond issued. These would include asset managers, insurance companies, hedge funds, banks, and even central banks and corporate treasurers.

Figure 4.4 DCM Value chain

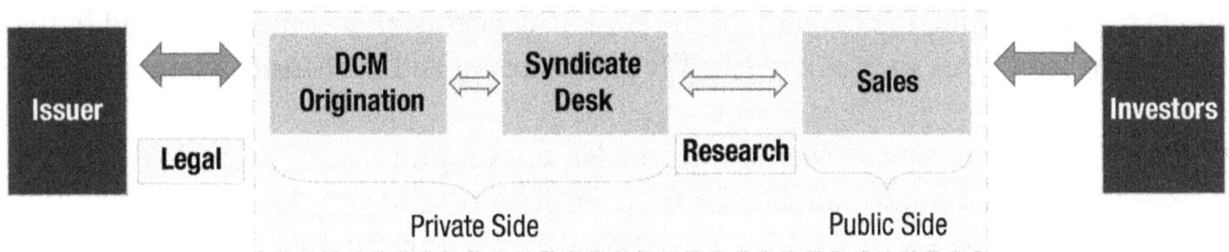

All these players act together forming the typical DCM workflow, that can be ideally divided into five different phases, summarized in **Figure 4.5**.

Phase 1 (Pitching, Analysis, and Mandate)

This phase is characterized by **a market and issuer analysis** and a **pitching activity**. DCM monitors market conditions closely, through a wide range of specialized information providers such Bloomberg, Reuters, etc. Via a full and continuous analysis of potential issuers, DCM tries to be as ready as possible to advise clients on funding opportunities in the market. A timely market/client approach is crucial to get Eurobond mandates.

The DCM origination team meets clients (SSA, corporates, FIG) on a regular basis to understand their needs and to propose efficient funding strategies based on the prevailing market conditions. During these meetings, DCM provides a full analysis of market conditions together with a comparables analysis. The main task of these activities, combined with a strong effort in pitching with clients, is to get the mandate. When an issuer decides to go ahead with a bond issue, it assigns a **mandate** to a group of banks (called joint bookrunners/joint lead managers) that will lead the whole process of the bond issue (from documentation to settlement). The mandate represents the starting point of the bond issue execution.

Figure 4.5 DCM Workflow

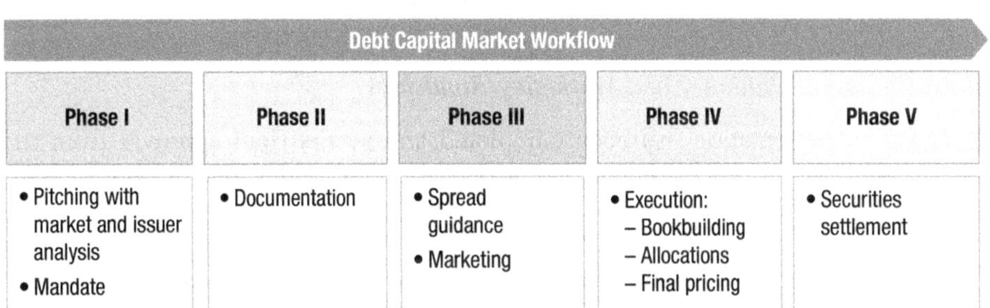

Phase 2 (Documentation)

Once the mandate has been assigned, the bookrunner(s) manage the **documentation** process, coordinating the creation of the Base Prospectus, that could be shaped in two alternative structures such as the **EMTN programme** and the **Stand-Alone** format.

- The EMTN (European Medium Term Notes) programme is an umbrella documentation programme suitable for frequent issuers, allowing for higher flexibility in terms of time-to-market and for a broader panel of funding opportunities (i.e. public Eurobond and opportunistic private placements).
- A Stand-Alone Prospectus is a one-off documentation, created and valid for a single transaction only (it expires with it). It cannot be used for multiple issuances.

A stand-alone bond issue requires more time to be completed compared to an EMTN issuance (up to six weeks from the kick-off meeting to the final settlement, particularly for the debut issuance, or "freshmen" issuers[6]), because there is no EMTN documentation ready to be used, but the Base Prospectus must be prepared ad-hoc. Differently, an EMTN issuance may require just two weeks to be completed (see the case studies below for a real example of timing).

An EMTN programme/Stand-alone base prospectus typically consists of key sections, such as: description of the issuer and overview, risk factors, form, governing law, terms and conditions, use of proceeds, taxation, etc. A bond issuance also includes other documents, besides the Base Prospectus: (i) programme/subscription agreement, that contains the contractual agreement between the issuer and the bookrunner(s), (ii) agency agreement, a contract between the issuer and the agent responsible for the settlement of the bond, (iii) comfort letter, that confirms the financial information within the prospectus and is provided by the issuer's auditor, and (iv) the legal opinion, prepared by law firms, a formal opinion that covers different aspects of the transaction.

Figure 4.6 summarized the documentation requirements under an EMTN programme. During this phase, syndicate also manages the filing process with the Stock Exchange. During the filing, the Stock Exchange may send comments or request additions to the Base Prospectus, before approving the revised draft. For stand-alone issuances, a preliminary prospectus is available for investors after the mandate announcement, also called the "preliminary offering circular."

Phase 3 (Spread Guidance and Marketing/Roadshow)

After the documentation has been completed and awaits final approval from the Market Authority/Stock Exchange, the next phase is to set the **spread guidance** for

[6] In DCM jargon it is possible to identify new issuers as "freshmen," that become "sophomores" when they launch a subsequent issuance with already outstanding bonds. After these two tiers, they can be classified as frequent issuers.

Figure 4.6 Documentation requirements for drawdown under EMTN programme

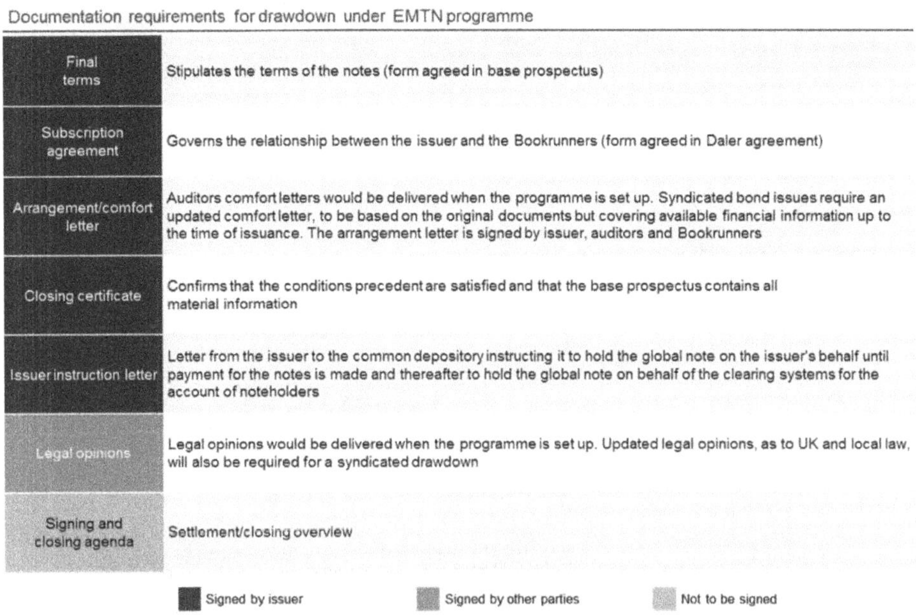

Source: Deutsche Bank DCM

the specific transaction, that is developed through the analysis of the issuer's sector and its peers. In order to price the bond, first the bookrunner has to carry out an analysis of the issuer's outstanding bonds as a benchmark reference. Secondly, it is important to define a comparables group to analyse their secondary curves as a relative value for the positioning of issuer credit within the sector. Subsequently, a selection of the same rated issues is made in order to understand the main market trends. As a final step, there is a definition of the spread area vs the benchmark rate (i.e. Mid-Swap) based on the outlined variables. Mid-Swap represents an average of all the rates of IRS fixed legs with identical maturities traded on the market. MS is used as a reference rate to price EUR fixed notes, while Euribor is used for floating notes. As can be seen in **Figure 4.7**, during the last twelve years there was a downward trend over all the IRS maturities, with negative values for most of the last two years.

Before an official deal announcement, **marketing** efforts will take place. Depending of the nature of the issuer and on the type of the transaction, a 2-4 full working days **roadshow** could be arranged in most financial European centres. This entails a mix of group presentations (breakfast or lunch) and one-on-one meetings with key potential investors. Alternatively, a 1-2 days investors' pre-sounding could be enough to gauge investors' interest. The bookrunners implement the best solution also based on the type of issuer (frequent vs one-off deal). The DCM team also prepare a so-

Figure 4.7 The Mid-Swap trend over the last decade. (*) as of 31 August 2020

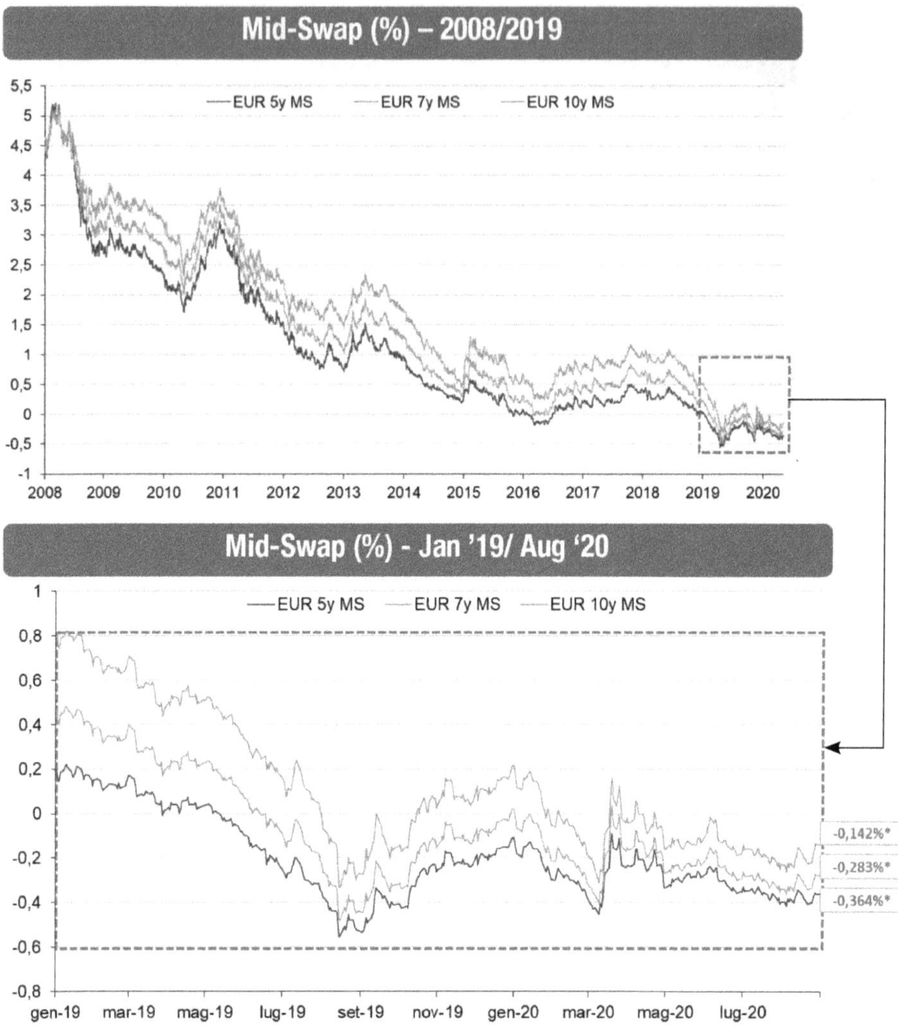

Source: Author's elaboration based on data from Bloomberg.

called "sales memo":[7] a brief summary of the new notes to be sent by syndicate to their sales force, in order to streamline all the relevant information for the trade. During the roadshow, the issuer presents its credit and financial profile, and in the case of a planned bond issue the main features of the transaction are outlined. The marketing strategy is a crucial element and paves the way for a successful bond issue execution.

[7] An example of a real sales memo will be provided in the subsequent case studies.

Especially for a debut issue (i.e. an issuer that goes to the DCM market for the first time), it is strongly recommended to stage a comprehensive roadshow in order to position its credit vis-à-vis sector peers/market comparables among fixed-income investors and enhance issuer recognition in the European market. Ahead of the beginning of the roadshow, a global sales force teach-in via conference call allows the issuer to conduct a sort of "rehearsal," and at the same time, develop knowledge among sales forces that are in charge of talking with the investors. The traditional meetings are held in the most important financial hubs like Paris, London, Frankfurt, and Milan, but other venues such as Zurich or Amsterdam can also be covered. The major topics for financial debt investors are usually Basel III, MREL, and Capital Requirements, while the major ones for corporate debt investors are typically credit profile, use of proceeds (CAPEX/acquisitions), debt and cash management, strategic business plan, shareholding structure, and economic and financial targets. The feedback gathered from investors during and after the roadshow will be a key driver in determining the correct spread, tenor, and size of the upcoming transaction. **Figure 4.8** shows an example of a timetable for European investors' meetings, combined with a selection of European fixed income investors. Consider that the final roadshow schedule and attendees depend on investors' feedback and availability. Usually the final approval of the base prospectus by Authority comes during or at the end of the roadshow. **Figure 4.9** displays the timing of a bond issue (EMTN), in days, from mandate to settlement.

Phase 4 (Execution/Syndication)

This phase is the most important part of the process, because the issuer and the bookrunners approach the market putting the transaction on a live status (public side). The key steps are:

- **Announcement**: the bookrunners announce the details of the bond issue through financial info providers (i.e. Bloomberg, Reuters, etc.).
- **Book-building**: bookrunners collect orders from investors and build the deal orderbook. Investment banks operate through internet-based book-building tools, that facilitate real-time order flow and allocation monitoring. These tools can provide bookrunners with detailed order information and they allow Excel download of the order book. In addition, an appreciated function is the analysis with distribution by investor type/region, spread sensitivity, and orders volume.
- **Final Terms**: bookrunners provide the final spread and size of the issue.
- **Allocation**: bookrunners allocate investors considering their features/quality (i.e. real money accounts vs hedge funds).
- **Final pricing**: once the book is agreed on and the re-offer spread fixed, the bookrunners and the issuer finalize the bond price.
- **Communication**: bookrunners publish new issue details on Bloomberg/Reuters etc.

The execution takes place intraday, with this indicative timetable (obviously, the exact time may vary depending on each transaction's features):

Figure 4.8 Indicative timetable for European investors' meetings, combined with a selection of the same

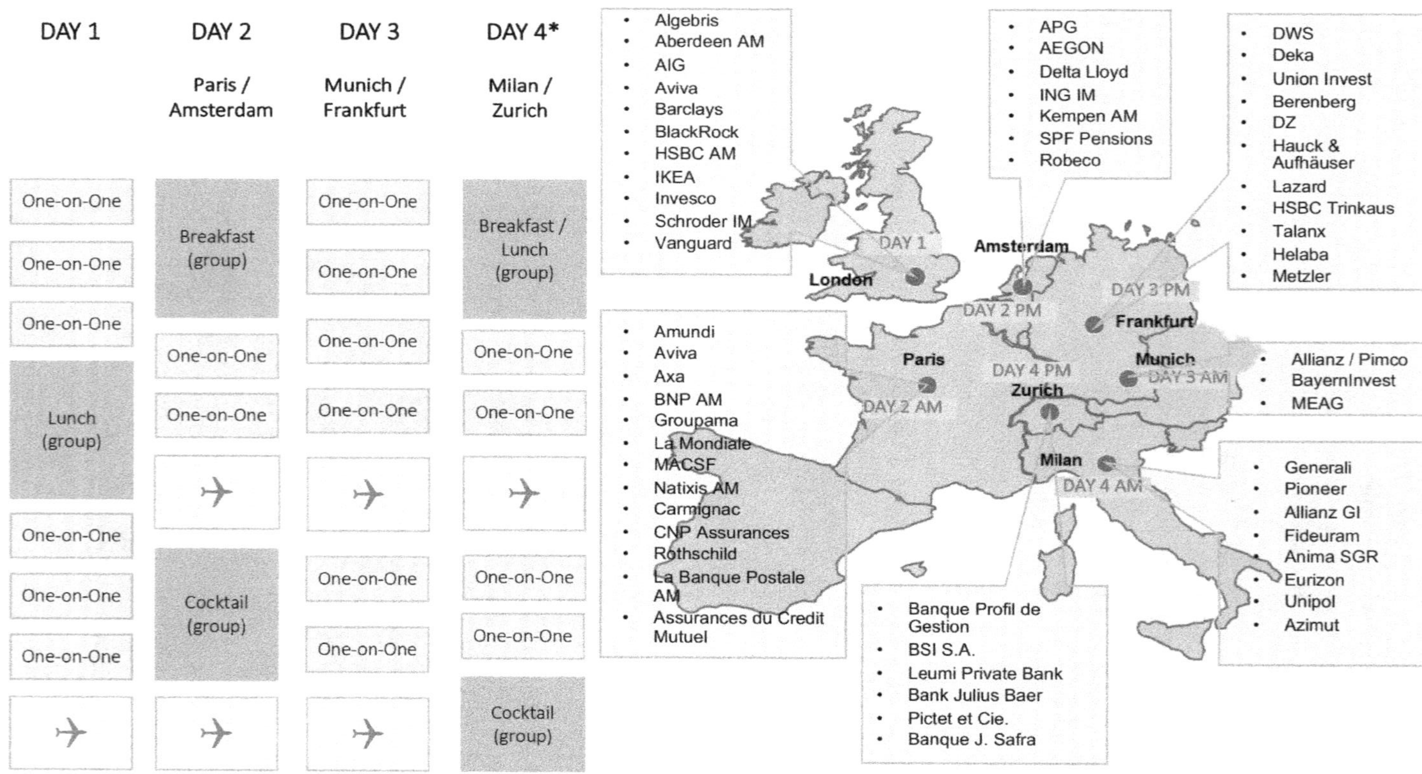

(*) It is also possible, for instance, to stage the roadshow in three days, doing Italy and Germany in one day and excluding Switzerland.

Figure 4.9 Timing of a bond issue (EMTN), in days, from mandate to settlement

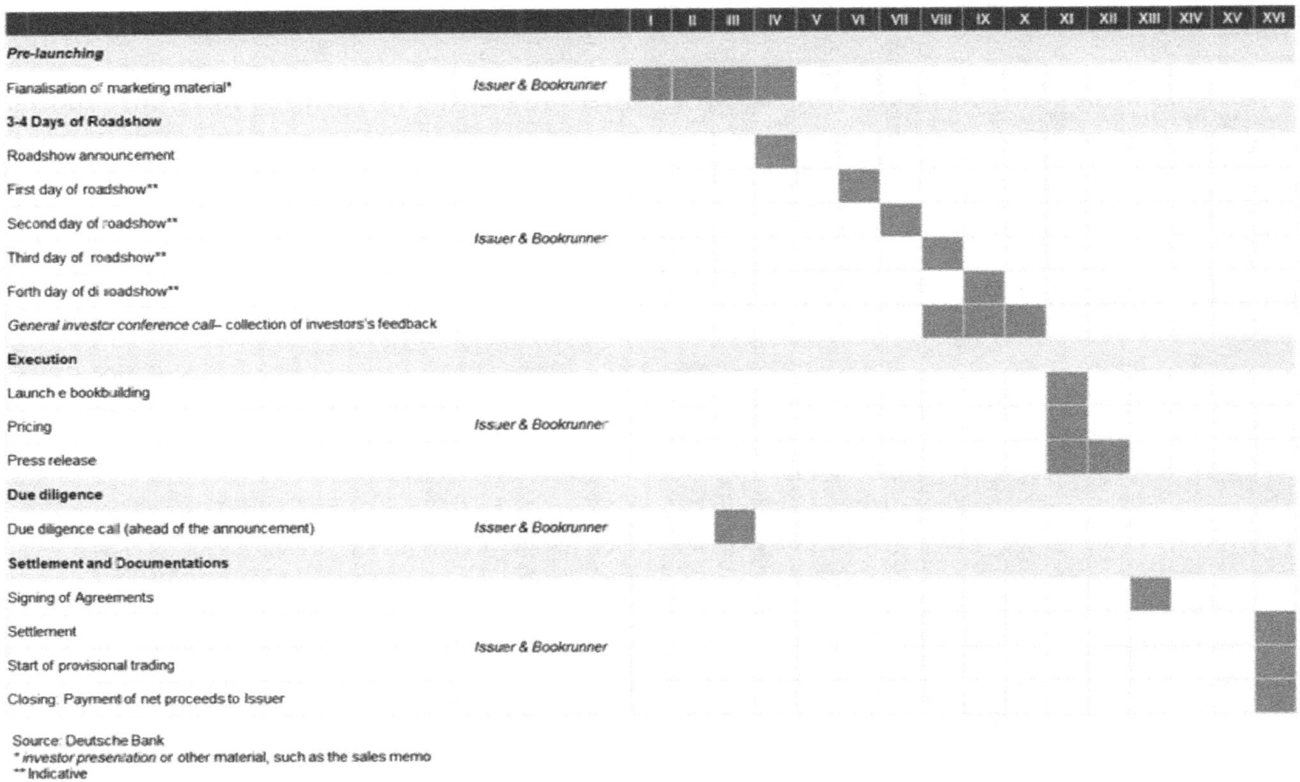

Source: Deutsche Bank DCM

- **9:15 a.m. – Go/No-Go Call**: before launching the transaction, bookrunners schedule a call to provide a market conditions update and get final approval from the issuer to proceed with the execution at the agreed terms (strategy, IPT, targets).
- **9:30 a.m. – Deal announcement with "Initial Price Thought"**: the deal is announced on Bloomberg screens and it becomes public. IPT is the first price indication provided to investors and it is the initial Reoffer Spread with which the new bond is announced to the market. It is generally expressed as range (90-95 bps) or area (90 bps area) + reference rate (i.e. MS+90bps area). Starting from the spread guidance, bookrunners consider many different parameters to the set the IPT. It is always broader than the fair value spread/yield of the new notes. The delta between the Reoffer Spread and the fair value is called **New Issue Premium (NIP)** at IPT and represents the economic incentive used to encourage investors' participation earlier in the process in the primary market. Books are now open and bookrunners can start gathering investors' orders; **the book-building begins.**
- **11:00 a.m. – Price guidance/Assess Orderbook**: bookrunners monitor orders in real time, and after an assessment of the orderbook and investor demand, they release the Price Guidance (or "spread guidance" or just "guidance"), which is the revised reoffer spread announced with IPT. Usually, if demand is strong, the spread can be tightened (i.e. Guidance MS+75-80 bps) vs the IPT.
- **12:30 a.m. – Final terms/Close Orderbook**: usually around an hour and a half after the Spread Guidance, the final terms are announced to the market, setting the final spread over the reference rate (i.e. MS+75bps), that is used to define the coupon and the reoffer price. Books are now closed.
- **3:00 p.m. – Release Allocation**: syndicate has prepared a draft allocation of the orders for the issuer's approval, in accordance with the allocation policy shared with the issuer before the book-building process started. This phase is important to find a good balance between real money investors (buy and hold) and other types of investors with different strategies (i.e. hedge funds).
- **04:00 pm – Pricing call**: once the allocation has been agreed on, the bookrunners and the issuer finalize the bond pricing through an official "pricing call": the parties agree on the trading level of the reference rate (MS) and calculate the reoffer yield (MS + final spread) and the coupon (that could be equal to the reoffer yield if the bond is priced at par).

The price of a bond is the sum of the present values of all expected coupon payments plus the present value of the Face value at maturity. All the future flows are discounted at the Reoffer Yield, under the following formula:

$$\textbf{Bond Price} = \sum_{t=1}^{T=\text{Maturity}} \frac{\textbf{Coupon}_t}{(1+\text{Reoffer Yield})^t} + \frac{\textbf{Face Value}}{(1+\text{Reoffer Yield})^T}$$

A key variable of the bond pricing is the Reoffer Yield, which is the sum of:

	%		*%*		*bps*		*bps*
Reoffer Yield	=		**Reference rate** (Euribor/Midswap)	+	**Issuer Fair Value** ("FV")	+	**New Issue Premium** ("NIP")
↓			↓		↓		↓
Risk/Return=			Interest rate risk		Issuer risk		Risk related to new issues

Generally, the standard fee applied by the bookrunners is up to the kind of issuer and issuance. On average, a total fee is equal to (type of issuer/% fee expressed in bps):

- SSA: 10 bps;
- IG: 30/80 bps depending on underling asset class (up to 100 bps for deeply subordinated notes in EUR);
- HY: 80/100 bps (also 200 bps for difficult HY issuances or "new comers").

The total amount of fees is usually split between the Global Coordinator(s) and Joint Bookrunners with a 80%/20% proportion. Please notice that in DCM jargon the term "Reoffer" is used (i.e. Reoffer spread, yield, price) because it is the price (agreed on with the issuer) at which the underwriting syndicate resells the bond to public investors (e.g. the syndicate purchases the bond from the issuer at 99.4 and "resells" it to the market at 100, thus the reoffer price - 0.6 is the profit for the syndicate, the fees applied).

Figure 4.10 provides a recapitulation of all the factors that combined form the Reoffer Yield.

Figure 4.10 Recap of all the factors that form the Reoffer Yield

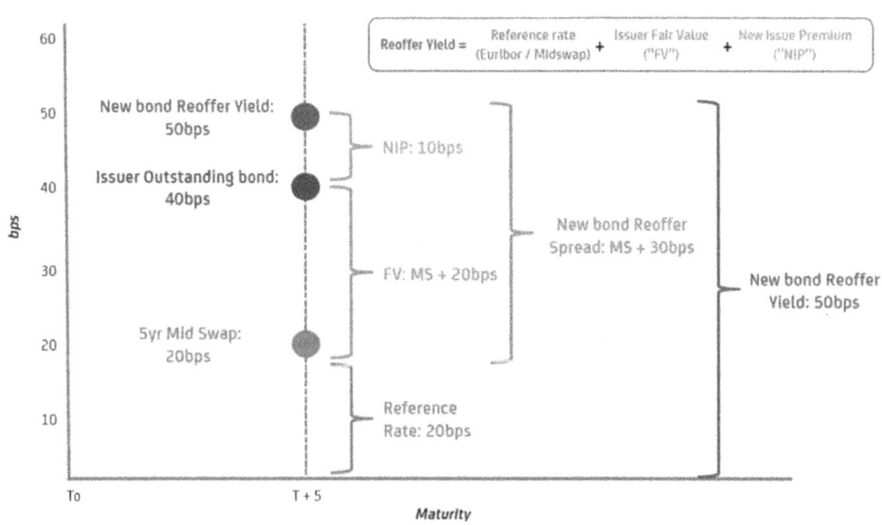

- **05:00 pm** – Free to trade, the bond is now on the secondary market (the grey[8] one, before the settlement is completed).

Phase 5 (Settlement)

The final phase is called settlement, that represents the end of the bond issue and usually takes place 5 days (T+5) after the pricing. Settlement is completed when funds have been transferred from investors to issuers against the delivery of the securities.

4.2.3 Credit ratings

A credit rating is an opinion on the creditworthiness of an issuer in general terms or with respect to a particular debt or financial obligation. An issue rating might be different from an issuer rating: obviously the former depends on the latter, but other elements are considered such as, for example, the seniority of the issue and the presence of collateral. Credit ratings impact directly on both credit spread (i.e. the interest rate the issuer has to pay to investors) and gross spread (i.e. the fee paid by the issuer to the syndicate/bookrunner). The better the rating, the lower both spreads are. The main function of ratings is to provide investors indications of the likelihood of receiving the money owed to them in accordance with the terms on which they invested. A worse credit rating is associated with higher risk of default and so investors require a higher return (i.e. higher coupon) and the investment bank requests a higher fee because it is relatively harder to price and place the bond. In addition, we might consider that in many jurisdictions, some financial institutions, such as insurance companies or pension funds, can only buy securities with a rating above a given level (i.e. investment grade).

The most important rating agencies are Standard and Poor's (S&P), Moody's, and Fitch. Their credit ratings cover the global spectrum of sovereign, corporate, insurance, bank, and public finance entities (i.e. supranational and sub-national entities) and the securities they issue, as well as structured finance securities backed by collateral (i.e. receivables, mortgages, loans, etc.). **Figure 4.11** reports the rating scales of the three most relevant agencies, for medium and long-term securities (maturity longer than 12 months). Ratings are conventionally classified into two main categories: (i) **investment grade** and (ii) **speculative grade**. The first category comprises those securities with rating equal to or above BBB- (the safest securities), while the second those below BBB- (the riskier ones).

It is important to underline that some issuers or issues are rated by more than one agency, and a split rating occurs when agencies assign different ratings to the same

[8] The grey (or gray) market is an Over-The-Counter (OTC) market for financial securities, where the bonds trade before the official trading begins on an exchange market, after the settlement.

Figure 4.11 Rating scales

Moody's		Fitch		S&P		Rating description	Investment type
Long-term	Short-term	Long-term	Short-term	Long-term	Short-term		
Aaa	P-1	AAA	F1+	AAA	A-1+	Prime	INVESTMENT GRADE
Aa1		AA+		AA+		High grade	
Aa2		AA		AA			
Aa3		AA-		AA-			
A1		A+	F1	A+	A-1	Upper medium grade	
A2		A		A			
A3	P-2	A-	F2	A-	A-2		
Baa1		BBB+		BBB+		Lower medium grade	
Baa2	P-3	BBB	F3	BBB			
Baa3		BBB-		BBB-	A-3		
Ba1	Not Prime	BB+	B	BB+	B	Non-investment grade	SPECULATIVE GRADE*
Ba2		BB		BB			
Ba3		BB-		BB-			
B1		B+		B+		Highly speculative	
B2		B		B			
B3		B-		B-			
Caa1		CCC+	C	CCC+	C	Substantial risks	
Caa2		CCC		CCC			
Caa3		CCC-		CCC-			
Ca		CC		CC		Extremely speculative	
		C		C		Default imminent	
C		RD	RD / D	SD	D	In default	
/		D		D			
/		/		/			
* Speculative grade securities are also known as **"high yield"** or **"junk"**.							

Source: Author's elaboration based on data from Moody's, Fitch and S&P websites

issuer/issue. An example is a bond rated BBB- by one agency and BB+ by another agency. A **split rating** is possible because one agency consider certain variables differently or because it assesses a particular item (such as a recent acquisition by the issuer) with a different methodology than the other agency.

Agencies apply a fee for ratings requested by issuers; these are called **solicited**. Normally, issuers solicit a preliminary rating and then, depending on the result, they decide whether to disclose it to the market or not. In contrast to solicited ratings, **unsolicited** ones are opinions about the creditworthiness of a borrower and are published by credit rating agencies without the request of the issuer. The issuance of this kind of evaluation does not require charging a rating fee. It should be noted that most ratings are solicited.

Case study Assicurazioni Generali, by Aldo Sioli, Managing Director DCM/ Structured Finance Italy and Chiara Campagner, Associate DCM, Deutsche Bank AG

Debt Capital Markets: The New Issue Process

In the following section, we will describe in detail the mechanics for issuing new debt securities on the primary market. We will present it through a real case study: Assicurazioni Generali's green Tier 2 subordinated issuance - 2.429% Eur 600 million, priced on July 6, 2020 with a bullet maturity on July 14, 2031.

1. The main players involved in a public primary bond issuance

The main players involved in the placement of a new bond would be: (i) the issuer looking to sell a new debt security, (ii) the investors willing to buy such a security, and (iii) the Bookrunner Banks that would support the issuer in the sales effort and function as a liaison between (i) and (ii).

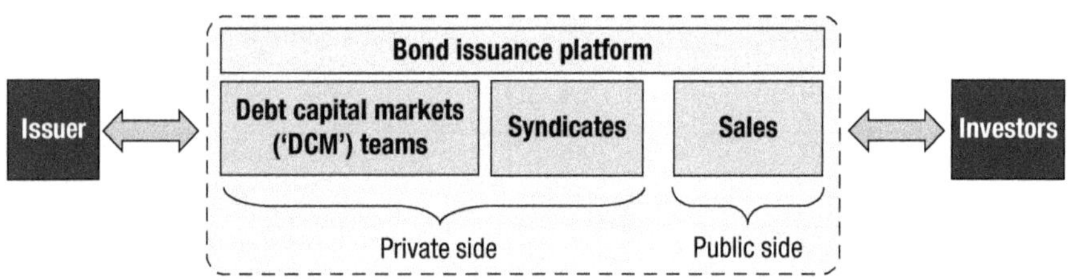

2. Execution flow

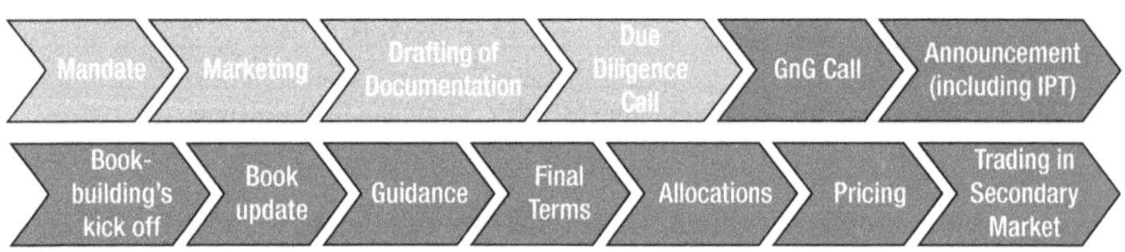

Activities performed in days preceding the execution
Activities performed in the same day (intra-day execution)

Execution starts once an Issuer decides to access the market to issue a new public bond and mandates the Bookrunners of its choice to lead such a process.

To present from a pragmatic perspective all the steps required for the execution of the new issue, we will take as an example Generali's Eur 600 million Tier 2 notes due in 2031 priced on July 6, 2020.[1]

As we will describe below, this transaction represents an important example of an extremely high quality issuer executing a state-of-the-art transaction under multiple metrics: record order-book size, extremely strong investor participation, and positive final economics achieved despite a volatile market during the Covid-19 pandemic:

Issuer: Assicurazioni Generali ("Generali," "ASSGEN")

Bookrunners: Barclays, BofAML, CITI, Deutsche Bank, Mediobanca, Natixis

[1] Note that this transaction was linked to a wider financial exercise but in this context we will focus our analysis on the primary new issue process only.

3. Before Announcing a Transaction

Once the mandate is received, the Bookrunners start monitoring the best market window for execution. The Banks perform multiple analyses, regarding: the general macroeconomic backdrop across credit, equity, and rates in the various geographies (including feedback from Asia overnight, European opening, and futures on the US market), the expectations for competing supply from other issuers, the performance of other deals recently brought into the market, the secondary market levels of the issuer's outstanding securities, and the main macro-events that could favor or jeopardize the execution.

The analysis would include the expected target coupon for different sizes of the deal, and the recommended strategy to achieve the best outcome to satisfy the issuer's needs. We will describe the different pricing references in detail afterwards.

Investment Banks have several tools at their disposal to perform a wide range of analyses: Bloomberg/Reuters or other data providers, internal research, or public feedback from investors (usually filtered by Syndicate). In particular, the team closely monitors the performance of other recent transactions by the issuer's peers and the trading levels of the issuer's already-existing notes.

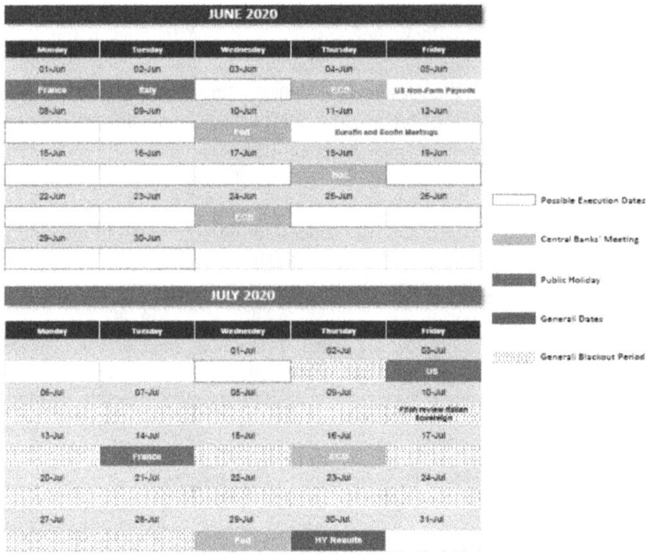

In this phase and until the official public announcement of the deal, the information on the new potential bond remains strictly private: DCMs and Syndicates are not allowed to share anything with the public-side (Sales, Investors, media, etc.).

3.1 Documentation

As mentioned, the DCM team would support the issuer and manage the documentation process, coordinating the preparation of the set of legal documents required for execution. The main document is the Base Prospectus (EMTN or Standalone) under which an Issuer is able to access the public markets (in this case the European market):

- **Standalone**: this documentation is created for a single transaction and expires with it, so it cannot be used for multiple issuances.
- **EMTN Programme**: a set of documents that can be used at any point over a one-year period, it needs to be updated annually and frequent issuers usually select it as a more cost-efficient documentation framework for more than one drawdown in the period.

A Base Prospectus of the EMTN programme/Standalone typically comprises the following key sections

Section	Description
Overview	– An introduction to the Prospectus, with a short summary of the different sections included in the Base Prospectus
Risk Factors	– A list of risks which are specific to the situation of the Issuer (business, industry, shareholders, etc.) and the securities, and which are material for making investment decision (which now have to comply with the new Prospectus Regulation) – Usually these are drafted by Issuer's legal team together with its legal counsel and it is reviewed by the Dealers' Counsel
Form of the Notes	– This section relates to the Form of the Notes that could be issued under this EMTN Programme/Standalone (Bearer form, Temporary Global Note or Permanent Global Note), which will be specify in the Final Terms
Terms and Conditions	– Section setting out all Terms and Conditions of the Notes to be issued under the Programme/Standalone. Typically it covers the status and security, form and denomination, negative pledge, interest, redemption and purchase, payments, taxation, events of default, enforcement, replacement of notes and coupons, notices to bondholders, etc.
Governing Law	– Governing law of the notes issued under the programme
Use of Proceeds	– Description of the use of proceeds of the Notes. – For a "green" issuance the use of proceeds will be used to finance or refinance Eligible Green Projects (i.e. Green Buildings, Energy Efficiency (storage, grid, infra), Clean Transportation, Renewable Energy, Water, Recycling and waste management).
Description of the Issuer	– In depth description of Issuer comprised by its different areas of business, historical financial information, significant recent financial events (dividends, M&A, etc.), recent developments, organizational structure, management board, share capital, etc. – Usually these are drafted by Issuer's legal team together with its legal counsel and it is reviewed by the Dealers' Counsel
Taxation	– General description of certain EU and Italian tax considerations relating to the Notes issued under the EMTN programme/Standalone that investors should be aware
Subscription and Sale	– Section related to restrictions on the distribution and sale of the Notes (i.e. Selling Restrictions to specific countries, retail investors, etc.)

An EMTN programme/Standalone typically comprises the following key documents, besides the Base Prospectus

Document	Description
Dealer agreement/ Subscription agreement	– Contains the contractual agreement between the Issuer and the Dealers that governs the establishment of the programme/standalone and the issuance of notes under the programme/standalone, and contains an agreed form of subscription agreement for each issue
Agency agreement/ global note	– Contains the contractual agreement between the issuer and the Agent (responsible for the settlement of the bond), setting out payment mechanics and timing, and responsibilities/liabilities for each party
Comfort Letter	– The offer document will contain financial information about Inditex and this will have to be confirmed by Issuer's auditor. The auditor will also provide a consent letter to this information being used in the offer document. The auditor's comfort letter will be issued as at the date of the offer document and will confirm that the financial information within the offer document is accurate
Legal Opinions	– A legal opinion is a formal opinion expressing a view on legal matters relevant to a transaction, which are drafted by Law Firms. They typically cover a number of different aspects of a transaction and the scope of the opinion will vary on a case by case basis

3.2 Marketing (Roadshow and Sales Memo)

Depending on the type of transaction, the Issuer's decision and timing, the Bookrunners may recommend launching a marketing exercise aimed at interacting with prospective investors: the Roadshow. If specifically linked to a transaction, we would define it as a "deal-related roadshow" which would be publicly announced together with the transaction. Often, a Roadshow is essential for first-time issuers or for complicated transactions that require adequate investor education. In particular, Investment Banks would arrange for the issuer to hold a comprehensive series of meetings in the most important financial centres. The roadshow would usually last 2 to 4 full working days and would entail a mix of group presentations (breakfast or lunch) and one-to-one meetings with key potential investors.

During the roadshow, the issuer presents its credit and financial profile along with the main features of the new bond, while Investors will take time to perform credit analysis and open new lines for the Issuer.

Selected list of European Fixed Income Investors

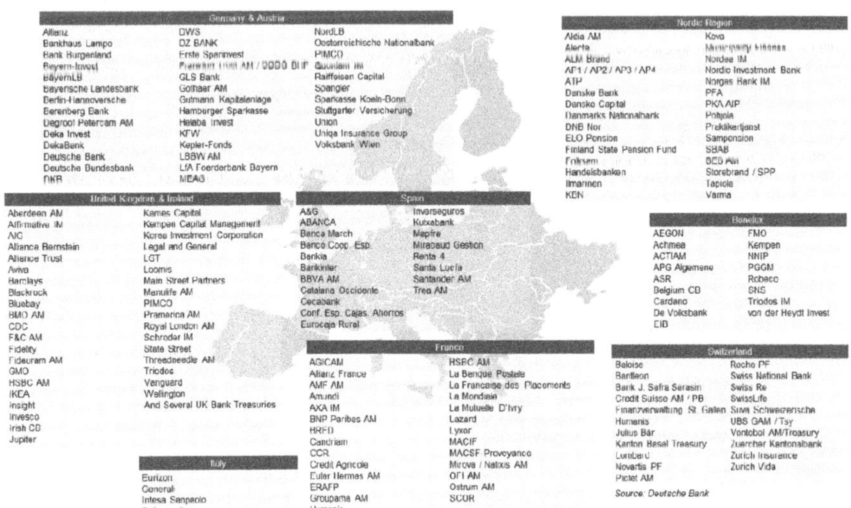

The DCM teams also prepare a so-called "sales memo": a brief summary of the new notes to be sent by Syndicates to their Sales Force, in order to streamline all the relevant information for the trade.

In the case of the Generali transaction, a roadshow was not envisaged, given a well-established EMTN programme and the important investments made by the company over the years to interact with investors through non-deal related meetings. In this way, the Investor Relations team – responsible for the interactions and the relationship between the Company and the investors – has built deep knowledge among investors of Generali's credit specifics. For this transaction, Generali organized a virtual presentation via a dedicated provider (the only way allowed due to the COVID), that consisted of a recorded video illustrating the company's last financial update and the main characteristics of the new transaction. The sales memo is presented below.

SALES MEMO

GENERALI

GENERALI NEW GREEN TIER 2 ISSUE

OFFER RESTRICTIONS: NOT FOR RELEASE, PUBLICATION OR DISTRIBUTION TO ANY U.S. PERSON OR IN OR INTO THE UNITED STATES, ITS TERRITORIES AND POSSESSIONS OR RESIDENT IN ANY OTHER JURISDICTION WHERE IT IS UNLAWFUL TO DISTRIBUTE THIS ANNOUNCEMENT.

New Notes Offering – to be issued in the form of green bonds	
Maturity	Due in 2031 subject to Conditions to Redemption and redemption would not result in / accelerate insolvency (postponement of Maturity Date if not satisfied)
Par Call	Any Business Day during the six months period preceding the Maturity Date, subject to regulatory approval, Conditions to Redemption and redemption would not result in / accelerate insolvency
Interest	Fixed rate payable annually in arrears from [ ] 2020 up to and including the date of redemption of the Notes
Expected Size	Up to €800 million
Interest Deferral	Mandatory: (i) Solvency Capital Event has occurred or would occur as result of payment (unless waived by regulator); (ii) payment would result in / accelerate insolvency; (iii) regulatory request
Optional Early Redemption	The Issuer may redeem the Notes in whole, but not in part, at par upon (i) Tax Event (loss of deductibility or imposition of withholding tax), (ii) Regulatory Event, (iii) Rating Event or (iv) Clean-Up Call (80%) subject to regulatory approval, Conditions to Redemption, redemption would not result in / accelerate insolvency and certain other conditions satisfied
Status	Senior Dated Subordinated Notes and constitute unconditional and unsecured subordinated obligations and rank (i) junior to unsubordinated obligations, (ii) at least equally with all other dated subordinated obligations which constitute Tier 2 Own Funds of the Issuer and (iii) senior to any obligations of the Issuer which rank, or are expressed to rank, junior to the Notes
Expected Issue ratings (M/F)	[Baa3 / BBB-]
Denoms / Listing	EUR100,000 + EUR1,000 / Luxembourg
ESG Framework	https://www.generali.com/investors/debt-ratings/green-bond-framework
Additional information about ESG Credentials	https://www.generali.com/it/info/download-center/sustainability/documents

Focus points

- **Generali's 2.124% 2030 Green Bond has been issued last October 2019 at MS+225bps vs an IPT today of MS+[300]. This compares to the Sub Inco Index and BTP/Bunds spread levels being substantially in line with last year**
- **This new security will add a new liquid benchmark to Generali's curve and provides a unique opportunity to invest in the name in size, as opposed to outstanding securities that remain hard to source given the bonds are tightly held by investors, especially in the recent directional (buying) market. The new bond will also help enhancing the liquidity across the curve.**
- **Zero net new issuance given concurrent matched tender. Replacing existing non-green bond with new green bond will bring incremental demand to Generali's curve rather than incremental supply, and will squeeze the premium of the new issue**
- **In line with the existing Green Tier 2 Bond, the new issue will be in bullet format, a more investor friendly structure that has proved to be more resilient to volatility shocks through Covid**
- **New issue calendar is expected to slow down over the next couple of weeks, while Investment Grade credit continues to see inflows, supply in general in the insurance sector is likely to be lower in H2 2020 vs H1 2020**
- **Green Bond investment plans/commitments and demand for ESG assets continue to grow**

Generali's Path to the Strategic Debt Targets

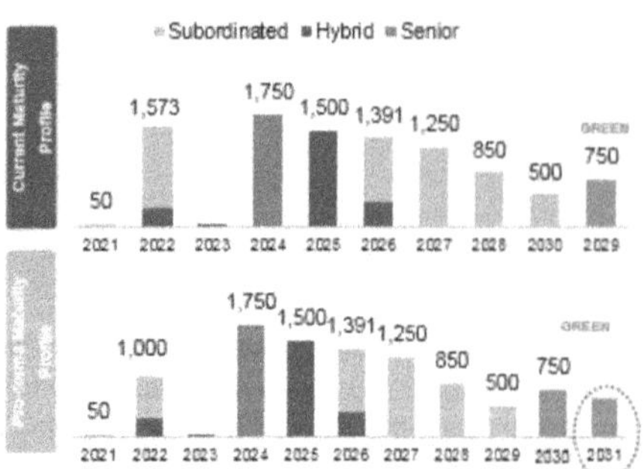

2019-2021 Strategic Plan:

Debt reduction so Far:

- EUR 250m in Jan 2019
- EUR 250m in Oct 2019
- EUR 1,250m in Jan 2020

EUR 1,750m so far

Annual interest expense:

- Already reduced by almost 165m vs the 70-140m strategic target

Debt Profile:

- More balance debt maturity profile, with the 2022 refinancing wall already reduced by 1bn last year and further with this transaction
- Following this transaction, the average maturity of Generali's debt profile is expected to extend from 5.5y to 6.7y

3.3 Due Diligence Call
Ahead of the new issue date, the Banks perform the "due diligence call" by sending and discussing with the issuer a certain set of questions ("Due Diligence Questionnaire") related to the issuer's business overview and potential risks that should be highlighted before the transaction is launched (including past performance and expected risk factors).
Usually, a 15-20 minutes due diligence call would be held ahead of announcing the transaction, during which the client has the opportunity to update the Bookrunners on any material information that could have an impact on the new issue.

4. Pricing Day
On Monday July 6, Assicurazioni Generali S.p.A. launched and successfully priced a new Eur 600m Tier 2[2] Green bond.
The "Green" format, following the so called "equivalence principle," means that an amount equal to the net proceeds from the issue will be used to finance or refinance, in whole or in part, eligible green projects meeting certain eligibility categories (i.e. green buildings, energy efficiency projects, clean transportation, renewable energy, recycling and waste management). This feature has been gaining considerable importance in capital markets within the wider ESG focus ("Environmental, Social and Corporate Governance topics).
During the offering process, described in detail below, the Joint Banks worked to guarantee the best possible outcome given the Issuer's targets in terms of size and final cost.

4.1 Initial Price Thoughts
In the morning of the pricing day, the Banks would suggest an Initial Price Thoughts (IPT) that is the earliest price indication given to investors.
The IPT may be expressed as:

- a fixed rate (for example: 3.5% or 5%);
- a spread (expressed in basis points; 1bp = 0.01%) vs a benchmark rate:
  - for Euro-denominated bonds the benchmark is generally the Mid Swap rate (referred to as MS in the following paragraphs) of the same maturity or call date of the new bond issued;
  - for issuance in USD, the spread is usually presented over the Treasury yield matching the new issue maturity.

The IPT is used to test the investors' willingness to buy the new issue notes, and it can be amended, generally tightened, during the course of the pricing day, based on investor feedback on the new bond visible in the number, amount, and quality of the orders that constitute the book during the book-building process. The "amended" IPT is called "Guidance" or "revised Guidance."
As such, the IPT is always wider than the fair value spread/yield of the new notes: the delta between IPT and fair value is called the New Issue Premium (NIP) at IPT and represents the economic incentive used to encourage investors' participation earlier in the process in the primary market.
How is the IPT set? The Bookrunners consider multiple parameters, such as the assessment of macro market conditions, the issuer's securities bid trading levels on the secondary market adjusted for the required duration gap of the upcoming transaction, and the relative value of secondary bid bond levels of the issuer's competitors.
A competitor is an entity active in the same business sector as the issuer, with a similar rating parameter and capital/asset size, and potentially operating within a similar macroeconomic backdrop.
For Generali's transaction, the IPT was set at MS+300bps. The Bookrunners used one of Generali's already-outstanding bonds (ASSGEN Tier 2 Green 2.124% - due in 2030) as a main reference on the secondary market as a starting point to build the fair value for the transaction.

[2] A detailed explanation on the capital structure of Banks and Insurance companies will be provided in a separate Chapter.

ASSGEN 2.124% Oct 2030 Green T2 was bid in the context of the i-spread[3] + 260bps pre new issue announcement, and Banks determined the fair value ("FV") to be MS+270bps for a new instrument after considering the tenor adjustment.
The Syndicate teams estimated that, in the specific particularly volatile market condition, a NIP of 30bps (IPT of 300bps - FV of 270bps) at IPT would guarantee strong investor engagement.

Generali's outstanding curve and other selected EUR notes issued by insurance companies
Execution Day - Timeline

Subject [/] DB FINS: EUR INSURANCE HYBRID/SUB RUN
Attached 97) Bloomberg Function (RUNZ)
Desk: + [illegible]
This Message is Firm-forwardable

Security			Next Call Dt	Bid Px - Ask Px	Bid Sprd / Ask Sprd	Sprd Chg	Bid ZSpd / Ask ZSpd	Bid Yield / Ask Yield	Bench	BLP RTG	ISIN
ACAFP	2⅝	48	01/29/28	102.250-103.250	295/281	0.120	256/241	2.30/2.15	6YR	NR	FR0013312154
ACAFP	4¾	48	09/27/28	118.375-119.375	293/281	0.335	252/239	2.27/2.15	6YR	NR	FR0013203734
ACAFP	4¼	PERP	01/13/25	109.000-110.000	283/261	0.250	250/227	2.14/1.92	DBR 1 24	NR	FR0012444750
ACAFP	4½	PERP	10/14/25	111.000-112.000	296/277	0.250	260/241	2.26/2.07	DBR 1 24	NR	FR0012222297
ACHMEA	6	43	04/04/23	110.250-111.250	282/247	0.270	250/214	2.11/1.75	DBR 1½ 23	BBB-	XS0911388675
ACHMEA	4¼	PERP	02/04/25	105.125-106.125	372/350	0.245	339/316	3.03/2.80	DBR 0½ 25	BBB-	XS1180651587
ACHMEA	2½	39	06/24/29	94.564-95.611	368/354	-1.760	339/325	3.19/3.05	9YR	BBB-	XS2056491660
AEGON	4	44	04/25/24	106.000-107.000	304/277	0.240	271/243	2.33/2.06	DBR 1¾ 24	BBB	XS1061711575
AGSBB	3¼	49	07/02/29	104.625-105.625	319/307	0.125	288/275	2.66/2.54	DBR 0¼ 29	BBB+	BE0002644251
AGSBB	3½	47	06/30/27	107.500-108.500	302/287	0.250	261/245	2.32/2.17	DBR 0½ 25	BBB+	BE6277215545
AGSBB	3⅞	PERP	12/10/29	95.000-96.000	507/494	0.000	469/455	4.51/4.38	8YR	BBB-	BE6317598850
ALVGR	5¾	41	07/08/21	104.625-104.909	184/156	0.105	132/104	1.08/0.80	DBR 2½ 21	A	DE000A1GNAH1
ALVGR	2.241	45	07/07/25	104.498-105.093	200/188	-5.000	166/153	1.31/1.19	DBR 0½ 25	A	DE000A14J9N8
ALVGR	3.099	47	07/06/27	111.065-111.783	208/198	0.000	171/160	1.43/1.32	6YR	A	DE000A2DAHN6
ALVGR	1.301	49	09/25/29	96.808-97.649	217/207	0.000	187/177	1.68/1.58	9YR	A	DE000A2YPFA1
ALVGR	3⅜	PERP	09/18/24	107.000-108.000	234/210	0.125	200/176	1.63/1.40	DBR 1½ 24	A	DE000A13R7Z7
ALVGR	4¾	PERP	10/24/23	110.250-111.250	225/196	0.000	192/162	1.53/1.24	DBR 2 23	A	DE000A1YCQ29
ASRNED	5⅛	45	09/29/25	114.250-115.250	289/270	0.250	255/236	2.21/2.02	DBR 1 25	NR	XS1293505639
ASRNED	3⅜	49	02/02/29	105.250-106.250	327/315	0.250	292/279	2.70/2.57	7YR	NR	XS1989708836
ASRNED	5	PERP	09/30/24	110.125-111.125	315/291	0.125	282/258	2.45/2.21	DBR 1 24	NR	XS1115800655
ASRNED	4⅝	PERP	10/19/27	101.250-103.250	512/480	0.250	470/438	4.47/4.15	6YR	NR	XS1700709683
	4⅛	26		110.500-111.500	289/272	0.250	251/233	2.18/2.01	DBR 1¾ 24	BBB-	XS1062900912
	10⅛	42	07/10/22	116.500-118.500	238/148	0.000	207/117	1.69/0.79	2YR	BBB-	XS0802638642
	5½	47	10/27/27	114.750-115.750	388/374	0.000	348/333	3.20/3.06	DBR 1 25	BBB-	XS1311440082
	5	48	06/08/28	112.250-113.250	389/376	0.125	348/334	3.22/3.09	DBR 0½ 26	BBB-	XS1428773763
	3⅞	29		109.125-110.125	319/307	0.000	290/277	2.67/2.54	DBR 0¼ 29	BBB-	XS1941841311
	2.124	30		97.000-98.250	295/281	0.250	262/247	2.46/2.32	9YR	BBB-	XS2056491587
	4.596	PERP	11/21/25	105.125-106.375	423/398	0.175	387/361	3.53/3.28	DBR 1 24	BB+	XS1140860534
ATRADI	5¼	44	09/23/24	104.375-105.625	480/448	0.125	446/414	4.09/3.78	DBR 1½ 24	NR	XS1028942354
AVLN	6⅜	43	07/05/23	113.500-114.500	219/188	0.250	187/155	1.48/1.17	DBR 1½ 23	BBB+	XS0951553592
AVLN	3⅞	44	07/03/24	107.250-108.250	267/242	0.250	234/209	1.97/1.72	DBR 1½ 24	BBB+	XS1083986718
AVLN	3⅜	45	12/04/25	106.786-107.423	273/261	-3.000	237/225	2.04/1.92	DBR 0½ 25	BBB+	XS1242413679
AXASA	5⅛	43	07/04/23	111.609-112.082	186/171	-1.000	154/138	1.15/1.00	DBR 1½ 22	BBB+	XS0878743623
AXASA	3⅜	47	07/06/27	110.401-111.235	245/233	-3.000	207/194	1.78/1.66	DBR 0½ 26	BBB+	XS1346228577
AXASA	3¼	49	05/28/29	110.147-111.179	258/246	-2.000	221/208	1.99/1.87	DBR 0½ 28	BBB+	XS1799611642
AXASA	3.941	PERP	11/07/24	109.000-110.000	246/224	0.000	213/190	1.76/1.54	DBR 1 24	BBB	XS1134541306
BNP	1	24		99.317-99.960	186/171	-5.000	153/137	1.16/1.01	DBR 1 24	NR	FR0013299641
CASSIM	4¼	47	12/14/27	97.750-99.750	526/494	0.000	488/455	4.61/4.29	6YR	NR	XS1733289406
CCAMA	6	27		121.125-122.125	311/297	0.250	277/261	2.46/2.31	6YR	NR	FR0013232444
CCAMA	3⅜	28		105.961-107.098	312/297	-1.380	280/265	2.56/2.41	8YR	NR	FR0013365640
CCAMA	2⅝	29		96.177-97.362	309/294	-2.130	280/264	2.60/2.45	9YR	NR	FR0013447125
CCAMA	7⅞	39		100.000-100.500		0.000			EUR003M	NR	FR0010815464
CCAMA	6⅜	PERP	05/28/24	111.375-112.375	391/366	0.000	359/333	3.21/2.96	4YR	NR	FR0011896513

Source: Used with permission of Bloomberg Finance L.P.

At 9.15 CET: before launch, Syndicate, DCM and issuer participated in a "Go/No-Go call (GnG)" providing the Issuer with the joint banks' recommendation (including strategy, targets, and IPT).

[3] The Interpolated Spread or I-spread or ISPRD of a bond is the difference between its yield to maturity and the linearly interpolated yield for the same maturity on an appropriate reference yield curve.

Below are the notes of the GnG call:
" Today ASSGEN 2.124% 2030 is opening 1bp tighter vs Friday's closing (at i+260 vs +261)*
** Euro markets are opening the week on a strong tone (+1.8%) as markets look past US C19 case rises over 4th of July holidays*
** Asia markets rally on hope of more CB/Gov Stimulus (+2.0%), with China (+5%) outperforming, thanks to a positive commentary on the stock market from Chinese state media*
** Rates higher, Cash tighter, CDS tighter*
** Texas, Arizona and Florida continue to see C19 infection rates climb*
** Reporting season blackouts will slow supply into the summer break (14 issuers in B/O ahead of 11 releases next week)*
** Other issuers in the capital market space might take advantage of this strong market window today*
** Given the heavy supply into Q2, we would expect July to be a sub 15bn/eur month, vs run-rate of 20bn/eur*
** Eco data follows the usual global post US-Payrolls lull, but today will see the release of Euro Area retail sales for May, and in US one of the main data releases will be the ISM non-manufacturing index, along with the services and composite p.m.Is*
** IPT: Mid Swap +300bps area."*

At 9.30 CET, following the issuer's green light for launch, the deal was announced on Bloomberg screens and from that moment on the transaction became "public."
The Banks announced all the relevant information on the new notes (please see below). In this case the final size was announced from inception, but an issuer can choose to provide a more general indication such as a "benchmark transaction" in order to maintain the full flexibility on the amount issued (a Benchmark transaction would be > Eur 350m).

```
Subject   €€€ Assicurazioni Generali EUR600mm (no-grow) Green 11yr Bullet T2 - IPTs MS
Attached  No Attachments
***************** DONT REPLY TO THIS ADDRESS !!!!! ****************************
€€€ Assicurazioni Generali EUR600mm (no-grow) Green 11yr Bullet T2  IPTs MS+300 area €€€

Issuer:                      Assicurazioni Generali S.p.A.
Legal Entity Identifier:     549300X5UKJVE386ZB61
Description:                 EUR Fixed Rate Green Senior Dated Subordinated Notes
                             (Tier 2)
Issuer Financial Strength:Baa1, Stable (Moody's) / A-, Stable (Fitch) /
                             A, Stable (A.M. Best)
Expected Issue Ratings:      Baa3 (hyb)(Moody's) / BBB-(Fitch)
Status of the Notes:         Senior Dated Subordinated Notes (as set out in
                             Condition 4.1 (Status - Senior Dated Subordinated
                             Notes) of the Terms and Conditions of the Tier 2
                             Notes
Amount:                      €600mm (no-grow)
Settlement Date:             14 July 2020 (T+6)
Scheduled Maturity Date:     Interest Payment Date falling on 14 July 2031,
                             subject to Conditions to Redemption below
Optional Redemption Call: At any time from (and including) 14 January 2031 to
                             Scheduled Maturity Date) to (but excluding) the
                             Scheduled Maturity Date subject to Conditions to
                             Redemption below
Initial Price Thoughts:      MS+300bps area
Coupon:                      Fixed payable annually in arrear
Mandatory Interest Deferral: Cash cumulative, non-compounding upon the
                             occurrence of a Solvency Capital Event (meaning non-
                             compliance with the SCR (or that payment of interest
                             or principal on the Notes would lead to such non-
                             compliance); any other event which would require a
                             deferral or suspension of payment of interest or
                             principal under the Applicable Regulations for Tier 2
                             Own Funds qualification); if interest payment would
                             result in or accelerate insolvency of the Issuer; or
                             if Lead Regulator determines that Solvency Margin
                             would fall below SCR in the short term
Arrears of Interest:         Compulsory payment of Arrears of Interest on the
                             earlier of (i) the first Interest Payment Date
                             following receipt by Fiscal Agent of notice that the
                             event or circumstance giving rise to interest
```

Source: Used with permission of Bloomberg Finance L.P.

Syndicate also shared the sales memo with the Sales Force, which immediately started engaging with fixed income Investors.

The books were now open and the Bookbuilding process kicked off: the Bookrunners started collecting all investor orders based on the cited IPT. Both the Bookrunners and the Issuer could easily monitor the growth of the book in real time.

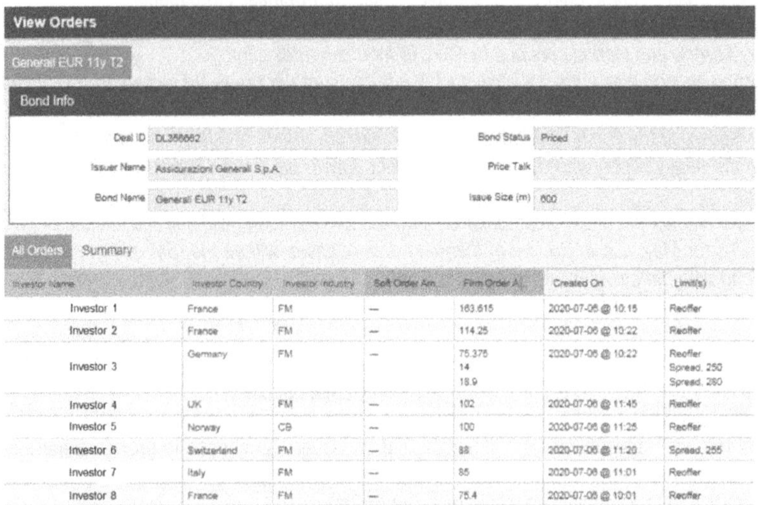

View Orders

Generali EUR 11y T2

Bond Info

Deal ID	DL356662	Bond Status	Priced
Issuer Name	Assicurazioni Generali S.p.A.	Price Talk	
Bond Name	Generali EUR 11y T2	Issue Size (m)	600

All Orders | Summary

Investor Name	Investor Country	Investor Industry	Soft Order Am...	Firm Order A...	Created On	Limit(s)
Investor 1	France	FM	—	163.615	2020-07-06 @ 10:15	Reoffer
Investor 2	France	FM	—	114.25	2020-07-06 @ 10:22	Reoffer
Investor 3	Germany	FM	—	75.375 14 18.9	2020-07-06 @ 10:22	Reoffer Spread, 250 Spread, 280
Investor 4	UK	FM	—	102	2020-07-06 @ 11:45	Reoffer
Investor 5	Norway	CB	—	100	2020-07-06 @ 11:25	Reoffer
Investor 6	Switzerland	FM	—	88	2020-07-06 @ 11:20	Spread, 255
Investor 7	Italy	FM	—	85	2020-07-06 @ 11:01	Reoffer
Investor 8	France	FM	—	75.4	2020-07-06 @ 10:01	Reoffer

Investor demand for Generali's new Tier 2 was extremely strong and the book started showing interest in excess of €2.0bn already at **10.45 CET**. This information was communicated to show how strong the deal was performing in terms of investor participation.

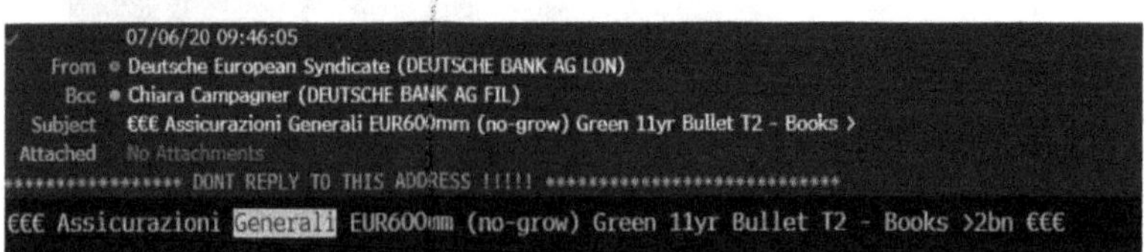

Source: Used with permission of Bloomberg Finance L.P.

Orders kept growing at record pace, to more than €4.4bn, and at **12.30 CET** the Guidance was announced at MS+250 +/-5bps area. Given such a strong investors' demand – substantially higher than the amount to be issued - Generali was able to considerably tighten the spread vs MS compared to the announced IPT.

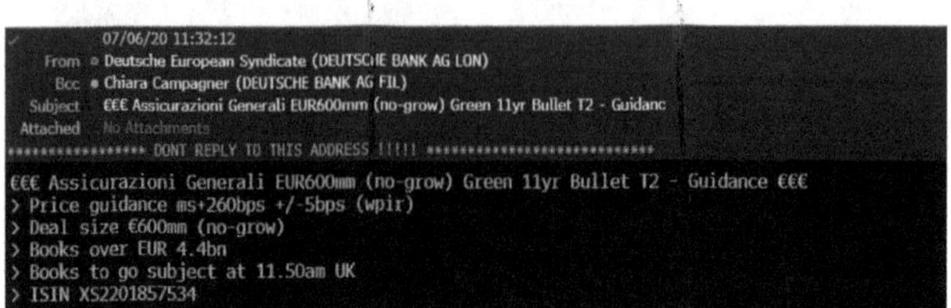

Source: Used with permission of Bloomberg Finance L.P.

At 12.50 CET, taking advantage of the booming demand for the trade, Generali set the final spread at MS+255bps, with the deal ending up ~7.5x times oversubscribed (Eur 4.500m orders/Eur 600m issued) with total orders from over 355 investors.
The outcome of this transaction was extremely strong and backed by the superior credit quality of the issuer and the "green" feature of the transaction. Generali was able to tighten the spread in the course of the bookbuilding process from the original MS+300 IPT to the final MS+255bps, within the original estimated Fair Value of MS+270bps and even within the ASSGEN 2030 secondary market level taken as a reference at the beginning of the process (effectively locking-in a negative NIP).

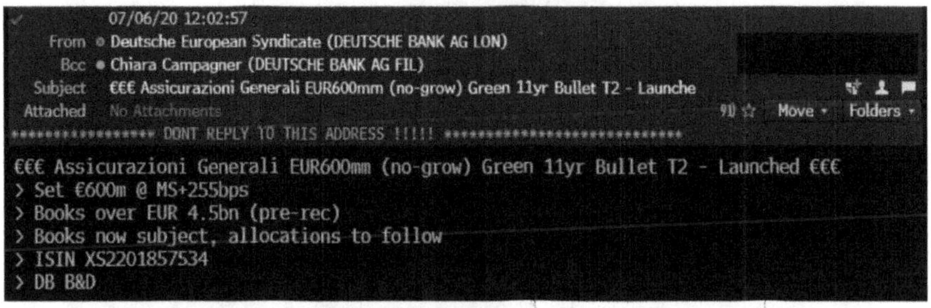

07/06/20 12:02:57
From ◦ Deutsche European Syndicate (DEUTSCHE BANK AG LON)
Bcc • Chiara Campagner (DEUTSCHE BANK AG FIL)
Subject €€€ Assicurazioni Generali EUR600mm (no-grow) Green 11yr Bullet T2 - Launche
Attached No Attachments
Move Folders
***************** DONT REPLY TO THIS ADDRESS !!!!! *****************************

€€€ Assicurazioni Generali EUR600mm (no-grow) Green 11yr Bullet T2 - Launched €€€
> Set €600m @ MS+255bps
> Books over EUR 4.5bn (pre-rec)
> Books now subject, allocations to follow
> ISIN XS2201857534
> DB B&D

Source: Used with permission of Bloomberg Finance L.P.

Final terms of the bond were now set and Syndicate started preparing a draft allocation of the orders for the issuer's approval based on an allocation policy shared with the issuer, as required by the MIFID directive, before the Bookbuilding process started.
Once the allocation was agreed on, the Bookrunners and the issuer finalized the bond pricing during an official "pricing call." During this call, the Bookrunners and the Issuer agreed on the trading level of the benchmark rate (MS and Bund) and calculated the yield (MS + Spread) and coupon (equal to the yield since the bond was priced at par in this case). The Allocation process is quite important, since the quality and the trading strategy of the investors receiving allocation will contribute to both the initial performance as well as the overall liquidity of the trade. A good balance should be found between real money investors (buy and hold) and other types of investors with different strategies. For an issuer it is important to have liquid and well-performing securities representing reliable trading levels for their curve.
The Bond was now on the **secondary market**.

```
07/06/20 17:32:13
From    • Deutsche European Syndicate (DEUTSCHE BANK AG LON)
Bcc     • Chiara Campagner (DEUTSCHE BANK AG FIL)
Subject   €€€ Assicurazioni Generali EUR600mm (no-grow) Green 11yr Bullet T2 - Priced
Attached  No Attachments
***************** DONT REPLY TO THIS ADDRESS !!!!! ****************************

€€€ Assicurazioni Generali EUR600mm (no-grow) Green 11yr Bullet T2 - Priced

Issuer:                     Assicurazioni Generali S.p.A.
Legal Entity Identifier:    549300X5UKJVE386ZB61
Description:                EUR Fixed Rate Green Senior Dated Subordinated Notes
                            (Tier 2)
Issuer Financial Strength:Baa1, Stable (Moody's) / A-, Stable (Fitch) /
                            A, Stable (A.M. Best)
Expected Issue Ratings:     Baa3 (hyb)(Moody's) / BBB-(Fitch)
Status of the Notes:        Senior Dated Subordinated Notes (as set out in
                            Condition 4.1 (Status - Senior Dated Subordinated
                            Notes) of the Terms and Conditions of the Tier 2
                            Notes
Amount:                     €600mm
Settlement Date:            14 July 2020 (T+6)
Scheduled Maturity Date:    Interest Payment Date falling on 14 July 2031,
                            subject to Conditions to Redemption below
Optional Redemption Call: At any time from (and including) 14 January 2031 to
                            Scheduled Maturity Date) to (but excluding) the
                            Scheduled Maturity Date subject to Conditions to
                            Redemption below
Reoffer:                    MS+255 / 100.00 / 2.429%
Benchmark:                  DBR 0 02/15/30 + 289.4bp (104.58)
Coupon:                     2.429% Fixed payable annually in arrear
Mandatory Interest Deferral: Cash cumulative, non-compounding upon the
                            occurrence of a Solvency Capital Event (meaning non-
                            compliance with the SCR (or that payment of interest
                            or principal on the Notes would lead to such non-
                            compliance); any other event which would require a
                            deferral or suspension of payment of interest or
                            principal under the Applicable Regulations for Tier 2
                            Own Funds qualification); if interest payment would
                            result in or accelerate insolvency of the Issuer; or
                            if Lead Regulator determines that Solvency Margin
```

Source: Used with permission of Bloomberg Finance L.P.

Case study summary

Assicurazioni Generali (Baa1/A-/A M/F/A.M.)

2.429% €600m Green Tier 2

The transaction represents a further step for Generali in fulfilling the Group's sustainability commitments, after having printed the first green subordinated notes issued by a financial issuer

The new issue is linked to tender of 3 legacy capital instrument

That allows to have zero net issuance, forcing investors to chase the trade to maintain credit exposure to the Italian national champion issuer

Distribution by investor type

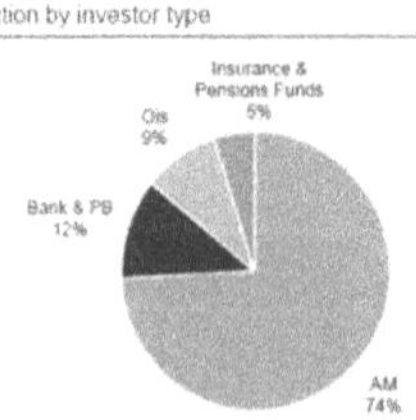

Distribution by geography

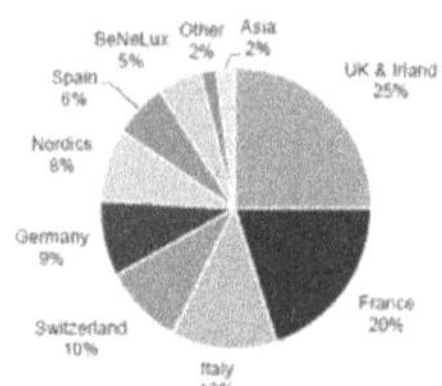

Transaction details

Issuer	Assicurazioni Generali S.p.A.
Description	EUR Fixed Rate Green Tier 2 Notes du
Optional Redemption Call	At any time from (and including) 14th Ja Scheduled Maturity Date) to (but exclud Scheduled
Form	RegS Bearer, TEFRA D
Second Party Opinion	Sustainalytics
Size	EUR750bn
Issue Rating (exp)	Baa3 (hyb)/BBB (Moody's/Fitch)
Amount	EUR 600mln
Launch / Pricing Date	06th July 2020
Settlement Date	14th July 2020 (T+6)
Maturity Date	14th July 2031
Coupon	2.429%, Fixed payable annually in arre
MS rate 11yr	-0.121
Re-offer spread	MS + 255bps
Issue Price	Par
Governing Law	Italian Law
Joint Bookrunners	Barclays, BofAML, CITI, DB, MEDIOBA
ISIN	XS2201857534

Transaction highlights

- On Monday July 6th Assicurazioni Generali S.p.A. successfully l priced a new EUR 600m WNG Tier 2 Green offering at MS+255b IPTs of MS+300bps area:
- The deal (linked to the tender of 3 legacy capital instruments) wa screens at 9.30CET in a supportive market backdrop. The syndic the outstanding ASSGEN 2.124% Oct 2030 Green T2 as the sta build FV for this transaction. The bond was bid in the context of t new issue announcement, thus evaluating FV at MS+270 for a n bullet T2 after considering curve extension
- The replacement of existing non-green bond with new green bon boost in the demand along with a strong investors' engagement market was extremely responsive and started showing interests €2.0bn already at 10.45CET. Orders kept growing to more than at 12.30CET the guidance was announced at MS+250 +/-5bps (
- Taking advantage of booming demand for green assets and rep for many issuers, final spread was set at MS+255bps, with the d ~7.8x times oversubscribed, with total orders form over 355 inve a landing price inside the calculated FV (estimated NIP at -15bp the trading level of the existing green Tier 2 due in Oct 2030

Source: Distributions based on allocations

Case study **BTP 10Y, by Luca Falco, Senior Vice President - Head of Global Syndicate & Capital Markets and Pietro Bianculli, Managing Director - Head of Global Syndicate & Capital Markets, UniCredit Bank AG**

Republic of Italy - BTP10 year €uro Benchmark in syndicated format

Intro

One of the biggest Issuers in €uroland is the Republic of Italy.

The MEF (Ministero dell' Economia e delle Finanze) via the Italian Department of the Treasury, through a dedicated directorate general, issues government securities and manages central government liabilities. The two main channels to issue new government securities are the auctions, with a precise calendar defined at the beginning of each year, and the Syndicated format.

Here, in particular, we report the case study of the **Republic of Italy**'s EUR14bn Dec 2030 (BTP) syndicated line. The new BTP 10yr attracted the biggest demand on record for any single tranche SSA transaction in euros, over EUR 107bn+, as reported below by one of the main market info providers (IGM – Informa Financial Intelligence).

IGM

Informa Financial Intelligence

Bondwatch Morning Insight (text version) Alert

Daily Close: Italy's record-breaking trade spearheads red hot session

Matthew Barrett

Wed Jun 03, 2020 3:02pm

** The **European primary bond market remained active** Wednesday ahead of Thursday's ECB meeting where the central bank is set to announce further stimulus measures to help combat the effect of the Covid-19 pandemic on the region's economies. In total we saw **EUR18.7bn print in the single currency**, led by **Italy**'s record-breaking EUR14bn Dec 2030 syndicated BTP (more in next bullet). For the full list of the day's euro trades see the IGM DAILY EUR NICS & BOOKS.

** **Republic of Italy**'s EUR14bn Dec 2030 syndicated line stole the show Wednesday, attracting the **biggest demand on record for any single tranche SSA transaction** in euros at EUR-107bn+, beating Spain's 10yr in April (see graph below). The deal landed 6bps inside IPTs at BTPs +9 which equated to a final pick-up of ~6bps versus the sovereigns existing curve.

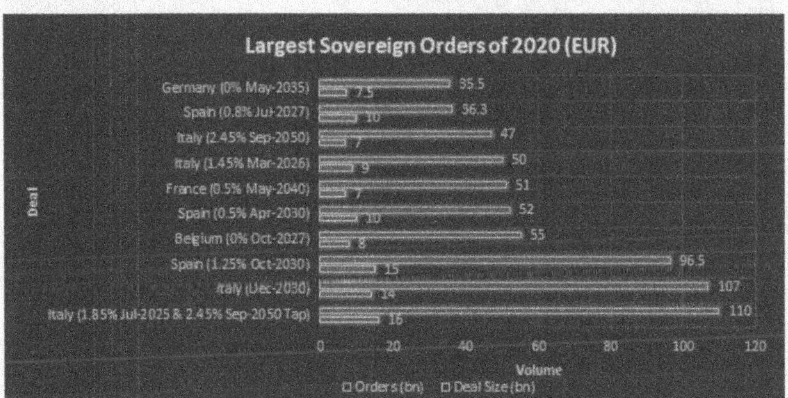

Source: IGM

Mandate

MEF selects the Bookrunners from among the list of Specialists (16 primary dealers, including top International, Euro area and Domestic banks).

Each Specialist, on top of participating in auctions and providing liquidity to the secondary market, has a constant bilateral dialogue with the MEF, on market development, clients views, secondary market turnover, and many other topics related to the SSA market, including pitching activity for potential syndicated mandates.

Once the MEF has decided to Issue via Syndicate and selected the Banks, the syndicate group is defined and the Banks (Joint Bookrunners = JBR) are mandated. The group starts to work together to optimize the outcome for the Issuer.

At this stage, the information is not yet public, and of course, all the compliance rules are applied considering how sensitive the mandate is in terms of potential market impact, in particular on the BTP outstanding curve.

The Joint Proposal

As the first step, the MEF asked the JBR to send a Joint proposal.

Below are some samples of the document sent by the JBR to the MEF (called here Italy DMO – Debt Management Office) in relation to the potential new BTP 10 year benchmark bond (as of Tuesday, June 2, 2020).

The joint proposal included the market view, the timing, the draft screen announcements, the bond terms, and the overall strategy/pricing methodology.

Dear Italy DMO,

*On behalf of (***to be decided if to report the names of banks***) BNP Paribas, Citi, HSBC, MPSCS, NatWest Markets and Unicredit, please find below our considerations and a joint recommendation for the transaction that you are evaluating.*

We remain available to discuss the points below at the next conference call.

I. *View on market developments* *(global picture, euro rates, Italian curve, flows, etc...)*

- *Market tone last week remained very strong in general and was reinforced by the announcement of the EC's Recovery Fund and stimulus plans which was slightly better than expected, providing relief for peripherals and a stronger support for the EU politically.*
- *The week started with a positive tone led by equity markets, but fairly rarefied activity due to holidays across Europe and investors waiting for the ECB meeting on Thursday.*
- *Yesterday, Italy May Manufacturing p.m. I rose to 45.4 (forecast 36.8) with a rebound larger than expected while industrial production fell 33.8% in May compared to the same month in 2019, providing an indication of the impact as activity restarted after almost two months of lockdown.*
- *Last week, BTPs had a series of very positive trading sessions with 10Y tightening from 210bps to 191bps vs Bund. Yesterday afternoon, Italy sold off after the MNI piece suggesting that maybe it's too early for an increase in the PEPP, but is recovering this morning with the IK recovering part of yesterday post-headline sell-off and BTP trading at around 188bps vs Bund.*
- *In terms of flows, the belly outperformed the wings and the same holds for the 10Y against 30y (10s30s is around 6bp steeper since last week). We saw good buying of 5Y BTP especially from internationals while domestics focused on maturities up to 3Y in anticipation of the upcoming ECB facilities.*
- *Given the overall market tone, we believe market conditions are conducive for Italy DMO to announce a new syndicated transaction.*

II. *Timing and Communication Strategy*

✓ *Screen mandate announcement on*

Tuesday, June 2 at 14:30 CET (ECB announcement on the composition of PEPP Programme is expected at 14:45 CET)

✓ *Proposed text of the announcement*

(English version)
The Republic of Italy, rated Baa3/BBB/BBB-/BBBH (stab/neg/stab/neg) has mandated BNP Paribas, Citi, HSBC, MPS Capital Services, NatWest Markets and UniCredit to joint lead manage a new euro 10 year benchmark with maturity date 1-December 2030 …… The issuance of the new 7y benchmark BTP announced in the Quarterly Issuance Programme will be moved to the third quarter.
The transaction is expected to be launched in the near future subject to market conditions.
All other Specialists will be invited as Co-Lead Managers.
Reg S, 144A Eligible, CACs. FCA/ICMA stabilisation.
Manufacturer target market (MIFID II product governance) is eligible counterparties, professional and retail (all distribution channels).

(Italian version)
Il Ministero dell'Economia e delle Finanze (MEF) comunica di aver affidato a BNP Paribas, Citigroup Global Markets Ltd, HSBC France, Monte dei Paschi di Siena Capital Services Banca per le Imprese S.p.A, NatWest Markets, UniCredit S.p. A. il mandato per il collocamento mediante sindacato di un nuovo BTP benchmark a 10 anni con scadenza 1 Dicembre 2020 ……………

✓ *Timing of opening of the IOIs*
Wednesday 3 June at 09:00 CET

✓ *Timing of opening of the book*
10:30 CET

✓ *Tentative pricing timing (looking at market movers)*
16:00 CET

III. Bond characteristic
✓ *Maturity*
Option A: 1-December-2030
Option B: ……….

✓ *Coupon (relevance of price being above or below par)*
XXX %, in order to price the transaction slightly below par

IV. Settlement Date
T+5 [10 June 2020]

V. Size Range

✓ *Size to be announced*
Benchmark transaction

✓ *Expected final size of the deal*
€10bn+

✓ *Demand composition (distribution by type of investor and geographical residence) …….*

✓ *Composition of orders in terms of type (outright, asw, switch, etc.): …….*

VI. Price Methodology and Guidance
✓ *Methodology to determine the fair value*
Fair Value for a new ***BTP Dec-30***
BTP Aug-30 + xxx bps (extrapolating curve steepness between BTP Apr-30 and BTP Aug-30)
……

BTP 1-December-30

✓ *Current fair value with the above-mentioned methodology*
BTPS 0.95% 1-Aug-2030 + xxx bps

✓ *Initial price thoughts (price range) for IOI*
BTPS 0.95% 1-Aug-2030 + xxx bps area

✓ *Final expected price spread*
BTPS 0.95% 1-Aug-2030 + xx bps/xxx bps [xxx bps New Issue Premium]

....

VII. *Syndicate structure and fees*

Assuming 6 JLM, we would recommend your standard pot structure with the following split:
- 90% to the Joint Lead Managers
- 10% to Co-Managers

✓ *We would indicate a level of fees in terms of xxxx %*

Execution

Based on the Joint recommendation, followed by conference calls between the MEF and the JBR to finalize the strategy, **the deal was publicly announced** on 2 June 2020 in the course of the afternoon, to start to engage all the potential Investors.

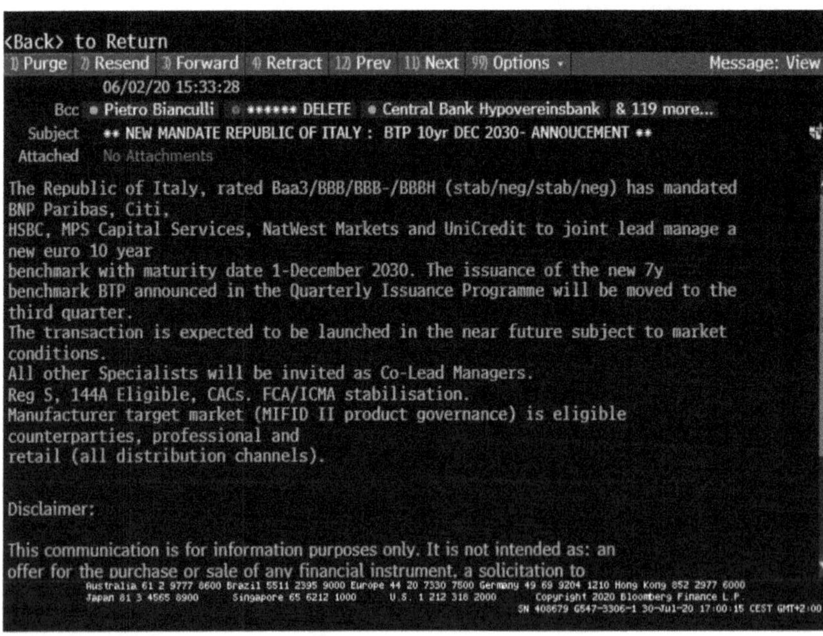
<Back> to Return
1) Purge 2) Resend 3) Forward 4) Retract 12) Prev 11) Next 99) Options · Message: View
06/02/20 15:33:28
Bcc • Pietro Bianculli • ****** DELETE • Central Bank Hypovereinsbank & 119 more...
Subject ** NEW MANDATE REPUBLIC OF ITALY : BTP 10yr DEC 2030- ANNOUCEMENT **
Attached No Attachments

The Republic of Italy, rated Baa3/BBB/BBB-/BBBH (stab/neg/stab/neg) has mandated BNP Paribas, Citi,
HSBC, MPS Capital Services, NatWest Markets and UniCredit to joint lead manage a new euro 10 year
benchmark with maturity date 1-December 2030. The issuance of the new 7y benchmark BTP announced in the Quarterly Issuance Programme will be moved to the third quarter.
The transaction is expected to be launched in the near future subject to market conditions.
All other Specialists will be invited as Co-Lead Managers.
Reg S, 144A Eligible, CACs. FCA/ICMA stabilisation.
Manufacturer target market (MIFID II product governance) is eligible counterparties, professional and
retail (all distribution channels).

Disclaimer:

This communication is for information purposes only. It is not intended as: an offer for the purchase or sale of any financial instrument, a solicitation to

Australia 61 2 9777 8600 Brazil 5511 2395 9000 Europe 44 20 7330 7500 Germany 49 69 9204 1210 Hong Kong 852 2977 6000
Japan 81 3 4565 8900 Singapore 65 6212 1000 U.S. 1 212 318 2000 Copyright 2020 Bloomberg Finance L.P.
SN 408679 G547-3306-1 30-Jul-20 17:00:15 CEST GMT+2:00

Source: Used with permission of Bloomberg Finance L.P.

The morning after, on 3 June 2020, based on market conditions and based on the preliminary conversation the JBR had with Investors after the public announcement, the IPT (Indicative Pricing Thoughts) was released to collect IOI (Indication of Interest) from the potential Investors. As usual, the reference point for the pricing was the previous BTP, the 0.95% 08/2030.

```
<Back> to Return
1) Purge  2) Resend  3) Forward  4) Retract  12) Prev  11) Next  99) Options ·        Message: View
          06/03/20 09:00:09
      Bcc  • Pietro Bianculli  • Central Bank Hypovereinsbank  • Martin Schwindack  & 119 more...
  Subject  €€€ NEW Italy 10YR EUR Benchmark - Taking IOIs @ BTPS+15bps area €€€
 Attached  No Attachments

€€€ NEW Italy 10YR EUR Benchmark - Taking IOIs @ BTPS+15bps area €€€

Issuer:        Republic of Italy
Ratings:       Baa3/BBB/BBB-/BBBH (stab/neg/stab/neg)
Format:        Buoni del Tesoro Poliennali (RegS in dematerialised
               book entry form), 144A eligible, CACs
Size:          EUR Benchmark
Settlement:    10 June 2020 (T+5)
Maturity:      1 December 2030
Coupon:        Fixed, S/A ACT/ACT. Full first coupon on 1 December 2020
IPTs :         BTPS 0.95 08/30 +15bps area
Listing:       Borsa Italiana S.p.A. (M.O.T.) (Regulated Market), also trading
on MTS
Denoms/Law:    €1k+€1k/Italian Law
Docs:          Domestic, Standalone
Target Market: The target market for the Bonds is eligible counterparties,
professional and retail (all distribution channels)
Bookrunners:   BNPP, CITI (B&D/DM), HSBC, MPSCS, NWM, UNICREDIT
Timing:        Taking IOIs, expect today's business.
```


Source: Used with permission of Bloomberg Finance L.P.

The reactions of the Investors were extremely positive: in less than 1.30 hours the amount of IOI collected were over 85bn.
The MEF, in agreement with the JBR, decided to officially open the book and released the official price guidance.

```
<Back> to Return
1) Purge  2) Resend  3) Forward  4) Retract  12) Prev  11) Next  99) Options ·        Message: View
          06/03/20 10:23:07
      Bcc  • Pietro Bianculli  • Central Bank Hypovereinsbank  • Martin Schwindack  & 119 more...
  Subject  €€€ NEW Italy 10YR EUR Benchmark - Books open @ BTPS +12bps area €€€
 Attached  No Attachments

€€€ NEW Italy 10YR EUR Benchmark - Books open @ BTPS +12bps area €€€

- IOIs over €85bn including JLM interest of €8.5bn

Issuer:        Republic of Italy
Ratings:       Baa3/BBB/BBB-/BBBH (stab/neg/stab/neg)
Format:        Buoni del Tesoro Poliennali (RegS in dematerialised
               book entry form), 144A eligible, CACs
Size:          EUR Benchmark
Settlement:    10 June 2020 (T+5)
Maturity:      1 December 2030
Coupon:        Fixed, S/A ACT/ACT. Full first coupon on 1 December 2020
Guidance:      BTPS 0.95 08/30 +12 bps area
Listing:       Borsa Italiana S.p.A. (M.O.T.) (Regulated Market), also trading
on MTS
Denoms/Law:    €1k+€1k/Italian Law
Docs:          Domestic, Standalone
Target Market: The target market for the Bonds is eligible counterparties,
professional and retail (all distribution channels)
```


Source: Used with permission of Bloomberg Finance L.P.

In the following hour, the book jumped over 100bn in total size: the final spread was set and the book closing hour communicated to the market.

<Back> to Return
1) Purge 2) Resend 3) Forward 4) Retract 12) Prev 11) Next 99) Options • Message: View
06/03/20 11:14:07
Bcc • Pietro Bianculli • Central Bank Hypovereinsbank • Martin Schwindack & 119 more...
Subject €€€ NEW Italy 10YR EUR Benchmark - Update#1 / Spread set €€€
Attached No Attachments

€€€ NEW Italy 10YR EUR Benchmark - Update#1 / Spread set €€€

- Books over €100bn incl. JLM interest of €9bn
- Spread set @ BTPS 08/2030 + 9bps
- Books to close 10.45 UKT / 11.45 CET

Disclaimer:

This communication is for information purposes only. It is not intended as: an offer for the purchase or sale of any financial instrument, a solicitation to participate in any trading strategy, or an official confirmation of any transaction. The information is believed to be reliable, but we do not warrant its completeness or accuracy. Prices are indicative only, and are subject to change without notice. We may hold a position or act as a market maker in any financial instrument discussed herein. Clients should consult their own advisors regarding any tax, accounting or legal aspects of this information.

Australia 61 2 9777 8600 Brazil 5511 2395 9000 Europe 44 20 7330 7500 Germany 49 69 9204 1210 Hong Kong 852 2977 6000
Japan 81 3 4565 8900 Singapore 65 6212 1000 U.S. 1 212 318 2000 Copyright 2020 Bloomberg Finance L.P.
SN 408679 G547-3306-1 30-Jul-20 17:18:11 CEST GMT+2:00

Source: Used with permission of Bloomberg Finance L.P.

By 2:00 p.m. Rome time, after a long analysis between the MEF and the JBR, the deal was LAUNCHED defining the final terms (the spread was already fixed previously, including the final size to be printed: it required a deep look into the book, to guarantee a balanced allocation).

<Back> to Return
1) Purge 2) Resend 3) Forward 4) Retract 12) Prev 11) Next 99) Options • Message: View
06/03/20 13:42:49
Bcc • Pietro Bianculli • Central Bank Hypovereinsbank • Martin Schwindack & 119 more...
Subject €€€ NEW Italy 10YR EUR Benchmark - LAUNCHED €14bn @ BTPS+9 bps €€€
Attached No Attachments

€€€ NEW Italy 10YR EUR Benchmark - LAUNCHED €14bn @ BTPS+9 bps €€€

Issuer:	Republic of Italy
Ratings:	Baa3/BBB/BBB-/BBBH (stab/neg/stab/neg)
Format:	Buoni del Tesoro Poliennali (RegS in dematerialised book entry form), 144A eligible, CACs
Size:	EUR 14 bn
Settlement:	10 June 2020 (T+5)
Maturity:	1 December 2030
Coupon:	Fixed, S/A ACT/ACT. Full first coupon on 1 December 2020
Spread:	BTPS 0.95 08/30 +9 bps
Listing:	Borsa Italiana S.p.A. (M.O.T.) (Regulated Market), also trading on MTS
Denoms/Law:	€1k+€1k/Italian Law
Docs:	Domestic, Standalone
Target Market:	The target market for the Bonds is eligible counterparties, professional and retail (all distribution channels)
Bookrunners:	BNPP, CITI (B&D/DM), HSBC, MPSCS, NWM, UNICREDIT
Timing:	Books closed in excess of €108bn (including €9bn JLM interest)
ISIN:	IT0005413171

Australia 61 2 9777 8600 Brazil 5511 2395 9000 Europe 44 20 7330 7500 Germany 49 69 9204 1210 Hong Kong 852 2977 6000
Japan 81 3 4565 8900 Singapore 65 6212 1000 U.S. 1 212 318 2000 Copyright 2020 Bloomberg Finance L.P.
SN 408679 G547-3306-1 30-Jul-20 17:21:44 CEST GMT+2:00

Source: Used with permission of Bloomberg Finance L.P.

Given the size of the book and the total number of the orders, the allocation process required over 2 hours and was released mid-afternoon, with the hedge terms.

```
<Back> to Return
1) Purge 2) Resend 3) Forward 4) Retract 12) Prev 11) Next 99) Options -        Message: View
           06/03/20 16:31:50
      Bcc  • Pietro Bianculli  • Central Bank Hypovereinsbank  • Martin Schwindack  & 119 more...
  Subject  €€€ NEW Italy 10YR EUR Benchmark - Allocations out €€€
 Attached  No Attachments

€€€ NEW Italy 10YR EUR Benchmark - Allocations out €€€

- Allocations out
- Final books over €107bn including €9bn JLM interest
- Hedge deadline 15.40 UKT / 16.40 CET
- HR 106% vs BTPS 0.950% 08/2030
- CITI B&D and DM

Disclaimer:

This communication is for information purposes only. It is not intended as: an
offer for the purchase or sale of any financial instrument, a solicitation to
participate in any trading strategy, or an official confirmation of any
transaction. The information is believed to be reliable, but we do not warrant
its completeness or accuracy. Prices are indicative only, and are subject to
change without notice. We may hold a position or act as a market maker in any
financial instrument discussed herein. Clients should consult their own
Australia 61 2 9777 8600 Brazil 5511 2395 9000 Europe 44 20 7330 7500 Germany 49 69 9204 1210 Hong Kong 852 2977 6000
Japan 81 3 4565 8900   Singapore 65 6212 1000   U.S. 1 212 318 2000   Copyright 2020 Bloomberg Finance L.P.
                                         SN 408679 G547-3306-1 30-Jul-20 17:27:40 CEST GMT+2:00
```

Source: Used with permission of Bloomberg Finance L.P.

At 5:10 p.m. CET the deal was finally priced.

```
<Back> to Return
1) Purge 2) Resend 3) Forward 4) Retract 12) Prev 11) Next 99) Options -        Message: View
           06/03/20 17:09:51
      Bcc  • Pietro Bianculli  • Central Bank Hypovereinsbank  • Martin Schwindack  & 119 more...
  Subject  €€€ NEW Italy 10YR EUR Benchmark - PRICED €€€
 Attached  No Attachments

€€€ NEW Italy 10YR EUR Benchmark - PRICED €€€
Issuer:        Republic of Italy
Ratings:       Baa3/BBB/BBB-/BBBH (stab/neg/stab/neg)
Format:        Buoni del Tesoro Poliennali (RegS in dematerialised
               book entry form), 144A eligible, CACs
Size:          EUR 14bn
Settlement:    10 June 2020 (T+5)
Maturity:      1 December 2030
Reoffer:       99.520  / 1.707% Ann.
Coupon:        1.650% Fixed, S/A ACT/ACT. Full first coupon on 1 December 2020
Benchmark:     BTPS 0.95 08/30 (Spot px 93.835%)  +9 bps
Listing:       Borsa Italiana S.p.A. (M.O.T.) (Regulated Market), also trading
on MTS
Denoms/Law:    €1k+€1k/Italian Law
Docs:          Domestic, Standalone
Target Market: The target market for the Bonds is eligible counterparties,
professional and retail (all distribution channels)
Bookrunners:   BNPP, CITI (B&D/DM), HSBC, MPSCS, NWM, UNICREDIT
Timing:        PRICED, TOE 17.05 CET/ FTT Immediately
Australia 61 2 9777 8600 Brazil 5511 2395 9000 Europe 44 20 7330 7500 Germany 49 69 9204 1210 Hong Kong 852 2977 6000
Japan 81 3 4565 8900   Singapore 65 6212 1000   U.S. 1 212 318 2000   Copyright 2020 Bloomberg Finance L.P.
                                         SN 408679 G547-3306-1 30-Jul-20 17:35:41 CEST GMT+2:00
```

Source: Used with permission of Bloomberg Finance L.P.

Here below is the official press release issued by the MEF including all the main figures in terms of Investor and Geographic breakdown.

Ministero dell'Economia e delle Finanze

PRESS RELEASE

Details on the new 10-year BTP placement

The Ministry of Economy and Finance announces the placement details of the new 10-year BTP, maturing on the 1st December 2030, with a 1.65% annual coupon.

About 490 investors have taken part to the transaction with a total amount requested of about 108 billion Euros, which represents the highest demand ever recorded for a single syndicated issuance. The highest share of the issuance has been allotted to fund managers (38.7%), while a share of 35.6% has been subscribed by banks. Investors with a long-term investment horizon have bought 19.7% of the issuance (in particular pension funds and insurance companies for 15.1%, while central banks and official institutions have been allotted for 4.6%). Hedge funds have subscribed 5.5% of the total amount issued. Also non-financial institutions (corporations) have taken part to the transaction with a residual share of 0.5%.

In terms of geographical residence of investors, the placement has been extremely diversified with the involvement of investors coming from about 40 countries: foreign investors have been allotted for 76% of the issuance, while domestic ones have bought a share of 24%. Among foreign investors, the most relevant share of the issuance, equal to 71.3%, has been allotted to investors from Europe, in particular from UK (23%), Germany, Switzerland and Austria (14.4%), Iberian Peninsula (11.1%), France (7.4%), Nordic countries (7%), Benelux (3.5%), Central and Eastern Europe (3.1%) and other European countries (1.8%). The rest of the issuance, equal to 4.7%, has been subscribed by investors from outside Europe, in particular from United States (3.3%), Asia (1.1%) and Middle East (0.3%).

The bond has been placed through a syndicate structured with six lead managers, BNP Paribas, Citigroup Global Markets Ltd, HSBC France, Monte dei Paschi di Siena Capital Services Banca per le Imprese S.p.A, NatWest Markets PLC and UniCredit S.p.A, while the remaining Specialists in Italian Government Bonds participated as co-lead managers.

Rome, June 4th, 2020

Here is the deal review prepared by UniCredit, summarizing the full process and the main figures of the transaction.

Deal Review – New Republic of Italy BTPs 1.650% EUR 14,000mn due December 2030

Transaction details

Issuer	Republic of Italy
Issue rating	Baa3 (Moody's) / BBB (S&P's) / BBB- (Fitch) / BBBH (DBRS)
Format	Buoni del Tesoro Poliennali (RegS in dematerialised book entry form), 144A eligible, CACs
Issue size	EUR 14bn
Launch date / Value date	3 June 2020 / 10 June 2020
Maturity	1 December 2030
Coupon	1.65% Fixed, S/A ACT/ACT, Full first coupon on 1 December 2020
Reoffer Price / Reoffer Yield	99.520% / 1.707% Ann.
Reoffer Spread	+9bp over BTPs 0.95 08/30
ISIN	IT0005413171
UniCredit Bank Role	Joint Bookrunner

Investor and geographical distribution (allocated)

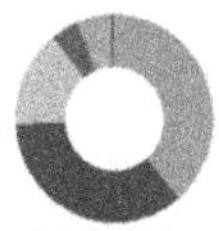

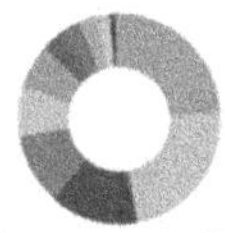

Execution Summary

- Republic of Italy successfully launched its new syndicated EUR 14bn 10Y BTPs due 1st December 2030. This transaction marks the first 10Y maturity to be launched in a syndicated format rather than the usual auction format and the biggest benchmark printed by Republic of Italy (excluding BTP Italia)
- Following a close market monitoring, the Italian Treasury together with the selected syndicate banks announced the mandate on Tuesday, 2nd June at 3:35 PM CET for an execution the day after
- The strong feedbacks received, both in terms of type and geographical presence, coupled with conducive market conditions, allowed the announcement of the Iols gathering on Wednesday, 3rd June at 9:00 AM CET with EUR Benchmark size wording at an IPTs of +15bps area over the reference BTPS 0.95 08/30
- At 10:23 AM CET, books officially opened at BTPs+12bps area with IOIs over €85bn including JLM interest of €8.5bn
- The first update was released at 11:15 AM CET on the back of an overwhelming demand and response with books over €100bn incl. JLM interest of €9bn that allowed to set the spread at BTPs 08/2030 +9bps
- The transaction was finally launched at 1:14 PM CET for a size of EUR 14bn
- Roughly 490 investors participated into the book with a final demand at circa EUR 108bn which is the largest book ever recorded by the Italian Treasury in a syndicated BTPs transaction and the largest book ever for a single tranche in Euro land
- The bulk of the allocations went into Fund Managers (38.7%) and Banks (35.6%) together with Pension Funds & Insurances (15.1%) and Central Banks & Official Institutions (4.6%)
- From a geographical point of view 76% went into foreign investors with 71.3% in Europe and 3.3% in US, 1.1% in Asia and 0.3% in Middle-East

Case study Snam, by Luca Falco, Senior Vice President - Head of Global Syndicate & Capital Markets, and Carolina Marazzini, Managing Director - Deputy Co-Head of Debt Origination, UniCredit Bank AG

Snam EUR 500mn 0.750% 10yr Transition Bond

Introduction

"On the 10th of June 2020, Snam SpA, exploiting a constructive market window driven by BTPS and credit spreads stabilization, rally in equities as well as the vast liquidity available, announced and successfully priced a new EUR 500mn 10yr bond. The new issue was structured as Transition Bond under the newly established Snam's Transition Bond Framework"

The following pages describe the placement process (from pitching to the settlement of the notes) completed by Snam and the Joint Bookrunners with respect to the June 2020 bond transaction, which represents the first **Transition Bond** ever issued by an Italian Company and the second ever in Europe. Before that, a brief description of Snam's business profile and a quick overview of the current debt capital market environment are provided.

Main features of Snam 2020 Transition Bond transaction

Transaction details	
Issuer	Snam SpA (Bloomberg Ticker: SRGIM, Country: ITA)
Issue Rating	Baa2 Stable (Moody's)/BBB+ Negative (S&P)/BBB+ Stable (Fitch)
ESG Rating	Sustainalytics: Medium Risk; 20.3 out of 100 // ISS ESG: Prime (B-) // Robeco: 81/100
Issue Size	EUR 500mn
Status	Senior, Unsecured, RegS Bearer, NGN
Format	Transition Bond
Maturity Date	17 June 2030 (10yr)
Settlement	17 June 2020
Coupon	0.750%
Issue Spread	Mid-Swap +80bps
Re-offer Price/Yield	99.856%/0.765%
Documentation	EMTN Programme/3m par call
Listing /Law	Luxembourg (regulated market)/English
Denom./Increment	EUR 100k/EUR 1k
Joint Bookrunners	Banca IMI/BBVA/BNPP (B&D)/BofA Securities/GSI / JPM/MUFG/Societe Generale/UniCredit

Snam at a glance

Snam SpA, headquartered in San Donato Milanese, Italy, is a leading European operator in the management and construction of gas infrastructure and one of the largest Italian listed companies in terms of market capitalization.

Snam in the Debt Capital Markets

Snam is one of the highest-rated corporate bond issuers in Italy. Being spun-off from ENI in 2012, the group made its debut in the Eurobond market and issued over EUR 9bn EUR-denominated senior bonds within an 18-month timeframe (from July 2012 to January 2014). Since then, Snam has relied on the Debt Capital Markets ("DCM") as the main source to fund both its capex and (re)financing needs.

The regulated nature of its operations and its role as a key strategic energy asset for Italy has allowed the company to retain a higher rating vs Italian Sovereign debt.
Since its debut in the DCM, Snam has historically enjoyed easy access to capital market funding, mainly due to a combination of a defensive and regulated business profile and a strong credit profile/rating.
Public ratings: Snam SpA shows strong investment grade ratings from the three main rating Agencies: (i) Moody's: Baa2 (Outlook: Stable), (ii) S&P: BBB+ (Outlook: Negative) and (iii) Fitch: BBB+ (Outlook: Stable).
Current Bond Maturity Profile: as represented in the below chart, Snam currently has c. EUR 8.9bn of bonds outstanding, spread over 11 different maturities (ranging from 2020 to 2034).

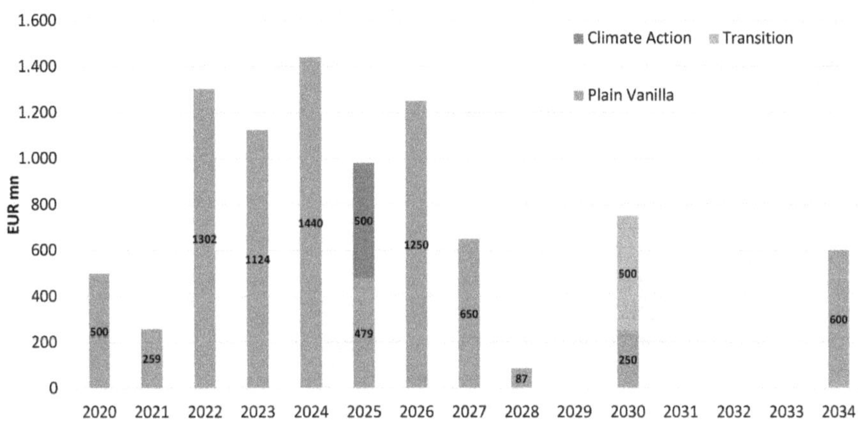

General Bond Market Backdrop
Following the Covid-19 global lockdown, the market was hit by high volatility, causing significant repricing of all asset classes. However, despite the market turmoil, primary activity in the corporate fixed income space has been highly functional, especially since March, when the ECB announced solid liquidity measures and additional purchase programme(s) in the form of higher amounts in the CSPP – Corporate Sector Purchase Programme - and the new PEPP - the "Pandemic Emergency Purchase Programme."
Execution strategies and marketing dynamics adapted surprisingly fast: a number of debut and non-frequent issuers successfully executed very efficient "virtual roadshows" that lead to excellent hit ratios and overall positive results highlighting the absence of any real drawback vs physical meetings and marketing exercises.

Snam case study
The process for issuing the Snam Transition bond started with the Debt Capital Markets teams (DCM) monitoring market developments and advising the client on funding opportunities based on prevailing market conditions, and (if everything goes according to plan), it will end with the execution of the transaction.
In the following pages you will find a detailed description of each of the steps (from the pitching activity to the settlement) which led to a successful execution of the Snam Transition bond.

Phase I – "Pitching with market and issuer analysis" & "Issuer gave the mandate to the banks"
In the "Pitching" phase, Snam received market updates and pricing indications from the DCM departments of Italian and international banks active in the capital markets, which are typically relationship banks of the client. Updates are sent on a regular basis, aiming at supporting the client in

selecting efficient funding strategies based on the prevailing market conditions. Once the Issuer decides that the pricing is satisfactory and the market backdrop is constructive, it can move to the next step by establishing a "Syndicate Group" for executing the new bond issuance.
In the case of Snam's Transition bond, the process followed the standard sequence (pitch, calls, and weekly market and pricing updates in the preliminary phase), and was significantly accelerated starting from the second half of May. Unicredit was ultimately awarded with a Joint Bookrunner (JBR) role for Snam's new bond transaction in Transition format, together with other banks (the "Syndicate Group" or the "Joint Bookrunner") on 9 June 2020.
Since Snam is a listed company with listed debt securities, the Market Abuse Regulation applied. This requires at least the immediate opening of an "Insider List" where all the employees that have access to the mandate information are reported. Such an insider list will be closed after the transaction is priced and the relevant insider information is made public.

Phase II – "Documentation"
Given its status as a frequent issuer, Snam has established a Euro Medium Term Note Programme (EMTN), which allows the issuer to swiftly bring new transactions to the market. In practice, Snam is allowed to issue all its capital market debt under this predefined documentation, thus materially reducing time to market. The review/update of the EMTN Programme and the Prospectus occurs once a year, while additional information (such as financial results) can be incorporated in the Prospectus through supplements.
For this new bond issue, Snam updated its EUR 11bn EMTN on 7 November 2019, while it added a first supplement on 9 June 2020. With this supplement, Snam also updated the section of the Base Prospectus related to the "Use of Proceeds" in order to include all new features of its Transition Bond Framework published the day before (8 June 2020).

Snam S.p.A.
(incorporated with limited liability in the Republic of Italy)
€11,000,000,000 Euro Medium Term Note Programme

Besides standard transaction documents, a Due Diligence questionnaire is answered by Snam during the day of execution.

Phase III – "Spread Guidance/Banks Joint Recommendation"
As a frequent issuer, the definition of Snam's spread guidance was based on 1. its outstanding secondary curve, and 2. an analysis of its closest comparable peers (i.e. Terna, Italgas, Enel etc.). In addition, the current market backdrop (BTPs, indexes, and equity trends) and recent relevant primary market transactions are taken into consideration (New Issue Premiums; Initial Price Talks/ Thoughts, final books, and oversubscription).
Once the Syndicate group has agreed on the best execution strategy, all the relevant information are shared with the issuer during a dedicated call. In the Snam Transition Bond, that call between the banks and the company took place in the evening of 9 June (the day before the public deal execution). The call was facilitated by a support document prepared by the JBRs and called the "Joint Market Tracker."
The key relevant information usually included in a Tracker are:

- JBRs joint view on achievable pricing levels;
- The company's secondary trading levels for the outstanding bonds;
- A short recap of recent transactions executed in the market.

The outcome of the pre-execution call with Snam can be summarized as follows:

- Target tenor: 10 years;
- Size: EUR 500mn expected;
- Initial pricing thoughts "IPTs": Mid Swap+115bps area (which given the 10yr Fair Value "FV" @ Mid Swap+82bps – linear interpolation based on Snam outstanding curve – implies a New Issue Premium "NIP" at IPTs of c. 33bps);
- Expected landing: MS+85-90bps (which implies a final NIP of ~ 3 to 8bps);
- Timing: next day "subject to a constructive market opening and general conditions";
- Pre-launch call ("Go/No-Go Call") among the JBRs set at 9:00 a.m. on the following day (execution day).

Phase IV – "Execution Day: Bookbuilding, Allocation, Final Pricing"
This is the most important part of the process as the issuer and the Bookrunners publicly approach the market. The main steps can be summarized as follows:

1. **Announcement**: the Bookrunners announce the details of the bond issue through financial info providers (i.e. Bloomberg, Reuters, etc.) and bilateral messages from sales to potential investors;
2. **Bookbuilding**: Bookrunners gather orders from investors and build the deal orderbook;
3. **Final terms**: setting of the final spread and the final size;
4. **Allocation**: Bookrunners allocate investors taking into account their nature/quality (real money accounts);
5. **Final pricing**: when the book is in an agreed form and the re-offer spread is fixed, the Bookrunners and the issuer finalize the bond price;
6. **Communication**: Bookrunners publish new issue details on Bloomberg/Reuters/IIIA.

Snam, leveraging its status as a frequent issuer, opted for an intraday execution which entails all steps of the issuance, from the opening of the book to the pricing, taking place in a single day, as per the timetable below:

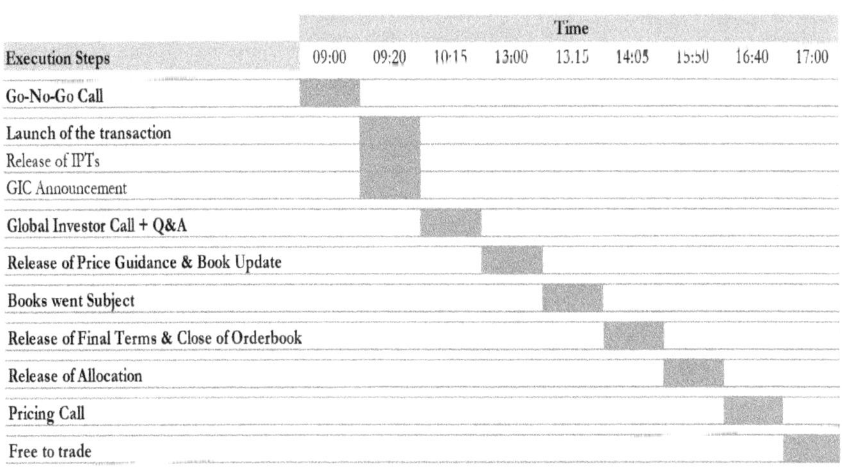

On 10 June, at 9:00 a.m., the GNG Call occurred and provided confirmation to Snam on the following market topics:

1. Presence of a constructive market backdrop;
2. Transaction economics with secondary and new issue levels unchanged vs the previous day;
3. Execution strategy confirmed.

Before launching the transaction, Snam agreed to the terms and gave its sign-off to the screen announcement. The transaction went live through the communication to the market of IPTs at MS+115bps area for a 10yr Transition Bond transaction with expected size of EUR 500mn.
All communications to the market related to a bond transaction customarily take the form of "screen/Bloomberg announcements." In Snam's Transition Bond, the first set of Bloomberg messages released at 9:20 a.m. comprised:

4. Transaction Announcement (IPTs + all the transaction terms);
5. Pre-announcement Snam levels (which help investors to determine the Fair value of the new bond and facilitate their relative value analysis);
6. The Global Investor Call (GIC) announcement invite, together with the link to the Investor Presentation (IP) and the link to the "Snam Transition Bond Framework" (Snam website).

10 June 2020 @9:20am

1) Transaction Announcement

```
*** SNAM €500m exp. 10-year Transition Bond: IPTs MS+115bp area

Issuer:                 SNAM S.p.A.  (Ticker: SRGIM, Country: IT)
LEI:                    815600EAD78C57FCE690
Issuer Rating:          Baa2 (stab) / BBB+ (neg) / BBB+ (stab) (Moody's / S&P / Fitch)
Expected Issue Rating:  Baa2 / BBB+ / BBB+
Format:                 Senior, Unsecured, RegS Bearer, (TEFRA rules apply, no
                        communications with or into the U.S.), NGN
Size:                   €500mn exp.
Settlement:             17 June 2020 (T+5)
Maturity:               17 June 2030 (10-year)
Coupon:                 Fixed (Annual, ACT/ACT)
IPTs:                   *** MS+115bp area ***
Docs:                   Lux listing regulated market / EMTN / €100k+1k / 3m Par
                        Call / English law
Jt Books:               Banca IMI / BBVA / BNPP (B&D) / BofA Securities / GSI /
                        JPM / MUFG / Societe Generale / UniCredit
UoP:                    Finance and/or refinance, in whole or in part, existing
                        and/or future Eligible Projects under Snam's Transition
                        Bond Framework
https://www.snam.it/
SPO:                    DNV GL
https://www.snam.it/

Target Mkt:             Manufacturer target market (MIFID II product governance)
                        is eligible counterparties and professional clients only
                        (all distribution channels).
                        No PRIIPs key information document (KID) has been
                        prepared as not available to retail in EEA or the UK
Advertisement:          https://www.snam.it/en/

Marketing:              URL: www.netroadshow      and enter Entry Code:
                        OR Direct Link:
                        https://www.netroadshow.
                        Global investor call to be held at 9:15GMT/10:15CET
                        Dial in:                  and Access Code:
Timing:                 Books open, today's business
```

Source: Used with permission of Bloomberg Finance L.P.

2) Pre-announcement Levels

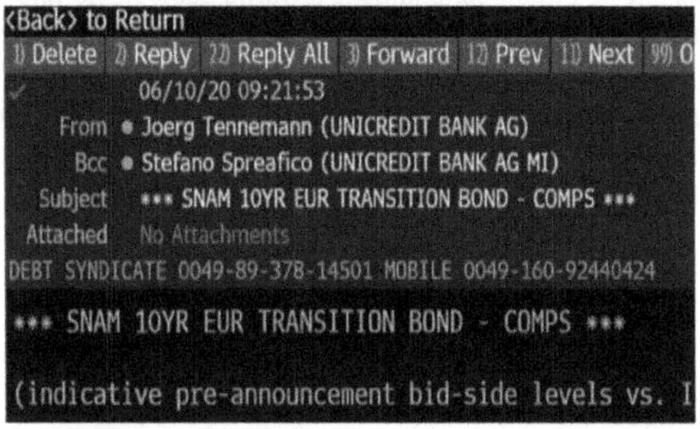

3) Global Investor Call Invite Announcement

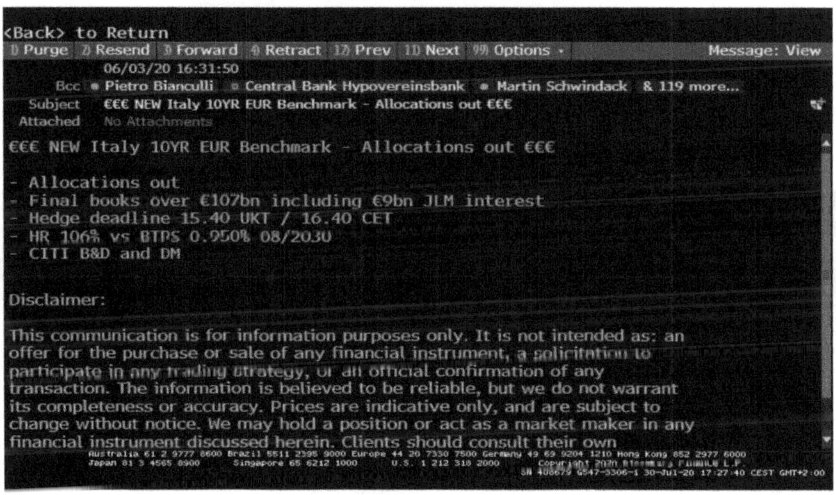

Source: Used with permission of Bloomberg Finance L.P.

Rationale & Execution of the Global Investor Call

Being Snam's debut in the Transition format, the Issuer was keen to arrange some marketing activities to highlight to the investor community the features of its newly-established Transition Bond Framework. The format was an intraday Global Investor Call (GIC) which took place after the announcement of the transaction on 10 June 2020 at 9:15 UKT/10:15 CET.

Execution of Global Investor Call (@10:15am) → Participation of ca. 50 investors

Net-Roadshow presentation

During the GIC, Snam had the chance not only to update investors on its latest financial developments but also to highlight its strong commitment towards sustainable finance and the transition to a low-carbon economy. Snam presented its new Transition Bond Framework, which laid out the guidelines for the issuance of future bonds aimed at financing sustainable investments.
As presented, the beginning of the bookbuilding phase started with the IPT release and ended with the closing of the books. During this process the Joint Bookrunners gathered orders from investors and built up the deal orderbook, that is an internet-based book-building tool. It shows:

- Detailed order-specific information;
- Excel download of the order book;
- Analysis in tabular and chart form with distribution by investor type/region, spread sensitivity, and order volume.

10 June 2020 @1:00pm

Spread Guidance Call
This call represents one of the most important steps towards a successful pricing of the transaction as it defines the span in which the bond will price and what level the issuer will pay in terms of yield. When setting the guidance, the JBRs' goal is to define the most suitable level in order to achieve both the Issuer's and the Investors' pricing targets.

```
*** SNAM 10YR EUR TRANSITION BOND - UPDATE & GUIDANCE ***

=> Books > €1.75bn
=> Guidance: MS+85-90bps
=> Size remains €500mln expected
=> Books subject at 12.15 UKT / 13.15 CET
```

Source: Used with permission of Bloomberg Finance L.P.

In the Snam Transition bond, based on a book in excess of EUR 1.75bn of orders, the JBRs (following Snam's sign-off/approval to proceed) decided to communicate to the market a guidance level of MS+85-90bps, which implied an NIP in the range of 3 to 8bps and a tightening of 25/30bps vs IPTs.
In the same message, it was also communicated to the market that the Books would go subject at 13:15 CET, setting the deadline for accepting new orders. After the books go subject no further orders can be accepted.

10 June 2020 @2:05pm

Final Terms (Spread Set + Books Closed)
About one hour after the communication of the Spread Guidance, the Final Terms announcement hit the screens with a spread set at MS+80bps and a book of EUR 1.5bn at guidance (books were closed).

The release of the final terms set the final premium over the reference benchmark (Mid-Swap) which (during the pricing call and once the reference Mid-Swap was spotted) was used to define the coupon and reoffer price.

```
*** SNAM 10YR EUR TRANSITION BOND - FINAL TERMS ***

=> Books closed > €1.5bn at guidance (pre-rec)
=> Spread set at MS+80bps
=> Size set at €500mln
=> ISIN: XS2190256706
=> BNPP to B&D
=> Allocations & Pricing to follow this afternoon
```

Source: Used with permission of Bloomberg Finance L.P.

10 June 2020 @3:50pm

Allocation Release

Once the orders were confirmed, the JBRs coordinated the allocation of the Snam bond. Usually the majority of orders are allocated pro-rata (e.g. a deal of EUR 1bn with a book of EUR 1.5bn may see allocations of around 66% per investor). With that in mind, during the Snam allocation the Syndicate group made reference to the so-called "allocation principles" which are shared with the issuer before the allocation process starts.

```
*** SNAM 10YR EUR TRANSITION BOND - ALLOCS OUT ***

- Allocations available
- HR 96% vs. DBR 0% 02/30
- Hedge deadline: 15.10 UKT
- BNPP B&D
- ISIN: XS2190256706
- Final book > 950m
```

Source: Used with permission of Bloomberg Finance L.P.

In this transaction, the Issuer opted for optimizing the pricing level with a final spread 35bps tighter versus the IPT levels. This decision had an impact on the book with some investors deciding not to take part to the transaction or reducing their orders (final books at EUR 950mn).

10 June 2020 @4:40pm

Pricing Call

During this last call, the JBRs defined the yield as the sum of issue spread plus the mid-swap rate (for the relevant tenor) and the issue price is defined as a mathematical relation between coupon and yield.

For Snam Transition Bond the Reoffer Yield was obtained as the sum between the Final spread (80bps) and the Reference Rate (10yr Mid Swap = -0.035%) to give = 0.765%. The coupon was then set 0.750% Issue Price was < 100% and equal to 99.856%.

*** SNAM €500m 10-year Transition Bond: Priced ***

Issuer:	SNAM S.p.A. (Ticker: SRGIM, Country: IT)
LEI:	815600EAD78C57FCE690
Issuer Rating:	Baa2 (stab) / BBB+ (neg) / BBB+ (stab) (Moody's / S&P / Fitch)
Expected Issue Rating:	Baa2 / BBB+ / BBB+
Format:	Senior, Unsecured, RegS Bearer, (TEFRA rules apply, no communications with or into the U.S.), NGN
Size:	€500mn
Settlement:	17 June 2020 (T+5)
Maturity:	17 June 2030 (10-year)
Coupon:	0.750% Fixed (Annual, ACT/ACT)
Reoffer:	99.856 / 0.765% / MS+80bps
Benchmark:	DBR 0% 02/30 (@103.180) +108.8bp, HR 96%
TOE:	15:22 UKT / 16.22 CET
FTT:	16.00 UKT / 17.00 CET
ISIN:	XS2190256706
Docs:	Lux listing regulated market / EMTN / €100k+1k / 3m Par Call / English law
Jt Books:	Banca IMI / BBVA / BNPP (B&D) / BofA Securities / GSI / JPM / MUFG / Societe Generale / UniCredit
UoP:	Finance and/or refinance, in whole or in part, existing and/or future Eligible Projects under Snam's Transition Bond Framework

Source: Used with permission of Bloomberg Finance L.P.

Before the settlement date, all the documentation is finalized and signed. In the Snam Transition bond, in line with the standard market practice, the documentation package was signed two days before the settlement, on 15 June 2020. Settlement date 17 June 2020.

Phase V – "Settlement"

The settlement of the Snam transaction took place on 17 June 2020, when the funds were effectively transferred to the Company's account. The settlement represented the end of the bond issue and took place 5 days (T+5) after the pricing. Settlement is deemed to be completed once the funds have been transferred from investors to issuers against the delivery of the notes to investors' custody accounts.

Execution Recap

See below a summary of the entire process which allowed Snam to issue its first Transition Bond (from the Mandate to the JBRs to the Settlement date), as well as a quick analysis regarding the book and the pricing evolution (from IPTs to guidance and final terms):

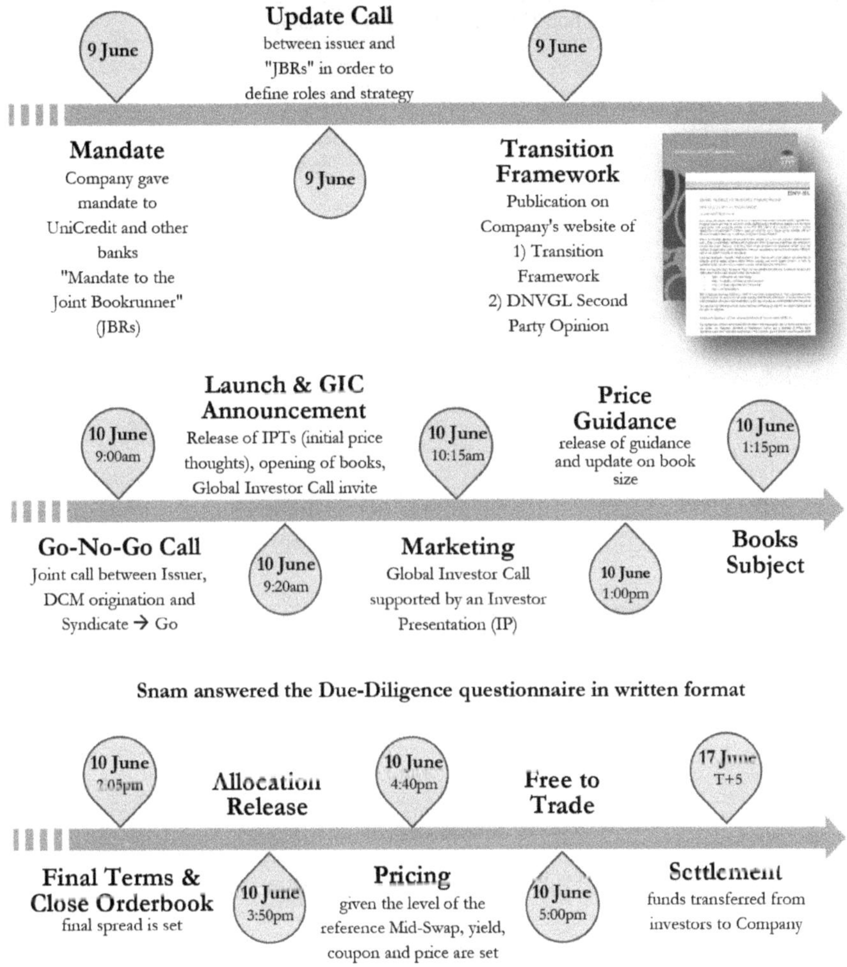
9 June
Update Call
between issuer and "JBRs" in order to define roles and strategy
9 June
Mandate
Company gave mandate to UniCredit and other banks "Mandate to the Joint Bookrunner" (JBRs)
9 June
Transition Framework
Publication on Company's website of 1) Transition Framework 2) DNVGL Second Party Opinion
10 June 9:00am
Launch & GIC Announcement
Release of IPTs (initial price thoughts), opening of books, Global Investor Call invite
10 June 10:15am
Price Guidance
release of guidance and update on book size
10 June 1:15pm
Go-No-Go Call
Joint call between Issuer, DCM origination and Syndicate → Go
10 June 9:20am
Marketing
Global Investor Call supported by an Investor Presentation (IP)
10 June 1:00pm
Books Subject
Snam answered the Due-Diligence questionnaire in written format
10 June
Allocation Release
10 June 4:40pm
Free to Trade
T+5
Final Terms & Close Orderbook
final spread is set
10 June 3:50pm
Pricing
given the level of the reference Mid-Swap, yield, coupon and price are set
10 June 5:00pm
Settlement
funds transferred from investors to Company

Book Evolution Through Execution & Pricing Dynamics

Book evolution through execution

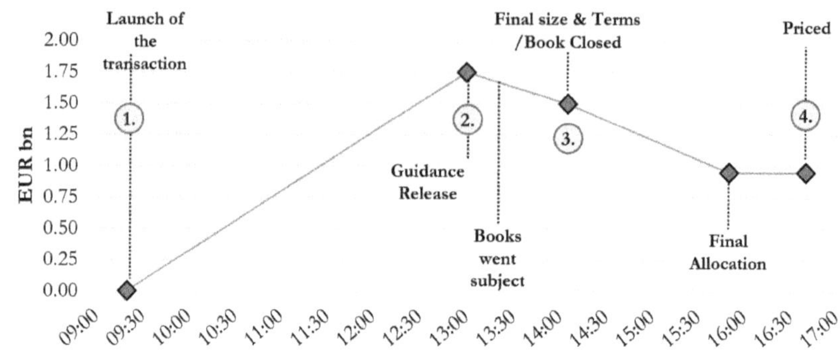

NIP	@IPTs	@guidance	@final terms
10yr	= 33bps	= 3/8bps	= -2bps

Pricing dynamics – from 33bps NIP @IPTs to -2bps

Annex – The Sustainable Finance Bon

Sustainability in Financial Markets is on the rise

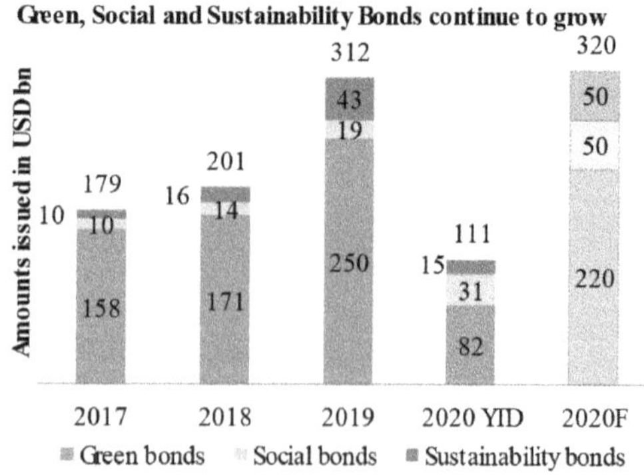

Source: Bloomberg, CBI, UniCredit Research, data as of June 2020

Sustainability in financial markets is achieved by integrating additional non-financial principles in investment decisions. The most commonly-used principles involve the identification and integration of Environmental, Social, and Governance (ESG)-related factors in investment strategies and decisions. In particular, a Socially Responsible Investment (SRI) approach considers ESG

factors in portfolio selection and management activities and favours responsible businesses by encouraging investors to take into account extra-financial criteria when selecting assets to invest in. In this regard, the Debt Capital Market has proven to be the perfect crucible for the creation of the concept of sustainable finance products driven by the broad spectrum of stakeholders involved and strong bottom-up attention to the topic.
Below we provide a brief overview of the different types of instruments available in the sustainable fixed income market.

Use of Proceeds-based				
Type	Green	Social	Sustainability	Transition
Principle			The Sustainability Bond	Under discussion by industry bodies
Use of proceeds	**Fund projects with environmental benefits, e.g.:** ✓ Renewable Energy & Energy efficiency ✓ Pollution prevention & control ✓ Clean Transportation ✓ Sustainable water and wastewater management ✓ Climate change adaption ✓ Green buildings ✓ Environmental sustainable management of living natural resources ✓ Biodiversity conservation ✓ Circular economy	+ **Fund projects with social benefits, e.g.:** ✓ Affordable basic infrastructure ✓ Access to essential services ✓ Affordable housing ✓ Employment generation ✓ Food security ✓ Socioeconomic advancement & empowerment	= A combination of Green and Social UoPs	**Eligible projects helping the transition to a carbon free economy, e.g** **Energy** ✓ Waste-to-energy ✓ Cogeneration plants ✓ Carbon Capture Storage ✓ Gas transport infrastructure (with lowe carbon intensity fuels) **Transportation** ✓ Gas powered ships ✓ Aircraft alternative fuels **Industry** ✓ Energy efficiency investments

General Corporate Purpose-based	
Type	Sustainability linked
Principle	The Sustainability-Linked Bond Principles
KPI selection and bond charact.	✓ Innovative solution as this Bond instrument is allowing investors to hold the company accountable for its sustainability strategy via the coupon step-up mechanism ✓ KPIs and Sustainability Performance Targets should be relevant, robust, reliable and ambitious ✓ Design of bond characteristics with inclusion of a financial and/or structural impact involving trigger events (i.e. non meeting the SPTs) ▫ Coupon step-ups are a clear example, but alternative structural/financial adjustments are allowed

A short introduction to the transition format
As of today, not all companies or industries are at a stage where they can finance environmental-friendly projects. However, this does not mean that they should not have the chance to do so in the future. To shift from their "brown" businesses to greener ones they need to go through a transition phase. This concept, although already identified and endorsed globally, found its maximum expression in the article published by AXA Investment Managers in June 2019, which followed Snam's issue of its Climate Action Bond (CAB) some three months earlier, effectively making Snam one of the precursors of the format.
The concept of Transition bonds is molded on the principles set out by Green Bonds, with some slight adjustments to allow room for the carbon-intensive industries they are addressing. In particu-

lar, use of proceeds from Transition bonds is conditional on investments in climate transition-related activities in energy, transportation, or heavy industry. The selection of the eligible projects is led by clearly defined objectives and criteria which are shared and endorsed by many investors. The possible negative externalities caused by the projects are also taken into account in the evaluation. An essential phase in implementing the projects is to keep track of the impact of the activities using appropriate indicators, often those described in the Green Bond Principles. The monitoring of the use of proceeds occurs not only internally, but is also independently audited, as well as publicly reported annually.

Snam transition bonds in a nutshell

Prior to the issue of its Transition Bond in June 2020 and with the introduction of its new Transition Bond Framework, Snam expanded the scope of its Climate Action Bond Framework from November 2018 to include the retrofitting of gas networks for the purpose of transmitting hydrogen and other green gases.

In particular, the conversion of the pipeline for transmitting hydrogen and green gases alongside traditional natural gas supports the shift towards more sustainable energy sources; this concept allowed the bond to be awarded the Transition label.

It should be noted that this specific activity is already recognized as eligible under the EU Taxonomy and it has been certified by DNV-GL, an accredited certifier with the Climate Bonds Standard and globally recognized Second Party Opinion (SPO) provider.

Because of the lack of a Green label, the bond cannot be included in Green indices. However, the Transition format should be well-received by broader ESG indices.

Integration of the overall corporate sustainability strategy

The proceeds from the new Transition Bond are aligned with Snam's strategy to contribute to the transition to a low carbon economy and decarbonisation goals as well as the company's improved environmental objectives related to CO_2 and CH_4 emissions.

Snam has communicated its commitment towards further aligning its activities with the 2015 Paris Agreement goals, and to that end the company is currently developing a 2050 net zero carbon strategy. DNV GL has also assessed the alignment of the company's strategy with the trajectory to pursue the Paris decarbonisation goals.

Snam's transition eligible projects

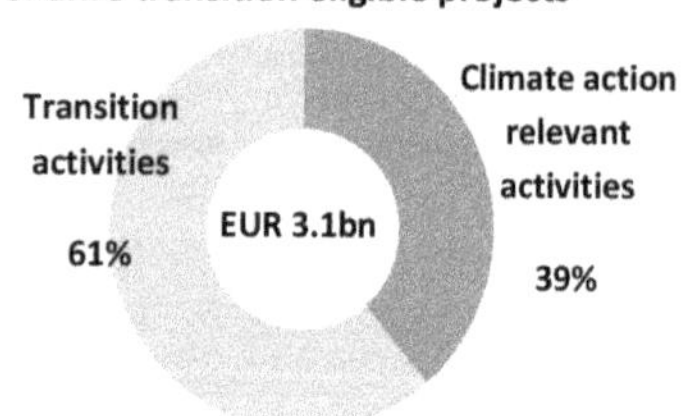

- Snam's current portfolio of eligible projects provides a buffer of >2x the size of the CAB and Transition bond combined

Focus on sustainability boosted by investors

During the Global Investor Call, there was a strong focus on ESG topics with a lively discussions on the breakdown of the use of proceeds, the group's strategy on decarbonisation, and development of the Hydrogen-ready grid and taxonomy aspects, demonstrating the central interest of investors towards these themes.

An analysis of the final allocation books showed that the transition feature drew attention from many investors with a strong focus on sustainability, driving the generation of additional demand.

Allocation of proceeds

The company has identified over EUR 3bn of eligible projects from their industrial plan for 2019-2023, providing a material buffer for Transition-eligible use of proceeds. More than 60% of the eligible projects will be dedicated to the retrofitting of the gas network, while the rest will be dedicated to green activities.

For the original Climate Action Bond, Snam identified c. EUR 700m of eligible categories (c. 1.4x the size of the CAB). The Transition bond relies on additional EUR 500m of new eligible projects which have been identified in the categories of carbon and emission reduction, renewable energy, green development, and energy efficiency, and on EUR 1.9bn which have been allocated to retrofitting activities and related R&D and pilot projects.

Overview of Snam's eligible categories and use of proceed allocation

Use of proceeds	Alignment with CAB UoP	Green Bond principles	EU Taxonomy alignment	CAB allocation (Dec 2019)	Transition bond exp. projects
Carbon & emission reduction	✓	✓	✓	c. EUR 190m	c. EUR 400m
Renewable energy	✓	✓	✓	c. EUR 180m	c. EUR 100m
Green Development	✓	✓	✓	c. EUR 40m	n.a.
Energy efficiency	✓	✓	✓	c. EUR 90m	n.a.
Retrofitting of gas transmission networks	X	X	✓	n.a.	c. EUR 1.9bn
Total				**c. EUR 0.5bn**	**c. EUR 2.4bn**

Case study **BP Capital, by Vittorio Ogliengo, Executive Chairman BNP Paribas Italy & Vice General Manager BNL S.p.A. and Giulio Baratta, Head of Corporate DCM EMEA, BNP Paribas**

COMPANY OVERVIEW

BP plc is one of the global leaders in Energy, whether measured by market capitalization, revenue or net income. BP is an integrated energy company operating in 79 countries globally across North and South America, Europe, Australasia, Asia and Africa, and it holds a large investment in Russia through its 19.75% stake in Rosneft. The company's operations are upstream focused, with a significant downstream business (refining, manufacturing and marketing) and a growing focus on low carbon initiatives and renewable energy. As of 2nd June 2020, the market capitalization of BP was $83.5 billion with the stock trading at £315, 35% lower than FY2019 levels of $126.6 billion and 37% higher than the local lows of £240 as of 19-March 2020

Introduction

This chapter of the textbook will aim to provide a deep dive into one of the most successful and landmark transactions within the Debt Capital Markets in 2020, if not in recent years. On 17 June 2020, BP plc priced c. $12bn-equivalent of "hybrid bonds," representing the largest multi-currency hybrid bond transaction ever carried out,[1] the previous largest being $6.5bn for BHP in 2015. BP managed to raise $5bn of USD notes, €4.75bn (c. $5.3bn-equiv.) of EUR notes and £1.25bn (c. $1.6 equiv.) of GBP notes from investors around the globe, successfully navigating a very challenging period, shaped by the impact of the COVID-19 pandemic.

The chapter will be divided in three sections following chronological order: the pre-execution, the execution, and the post-execution phases.

1. Pre-Execution

a. Sector Landscape

The Oil & Gas ("O&G") sector has always been a challenging environment with fierce competition between the oil majors. While most analysts identified the biggest challenges in 2020 as weakening economic growth, intensifying trade tensions, and global political risks, a sudden pandemic swept across the world: the COVID-19 virus.

The spread of COVID-19 has disrupted global financial and commodity markets, as well as the US oil and gas industry, now showing an unparalleled decline in energy demand. In an industry used to the highs and lows of economic and commodity price cycles, 2020 poses great challenges to O&G companies.

With the barrel price dropping to the lowest level ever in the second quarter of the 2020 (the price reached a negative value for the first time in history on 20 April!), the oil majors had one more challenge to face in addition to the coming disruptive forces associated with this century's energy transition. The O&G majors have had to deal with the reduction in revenues and the cut in the capex program, as well as the pressure on the main financial ratios (the gearing ratio,[2] among others) due to the current market conditions.

Most of them raised funds in the capital markets in 2020, with BP, Shell, Total, Exxon, Repsol, and OMV successfully pricing bonds in all the markets and in all the currencies despite the financial differences among them (**Table 1**).

[1] As we are writing.

[2] Gearing ratio defines the amount of debt – in proportion to equity capital – that a company uses to fund its operations.

Table 1 **Oil Majors' Financial Metrics**

($ in millions)	BP	Shell	Total	Exxon
Moody's	A1	Aa2	Aa3	Aa1
S&P	A-	AA-	A+	AA
Market Cap	$ 64,111	$ 114,746	$ 85,867	$ 191,834
EV	156,612	305,689	151,308	387,934
LTM Income Statement Summary				
Revenue	$ 270,400	$ 321,171	$ 169,702	$ 249,071
EBITDA	23,602	41,955	27,016	28,253
EBIT	2,276	16,444	13,476	8,669
Net Interest Expense	(1,925)	(4,094)	(1,723)	(898)
Balance Sheet (as of)	**Mar-20**	**Mar-20**	**Mar-20**	**Mar-20**
Cash and Equivalents	$ 18,139	$ 21,811	$ 21,634	$ 11,412
Total Assets	273,864	393,961	263,184	355,804
LT Debt	56,741	50,008	48,896	31,857
Total Debt	69,117	65,775	54,388	31,857
Total Equity	90,480	183,379	114,434	188,743
Key Credit Ratios				
EBITDA Margin	8.7 %	13.1 %	15.9 %	11.3 %
EBITDA/Net Interest Expense	12.3 x	10.2 x	15.7 x	31.5 x
(EBITDA - Capex)/Net Interest Expense	4.2 x	4.8 x	9.0 x	3.5 x
Total Debt/EBITDA	2.9 x	1.6 x	2.0 x	1.1 x
Net Debt/EBITDA	2.2 x	1.0 x	1.2 x	0.7 x
LTM Capex	(15,512)	(22,113)	(11,470)	(25,107)

b. BP's Rationale

Before diving into a deeper description of the reason why BP decided to issue such a jumbo transaction, we need to better identify and understand the main features of a hybrid bond (further details will be provided in the next section).

Unlike plain-vanilla senior bonds, hybrid bonds are subordinated debt instruments. They are known as 'hybrids' because they combine features of bonds (payment of a coupon) and of equities (perpetual or super-long maturity date and the possibility to suspend/delay the obligation to pay coupons, as is the case for dividends). For these reasons, they get an "Equity Credit" from the Rating Agencies (generally in the context of 50%) and, if perpetual, they are accounted for as equity under IFRS. As a result of their nature as deeply subordinated debt, hybrids are assigned a rating which is lower (generally 2 notches) than the issuer rating or the senior unsecured rating.

BP, like most O&G companies, has been facing challenging global market conditions, including the energy transition, low oil price environment, COVID-19 related shocks, and more generally challenging macro-economic headwinds impacting the wider world as well as the sector specifically.
In addition to the above, BP was planning a significant cut to capex, opex reductions, and a $15bn disposal programme.

All these new challenges have strained the on-going need to balance the demands of capital across the business in order to fulfil the needs of all the Company's stakeholders:

- **Equity holders** are primarily focused on returns, principally through the delivery of the dividend;
- **Credit investors** are largely focused on the strength of the balance sheet and the ability to service debt;
- **Capital for investment** is required to support the long-term health of the business including new energies and renewables, but can be flexed to an extent.

In this contest, the hybrid issuance was part of this wider package; it provided a tranche of long-term equity-accounted capital and bolstered the strategic flexibility of the business as it looks to navigate these challenging times.

Issuing a hybrid bond can benefit all stakeholders.

- **For current investors, a hybrid bond:**
  1. issuing from a position of strength, it will be seen as a positive, proactive measure to allow BP to continue to invest in the business for the future;
  2. reinforces BP's financial structure, facilitating investment in the long-term future of the group and delivery on the growth agenda;
  3. underpins the gearing ratio while providing a 50% rating agency equity credit;
  4. reiterates BP's commitment to the energy transition, supporting sustained investment through the oil price cycle;
  5. improves financial flexibility, creating additional capital that can be allocated towards New Energy investments;
  6. reaffirms the new CEO and CFO's vision for BP, providing an additional and sustainable layer of long-term capital;
  7. is non-dilutive for existing shareholders, with tax deductible coupons and full equity accounting (100% IFRS) on the balance sheet.

- **For debt investors and rating agencies, a hybrid bond:**
  8. shows a commitment to strong balance sheet and current ratings;
  9. improves rating agency metrics and demonstrates a commitment to balance sheet strength through the cycle;
  10. supports and reinforces the <30% Gearing target;
  11. supplements the broader package of measures BP has announced including Capex, Opex cuts, and the disposal programme;
  12. validates the fact that BP is taking 'decisive and effective steps to protect its assets, cash generation, and credit metrics' (S&P, 25 March 2020);
  13. protects senior bondholders by introducing an additional capital "buffer";
  14. diversifies the investor base, bringing in a new group of long-term stakeholders.

- For equity investors, a hybrid bond:
  15. is non-dilutive for shareholders even though the financial impact on the balance sheet is similar to issuing equity;
  16. has a counter-cyclical, anti-dilution mechanism;
  17. the Hybrid coupon will have less impact on EPS as oil prices rise; has the exact opposite impact of issuing equity/equity linked instruments;
  18. coupons are fully tax deductible;
  19. increased financial flexibility allows BP to continue to invest in the business and not have to cut Opex/Capex further, ensuring the long term future of the group;
  20. creates optionality on the disposals; allows BP to sell assets at the right time and price;
  21. protects and supports the dividend;
  22. provides opportunistic access to an attractive asset class with a deep pool of liquidity available at attractive rates.

Figure 1 **Main Objectives of the BP's Hybrid Issuance**

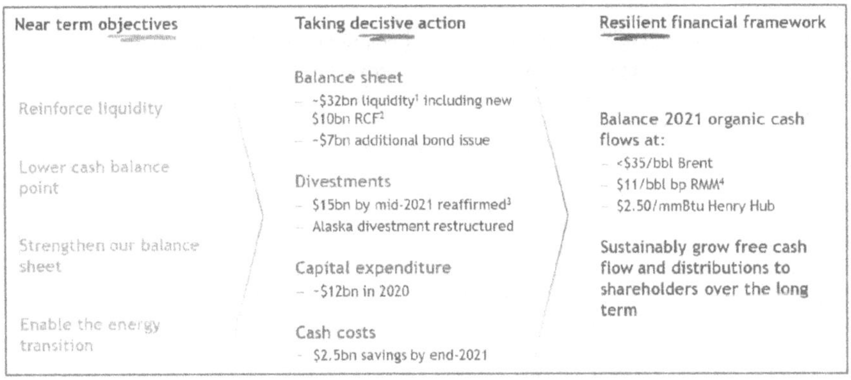

The hybrid notes are therefore part of the broader toolkit of measures that BP has chosen to deploy as part of building resilience in a challenging environment. This further demonstrates that BP is taking decisive action to support its near-term objectives, creating a resilient long-term financial framework through the addition of a layer of subordinated equity-accounted hybrid capital, that provides stability to operate through challenging market conditions while creating the strategic flexibility to enable the energy transition towards a net zero company (**Figure 1**).

c. Bank groups
The decision on the composition of the bank groups was crucial to ensure the smoothest execution process possible.
As often happens for structured transactions, the issuer prefers to select different bank groups based on the role they play in the transaction and to appoint them at different times. The advantage of this approach is certainly to make the leading bank group as limited as possible, and to make the process and the communication among the banks and the issuer more efficient.

BP opted to split the banks into the following groups:
(i) **Structuring Agents:** BNP Paribas and BofA Securities;
(ii) **Global Coordinators:** BNP Paribas, BofA Securities, Citi, and Goldman Sachs;
(iii) **Joint Lead Managers:** BNP Paribas, BofA Securities, Credit Agricole CIB, Citi, Goldman Sachs, and Societe Generale on the EUR and GBP tranches; BNP Paribas, BofA Securities, Citi, Goldman Sachs, J.P. Morgan, and Morgan Stanley on the USD tranches.

The **Structuring Agents** are appointed first – generally a couple of months prior to the launch of the transaction as they have the most important role in the process. With the help of the company and the lawyers, they determine the Terms & Conditions and the overall structure of the hybrid notes, and are in the middle of the dialogue with the Rating Agencies. As already mentioned, a hybrid bond is an instrument halfway between an equity and a debt instrument. For these reasons, a constant dialogue with the Rating Agencies is critical to ensure the issuer will get the Equity Credit and to obtain confirmation of the rating of the notes.

The **Global Coordinators** are added to the process closer to the execution date – as they are mainly responsible for coordinating all activities involved with the issuance. These activities include the documentation of the notes (drafting of legal contracts, including the Offering Circular), the investor presentation (together with the Offering Circular, this is used to market the company and the deal to investors, in order to gather their interest in the notes), the marketing logistics, screen announcements, etc.

The **Joint Lead Managers** are added about a week before the launch of the transaction and work together to support the process. **Co-managers** are also added closer to the transaction date, having more of a passive role in the process.

2. Execution

a. Structuring

Hybrid bonds typically have perpetual (or super-long dated) maturities. The issuer can opt to delay the payment of coupons and – if they are perpetual – they are classified as equity under IFRS (despite not creating any shareholder dilution, as the notes do not carry voting rights).

The structure of BP's hybrid bonds followed the market standard features in all material aspects (Table 2). The bonds included the main clause with respect to subordination, coupon deferability, and coupon step-ups for issuers seeking to achieve 50% equity credit from S&P and Moody's. Moreover, given their hybrid nature, they were ranked junior to all BP's other debt (and specifically all senior unsecured debt) and have sat senior only to BP's ordinary shares.
Despite being long-dated or perpetual (as in the case of BP), hybrid bonds are "callable" from a certain date since their issuance (note below "non-call 6" or NC6, for example, referring to the bond being callable from year 6, and not earlier). If not called, and as per Rating Agency methodologies governing the treatment of such notes, the bonds may lose the Equity Credit treatment. This feature creates a strong incentive for issuers of hybrid bonds to exercise such calls, and refinance the notes with new hybrids, to be issued at the prevailing market conditions, or to refinance them with senior debt – or cash – should the company at that time cease to need such a layer of capital to support ratings.

Table 2 Terms & Condition of the Hybrid Notes

Issuer:	BP Capital Markets p.l.c. (Ticker: BPLN)				
Guarantor:	BP p.l.c.				
Guarantor Rating (M/S):	A1 (negative) / A- (stable)				
Senior Rating (M/S):	A1 (negative) / A- (stable)				
Exp. Notes Rating (M/S):	A3 / BBB				
Exp. Equity Credit (M/S):	Moody's 50% / S&P 50% until First Reset Date				
Status of the Notes:	Unconditional, unsecured and deeply subordinated obligations, senior only to the Issuer's Ordinary Shares				
Status of the Guarantee:	Unconditional, unsecured and deeply subordinated obligation, senior only to the Guarantor's Ordinary Shares				
Settlement Date:	22 June 2020 (T+3)				
Tranche:	EUR 2.5bn	EUR 2.25bn	GBP 1.25bn	USD 2.5bn	USD 2.5bn
Maturity:	Perp. NC6	Perp. NC9	Perp. NC7	Perp. NC5.25	Perp. NC10
First Call Date:	22 March 2026	22 March 2029	22 March 2027	22 June 2025	22 March 2030
First Reset Date:	22 June 2026	22 June 2029	22 June 2027	22 September 2025	22 June 2030
Initial Coupon/Yield:	3.250%	3.625%	4.250%	4.375%	4.875%
Re-Offer Price:	100.00	100.00	100.00	100.00	100.00
Initial Margin:	352.0bp (vs MS)	378.0bp (vs MS)	417.0bp (vs Gilt)	403.6bp (vs UST)	414.8bp (vs UST)
Spread to Benchmark:	388.0bp	412.0bp	417.0bp	403.6bp	414.8bp
Interest:	3.250% until FRD; on FRD and each 5 years thereafter resets to 5yr MS Rate + Initial Margin + Step-Up, ann. act./act	3.625% until FRD; on FRD and each 5 years thereafter resets to 5yr MS Rate + Initial Margin + Step-Up, ann. act./act	4.250% until FRD; on FRD and each 5 years thereafter resets to 5yr Gilt + Initial Margin + Step-Up; ann. act./act	4.375% until FRD; on FRD and each 5 years thereafter resets to 5yr UST + Initial Margin + Step-Up, s.a. 30/360	4.875% until FRD; on FRD and each 5 years thereafter resets to 5yr UST + Initial Margin + Step-Up, s.a. 30/360
First Step-up (+25bp):	22 June 2031	22 June 2034	22 June 2032	22 September 2030	22 June 2030
Second Step-up (+100bp):	22 June 2046	22 June 2049	22 June 2047	22 September 2045	22 June 2050
Interest Payment Date:	22 June each year commencing 2021	22 June each year commencing 2021	22 June each year commencing 2021	22 March and 22 September each year commencing 2020 (short first coupon)	22 June and 22 December each year commencing 2020
Format:	RegS Bearer	RegS Bearer	RegS Bearer	SEC-registered	SEC-registered
Denominations:	€100k x €1k	€100k x €1k	£100k x £1k	$1k x $1k	$1k x $1k
Docs / Law / Listing:	Standalone – Preliminary Prospectus / English law / LSE			Prospectus Supplement and Base Prospectus / New York law / NYSE	
Special Event Redemption:	Accounting Event, a Rating Agency Event or a Tax Deduction Event: at 101% of the principal amount until the FCD, and 100% thereafter; Gross-Up Event and Substantial Purchase Event (≥75%) at 100% of the principal amount			Accounting Event, a Rating Agency Event or a Tax Deduction Event: at 101% of the principal amount until the FCD; 100% thereafter, Gross-Up Event at 100% of the principal amount	
Optional Interest Deferral:	Optional cumulative, in whole or in part, and compounding for an unlimited period, cash settled anytime at the option of the Issuer and mandatory payment in accordance with the provisions on Mandatory Payment of Arrears of interest				
Optional Redemption:	FCD and on any day thereafter to (and including) the FRD (3 month par call) or on any Interest Payment Date thereafter at their outstanding principal amount plus any accrued but unpaid interest				
Replacement Language:	Replacement intention (subject to customary carve-outs)				
Sub. and Variation:	Upon, amongst others, occurrence of Accounting Event, Gross-Up Event, Rating Agency Event or Tax Deduction Event				
Use of Proceeds:	General corporate purposes, including working capital for BP or other companies in the BP Group and the repayment of existing borrowings of BP and its subsidiaries				
Structuring Agents:	BNP Paribas, BofA				
Global Coordinators:	BNP Paribas, BofA, Citi, GS				
Joint Lead Managers:	BNP Paribas (B&D), BofA, CACIB, Citi, GS, SG			BNP Paribas, BofA (B&D), Citi, GS, JPM, MS	

b. Marketing
Given the complexity of the transaction, mainly due to (i) the debut nature of the notes, (ii) the notes being issued in 3 different currencies (EUR, GBP and USD), and (iii) the distribution of the notes (RegS vs SEC), the marketing strategy was critical to ensure investors received extensive and accurate information for them to make a sound investment decision.

(i) The debut nature of the notes implied that an extensive marketing exercise was preferred in order to educate investors on this new instrument (rationale of the issuance, structure of the notes, etc.). BP, being a recurrent issuer of senior notes in the market across currencies, opted for a full one-day marketing, which consisted of group calls. An intraday execution (as usually done for senior notes) would have not given investors sufficient time to learn about the new instruments, and more than one day of marketing would have added unnecessary market risk. Alongside the calls, BP also provided investors with an Investor Presentation published on an online platform, NetRoadshow.[3]

(ii) The objective of the transaction being to issue the notes in EUR, GBP, and USD brought forward two challenges. The first challenge regarded the structuring of the notes. While the main Terms & Conditions apply for all currencies (issuer, rating, status, etc.), there are significant distinctions to be made when structuring the EUR and GBP notes vs the USD notes (law, listing, minimum denominations of the bonds, etc.)

(iii) Typically, EUR and GBP notes are issued under the RegS (or "Medium Term Note") format, as regulated by the European Prospectus Directive, whereas USD notes are "SEC-registered." The main difference between such formats is that RegS notes may be sold to European investors only (not US) while SEC notes can be sold to both. As a result of this regulatory obligation, the marketing documents such as the Investor Presentation, the documentation of the notes, and the announcements to the market were each made in two versions: one respecting the RegS regulation, and another one respecting the SEC regulation.

c. Execution
After several weeks of preparation, on 15 June 2020, BP announced the mandate for the two legs of the transaction (SEC for the USD tranches and RegS for both EUR and GBP tranches) through two Bloomberg messages (**Figure 2**) at both the Asian and European market opening.

In the announcement message sent by the appointed banks, BP stated its intention to issue its inaugural multi-currency hybrid transaction, making a clear reference to the maturities they were willing to consider. In addition to the Investor Presentation uploaded on NetRoadshow, the BP Treasury, Capital Markets, and Investor Relations teams made themselves available for potential 1-to-1s or group calls in the case investors were willing to learn more about the Company and the transaction.
As expected, the announcement of the transaction had an international resonance, with several investors asking for 1-to-1 calls. In order to manage the huge amount of requests from investors, BP appointed BNP Paribas and Citi as marketing logistics coordinators.
Given the high engagement from investors, the two banks filled all the available slots for the calls with the BP management on 16 June 2020 (**Table 3**).

[3] NetRoadshow is one of the most popular marketing platform providers, where the issuer can upload all the documents related to a specific transaction.

Figure 2 Bloomberg Mandate Announcement

*** BP p.l.c. Inaugural EUR/GBP/USD Hybrid Mandate / Marketing ***

BP Capital Markets p.l.c., guaranteed by BP p.l.c., rated A1/A- (Neg/Sta) by Moody's/S&P, has mandated BNP Paribas and BofA Securities as Joint Structuring Agents and BNP Paribas, BofA Securities, and Goldman Sachs International as Joint Global Coordinators to arrange a series of global fixed income investor calls from Tuesday 16th June.

An inaugural multi-currency hybrid transaction comprising RegS Bearer EUR PerpNC6 and PerpNC9, RegS Bearer GBP PerpNC7 (the RegS notes) and SEC-registered USD PerpNC5.25 and PerpNC10 tranches (the with expected ratings of A3/BBB by Moody's/S&P is expected to follow, subject to market conditions. Additional Joint Lead Managers on the RegS notes will be Crédit Agricole CIB and Societe Generale additional Joint Lead Managers on the USD notes will be J.P. Morgan and Morgan Stanley.

Use of proceeds will be for general corporate purposes of BP p.l.c. and its group. A NetRoadshow presentation has been made available and a stand-alone Preliminary Prospectus will be made available

Marketing logistics coordination:
Europe - BNP Paribas
Asia - BNP Paribas & Citigroup

Relevant stabilisation regulations including FCA/ICMA will apply. MiFID II professionals/ECPs-only - Manufacturer target market (MiFID II product governance) is eligible counterparties and professi clients only (all distribution channels). No PRIIPs key information document (KID) has been prepared as not available to retail in EEA or UK.

Advertisement: The final RegS prospectus in relation to the RegS notes, when published, will be available on BP's website at www.bp.com/debtissuance and on the website of the London Stock Exchange (http://www.londonstockexchange.com).

** BP - INVESTOR CALLS SCHEDULE **
Available call slots from:

Asia 13:30 HKT (16th June)
Europe 10:00 CET (16th June)

Investor calls will be hosted by two teams and BP p.l.c. will be represented by:

Team 1
Kate Thomson, Group Treasurer
Gary Admans, Head of Liquidity & Capital Markets
Craig Marshall, Group Head of Investor Relations

Team 2
Richard Wheatley, Vice President - Liquidity
Patrick Halpin, Manager Equity & Capital Markets
Mark Bloomfield, Senior Investor Relations Manager

** BP - NETROADSHOW DETAILS **

Link for USD SEC-registered tranches: www.netroadshow.com
Link for EUR & GBP RegS tranches: www.netroadshow.com/nrs

Source: Used with permission of Bloomberg Finance L.P.

Table 3 Investor Calls Schedule

UKT	NYT	HKT	Team A Kate Thompson, Group Treasurer Gary Admans, Head of Liquidity & Capital Markets Craig Marshall, Head - Investor Relations	Team B Richard Wheatley, Vice President - Liquidity Patrick Halpin, Manager Equity & Capital Markets Mark Bloomfield, Investor Relations
06:30-07:00	01:30-02:00	13:30-14:00	-	Asia
07:15-07:45	02:15-02:45	14:15-14:45	-	Asia
08:00-08:30	03:00-03:30	15:00-15:30	-	Asia
08:30-09:00			-	**Break**
09:00-09:30	04:00-04:30	16:00-16:30	Asia / Europe	Asia / Europe
09:45-10:15	04:45-05:15	16:45-17:15	Asia / Europe	Asia / Europe
10:30-11:00	05:30-06:00	17:30-18:00	Europe	Europe
11:15-11:45	06:15-06:45	18:15-18:45	Europe	Europe
12:00-12:30	07:00-07:30	19:00-19:30	Europe	Europe
12:30-13:00			**Break**	**Break**
13:00-13:30	08:00-08:30	20:00-20:30	US	Europe
13:45-14:15	08:45-09:15	20:45-21:15	US	US / Europe
14:30-15:00	09:30-10:00	21:30-22:00	US	US / Europe
15:00-15:45			**Break**	**Break**
15:45-16:15	10:45-11:15	22:45-23:15	US	US / Europe
16:30-17:00	11:30-12:00	23:30-00:00	US	US
17:15-17:45	12:15-12:45	00:15-00:45	US	US
18:00-18:30	13:00-13:30	01:00-01:30	US	US
18:30-19:15			**Break**	**Break**
19:15-19:45	14:15-14:45	02:15-02:45	US	-
20:00-20:30	15:00-15:30	03:00-03:30	US	-
20:45-21:15	15:45-16:15	03:45-04:15	US	-
21:30-22:00	16:30-17:00	04:30-05:00	US	-

Following the success of the marketing exercise, on Wednesday, 17 June 2020, BP Capital Markets p.l.c. (issuer rating A1 negative/A- stable by Moody's/S&P) successfully priced its debut multi-currency hybrid offering consisting of €2.5bn PNC6, €2.25bn PNC9, £1.25bn PNC7, $2.5bn PNC5.25, and $2.5bn PNC10 notes. The corresponding coupons/yields are 3.250%, 3.625%, 4.250%, 4.375%, and 4.875%, respectively.

Figure 3 IPTs Bloomberg Message – SEC Hybrid Notes

** BP CAPITAL MARKETS US$ SEC-REGISTERED PNC5.25 & PNC10 - IPT **

Issuer:	BP Capital Markets p.l.c. (Ticker: BPLN)	
Guarantor:	BP p.l.c.	
Guarantor Rating (M/S):	A1 (negative) / A- (stable)	
Senior Rating (M/S):	A1 (negative) / A- (stable)	
Expected Instrument Rating (M/S):	A3 / BBB	
Expected Equity Credit (M/S):	Moody's 50% / S&P 50% until First Reset Date	
Country of Risk:	GB	
Status of the Notes:	Unconditional, unsecured and deeply subordinated obligations, senior only to the Issuer's Ordinary Shares	
Status of the Guarantee:	Unconditional, unsecured and deeply subordinated obligation, senior only to the Guarantor's Ordinary Shares	
Format:	SEC-registered	
Currency:	USD	USD
Maturity:	Perp. NC5.25	Perp. NC10
Size:	Benchmark	Benchmark
IPTs (semi-annual yield):	4.625-4.750%	5.25% area
Settlement Date:	22 June 2020 (T+3)	22 June 2020 (T+3)
First Call Date:	22 June 2025	22 March 2030
First Reset Date:	22 September 2025	22 June 2030
Interest:	[ ]% until the First Reset Date; on the First Reset Date and each 5 years thereafter resets to the sum of Five-Year Treasury Rate + initial margin + Step-Up (when applicable); semi-annual rate 30/360	[ ]% until the First Reset Date; on the First Reset Date and each 5 years thereafter resets to the sum of Five-Year Treasury Rate + initial margin + Step-Up (when applicable); semi-annual rate 30/360
First Step-up (+25bps):	22 September 2030	22 June 2030
Second Step-up (+100bps):	22 September 2045	22 June 2050
Interest Payment Date:	22 March and 22 September in each year commencing on 22 September 2020 (short first coupon)	22 June and 22 December in each year commencing on 22 December 2020
Optional Interest Deferral:	Optional cumulative, in whole or in part, and compounding for an unlimited period, cash settled anytime at the option of the Issuer and mandatory payment in accordance with the provisions on Mandatory Payment of Arrears of Interest	
Optional Redemption:	First Call Date and on any day thereafter to (and including) the First Reset Date (3 month par call) or on any Interest Payment Date thereafter at their outstanding principal amount plus any accrued but unpaid interest	
Special Event Redemption:	Accounting Event, a Rating Agency Event or a Tax Deduction Event: at 101% of the principal amount until the First Call Date; 100% thereafter	
Optional Tax Redemption	100% of the principal amount of the Notes	
Substitution and Variation:	Substitution or variation option upon, amongst others, occurrence of an Accounting Event, an event that permits an Optional Tax Redemption, a Rating Agency Event or a Tax Deduction Event, subject to certain conditions, so that the Notes remain or become Qualifying Securities	
Replacement Language:	Replacement intention (subject to customary carve-outs)	
Documentation / Governing Law:	Prospectus Supplement dated 15 June 2020 and Base Prospectus dated 1 August 2018 / New York law (subject to subordination provisions and waiver of set-off governed by English law)	
Listing:	New York Stock Exchange	
Clearing:	DTC (including Euroclear / Clearstream as participants)	
Denominations:	$1k X $1k	
Joint Structuring Agents:	BNP Paribas, BofA Securities	
Joint Global Coordinators:	BNP Paribas, BofA Securities, Citigroup, Goldman Sachs	
Joint Lead Managers:	BNP Paribas, BofA Securities (B&D), Citigroup, Goldman Sachs, JP Morgan, Morgan Stanley	
Use of Proceeds:	General corporate purposes, including working capital for BP or other companies in the BP Group and the repayment of existing borrowings of BP and its subsidiaries	
PRIIPs:	No PRIIPs key information document (KID) has been prepared as not available to retail in EEA or the UK	
Marketing:	www.netroadshow.com | Passcode: energy41	
Timing:	Books open, today's business	
Sales into Canada	No	

Source: Used with permission of Bloomberg Finance L.P.

Initial Price Thoughts ("IPTs") for the SEC leg of the transaction were announced at the Asian open at 4.625%/4.750% for the PNC5.25 and 5.250% area for the PNC10 (**Figure 3**).
IPTs for the RegS tranches followed at the London open at 3.500% area, 4.000% area and 4.500% area for €PNC6, €PNC9 and £PNC7 respectively (**Figure 4**).

Figure 4 IPTs Bloomberg Message – RegS Hybrid Notes

*** NEW CORP HYBRID: BP - EUR PNC6 & PNC9 & GBP PNC7 ***

IPTs EUR Bmk PNC6 (Jun 2026) *** 3.5% area *** (Annual Yields)
EUR Bmk PNC9 (Jun 2029) *** 4% area ***
GBP Bmk PNC7 (Jun 2027) *** 4.5% area ***

BNPP (B&D) / BofA / CACIB / Citi / GS / SG

Books open, today's business

Issuer:	BP Capital Markets p.l.c. (Ticker: BPLN)		
Guarantor:	BP p.l.c.		
Issuer LEI:	549300CRVT18MXX0AG93		
Guarantor Rating (M/S):	A1 (negative) / A- (stable)		
Senior Rating (M/S):	A1 (negative) / A- (stable)		
Expected Instrument Rating (M/S):	A3 / BBB		
Expected Equity Credit (M/S):	Moody's 50% / S&P 50% until First Reset Date		
Country of Risk:	GB		
Status of the Notes:	Unconditional, unsecured and deeply subordinated obligations, senior only to the Issuer's Ordinary Shares		
Status of the Guarantee:	Unconditional, unsecured and deeply subordinated obligation, senior only to the Guarantor's Ordinary Shares		
Format:	Reg. S, bearer form (TEFRA rules apply, no communications with or into the U.S.)		
Currency:	EUR	EUR	GBP
Size:	Benchmark	Benchmark	Benchmark
Maturity:	Perp. NC6	Perp. NC9	Perp. NC7
IPTs (annual yield):	3.500% area	4.000% area	4.500% area
Settlement Date:	22 June 2020 (T+3)	22 June 2020 (T+3)	22 June 2020 (T+3)
First Call Date:	22 March 2026	22 March 2029	22 March 2027
First Reset Date:	22 June 2026	22 June 2029	22 June 2027
Interest:	[ ]% until the First Reset Date; on the First Reset Date and each 5 years thereafter resets to the sum of 5 year Swap Rate + initial margin + Step-Up (when applicable); annual rate act./act	[ ]% until the First Reset Date; on the First Reset Date and each 5 years thereafter resets to the sum of 5 year Swap Rate + initial margin + Step-Up (when applicable); annual rate act./act	[ ]% until the First Reset Date; on the First Reset Date and each 5 years thereafter resets to the sum of 5 year Gilt + initial margin + Step-Up (when applicable); annual rate act./act
First Step-up (+25bps):	22 June 2031	22 June 2034	22 June 2032
Second Step-up (+100bps):	22 June 2046	22 June 2049	22 June 2047
Interest Payment Date:	22 June in each year commencing on 22 June 2021	22 June in each year commencing on 22 June 2021	22 June in each year commencing on 22 June 2021
Denominations:	€100k X €1k	€100k X €1k	£100k X £1k
Optional Interest Deferral:	Optional cumulative, in whole or in part, and compounding for an unlimited period, cash settled anytime at the option of the Issuer and mandatory payment in accordance with the provisions on Mandatory Payment of Arrears of Interest		
Optional Redemption:	First Call Date and on any day thereafter to (and including) the First Reset Date (3 month par call) or on any Interest Payment Date thereafter at their outstanding principal amount plus any accrued but unpaid interest		
Special Event Redemption:	Accounting Event, a Rating Agency Event or a Tax Deduction Event: at 101% of the principal amount until the First Call Date, and 100% thereafter; Gross-Up Event and Substantial Purchase Event (≥75%) at 100% of the principal amount of the Notes		

Substitution and Variation:	Substitution or variation option upon, amongst others, occurrence of an Accounting Event, a Gross-Up Event, a Rating Agency Event or a Tax Deduction Event, subject to certain conditions, so that the Notes remain or become Qualifying Securities
Replacement Language:	Replacement intention (subject to customary carve-outs)
Documentation / Governing Law:	Standalone - Preliminary Prospectus dated 15 June 2020 / English law
Listing:	London Stock Exchange
Clearing:	Euroclear / Clearstream
Joint Structuring Agents:	BNP Paribas, BofA Securities
Joint Global Coordinators:	BNP Paribas, BofA Securities, Citigroup, Goldman Sachs International
Joint Lead Managers:	BNP Paribas (B&D), BofA Securities, Citigroup, Crédit Agricole CIB, Goldman Sachs International, Société Générale
Use of Proceeds:	General corporate purposes, including working capital for BP or other companies in the BP Group and the repayment of existing borrowings of BP and its subsidiaries
MiFID II Target Market:	Eligible Counterparties and Professional Clients only (all distribution channels). No PRIIPs key information document (KID) has been prepared as not available to retail in EEA or the UK
Selling Restrictions:	Regulation S (Cat 2), TEFRA D rules apply, no communications with or into the U.S., no sales into Canada
Marketing:	www.netroadshow.com | Passcode:
Timing:	Books open, today's business
Advertisement:	The final prospectus, when published, will be available on the website of the London Stock Exchange (http://www.londonstockexchange.com)

Source: Used with permission of Bloomberg Finance L.P.

The transaction was well-received by investors from the time of launch. The orderbooks grew rapidly, enabling BP to set the yields at an early stage while keeping flexibility on size to gauge the dynamics between the different markets (**Figure 5 and 6**).

Figure 5 Guidance Bloomberg Message – SEC Hybrid Notes

```
** BP CAPITAL MARKETS US$ SEC-REGISTERED PNC5.25 & PNC10 - GUIDANCE **
Perp. NC5.25: 4.375%#
Perp. NC10:   4.875%#
```

Source: Used with permission of Bloomberg Finance L.P.

Figure 6 Guidance Bloomberg Message – RegS Hybrid Notes

```
*** BP EUR/GBP Hybrid - Update / Guidance ***

>> EUR/GBP books north of €7.3bn / €8.7bn / £4bn

>> Guidance:   EUR PNC6 - 3.250% the # - Expect €2bn+
               EUR PNC9 - 3.625% the # - Expect €2bn+
               GBP PNC7 - 4.250% the # - Expect £1.25bn+

>> Books subject 13.50 UKT / 12.50 CET

>> Expect final terms mid-afternoon
```

Source: Used with permission of Bloomberg Finance L.P.

Thanks to a solid orderbook, the final size was set to c. $12bn eq. for the transaction, split into the following tranches:

- €2.5bn Perpetual NC6
- €2.25bn Perpetual NC9
- £1.25bn Perpetual NC7
- $2.5bn Perpetual NC5.25
- $2.5bn Perpetual NC10

The deal represents a landmark transaction for BP. While more expensive than senior bonds, the hybrid issuance allowed BP to diversify its long-term capital structure, to support its credit metrics, and to further strengthen its liquidity position in what is admittedly still a highly uncertain macro backdrop.
It also represents the largest multi-currency hybrid transaction ever (the previous largest was $6.5bn for BHP in 2015) and the largest GBP single-tranche hybrid issuance ever (jointly with EDF's 6% transaction from 2013).

Table 4 shows a brief summary of the execution timeline in order to recap all the work streams behind this successful deal.

3. Post-Execution

The transaction caught the eyes of the entire financial community. The news bounced everywhere, with newspapers and websites reporting the success of BP's inaugural jumbo deal (Figure 7).
BP's mandate announcement appeared perfectly timed with the Company's needs and the mood swinging back to buying risk assets, after the US Federal Reserve had said it would start purchasing corporate bonds in secondary markets, and the strong investor response seemed to confirm our thoughts.
Although BP was a late arrival when it comes to issuing hybrid bonds, since most of its O&G peers

Table 4 Execution Timeline

UKT		EUR & GBP		NYT		USD		HKT
		Monday 15th June				Monday 15th June		
19:45		Announcement of global marketing exercise		14:45		Announcement of global marketing exercise		02:45 (Tue)
		Tuesday 16th June				Tuesday 16th June		
06:30 – 10:15		Asian Investor Calls		01:30 – 05:15		Asian Investor Calls		13:30 – 17:15
09:00 – 15:00		European Investor Calls		04:00 – 10:00		European Investor Calls		16:00 – 22:00
13:00 – 22:00		-		08:00 – 17:00		US Investor Calls		20:00 – 05:00 (Wed)
		Wednesday 17th June				Wednesday 17th June		
02:15		-		21:15 (Tue)	USD PNC5.25 4.625% - 4.750% Benchmark size	**IPTs**	USD PNC10 5.250% area Benchmark size	09:15
07:45	EUR PNC6 3.500% area Benchmark size	**IPTs** EUR PNC9 4.000% area Benchmark size	GBP PNC7 4.500% area Benchmark size	02:45		-		14:45
13:30	EUR PNC6 3.250% the # Books > €7.3bn Expect €2bn+ size	**Guidance** EUR PNC9 3.625% the # Books > €8.7bn Expect €2bn+ size	GBP PNC7 4.250% the # Books > £4bn Expect £1.25bn+ size	08:30		-		20:30
13:50		**Books Subject**		08:50		-		20:50
16:20	EUR PNC6 3.250% €2.5bn Books €7.35bn	**Final Terms** EUR PNC9 3.625% €2.25bn Books €8.5bn	GBP PNC7 4.250% £1.25bn Books £4bn	11:20		-		23:20
16:45		-		11:45		**Books Subject**		23:45
17:35		-		12:35	USD PNC5.25 4.375% the #	**Guidance**	USD PNC10 4.875% the #	00:35 (Thu)
18:15		**Allocations Out**		13:15	USD PNC5.25 4.375% $2.5bn	**Launch**	USD PNC10 4.875% $2.5bn	01:15 (Thu)
18:45	EUR PNC6 Final Books ~ €7.1bn	**Priced** EUR PNC9 Final Books ~ €8bn	GBP PNC7 Final Books ~ £4.1bn	13:45		-		01:45 (Thu)
20:25		-		15:25		**Allocations Out**		03:25 (Thu)
21:00		-		16:00		**Priced**		04:00 (Thu)

Figure 4.7 Press coverage

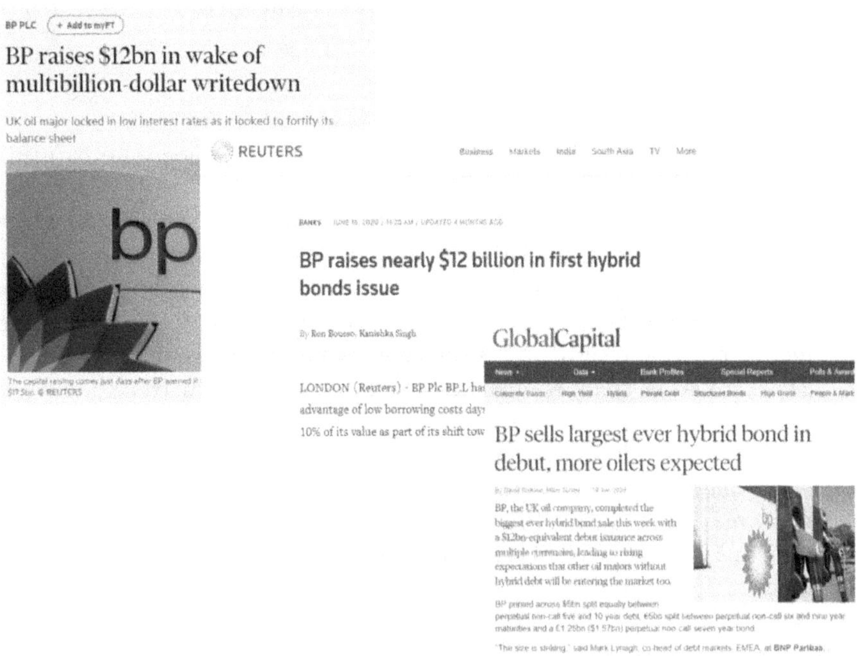

BP PLC + Add to myFT

BP raises $12bn in wake of multibillion-dollar writedown

UK oil major locked in low interest rates as it looked to fortify its balance sheet

REUTERS

BP raises nearly $12 billion in first hybrid bonds issue

By Ron Bousso, Kanishka Singh

LONDON (Reuters) - BP Plc BP.L has ... advantage of low borrowing costs days ... 10% of its value as part of its shift tow...

GlobalCapital

BP sells largest ever hybrid bond in debut, more oilers expected

BP, the UK oil company, completed the biggest ever hybrid bond sale this week with a $12bn-equivalent debut issuance across multiple currencies, leading to rising expectations that other oil majors without hybrid debt will be entering the market too.

"The size is striking," said Mark Lynagh, co-head of debt markets, EMEA, at BNP Paribas.

(i.e. OMV, Repsol and Total) already have hybrid bonds outstanding, the success of the transaction paved the way for more corporates to utilise hybrids to strengthen their capital structure.

As an example, again in the Oil & Gas sector, another major decided to tap the hybrid bond market for the first time. Italy's ENI (Baa1/A-/A-) successfully priced its inaugural EUR dual-tranche hybrid transaction on 6 October 2020 consisting of €1.5bn PNC5.25 notes and €1.5bn PNC9 notes that priced at yields of 2.625% and 3.375%, respectively.

In line with BP's rationale, ENI exploited the ability of the instrument to be 100% equity-accounted as per IFRS principles, thus adding an extra capital buffer and reducing the financial leverage, without diluting existing shareholders.

The issue received strong support across the investor community, allowing ENI to further diversify its capital structure and support its strong investment grade rating thanks to 50% Equity Credit assigned by the rating agencies. BNP Paribas, Goldman Sachs International, and Barclays acted as Global Coordinators for the transaction, together with a pool of an additional five Active Bookrunners.

Questions and answers

1. *How many Credit Rating categories are there in bond offerings? Please describe them.*
   There are four categories, as follows:

   1. Investment Grade - IG (>BBB-, Baa3).
   2. High Yield - HY (<BBB-, Baa3); in credit agency jargon, also defined as Speculative Grade or Junk.
   3. Cross-Over - XO (one IG rating and one HY rating). A situation in which a bond is speculative grade but very close to investment grade, or vice versa. It often refers to a split rating in which one credit rating agency gives the bond an IG rating and another gives it a junk rating. Generally speaking, regulators require bonds to receive investment grade ratings from two different agencies. Thus, crossover credit is often not strong enough to allow banks to invest in them.
   4. Not Rated - NR. Bonds with issuers that have not received a credit rating from one or more of the major credit rating agencies. A bond may be not rated for many reasons, including simply not wishing to pay the fee to the credit rating agency. This kind of bond is not necessarily risky, but it cannot be investment grade.

2. *What are the most common maturities in EUR bonds?*
   The 5, 7 and 10-year tenors remain the most sought-after tenors by investors on the EUR fixed-rate market as the best suited for their portfolios requirements. However, any maturity between 1y-30y is generally achievable. Floating-rate notes typically have shorter maturities (e.g. 2-4 years).

3. *What are the New Issue Premium, the Initial Price Thought, and the Reoffer Spread?*
   The New Issue Premium is the spread that an issuer will overpay (or underpay, if negative) in the offering of a new bond vs the fair value of its bonds outstanding (if any).
   The Initial Price Thought is the initial Reoffer Spread with which a new bond is announced to the market. It is generally expressed as a range (90-95 bps) or an area (90 bps area).
   The Reoffer Spread is the final Spread vs the Reference rate which is used to price the bond. It is expressed as a precise number (e.g. 90 bps).

4. *How many types of issuers are there and what are the product types linked to each issuer?*
   There are three types of issuers: Corporates, Financial Institutions Group and SSAs.

- SSAs: Sovereign, Supranational, and Agencies. For this kind of issuer, there are three bond placements options:
  1. Syndicated Issues;
  2. Auctions;
  3. Private Placements.
- FIG: from the most senior to the most junior, the DCM solutions for this type of issuer are:
  1. Covered Bonds;
  2. Senior Unsecured Bonds;
  3. Subordinated Bonds (Tier 2 and 1 for banks/Tier 3, 2, Hybrid and 1 for Insurance companies).
- Corporates: all issuers which are not FIG or SSAs:
  1. Senior Unsecured Bonds (Investment Grade/High Yield/Unrated);
  2. Hybrid Bonds;
  3. Private Placements.

5. *What is the difference between Senior Preferred and Senior Non-Preferred bonds?*
   Senior Preferred and Senior Non-Preferred are two types of Senior Unsecured bonds issued by banks. Senior Non-Preferred bonds can absorb losses, meaning they are part of TLAC. These bonds have the status of senior debt but are nevertheless more risky than Senior Preferred notes. They are considered as "junior" senior debt, because in the event of default, priority for repayment is given to traditional senior debt. These notes do not replace senior debt, but simply introduce an additional layer in the hierarchy of creditors.

6. *What is a Covered Bond?*
   A Covered Bond is a bond issued by a financial intermediary backed by a segregated cover pool (i.e. a package of loans/mortgages), usually with benchmark size (i.e. EUR 750mn–1bn), a fixed or floating rate, a bullet format, a higher rating compared to the senior level, placed on a public or private basis, and listed on a regulated market.

7. *What type of issuer may issue Restricted Tier 1 bonds? Please describe the main features.*
   "Restricted" Tier 1 bonds, also known as Hybrid bonds, are issued by insurance companies within the broader FIG issuers space. These are securities usually with benchmark size, dated or undated, usually with fixed or resettable coupons, callable format (sometimes also bullets), limited coupon payment flexibility (optional/mandatory/cumulative/dividend pushers), subordinated reimbursement, no principal loss absorption, with limited incentives to redeem, notch-down rating vs senior, placed on a public or private basis, and listed on a regulated market.

8. *What is the EMTN Programme?*
   The EMTN (European Medium-Term Notes) programme is an umbrella documentation suitable for frequent issuers, allowing for higher flexibility in terms of time-to-market and for a broader panel of funding opportunities (i.e. public Eurobonds and opportunistic private placements).

9. *Who are the main actors involved in the placement of a new bond?*
   The main actors involved in the placement of a new bond are:

   - the issuer;
   - the bookrunners (via their DCM origination team, syndicate desk and sales force);
   - fixed-income investors.

10. *In how many phases can the typical DCM workflow ideally be divided?*
    The typical DCM workflow can ideally be divided into five different phases:

    1. Pitching, Analysis and Mandate;
    2. Documentation;
    3. Spread guidance and Marketing;
    4. Execution (Bookbuilding/Allocations/Final pricing);
    5. Securities Settlement.

11. *What is the standard fee applied by bookrunners and how is it determined and split?*
    Generally, the standard fee applied by the bookrunners is up to the kind of issuer and issuance. On average, a total fee is equal to (type of issuer/% fee expressed in bps):

    - SSA: 10 bps;
    - IG: 30/80 bps depending on underlying asset class (up to 100 bps for deeply subordinated notes in EUR);
    - HY: 80/100 bps (also 200 bps for difficult HY issuances or "new comers").

    The total amount of fees is usually split between the Global Coordinator(s) and Joint Bookrunners with a 80%/20% proportion.

5 Corporate Lending and Syndicated Loans

by Stefano Caselli and Kim Salvadori

5.1 Introduction

One source of income for banks are the fees related to the advisory services they offer clients on the best way to raise debt capital (such as governments, corporations, and private equity funds). Clients may need additional debt for several reasons, including the execution of an Initial Public Offering (**"IPO"**), the distribution of a dividend to shareholders, the refinancing of existing debt approaching the maturity date, M&A-related events (including leveraged buyouts), or when a company is undergoing restructuring or finds itself in a situation of distress.

In addition to advisory services, banks arrange the syndication of the debt and can also use their own balance sheet to underwrite the issuance before it gets sold to investors in the market; underwriting and arranging a syndication in the so-called "primary" market is a further source of fees for investment banks. As banks place the debt raised on behalf of their clients to third-party investors, they are also referred to as the "sell-side," with the "buy-side" represented by investors buying the debt.

The investor base for debt products sold by banks is broad and includes several types of institutions:

- *Insurance companies, mutual/prime funds and pension funds:* also known as "real money," these are "traditional," long-only players that invest the capital raised with little to no leverage. Their primary goal is to avoid defaults rather than maximize absolute fund returns. In recent years, several funds previously focused on private equity investments also expanded into credit funds, including KKR, EQT, and Bain Capital;
- *Hedge Funds*: investors whose primary goal is to maximize absolute returns. They often employ more aggressive strategies than those of "real money" investors, that might include leverage. These funds are backed by a pool of sophisticated individual and institutional investors;
- *Collateralized Loan Obligations ("CLOs")*: CLOs are asset-backed special purpose vehicles that invest and manage portfolios of loans. CLOs raise funds by issuing bonds (split into senior and subordinated tranches) backed by the payment flows of the portfolios of loans they buy in the market. These vehicles can have significant leverage;

- *Banks*: their investments are often relationship-driven. They participate with take-and-hold tickets in certain debt tranches with the expectation of securing further business with a client. Several major central banks also play in Government and corporate bond markets through asset purchase programs such as the ECB's PEPP (Pandemic Emergency Purchase Program);
- *High Net Worth Individuals.*

Syndicated Loans are part of the "straight debt" (i.e. non-hybrid) products that banks offer their clients. A Syndicated Loan is a commercial loan provided to a borrower by a group of lenders and structured and arranged by a group of commercial or investment banks (the **"syndicate"**). Not all loans are syndicated, as loan facilities can be negotiated individually or bilaterally with a counterparty.

5.2 Types of loans

Loans can be classified according to their different features. The main categories are the following:

1. Revolving Credit Facilities ("RCF");
2. Acquisition/Capex Facilities;
3. Letters of Credit and Commercial Paper;
4. Term Loan Facilities.

5.2.1 Revolving Credit Facilities (RCF)

A **Revolving Credit Facility** is a loan that funds a company's intra-year working capital needs, letters of credit and small investments (including M&A) and represents a "quick" source of funding to corporates for their own strategic needs. In loan documentation, these uses for the proceeds of RCFs are grouped under the umbrella definition of "general corporate purposes." An RCF works like an overdraft facility and can be repaid and drawn down multiple times and in different currencies across the life of the instrument. In the case of M&A or capex-related drawdowns, the drawn RCF is often replaced at a later stage by more permanent sources of funding, such as term loans or bonds, with the intention of keeping the RCF available as a liquidity buffer for the company's day-to-day operations.

Banks do not usually syndicate such facilities, and hold their commitments until the maturity of the RCF. However, there can be instances when underwriting banks are not able to keep the full commitment on their own balance sheets for various reasons, including: (i) size of the commitment, (ii) currency (e.g. the bank may not be able to fund a specific currency), and (iii) risk management policies that may dictate a reduction of the bank's balance sheet exposure to certain types of credit in order to preserve its profitability and/or creditworthiness. These RCF tickets are syndicated

Table 5.1 Revolving credit facility: Key features

	Revolving Credit Facility
Investor Base	Banks
Maturity	Generally, 5-6 years, but can have bespoke tenors (e.g. 6.5 years, 3 years, etc.)
Repayment Schedule	Can be borrowed and repaid anytime over the life of the facility, like a credit card
Pricing	Floating rate: set margin over base rate (e.g. EURIBOR+250bps, LIBOR+100bps), with margin stepping down at pre-agreed leverage- or rating-based thresholds
Undrawn Fee	Fee paid by the Borrower on the amount that is left undrawn to compensate Lenders that make the funds available. In Europe, this is mostly set as percentage of margin (e.g. 35% of applicable margin); in the US, it is mostly set as a flat figure (e.g. 50bps)

to banks and not to other institutional investors, as it is not common for credit funds to be able to invest in facilities with "overdraft-like" mechanisms.

Table 5.1 lists the main features of these loans.

5.2.2 Acquisition (or Capex) Facilities

An **Acquisition (or Capex) Facility** is a loan that is earmarked for capex or acquisition purposes. The use of proceeds for these facilities is clearly specified in the loan documentation and cannot be amended without lender consent. These loans are common in capital-intensive or acquisitive sectors, such as telecom operators, restaurant chains, lab or dental services networks. The amount available to the Borrower under the loan agreement is not always drawn at closing, but can be drawn at any time during a so-called **"Availability Period,"** which is usually set at 2-3 years after the closing of the transaction. If an Acquisition Facility is partially drawn at the end of the Availability Period, the undrawn amount cannot be drawn by the Borrower. Drawn amounts, once repaid, cannot be redrawn, and follow an amortizing schedule until maturity.

Albeit some credit funds are able to invest in these instruments, Acquisition Facilities are usually syndicated to banks, like RCFs.

Table 5.2 lists the main features of these loans.

5.2.3 Letters of Credit and Commercial Paper

Letters of Credits and Commercial Paper are products that cover short-term corporate funding needs.

A **Letter of Credit ("LoC")** is a guarantee that is provided by one of the Lenders (**"Issuing Bank"**) in case the Borrower cannot fulfil an obligation, or a direct pay-

Table 5.2 **Acquisition/Capex facility: Key features**

	Acquisition/Capex Facility
Investor Base	Mostly banks
Maturity	5-6 years
Repayment Schedule	• The full amount of the loan can be borrowed at any time until the end of the Availability Period (usually 2-3 years from closing); • Drawn amounts cannot be re-borrowed and are repaid in instalments over the life of the facility according to an amortization schedule set in the loan documentation (e.g. 33% amortization *per annum*)
Pricing	Floating rate: set margin over base rate (e.g. EURIBOR+250bps, LIBOR+100bps), with margin stepping down at pre-agreed leverage- or rating-based thresholds
Undrawn Fee	Paid by the Borrower on the amount that is left undrawn to compensate Lenders that make the funds available, like an RCF

ment that the Issuing Bank makes on behalf of the Borrower. It is commonly used to facilitate payments during the company's normal course of business (especially in international trade) and can also be used to provide credit support to the Borrower.

Commercial Paper ("CP") is short-dated debt that matures within 1 year (the tenors of these facilities do not usually exceed 270 days). This financing instrument is available only to the most creditworthy and sizeable companies and is not common for sub-investment grade[1] companies. Commercial paper is issued as part of so-called "programs" that set a framework of terms and conditions and a maximum borrowing amount to be raised over a certain time period; the Borrower can then issue CP within the stated time period at the pre-agreed terms with short-form documentation, reducing the time-to-market.

5.2.4 Term Loan Facilities

A **Term Loan** is an agreement between Borrower and Lender(s) to borrow a set amount of money to be repaid in instalments according to a set amortization schedule or as a lump sum at maturity, in exchange for a series of interest payments over the life of the facility.

[1] The credit risk of companies and debt tranches is measured by independent rating agencies, the most famous of which are S&P, Moody's, and Fitch. Rating agencies analyze a company's business and financial risk and summarize the overall credit risk in a score expressed on a scale from AAA to D (or equivalent). "Investment Grade" ratings are the highest of the range; issuers in this group have lower probability of default and can finance new debt at low rates. "Speculative Grade"/"High Yield" issuers are the riskiest end of the rating spectrum; debt issued by these companies bears higher rates that reflect the greater credit risk. It is worth noting that not all debt issuances across different products (loans, bonds, etc.) have or need a rating.

Term loans are the most broadly-used permanent source of funding across the different loan products and their proceeds can serve any purpose. The amount of a loan is generally drawn at closing and does not require an undrawn fee; **"delayed draw"** loans can also be issued in specific situations, such as acquisitions that are expected to close with some delay after the loan is allocated to investors (e.g. because of Antitrust reviews, which can take up to several months). When investors expect a significant gap between allocation and closing (i.e. settlement) of the loan, they require compensation for making funds available without receiving interest payments. This compensation takes the form of a **"ticking fee,"** paying a pre-agreed percentage of the margin that steps-up over time.

For instance, a ticking fee can pay no margin in days 0-45 from allocation ("holiday period"), then 50% of margin in days 46-90 from allocation and 100% of margin from day 91 until the loan is drawn. Assuming the loan pays a margin of E+400bps and is funded on day 120, investors will receive the following fees:

Loan Pricing:	**E+4.00%**
Loan Amount (€m):	**500**
Funding:	**Day 120**

Day		**#days**	**Margin %**	**Margin**		**Ticking Fee (€ '000)**
0	45	45	0%	0.00%		0
46	90	44	50%	2.00%		1,205
91	120	29	100%	4.00%		1,589
					Total	2,795

An investor with an allocation of €50m in the loan would then receive €279,500 in ticking fees.

Term Loans can be split according to their amortization schedules (amortizing vs bullet):

- *Amortizing or Term Loan A ("TLA"):* a loan the drawn amount of which is repaid through an agreed schedule of instalments detailed in the loan documentation. Since amortizing instruments through instalments create reinvestment risk for institutional investors, TLAs are syndicated almost entirely to banks, which instead consider the amortization as a way to gradually de-risk their own balance sheets. As a function of the investor base skewed towards banks, these loans require strict covenant packages. On the other hand, the result of their amortizing features and stricter covenant packages make TLAs often the cheapest term loan in the capital structure because they are perceived as less risky;
- *Bullet or Term Loan B ("TLB"):* a loan the drawn amount of which is repaid fully at maturity (in Europe) or is subject to nominal amortization of 1.00% *per annum* (in the US). TLBs were originally introduced for institutional investors, who pre-

fer non-amortizing products with long tenors that can generate attractive yields. TLBs are structured to mature outside (i.e. later than) any existing bank debt in the capital structure, such as a TLA or an RCF. As a result of the longer tenor and slower de-risking (the majority of the principal is repaid at maturity), investors require a certain premium (around 50bps) on TLB margins compared to TLA and RCF margins. The recommended minimum size for a new TLB offering to institutional investors is between €200-250m to ensure tranche liquidity and optimal pricing, i.e. to avoid paying a liquidity premium to investors in the form of a higher margin or a lower original issue discount. In more complex capital structures with multiple loan tranches outstanding and multiple sets of financial documentation backing the different loans, TLB tranches can be issued in alphabetical order (TLC, TLD, etc.).

Table 5.3 lists the main features of these loans.

TLAs and TLBs issued by sub-investment grade companies are secured by a collateral package that grants the Lender(s) first priority claims on the assets of the Borrower identified in the loan documentation, which can include cash deposits, inventory, accounts receivables, or real estate; these tranches are also known as "senior secured" or "first lien" debt.

Not all loans secured by collateral have first priority claims over the Borrower's assets: this is the case of "junior" loans that share the same security as first lien loans, but with second priority claims. If the Borrower defaults, the holders of these loans can only exercise their claims over the Borrower's assets included in the security package after the first lien creditors are satisfied. These facilities are called Second Lien Loans to differentiate them from "traditional" first lien debt.

Second Lien Loans, like TLBs, are sold to institutional investors and have similar features. They do not require any amortization and mature outside first priority debt (usually 12 months after). Generally issued as part of LBO financings, the

Table 5.3 Term loan: Key features

	Term Loan	
Investor Base	Banks (TLA + TLB), funds and Collateralized Loan Obligations ("CLOs") (mostly TLB)	
Maturity	5-7 years	
Tranche	**TLA (Amortizing)**	**TLB (Bullet)**
Repayment Schedule	Amortizes over a set, gradually increasing schedule (e.g. 5% of total amount/10%/20%/30%/35% in years 1-5)	Repaid in full at maturity, with no amortization (European TLB) or 1% amortization p.a. (US TLB)
Pricing	• Floating rate: set margin over base rate (e.g. EURIBOR+250bps, LIBOR+100bps), with margin stepping down at pre-agreed leverage- or rating-based thresholds • Base rate has a floor of at least 0% (especially in Europe)	

Table 5.4 Second lien loan: Key features

	Second Lien Loan
Investor Base	Institutional investors (funds, CLOs, etc.)
Maturity	6-8 years (generally 12 months after TLB maturity)
Repayment Schedule	No amortization
Pricing	Floating: set margin over base rate, e.g. E+250bps, L+100bps (no step-downs) Base rate has a floor of at least 0% (esp. in Europe)

subordination of Second Liens to first lien debt and the implied higher credit risk of these instruments requires a pricing premium vs senior loans (which can be as high as >300bps). The market for these facilities is less liquid and these facilities do not have minimum size requirements, as not all institutional investors are willing to face greater credit risks to obtain higher yields. It is not uncommon for Second Lien Loan tranches to be allocated to a very small number of investors and for the terms of the loan agreement to be negotiated directly with investors.

Table 5.4 lists the main features of these loans.

5.2.5 Other loan products

Other, non-standard loan products include the following instruments:

- *Mezzanine:* this is a junior term loan with equity like features, such as equity warrants or equity conversion triggers
- *Payment In Kind ("PIK")*: term loan that pays interest "in kind," i.e. interest that accrues over the life of the facility and is paid at maturity. Some of these loans can be structured to pay cash interest and switch to PIK interest when the Borrower falls below certain liquidity or leverage thresholds ("PIYC" or "Pay If You Can") or at the Borrower's discretion ("PIYW" or "Pay If You Want"). These loans are called "PIK Toggles" due to their ability to toggle between cash-pay and PIK interest.

All these instruments are positioned between cash-pay debt and equity products and they are introduced in a capital structure to minimize the upfront equity injection of a financial buyer in the context of a leveraged buy-out ("LBO"). These are heavily subordinated debt products that are common in borrower-friendly ("bull") markets. Very illiquid and often directly placed by the buyers with interested funds with no intermediation from banks, they have bespoke features and their documentation is negotiated directly between the parties.

5.3 Basics of loan covenants

Loans are private securities, financing arrangements between the Borrower and the Lender(s) that are traded over the counter. Loan documentation originates from the US bank market, where syndicated loans to institutional investors developed since the 1980s.

Most terms, concepts and structures born in the US leveraged loan market have since been "translated" into European loans, with certain added features that consider the specificities of the European market, such as the lack of unified restructuring procedures like Chapter 11 in the United States.

Covenants are a promise of the Borrower to take (or not to take) a specific action that may result in a deterioration of the Borrower's credit quality, such as an increase in debt, dividend distributions, asset sales and changes in the company's majority ownership; they also protect Lenders against a reduction in value of the assets constituting the collateral of the loans.

The covenant package of a loan must be strict enough to give protection and tools to Lenders to keep an eye on the Borrower's activities (and restrict its actions, where appropriate) and be loose enough to ensure the Borrower has enough flexibility to operate its business.

Covenants can be split into three categories, according to their nature: (i) Affirmative Covenants, (ii) Negative Covenants, and (iii) Financial Covenants.

- **Affirmative Covenants**: list what the Borrower must do and are usually a set of standardized obligations, including payment of taxes, financial reporting, compliance with laws, compilation of budget, etc.
- **Negative Covenants**: list what the Borrower is not allowed to do (and any related exceptions). These provisions are tailor-made to the Borrower's financial situation and capital structure. They include limitations on new debt issuance, asset sales, type and amount of investments, M&A and Joint Ventures, dividend distributions, prepayment of junior debt, etc.
- **Financial Covenants**: list certain performance measures with which the Borrower must comply. The main financial covenants included in loan agreements are:
  - *Leverage*. It is customary for European loan agreements to set the maximum threshold as the ratio of Net Debt over EBITDA, whereas in the US it is calculated as Gross Debt/EBITDA. The ratio can be set as flat or step-down over the life of the loan to incentivize deleveraging;
  - *Interest Coverage*. Calculated as EBITDA/Annual Interest Expense, it needs to be above an agreed threshold. Like leverage, it can step up over the life of the loan;
  - *Cash Flow Covenants*. The most common are Debt Service Cover Ratio ("DSCR"), calculated as Cash Flows Before Debt Service/(Debt Service, i.e. Annual Interest Expense + Annual Principal Repayment) or Fixed Charge Cover, calculated as Cash Flows Before Debt Service/(Debt Service + Lease Obligations);

- *Minimum Liquidity*. Sets the minimum liquidity that the Borrower must maintain at any testing period;
- Other less common covenants include: (i) limitations on annual capex spend, (ii) maximum debt to equity ratio, (iii) other liquidity covenants (e.g. quick and current ratios, which compare the ratio of liquid assets to current liabilities and of current assets to current liabilities, respectively), and (iv) minimum tangible net worth.

Loans can be classified by the type of covenant package they bear. The main distinction across loan agreements is between maintenance and incurrence covenants:

- **Maintenance Covenants** require the Borrower to comply with financial covenants that are tested at regular intervals (usually at the end of each quarter) throughout the life of the facility. These covenants allow Lenders to constantly monitor the activity of the Borrower but may leave Borrowers at the risk of breaching them more frequently, especially in the case of temporary operational underperformance.
- **Incurrence Covenants** are financial covenants that are tested only when a certain "trigger" action is performed by the Borrower, for instance the issuance of new debt, the distribution of a dividend, or the drawing of the RCF above a certain percentage of the total facility. If the Borrower does not perform any of the trigger actions laid out in the loan agreement, the covenants are not tested. While the Borrower enjoys greater operational flexibility with these covenants, they also translate into less effective monitoring tools for the Lenders.

A key covenant regulates Debt Incurrence. Under this covenant, a Borrower cannot incur additional debt. It may only be allowed to raise new debt if the leverage ratio, pro forma for the new tranche, stays below a certain threshold.

Box 5.1 Example

A company is looking to acquire a €15m EBITDA target for a purchase price multiple of 10x EV/EBITDA. The company's existing loan agreement states that the company can incur debt up to 4.50x net total leverage.

Assumptions:	
Target EBITDA (€m)	15
EV / EBITDA	10.0 x
Target EV (€m)	150
Existing Debt	300
Existing Cash	25
EBITDA	80
Max Tot. Leverage	4.50 x

Sources	€m	Uses	€m
New TLB	150	Purchase Target	150
Total Sources	150	Total Uses	150

€m	Current Debt Stack Amount	Current Debt Stack xEBITDA	Adj.	Pro Forma Debt Stack Amount	Pro Forma Debt Stack xEBITDA
Cash	(25)		-	(25)	
Existing Debt	300		-	300	
New TLB	-		150	150	
Net Total Debt	275	3.44 x		425	4.47 x
Combined EBITDA		80			95
o/w Bidder		80			80
o/w Target		-			15

As the pro forma capital structure stays below 4.50x, the Borrower can fund the acquisition with 100% debt. But what if the Borrower had a more complicated capital structure in place?

Example: a company is looking to acquire a €50m EBITDA target for a purchase price multiple of 10x EV/EBITDA. The company has both senior and junior debt on its balance sheet and the company's existing loan agreement states that the company can incur debt up to 4.50x net senior leverage and up to 6.50x net total leverage.

Assumptions:	
Target EBITDA (€m)	50
EV / EBITDA	10.0 x
Target EV (€m)	500
Existing Sr. Debt	1,000
Existing Jr. Debt	300
Existing Cash	80
EBITDA	225
Max Sr. Leverage	**4.50 x**
Max Tot. Leverage	**6.50 x**

Sources	€m
New TLB	500
Total Sources	500

Uses	€m
Purchase Target	500
Total Uses	500

	Current Debt Stack			Pro Forma Debt Stack	
€m	Amount	xEBITDA	Adj.	Amount	xEBITDA
Cash	(80)		-	(80)	
Existing Senior Debt	1,000		-	1,000	
New TLB	-		500	**500**	
Net Senior Debt	**920**	**4.09 x**		**1,420**	**5.16 x**
Existing Junior Debt	300			300	
Net Total Debt	**1,220**	**5.42 x**		**1,720**	**6.25 x**
Combined EBITDA		**225**			**275**
o/w Bidder		*225*			*225*
o/w Target		-			*50*

In this case, raising all the debt as a single tranche of senior secured debt does not work, because the net senior leverage at 5.16x breaches the maximum senior leverage set at 4.50x.
On the other hand, the Borrower is compliant with the total leverage covenant, at 6.25x (vs maximum total leverage of 6.50x). This last point demonstrates that a fully debt-funded acquisition is still feasible with a retranching of the new debt:

Assumptions:	
Target EBITDA (€m)	50
EV / EBITDA	10.0 x
Target EV (€m)	500
Existing Sr. Debt	1,000
Existing Jr. Debt	300
Existing Cash	80
EBITDA	225
Max Sr. Leverage	**4.50 x**
Max Tot. Leverage	**6.50 x**

Sources	€m
New TLB	300
New Second Lien	200
Total Sources	500

Uses	€m
Purchase Target	500
Total Uses	500

	Current Debt Stack			Pro Forma Debt Stack	
€m	Amount	xEBITDA	Adj.	Amount	xEBITDA
Cash	(80)		-	(80)	
Existing Senior Debt	1,000		-	1,000	
New TLB	-		300	**300**	
Net Senior Debt	**920**	**4.09 x**		**1,220**	**4.44 x**
Existing Junior Debt	300			300	
New Second Lien	-		200	**200**	
Net Total Debt	**1,220**	**5.42 x**		**1,720**	**6.25 x**
Combined EBITDA		**225**			**275**
o/w Bidder		*225*			*225*
o/w Target		-			*50*

Splitting the new debt into a senior secured tranche (TLB) and a junior tranche (Second Lien) results in the Borrower being compliant with both covenants, at 4.44x and 6.25x.

Covenant packages change according to the target investor base for the loan being raised:

- Loans syndicated to banks, such as club loans and loans to investment-grade borrowers have at least two maintenance covenants and are therefore called **"Covenanted"** or **"Fully Covenanted"**;
- Institutional investors, who don't require maintenance covenants, created demand for so-called **"Covenant-lite"** or **"cov-lite"** loans. Like the covenant packages commonly found in high-yield bonds, these facilities have just incurrence covenants in their loan agreement and no maintenance covenants. As shown in **Figure 5.1**, more than 80% of the total volume of institutional loans issued in 2018 in Europe were cov-lite;
- A third type of loans is represented by the in-between category of **"Cov-loose,"** i.e. loans with one maintenance covenant, usually set at a wide headroom over the Borrower's business plan. This covenant may be required due to specificities of: (i) the reference market (for instance in Italy, where corporate lending regu-

Figure 5.1 Cov-lite loans (% total institutional loan volumes)

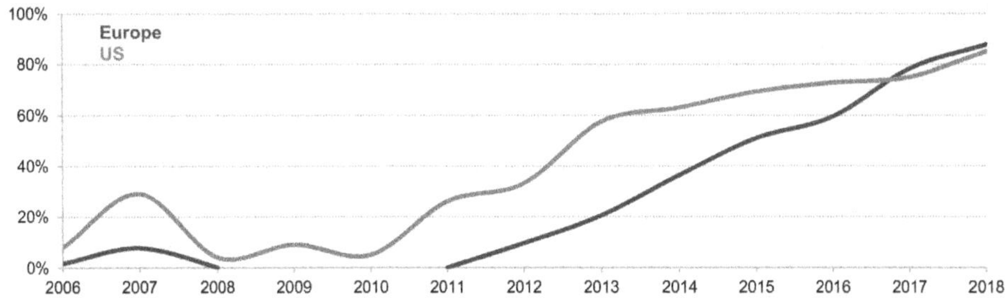

Source: Adaptation based on data from LCD/S&P Global Market Intelligence.

lations limit the participation of institutional investors and the investor base for term loans still includes a significant portion of banks, or for GBP-denominated facilities, given the limited number of funds that can commit capital in that currency), or (ii) the Borrower's credit standing, as investors may request stricter monitoring via one maintenance covenant after operational underperformance or recent restructurings.

In addition to the presence of maintenance covenants, an important loan feature for Borrowers is the **"call protection"** of the loans, which represents any premium or penalty that the Borrower must pay when making a voluntary prepayment of the facility. Call protection shields investors from early downward adjustments to margins via full refinancings or amendments to the loan agreement ("repricings") that leverage strong market conditions.

Loans syndicated to banks, such as TLAs, RCFs, or other club loans, carry no prepayment penalty and can be totally or partially repaid any time before maturity at no additional cost. On the other hand, institutional loans carry a **"soft[2] call"** protection, usually set at 101% for 6 months (sometimes up to 12). This feature implies that any voluntary prepayment made within 6 months from closing of the transaction will result into a penalty paid by the Borrower and calculated as 1% of the face value of the loan being repaid early (e.g. €4.4m when repaying €440m).

Junior loans also carry some form of call protection. Since their terms are more bespoke, the structure of the call protection is a result of negotiations and differs by tranche. The most common structures are NC1, 102, 101 or 102, 101.

A "NC1" (i.e. **"non-call one"**) feature means that, within the first year from closing, a voluntary prepayment of the facility is possible, but the repayment price is calculated with a **"make-whole"** mechanism and results in a significant penalty.

[2] The difference between "soft" and "hard" calls lies in the trigger event for such penalties; the former only applies to voluntary loan prepayments, the latter applies to both voluntary and mandatory prepayments.

The "make-whole" price equals the NPV of the interest payments that the Lender will not receive due to the early redemption, plus the redemption of the principal at expiration of the non-call period (e.g. 2 years after closing if NC2, also called the "first call date").

The mathematical formula is set out below:

$$Makewhole\ Price = \sum_{t=1}^{First\ Call\ Date} \frac{Debt\ Service_t}{(1 + Ref.\ Rate + Fixed\ Spread)^t} + \frac{First\ Call\ Price}{(1 + Ref.\ Rate + Fixed\ Spread)^{Years\ to\ Maturity}}$$

Market rates are an input for the discount rate in the formula and are specified in the loan agreement as the current yield of a reference security (*Bundesanleihen* for Euro-denominated loans, Gilts for Sterling-denominated loans, etc.) that matures close to the expected settlement date of the early repayment. The loan agreement details the features of the reference rate, which for instance can be augmented by a fixed spread (usually 50 basis points) and can be assumed equal to zero if negative. In low interest rate environments, the Borrower can incur significant prepayment penalties until the loan enters the first call date. This is an effective deterrent to the early repayment of the loan, because the high penalties are likely to outweigh the savings on interest that a new loan at more attractive rates could generate.

Box 5.2 Example

A €300m Second Lien Loan issued on 22-Dec-20 gets fully repaid on 24 May 2021. What is the difference in prepayment penalties due to Lenders between a NC1, 102, 101 and a 102, 101 structure?*

Loan Size (€m):	300
Loan Pricing:	E+8.50%
EURIBOR:	0.00%
All-in Rate:	8.50%
Settlement:	22-Dec-20
Maturity:	22-Dec-25
Ref. Rate:	Current yield of Bund maturing in May-21 (Assumed 0% if < 0%)

EARLY LOAN REPAYMENT - WITHIN YEAR ONE

Structure A: NC1, 102, 101		
Call Protection Structure:	NC1, 102, 101	
1st Callable Date:	22-Dec-21	
1st Call Price (% of Par):	102	
Repayment Date:		24-May-21
Reference Rate (Bund due May-21):		0.00%
Spread Over Reference Rate:		0.50%
Price (% of Par)[1]:		106.60
Prepayment Penalty (€m):		**19.8**
Delta vs. Structure B (€m):		*13.8*

Structure B: NC1, 102, 101		
Call Protection Structure:	102, 101	
1st Callable Date:	22-Dec-20	
1st Call Price (% of Par):	102	
Repayment Date:		24-May-21
Price (% of Par):		102.00
Prepayment Penalty (€m):		**6.0**

The delta between the two prepayment penalties is 4.60% of the face value of the loan, which totals €13.8m in the case of a €300m facility.

* The price is calculated with the make-whole formula, i.e. $\sum_{t=1}^{24\ May\ 21} \frac{(8.50\% * 300)_t}{(1 + 0.00\% + 0.50\%)^t} + \frac{102.00\% * 300}{(1 + 0.00\% + 0.50\%)^{4.58}}$. In Excel this can be calculated with a "PRICE" function.

A 102, 101 structure means that within the first year from closing prepayment penalties will total 2% of the face value, then 1% for the following 12 months; thereafter, the loan will be prepayable at par.

A NC1, 102, 101 call protection structure is more Lender-friendly than a 102, 101 structure, as it provides a disincentive for Borrowers to repay the loan during the first year of the facility, ensuring protection for Lenders' returns.

5.4 Loan syndication

The needs of the Borrower driving the choice of a specific deal structure affect several features of loan syndication, including the length of the process, the fees paid to investors and/or to the syndicate of banks, and management attendance.

From the point of view of the arrangers of the loan (i.e. the investment banks placing the loan to investors), a given deal structure differs by: (i) the **level of risk** carried by the bank on its balance sheet, (ii) the **fees** generated by the transaction, and (iii) the targeted **investor base** for syndication.

Deals can be classified according to the **risk on balance sheet** carried by the arrangers.

5.4.1 Underwritten vs Best efforts deals

The longest risk carried by the arrangers lies with **underwritten or "committed"** deals, in which the arrangers underwrite on their own balance sheet the amount that the client needs to raise.

The commitment provided by the syndicate ensures that the amount needed by the Borrower will be raised no matter what. If there is not enough demand for the paper in the market, the arrangers will anyhow issue new debt for the full amount required. The unsold portion will then be kept on the banks' balance sheet or sold in the secondary market (usually at a steep discount), causing losses for the arrangers. In the case of a discount sale, the bank incurs a loss once the sale is settled. In the case of an on-balance sheet commitment, upfront losses are a function of the bank's own accounting policies and can be lower than a discount sale, but there are additional upfront opportunity costs of the cash reserves set aside to counterbalance the risk profile of the loan.

The terms of the commitment provided by the arrangers, including loan features such as maturity and pricing, are set out in the commitment documentation. When underwriting a deal, banks are subject to a certain degree of market risk, which can be exacerbated for example by periods of high market volatility or by long gaps between the commitment date and the launch date. In order to mitigate the market risk resulting from the commitment (in jargon, the risk that markets can "move away" from the terms agreed on in the commitment documentation), arrangers have two main levers: (i) documentation "flex" and (ii) fees.

The term **"Flex"** defines a series of potential changes to the underwritten terms of a loan financing that arrangers can exercise to enhance syndication and make the deal more attractive to investors (i.e. generate additional demand in the market).

These terms are pre-agreed with the Borrower and set out in the commitment documentation. Typical flex items include:

- **Currency flex**: grants the ability to shift amounts of the new debt from one currency to another, e.g. flex of £500m of TLB into $-equivalent. This allows arrangers to access other debt markets in case of low demand expected from the base currency (e.g. because of significant size of the new tranche);
- **Structure flex**: grants the ability to shift amounts of the new debt across seniority of claims (usually from senior to junior), e.g. flex to raise a portion of new TLB as Second Lien. This allows arrangers to de-risk the senior debt lenders by lowering the net senior leverage, pro forma for the transaction;
- **Flex to bond/loan**: grants the ability to shift amounts of new loans being raised into a new bond tranche (or vice versa, with flex to loan), e.g. flex to raise a portion of new TLB as fixed or floating rate notes with the same maturity as the TLB. This allows arrangers to access other debt markets in case of expected low demand (e.g. because of significant size of the new tranche or temporary weakness of the loan/bond market);
- **Maturity flex**: grants the ability to amend the maturities of a loan tranche (usually to reduce them by a stated number of months)
- **Market flex**: grants the ability to increase the yield of a loan up to a maximum amount by raising the margin and the Original Issue Discount of the facility;
- **Other flex items**: other changes allowed to the clauses of the loan agreement that do not necessarily affect the structure of the financing (e.g. tighter restrictions on dividend payments, longer call protection for the loan, potential introduction of financial maintenance covenants, etc.)

Market Flex is the most important flex item, as it defines the breakeven level of an underwritten loan for the arrangers. It is quoted in basis points (e.g. 150bps). It can be fully used to increase the underwritten margin of a loan, but a set portion can alternatively be used to increase the **Original Issue Discount ("OID")**[3], i.e. the discount at which the loan is offered to investors during syndication.

Every deal has a different market flex, as average levels can compress and expand according to the market risk perceived by the arrangers at the time of commitment and are subject to negotiations between the arrangers and the Borrower. Certain commitment documents can allow for step-ups in the market flex based on ratings (e.g. if the rating feedback obtained is below a certain rating threshold) or time (e.g. if the deal is not launched in the market by a certain date).

[3] OID is expressed as % of face value. One point of OID is expressed as 99.00 and means that investors will pay 99¢ to purchase a commitment of $1 from the arrangers.

Box 5.3 Example

A bank underwrites a EUR TLB at E+400 with an OID of 99.50. The agreed fee and flex structure is as follows:
Upfront fees to arrangers: 1.75%
Market flex: 150bps, of which up to 50% (i.e. 62.5bps) usable as OID under 3-year convention
The breakeven level is calculated as follows:

	Margin (bps)	OID (%)	Fees to Arrangers (%)
Original Underwritten Levels	(EURIBOR +) 400.0	99.500%	1.75%
+ Full Flex (150bps)	+ 62.5	– (0.625% × 3 =) 1.875%	
After Full Flex	(E +) 462.5	97.625%	1.75%
+ Underwriting Fees	—	– 1.75%	
Breakeven Levels	(E +) 462.5	95.875%	—

Arrangers will "own" the TLB at a margin of E+462.5bps with OID of 95.875. If they sell the loan to investors at these levels, they make no fees (they pass them on to the market), but they also do not incur any losses. If the price of the loan moves higher or lower this will generate a profit or a loss for the arrangers, respectively.

In Europe, up to 50% of the market flex can generally be used as OID. The upfront OID for investors is conventionally calculated by multiplying the OID flex by a factor of 3, e.g. 50bps of OID flex × 3 = 150bps of upfront OID (98.50). In the US, banks use a 4-year convention, hence 50bps of OID flex × 4 = 200bps of upfront OID (98.00).

Arrangers try and negotiate market flex terms that allow them to place the loan in projected worst-case scenarios without the need to give away their underwriting fees. Incorrect estimates on investor appetite or sharp and unexpected market movements (such as those registered in March 2020 after the first Covid-19 outbreak in Europe) can hurt the profits of an underwritten deal.

From a fee perspective, an underwritten deal comes at a cost for the Borrower because banks partially compensate for the market risk with higher fees. Despite the higher cost, companies may request an underwrite from banks in one of the following situations:

- **M&A/LBO**: in European M&A processes, the Vendor requests that the Acquiror show proof that it has the required funds to complete the transaction (also called "certainty of funds"). In practical terms, this means that at the time of the final bid, the Acquiror will have to present a commitment letter signed by banks, stating that they have committed to issue the full amount of debt (also stated in the letter) at the Closing Date. In US M&A processes, certain funds are not required and avoid an underwrite;

- **Certainty of execution**: in highly volatile markets or when debt tranches have upcoming maturities, the Borrower might require certainty on the amount raised. In addition, the yearly interest rate and the OID required by the Borrower at Closing have a maximum threshold, a worst-case scenario, set by the fully flexed pricing in the loan documentation.

When a deal is not underwritten, it is referred to as **"best efforts."** This is because the arrangers will use their "best efforts" to arrange and syndicate a deal for the Borrower. Loan terms are usually pre-agreed with the Borrower before launch, but in no way "guaranteed" by the arrangers. If market demand is lower than expected, this will result in a slightly different outcome (e.g. lower amount raised or loan priced at higher interest rate vs what was originally agreed) at no additional cost for the arrangers. The Borrower in any case retains the option to withdraw the offering from the market before the loan gets allocated to investors.

As the arrangers of a best efforts deal carry no balance sheet risk if the deal does not happen, the fees they charge are lower than those for committed deals.

Fees charged by arrangers in a debt transaction are driven by several factors; as mentioned above, the nature of underwritten vs best efforts deal will play a significant part in defining the fee structure. In general, the higher the complexity of the deal for the arrangers, the greater the fees that the Borrower will have to pay. Overall deal factors include: (i) the lead time from the signing of the deal to its launch (in jargon, "time to market"), (ii) the size of the amount of debt to be raised, (iii) the deal structure itself (e.g. when it involves a large number of parties and subsidiaries of the Borrower), (iv) the operating performance of the Borrower and its general creditworthiness (e.g. corporate credit rating, cyclical vs noncyclical operations, distress or significant recent underperformance), (v) the track record of the Borrower in the debt capital markets (i.e. first time vs repeat issuer), and (vi) general market conditions (a deal underwritten in volatile markets will be more costly than a deal underwritten in "quiet" markets).

Lastly, the fee structure of a deal is a function of its **syndication process**, which changes with the type of investors targeted and can be split into: (i) club deals (also referred to as bank syndication) and (ii) institutional deals (also referred to as "general" syndication).

5.4.2 Club deals: Fees, process and structure

A **club deal (bank syndication)** happens when the syndicate of underwriters looks to sell down their original commitments to other commercial banks. Sometimes the underwriters will not proceed with syndication and will instead keep the original commitments on their own balance sheet until maturity, in what is defined as a "buy and hold" position.

Club deals are a common type of loan product for investment grade companies, companies that refinance their capital structure in the context of an Initial Public Offering, and small or non-EUR denominated loans for sub-investment grade issuers. This is because club loans produce lower profitability compared to other products, such as institutional loans or bonds.

The route of bank syndication is often chosen when:

- general syndication is not a viable execution route, for instance when the size of the loan is too small to ensure enough liquidity to institutional investors or when the loan is in a local currency, or
- the original underwriters act as main relationship bank(s) to the Borrower, with the expectation of generating further revenues through ancillary business (e.g. hedging, advisory, etc.); this strategy generally implies that the original underwriters will buy and hold the biggest commitments as a % of the total.

From a fee perspective, the banks that are part of the original underwriting syndicate receive the following compensation:

- **Commitment (or Underwriting) Fee:** paid to all the banks in the syndicate to compensate for the capital made available and the use of their own balance sheet. This fee is paid upfront at the closing of the deal;
- **Structuring (or Coordination) Fee:** often included in the fee package, it is paid only to the lead bank(s) in the syndicate and compensates the lead bank(s)' coordination efforts throughout the execution of the deal. This fee is paid upfront at the closing of the deal.

When the underwriters decide to sell down their original commitments in full or in part, the **bank syndication** phase starts. The targeted banks are invited to take part in the syndication by the underwriters' debt syndicate teams and receive materials to conduct their due diligence (usually in the form of a corporate presentation and historical accounts of the Borrower, but often including due diligence reports prepared by third party advisors). Commitment "tickets" are offered to the targeted banks in a set of decreasing amounts; this differentiates the committing banks by the different tiers.

Banks committing to a ticket receive a **Participation Fee** that is proportional to the size of the ticket committed (e.g. a "tier 2" ticket will not receive the maximum fee, but a "tier 1" ticket will). This fee is paid upfront at the closing of the deal. The Participation Fee is not paid directly by the Borrower, but is instead carved out ("passed through") by the syndicate banks from the Commitment Fee that they are expected to receive. In addition to the participation fee, participating banks usually receive a title that may grant them the opportunity to be listed on the loan marketing materials as the arranging bank. "Tier 1" titles allow banks to claim league table credit for loan transactions. This is important for marketing purposes as league tables are a common marketing tool for banks and provide a ranking of the most active bookrunners by volume or number of deals in a given product and period of time.

Figure 5.2 Club/Bank deal: Example of syndicate composition and roles, sample ticket structure for participating banks

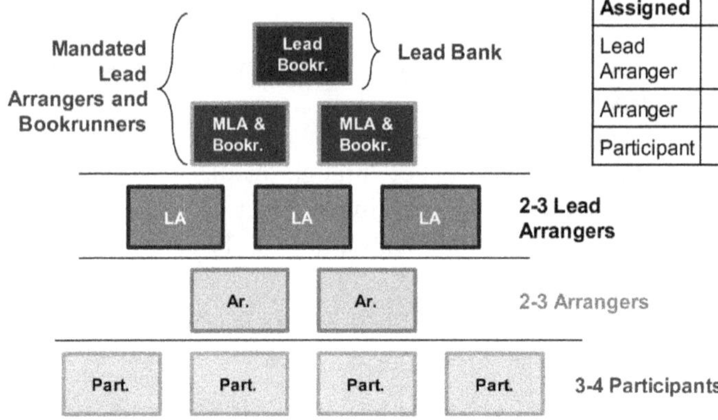

Role Assigned	Commitment Size (€m)	Participation Fee (bps)
Lead Arranger	€80m	55 bps
Arranger	€50m	45 bps
Participant	€30m	35 bps

Participating banks choose the tier in which to play depending on the economics of the deal (ticket size vs participation fee and title) and their relationship with the Borrower. A bank that wants to build a relationship with a new client will look to lend sizeable commitments in order to facilitate the commercial dialogue going forward.

Figure 5.2 outlines a sample syndicate and ticket structure for a sizeable club loan.

5.4.3 Institutional deals: Fees, process and structure

When arrangers target the broader category of institutional investors, the loan is sold via **institutional (or general) syndication**. This process is the most common for sub-investment grade credits.

From a compensation perspective, the fee structure of an institutional syndication does not include a pass-through of commitment fees by arrangers and includes the following:

- **Commitment (or Arranging) Fee:** paid to the syndicate of arrangers, it compensates the availability of capital (in committed deals) or the coordination effort of the arrangers (in best efforts deals). This fee is paid upfront at the closing of the deal. The amount paid by the Borrower varies significantly depending on whether the deal is best efforts or committed; a TLB for a sub-investment grade issuer in Europe can pay around 1.50-1.75% of the face value of the loan for an underwritten deal, but only 0.50-0.75% for a best efforts deal;
- **Original Issue Discount ("OID"):** paid to the institutional investors, this is the discount at which the loan is sold in the market. This fee is paid upfront at the

closing of the deal. TLBs are generally underwritten by arrangers at an OID range of 98.00-99.50. In order to make the deal attractive to investors, arrangers generally launch the deal at a discount and "tighten" the OID, moving it as close to par as possible towards the end of the syndication process, once they have a sense of the strength of the investor order book. As explained above, further OID can be paid to investors by exercising market flex. An upward revision of the OID (e.g. from 99.50 to 99.75) is called **reverse flex** (as opposed to the "normal" flex, i.e. a downward revision of the OID); in certain instances, depending on the terms negotiated with the Borrower, this OID which is not given out to investors can be retained by the arrangers, increasing their total upfront fees;

- **Ticking Fee:** paid to the institutional investors, and common in deals where there is a significant delay between allocation (i.e. when arrangers assign a share of the loan to each investor) and closing (i.e. when the loan funds). This fee is paid upfront at the closing of the deal. It has a mechanism that is similar to that of undrawn fees for RCFs, in that it starts accruing from a certain point in time (generally at allocation) until the loan funds. It can allow for a set "holiday period" (usually up to 90-120 days) and then starts charging an increasing % of margin as time passes. For instance, a ticking fee structure for a TLB paying E+400bps of: 0-45 days = 0% of margin, 46-90 = 50%, 91+ = 100% will mean that if the deal closes within day 45 from allocation there will be no additional cost for the Borrower; if the deal closes between days 46-90 from allocation, the Borrower will have to pay 50% of margin (i.e. 2.00%) times the number of days from day 46 until funding; if the deal closes after 90 days then the Borrower will have to pay 50% of margin for 45 days (i.e. covering the days 46-90 period) plus 100% of margin (i.e. 4.00%) for the number of days from day 90 until funding. This fee is common in M&A transactions, especially in complex cases such as carve-outs or acquisitions requiring lengthy anti-trust reviews.

Across the deal preparation and the deal syndication phase, a loan execution process can take from as little as a couple of weeks up to several months. Figure 5.3 shows a simplified standard execution timetable of an institutional deal for a first time sub-investment grade issuer.

The preparation of a loan financing always starts with a due diligence phase carried out by the arrangers, regardless of whether the transaction will require a commitment or not. The major part of the due diligence phase concludes once the arrangers obtain the required internal approvals to proceed with the transaction and start executing the deal, and it fully concludes before launching the deal on the market. Any major developments in the operations or the business of the Borrower that occur between the committee approval and the launch of the transaction may require additional internal committee sign-offs, according to the internal policies of each arranger.

Before announcing the deal to institutional investors, the Borrower has to complete a rating process in order to obtain credit ratings. Institutional loans in the sub-investment grade space require credit ratings because the institutional investors

Figure 5.3 Institutional deal: Illustrative execution timetable (first time sub-investment grade issuer)

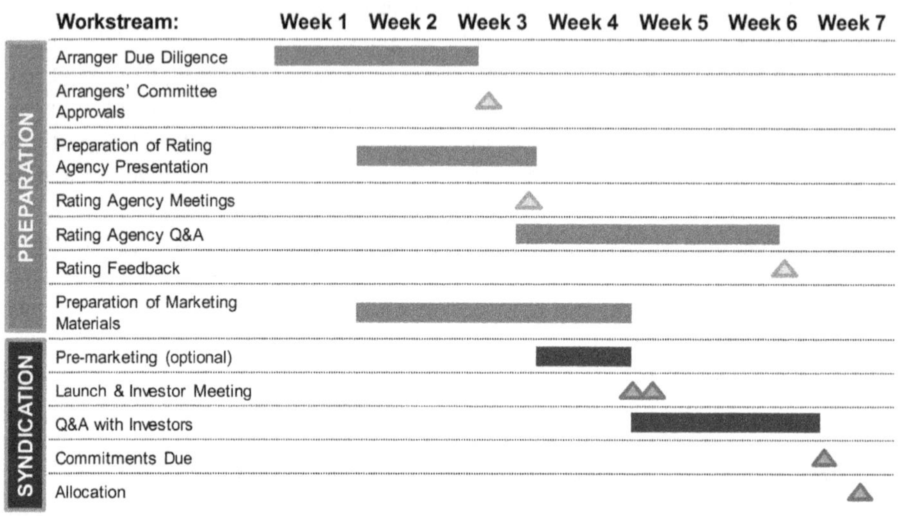

that buy this debt have minimum rating requirements for their potential investments. Several institutional investors require feedback from at least two different agencies. Ratings obtained by Borrowers can be publicly available as press releases on the rating agencies' websites ("public ratings") or shared with a limited number of parties in private data rooms by rating agencies ("private ratings"). Ratings for smaller institutional issuances (sub-€300m) do not need to be public; however, the recent market standard is to obtain a public rating regardless of deal size.

Rating agencies meet in person with the management of the Borrower during a 3-hour presentation where they explain the nature of the envisaged transaction, business and industry dynamics and the key selling points of the Borrower from a credit perspective (also called "credit highlights"). The presentation is followed by a Q&A period that can last up to four weeks after the initial meeting, in which the rating analysts gather the data to conduct their valuations. At the end of the process, the agencies provide feedback on corporate and tranche ratings, and if the Borrower requests a public rating they also publish their press releases and credit reports on their own websites.

First time sub-investment grade issuers often contact a few selected key debt investor accounts before the official launch of the deal to pre-sound general market interest and have a better sense of the reception of the deal at announcement by investors. This phase is called **"pre-marketing" (or "early bird")** and occurs on average one week before the launch of general syndication. The targeted investors sit through a presentation by management covering the envisaged transaction and the business and have the opportunity to ask questions during and after the meeting. The goal of this process is to collect early investor feedback on pricing and key areas of concern (such as the Borrower itself, the deal structure, industry dynamics, etc.) and anchor orders to support general syndication. If investor demand is strong enough, the loan can be fully allocated in this phase and skip the general syndication phase.

In order to present the transaction in the most efficient way, the arrangers and the Borrower prepare a set of **marketing materials** to be shared with investors. These usually include a business plan ("syndication model"), a 30+ page lender presentation and a 60+ page information memorandum covering the business and industry, key credit highlights (i.e. the "sales pitch" for debt investors) and the Borrower's historical and projected financials. Unlike corporate bonds or shares of a listed company, loans are not classified as public securities and as such bear less stringent marketing requirements; for instance, they do not require the preparation of an Offering Memorandum.

In European syndication processes, non-listed companies might also share with investors third-party due diligence reports focusing on legal, industry, financial, and other matters that help investors to gather the required information for their credit analysis. An important analysis included in the financial due diligence (and sometimes presented in a separate report) is called **"Quality of Earnings"** and provides details on all the adjustments to the reported EBITDA that result in the financing EBITDA. The financing EBITDA is the base for the leverage shown in the syndication materials and is subject to scrutiny by investors, who take their own view on the number of adjustments to accept in the leverageable EBITDA. US-style syndication processes do not include additional due diligence reports to be shared with investors.

Marketing materials used in loan syndications are classified as either "public" or "private." All materials including material non-public information on the Borrower, such as financial projections, are deemed "private." Investors reviewing materials that include material non-public information are restricted from trading in the Borrower's securities; therefore, the distinction exists for investors to gather information about the transaction while maintaining their freedom to trade (in this case, they opt to remain "public only" and not to receive private-side information). The lender presentation and the information memorandum include a separate section called "private addendum," which usually includes a detailed overview of the business plan and its assumptions. Before presenting this section during investor meetings, there is a break for public investors to exit the room.

At the launch of the deal, the syndicate desks of the arrangers send out invite letters to the targeted investors, publish a short announcement on Bloomberg, and brief their own internal sales teams on the transaction. The sales teams have the task of getting in touch with their accounts and gather sign-ups for the group investor meeting and for any separate Q&A sessions with management.

The **investor meeting** takes the form of a group in-person meeting or a call, the latter usually for repeat and investment grade Borrowers. The management team walks the group of investors through the lender presentation and arrangers communicate initial price indications ("price talk") on the margin and OID of the loan. The meeting lasts around two hours including investor Q&A and a session for private investors at the end outlining the contents of the private addendum. The presentation is followed by several one-on-one meetings where key investors can separately discuss their own questions with management. Unlike a bond roadshow where the management team holds several group meetings across Europe, there is only one investor meeting for loan syndications. If the deal is marketed to both European and US investors, arrangers could require management to also host a second meeting in the US.

Once the investor meeting and one-on-one sessions are completed, the sales and the syndicate teams of the arrangers start reaching out to investors to draw their attention to the deal and to get feedback on potential order size and price ahead of the investors' credit committees. Investors review the materials made available in a virtual data room and contact the arrangers with business and industry questions, while they prepare the memos for their internal credit committees.

While the deal is in the market, arrangers monitor market feedback and start gathering indications of interest and orders from the sales teams. As the order book develops and the deadline for final investor commitments approaches, they will form a view on the outcome of the deal. If they fear undersubscription, they will exercise market flex and communicate a revised price guidance to investors ahead of the commitment deadline (this is also called a "widening" of the price talk, as the new guidance will have a higher yield). Vice versa, if the deal is going well, "tighter" guidance (i.e., at lower yield) can be issued to the market.

Once investors' credit committees approve order sizes and a combination of price and OID, investors place their orders with sales ahead of the commitment deadline. On average, a loan offering remains in the market for two weeks after launch.

For the syndication to be complete, the order book has to cover at least the amount being raised in the market, but in order to be successful the order book will have to be greater than the amount offered, as it is market practice that investors expect to be assigned only a portion of the order they submit.

Once the arrangers collate the orders from sales at the margin and OID combination preferred by the Borrower in the order book, the sales and the syndicate teams work on a proposed list of allocated shares of the loan for each investor, which is then sent to the Borrower for sign-off (the **"allocation phase"**). As the order book is usually oversubscribed, investor commitments are scaled down. The aim of the allocation exercise is to create a base of investors that will look to be stable, long-term holders (instead of selling down their exposure and negatively impacting the price). A loyal investor base is important as the relationships built between investors and the management team can support borrowers throughout their strategic milestones. The Borrower has a final say on the investor list and can increase or decrease allocations at its own discretion, for instance favouring "relationship" accounts or rewarding investors that showed constructive behaviour during syndication. Once the Borrower accepts the allocation proposal and the deal fully allocates, syndication is complete.

From a syndicate structure perspective, institutional deals are less complex than club deals: there is no fee "pass-through" across arrangers, but banks with junior (i.e. passive) roles are assigned a low commitment percentage of the total (also called "economics") and in turn receive lower fees. While US deals carry the concept of a

Figure 5.4 Institutional deal: Example of syndicate composition and roles

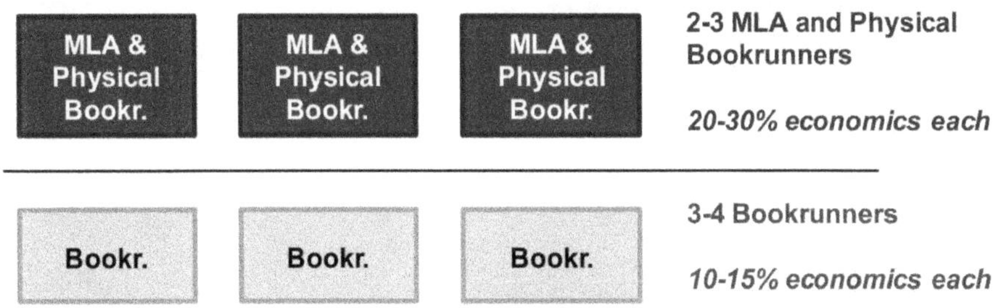

"lead bank" that has the highest economics of the syndicate and is the only one in charge of the execution of the deal and the only one to receive league table credit (similar to what happens in bond syndications), in Europe this role does not exist and the active bookrunners split both execution tasks and league table credits.

Questions and answers

1. *Please explain the concept of "ticking fee."*
   a. *An investor is allocated a €45m ticket in a new TLB priced at E+3.25%. The TLB has the following ticking fee schedule: 0-60 days from allocation: 0% of applicable margin / 61-120 days: 50% of applicable margin / 121+ days: 100% of applicable margin. The TLB funds after 165 days. Calculate the ticking fee due to the investor.*

   The ticking fee is a fee paid to investors that starts accruing from a certain date and steps up over time, which compensates investors in the case of significant gaps between the date of allocation and the funding date of the loan (for instance, due to delays in an M&A process). The ticking fee is calculated as percentage of the margin paid by the loan.

   a. The investor is due c. €240,000.

Loan Pricing:	**E+3.25%**
Loan Amount (€m):	**45**
Funding:	**Day 165**

Day		#days	Margin %	Margin		Ticking Fee (€ '000)
0	90	90	0%	0.00%		0
91	120	30	50%	1.63%	=(30/365)×1.63×45,000	1,205
121	165	45	100%	3.25%	=(45/365)×3.25×45,000	1,589
					Total	**2,795**

b. *Ceteris paribus, what would the difference (in €m) be for the investor if the TLB had a ticking fee schedule of 0-45 days from allocation: 0% / 46-90 days: 50% / 91+ days: 100% of applicable margin?*

b. The investor is due c. €391,000, i.e. c. €150,000 more than in the previous case.

Loan Pricing:	**E+3.25%**
Loan Amount (€m):	**45**
Funding:	**Day 165**

Day		#days	Margin %	Margin			Ticking Fee (€ '000)
0	45	45	0%	0.00%			0
46	90	45	50%	1.63%	=(45/365)×1.63×45,000		90
91	165	74	100%	3.25%	=(75/365)×3.25×45,000		301
						Total	**391**

2. *Please outline the main differences between a TLA and a TLB.*
A Term Loan A is a term loan that amortizes through scheduled instalments over the life of the facility. It is generally syndicated to banks and this results in the TLA having strict covenant packages (e.g. maintenance covenants). This tranche is often cheaper compared to a TLB due to its amortizing features and good level of investor protection granted by the strict covenant package. TLAs are prepayable at par at any time. On the other hand, TLBs have little to no amortization (US TLBs have 1.00% annual amortization, European TLBs do not amortize). TLBs are mostly syndicated to institutional investors and as a result have minimum size requirements (€200-250m in Europe), more expensive rates but looser covenant packages (e.g. covenant-lite). TLBs usually include call protection features that expire after a certain period. Both TLA and TLBs are floating rate instruments priced with a set spread over a base rate (EURIBOR, LIBOR, etc.) and have a floor to the base rate.

3. *Please describe the three main categories of covenants and provide examples.*
Covenants can be split into three categories. Affirmative covenants, stating the obligations of the Borrower: these are quite standardized in nature, with examples including the preparation of a budget, payment of taxes, financial reporting, and compliance with laws. Negative covenants state what the Borrower cannot do (including exceptions). These provisions are more specific to the Borrower's financial situation and existing capital structure. Examples include limitations on asset sales, limitation on investments, M&A and joint ventures, limitation on new debt issuance, limitation on the payment of distributions to shareholders, and limitations on the prepayment of junior debt. Financial covenants represent minimum performance thresholds (mostly related to liquidity and solvency) that the Borrower must not breach. Examples include leverage (Net or Gross Debt/

EBITDA), interest coverage (EBITDA/Annual Interest Expense), Debt Service Cover Ratio or DSCR (Cash Flows Before Debt Service/Debt Service, i.e. Annual Interest Expense + Annual Principal Repayment), Fixed Charge Cover (Cash Flows Before Debt Service/[Debt Service + Lease Obligations]), and minimum liquidity covenants.

4. *Please explain the concepts of "call protection" and "make-whole" price.*
   a. Company X has two Second Lien tranches with the features below:

	Tranche 1	Tranche 2
Loan Size (€):	250 million	450 million
Loan Pricing:	E+7.25%	E+8.50%
Settlement:	11-Nov-20X0	25-Mar-20X1
Maturity:	8 years	8 years
Call Protection:	NC1, 102, 101	102, 101

   Assuming a make-whole price for Tranche 1 of 112%, what would the total prepayment penalties be (in € millions) if Company X decided to refinance both tranches on 22-Jun-20X1? And on 30-Nov-20X2?
   A call protection is a common feature for institutional loans and consists of a premium or penalty that the Borrower is obliged to pay when it voluntarily prepays a loan. This feature protects lender returns on the loan as it discourages early loan repayments or repricing transactions. The "make-whole" price of a loan is the NPV of the interest payments not paid to the Lender as a result of the early repayment, plus the redemption of the principal at expiration of the non-call period.
   a. Prepayment penalties for the two tranches follow the schedule below:

Tranche 1		Tranche 2	
11-Nov-20X0	112.0% (MW price)	25-Mar-20X1	102.0%
11-Nov-20X1	102.0%	25-Mar-20X2	101.0%
11-Nov-20X2	101.0%	25-Mar-20X3	100.0%
11-Nov-20X3	100.0%		

   In June 20X1, Tranche 1 would still be within the NC1 period and similarly, Tranche 2 within the 102 period, therefore Company X would pay the highest prepayment penalties: €250 × (112% – 100%) + €450 × (102% – 100%) = 30 + 9 = €39 million. On 30-Nov-20X2, both tranches would be prepayable at 101%, with penalties totalling €250 × (101% – 100%) + €450 × (101% – 100%) = 2.5 + 4.5 = €7 million.

5. *Please elaborate on the key differences between underwritten and best efforts deals, including the implications for the Borrower and the syndicate of banks.*

An underwritten or committed transaction is a deal where banks "secure" the amount to be raised for the Borrower using their own balance sheets, whereas in best efforts deals the syndicate banks help the Borrower to place the debt with investors (without the use of their own balance sheet). Underwritten deals are riskier for banks than best efforts deals, because they put banks' balance sheets at risk. Unsuccessful deals that fail to generate enough investor demand for the loan can translate into upfront costs (if the remainder of the loan is sold at a significant discount) or higher capital requirements (if the remainder of the loan is kept on the bank's books). From a Borrower perspective, underwritten deals guarantee certainty of the financing (required mostly in M&A situations) but carry more expensive fee provisions and additional flexibility on the agreed loan terms through market and documentation flex. Flex and fees are the two levers that compensate the underwriting banks for the higher risk incurred with their commitment.

6. *Please explain the concept of "flex."*
   a. *Assume that Company X is looking to raise a €680m TLB and a \$225m Second Lien with the following flex features:*

EUR TLB	
Loan Size:	€680m
Loan Pricing:	E+3.75%
OID:	99.50
UW Fees:	1.75%
Mkt Flex:	1.50%
o/w usable as OID:	50%

USD SECOND LIEN	
Loan Size:	\$225m
Loan Pricing:	L+8.50%
OID:	97.50
UW Fees:	2.50%
Mkt Flex:	1.75%
o/w usable as OID:	100bps

At which levels would the underwriters "own" the loans?

The term "flex" indicates a series of potential changes to the loan documentation of an underwritten deal pre-agreed with the Borrower. Arrangers can request these changes to the underwritten terms during syndication to make a transaction more palatable to potential investors. Flex provisions are of various natures, including currency, structure, and maturity. The most important type of flex is the so-called "market flex," that sets the maximum amount of margin and OID that will be paid by the Borrower (and, conversely, the break-even levels of the loan for the underwriting banks).

a. Underwriting banks would own the €680m TLB at E+4.50%, 95.50 OID and the \$225m Second Lien at L+9.25%, 90.50 OID. See calculations below:

	TLB - EUR		USD - 2L	
	Margin	OID	Margin	OID
Original UW Levels	E+3.75%	99.50	L8.50%	97.00
+ Full Flex	= 50% × 1.5% = 0.75%	= 50% × 1.5% × 3 = 2.25%	= 1.75% – 1.00% = 0.75%	= 1.00% × 4 = 4.00%
Fully Flexed Levels	E+4.50%	97.25	L+9.25%	93.00
+ UW Fees		1.75%		2.50%
Break-even Levels	**E.4.50%**	**95.50**	**L+9.25%**	**90.50**

b. Company X decides to raise the Second Lien tranche in EUR (€225m) instead of USD. It lowers the UW fees to 2.25% but otherwise leaves flex, OID, and margin unchanged. Syndication proves challenging due to unexpected market turmoil and the underwriters end up allocating the loan at E+9.25%, 90.75 OID. Would the underwriting banks break-even or lose/make money on the deal? If so, how much money would they lose/make?

By allocating the tranche at E+9.25%, 90.75 OID, underwriting banks would lose money on the transaction:

	EUR - 2L	
	Margin	**OID**
Original UW Levels	E+8.50%	97.00
+ Full Flex	= 1.75% – 1.00% = 0.75%	= 1.00% × 3 = 3.00%
Fully Flexed Levels	E+9.25%	94.00
+ UW Fees		2.25%
Break-even Levels	**E+9.25%**	**91.75**

As the OID flex multiplier for EUR-denominated tranches follows a 3-year convention, the break-even levels for the €225m Second Lien are E+9.25%, 91.75 OID. The allocated price is therefore 1.00% lower than break-even level. The underwriting bank syndicate as a whole would lose €(2.25)m on the transaction (i.e. €225m × 1.00%).

7. *Company X is raising a new €1,250m loan in the form of a club deal. The initial underwriters (with commitments of equal size) are Bank DTMG (acting as the lead bank) and Pierce & Pierce. The fee structure of the deal includes a commitment fee of 1.00% and a structuring fee of 0.25% (payable to the lead bank only). The tickets to participating banks are allocated as per the following schedule:*

Role Assigned	**Commitment Size**	**Participation Fee**
Lead Arranger	€150 million	85 bps
Arranger	€100 million	60 bps
Participant	€75 million	35 bps

Final allocations result in two Lead Arrangers, five Arrangers, and six Participants. Assuming both Bank DTMG and Pierce & Pierce fully sell down their initial exposure, what is the average participation fee paid to the syndicate of 13 banks? What is the P&L of the transaction for Bank DTMG and for Pierce & Pierce?

Based on the allocations, the syndicate of banks is split into the following tiers:

Role Assigned	Commitment Size	Participation Fee	# of Banks	Total Commitment by Tier
Lead Arranger	€150 million	85 bps	2	€300 million
Arranger	€100 million	60 bps	5	€500 million
Participant	€75 million	35 bps	6	€450 million
Total			**13**	**1,250 million**

Each tier is due a different participation fee:

- Lead Arrangers: €300m × 0.85% = €2.55m
- Arrangers: €500m × 0.60% = €3.00m
- Participants: €450m × 0.35% = €1.575m

By summing up the three figures, total participation fees paid to the syndicate are 2.55 + 3.00 + 1.575 = €7.125m, i.e. 0.57% of the €1,250m loan. The average participation fee paid to the syndicate is therefore 57bps.

Participation fees are paid away from the commitment fee that is due to the initial underwriters. As the commitment fee is 1.00% × 1,250 = €12.5m, the portion that Bank DTMG and Pierce & Pierce will be able to retain is €12.5 – €7.125 = €5.375m, i.e. 1.00% – 0.57% = 0.43% of the of the €1,250m loan. In addition, Bank DTMG is entitled to 100% of the structuring fee of 0.25%, i.e. €3.125m. The P&L for the two banks is the following:

- Bank DTMG (Lead): 50% of retained commitment fee + 100% of structuring fee = 50% × 5.375 + 3.125 = €5.81m. This represents 0.47% / 47bps of the €1,250m loan
- Pierce & Pierce: 50% of retained commitment fee = 50% × 5.375 = €2.69m. This represents 0.22% / 22bps of the €1,250m loan.

The following table summarizes the key calculations:

	#Banks	Total Size (€m)	Fees (€m)	Fees (%/bps)
Lead Arrangers (85bps)	2	300	2.550	
Arrangers (60bps)	5	500	3.000	
Partecipants (350bps)	6	450	1.575	
Total	**13**	**1,250**	**7.125**	**0.570%/57bps**
Total Commitment Fee (100bps)		1,250	12.500	
(-) Less Partecipation Fee Payaway			(7.125)	
Commitment Fee due to Inizial UWs			**5.375**	**0.430%/43bps**
Structuring Fee (25bps) - Lead Bank Only		1,250	3.125	
Bank DTMG (Lead Bank) - P%L			5.813	0.465%/47bps
Pierce & Pierce - P&L			2.688	0.215%/22bps

8. *Please describe the main types of fees paid by the Borrower in an institutional deal, with specific reference to the recipient of each fee and the way each fee is calculated.*
   A typical fee structure of an institutional loan deal includes a commitment/arranging fee and an Original Issue Discount (OID). The commitment fee (or arranging fee in the case of best efforts deals) is paid to the syndicate of arranging banks as compensation for the execution and the use of balance sheet (the latter in underwritten deals only). This fee is calculated as a percentage of the face value of the loan. The OID is paid to investors and represents an initial discount at which the loan is sold in syndication. This fee is calculated as a percentage of the face value of the loan. In deals where a significant delay is expected between allocation and funding of the loan (mostly due to the structure of M&A processes), investors are also paid a ticking fee, which starts accruing from a certain date and steps up over time. This fee is calculated as a percentage of the margin paid by the loan.

9. *Please elaborate on the marketing documents required for an institutional syndication. What is the difference between "public" and "private" materials?*
   Marketing materials prepared for institutional syndications include a lender presentation and an information memorandum that cover the main aspects of the deal and the key selling points of the Borrower (transaction summary, business and industry overview, key credit highlights, and historical and projected financials), plus the Borrower's business plan (also called the "syndication model"). In addition, and more commonly in Europe, the Borrower may share with investors third-party reports on various due diligence topics (legal, commercial, financial, insurance, environmental, IT, etc.), the most important of which is the so-called "Quality of Earnings," that includes details on the adjustments to the reported EBITDA that are the basis of the financing EBITDA. Private side marketing materials include material non-private information on the Borrower. They are kept separate from public-side marketing materials because they restrict the trading in the Borrower's securities for investors that review them. An example of private-side marketing materials is the syndication model, because it includes financial projections. Investors can choose not to review private-side marketing materials in order to avoid trading restrictions.

6 Equity Capital Market: Primary Offerings – The IPO

by Andrea Tortoroglio

6.1 Introduction

The Equity Capital Market (ECM) covers a wide range of financial instruments and activities. As the Goldman Sachs website reports: "ECM team works closely with public and private companies, governments and financial sponsors to originate, structure and execute equity and equity-linked financings such as initial public offerings, follow-on offerings, convertibles and derivatives."[1]

In this first chapter dedicated to ECM, we provide a complete overview of the primary market, which is where companies list shares not previously traded on any exchange. The offering has the aim to raise funds for various purposes and the securities are issued directly by companies to investors through either an Initial Public Offering (IPO) or a private placement (or "non-public offering"). The latter is a funding round of securities which are sold not through a public offering, but rather through a private one, mostly to a small number of selected investors (typically these include accredited and institutional investors and family offices).

An IPO is the first sale of a company's shares to the public and the listing of the shares on a stock exchange, certainly one of the most prestigious operations for an investment bank in terms of revenues and reputation.

First, we have to understand why a company decides to go public (section 6.2), even though we will not analyse in depth the reasons and the implications with a "corporate finance" approach, as we will focus on the key features under an "investment banking" perspective. It is important to describe the offering structure (section 6.3), as there are many possible alternatives depending on the kind of shares, to whom the offer is addressed, and where the company is listed. Section 6.4 is dedicated to American Depository Receipts (ADRs).

After these preliminary sections, we will go into the IPO process (section 6.5), describing the main actors and how the process of going public works. Then our attention will move to the Syndicate (section 6.5.4), a key element of the listing along with the price-setting mechanism (section 6.5.5).

The goal of this chapter is to combine a theoretical set of skills with an "applied" approach to learning, thanks to the contributions of important investment banks that

[1] https://www.goldmansachs.com/what-we-do/investment-banking/

provide selected case studies helpful to understand how a real IPO is executed. This is why the chapter proceeds with three case studies, that allow students to follow the listing process through real successful IPOs carried out by top players in the investment banking industry: Ferrari with UBS, Nexi with Goldman Sachs, and San Lorenzo with UniCredit (sections 6.5.7 and beyond).

6.2 Why go public

In order to understand the reasons why a company gets listed on the stock exchange, we might face the question from the firm's perspective versus that of the shareholder, considering that a common factor is "cash." From the firm's perspective, listing has four main objectives:

1. **Financial structure**: it comprises the fundraising for development plans, financing future growth, or the improvement of the cost of capital in relation to the risk of financing sources (equity versus debt).
2. **Acquisition currency**: listed shares could be the payment method in an M&A transaction. A company can buy another one by paying either cash or stock, i.e. paying with the shares of the acquiring firm. In general, a listed company has more chances to pursue a strategy of external growth, and an IPO is a perfect way to enhance the payment alternatives.
3. **Reputation:** a firm might also decide to go public to improve its status and develop a positive image. A listed company benefits from visibility deriving from the stock market, especially if it is an important one where many competitors are also listed. The positive effects come also from the presence of institutional investors and the credibility the listing process gives to the company, also as regards credit standing.
4. **Management compensation and discipline:** listing allows the company to attract the best managers and to set up compensation schemes. Stock options and other similar performance-based plans provide the right incentive to management, and these kinds of structure are possible only if a company is listed. In addition, listing generates the adoption of best practice standards regarding corporate governance topics, due to the strengthening of the corporate structures responsible for risk management (i.e. investor relators, internal control, etc.).

From the shareholders' perspective, as previously mentioned, the decision to be listed basically is related to cash. We can find the following three main reasons:

1. **Disinvestment**: through an IPO, the founder can obtain liquidity if he wants to monetise a part or the whole stake in the firm. It might be also a way to deal with the succession plan, if the first entrepreneurial generation doesn't have a second generation available or willing to manage the company. Another example is the exit strategy for private equity funds, where the IPO is one of the favourite ways to cash out investments. Zingales (1995) says that IPOs facilitate the acquisition of companies at a higher value compared to a trade sale.

2. **Privatization**: budgetary policy may lead a country to generate cash through an IPO (i.e. the period of privatizations experienced in Italy in the early 1990s). A modification of current legislation (i.e. European Union rules regarding the presence of the state in private companies) may be a reason to go public.
3. **Agency problems** refer to a conflict of interest between a company's management and the company's shareholders. The manager, acting as the agent for the shareholders, or principals, is supposed to make decisions that will maximise shareholder wealth even though it is in the manager's best interest to maximise his own wealth. Thanks to listing, the firm may solve this typical problem by aligning the interests of shareholders with those of managers, for example through stock options plans.

Having analysed the motivations for going public, we must consider that IPOs do not come without drawbacks. Typically, we can identify the following risks and limits relating to the listing process:

- **Increased formalization of the decision-making process**. A listed company must comply with many rules to protect minorities, to avoid conflicts of interest, and to guarantee market integrity. The impact on corporate governance might be relevant.
- **Burden of disclosure requirements and compliance costs**. Once the firm is public, it is like living in a "fishbowl," with stakeholders, authorities, analysts, and institutional investors all focused on continuous screening of the firm's activities. An example is the introduction of the Sarbanes-Oxley Act (2002) in the United States, which significantly raised the level of governance and market disclosure requirements for listed companies.
- **Pressure on short-term performance**. Quarter by quarter, the company is exposed to a rising pressure regarding performance and analyst expectations. This may not be coherent with medium/long-term development plans.
- **Exposure to takeover risk**. This is present in markets where the public company model prevails, when, post-IPO, the controlling stake is contestable.

The last, but not least, factor to consider is that IPOs are not free of both direct and indirect costs. The direct costs are divided into two categories:

- **"One-off" costs** which include fees paid to lawyers, accountants, advisors, and most importantly, investment banks. The last kind of fees vary according to country, the IPO size, and many other factors, but usually 1.5%-4%[2] of the amount raised (i.e. the proceeds) is a balanced range.

---

[2] Fees are obviously related to many factors. The key ones are the quality of the issuer and the complexity of the operation. The more difficult it is to place the shares, the more expensive the IPO is for the issuer.

- **Recurring costs** refer to operating costs for new corporate structures, public information, investor relations, and market and compliance charges.

The indirect costs are probably more significant, even if often less evident. IPOs are usually underpriced, it means that the first-day return could be in general positive. Underpricing is a cost because it is money that the issuer doesn't get ("left on the table") and it is related to the price-setting mechanism, that will be discussed in the next sections. If you sell 100 shares on the market for € 1 per share and on the first day of listing the price goes up to € 1.1 per share, this 10% underpricing represents a cost for the issuer, albeit an indirect one.

6.3 The offering structure

When we talk about offerings, we must consider that they can be classified according to different criteria, which we can sum up as answers to the following four different questions.

1) Which shares?
Considering the shares sold, if they are issued for the first time, and hence the proceeds go directly to the company, it is a **primary offering**. Alternatively, if existing shares are for sale (the proceeds go to the shareholders) it is a **secondary offering**.

Primary and secondary offerings are international terms which assume different translations in different jurisdictions. For example, in Italy an "Offerta Pubblica di Sottoscrizione" (OPS) is a primary offering, while an "Offerta Pubblica di Vendita" (OPV) is a secondary one. Usually, most of the IPOs are a combination of primary and secondary offerings (i.e. in Italy this kind of mixed offering is called "Offerta Pubblica di Sottoscrizione e Vendita" – OPSV). There is no standard rule regarding the ideal proportion of primary versus secondary. For example, if a private equity fund is using an IPO as an exit strategy, existing shares sold will be probably represent the entire offer or the most important stake. Note that sometimes Seasoned Equity Offerings (SEOs, that will be analysed in the following chapter), i.e. offerings of shares issued by an already-listed firm, are also called secondary offerings or follow-ons.

In American and British markets a primary offering is an "offer for subscription," while a secondary offering is an "offer for sale."

2) To Whom?
Another key aspect is the type of investors the offering is addressed to. If it is directed to all investors (i.e. including retail investors) it is a ***public*** **offering**, while if it is targeted just to institutional investors (mutual funds, banks, pension funds, insurance companies) it a ***private*** **offering**. IPO refers to a public offering (otherwise we talk about a private placement), with an involvement of all types of investors. The typical IPO has a **retail tranche** and an **institutional tranche**, and the proportion may vary

deal by deal, even though usually the latter is 70-80% of total offerings. Consider that sometimes, for example during privatizations, a "clawback" mechanism is applied if retail demand is strong. It means that the investment bank managing the operation reduces the institutional tranche in favour of the retail tranche, for instance when the retail tranche is more than three times oversubscribed. **Figure 6.1** shows a sample of Italian IPOs of the past years: the percentage is the maximum retail tranche, whereas the €/mn amount is the retail demand received during the bookbuilding. On average, the retail allocation is about 15% (from a typical 10% to the 30% of Poste Italiane). If we consider the Anima IPO, the retail demand was equal to € 366mn (over 5x oversubscribed), while the amount allocated to retail investors was € 69mn, equal to 10% of the total offering. The reason why the retail tranche may vary considerably is found in four main drivers: 1) the issuer's brand: a well-known B2C company usually has a much greater chance to attract retail investors; 2) press and media coverage: the more an issuer invests in media and press campaign, the greater the likely percentage of the retail tranche; 3) general condition of market: if the market conditions get worse, the retail tranche may usually be reduced because in tough markets retail investors drastically reduce their risk appetite; 4) incentives: in order to incentivize retails to invest, the offer may provide bonus shares that means the investor receives one share for each five held continually at least one year, or other compensation schemes, such as an "employee tranche" discount.

It is important to consider that the institutional tranche is crucial in the price-setting mechanism (as we will see later in the chapter). Moreover, the retail tranche requires the so-called "prospectus," the offering document that contains much more detailed information, as the investors are less sophisticated than those of the institutional tranche. That's why the latter requires lighter documentation, the so-called "offering circular."

Figure 6.1 Retail Tranche Size in Italian IPOs since 2006 (includes IPOs > € 400mn)

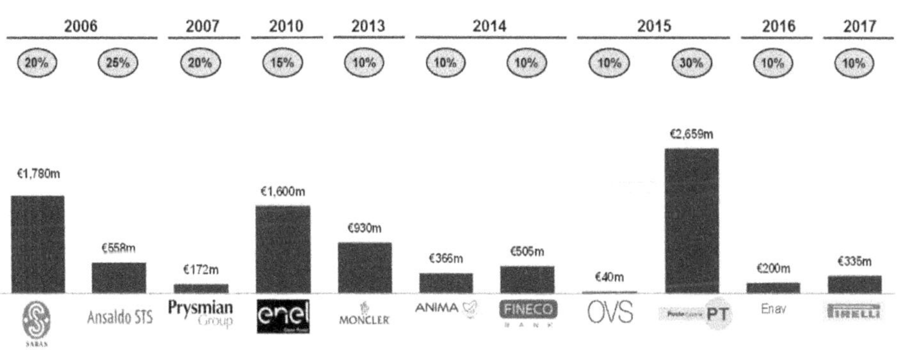

Source: Authors' elaboration based on data from Goldman Sachs, Borsa Italiana as of Jan-2019.

3) Where?
A German company might complete an international offering (e.g. selling shares to German as well as foreign investors), being listed only on the Frankfurt Stock Exchange. This example shows that equity offerings may be domestic or international, depending on where the shares are offered and not relating to the market of listing. Usually, international offerings are dedicated just to foreign institutional investors, because of the complexity and compliance costs that an involvement of international retail investors would require (only a few big issuers can afford these). Having said this, the most common structure is a domestic public offering plus an international private offering, while larger firms tend to structure the IPO with a combination of multiple public offerings (i.e. directed to all types of investors in different countries) and an international private offering.

If we want to approach US investors, a special mention might be dedicated to a particular type of placement: **Rule 144A**. In the US (as in other countries), a private placement involves the sale of securities in a specific transaction that is exempt from registration requirements imposed by federal securities law (Section 5 of the Securities Act of 1933). Even if the shares are sold via a private placement to "accredited investors" (typically individuals or institutions that meet certain wealth and income requirements), these must be registered before they can be freely resold. Rule 144A provides a private placement exemption for **Qualified Institutional Buyers** and allows them to trade privately placed securities among themselves.

In summary, a Rule 144A equity offering is an unregistered offer and sale of equity securities issued by a US or foreign company, the shares of which are neither listed on a US exchange nor quoted in the US. A 144A offering allows the Company to access US demand without the additional burden of the US registration process under SEC requirements. There are minimal additional costs or time for the Company but it allows for targeting Qualified Institutional Buyers in the US, which make up the bulk of the target US institutional investment community. It is also important to mention the **Regulation S** (or just "Reg S"), the second primary exemption from registration requirements imposed by US Security Act. **Reg S** is used in international securities offering with sales to investors outside the United States in offshore transactions. **Box 6.1** shows pros and cons of a 144A offering.

Box 6.1 Pros and Cons of a 144A offering

- ✓ Access to the most important international pool of equity funds
- ✓ Considerable additional potential demand for Issuer shares, which is key to create additional price tension during bookbuilding
- ✓ Internationalisation of the shareholder base
- ✓ Greater name recognition and higher visibility for Issuer in the US
- ✓ Increased potential to broaden the investor base post-IPO

- ✗ Exposure to more litigious US investors
- ✗ Due diligence process documented and reported to a greater extent

4) Which market?

The last factor we have to consider in analysing the offering structure is in which market the firm could be listed: **home market**, **foreign market,** or even a **dual/multiple listing**. The vast majority of companies usually decide to list in their home country, because it is easier and less expensive. A company decides to list in a foreign market for the following three main reasons:

1. The issuer operates in a niche and all the main competitors are listed in a specific market (e.g. tech companies on the NASDAQ): investors, analysts, and trading activities for that kind of industry are concentrated in that market, and thus the firm might have a strong preference to be listed there.
2. The issuer needs to obtain visibility on a foreign market because it is pursuing an M&A strategy and as we have seen, listed shares are an acquisition currency. Alternatively, the company might choose a specific foreign market because of the revenues generated or the potential developments that may arise from that geographical area.
3. The issuer is looking for a more liquid/well-known market because its domestic market is small or lacks credibility. In the past this was a pronounced trend, but with the increasing development and globalization of stock markets, there is no reason to go abroad to become public.

As investors and stock markets become global, dual/multiple listings are less preferred: technological development has contributed to easing access to international platforms, reversing the trend and marking a return to the domestic market.

6.4 American Depository Receipts (ADRs)

American Depositary Receipts (ADRs) are US dollar-denominated negotiable instruments issued by a depositary bank, representing ownership of the underlying ordinary shares of a non-US issuer. Trading in ADRs permits US investors to trade in non-US companies directly in the US equity markets. ADRs are quoted in US dollars and trade just like any other US domestic security. US investors can acquire and trade non-US securities without the concern for different settlement times and other problems typically associated with investing directly in overseas markets. The instrument is designed to be US shareholder-friendly. ADRs are issued, settled, and cleared through the US settlement system in US dollars known as The Depositary Trust Company (DTC). The payment of dividends is also made in US dollars. Compliance and disclosure requirements are the reasons why many issuers tend to avoid direct listing in the US, explaining why most European issuers prefer to approach US investors through ADRs.

US Banks can purchase stock of foreign companies in bulk and reissue them on the US market. ADRs are listed on the NYSE, NASDAQ, and AMEX and can be sold over-the-counter. The introduction of ADRs dates back to 1927, when JP Morgan launched the first instrument of this kind in the US market, issuing a dollar-denominated security for the UK chain of high-end department stores, Selfridges.

Investors willing to invest in ADRs can purchase them from brokers or dealers, that obtain ADRs by buying already-issued ADRs in the US financial markets or by creating a new ADR, that involves buying the stock of the foreign company in the issuer's home market and depositing the acquired shares in a depository bank in the overseas market. The bank then issues ADRs that are equal to the value of the shares deposited with the bank, and the dealer/broker takes the ADR to US financial markets to sell them.

There are several types of ADRs, each involving a different level of disclosure of information and compliance with SEC regulations. But perhaps the most important distinction for issuers of ADRs is that some structures allow the company to raise capital in the US, while others simply provide a mechanism which makes it easy for US investors to buy and trade existing shares.

ADRs can be either sponsored or unsponsored, generating four different levels of ADR programs:

1. **Unsponsored ADR program**
   An unsponsored ADR program is initiated by a depositary bank without the contractual involvement of the company. The establishment of an unsponsored ADR program is driven by broker/investor demand. The ADRs are traded on the over-the-counter ("OTC") market in the US. Once the depositary bank confirms that a company meets its 12g3-2(b) requirements, the depositary bank makes an initial F-6 filing to the SEC and is classified as "first filer." The filing is usually mirrored by the other depositary banks in the form of "piggy-back" filings. All four depositary banks may establish unsponsored ADR programs for a given company.
2. **Sponsored Level I ADR program**
   A Level I ADR program is the simplest way for a company to sponsor an ADR facility. The ADR program is initiated by the company and involves the filing of an F-6 registration statement but allows for an exemption from full SEC reporting requirements under Rule 12g3-2(b). The company has a degree of control over the ADRs issued under a sponsored Level I program, since a deposit agreement is executed between the company and one selected depositary bank. Level I ADRs can only be traded on the OTC market and not on a US stock exchange.
3. **Sponsored level II ADR program**
   A sponsored Level II ADR must comply with the SEC's full registration and reporting requirements. In addition to filing an F-6 registration statement, the company is also required to file SEC Form 20-F and to comply with the SEC's other disclosure rules, including submission of its annual report, which must be prepared in accordance with US Generally Accepted Accounting Principles (US GAAP) or International Financial Reporting Standards (IFRS). Compliance with Sarbanes-Oxley is required, including certifications by management regarding the effectiveness of the company's internal controls over financial reporting and disclosure controls and procedures related to annual reports filed on Form 20-F.

Registration allows the issuer to list its ADRs on a major US stock exchange, namely the New York Stock Exchange (NYSE Euronext) or NASDAQ Stock Market, each of which has further reporting and disclosure requirements.
Level II sponsored programs are initiated by non-US companies to give US investors access to their stock in the US. As with a Level I program, a depositary agreement is signed between the issuer and a depositary bank. The agreement defines the responsibilities of the depositary, which usually include extending corporate actions to ADR holders, mailing annual reports and other important material to shareholders, and maintaining shareholder records. A Level II allows the company's ADRs to have greater visibility in the US but without raising capital.

4. **Sponsored level III ADR program**
Level III sponsored ADRs are similar to Level II ADRs in that the issuer initiates the program, deals with one depositary bank, lists on a major US exchange, and fully complies with SEC reporting requirements. The major difference is that a Level III program allows the issuer to raise capital through a public offering of ADRs in the US and this requires the issuer to submit a Form F-1 registration statement to the SEC.

Table 6.1 summarises the types of American Depositary Receipt programs.

A typical problem of ADRs and more in general of foreign listing is the "flowback" effect. Over time liquidity tends to migrate to the "home" market and this effect may occur because of price discrepancies when a company is listed on more than one global exchange. Arbitrageurs will sell the overpriced shares and purchase the underpriced ones.

In order to illustrate how ADRs are created, assume that ZIBRA SpA, a listed Italian company, wants to establish an ADR program for its shares on the NASDAQ. The firm asks an ALFA Bank to handle the issue, consider the following data:

Table 6.1 Types of ADR

Type of program	Description	Capital raising
Unsponsored	ADRs traded on the US OTC market, using existing shares. No contractual relationship with company. Up to four depositary banks can establish	No
Sponsored Level I	ADRs traded on the US OTC market, using existing shares. Company forms contractual relationship with single depositary bank	No
Sponsored Level II	ADRs listed on a recognized US exchange (NYSE or NASDAQ), using existing shares	No
Sponsored Level III	ADRs initially placed with US investors and listed on a recognized US exchange (NYSE or NASDAQ)	Yes

Source: https://www.adr.db.com/drwebrebrand/about-drs/adrs/types-of-adrs

- ZIBRA's shares trade on the Borsa Italiana at € 10 per share.
- The €/$ exchange rate is 1.15 (i.e. 1.15 dollars for 1 euro).
- ALFA Bank believes the ideal price to trade on the NASDAQ is $23.

Given the target ADR price and the $ equivalent ZIBRA price per share ($11.5 = € 10 × 1.15 €/$), the ADR ratio (number of shares per ADR) is 2 (23/11.5). Now assume that ZIBRA is willing to raise € 200 million through an ADR program, which corresponds to 20 million shares and consequently to 10 million ADRs (i.e. 20 million divided by 2). ALFA will implement this ADR program by implementing the following actions:

1. Purchase 20 million shares issued by ZIBRA at € 10 per share, paying € 200 million. For ALFA Bank this represents an investment of $ 230 million (€ 200 million × 1.15 €/$).
2. Create 10 million ADRs for listing on the NASDAQ, each ADR representing ownership of 2 ZIBRA shares.
3. Sell the 10 million ADRs to American investors at a price of $ 23 per ADR. This is the dollar price implied by ZIBRA's price in €, the current €/$ and the fact that each ADR is worth two ZIBRA shares: € 10 × €/$ 1.15 × 2 = $ 23.

Obviously, ADRs reflect any changes in ZIBRA's stock price, avoiding possible arbitrage between the two different instruments/markets. Let's assume that ZIBRA's shares increase by € 2 per share (to € 12 each) during the opening trading session in Italy. We can easily affirm that the ADRs should rise by $ 4.6 (€ 2 per share x 1.15 €/$ x 2 shares per ADR) to $ 27.6 per ADR when the NASDAQ trading session begins later that day. Also, any exchange rate movements will be reflected in ADR's price: if ZIBRA's price remains unchanged at € 10 per share but the € appreciates from 1.15 to 1.30 just before trading begins in New York, the ADRs should begin trading at $ 26 (€ 10 x 1.30 €/$ x 2).

6.5 The Initial Public Offering (IPO)

6.5.1 Definitions

As we have seen in the introduction to this chapter, in an initial public offering (IPO) a private company gets listed on the stock exchange for the first time (i.e. Milan Stock Exchange). Shares can be offered to institutional and private investors. Two types of shares can be offered in an IPO: primary shares are new shares offered by the issuer to raise new capital, and secondary shares are offered by existing shareholders to monetize part or all of their stake in the company. An IPO is a fully documented offering: an approved prospectus is required by the market authorities (i.e. in Italy the Italian Securities and Exchange Commission – Consob). Banks support the issuer during and after the IPO process conducting business due diligence, structuring the offering, providing research, supporting the key authorities' approval process (i.e. Borsa and Consob in Italy), marketing the transaction, and selling the shares to the market. Banks also provide post-IPO services like acting as a specialist on the stock, research coverage, market making etc. An IPO process usually takes around 6 months to complete (starting from the kick–off meeting).

On top of financing future growth, development plans, or M&A, the IPO also represents a first step for further multiple financing opportunities: convertible debt, access to bond markets, and the possibility to use listed shares for "paper" M&A. An IPO gives the issuer broader access to investors, transforms a company into a liquid asset, and improves the Company's visibility. Selling shareholders use an IPO to monetize part of its investment, enlarging the investor base. A parent company can also structure an IPO as a spin-off of certain business operations. The transaction gives the possibility to develop management incentive schemes and to solve generational turnover issues.

A successful IPO candidate usually operates in an attractive industry with good future earnings and growth potential. The company should have a convincing Equity Story: market leading position, a sustainable competitive advantage, an established customer base, and high product and service quality. The management is expected to be capable and experienced and should have a comprehensible business strategy. Ideally, the company should have a sustainable earnings perspective and stable positive cashflows with high margins and good payout potential.

6.5.2 Overview of the key participants

Several parties are involved under a holistic coordination by an investment bank that assumes the role of Global Coordinator(s) (GC), which allows the process to be tightly managed while the Shareholders/Issuer are in control at all times. In general, the key objectives of the GC and other advisors can be summarized as follow:

- introduce the Issuer to the widest investor universe;
- position the equity story for the long-term;
- narrow the information gap between buyer and seller;
- set the Company up for "no surprises";
- provide guidance on the balance between value maximisation and further upside;
- manage regulatory challenges and disclosure.

In **Figure 6.2** we provide a complete overview of all the main actors:

1. Global Coordinator(s) – Syndicate;
2. Issuer's counsels;
3. Underwriters' counsels;
4. Business consultant;
5. Auditors;

Figure 6.2 **The main actors**

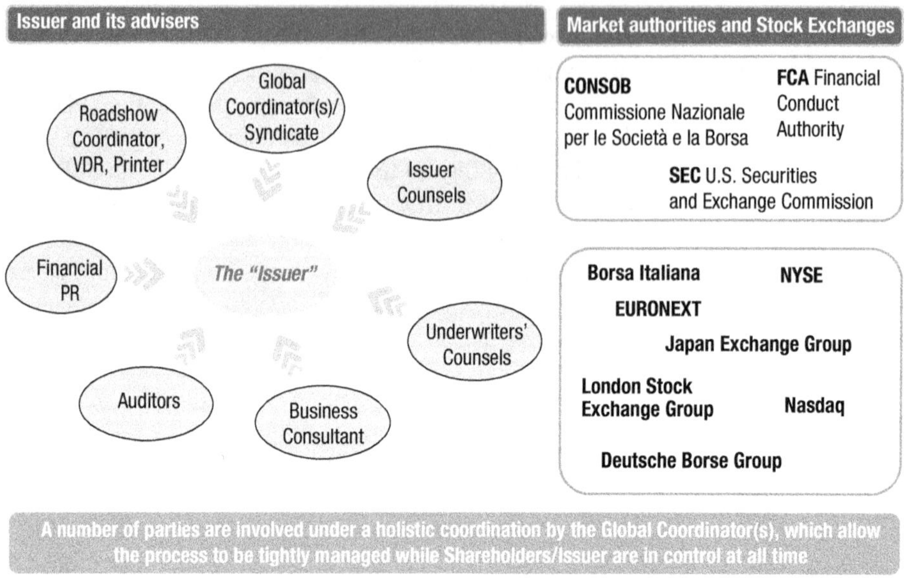

6. Financial PR;
7. Roadshow coordinator, Virtual Data Room (VDR) provider, and Printer.

A number of functions and professionals from the Issuer will work together throughout the process, each one providing a vital contribution under the coordination of a project management team (internal and external). Each party is expected to lead or provide support according to its competences. Within the Issuer's organisation, it is advisable to appoint an internal project manager enabling access to necessary information on a timely basis, supported by various internal functions. An efficient process will aim to update the top management and shareholders on a weekly basis, while allowing them to still drive business operations successfully for the "IPO year" and beyond (see **Figure 6.3**).

Assuming an Italian IPO, Borsa Italiana and Consob are the key **market authorities** involved in the process. Their primary responsibility is the review and sign-off on the IPO documentation package. Issuer's counsels and the Italian sponsor (together with JGCs) are typically the primary coordinators of discussions with Consob and Borsa Italiana. Every Stock Market has different segments depending on the characteristics of the Issuer and the transaction. **Figure 6.4** summarizes the key authorities' roles and main documents in Italian IPOs.

Continuing with the analysis of the main actors, a key role is definitely attributed to the **Global Coordinator**(s), that may be sole or joint. The GC coordinates and manages the underwriters which constitute the Syndicate (in the next section we will

Figure 6.3 Parties involved and working framework

	Parties	Degree of involvement in the process	Advisors	Key counterparts – Issuer: PM	FA	L	BD	COMM / IR
Authorities	CONSOB	●	IC, B	◑	◕	◕	◔	◔
Authorities	Borsa Italiana	◕	IC, B	◑	◕	◕	◔	◔
Advisors	Underwriters/Sponsor (B)	●	All	●	◕	◕	●	◑
Advisors	Issuer Counsels (IC)	●	A, UC	◕	◕	◕	◑	
Advisors	UW Counsels (UC)	◕	IC, B	◔		◔		◑
Advisors	Business Consultant	◔	B, IC	◑	◕		●	
Advisors	Auditors (A)	◑	IC, UC, B	◔	●			
Advisors	Financial PR	◔	B	◔	◑			●
Advisors	Roadshow Coordinator	◔	B	◔				●
Advisors	VDR/Printer	◔	IC, B	◔				

PM: Project Manager FA: Finance and accounting L: Legal ● High ○ Low

BD: Business development COMM / IR: Communication & Investor Relations

Figure 6.4 Market authorities

Key authorities in Italian IPOs	
CONSOB Commissione Nazionale per le Società e la Borsa	• Market Authority: primary responsibility regarding the review of prospectus • Up to 60 days review period (at times longer).
Borsa Italiana	• Due diligence on the company: business plan document, Management Information and control System (MIS), in conjunction with prospectus, etc

Source: Author's elaboration based on Borsa Italiana, Consob.

analyse in detail the Syndicate structure and functions) and carries out fundamental activities:

- Project management;
- Transaction structure;
- Capital structure, dividend policy and financial benchmarking;
- Coordination of due diligence;
- Coordination and review of prospectus and disclosure documents;
- Coordination with stock exchange and counsel;
- Investment case;
- Market, sector, and peer monitoring;
- Valuation;
- Analyst Presentation;
- Identification of and engagement with key investors;
- Comprehensive multiphase marketing plan;
- Demand discovery globally;
- Roadshow presentation;
- Coordination/preparation of roadshow/marketing/PR;
- Underwriting and other relevant legal agreements;
- Syndicate management (banks & analysts);
- Pricing/trading/settlement/stabilisation;
- Aftermarket support.

All these activities involve several teams of the appointed GC(s), that assist the ECM in different areas of the process. Typically, the Industry & Coverage team and ECM Syndicate work closely with ECM Origination in the so-called "private side," because they have access to inside company information that is not available to the public.

This is separated from the public side by a "Chinese wall."[3] These groups deal directly with the issuer and have access to all inside information. Note that bankers on the private side of the business are strictly prohibited from using any of that knowledge for their own benefit or the benefit of others. So whenever you hear that there was some case of insider trading, that means that some type of private information was leaked and someone took advantage of it. The public side has access only to the information an average person has access to (e.g. information found in the annu-

[3] The term Chinese wall is used in finance to describe a virtual barrier intended to block the exchange of information between different departments, if it might result in business activities that are ethically or legally questionable. Investment bankers frequently have access to non-public information concerning a publicly-traded company or a company that is about to become public through an IPO. So they are strictly responsible for developing information barriers that control the transfer of confidential information from one department of the bank to another and to other business units within the bank. After many "headline episodes," several regulations were designed to prevent abuses stemming from pressure by investment bankers on analysts to provide "favourable" appraisals.

al reports, SEC filings, etc.). This side includes equity sales and equity research. Although these professionals work in the same building with their colleagues sitting on the private side, they are not exposed to private information. There are strict regulations within every bank to ensure that their sales and research staff does not take advantage of that information. Therefore, employees take this very seriously. **Figure 6.5** shows the different teams involved.

Legal counsels supporting the Issuer and the Syndicate are a key component for a smooth process. As legal advice needs to cover both domestic and international law, the Issuer can choose to appoint one integrated firm or to have a local firm team up with an international UK/US practice. We can divide the legal counsels in two groups, based on the support they provide to the Issuer or the Underwriters, with different specific tasks.

1. **Issuer's Counsels**:
- Corporate and regulatory actions
- Drafting of the Prospectus and IOC (International Offering Circular)
- Due diligence
- Review underwriting and other relevant legal agreements

Figure 6.5 **Who is involved from within the Global Coordinator(s)**

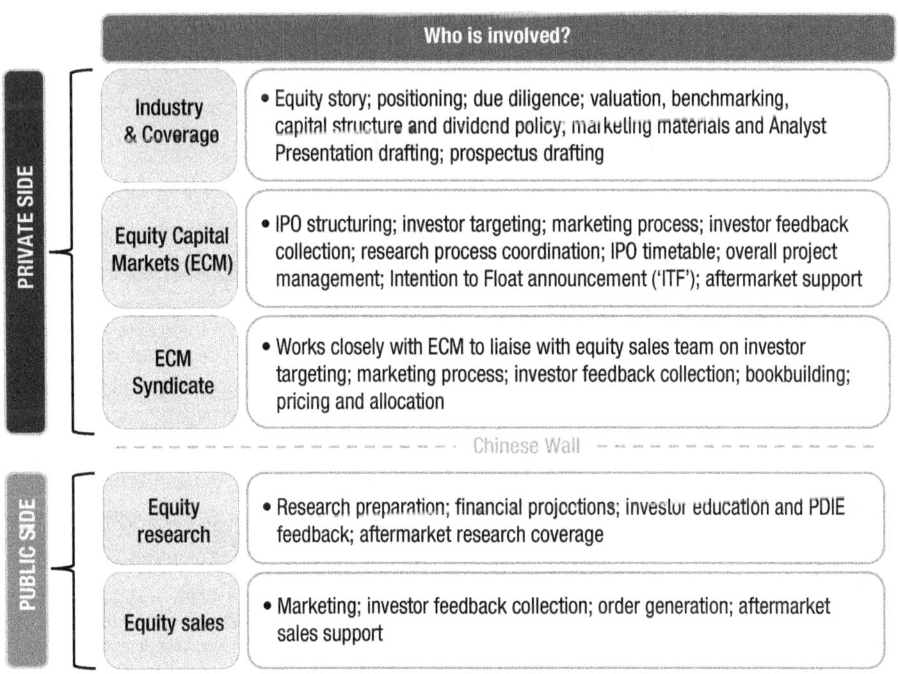

- Publicity guidelines
- Verification of roadshow and marketing materials
- Liaising with printer
- Legal opinions
- Coordination with regulators.

2. Underwriters' Counsels:
- Review of and contribution to prospectus and IOC
- Due diligence
- Underwriting agreements and other relevant legal agreements
- Research guidelines
- Review and input into publicity guidelines
- Verification exercise/review of the analyst presentation as well as other marketing presentations
- Legal opinions.

Legal counsels might be domestic (e.g. Italian), combined (international law firms with local branches), or international only.

Additional advisors complete the team of professionals that assist the Issuer and the investment bank(s) in completing the IPO process, with complementary roles that are crucial. A brief description of the main functions of each advisor follows (see **Figure 6.6**).

As discussed in section 6.2, IPOs are not free of both one-time and ongoing costs. In **Tables 6.2** and **6.3** we provide an estimation regarding an example of an Italian IPO and ongoing costs as a public company. All amounts were estimated by collect-

Figure 6.6 **Additional advisors and their main functions**

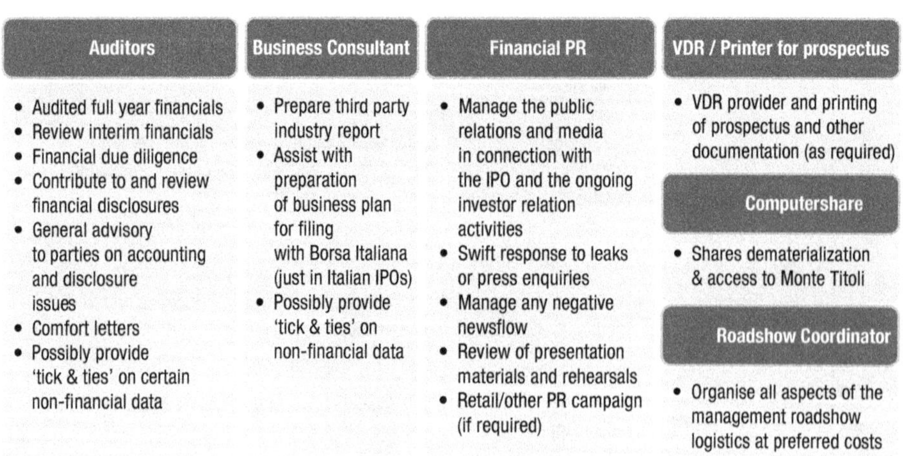

Table 6.2 One-time IPO expenses: an Italian IPO simulation*,**

Listing fees* (market authorieties e.g. Borsa Italiana, CONSOB, Monte Titoli)	€ 120,000 - € 180,000
Issuer's legal counsels	€ 400,000 - € 600,000
JGCs & Bookrunners' legal counsels	€ 300,000 - € 500,000
Auditors	€ 500,000 - € 650,000
Business consultant	€ 150,000 - € 250,000
Roadshow (consultant & live expenses)	€ 150,000 - € 250,000
PR / IR consultant	€ 50,000 - € 200,000
Financial printer & VDR	€ 25,000 - € 50,000
Retail / other advertising campaign (*optional*)	[TBC]
Representation & Warranties insurance (*optional*)	[TBC]
Other out of pocket expensens	€ 75,000 - € 150,000
Total	**~ € 1,770,000 - € 2,830,000**

* Excludes gross spread to JGCs & Bookrunners; ** Based on €0.8-1.2bn market cap. Additional marginal one-off costs towards Monte Titoli and Consob

Note: Estimated for a Reg S + 144A offering

Table 6.3 Ongoing annual expenses post listing: the Italian case simulation*,**

Audits / Interrim reviews	Expected increase limited to interim review vs status quo
Director & officer insurance	If already in place, limited additional cost to reflect Board size
Investor relations activities (marketing, travelling, investors, website)	€100,000 – €150,000
PR / IR consultant (*optional*)	€25,000 – €50,000
Listing fees** (market authorieties e.g. Borsa Italiana, CONSOB)	€34,000 – €46,000
Monte Titoli	
–Regular services and extraordinary actions (min c.€2,000)	€5,000 (depending on number and nature of corporate actions)
Costs for Independent Non-Executive Directors (INED) & governance (additional committees)	Not expected to be material / typical INED €25,000 – €40,000
Financial printer (publish annual/interim reports, shareholder notices, marketing presentations, etc.)	€25,000 – €50,000
Computershare	€5,000 one-off and €10,000 – €15,000 ongoing
Total	**~ € 229,000 - € 361,000**

* Does not include expenses involved for any corporate actions like further issuance, share buy-backs etc.;
** Based on €0.8-1.2bn market cap. Additional marginal one-off costs towards Monte Titoli and Consob

Note: Estimated for a Reg S + 144A offering

ing data from IPOs prospectuses and info from Investment Banks that have been involved in many domestic deals. Actual amounts will vary based on offering size, nature and length of market authorities review and other processes, as well as the extent to which the existing reporting and auditing can be leveraged. It is important to note that an IPO is a costly process, a "binding" decision in terms of financial commitment, also because of the structural costs that the listing generates in the issuer organization. In addition, a listed company has to continuously share information and data with market, (for instance, reporting on a quarterly basis). That's why so many ideal candidates for an IPO avoid approaching the market; they don't want to incur these kinds of controls and costs. Let's say sometimes the market is an "uncomfortable" partner, particularly for those companies that are family-owned, which generate robust cashflow and have strong growth potential even without the support of equity capital markets.

In **Figure 6.7**, we provide an illustrative example of listing and admission fees regarding the Italian stock exchange. Borsa Italiana fees mainly comprise: (1) a one-time fee linked to first time admission to listing or trading, and (2) a half-yearly fee which is payable twice per year on an ongoing basis following the IPO. For both fees,

Figure 6.7 Indicative Borsa Italiana listing and admission fees as of 22 July 2020

One-time admission fee [(a)]

Fee for every €1,000,000 of capitalisation
- €180.00

Cap
- €500,000

Floor
- Capitalisation<€1bn: €35,000
- Capitalisation>€1bn: €100,000

Illustrative example

Data in Euro

Market Capitalization (A)	800,000,000	1,000,000,000	1,200,000,000
Reference market cap unit (B)	1,000,000	1,000,000	1,000,000
Implied units (C = A / B)	800	1,000	1,200
Fee for each unit (D)	180	180	180
Total one time listing fees (C x D)	**144,000**	**180,000**	**216,000**

- For MTA and MIV markets, an advance payment, corresponding to the Floor, will be due on applying for the admission procedure which is not reimbursable if the company decides not to proceed with its application for admission or the application is not formalised within three months of the fee being billed
- This fee will be billed the first time a company applying for admission submits documentation

\+

Half-yearly fee[(b)]

Fee for every €1,000,000 of capitalisation
- Capitalisation<€1bn: €22.00
- Capitalisation>€1bn: €20.00

Cap
- €215,000

Floor
- €10,000

Data in Euro

Market Capitalization (A)	800,000,000	1,000,000,000	1,200,000,000
Reference market cap unit (B)	1,000,000	1,000,000	1,000,000
Implied units (C = A / B)	800	1,000	1,200
Fee for each unit (D)	22.00	20.00	20.00
Total hal-year listing fees (E = C x D)	17,600	20,000	24,000
Total annual listing fees (F = E x 2)	**35,200**	**40,000**	**48,000**

- This fee (payable twice per year, invoiced in January and July for next 6 months) includes also the provision to Issuer of following services:
  - Network Information System technological and operational structure
  - assistance in compliance with regulatory duties, with particular reference to the management of price sensitive information
  - assistance and support in the technical management of operations of: merger / spin-off, conversion, listing of separate lines, dividend payment, split / reverse split, free allotment, financial instruments duration extension

(a) Capitalization is calculated on the basis of the offering price.
(b) Capitalization is calculated on average market cap of preceding 6 months. IPO semester waived

Source: Author's elaboration based on Borsa Italiana.

the amount to be paid varies based on market capitalization and listing segments (e.g. MTA vs AIM). In this example we consider only the MTA segment and we took the last available version of the document from Borsa Italiana website (effective from 2 January 2020, version of 22 July 2020).

6.5.3 *The listing process and timetable*

After the decision to go public is taken and the Global Coordinator(s) gets the mandate from the issuer, a series of workstreams and documents are required for listing. However, the main items that typically drive the timetable are the preparation of documents for filing, the financials, the market authorities review process of the prospectus, and the market conditions at the time of launch. **Figure 6.8** presents the key workstreams, combined with the issuer management involvement for each phase.

The IPO process usually takes around 6 months to complete, without considering pre-IPO preparation, an additional period that may last 4-6 months, where the issuer has to set-up the company organization in order to be compliant with the market requirements, once the decision to go public has been taken by the management. **Figure 6.9** provides an indicative timetable for an Italian IPO, showing the

Figure 6.8 Key workstreams and management involvement

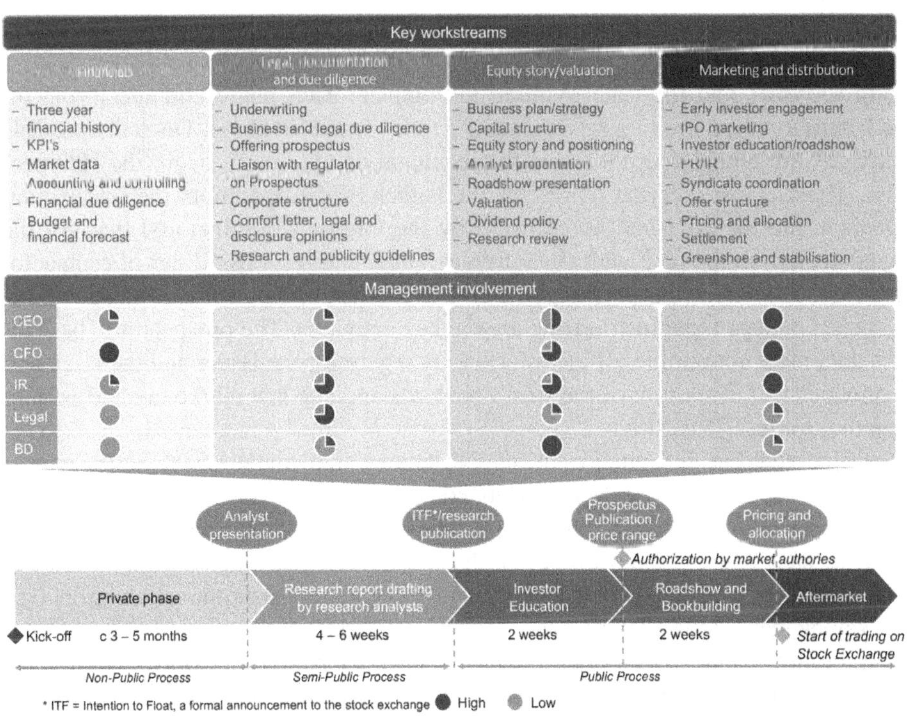

Figure 6.9 Indicative timetable for an IPO: the Italian example

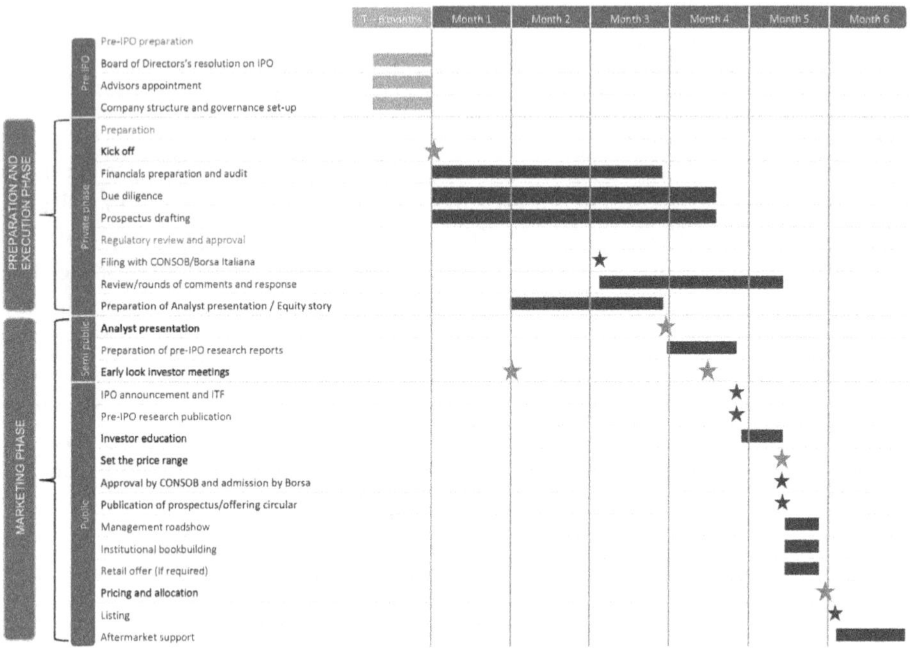

main activities and the time required to complete each phase and specifying for each activity if we are in a private, semi-public, or public phase. Once the pre-IPO activities are completed, there are the technical conditions to begin the IPO process. The kick-off meeting represents the launch of the operation: the issuer management and the advisors, coordinated by the Global Coordinator(s) that got the mandate, define the plan with the activities, time, and responsibilities of each actor involved. We are in the **preparation and execution phase**, where financials, due diligence, and **prospectus** drafting are the key activities. The prospectus is basically a document containing all the information regarding the issuer and the issue and it provides full disclosure of the firm's business and is a key marketing and protection tool for retail investors.

It also contains information about risk factors that might affect future performance, the strategy of the company, its competitive advantage, the quality and experience of the management and the use of proceeds (growth, acquisition, debt reduction, etc.) A simplified version of the prospectus, the **International Offering Circular (IOC),** is prepared in English and addressed to institutional investors (see the key elements in the **Figure 6.10**). Then there is the filing, that is the formal application to the market authority and to the stock exchange (e.g. Borsa Italiana) for listing. The latter has a period to assess the proposal and authorize the admission, and once done, the market authority (e.g. CONSOB) gives approval for publication of

Figure 6.10 IOC indicative outline and key sections

International Offering Circular - IOC (english prospectus)

Indicative outline

- Disclosure determined and governed by the Prospectus Directive
- Cover
- Placing restrictions etc
- Summary
- Risk factors
- Placing statistics
- Directors, officers and advisers
- Part I – Overview of the sector
- Part II – Information on the company's operations
  - business description
  - market opportunity
  - strategy
  - use of proceeds (if applicable)
  - dividends and dividend policy
- Part III – Corporate structure and management
  - directors and senior management
  - related party transactions
- Part IV – Operating and financial review
- Part V – Selected statistical information
- Part VI – Accountant's report
- Part VII – Capitalisation and indebtedness
- Part VII – Historical financial information
- Part VII – Expected timetable of principal events
- Part IX – Pro-forma
- Part X – The Offer
- Part XI – Additional information
- Definitions
- Glossary

Key sections

Operating and financial review ('OFR')	– Investors will look to this section for key business trends and developments – Three years financials, audited under IFRS – Potentially interim/quarterly financials for the current year and the previous year for comparison purposes – Financials must be no more than 135 days old for 144A offering into US (but can be reviewed rather than audited)
Risk factors	– Risks must be specific to the Issuer, its industry and the securities being offered – Risks must not undermine other rule requirements (e.g. working capital statement) or listing principles (e.g. maintaining adequate systems and controls)
Sector overview	– This section describes and discusses the industry's trends and the Issuer's positioning in the sector – Commonly drafted by the Global Coordinator(s)
Working capital and no significant change	– The directors must make a working capital statement that the company has sufficient working capital for the requirements of its group for the 12 months following publication of the Prospectus – In addition, the prospectus must include a statement confirming that there has been no significant change in the financial or trading position of the group since the end of the last annual or interim financial period
Pro forma	– As well as the historical financial information, the prospectus must include a 'pro forma' table, illustrating the effect of the IPO on the balance sheet and income statement – The company will be obliged to include an audited profit forecast if it has previously published one that remains current

the prospectus. The prospectus review by market authorities usually requires approximately 8-10 weeks.

After filing has been completed, and while regulators are assessing the application, the issuer and its advisors prepare the so-called **equity story**, in preparation for communicating the listing project to analysts. This is a detailed presentation of the company containing all the considerations that make investing in the issuer appealing. It is therefore an important starting point for the entire evaluation process, whose successive stages will include meetings with analysts and the production of research reports. Before the publication of the prospectus, this will be the fundamental information available to the market and investors. We can say that the equity story represents a key element in the pricing process. After the preparation and execution phase, the marketing phase starts with the analyst presentation and the preparation of the pre-IPO research report, that is subsequently published with the IPO announcement. Before this report is released, the prospective IPO is undisclosed to the public. The research report is prepared by the analysts of the Global Coordinator(s). Before the research report is released, it is typical in Europe to have one or two rounds of early look investor meetings.

The first round is in the preparation and execution phase, called "**pre-marketing**," while the second one is optional. This "early" marketing process (or "early look investor meeting") is a confidential pre-sounding of the planned IPO with selected and trusted investors (also called "pilot fishing"), that allows banks to gauge the institutional investors' feelings about the issue.[4] After the investor education phase is concluded, a price range is set. The width of the range is quite variable, ranging from 10% to 20% or more of the mid-price. The valuation reflects the sentiment assessed during the investor education meetings. After the publication of the prospectus, the roadshow begins. It takes usually just a couple of weeks, but it is a quite intense time for the issuing company and the syndicate. During this period the issuer and the investment bank(s) present the issue to institutional investors. The roadshow combines presentations to audiences of potential investors with meetings with small groups and "one-to-one" with the most important and selected investors. In this crucial phase, many investors prefer to ask their questions in the private one-to-one, to prevent other investors from free riding on the info they obtain. During the roadshow, non-binding bids are requested and the international bookbuilding opens, and the book is built. When the book is still open, a maximum IPO price is announced, and the retail offer begins (if present). Once the book is closed, the issuer and the syndicate set the offer price during the so-called "price meeting." It is a crucial moment: the issuer wants to maximise the proceeds, the investors want to get a good deal, and the global coordinator(s) is in between. In the institutional tranche the allocation is made on a discretionary basis. In contrast, within the retail tranche the allocation is usually made on a non-discretionary basis: depending on the country, it will be a scale down allocation on a pro-rata basis or a random allotment using a ballot. Pricing and share allocation trading then begins, but the work of the syndicate is not over; the final effort is represented by the aftermarket support, which consists of stabilizing or maintaining the price of shares during the first days of trading.

6.5.3.1 The marketing phase

As we have seen in the previous section, the preparation and execution phase, essentially focused on preparation of the prospectus & offering structure, due diligence, and pre-marketing activities, leads to the marketing phase, that de facto opens the doors to the heart of the listing process. **Figure 6.11** summarizes the four main steps of the marketing phase, describing the typical activities.

(1) The **analyst presentation** is a pivotal element of the IPO marketing process, led by the top management team. In several cases, it will be the first opportunity to test the overall equity story against market views. The management team (including divisional heads) will need to rehearse for it intensively in order to convey clear messages and be prepared for any questions the research analysts may have. Delivering a good

[4] The 'early' marketing process provides an overview of the company, its history, strengths, market opportunity, high level strategy, and operational and financial historical performance to a select group of 25-30 institutional investors. Thanks to this activity, it is possible to enable management to build early relationships with key thought leaders, begin the education process with investors, and gather early feedback, that is vital in structuring the IPO.

Figure 6.11 The marketing phase

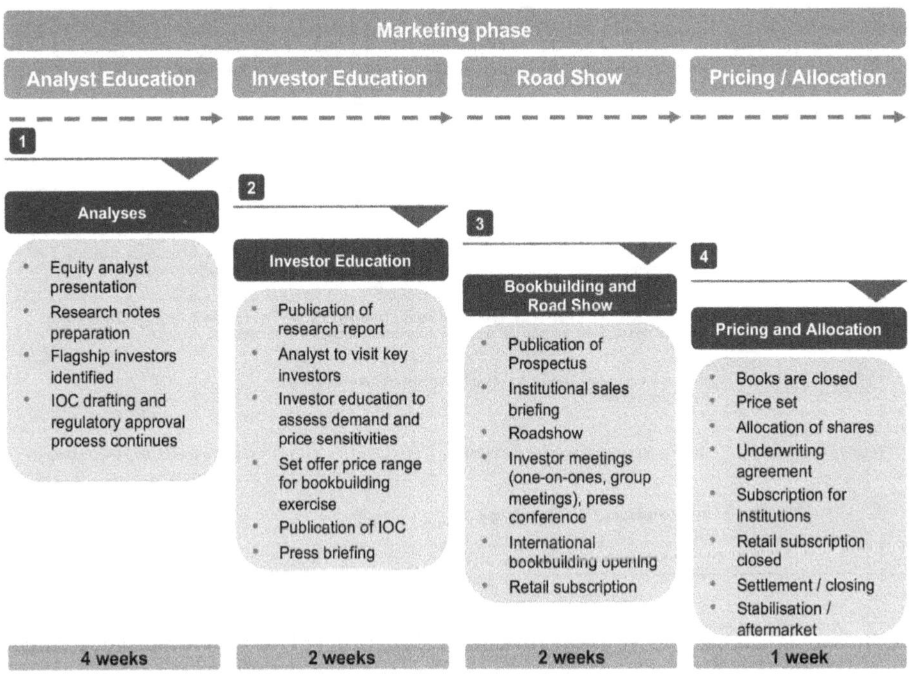

presentation will not only increase the analysts' awareness, but raise their confidence to market the story to investors. In this phase, the role of investment banks is to carry out extensive drafting of the analyst presentation, including Q&A with the most experienced senior banking professionals, conducting many rehearsals of the analyst presentation with them. **Figure 6.12** presents an illustrative agenda of a typical analyst presentation, also citing the issuer team involved for each section approached.

The valuation contents of the analysts' research reports are subject to strict restrictions, as is the guidance that issuers are allowed to give to the analysts. Early and continuous engagement with the research analysts, not just at the analyst presentation, is key to provide guidance that enables the analysts to build a model and valuation reflective of the issuer. Key areas to focus on in terms of guidance are: (i) peer group for valuation, (ii) historical trends in financials, (iii) size of, growth rates of, and market share position in the key markets in which the issuer is present or plans to expand in line with its strategy. Although the analyst presentation is a key forum for communication, follow-up or Q&A sessions may take place in person or by phone.

(2) After the publication of the research report and the IPO announcement, the syndicate **research** analysts will independently educate fund managers on the issuer invest-

Figure 6.12 Analyst presentation preliminary overview

Section	Summary of contents	Issuer team involved
Overview of the offering	Key offering terms and indicative research timetable	✓ Shareholders
Introduction to Issuer	Company overview, including key figures, main products, end-markets and historical development	✓ Top management, Business Development
Investment highlights	Overview of the key strengths of the Company and reasons for investing	✓ Top management, Business Development, Finance
Market overview	Detailed description of the addressable market, competitive landscape, Issuer positioning and key market trends	✓ Business Development, Marketing, Commercial, Operations
Business model overview	Description of Issuer business model, industry value chain, customers and suppliers, manufacturing, geographical footprint and innovation approach	✓ Operations, R&D, HR, Commercial and Marketing
Financial performance	Detailed description and commentary of key P&L, Balance Sheet and Cash Flow financials items	✓ Finance
Issuer long-term strategy	Overview of the key pillars of the growth strategy	✓ Top management, Business Development
Closing remarks and Q&A	Final summary of the equity story and Q&A	✓ Top management

ment case: this is called **Pre-Deal Investor Education (PDIE)**, an important element in disseminating the equity story to investors. It will be the first time the investor community hears the overall issuer story; therefore, credibility of research will be key for the success of the issuer's offering. The main focus from PDIE should be to obtain quality feedback in order to establish the **price range** for bookbuilding and to prepare the management for the roadshow. Syndicate analysts/sales specialists typically meet up to 200 potential institutional investors over a two-week period before the management roadshow commences, educating investors on the equity story. Rules on pre-IPO research education are different: in Europe, research analysts cannot give any recommendations with regard to the stock nor can it show any valuation on a per share basis (no target price). In the US, pre-IPO research distribution is not allowed. Notice that the research analysts are not allowed to participate in the management roadshow. **Figure 6.13** shows the typical Chinese wall existing between investment banking and research departments, in order to avoid any potential conflict of interests.

(3) The marketing process continues with the management **roadshow**, the backbone of the marketing strategy, which represents the chance for senior management to communicate the investment case to the broad investor community. The ability of the management to deliver in the roadshow meetings will drive the momentum in the book of demand. During this crucial phase, management presents the investment case and the equity story to a broad universe of investors, in "one-on-one" and group meetings. The aim is to achieve the highest meeting-to-order conversion ratio, maximising the demand and driving the pricing debate. The Global Coordinators have a

Figure 6.13 Chinese wall and information flow

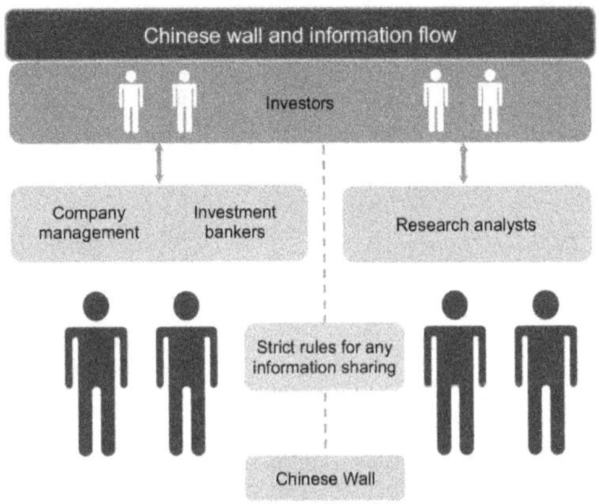

key role in preparing the roadshow presentation, in close cooperation with the issuer management. Generally, a two-week roadshow programme is established, with presentations in Europe and the US, which are tailored based on feedback obtained in the investor education process. Detailed feedback and price sensitivity will be sought from investors through the course of the roadshow. The Global Coordinators host the majority of "one-on-one" meetings, while junior syndicate members, if any, could be given the opportunity to host a limited number of "one-on-one" meetings, in order to maintain maximum motivation for the transaction. **Figure 6.14** displays the indicative agenda of a roadshow day, whereas the **Figure 6.15** provides an example of international roadshow schedule.

Figure 6.14 Indicative agenda of a roadshow day

Indicative agenda of a roadshow day	
8:00	Group breakfast
9:30	One-on-one
11:00	One-on-one
12:30	Group lunch
14:30	One-on-one
16:00	One-on-one
17:30	One-on-one
19:00	Market and bookbuild update with Global Coordinator (call)
20:00	Flight to next destination

Figure 6.15 International roadshow schedule

Management roadshow – week 1

London		London		London		Milan		Milan	
Monday		Tuesday		Wednesday		Thursday		Friday	
08:00	Group Breakfast	08:00	Group Breakfast	08:00	Group Breakfast	08:00	Group Breakfast	08:00	Group Breakfast
09:30	One-on-One	09:30	One-on-One	09:30	One-on-One	09:30	One-on-One	09:30	One-on-One
11:00	One-on-One	11:00	One-on-One	11:00	One-on-One	11:00	One-on-One	11:00	One-on-One
12:30	Group Lunch	12:30	Group Lunch	12:30	Group Lunch	12:30	Group Lunch	12:30	Group Lunch
14:00	One-on-One	14:00	One-on-One	14:00	One-on-One	14:00	One-on-One	14:00	One-on-One
15:30	One-on-One	15:30	One-on-One	15:30	One-on-One	15:30	One-on-One	15:30	One-on-One
17:00	One-on-One	17:00	One-on-One	17:00	One-on-One	17:00	One-on-One	17:00	One-on-One
					Fly to Milan				Fly to

Management roadshow – week 2

New York		New York / Boston		Geneva/Zurich		Frankfurt		Paris	
Monday		Tuesday		Wednesday		Thursday		Friday	
08:00	Group Breakfast	08:00	Group Breakfast	08:00	Group Breakfast	08:00	Group Breakfast	08:00	Group Breakfast
09:30	One-on-One	09:30	One-on-One	09:30	One-on-One	09:30	One-on-One	09:30	One-on-One
11:00	One-on-One	11:00	One-on-One	11:00	One-on-One	11:00	One-on-One	11:00	One-on-One
12:30	Group Lunch		Fly to Boston		Fly to Zurich	12:30	Group Lunch	12:30	One-on-One
14:00	One-on-One	15:00	One-on-One	15:00	One-on-One	14:00	One-on-One	14:00	One-on-One
15:30	One-on-One	16:30	One-on-One	16:30	One-on-One	15:30	One-on-One		
17:00	One-on-One	18:00	One-on-One	18:00	One-on-One	17:00	One-on-One		
			Fly to Geneva		Fly to Frankfurt		Fly to Paris		

During the roadshow period, bookrunners collect non-binding bids from institutional investors through their sales force, that solicit orders from investors, starting the so-called **bookbuilding** (see section 6.5.5.1 for a deep dive into the bookbuilding approach).

(4) At the end of the roadshow, when the book is closed, the marketing phase ends with the final IPO price-setting and shares allocation & settlement. This final part will be analysed in section 6.5.5.

6.5.4 The syndicate structure

In the previous section we referred to the Global Coordinator(s) as managing the issue. However, more than one investment bank is involved in the IPO process. Issuers select various banks with different roles that combined form a syndicate of banks in the origination (set-up and pricing), underwriting, and distribution of the offering. Typically, the structure is pyramidal: the Global Coordinator[5] (often more than one if the deal is complex, called "Joint GC") is on the top, and moving down we find banks with less important roles and responsibilities. The upper part of the syndicate has a management function, while the lower one is dedicated to distribution activity in the strict sense; the top positions benefit from higher fee levels. The syndicate is bound by a set of formal contracts ("inter-syndicate agreement") and upon the completion of the offering, it is dissolved.

The typical syndicate is composed of three parts (in order of importance) and the first two are called "the underwriting group" (see **Figure 6.16**):

1. **the managing group:** composed by the Global Coordinator(s), book-runner, and joint book-runner(s). These banks manage the syndicate and have the responsibility for the deal origination. Moreover, they underwrite the issuance and also have placement functions. The Global Coordinator(s), which gets the largest portion of fees, is responsible for: (1) due diligence, (2) roadshow, (3) bookbuilding, (4) allocation, and (5) aftermarket. It is common to see multiple bookrunners, in particular for the largest IPOs.
2. **the non-managing underwriters**: the group of banks, called co-lead managers, that underwrites part of the shares, the proportion of which is determined by the managing group under the "underwriting agreement," and executes the placement activity.

[5] The use of the term Global Coordinator to indicate the leading role in the coordination and management of the IPO is relatively widespread, especially in European and Italian practice. However, often with reference to the American market, the terms bookrunner, book manager, and lead bank are also used to define a coordination role. In other cases, bookrunner indicates a role within the syndicate and coexists with the presence of a global coordinator; it is often the same bank that covers two positions.

Figure 6.16 **The typical syndicate structure**

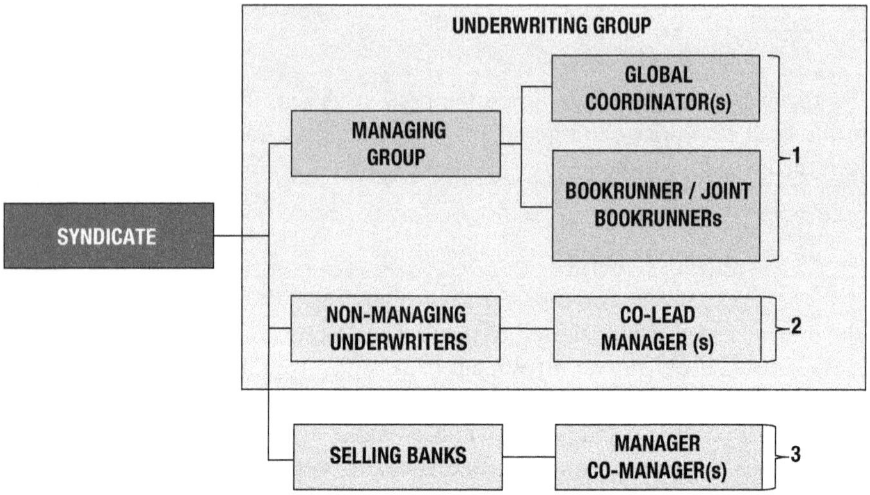

3. **the selling group:** the banks that just put their best effort into selling the shares, without underwriting them. In other words, they do not guarantee the allocation (typically they are present just in the retail tranche).

The syndicate concentration differs depending on the tranche: the retail tranche is usually more crowded and includes a selling group (up to 20 banks), while the institutional tranche usually has 3-6 banks and rarely has a selling group. Obviously, the underwriting group and the selling banks are chosen as a function of the markets and potential investors they are able to cover. Recently, IPOs have been distributed mainly to institutional investors only, with the retail tranche becoming a less used feature than in the past.

The **Figure 6.17** shows the syndicate structure of the 2007 Prysmian IPO, executed on the Milan Stock Exchange. As you can see, there are two kinds of offerings: the global institutional one (80% of underwriting) and the Italian retail one (20% of underwriting). Goldman Sachs and Mediobanca acted as joint bookrunners for the institutional offering, while the latter was also responsible for the placement of the retail tranche ("responsabile del collocamento" in Italian). Note that the two banks are also joint global coordinators with JP Morgan; indeed, an investment bank may act with many roles in the syndicate.

6.5.4.1 The functions

Why would an investment bank invite others and share its business? To reduce risks is probably the main reason, and around this key element, we can identify the following points:

Figure 6.17 The Prysmian 2007 IPO: the syndicate structure

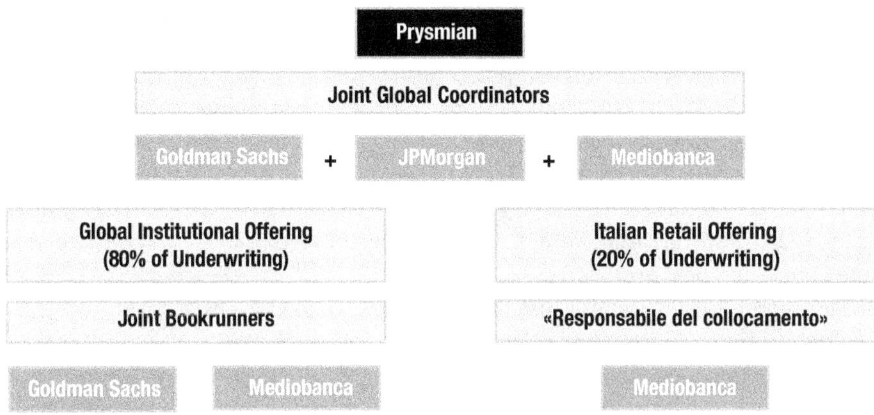

Source: Author's elaboration based on IPO prospectus – Borsa Italiana website

- it needs to share the capital commitment necessary to underwrite the security issue;
- it needs to share the marketing effort to place the shares;
- it needs to share expertise and skills to price the shares more accurately;
- it needs to establish business relations since those invited to the syndicate will likely invite it when they win future IPO mandates.

Sometimes it is the issuer that desires to include a specific investment bank(s) in the syndicate, usually for related business purposes.

In theory, there are several formulas of syndicate, typically based on different levels of commitment. The most common are three: (1) **best effort**, (2) **standby underwriting**, (3) and **firm commitment underwriting**. In each case, the issuer selects the banks and enters into an underwriting agreement, but with a different guarantee commitment by the syndicate. Under a best effort contract, the syndicate makes its best effort to sell the offered shares and the issuer gets its capital net of underwriter compensation (called "gross spread") as each share is sold. In investment banking jargon, it is a "commitment to procure purchasers." The syndicate's responsibilities are managing the issue, from the origination phase, through the marketing and up to the distribution/selling and final settlement. The syndicate is not liable for any unsold securities. Most of the IPOs are conducted under this framework, with the other options representing a divergence from market standards. Under a standby underwriting agreement, the syndicate agrees to purchase whatever shares remain after it has sold all of the shares it can to the public. In order to guarantee the amount received through the issue, the company gets a backstop from the syndicate, a form of insurance. Under a firm commitment contract (also called a "bought deal"), the underwriters buy the security from the issuer and sell them to the public. The banks guarantee all of the issuer's money right away. The issuer gets its proceeds immediately (net of underwriters' compensation) and the risk of distribution is shouldered by the syndicate members. The investment banks underwrite, manage, and sell the issue. Due to the potential high risk of a firm commitment contract, the underwriters often insist on including a market-out clause in the underwriting agreement. This clause allows the syndicate members to be free from their obligation to purchase all of the securities in case there is a development that impairs the quality of the issue. Poor market conditions, though, are not a qualifying condition. One example of when a market-out clause might be invoked is if the issuer were a biotech company and the FDA (Federal Drug Administration – the US Authority) just denied approval of the company's new drug.

Market practice, especially in European IPOs, is to use "best effort" contracts: given the primary nature of the offering with no reference market price before bookbuilding is commenced, banks involved in the syndicate usually commit to procure purchasers and distribute shares on the market. In fact, the deal is only underwritten once the syndicate knows there is enough demand for the shares on offer. If there is insufficient demand on the planned pricing day, the offering price is reduced, or the size of the offer is scaled down. If it is not possible to reach the minimum offer size, the offering is abandoned. In financial jargon, this kind of syndicate is also called soft underwriting. In contrast, considering the secondary offerings, described in the next chapter, the fully underwritten formula (or "backstop formula") is common for rights issues and may also be applied for Accelerated Bookbuilding (ABB).

The official version of a listing prospectus, including deal terms, is usually available only after the closing of the transaction, while a draft of the prospectus is distributed to investors during the roadshow. Such a draft contains all the key terms of the offer still in brackets (number of shares to be sold, price per share, etc.) while all the other information provided are then confirmed in the final version. In financial jargon, such a draft version of the prospectus is called a "Red Herring," as the front page shows a bold red disclaimer stating that the document may still be subject to amendments. It may also be referred to as a "pathfinder" version.

Figure 6.18 shows the front page of the prospectus for the IPO of Knorr-Bremse, the second-largest German IPO in 2018 (3.9 billion euros in proceeds from the sale of a 30 percent stake went to the owners Heinz Hermann Thiele and his daughter). The syndicate structure is shown, where the Joint Global Coordinators (Deutsche Bank, JP Morgan and Morgan Stanley) also act as joint bookrunners. **Figure 6.19** reports the underwriting agreement, with the number of shares each bank commits to underwriting, after the closing of the bookbuilding. Note that section 20.4, "Termination/Indemnification," states that:

> the underwriting agreement provides that the underwriters may under certain circumstances terminate the underwriting agreement, including after the shares have been allotted and listed, up to delivery and settlement. Grounds for termination include in particular: (1) a material adverse change in the economic position of the Company or the Knorr-Bremse Group or (2) an event that has material adverse effects on the financial

Figure 6.18 The Knorr-Bremse IPO prospectus

KNORR-BREMSE

Prospectus
for the initial public offering
in the Federal Republic of Germany and in the Grand Duchy of Luxembourg

of

35,043,479 bearer shares with no par value from the holdings of the Selling Shareholder, of

8,060,000 bearer shares with no par value from the holdings of the Selling Shareholder, with the number of shares to be actually placed with investors subject to the exercise of an Upsize Option upon decision of the Selling Shareholder, in consultation with the Joint Global Coordinators on the date of pricing, and of

up to 5,256,521 bearer shares with no par value from the holdings of the Selling Shareholder to cover potential over-allotments,

and at the same time

for the admission to trading on the regulated market segment (*regulierter Markt*) of the Frankfurt Stock Exchange (*Frankfurter Wertpapierbörse*) with simultaneous admission to the sub-segment of the regulated market with additional post-admission obligations (Prime Standard) of the Frankfurt Stock Exchange (*Frankfurter Wertpapierbörse*)

of

161,200,000 bearer shares with no par value (existing share capital)

— each such share with a notional value of EUR 1.00 in the share capital and with full dividend rights as from January 1, 2018 —

of

Knorr-Bremse Aktiengesellschaft
Munich, Germany

Price Range: EUR 72.00 — EUR 87.00

International Securities Identification Number (ISIN): DE000KBX1006

German Securities Code (*Wertpapier-Kenn-Nummer*) (WKN): KBX100

Common Code: 186559398

Trading Symbol: KBX

Joint Global Coordinators and Joint Bookrunners

Deutsche Bank **J.P. Morgan** **Morgan Stanley**

Joint Bookrunners

Berenberg **COMMERZBANK** **UBS Investment Bank** **UniCredit Bank AG**

The date of the Prospectus is September 28, 2018

Source: issuer's website.

Figure 6.19 The Knorr-Bremse IPO underwriting agreement

20. UNDERWRITING

20.1. Subject of and Arrangements on Underwriting

The Company, the Selling Shareholder, Ursus and each of the Underwriters have entered into an underwriting agreement with respect to the offer and sale of the shares offered hereby (the Underwriting Agreement) on September 28, 2018.

In the Underwriting Agreement, the Underwriters have agreed to acquire a total of 35,043,479 Base Shares as well as up to 8,060,000 Additional Base Shares to the extent the Upsize Option is exercised and up to 5,256,521 Over-Allotment Shares from the holdings of the Selling Shareholder, with a view to offering them to investors in the Offering, subject to certain conditions. The Underwriters have agreed to remit to the Selling Shareholder the purchase price for its Base Shares and its Additional Base Shares, if and to the extent the Upsize Option is exercised and, in addition, to remit to the Selling Shareholder the purchase price for the Over-Allotment Shares being sold, if and to the extent the Greenshoe Option is exercised, in case of the Base Shares and the Additional Base Shares at the time the shares from the holdings of the Selling Shareholder are delivered and in case of the Over-Allotment Shares one day after the Greenshoe Option is exercised.

The following table presents the percentage of Base Shares, Additional Base Shares and Greenshoe Shares that will or may be purchased by the respective Underwriter pursuant to the Underwriting Agreement:

Underwriter	Maximum number of Base Shares to be purchased	Maximum number of Additional Base Shares to be purchased	Maximum number of Greenshoe Shares to be purchased	Percentage of purchased Base Shares, Additional Base Shares and Greenshoe Shares(*) (in %)
Deutsche Bank Aktiengesellschaft Mainzer Landstraße 11-17 60329 Frankfurt am Main, Germany Joint Global Coordinator and Joint Bookrunner	8,760,871	2,015,000	1,314,131	25.00%
J.P. Morgan Securities plc 25 Bank Street, Canary Wharf London, E14 5JP, U.K. Joint Global Coordinator and Joint Bookrunner	8,760,870	2,015,000	1,314,131	25.00%
Morgan Stanley & Co. International plc 25 Cabot Square, Canary Wharf London, E14 4QA, U.K. Joint Global Coordinator and Joint Bookrunner	8,760,870	2,015,000	1,314,131	25.00%
Joh. Berenberg, Gossler & Co. KG Neuer Jungfernstieg 20 20354 Hamburg, Germany Joint Bookrunner	2,190,217	503,750	328,532	6.25%
COMMERZBANK Aktiengesellschaft Kaiserstraße 16 60311 Frankfurt am Main, Germany Joint Bookrunner	2,190,217	503,750	328,532	6.25%
UBS Limited 5 Broadgate London, EC2M 2QS, U.K. Joint Bookrunner	2,190,217	503,750	328,532	6.25%
UniCredit Bank AG Arabellastraße 12 81925 Munich, Germany Joint Bookrunner	2,190,217	503,750	328,532	6.25%
Total	35,043,479	8,060,000	5,256,521	100.00%

(*) Assuming the placement of the maximum number of Offer Shares (*i.e.*, assuming full exercise of the Upsize Option and full exercise of the Greenshoe Option).

The Offering comprises a public offering in Germany and Luxembourg and private placements in certain jurisdictions outside Germany. In the United States, the Offer Shares will be offered and sold only to Qualified

Source: IPO prospectus on issuer's website.

markets in Germany, the U.K. or the US If the underwriting agreement is terminated, the offering will not take place, in which case any allotments already made to investors will be invalidated and investors will have no claim for delivery.

This "market-out" clause features in all underwriting agreements between banks and issuers, protecting the syndicate against sudden adverse changes in market. The underwriting agreement is also used to split commissions between the syndicate participants, based on the stake each bank commits to purchasing. In the Knorr example, the three Global Coordinators underwrite 75% of the offer, while the remaining 25% is divided equally among the other four joint bookrunners, that having a "minor" role in the syndicate, get lower fees.

Looking at the more technical features of the IPO, we could state that the three main functions of the syndicate are the **origination, underwriting**, and **placement**. But if we go beyond this technical classification of the syndicate's activities, the question we must ask is: why is an IPO executed by a syndicate instead of a sole investment bank? Trying to answer this question, it is possible to identify the "economical" functions of the syndicate, which may not be carried out by a single investment bank, and vice versa, in a syndicate formula, are performed perfectly. The four different functions are:

1. **Information**
   The key element of an IPO is the price setting, that is based on valuation methods, but also on determining the market's interest in the offering.[6] Different banks cover different clients, thus conveying different information. As we have seen in the execution phase, pre-marketing early look meetings take place in order to get initial feedback and feelings about the IPO, from selected potential investors. The information contribution is very important in defining the price range, that is the base of roadshow and the bookbuilding process. The valuation methods are considered less discriminant, because they are market practice and usually more banks don't add significant value to the final result, while the composition and mix of the banks forming the syndicate might be a relevant aspect regarding the investors' feedbacks. In fact, each bookrunner has its specific characteristics: some may be focused on institutional clients, others have a better sales force or are stronger in a certain geographical area, etc. In conclusion, it follows that a key role of the Global Coordinator is to strengthen as much as possible the syndicate's ability to provide information.

2. **Certification**
   Another important function of the syndicate is to certify the quality of the issuer, meaning that reputable investment banks in the syndicate reduce uncertainty and

[6] "[...] pricing an IPO is "part art and part science." The science is using comparable traded companies to assign a price to the IPO. The art is determining the market's interest in the offering." (s.A. Corwin, P. Schultz, "The Role of IPO Underwriting Syndicates: Pricing, Information Production, and Underwriter Competion," *Journal of Finance*, February 2005, p. 448).

underpricing. The Global Coordinator and other bookrunners put their reputation in the deal, that may be damaged if they are involved in mispriced IPOs. Reputation is a crucial element if we consider that an IPO is characterized by asymmetric information; that is why investors often base their investment decisions more on the reputation of the investment banks involved than on the valuation of the issuer. The syndicate faces a trade-off during the price setting: overpricing vs the underpricing. In the first case, the advantage is for the issuers, creating financial damage to the investors, while in the second case the contrary is true. In both hypotheses, the investment banks incur a reputational problem, because their name is associated with unsuccessful deals, considerably reducing the probability of being selected by potential new issuers in the future. After these assumptions, we can now understand why league tables are so important for investment banks: the higher the ranking, the more likely they are to get new mandates.

3. **Research**
   Research services (i.e. analyst coverage) are usually provided by syndicate members in the aftermarket. This is important for the issuer because the analyst's coverage guarantees trading activities and thus liquidity for the securities on the secondary market. Usually, investment banks with top-ranked research teams are more likely to be included in a syndicate.

4. **Market making**
   Market makers[7] provide continuous trading activity for the shares of the listed company, generating a fundamental feature for any stock: liquidity. Especially when the IPO is executed in a quote-driven market (i.e. NASDAQ), the bookrunner is crucial as a market maker, together with the other syndicate's members, that play the same key role in market making. In conclusion, a possible effect is that an investment bank with no market marking division (or with a low-ranked one) has less opportunities to be appointed to the syndicate, because of the lack of aftermarket support in providing liquidity.

6.5.4.2 Fees

In equity offerings, the syndicate receives a fee, also called "gross spread." This amount depends on the issue characteristics and varies across countries. First of all, the riskier the securities offered, the higher the percentage charged by the underwriter(s). The information asymmetry and the difficulties in price-setting explain why investment bank fees are much higher in IPOs than in bond offerings, for example

[7] A market maker is a dealer available to trade a security on its own account on a continuous basis at the quoted price. The role of this financial intermediary is to promote liquidity for a security, buying and selling it for one's own account. Market makers may also be called "specialists" on the organized stocks exchanges.

(where the pricing is usually easier if the issue is rated), or in some Seasoned Equity Offerings.

Some market trends: in the US we observe higher fees than in Europe (up to 7%), while large privatizations are usually charged lower fees (below 1%). On average, fees applied on larger IPOs (above EUR 1bn) are in the range of 1.5% to 2.5%, whereas medium-sized IPOs (from EUR 50mn to EUR 600mn) have an average gross fee of c. 3.5% (from 2.7% up to 4.5%[8]). It is important to stress that these percentages are to be meant just as a general benchmark; in fact, the gross spread may vary deal by deal, depending on different factors.

Usually, fees applied in equity offerings have three components: management fee (20%), underwriting fee (20%), and selling concession (60%). This 20-20-60 is a market standard, but sometimes significant variations from these standard percentages are observed. **The management fees** compensate the global coordinator(s) for structuring the offering, drafting the prospectus, organizing the syndicate, managing the roadshow, dealing with regulators, overseeing the due diligence, etc. **The underwriting fee** is meant to compensate the underwriting group for the underwriting risks, which anyway are minimal (for example, thanks to the "market-out" clause already mentioned, and the bookbuilding procedure, that will be analysed in the next sections). As we have seen in Figure 6.19, after deducting all expenses, this fee is shared according to the number of shares underwritten. Lastly, **the selling concession** is split among syndicate members, based on the number of shares underwritten by single bank.[9] In practice, the selling concession is paid to the bank under pre-agreed economics, that usually match the same underwriting percentage, thus not considering the number of shares actually allocated by the bookrunners. In fact, it is important to note that a bookrunner has significant discretion in the allocation of shares, and for this reason, it would be very difficult to allocate orders if each bank had a selling concession directly related to the shares actually sold (the syndicate members would spend a lot of time in discussions, in order to get a higher allocation percentage, equivalent to higher selling commissions). Some institutional clients tend to split their orders among the syndicate members for two main reasons: (i) to be sure to receive a satisfying allocation, and (ii) to keep good relationships with the investment banks (necessary in order to receive decent allocations in future IPOs).

Geddes (2003) reported that a banker once said: "For every minute we spend negotiating the gross spread with the client, we probably spend well over 20 times negotiating the split of the gross spread among the various underwriters and co-managers."

Investment Banks usually put a clause in the contract that gives the issuer the discretion to pay underwriters an extra sum, called the "incentive fee," if the listing goes well.

---

[8] Italian IPO Prospectuses as of September 2020, on MTA since 2012 and with a deal size of EUR 50-600mn, excluding privatizations.

[9] In retail tranches, if any, selling banks get just a portion of selling concession based on the shares sold. Also in this case, a minimum amount of fees can be pre-agreed.

Table 6.4 Fee distribution: a simplified example with institutional tranche only

		Underwritten shares %		20% Management Fee	20% Underwriting Fee	60% Selling concession	Total fees
UNDERWRITING GROUP / MANAGING GROUP	Joint Global Coordinator 1	30%	15.000.000	2.500.000 €	1.500.000 €	4.500.000 €	8.500.000 €
	Joint Global Coordinator 2	30%	15.000.000	2.500.000 €	1.500.000 €	4.500.000 €	8.500.000 €
	Joint Bookrunner 1	10%	5.000.000		500.000 €	1.500.000 €	2.000.000 €
	Joint Bookrunner 2	10%	5.000.000		500.000 €	1.500.000 €	2.000.000 €
	Joint Bookrunner 3	10%	5.000.000		500.000 €	1.500.000 €	2.000.000 €
	Co-Lead Manager 1	2,50%	1.250.000		125.000 €	375.000 €	500.000 €
	Co-Lead Manager 2	2,50%	1.250.000		125.000 €	375.000 €	500.000 €
	Co-Lead Manager 3	2,50%	1.250.000		125.000 €	375.000 €	500.000 €
	Co-Lead Manager 4	2,50%	1.250.000		125.000 €	375.000 €	500.000 €
	Total	100%	50.000.000	5.000.000 €	5.000.000 €	15.000.000 €	**25.000.000 €**

To illustrate how the fee distribution mechanism works, consider the simplified example provided in **Table 6.4**. The assumptions are:

- total shares offered: 50mn (including Green Shoe shares, analysed in the sections below);
- institutional tranche only (no selling banks in the syndicate);
- offer price: EUR 20 per share;
- total proceeds: EUR 1bn (50mn shares × 20 EUR);
- fees: 2.5%;
- total fees: EUR 25mn;
- fee structure: a standard 20-20-60%.

Under the above assumptions, the example shows how each syndicate member receives a portion of fees in relation to its role. Note that:

- the two Joint Global Coordinators get a higher amount of the total fees, which is why this role is the most prestigious one in a syndicate;
- each syndicate member guarantees the proceeds related to the number of shares it underwrites;
- the 20% management fee, corresponding to EUR 5 million, is distributed among the two Joint Global Coordinators;
- the 20% underwriting fee (another EUR 5 million) is distributed between the underwriting group members according to the proportion of shares underwritten. Note that distribution of the underwriter fee is totally independent from the number of shares actually sold by each syndicate member;

- the selling concession (EUR 15 million) is distributed according to sales credited to each bank of the syndicate, in this case equal to the underwritten share percentage.

6.5.4.3 Stabilisation

Once shares are listed and start to trade, their price movements will depend on a variety of factors: as happens for any share, some of these factors are systemic (e.g. market sentiment, economic growth, etc.) while others are idiosyncratic (e.g. company results, equity research publications, etc.). However, some features of the IPO process allow for minimising the impact of such factors straight after the listing, resulting in a price stabilisation mechanism which, either directly or indirectly, helps to reduce the short-term volatility of the share price. The main stabilisation techniques include the following:

- Pricing stabilisation via overallotment and Greenshoe option;
- Lock-up and bonus share.

The US Securities and Exchange Commission (SEC) defines stabilisation as "the buying of a security for the limited purpose of preventing or retarding a decline in its open market price in order to facilitate its distribution to the public."

6.5.4.3.1 Overallotment and Greenshoe option

When an IPO is successful, the overall demand for shares is generally higher than the offering size, with the IPO book being oversubscribed. As a result, the banking syndicate has to scale back at least some of the original orders. To compensate at least partially for the extra demand, one or more Global Coordinators within the banking syndicate can decide to act as a stabilisation agent and implement a strategy called "overallotment."

Overallotment is the allocation of extra shares on top of the base IPO size: practically speaking, it is a "short" position of the stabilisation agent towards IPO subscribers, since the stabilisation agent does not have the ownership of such additional shares and the stabilisation agent is responsible for the additional amount offered. The overallotment is generally capped at 15% of the IPO size and is technically implemented via stock lending: the issuer and/or the selling shareholder(s) lend the overallotment shares to the stabilisation agent, with a maturity of up to 30 days (see **Figure 6.20**).

As a result of the short position established via the overallotment, the stabilisation agent is then able to implement a stabilisation strategy: specifically, if the shares come under pressure when they start to trade, the stabilisation agent can buy them in the market to reduce its short position, and consequently, stabilise the share price via such purchases. Given the sensitivity of the stabilisation process, there are clear and specific regulatory issues to be taken into account, including the following:

Figure 6.20 Overallotment mechanics

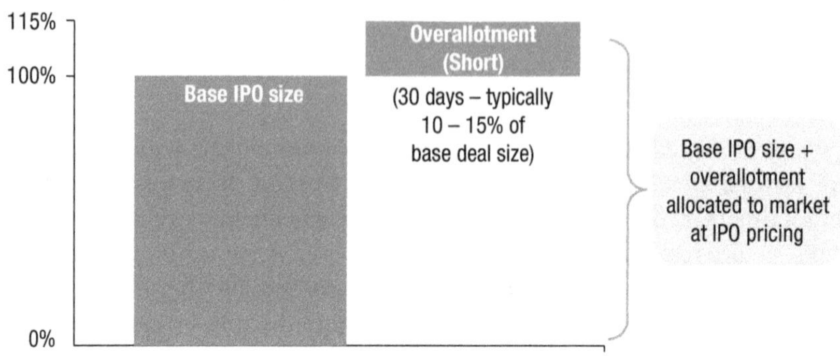

- Size and duration: overallotment typically capped at 15% of the base issue size, stabilisation period up to 30 days;
- Buying price subject to restrictions: has to be equal to or lower than issue price and cannot lead to upward pressure on the share price.

However, what if the stabilisation agent implements the overallotment strategy and the share price is above the IPO price? In such a situation, the short position would cost money; the stabilisation agent would not implement a stabilisation strategy, but would still have to buy back shares in the market at a price above the IPO price at which the shares were sold. In order to prevent such a loss-making scenario, a greenshoe option can be added to the IPO terms.

A greenshoe option, also referred to as an overallotment option, is a call option sold by the issuer and/or selling shareholder(s) to the stabilisation agent for an amount of shares up to the overallotment at a price equal to the IPO price. If the shares trade above the IPO price, the short position of the stabilisation agent generated by the overallotment can be covered by exercising that option. If the greenshoe option is not exercised (either partially or fully), the whole short is bought back in the market and only the initial IPO size remains outstanding.

The term "greenshoe option" is a jargon term which has become technical and stems from the first company implementing such a strategy: Green Shoe Corporation, which in its IPO process included such a technique for the first time.[10] As a result, overallotment is sometimes inappropriately referred to as "greenshoe," whereas the greenshoe option is effectively an overallotment option (i.e. a call option on the overallotment size).

The post-IPO share price can be more volatile than expected: trading patterns and

[10] The Green Shoe Manufacturing Company (today part of Stride Rite) was a U.S. company which in February 1963 conducted a public offering, using the overallotment option for the first time.

Figure 6.21 Stabilisation scenarios in the aftermarket

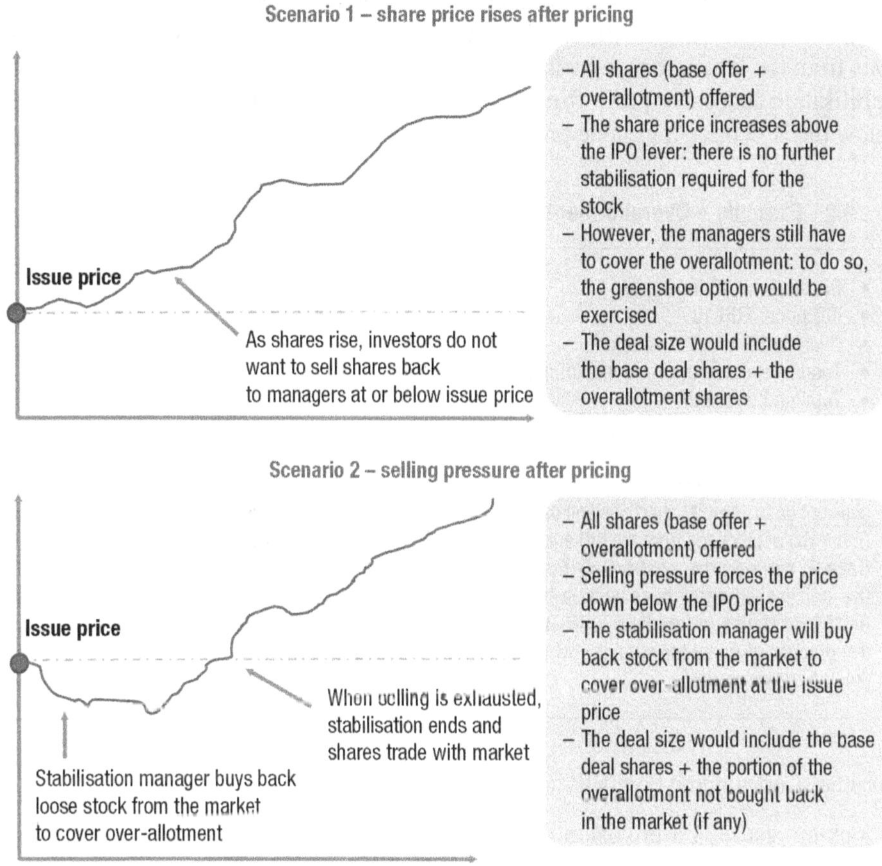

normal market volumes still have to be established, and simultaneously, some investors might want to realise a quick profit while others might have been scaled down in the allocation process and could opt for increasing their holdings. Moreover, market volatility itself could bring systemic shifts in the share price from the IPO level. Therefore, implementing an overallotment strategy, and potentially adding a greenshoe option, presents various advantages, including the following:

- Providing support for the issue immediately after the offering;
- Increasing confidence for the issuer and/or selling shareholder(s), the listed entity and investors participating in the IPO process;
- Improving the success probability of the offering;
- Enabling a safety net against temporary market turbulence;
- Enhancing the ability to improve pricing.

Figure 6.21 describes two alternative stabilisation scenarios in the aftermarket. From the revenue perspective of the stabilisation agent, there is a difference between exercising the greenshoe option and buying back the overallotment size in the market at a price below the IPO level. In the first case, the stabilisation agent will generate revenues from the fees associated with the extra size placed, while in the second case, the stabilisation agent will profit from buying back the overallotment at an average price below the IPO price (i.e. same profit mechanism as a short sale).

Box 6.2 **Example – Overallotment/greenshoe**

- Base offer: 100mn shares
- IPO price: EUR 10
- Overallotment: 10mn shares
- Total offer (base offer + overallotment) 110mn shares
- Total proceeds EUR 1.1bn
- IPO fees: 5%

Case 1: market price post-IPO @ EUR 11. In this case, the stabilisation agent fully exercises the greenshoe option to cover its short position of 10mn shares. The final result will be 110mn shares of free float, EUR 1.1bn of proceeds from the IPO and EUR 55mn in fees from the IPO process (5% of EUR 1.1bn).
Case 2: market price post-IPO @ EUR 9. In this case, the greenshoe option is not exercised and the stabilisation agent buys back in the market 10mn shares @ EUR 9/share. The final result will be 100mn shares of free float, EUR 1bn of proceeds from IPO and EUR 60mn in revenues from the IPO process given by the sum of EUR 50mn fees (5% of EUR 1bn) and EUR 10mn trading profit (EUR (10-9) x 10mn shares).

6.5.4.3.2 Lock-up and bonus share

A lock-up clause is a provision which regulates and limits the ability to offer additional equity of the company shortly after the IPO, in order to avoid the share price disruption which would be generated by such an event. Lock-ups are generally set between 180 and 365 days, and the longer the period, the more the clause might be seen by the market as a signal of confidence towards the future of the company. The overall lock-up clause can involve one or more of the following:

- Issuer lock-up: immediately post-IPO, investors would not expect any additional equity offering from the company and an issuer lock-up clause formalises such expectation. Generally, the issuer lock-up is 180 days long;
- Management lock-up: in the case of managers who are also shareholders in the company, a management lock-up clause can be implemented to signal support for the strategy, belief in the long-term vision of the company and alignment of interests with those of investors. Lock-up for management tends to be longer and is generally set at 360-365 days.
- Shareholder lock-up: in order to limit the potential amount of selling flow on top of the offering, a shareholder lock-up might be implemented to limit the ability of

selling shareholders to sell additional shares. Typically, shareholder lock-up is set at 180 days.

While there are no clear indications about the ability of lock-up to make the share performance more stable following the IPO, it is interesting to notice on average a negative impact on share price around the lock-up expiration date as investors price in the increased probability of a placing in the market by one or more of the locked-up entities.

Another indirect technique to achieve higher stability in the market following the IPO is the use of a bonus share provision when the IPO is a retail offering (i.e. not limited to institutional investors). A bonus share provision is a clause which offers free additional shares to retail investors (and potentially to employees) if they retain ownership in the shares acquired via the IPO process for a determined period of time. The bonus share provision encourages a longer holding period by the retail investor base, increases the appetite for the offering and reduces selling pressure immediately after-market; at the same time, it is possible to experience future downward pressure in the share price when the holding period expires.

Box 6.3 Enel Green Power IPO and bonus share provision

In November 2010, Enel completed the IPO process of its green energy unit, called Enel Green Power, listing 33% of the capital on the Milan and Madrid stock exchanges. Starting from an initial price range of EUR 1.9 – 2.4, Enel had to cut the IPO price to EUR 1.6 given lower-than-expected interest from institutional investors, which took only 22% of the offering.
At the same time, however, the offering received massive interest from small retail investors: one of the key elements to achieve such support was the bonus share provision included in the offering, which granted retail investors the right to obtain one bonus share for every 20 shares held continuously for one year from the IPO. As a result, the bonus share provision helped the company to smoothly cover the offering despite lower-than-expected support from institutional investors and to achieve price stability in the after-market thanks to the stable retail investor base.

Source: Reuters website.

6.5.5 Price-setting mechanisms

The price-setting mechanisms in an IPO process are the final step in the long path from the initial equity story to setting a clear value for the offering, which includes the following moments (**Figure 6.22** summarises the valuation and IPO price discovery process):

- Corporate finance valuation;
- Indicative investor valuation;
- Research valuation range;
- Marketing range;
- Final valuation.

The process starts even before the intention to float, with a valuation analysis performed by the Corporate Finance desk of the banks involved in the IPO process, based on comparable trading metrics and fundamental valuation models. Such valuation remains confidential between the banks and the company and no information is given to the market; it is a purely indicative number for the company and its shareholders. Having received such valuation and before submitting a formal intention to float, the company generally meets with selected institutional investors which provide the banking syndicate with an indicative level at which they would be willing to place orders in the case of an IPO. Such indicative levels are considered purely indicative and subject to a variety of factors, including further refinements after the investor education process and the prevailing market conditions at the time of potential listing. At this point, the research analysts of the banking syndicate are included in the process: they prepare research reports on the company which can be used on pre-deal "investor education" meetings and which have specific and stricter compliance requirements than a traditional research report (e.g. no views on price target/specific valuation, only wide valuation range allowed).

After the investor education process has taken place and based on the feedback received during the process, if the company formally communicates its intention to float ("ITF") it has to indicate an initial price range in which it intends to sell the offered shares. The initial price range is used to market the transaction during the management roadshow and helps investors assess their actual interest in the offering by setting a floor and a ceiling to the offer price, as the final price would typically be within such a range. The price range is set as follows:

- The bottom end of the price range is set to catch the attention of major investors, creating early momentum by allowing them to focus on the equity story and not on the pure price number. It also provides a buffer against the risk of adverse systemic and/or idiosyncratic news;
- The width of the price range is generally around 20-30%. A wider range, despite giving the idea of extra comfort, could signal uncertainty and/or weakness;
- The top end of the price range should be set at a level which is demanding but still achievable in case of favourable conditions. Setting it too high means investors will disregard it and focus only on the bottom number.

The subsequent step is to actually set the IPO price via a technical pricing mechanism: bookbuilding and auction are the two most common strategies implemented to achieve price discovery.

It is important to highlight that the listing price is the key variable in an IPO process. As the uncertainty level is higher than in other capital market transactions (e.g. secondary offerings, bond issuances), the price shows the efficiency level of the primary market and is based on the ability to achieve a smooth equilibrium of interests between the issuer (and/or selling shareholders) and investors. In such respect, the banking syndicate (especially the Global Coordinator(s)/Bookrunners) has a very important role, thanks to:

Figure 6.22 Valuation and IPO price discovery process

	Corporate finance valuation (Desktop valuation)	Indicative investor valuation views	Research valuation range	Marketing range	Final valuation
Input	– Business plan	– Early-look marketing presentation, financials and guidance	– Analyst Presentation	– Investor feedback from research education	– Bookbuilding
Key considerations	– Based on comparable trading metrics and fundamental valuation – Takes into account subjective views of the sector and market – Remains confidential and information is not given to the market – Purely indicative value for the Company and shareholders	– Preliminary valuation views from accounts met in early engagement – Indicative level at which investors would be willing to place orders during bookbuilding – Subject to further refinements post research investor education process	– Research reports contain a wide fully distributed valuation range–no views of price target/specific valuation allowed – Used by syndicate analysts on the Pre-Deal Investor Education exercise	– First time the Company declares a range in which it intends to sell – Initial range used to market the transaction during management roadshow – Sets a floor and ceiling on offer price – Final price would typically be within this range	– Blends quality of new shareholder list with value for selling shareholder – The success of an IPO is measured by the level and quality of demand in the book and aftermarket performance – IPO offer price based on highest point in range where deal is 'allocable'
Public announcements			ITF	Price range	Pricing

Corporate Finance → Research Analysts → Investors

- Direct impact on the different drivers of IPO success;
- High discretion in achieving such equilibrium of interests;
- Strong sensitivity to a successful IPO for all agents involved as it improves the reputation of the banks managing the IPO process.

6.5.5.1 The bookbuilding approach

In order to set the official IPO price, the bookbuilding approach is by far the methodology most used, for various reasons, including the following three:

1. It has historically been the preferred price-setting method in the United States, and as such, it has been spread widely in Europe and Asia by the dominant presence of US Investment Banks;
2. It is considered the most efficient process in order to generate relevant price discovery information via interaction with the potential investors;
3. It combines three key element for the success of an IPO: informed pricing, discretionary allocation and the ability to select a stable investor base.

In the bookbuilding process, that takes place during the management roadshow, the banking syndicate literally builds an order book with all the orders collected from the investors via the sales & trading franchise (see **Figure 6.23**); such orders result in a demand function which links different levels of demand to different levels of IPO price, clearly with larger demand at lower prices (see **Figure 6.24**, an example of demand curve, with three alternative scenarios). Each investor can submit different kinds of orders, in different moments, revising some previous bids, or even withdrawing them.

The final IPO price will then be determined by the Bookrunners and the issuer and/or selling shareholder(s), starting from this function and also considering the potential allocation outcomes at different price levels. The demand generation process in the days before the final pricing date provides the required information on which that decision is based: capturing early orders from investors which met the company before the formal intention to float is key to create early momentum and to drive all investors interested in the IPO to place their orders, by increasing transparency towards the potential final IPO price level. **Figure 6.25** shows an example of demand generation process

The allocation process will generally be set in a way which provides a stable investor base and accommodates preferences of both the issuer/seller(s) and the banking syndicate. In this respect, the order book can also be analysed by classifying accounts into three tiers:

1. Tier 1: high quality, long term investors such as large long-only funds, sector specialists, large pension funds, sovereign wealth funds, and top tier hedge funds;
2. Tier 2: other long-only investors including generalist investors;
3. Tier 3: middle market funds, momentum driven hedge funds.

Figure 6.23 **Example of orders received by the syndicatte**

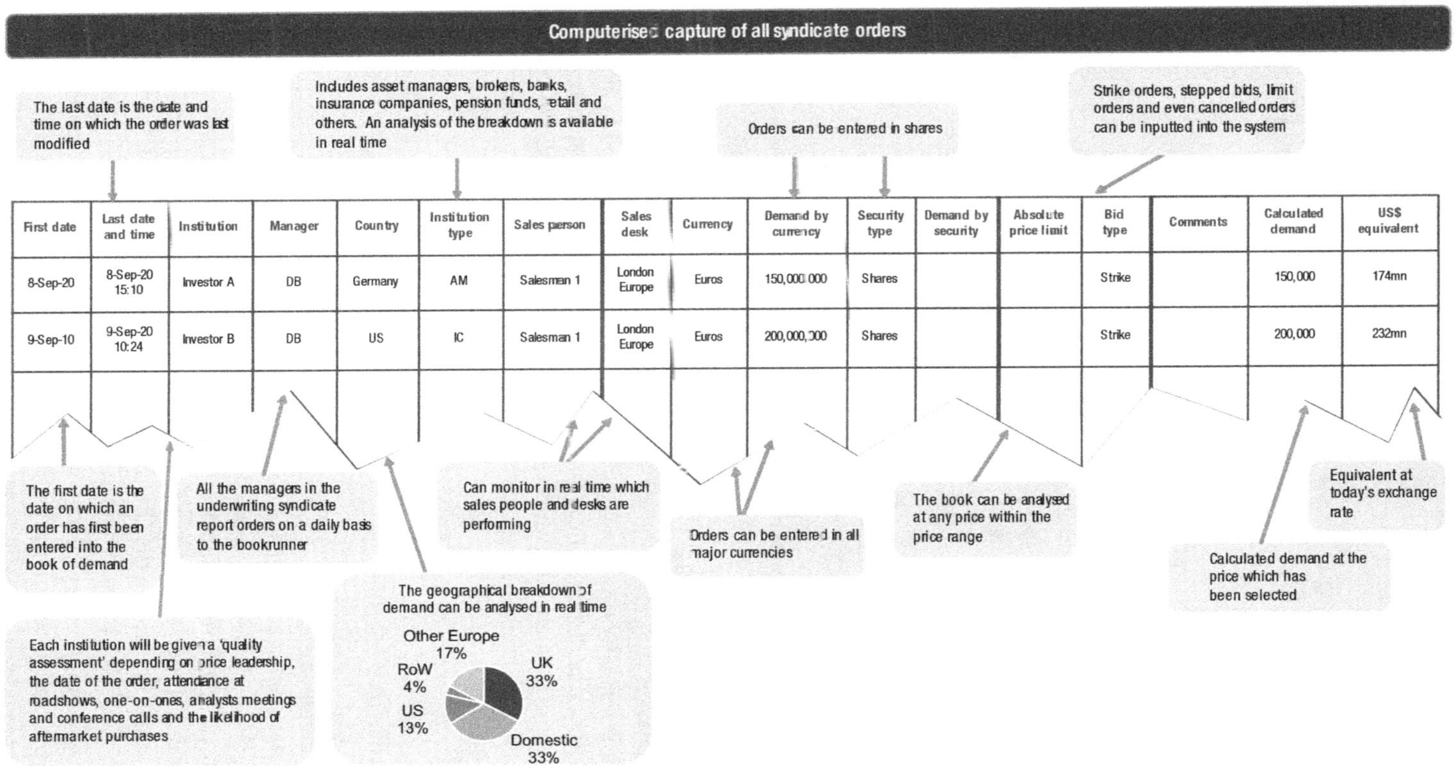

First date	Last date and time	Institution	Manager	Country	Institution type	Sales person	Sales desk	Currency	Demand by currency	Security type	Demand by security	Absolute price limit	Bid type	Comments	Calculated demand	US$ equivalent
8-Sep-20	8-Sep-20 15:10	Investor A	DB	Germany	AM	Salesman 1	London Europe	Euros	150,000,000	Shares			Strike		150,000	174mn
9-Sep-10	9-Sep-20 10:24	Investor B	DB	US	IC	Salesman 1	London Europe	Euros	200,000,000	Shares			Strike		200,000	232mn

Figure 6.24 The demand curve

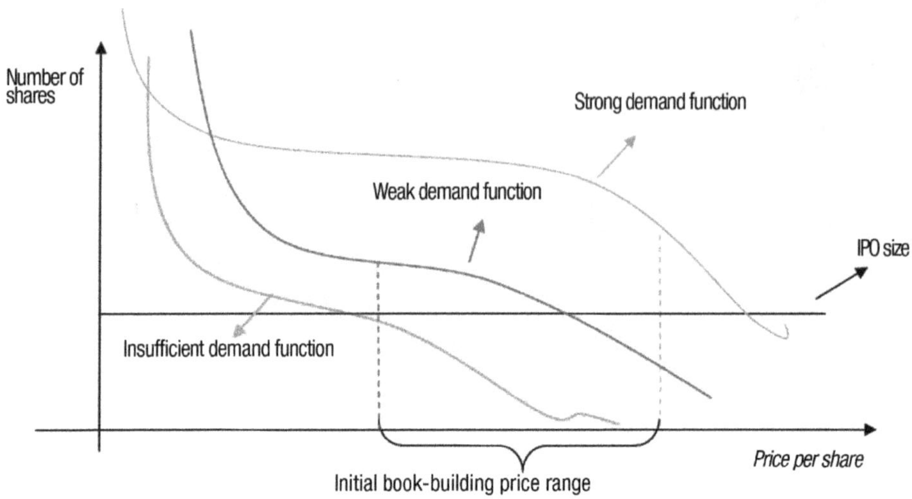

Generally, the tier 1 accounts will cover the bottom of the price range and be more price sensitive; this raises a potential trade-off between optimising the IPO price level and maximising the quality of the investor base, as setting the IPO price too high would lead to a larger share of lower quality investors with potential consequences in the aftermarket (e.g. more selling flow straight after the IPO). In a successful IPO, the book is typically oversubscribed at least at the lower end; the key is to determine the true allocable demand at the best mix between different investor tiers, in order to find an optimal balance between quality of the investor base and proceeds from the IPO process. A disciplined allocation process, therefore, should maximise the aggregate benefit in terms of:

- Offer price;
- Aftermarket performance;
- Quality of the investor base;
- Geographic diversification of the investor base;
- Split between institutional and retail orders (if applicable).

Investors clearly have an interest in buying at the lowest possible price. However, the bookbuilding process follows a peculiar pricing and allocation technique by mixing underpricing (i.e. pricing the IPO below the level where the book is just covered, for example at EUR 2.15 instead of EUR 2.30 in **Figure 6.26**) and discretionary allocation (i.e. providing better allocations to the most cooperative investors). In terms of order types, the bookbuilding process is characterized by three different bid styles. **Table 6.5** provides a simplified example of a book, that facilitates understanding:

Figure 6.25 Illustrative bookbuilding demand generation process

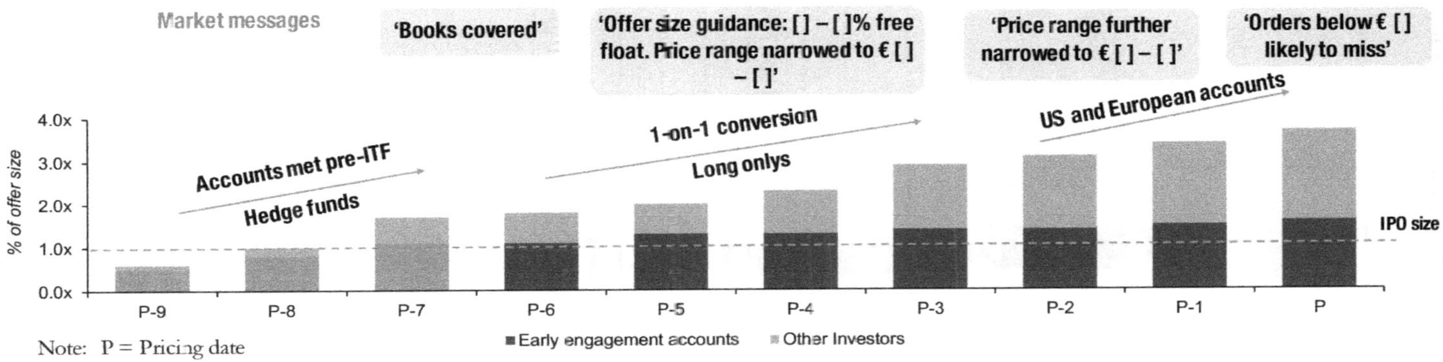

Note: P = Pricing date

Figure 6.26 Illustrative order book analysis: an example of demand at various prices

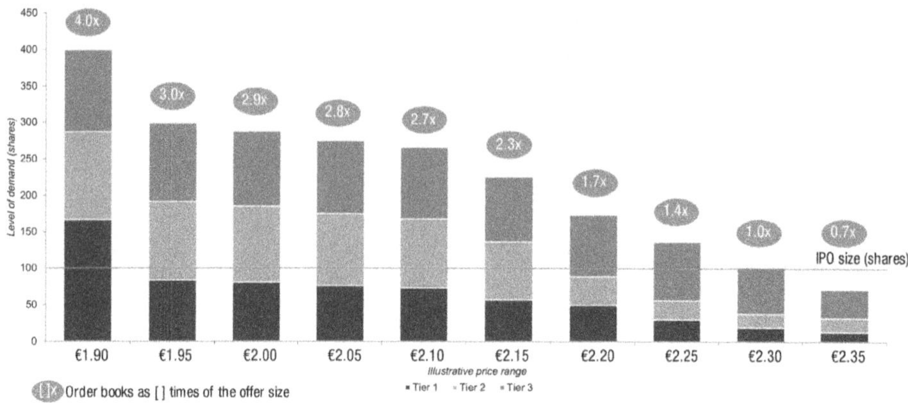

Table 6.5 A simplified example of a book

order #	Bid Quantity	Bid Type	Limit Price
1	30,000,000 USD	**Strike (currency)**	
2	20,000,000 EUR	**Strike (currency)**	
	9,000,000 EUR	**Strike (currency)**	
	5,000,000 EUR	**Strike (currency)**	
3	250,000 Shares	**Step 1**	10 €
	150,000 Shares	**Step 2**	12 €
4	300,000 Shares	**Limit**	9 €
5	200,000 Shares	**Strike**	

1. **Strike bid**: order without a price limit. An investor placing an order at strike will only signal its interest in terms of size (either notional or number of shares), implicitly committing to the final IPO price (in **Table 6.5** *orders 1 and 2* – revised twice – are currency strikes, while order 5 is a non-currency strike, because it is expressed as a number of shares).
2. **Limit bid**: order with a specific price limit. An investor placing a limit order will express an interest which is subject to the final IPO price being below a specific level; in other words, if the final IPO price is set higher than such limit, the order will be excluded from the book *(order* ***4****)*.
3. **Step bid**: multiple orders at different price levels. An investor placing a step order will express different levels of interest at different prices, with higher quantities

at lower prices; basically, it is a partial representation of its demand function. A step bid may or may not also include a size "at strike" within the various levels of interests expressed *(order* ***3****).*

A strike bid is the easiest order type to be managed, as the only potential issue lies with the amount actually allocated if the IPO is oversubscribed; at the same time, it carries the lowest level of information for the book runners. A limit order is a binary input, with a clear exclusion level preference but also with a harsh limit which can present difficulties when the IPO price is set just above such limit (imagine the following scenario: price range of EUR 72 – 88, your biggest client gives you an EUR 80 limit order for a large size, the IPO price is then set at EUR 81 but you experience difficulties in reaching the client to double-check if there is really zero interest at EUR 81). A step bid has the highest information content, but also comes with the most significant operational risk (more orders to be manually entered into the book, more orders to be amended if the client wants to change them, etc.).

As already mentioned, an IPO is generally oversubscribed and the allocation process requires a rationing exercise. While retail orders need to be allocated in a transparent and determined way (e.g. pro-rata filling), the bookrunners have some sort of discretion on allocation to institutional investors: generally, higher tier clients will see a larger allocation in terms of percentage of their original order. There are a variety of allocation drivers, including order size, order type, frequent participation in IPO transactions, nationality of the client (same/different from issuer), and whether the order was submitted directly to the bookrunners.

6.5.5.2 Auctions

The auction pricing methodology allows for pricing an IPO in a straight way, directly relying on clients' orders. While such a methodology is of significant importance in the academic world, it is actually much less frequent than the bookbuilding approach due to a variety of practical implications:

- Bookbuilding permits discretionary allocation, and as such, allows for actively designing the investor base in order to favour the most appealing shareholder mix;
- The auction bidding process often sees the winning bid being higher than the "true value" of the IPO ("winner's curse hypothesis");
- The auction bidding process can be subject to free riding as orders can be placed and filled regardless of the actual time and effort spent by the single investor with the syndicate around the IPO process.

At the same time, auctions are cheaper for the issuer and/or selling shareholder(s) as they allow for much lower remuneration for the Investment Banks involved in the listing process. Also, an auction process has the benefit of being fully transparent, while the discretionary allocation of bookbuilding could lead to a lack of transparency and potential abuse.

There are two main auction pricing approaches: the "Dutch" auction and the competitive auction. A Dutch auction is a single price auction, where every investor directly places an order for a certain amount of shares at a specific price; the highest price at which every available share can be sold becomes the single price at which all the shares are allocated to the orders, at or above such price. In a competitive auction the starting process is the same, as bids are selected in a decreasing price order until the whole offer can be covered. However, in this case, each order considered is filled at its original limit price. Given the same order book, a competitive auction increases the overall proceeds from the offering. However, a Dutch auction process could potentially lead to higher limit prices than a competitive auction given the much smaller incentive in trying to bid the lowest possible successful price.

Box 6.4 Example – Auction pricing methodologies

- Offer size: 10mn shares
- IPO pricing: auction

Investor	Bid level (EUR)	Number of Shares (mn)	Allocation (%)	Cumulative number of shares (mn)
A	13.00	1.00	100%	1.00
B	12.50	1.50	100%	2.50
C	12.00	1.00	100%	3.50
D	11.50	2.00	100%	5.50
E	11.00	2.50	100%	8.00
F	10.50	4.00	50%	12.00
G	10.00	3.50	0%	15.50
H	9.50	3.00	0%	18.50

Case 1: Dutch auction. The IPO final price is the highest single price at which the whole offer size can be covered: the 10mn shares threshold is reached at a price of EUR 10.50. Investors A, B, C, D, and E will be allocated 100% of their orders at EUR 10.50/share, while investor F will be allocated 50% of its order at the same level (i.e. the size required to reach 10mn shares). Investor G and investor H will not be allocated any shares. All shares offered at EUR 10.50, overall proceeds from the listing @ EUR 105mn.
Case 2: competitive auction. Each order is filled at its original price until the offer size is covered, ranking bids in decreasing price order. Investors A, B, C, D, and E will be allocated 100% of their orders, each at its limit price; investor F will be allocated 50% of its order at EUR 10.50/share (i.e. the size required to reach 10mn shares). Investor G and investor H will not be allocated any shares. Average offer price EUR 11.525, overall proceeds from the listing @ EUR 115.25mn.

Although much less frequent than the bookbuilding process, auctions have seen a good level of interest from a specific type of issuers: big technology companies with a well-known brand and large retail customer base, for which the possibility to directly address the wider retail population in a "tech-friendly" style makes the auction process very appealing as the cost saving opportunities on the listing process are matched by an equally significant (if not more important) perception of the offering style. For example, Google used a modified Dutch auction process when going public in 2004.

6.5.6 Life after the IPO

The first day of trading is the last moment of the IPO process and, at the same time, the initial moment of the company's life as a listed entity: this means a whole new step for the company, since being listed brings higher reputation but also increased scrutiny.

Table 6.6 Private company vs public company: a comparison

	Private Company	Public Company
Strategy execution	Limited to a selected number of stakeholders	Scrutinised by and communicated to a wide audience
Financial results	Benchmarked only against internal objectives	Benchmarked against previous guidance, public expectations and competitors' achievement; includes segmental reporting and KPIs
External influences	Limited to the concerns and adjustments of key shareholders	Daily impact on share price
Timing of reporting	Adjustable to internal needs	Dictated by regulatory authorities and market expectations
Equity marketing	Not applicable	Requires constant dedication to address investor's needs
Corporate governance	Limited to internal relationship needs	Must comply with regulatory rules to protect minority shareholders

Once a company is public and its shares are listed on the exchange, any relevant information will have an impact on the share price and signal the way the market is incorporating such information. As a result, stakeholders such as shareholders, new potential investors, analysts, press, employees, and clients will take a much more active interest around the company. Hence, some key post-IPO considerations include how the company and its Investor Relations team will deal with the first set of analyst interactions, the first results presentation (including the challenges around setting a track record of effective and efficient communication to the market, as well as addressing potential key issues raised from the IPO feedback), the communication of any relevant strategy update, and the need to establish broad shareholders' support within the market. **Table 6.6** summarises the comparison between a private and a public company.

Case study Ferrari IPO, by Riccardo Mulone, Country Head UBS Italy

Ferrari NYSE IPO - case study
"The stuff dreams are made of"

Introduction

The bell rings in the New York Stock Exchange on a warm and sunny morning in October 2015. Overcoming a period of extreme volatility in the US and global equity markets, Ferrari IPO is successfully priced at the top of the $48-$52 range.
Ferrari is valued 12x EV/EBITDA 2016E and 27x P/E 2016E, at premium vis-à-vis most of European luxury peers and substantially in line with Hermès and Brunello Cucinelli, two of the most exclusive high-end luxury players; a premium valuation not typically associated with carmakers, which only trade at low single-digit multiples.
Ferrari's enterprise value at IPO is $10.8bn, over $6bn more than the average value attributed by equity research analysts prior to the announcement of the intention to IPO in October 2014, which was approximately $4.7bn.
To date, Ferrari represents the only case of an automotive business listed in the stock markets and successfully positioned as a pure luxury player: a clear example of value creation via IPO and demerger. *"For defying a background of woeful new markets and still achieving a premium valuation – based on a purveyor of scarves rather than motor cars"* Ferrari's NYSE flotation was recognised as IFR's US IPO of the Year 2015.
UBS acted as Sole Global Coordinator and Lead Left Bookrunner on the IPO, ultimately responsible for every key workstream during the IPO process in the New York Stock Exchange.
As of 21 February 2020, prior to the Covid-19 outbreak, Ferrari's share price was $172.9, up more than 230% vs the IPO, outperforming all luxury peers over the same period and clearly standing out as one of the most premium listed players in the sector. This was underpinned by an outstanding financial performance: from FY15 to FY19 revenues increased from €2.9bn to €3.8bn (CAGR of 7.2%), EBITDA almost doubled, rising from €719m to €1,269m (CAGR of 15.3%), EBITDA margin improved c. 850bps from 25.2% to 33.7%, and net income grew almost 2.5x to €696m.
All this, however, was not as straightforward as it looks today when UBS was appointed to lead the overall IPO process in the New York Stock Exchange in July 2015.

Ferrari – business overview

Ferrari is the preeminent global performance and luxury car brand. Its sales, pricing, and growth trajectory are driven by the increasing number of high net worth individuals globally, capable of purchasing luxury high performance vehicles.
In 2014 (the year prior to the IPO), Ferrari generated net revenues of €2,762m, Adjusted EBITDA of €693m, net profit of €265m, and shipped 7,255 cars. Ferrari sold its vehicles through a worldwide distribution network of approximately 180 dealers.
Ferrari's heritage can be traced back to 1929 when Enzo Ferrari created the "Scuderia Ferrari" racing team. Ferrari is the only car producer to have competed continuously in the Formula 1 World Championship since its inception in 1950. Scuderia Ferrari is the most awarded F1 team, having won 16 Constructors' Championships and 15 Drivers' Championships.
Ferrari's relationship with Fiat began in 1969 when the Agnelli family's proprietary carmaker acquired 50% of Ferrari; in 1988, after the death of Enzo Ferrari, Fiat expanded its stake to 90% ownership. Prior to the IPO, Ferrari was 90% owned by Fiat Chrysler Automobiles and 10% owned by Piero Ferrari (son of the founder, Enzo)

At the time of the IPO, Ferrari's street car division produced seven models of luxury performance cars, including five sports cars (458 Italia, 458 Spider, F12berlinetta, and the special series 458 Speciale and 458 Speciale A) and two GT cars (California T and FF). Ferrari also produced a limited edition supercar, LaFerrari, very limited editions series (Fuoriserie), and one-off cars.
Ferrari introduces new models in standard, four-year cycles. This continuous renewal process enhances vehicular content and is responsive to client expectations.
Ferrari pursues a low-volume production and sales strategy in order to maintain a reputation of exclusivity among clients and deliberately monitors and maintains its production volumes and delivery wait-times to promote this reputation.
In recent years Ferrari has allocated a higher proportion of shipments to the Middle East and Greater China, and to a lesser extent, the Americas, and a lower proportion to Europe, reflecting changes in relative demand as part of its strategy to manage waiting lists and maintain product exclusivity.
At the time of the IPO, Ferrari's exposure towards APAC and Greater China was still quite limited (21% of sales), with EMEA being the largest market (45% of sales) followed by the Americas (34% of sales).
Ferrari's primary marketing and promotion efforts are made through investments in racing activities and specifically Scuderia Ferrari's participation in the Formula 1 World Championship: the Formula 1 World Championship is indeed one of the most watched annual sports events in the world.

Why an IPO

The decision to list and spin-off Ferrari was taken during the first Board of Directors meeting of Fiat Chrysler Automobiles on 29 October 2014, in London; Fiat had just completed the merger with Chrysler, creating FCA.
Under Sergio Marchionne and John Elkann's stewardship, in 2011 Fiat successfully completed the demerger of its industrial operations (Fiat Industrial – manufacturer of heavy trucks, buses, as well as construction and agricultural equipment such as tractors and excavators).
As a result, at the time of the IPO, FCA group mainly operated through the following divisions:

- Automotive: mass-market brands such as Fiat, Chrysler, Jeep, Alfa Romeo, Lancia, Dodge, RAM, with core operations in EMEA, North America, and LatAm;
- Components: car parts and components, though Magneti Marelli, Comau, Teksid;
- Luxury cars: high-end, luxury/sports cars, through the Ferrari and Maserati brands.

As explained in more detail in the paragraphs below, mass-market carmakers have much lower profitability and return on capital compared to luxury companies. As a result they only trade at low single-digit multiples, while luxury companies trade at double-digit multiples.
The ultimate aim of an IPO and demerger of Ferrari was therefore to create value for FCA shareholders, by separating businesses which are subject to different industry dynamics and enjoy different underlying valuations that were not fully reflected in FCA's market valuation.
The parent company FCA, by selling Ferrari shares to the market, would also use the proceeds to reduce financial leverage at the FCA level.
The IPO of Ferrari on the NYSE and subsequent demerger from FCA was to be carried out in three steps, as indicated beforehand:

- Step 1: FCA to execute an organizational restructuring whereby Ferrari S.p.A. is reincorporated into a Dutch entity, Ferrari N.V.
  - Ferrari to continue to be organised under Italian law and to serve as a tax resident in Italy, but the relocation allowed its shareholders to benefit from enhanced governance rights, such as a loyalty voting rights mechanism, not envisaged in Italian regulations.
  - Prior to the IPO, Ferrari to issue a special dividend of €2.5bn to its shareholders (FCA and Piero Ferrari).

- Step 2: FCA to IPO 10% of Ferrari from its 90% holding (100% secondary shares, with FCA as the selling shareholder).
  - Ferrari to be listed on the NYSE, remaining controlled by FCA (80% stake, corresponding to c. 84% voting rights), with Piero Ferrari owning a 10% stake (10.5% voting rights) and public shareholders keeping the remaining 10% (c. 5% voting rights), i.e. the stake sold by FCA during the IPO.
- Step 3: At the beginning of 2016, Ferrari to be demerged from FCA, which entailed FCA issuing a dividend of all FCA ownership in Ferrari (80% stake) to FCA's shareholders in the form of Ferrari individual shares.
  - As a result Exor to keep a 24% economic stake in Ferrari (c. 33% voting rights), public shareholders a 66% stake (c. 51% voting rights) and Piero Ferrari the remaining 10% (c. 15% voting rights).

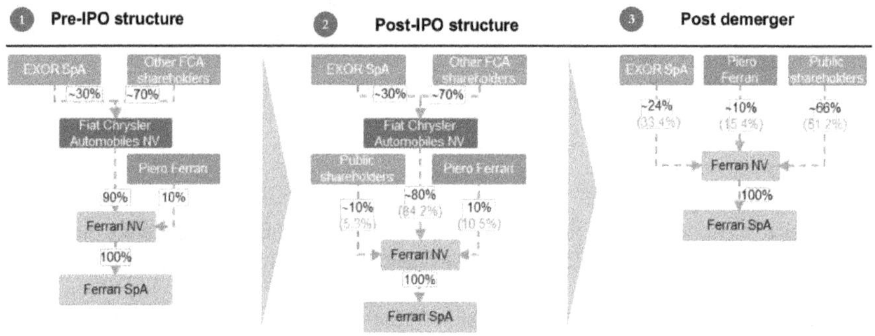

(#%) represents voting rights as per Ferrari loyalty voting program
Source: F-1 Prospectus

The Ferrari US IPO process on the NYSE – overview

The Ferrari IPO priced on 20 October 2015, with the first day of trading on 21 October 2015. UBS was appointed as the Sole Global Coordinator in July 2015, managing and coordinating the overall listing process on the New York Stock Exchange. The IPO process in the US envisages four main stages:

1. **Preparation (July-September 2015 – 10 weeks)**
   a. Draft the Prospectus (F-1) identifying equity story, areas of concerns, positioning, and comparable companies;
   b. Assess the business plan prepared by the company;
   c. Prepare the Analyst Presentation;
   d. Assess the best timing for the transaction.
2. **Analyst presentation (September 2015 – 10 days)**:
   a. Analyst presentation, to educate equity research analysts on the positioning of the company in order for them to write equity studies and ultimately build their financial model;
   b. Model template collection from research analysts and consensus definition;
   c. Price range definition.
3. **Roadshow and bookbuilding (October 2015 – 7 days)**:
   a. Roadshow;
   b. Bookbuilding;
   c. Feedback on price setting.

4. Pricing and aftermarket (October 2015 – 1 day):
   a. Final pricing definition;
   b. Shares allocation;
   c. First day of trading.

1. Preparation

The most time consuming phase, which lasted from July 2015 to September 2015, entailed intensive work together with the company's top management team to define a solid and compelling equity story, identifying the most appropriate investors to target and preparing the Analyst presentation to educate equity research analysts. Key activities in the preparation phase include: (i) definition of equity story and investment case; (ii) assessment of key potential areas of investor concern; (iii) positioning; and (iv) comparable companies selection and benchmarking.

Definition of equity story and investment case
The equity story includes a list of the key highlights which makes an investment in the company particularly compelling, emphasizing the key strengths of the business, in order to support a clear positioning of Ferrari in the luxury sector, hence commanding a premium valuation. For Ferrari, the highlights below were developed:

1. *Iconic brand with superior, enduring power, benefitting from a loyal customer base*
   - Ferrari brand is one of the most iconic and recognizable in the world and is a symbol of luxury, exclusivity, innovation, state-of-the-art sporting performance, and Italian design and engineering heritage. Ferrari has regularly been ranked as one of the world's most powerful brands, leveraging decades of success in racing and the performance and styling of luxury cars.
   - Brand power is preserved and enhanced by a rigorous production and distribution model, which promotes hard-to-satisfy demand and thus scarcity value.
2. *Global access to growing wealth creation*
   - Size and spending capacity of target client base (the wealthiest segment of the population) has grown significantly and is expected to further expand, particularly in emerging markets, proving to be relatively insulated from short-term economic downturns.
   - The low-volume strategy allows for quickly responding to economic developments and benefitting from patterns of wealth creation and demand for luxury products in different regions.
3. *Exceptional pricing power and value resilience*
   - The allure of the Ferrari brand and its controlled production and distribution model promote premium pricing in the new car and resale markets.
   - Constantly increasing average selling price, driven by focus on quality, performance and craftsmanship of cars also through extensive personalization.
4. *Racing heritage*
   - Ferrari implements cutting-edge innovations directly derived from its racing experience to deliver best-in-market performance cars.
   - With over 425 million viewers in 2014, Formula 1 races are the world's most watched sport series, giving Ferrari a strong marketing advantage and avoiding more common product advertising.
5. *Leading-edge engineering capabilities*
   - Ferrari's cars are the epitome of car performance, luxury, and styling and integrate industry-leading technological capabilities, from pure performance to luxurious interiors for comfort and drivability.
   - The cars' distinctive designs, performance, and luxury status provide Ferrari with a unique character, which contributes to increased brand strength.
6. *Flexible and efficient development and production process*
   - Racing heritage, with annual design, develop and build schedule enables Ferrari to bring

new models to market in just ~40 months, with models typically having a four-year lifecycle, ensuring that products remain responsive to client expectations.
- Recently-renovated production facilities, accommodating meaningful increases in production.

7. *Strong and resilient financial performance and profile*
   - Exceptional financial performance track record, not just as a leading luxury automaker, but as one of the world's leading absolute luxury brands.
   - Sales growth of 34% in the last 10 years (CAGR: 6%), suffering only a single year of modest revenue decline during the global financial crisis, 2014 Adjusted EBITDA margin of 25.1%, representing an increase of 690bps since 2005.
8. *Superior talent*
   - Ferrari's brand and technological heritage have allowed it to attract the best technical talent from a wide range of fields: employees include a large number of highly-skilled engineers, designers, technicians, and artisans.
   - The CEO, Amedeo Felisa, with over 40 years of automotive technical experience, and the Chairman, Sergio Marchionne, who engineered the operating and financial turnaround of Fiat and Chrysler.

Positioning Ferrari as luxury player

While it is now clear that Ferrari fully belongs to the luxury sector, positioning the company as a pure luxury player was one of the most delicate and complex exercises of the entire listing process, which required extensive and well-structured investor education. Indeed, ultimately Ferrari produces motor cars, not luxury shoes, scarves, or bags.

The implications in terms of valuation are extremely significant, as mass-market carmakers only trade at low-single digit multiples, while luxury players trade at double-digit multiples.

More specifically, while luxury players at the time of the IPO traded on average at 10.8x EBITDA 2016E, mass carmakers traded at only 2.3x EBITDA 2016E, that is 8.5x less.

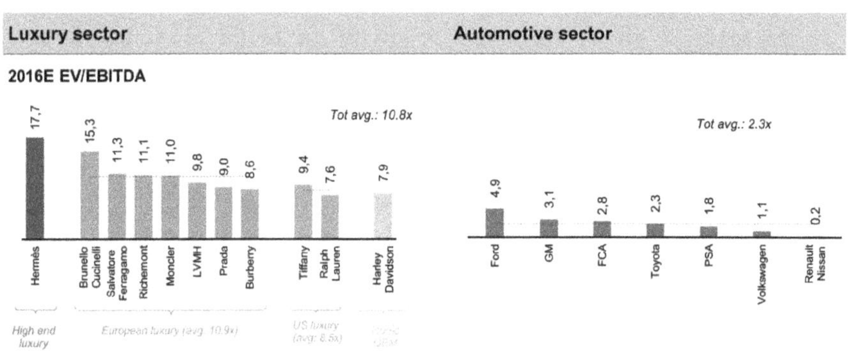

Such a difference in valuation multiples is due to different growth prospects, profitability profile, and capital intensity requirements, ultimately resulting in completely different return on invested capital (ROIC). Indeed mass-market carmakers have shorter earnings cycles, with higher volatility and cyclicality as well as much higher capital intensity requirements, ultimately resulting in a much lower return on capital.

Based on Ferrari 2016E EBITDA of approximately $900m, the difference in valuation multiples would translate into a change in enterprise value for Ferrari of $7.7bn.

To date, Ferrari represents the only case of a carmaker listed and successfully positioned to investors as a pure luxury player.

A number of qualitative elements were identified to support the positioning of Ferrari in the luxury segment:

World's most powerful brand (according to Brand Finance):
Similarly to luxury players, Ferrari is a global brand, whose products anyone dreams of owning regardless of class and social background, a unique blend of Italian craftsmanship and advanced technology. The only founding Formula 1 team still racing and winning, Ferrari has an ultimate collection of cars which increases its value over time, coupled with a multi-year waiting list for new models.

Top-line strength
Extremely resilient business, with 17 years of growth out of the last 19, supported by a strong pricing power and product mix as the main drivers of top-line growth. Ferrari enjoys strong revenue visibility, with a multi-year order book and long-term sponsorship/TV rights contracts. Ferrari's core business leaves plenty of room for growth (e.g. underpenetrated Asia) and could be further developed through unconventional sources of revenues (licensing, vintage restoration).

Superior operating performance
A lean cost structure, with low SG&A, strong operating leverage to support margin expansion as well as "pure margin" opportunities (e.g. licensing) still to be fully exploited. Ferrari enjoys an efficient asset base, with low working capital requirements and best-in-class return on invested capital.

ROIC – EBITDA margin correlation
However, to substantiate these qualitative items, the main quantitative item to prove to equity research analysts and investors that Ferrari clearly belongs to the luxury segment, while ultimately remaining an industrial business, is the correlation between profitability profile (represented by EBITDA margin) and the return on invested capital (ROIC).
The chart below shows two clearly separated buckets with similar profiles: (i) mass-market carmakers (Auto OEMs) with low profitability/returns and (ii) luxury players, with high profitability/return profile. Ferrari clearly belongs to the second bucket: indeed, as explained in more detail in the section below, Ferrari has a similar profitability profile vis-à-vis luxury peers, coupled with a lighter capital base.
In terms of profitability, Ferrari's lower gross margin – linked to the industrial nature of its business – is compensated by lower Selling, General & Administrative expenses, as most of the advertising activities are carried out through participation in Formula 1, lowering marketing expenses.
On the other hand, Ferrari enjoys a lighter asset base vis-à-vis luxury players, with a similar incidence of tangible assets but enjoying a negative net working capital, which benefits from cash advances to purchase new cars and from the peculiar "made-to-order" approach – which allows for reducing inventories.

ROIC/EBITDA margin correlation

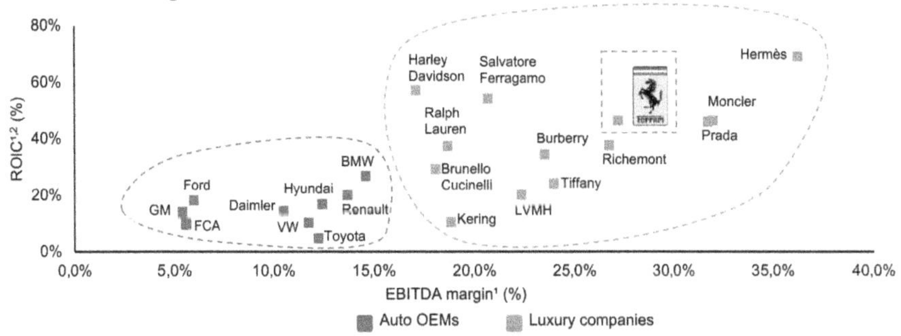

Notes: 1 Based on the latest available FY financials during the preparatory phase of the IPO; 2 Calculated as EBIT/Net invested capital (defined as PP&E + intangible assets excl. goodwill + Net working capital)

Comparable companies selection and benchmarking

The following step is to identify a bucket of listed comparable companies to Ferrari in terms of business model and financial dynamics as well as sector and geographic exposure: these peers will represent important reference points to anchor Ferrari's valuation relative to companies which are already listed, and as such, have a prevailing market value.

The following companies were selected as Ferrari peers:

- High-end luxury: Hermès, the ultimate luxury player with an exclusive product portfolio, outstanding return on capital, and profitability resulting in the highest multiples in the sector.
- European luxury: Burberry, LVMH, Brunello Cucinelli, Richemont, Salvatore Ferragamo, Prada, and Moncler, key luxury players headquartered in Europe.
- US luxury: Ralph Lauren, Tiffany. Given that the listing took place on the NYSE, it was key to give US investors references to US luxury players with which they were more familiar.
- Iconic OEM: Harley Davidson. The only "industrial" company which shared an iconic brand and heritage with Ferrari.

Ferrari's effective positioning as a pure luxury player was further validated by an extensive benchmarking exercise, highlighting the Key Performance Indicators supporting such positioning.

	Hermès	**Prada**	**Richemont**	**LVMH**	**Ferrari**
Brand					
Heritage	✓✓✓✓	✓✓✓✓	✓✓✓✓	✓✓✓✓	✓✓✓✓
Quality	✓✓✓✓	✓✓✓✓	✓✓✓✓	✓✓✓✓	✓✓✓✓
KPIs					
Gross margin	68.9%	73.8%	63.4%	65.0%	29.6%
SG&A	32.3%	47.7%	40.0%	46.1%	6.0%
EBITDA margin	36.2%	31.7%	26.7%	22.3%	27.2%
PPE (% of sales)	*27.2%*	*34.3%*	*18.5%*	*26.6%*	*25.4%*
OWC (% of sales)	*17.1%*	*11.4%*	*38.2%*	*28.8%*	*(2.8%)*
Asset base (% of sales)	44.3%	45.7%	59.4%	55.3%	22.6%
Capex + R&D (% of sales)	5.6%	15.3%	6.8%	6.0%	19.7%
OpFCF margin[1]	28.2%	17.2%	17.5%	16.0%	14.3%
ROIC[2]	69.0%	43.7%	37.7%	20.0%	46.6%

[1] Defined as (EBITDA – Capex – change in NWC)/revenues. Refers to 2015E

[2] Defined as EBIT/Invested capital (defined as PP&E + Intangible assets excluding goodwill + Net working capital)

Source: Companies' information and filings

Brand: Ferrari is one of the most powerful and recognizable brands, thanks to a rich racing history and a strong heritage, a symbol of Italian craftsmanship.

Company: Ferrari's growth profile is aligned with the average of its peers, but slightly below high-end luxury; profitability is aligned with peers while returns are fully comparable with high-end players. Ferrari enjoys a balanced geographic split and a strong growth potential given the lower exposure to Asian markets.

KPIs: given its industrial business model, Ferrari's Gross margin is less than half that of its luxury peers. However, Ferrari enjoys much lower advertising and selling costs vs luxury players, as most of its advertising activities are carried out through participation in Formula 1. As a result, its EBITDA margin profile is fully in line with luxury peers.

Ferrari's asset base is overall lighter compared to luxury peers, with incidence of PP&E comparable to that of its peers, despite having a completely different qualitative split (industrial assets vs stores) but enjoying much lower net working capital absorption: Ferrari has no inventories given the peculiar "made-to-order" approach, and cash advances to buy new cars reduce NWC absorption. Despite higher capex and R&D, as Ferrari is a more capital intensive business, the favourable NWC dynamics allow Ferrari's OpFCF margin to be aligned with luxury peers.

2. Analyst Presentation – 16-17 September

The Analyst Presentation is an interactive full-day round table session between top managers and equity research analysts. During the event, the company management team meets for the first time the research analysts who will write the equity research reports that will ultimately provide an indication of the expected valuation of the company and the target price once listed.
A comprehensive document is presented by the company management team, providing an extensive overview of the business. Key sections include:

- Equity story and investment highlights;
- Overview of the industry where the company operates and its growth prospects;
- Overview of the product portfolio, key business units, and activities;
- Analysis of historical financial performance;
- Management strategy to grow the business and financial targets.

The document is prepared through several drafting sessions with top management and the investor relations team, with ad hoc drafting sessions with other senior managers to prepare sections of the document related to the key business functions.
Rehearsal sessions are held with top management together with Q&A sessions in order to properly address any potential questions arising from analysts.
For the Ferrari Analyst Presentation, the choreography of the event was also carefully evaluated, with a visit to the Company's factory in Maranello and hot laps "track experience" in Florano.
Together with the analyst presentation, equity research analysts also received a model template to fill in providing the key financials forecasts and valuation indications and methodologies.
Following the analyst presentation, analysts had the opportunity to attend conference calls with Ferrari management to address any outstanding concerns/questions. Therefore, keeping a fluent and effective dialogue between the company's management and the analysts is crucial to ensure that research reports most accurately reflect the business and its strategy.

3. Roadshow and bookbuilding – 12-20 October

During the roadshow, the company top management meets the investors in a series of one-to-one and group meetings. A comprehensive document is presented by the management, providing an extensive overview of the business, its positioning and its strategy.
Ferrari's roadshow lasted for 1 week (from 12 to 20 October) during which more than 500 investors were met in either 1-on-1 meetings or group events across eight key locations in the US and Europe.
The roadshow started on the US East coast with more than 280 investors met in New York, Boston, and Baltimore.
The roadshow then moved to Europe, with more than 175 investors met between London, Milano, and Maranello, where a small group event was also organized at Ferrari facilities.
Finally, management flew back to the US West Coast, where the last 40+ investors were met between San Francisco and Los Angeles.
During the roadshow, investors provide feedback on the valuation anticipated for the business and potentially submit the orders that will be used to build the book of demand, one of the most important tools to set the IPO pricing.

4. Pricing and aftermarket – 20-21 October

The Ferrari IPO price range was set at $48-52 per share, corresponding to an implied EV/EBITDA 2016E multiple of 11.2-12.0x and a P/E 2016E multiple of 24.7x-26.8x. Ferrari was successfully priced at the top end of such range.
The definition of the price range and the setting of the IPO price take into account a number of different, sometimes contrasting elements: while selling shareholders aim to maximise the value at IPO, increasing the desired range, pricing below the range is significantly unattractive, as it signals a failed transaction, tarnishing the company in its "listed life" and ultimately putting the deal execution at risk in difficult market conditions.
Key factors taken into consideration in setting the price range and the IPO price include:

- Fundamental and relative valuation: represented by company DCF and by comparable companies' trading multiples, respectively;
- Analyst and investor feedback: collected from equity research reports and during the pre-marketing activity and roadshow;
- Company objectives and market conditions.

At the lower end of the range, valuation should reflect the majority of investors' views, generating early momentum and offering some insurance against market volatility and a sense of certainty of execution to investors. The higher end of the range represents an "aspirational" valuation, with an opportunity to drive value for selling shareholders if market conditions should further improve.
The book of demand, which includes the orders collected during the roadshow and bookbuilding phase, represents one of the key tools to set the IPO price: ideally, pricing should leave a reasonable discount to the fair trading value of the company.
At the IPO, Ferrari's enterprise value was $10.8bn, valuing the company 12.0x EV/EBITDA 2016E and 26.8x P/E 2016E, implying a premium of 10.7% vs European luxury peers on a EV/EBITDA basis and a P/E substantially in line with Hermès and Brunello Cucinelli.
This was the result of successful, extensive, and well-structured investor education to position the company as a pure luxury player.

2016E EV/EBITDA

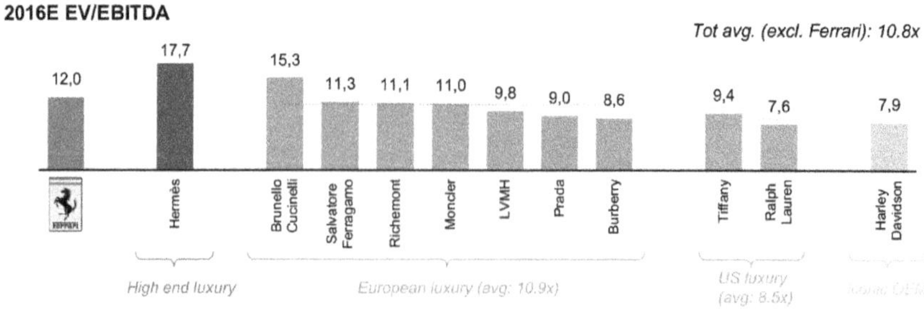

2016E P/E

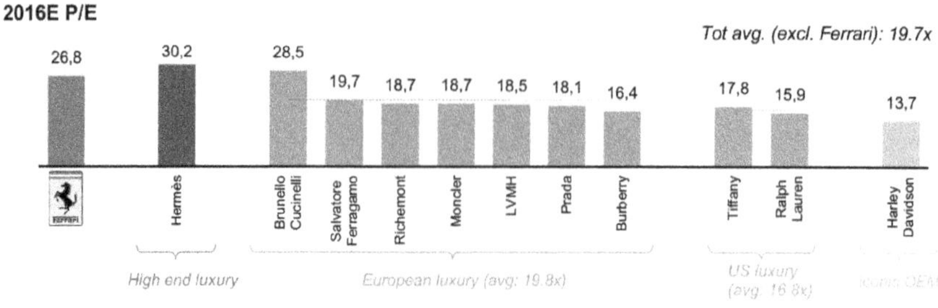

Source: Company information and filings, FactSet as of 21 October 2015

Ferrari shares closed at $55.00 during the first day of trading (+5.8%), with a strong rally shortly after opening (reaching an intra-day high of $60.97). At the closing price, the stock traded at a P/E 2016E of 30.0x, at premium compared to the 29.6x for Hermès.
The Ferrari IPO was successfully priced at the top end of the range despite a period of extreme volatility in the US equity market: volatility - measured by the VIX index - which normally remains in the ~20 area, peaked at 40.7 just a couple of days before the IPO.
The US equity capital markets also proved to be particularly challenging in 2015, with six of the previous seven IPOs pricing below the range or withdrawn prior to pricing, and six of the previous ten IPOs greater than $200m breaking issue and trading down on their first day of trading. Before the pricing, almost 60% were trading below their IPO price (12 down more than 10% and 5 down over 30%).
The Ferrari IPO was oversubscribed within two hours of launch and the final book was c. 20x oversubscribed at the top of the range at the end of the offering.
At the top of the price range, orders worth $17.6bn were collected and had to be allocated to investors against an envisaged offer of $982m. Offer allocation is a difficult and delicate process, whose main objectives are to:

- create a base of stable shareholders that fully understand the business, its positioning, and equity story;
- provide sufficient liquidity for the shares in the market;
- ensure a positive aftermarket once the stock is listed.

A number of elements are assessed when deciding the offer allocation, including the quality of the work done by each investor during the entire IPO process in order to understand the company business model and its positioning, the type of order placed (including timing and any price limit), the participation in the roadshow, as well as the track record in previous IPOs.
Ferrari being listed on the NYSE, a larger proportion of the offer was allocated to US-based investors (approximately 70%), with European investors receiving 25% and the remaining 5% allocated to other investors.
While hedge funds represented more than 50% of the overall demand, 50% of the offer was allocated to Long-Only funds, providing 20% to Retail investors (whose orders were also collected through UBS Wealth Management platform) and the remaining 30% to Hedge funds.
This type of allocation, focused on Long Only and retail investors, created a solid and stable shareholders base for Ferrari: this proved to be crucial once the envisaged demerger from FCA took place, in January 2016. Eighty per cent of Ferrari shares were re-distributed to FCA shareholders, mainly represented by investors focused on mass-market automakers with little experience – and in some cases – no mandate to invest in luxury players like Ferrari.
As a result, in the weeks following the IPO, the Ferrari share price was affected by the expectation of a significant redistribution of shares, but thanks to an allocation that created a stable and solid shareholder base, the share price overhang on Ferrari was absorbed more quickly.

Value creation
The IPO and demerger of Ferrari has been highly value accretive for both FCA and Ferrari shareholders and represents one of the brightest examples of value creation through IPO and M&A.
Prior to the Ferrari demerger announcement (29-Oct-14) equity research analysts attributed a valuation to Ferrari ranging between $3.5bn and $5.7bn, with a median value of $4.7bn. Such valuations were based on a sum-of-the-parts valuation of the parent company FCA.
At the IPO price ($52 per share) Ferrari's EV is valued at $10.8bn, ultimately more than double the average value attributed by the financial community to Ferrari prior to the announcement of the transaction. This translates into a $6.1bn value creation at IPO.

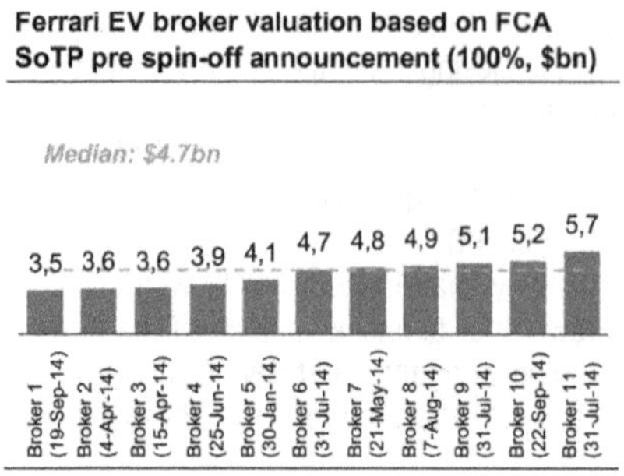

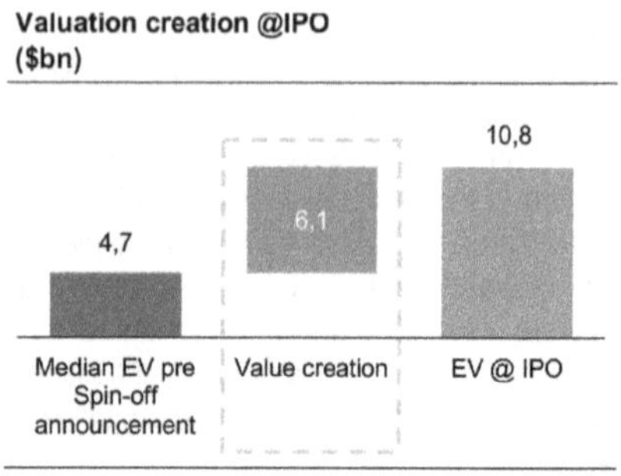

Note: Values converted at EUR/USD FX rate of 1.10; SoTP stands for "Sum-of-the-Parts"
Source: Research reports

Both FCA and Ferrari shareholders have largely benefitted from the transaction. Prior to the announcement (29-Oct-14), FCA's market cap was $14.7bn: by the time of the IPO (21-Oct-15) FCA's market cap was increased to $23.0bn, +56% or $8.3bn more. The share price of FCA peers (VW, Renault, PSA, Toyota, GM, and Ford), over the same period, has increased on average by just 20%. By the time of the demerger (3-Jan-16), FCA and Ferrari's market capitalization was $13.6bn and $9.0bn, respectively. For FCA shareholders, owning a total of 80% of Ferrari and 100% of FCA, that translates into an aggregated value of $20.8bn, corresponding to a value creation of $6.1bn vs FCA market value prior to the announcement of the transaction.
On 21 February 2020 (prior to the Covid-19 outbreak), Ferrari's share price was $172.9, up by more than 230% vs IPO, and the company traded at ~22x EV/EBITDA '20E, an impressive ~10x re-rating vs IPO levels, outperforming all luxury peers over the same period and clearly standing out as one of the most premium listed players in the sector.

	EV/EBITDA FY+1 (@ IPO)	EV/EBITDA FY+1 (today–21-Feb-20)	Δ EV/EBITDA vs IPO	Share price performance (since IPO)
Ferrari	12.0x	21.9x	+9.9x	+232.5%
High end luxury	17.7x	24.5x	+6.8x	+102.7%
European luxury	10.9x	13.0x	+2.1x	+52.9%
US luxury	8.5x	13.6x	+5.1x	+35.5%

Conclusions

- A distinctive example of value creation via IPO and demerger.
- A unique case of successful positioning of a carmaker as a pure luxury player, with a focus on exclusivity, pricing power, and customer loyalty.
- Achieved a premium valuation characteristic of most luxury companies, not typically associated with an auto business.
- Valued by the market more than double the average value attributed by the financial community prior to the announcement of the transaction.
- Successfully priced in a period of extreme volatility in the US and global equity markets.
- Strong demand enabled delivery of a "books covered" message within hours of opening, c.20x oversubscription and ultimately to price the deal at the top of the range.
- Bespoke global investor targeting effort that reached unique pockets of demand in every region of the globe to find the right investor base for the Ferrari stock.

Case study **Nexi IPO, by Francesco Papa, Managing Director ECM, Goldman Sachs**

1. Introduction to the Nexi IPO

Nexi SpA ("Nexi") – The leading Payment Technology Company in Italy – went public on the Milan Stock Exchange in April 2019 via an Initial Public Offering of €2.3bn that represented the 2nd largest IPO in Europe in 2019 and the 3rd largest IPO globally in the Payment Technology sector to date.

Nexi is active in numerous segments of Payment Technology, from Card Issuing to Merchant Services, ATM management, Interbank Corporate Banking, and Clearing & Settlement. The company provides best-in-class payment solutions to support Banks, Financial Institutions and Insurance Companies, Businesses and Public Administrations: from Cards to payment acceptance technologies, money transfers between Companies and Private Individuals, and the management of highly complex technical services such as Corporate Banking.

The history of the Company dates back to 1939 when six Italian banks founded a joint undertaking to provide essential banking infrastructure to the entire network of Italy's cooperative banks called the Istituto Centrale delle Banche Popolari Italiane S.p.A., or ICBPI. While pursuing such objective, ICBPI gradually expanded the service offering, both organically and through a series of acquisitions, positioning the company at the forefront of developments in payment technology and enabling it to drive innovation in the Italian market.

In 2015, ICBPI was acquired by a company owned by several Private Equity investors, Advent International, Bain Capital, and Clessidra, which invested significant capital and appointed a best-in-class management team allowing the group to further grow organically as well as consolidate via acquisitions.

In 2017, ICBPI changed its name to Nexi S.p.A. and adopted the Nexi brand as part of a broad reorganisation effort and transformational plan that led the company to change from a Banking group to a Technology group and undertake several major acquisitions in the Payment Technology sector, such as Setefi from Intesa Sanpaolo and Bassilichi from Monte dei Paschi. More than €300m were invested by Nexi in IT and Technology over the 3 years between 2016 and 2018.

Towards the end of 2018, once the main acquisitions had been completed and the internal re-organisation was underway, the company and its shareholders decided to kick-off the path towards an IPO.

2. Execution Set-up: Syndicate Structure and Timetable

Once the initial decision was taken towards the end of 2018, the Company started to appoint the working group of different advisors and kicked-off the more time-consuming activities, such as (1) Prospectus drafting and other legal documentation checklist, (2) review and audit of the financial disclosure set, and (3) preparation of the investor and analyst presentation.

2.1 Syndicate structure

Given the multiple business relationships of Nexi with its banking network, the Company and its Shareholders decided to appoint a large syndicate of 14 banks to reiterate the spirit of partnership with its banking relationships.

The syndicate was coordinated by 5 Joint Global Coordinators (Goldman Sachs, Bank of America, Credit Suisse, Intesa Sanpaolo, and Mediobanca) that took the lead on each of the execution workstream and the distribution efforts, managing communication with the rest of the syndicate.

Evercore was appointed as Financial Advisor.

Exhibit 1 shows the overall working group appointed on the IPO.

Exhibit 1 Full Working Group List for the Nexi IPO

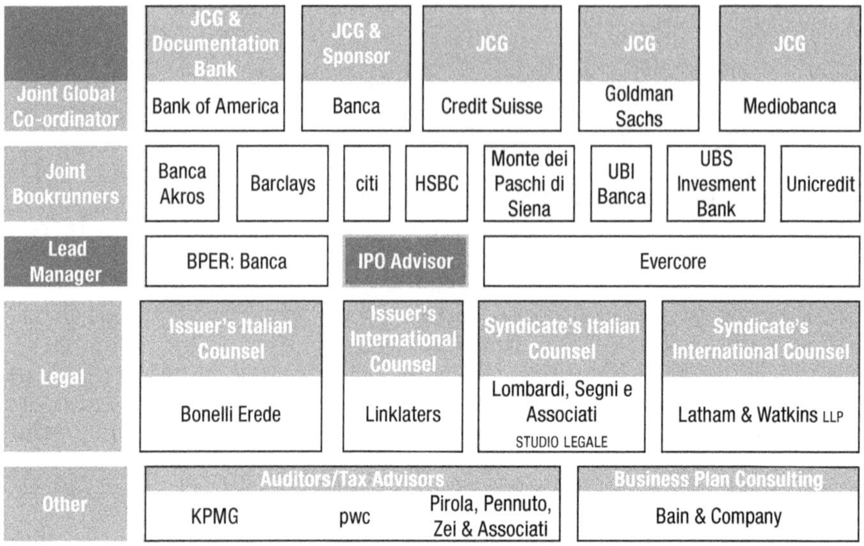

Source: IPO Prospectus.

2.2 IPO timetable

Following the preliminary work, the execution timetable for the IPO was highly compressed between February and April, in order to be able to access the window prior to Easter weekend, minimize exposure to market volatility, and pre-empt potential instability from the European Elections of May 2019.

Despite the short execution timeframe, the execution timetable included several rounds of investor interactions via pilot fishing meetings and a site visit ahead of the publication of the pre-deal research report, as discussed in further detail in section 4.

Exhibit 2 shows the timetable of the NEXI IPO.

Exhibit 2 NEXI IPO timetable

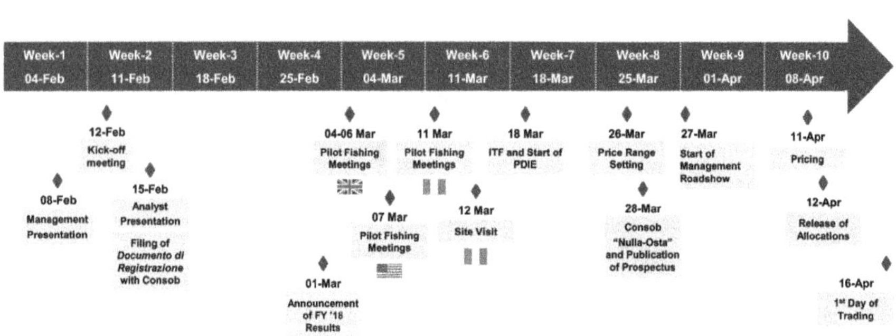

Source: Goldman Sachs, Company Press Releases.

3. Presenting Nexi and the IPO to the market: Equity Story, Financial Information Set, and Offer Structure

3.1 Framing the Equity story

Nexi's equity story and investment case were built on a comprehensive set of pillars, from macro to micro themes, covering the favourable structure and under penetration of the Italian market, the company's sustainable leadership position, and the significant operating leverage from the integration of the acquired assets, transformational projects, and re-organisation initiatives.
Below we report the seven points into which the NEXI equity story was articulated:

[1] *Europe's most attractive payments market with strong secular growth drivers*
[2] *Established market leader at scale with extensive payments ecosystem coverage*
[3] *Long-term, extensive, and value-oriented partnerships with Italian banks*
[4] *Superior products driving multiple growth opportunities*
[5] *Leading technology capabilities driving innovation and Next Generation Platform deployment*
[6] *Attractive financial profile combining profitable growth, resilience, operating leverage, and strong cash-flow generation*
[7] *Strong leadership team with proven track record across all value creation levers.*

Each of the equity story points was supported by quantitative data as part of the information set included in the Prospectus.

3.2 Financial information set for the IPO

Given the multiple acquisitions and re-organisation initiatives undertaken in a short timeframe leading to the IPO, the financial information set to be included in the Prospectus and all the offering documentation (e.g. roadshow presentation, sales memos etc.) were structured with the objective to be able to provide the investors with a consistent and accurate representation of the business, both *pro forma* and adjusted for all the one-offs that it had been facing.
Moreover, the management developed a set of forward-looking targets covering both the short and the medium-term in order to help the investor community to understand the key drivers within the P&L, cash flow generation, and leverage profile.
With respect to the broader industry trends, the company provided a number of reference data points leveraging different external and internal sources, with the aim of providing further visibility on the level of penetration of digital payments in Italy vs other European countries and sizing estimates for the different relevant segments.
Given the familiarity of the investor community with the payment technology market, Nexi did not need to commission an ad hoc report to an external consultant to include estimates of growth trends at the Industry level.

Exhibit 3 Summary of the Information Set Provided by Nexi at IPO

Historical financials	• Carve-out financial statements based on IFRS for 2016/2017/2018 to illustrate the effects of the re-organisation of the different businesses completed on 1 July 2018 • Pro-forma financials for 2018 to illustrate the effects of the Re-organisation and the different M&A transactions executed • Non-GAAP aggregate statements of P&L for 2016/2017/2018 to show the effect of the main acquisitions as if they had all happened on the first day of such periods in order to present a reference of how the main drivers of the business appear on an aggregate basis throughout the 3-year timeframe

	• Non-GAAP financial metrics such as Normalised EBITDA, Operating EBITDA, and other metrics used by management to assess financial and operating performance
Forward looking indications/ guidance	• Medium-term Net Revenues growth target as % range and expected % growth for 2019 • Medium-term Normalised Pro-forma EBITDA growth % range and €m expected amount for 2019 • % reduction in non-recurring items in the reported EBITDA for 2019 • Long-term target of Ordinary Capex as % of net revenues (range) with expected total CapEx in 2019 • Medium to long-term target for Net Debt to Normalised EBITDA • Dividend policy in the medium to-long term
Industry Data	• Dedicated section in the Prospectus covering the reference market and its different segments, leveraging external sources (e.g. Euromonitor, Eurostat, Bank of Italy) and internal company data

Source: IPO Prospectus.

3.3 Offer structure

The offer was structured to include: i) a significant primary component to allow the company to de-lever according to the financial targets provided to the market, and ii) a secondary offer from the existing shareholders.
As shown in the table below, as part of the offer structure, different lock-up arrangements were set for the Company, Shareholders, and Management, with the longer restriction applied to the Management given their critical role in the delivery of the Company strategy.
The table below summarises the offer structure of the NEXI IPO.

Exhibit 4 Offer Structure and Key Offer Terms

Issuer	• Nexi S.p.A
Offering	• Initial Public Offering of ordinary shares
Base Offer	• 228m shares, including greenshoe • Base offering of 223m, of which: – 35% primary (€700m) – 65% sell-down by Mercury HoldCo UK and other minorities
Greenshoe	• Up to 33.5m shares (15% of base deal size/100% secondary by Mercury HoldCo) – Greenshoe exercised: c.5m shares (2.2% of the base offer size)
Free Float at IPO	• Free-float: 36.4% incl. Greenshoe
Selling Shareholders	• Mercury UK Holdco: funds managed and controlled directly or indirectly by Advent International, Bain Capital, and Clessidra SGR • Minority Holders: Banco BPM, Banca Popolare di Sondrio, Banca di Cividale, Credito Valtellinese, Iccrea Banca
Lock-up	• 180 days for Mercury UK Holdco • 180 days for the Company • 90 days for Minority Holders • 12 months/24 months for Management

Listing	• Listing on the Mercato Telematico Azionario ("MTA") of Italian Stock Exchange
Distribution/ Retail	• 144A • Institutional investors only • No retail tranche envisaged

Source: Goldman Sachs, Press Releases, IPO Prospectus.

4. Investor Engagement Effort

A targeted plan of investor interactions was devised, through a targeted effort of Pilot Fishing meetings ahead of publication of the Research Reports.
During this phase, 41 investors were met in London, New York and Milan, between the 4th and the 12th of March 2019.
These meetings were followed by an onsite visit at Nexi Headquarters in Milan with management for selected Portfolio Managers, with the objective of building a closer and more personal interaction with selected investors that could play an important role in the context of the IPO, providing them access to the first line of management, and therefore increasing the quality of feedback received and visibility on the likelihood of participation in the IPO.

5. Pre-Deal Investor Education (PDIE) and Investor Feedback

Given the number of research analysts involved, the breadth of the investor education effort was very significant, leading to c. 1,250 investor meetings across 28 different locations in Europe and the US over the course of 8 days.
C. 2,000k lines of feedback were aggregated by the syndicate, with prevalence of UK investors (43%), followed by US (18%), Italian (9%), other European (25%), and rest of the world. By style, c. 55% of the feedback came from traditional Long-Only Funds, with the remainder provided by HFs (40%) and Sovereign Wealth Funds (5%).
The feedback gathered from investors in the PDIE process can be summarised in the following key themes:

Key positives
- Unanimous support and endorsement by investors of the structural trends and growth opportunity provided by the underpenetrated Italian digital payments market
- Recognition of Nexi leadership in the Italian market, albeit with limited track-record as a "fully-fledged" group given the numerous acquisitions and profound reorganization/transformation undertaken
- Defensive business model, with high barriers to entry, continuous focus on product and technology innovation, and top-class profitability across the sector, with further expansion potential
- Strategic opportunity to grow externally via M&A and to position itself as an in-market consolidator, but also to attract strategic interest from global players

Areas of focus and diligence
- Commercial relationships with banks a key area of diligence by investors to better understand risks and opportunities
- De-leveraging considered a key driver of further growth and strategic flexibility, although leverage profile does not represent a substantial pushback at IPO, given the primary component and the target indebtedness ratio communicated to the market.

From a quantitative perspective, all the valuation indications provided by investors were analyzed in-depth and extensively discussed in order to develop the best judgement on the price range setting as discussed in detail in the following section.
Please refer to Exhibits 5-7 for an overview of PDIE activity and the investor feedback gathering process.

Exhibit 5 Overview of PDIE Meetings by Location

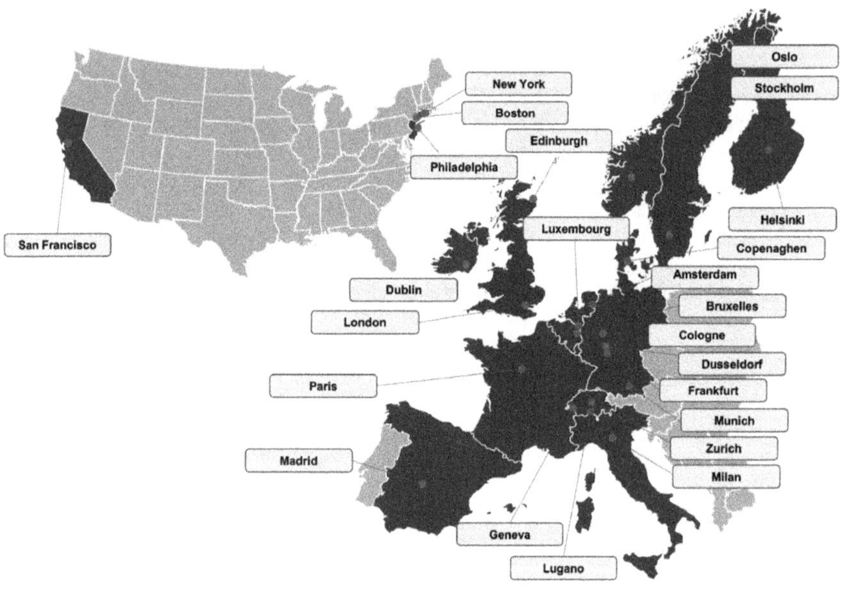

Source: Goldman Sachs.

Exhibit 6 Overview of Investor Feedback Gathering Effort

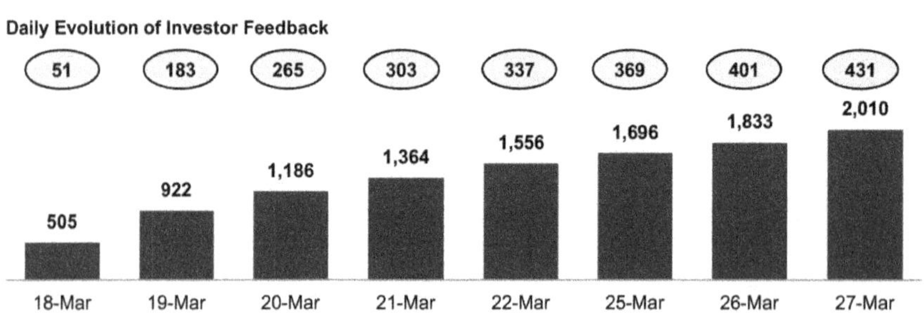

Source: Goldman Sachs.

Exhibit 7 Breakdown of PDIE Feedback by Geography and Type of Investors Met

Source: Goldman Sachs.

6. Price range setting, Roadshow, and Bookbuilding

6.1 Price Range Setting

The price range for the IPO was defined taking into account all the valuation feedback gathered from investors based on the Early Engagement Activities and Pilot Fishing meetings (see section 4) and during the Pre-Deal Investor Education phase.

The valuation indications were screened by (1) metric adopted and (2) reference year. The majority of investors focused on EV/EBITDA as the primary metric and 2020 as the reference year – therefore c. 20 months forward from the IPO, in order to give credit for the ongoing initiatives being implemented by Nexi to further expand profitability and margins in the year following the IPO.

The EV/EBITDA was then triangulated with the FCF yield, given the elevated Capex (with some adjustments for higher leverage, tax rate and Capex vs peers) and the P/E (to a lesser extent).

In terms of valuation indications, the feedback was also screened on the basis of the investor profile, in order to give more relevance to inputs provided by those investors that had spent more time and that could provide a leading role in the context of the overall demand generation:

1. **Early Look Investors and other High Quality Long-Only**: investors who had engaged with the Company since the early stages, maintaining an ongoing dialogue and interaction with management throughout the process, and thus forming a view on valuation ahead of the others
   - This cluster typically plays a key role as opinion leaders and influencers when approaching price-range discussions, given their depth of knowledge of the Company, the level of engagement, and the estimated real demand in the bookbuilding phase, including the potential to act as anchor.

2. **Smaller Long-Only and Fundamental Hedge Funds**: mix of Pan-European, domestic, and US Long-Only investors, as well as long-term oriented Hedge-Funds who had met one or more Research Analysts from the syndicate during PDIE and had provided punctual valuation indications
   - This cluster is supplementary to the previous one and provides additional comfort when setting the price range by incrementing the reference data points that support the decision around the initial bottom and top of the IPO price.

3. **Others**: residual category including the accounts interested but less engaged compared to the other two buckets. They typically provide only preliminary valuation indications during PDIE although not expressing any shadow demand/interest ex-ante. The relevance of these investors is lower in the context of the price range setting, although they help to provide volume in the book

during the bookbuilding phase, usually coming in with orders that are smaller but equally helpful to maximise the overall coverage level throughout the range.

In light of the above, the price range was set between €8.50 and 10.35 per share (implying a market capitalization of Nexi, including the primary component, of between €5.4 – 6.4bn), corresponding to a width of c.22%, broadly in line with European IPO standards.
The implied valuation at those levels was equivalent to 12.6x – 14.4x EV/EBITDA 2020 or 22.1x – 26.3x P/E 2020, based on the consensus of research analysts' reports.[1]

6.2 Management Roadshow

The management roadshow started on 29 March, immediately following the announcement of the price range, and included 315 investors met (through 1-to-1 and group sessions) across six different locations between Europe and the US over 9 days.
The primary objective of the roadshow was to allow investors to meet with Nexi's top management to further discuss the equity story and any Q&A from PDIE, with the aim of crystallizing their interest and locking in their participation commitment, to be then converted into an order in the book of demand.
Exhibits 8-9 below provide a comprehensive recap of the locations and number of 1x1/group meetings held.

Exhibit 8 Overview of the Nexi Management Roadshow Locations and Meetings Held

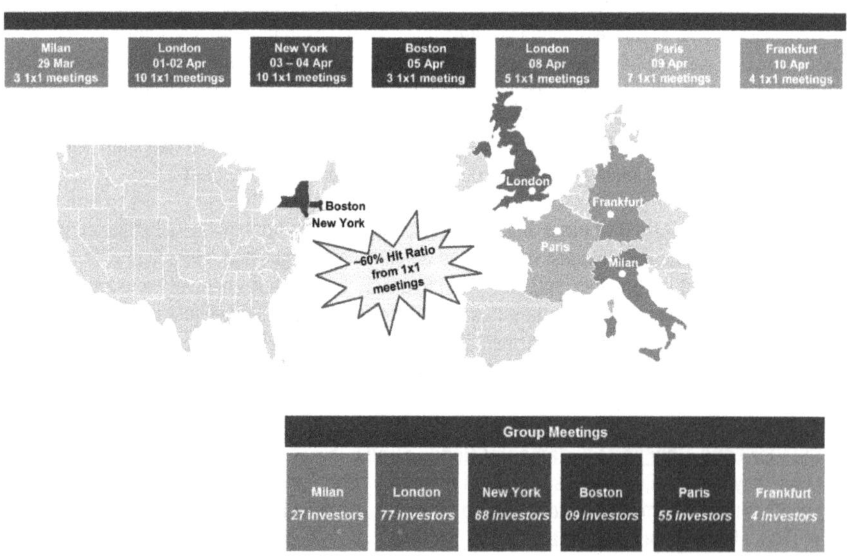

Source: Goldman Sachs.

Exhibit 9 Breakdown of Roadshow Meetings by Geography and Type of Investors Met

Source: Goldman Sachs.

6.3 Bookbuilding

The Bookbuilding commenced on 29 March, alongside the Management Roadshow, and lasted for 10 days, until 11 April.

The offer started with very strong momentum and was covered on day 1 at the bottom of the range, thanks to the conversion into orders of the indications of interest that many investors had provided during the weeks ahead of launch; it continued to grow organically over the following days, resulting in the offer being multiple times covered after the first week.

Ahead of the conclusion of the bookbuilding, the initial price range was narrowed to provide more precise guidance to investors and consolidate demand indications: the updated price range guidance was set at €9.0 – 9.50 per share on 8 April.

Looking at the hit ratio between the roadshow meetings held and the orders in the book, the final conversion ratio amounted to c.60%, in line with previous large European IPOs. Most of demand came from the UK and other Pan-European investors, with a decent split between Long-Only and HFs, and strong participation from early-engaged accounts.

Please see Exhibit 10 – 11 below for further details on the bookbuilding activity and final demand composition.

Exhibit 10 Daily Evolution of the Book

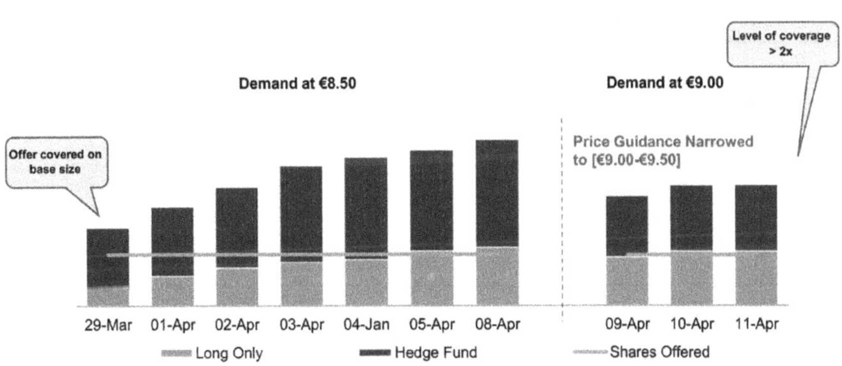

Source: Goldman Sachs.

Exhibit 11 Overview of Final Demand – Split by Geography and Type

Split by Geography

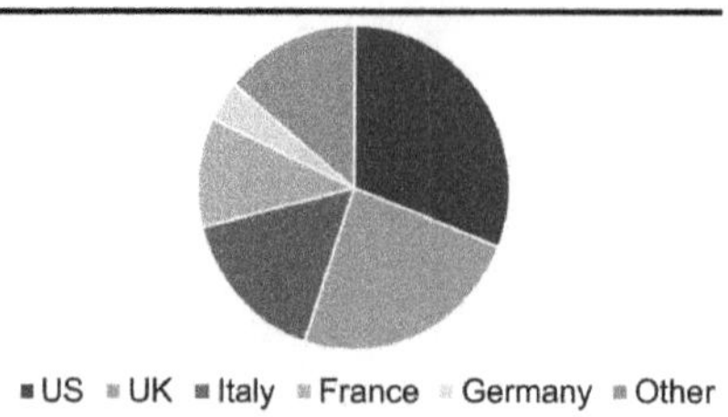

Split by Type

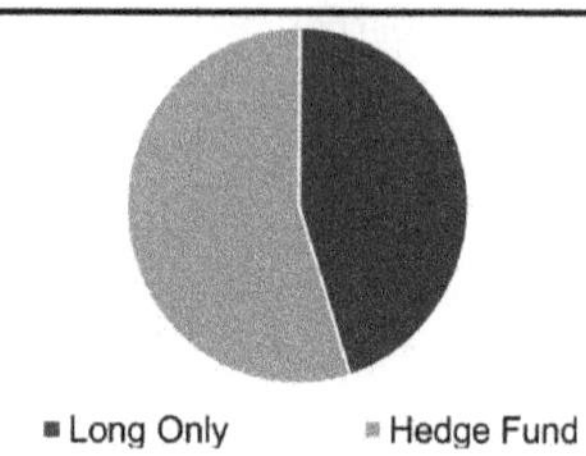

Source: Goldman Sachs.

7. Pricing and Allocation

Once the order book was closed on 11 April, the Company and Shareholders gathered to set the final price of the IPO on the basis of the several billions of demand orders received.

The price was set at €9.00 per share, implying an Equity Value post-money of €5,650m and an Enterprise Value of €7,358m. From a relative valuation perspective, the IPO price corresponded to 13.0x EV/EBITDA 2020 and 23.3x P/E 2020[2].

Once the price was set, the syndicate desks of the Joint Global Coordinators developed an allocation proposal for the Company and the Shareholders to review. Overall, allocations were skewed towards Long-Only and fundamental demand (>75%), with the aim of supporting the stock in the aftermarket and guaranteeing a blue-chip institutional base to support Nexi in the long-term. The top 25 allocations received more than 65% of the deal.

While US participation was lower than the historical average amid the highly volatile backdrop (further explained in the paragraph below), domestic representation came up at the high-end of historical records.

Exhibit 12 Overview of Allocations – Split by Geography and Type

Split by Geography

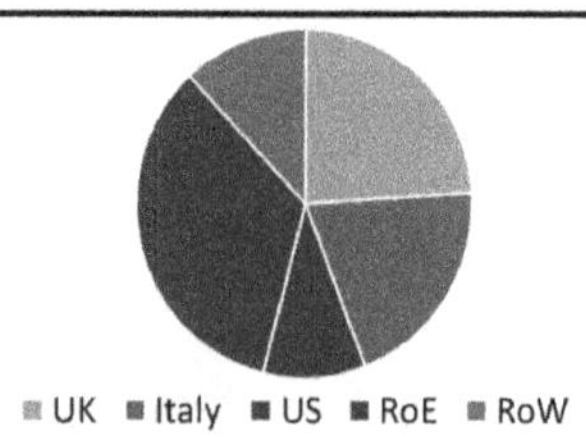

Split by Type

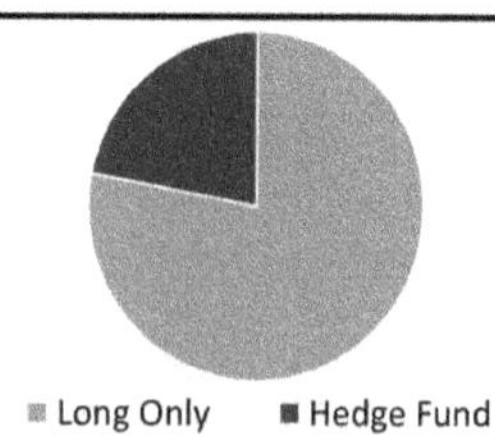

Source: Goldman Sachs.

8. Aftermarket Performance and Stabilisation Activity

Looking at the aftermarket performance of Nexi over the first month of trading, it is key to put the price pattern in the context of the market backdrop. As a matter of fact, despite a successful IPO execution, the political calendar and a deteriorating macro environment (Italian political instability, escalating Trade War concerns, and European elections) had a negative read-across on the stock during the stabilisation period, causing some initial volatility and dislocation away from the IPO price.

However, the announcement of a strong set of Q1 19 results on the 13 May, alongside the research initiations on the stock, served as the catalysts that the market was waiting for to further engage on the name, thus stimulating the stock's route back to the IPO price. Since then, Nexi's trading pattern has followed a continuous upward trend, with the stock ending up 53.07% in the first year since the IPO.

In order to provide some support to the stock and limit the downward moves, the Joint Global Co-ordinators undertook some stabilisation activities over the first 30 days of trading (the "stabilisation period") buying back some shares on the secondary market. Specifically, Credit Suisse, in their role of Stabilisation Agent on behalf of the JGCs, bought back 28,483,968 shares.

On 15 May 2019, the Joint Global coordinators announced to the market the partial exercise of the Greenshoe Option for the residual amount of 5,026,790 Nexi ordinary shares. Including the shares purchased in the exercise of the Greenshoe Option, the final offer size comprised 228m shares, corresponding to a free float of c. 36.4% of the share capital. As a result, the controlling shareholder, Mercury UK, retained a stake of c.60.15% of the share capital post-IPO.

Exhibit 13 Nexi Performance during Stabilisation Period (16 Apr – 16 May)

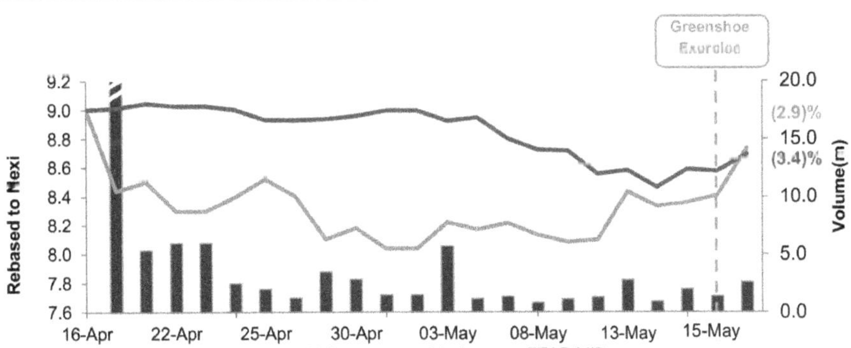

Source: Bloomberg.

[1] Based on the first available reported consensus on Bloomberg post-IPO
[2] Based on the first available reported consensus on Bloomberg post-IPO

Case study Sanlorenzo IPO, by Antonio De Luca, Managing Director ECM, UniCredit Bank AG

Introduction

Sanlorenzo is an Italian yacht manufacturer operating in the high-end luxury yachting segment. The group has a 'made-to-measure,' unique monobrand approach and a strong product portfolio covering both yachts (boats in composite between 24-38mts) and superyachts (boats in metal over 40mts). Sanlorenzo, with a strong reputation for superior quality, comfort, and reliability, has an excellent track record in innovation and this approach has resulted in above-market growth in recent years with solid resiliency across industry cycles. The company was listed on the Italian stock market - Mercato Telematico Azionario organised and managed by Borsa Italiana ("MTA"), STAR segment, on 5 December 2019. The transaction ("Initial Public Offering" or "IPO") envisaged a partial monetization by the reference shareholder (secondary component, c. 60% of the shares offered), and the issuance of new shares (primary component, c. 40% of the shares offered).

Transaction review

Transaction Summary

Issuer	SANLORENZO
1st day of trading	• December 10th, 2019
Pricing date	• December 5th, 2019
Listing	• Milan (Italy), STAR segment
Size	• EUR 176mn – Base Offer • EUR 194mn – Including GS
N. of shares	• 12.1mn shares incl. GS - o/w 4.5mn shares primary - o/w 7.6mn shares secondary incl. GS
Greenshoe	• 10% / 1.1mn shares (all secondary)
Issue price	• EUR 16 p.s.
Free Float	• 31.9% (Pre-GS) • 35.1% (Post-GS)
Market Cap	• EUR 552mn (including EUR 72mn capital increase)
Split Inst./ Retail	• 100% institutional. No retail tranche
Syndicate	• JGCs: BIMI, BofA and UniCredit

Demand by Style

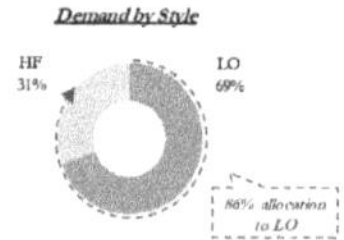

Marketing Activity Summary

Early Marketing *Jun-Jul / Oct-Nov*	• 60 investor meetings done over two rounds of ELs (in London, Milan, Paris and NY) + site visits across La Spezia and ad-hoc boat show events (Genova and Fort Lauderdale)
PDIE *12 Nov – 22 Nov*	• c. 200 meetings mainly across UK, US, Italy and Continental Europe and c. 380 lines of feedback gathered
Roadshow *26 Nov – 5 Dec*	• 31 1x1s / conf calls and 7 group sessions • More than 90 meetings across UK, US, Italy, France, Belgium and Germany
Roadshow Hit Ratio (1x1s)	• 55% (58% from accounts engaged in EL)

Demand by Geography

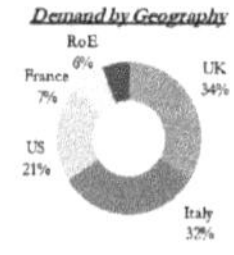

Transaction highlights

- **Sanlorenzo** ("SL" or the "Company") is a **leading global brand** in the **niche of luxury yachts over 30 meters,** manufacturing "made to measure" boats characterized by a distinctive and timeless design
- The deal was **successfully priced in a challenging market environment** for European IPOs, with **11 transactions postponed / cancelled post summer,** including **Ferretti,** the Italian yacht maker and SL competitor, amid increasing investor selectivity and price sensitivity due to volatile geopolitical scenario and lower appetite for less liquid SMEs approaching year end
- A **tailored pre-IPO investor approach** coupled with an **extensive pre-marketing activity** allowed to gather significant interest by key anchor investors ahead of deal launch, further increasing investor confidence during bookbuilding
- Strong demand collected from high quality long only investors allowed the banks' syndicate to announce a **book covered message** on the full deal size on the 6th day of offering, **fueling deal momentum** and **helping to convert additional orders ahead of pricing**
- The high visibility granted by a strong order backlog allowed **investors to focus on 2020E figures,** resulting in a compelling EUR 552mn valuation

Selection of banks (18 April 2019)

After having decided to become a public company by listing its shares on the market, the IPO candidate needs to select a syndicate of investment banks that will support the company during the transaction. Given the one-time nature of the IPO process, most SMEs decide to select an advisor that, thanks to its experience, will facilitate the dialogue with all the parties involved. At the start of the process it is crucial to involve a small number of banks, asking them for a structured pitch that will be evaluated in order to select the syndicate that will lead the transaction. Alantra and Lazard were selected as advisors for the transaction, and on 18 April they sent out a Request for Proposal (RfP).

The request usually covers topics such as the following: (i) credentials, track record, and team

involved; (ii) commercial issues and investment case; (iii) offer structure and fee proposal; (iv) investor knowledge and marketing approach; and (v) other matters (among which are disclosures of conflicts of interest and potential competing transactions). The proposal, following the request, usually has to be sent to the company in a very short timeframe and the terms of the same are discussed with the company and its advisor during an ad hoc meeting.
A complementary and highly-motivated syndicate of banks is critical for the execution of the transaction. Among the key factors to be considered are: bank commitment, ECM track record, institutional distribution platform, equity research capabilities, reach to a broad audience of investors, and corporate access platform.

Overview of key parties involved

An IPO is a complex process that requires interaction between many actors, with different responsibilities across the project. The parties involved in the Sanlorenzo IPO were the following:

Figure 1 Overview of the parties involved

Issuer	SANLORENZO			
Financial Advisors	Alantra (to the Issuer)		Lazard (to the Selling shareholder)	
Joint Global Coordinators	Banca IMI (Sponsor)	Bofa Securities		UniCredit
Legal Counsel	Issuer's Legal Counsel: Latham & Watkins (as to United States and English law)	Issuer's Legal Counsel: Musumeci, Altara, Desana e Associati - Studio Legale (as to Italian law)	Underwriters' Legal Counsel: White & Case	
Other Counsel	MIS/SCG: KPMG	Accounting Data: KPMG	Dataroom Provider/Printer: Intralinks	PR: Weber Shandwick
	Industrial Advisor & BP: Deloitte	Fiscal Advisor: RSM	Non-Accounting Data: RSM	Roadshow coordinator: B1

After the company has officially appointed the team that will support it with regard to the transaction, it is common to schedule a kick-off meeting where the company and all its advisors can align the teamwork to be done ahead of the start of the process. Once the team is determined, two different workstreams are set up in parallel: the legal documentation one and the marketing one. The first workstream is aimed at coordinating the activities necessary to finalize the legal documentation package, in line with the best market practices for this kind of transactions, on one side, and at drafting and finalizing both the Italian Prospectus and the Offering Circular, on the other. The Italian Prospectus has to be filed with and reviewed by Consob and Borsa Italiana before, respectively, the final approval ("Nulla Osta") by Consob and the admission to listing ("Ammissione alle negoziazioni") by Borsa Italiana. The International Offering Circular does not need to be approved by Consob and it is used to market and disclose the offering outside of Italy. To that end, the legal advisors must ensure consistency between the Italian Prospectus and the International Offering Circular content.
The marketing workstream is aimed at gathering potential interest from market investors towards the equity story, that will hopefully be converted into tangible orders once the book opens.
Below is a brief overview of the key responsibilities for each party:

Figure 2 Overview of the respective key responsibilities of each party

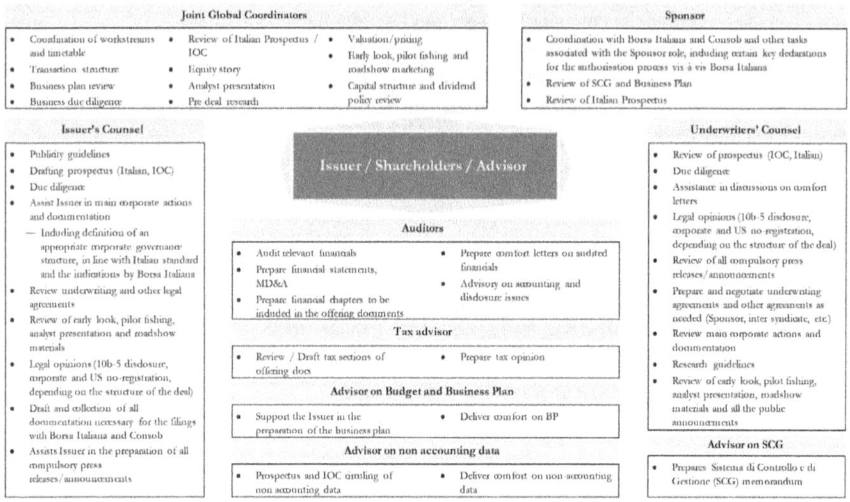

Management presentation (5 June 2019)

The first step for both the marketing and legal workstreams is a presentation from the management to banks and lawyers, that will be key to convey the key strengths and selling points that will have to be highlighted in front of investors and regulators. On 5 June, Sanlorenzo invited the whole working group to the La Spezia shipyard where the key managers gave a comprehensive presentation followed by a shipyard tour and a brief yacht cruise. The management presentation is a crucial moment, because it lays the foundation for all the documents that will be used with investors in order to successfully sell the company's shares. It is really important for all the parties involved to fully understand the business model, market dynamics, competitive scenario, future strategy, and the company's historical financials. Clear communication will help when preparing both the prospectus and investor material.

Figure 3 Sample management presentation agenda, detailed

Main Topics to be Covered

- **History and background**
  - Main events and evolution
- **Organisational structure**
  - Corporate structure
  - Management structure
- **Group overview / Business Model**
  - Different segments of activity / Business Units / Geographies
  - Products / Services offered
  - Customer base
  - Suppliers / Partnership agreements
  - Distribution network (agents, distributors, etc.)
  - Production footprint
  - Key lean manufacturing principles adopted
- **Competitive scenario (Product / Geography)**
  - Sector trends and major dynamics
  - Market positioning
  - Key competitors
  - Barriers to entry / exit
  - Regulatory framework
- **Financial overview**
  - Financial overview by Business Segment
  - Key highlights on historical performance
  - Details on current capital structure
  - Update on current trading (NWC dynamics / seasonality)
  - Business plan and key assumptions
- **Group strategy (Product / Geography)**
  - Key financial targets and business focus
  - Expansion / Growth strategies
  - Product development
  - Marketing strategies
  - Expected operating short and long term plans
  - Update on M&A activity
- **Research & Development**
  - Organization
  - R&D Investments
  - Patents
- **Human resources**
  - Highlights on personnel composition
  - Performance Indicators
  - Incentive structure
- **Corporate Governance**
  - Shareholders' structure
  - Existing shareholders' agreements
- **Legal issues**
  - Related parties transactions
  - Outstanding significant litigations
  - Others

Legal documentation

The first workstream, that will last from the start of the process until the pricing of the transaction, is the one related to the legal documentation. The main actors are the legal counsels for the issuer and the banks. The main documents are:

Figure 4 Legal documentation overview

Document	Description	Primary Responsibility
BUSINESS PLAN AND SCG MEMO	• Listing documents required by Borsa Italiana at filing (these docs will not become public but are provided solely to Borsa as part of its due diligence process), including – 3-year business plan including assumptions, key drivers, forecasts, sensitivity analysis, achieved and future strategy, action plan – Description of company's internal auditing and reporting system, including description of KPI ("key performance indicators") and highlighting, as appropriate, potential weaknesses and actions planned to address them	• Lead: Company, Consultant • Key parties: Sponsor, JGC
ITALIAN PROSPECTUS	• Offer document that describes the plan of distribution and contains a description of Company, its business, risks, management and financial statements and certain information about the shareholders • Historical and interim financials • The minimum required information is governed by EU Regulation (2017/1129 as amended) and best practice	• Lead: IC, Company • Key parties: JGC, UC, A
INTERNATIONAL OFFERING CIRCULAR	• International standard disclosure document used to market and disclose the offering outside Italy • Factual content to be aligned with the Italian prospectus • Preliminary IOC (with no IPO price detail) to be ready ahead of bookbuilding	• Lead: IC, Company • Key parties: JGC, UC, A
UNDERWRITING AGREEMENTS	• Provides standard representations, warranties and indemnity • Executed upon pricing between JGC, Company and Selling Shareholders–draft agreed before bookbuilding	• Lead: UC, IC • Key parties: JGC, Company, selling shareholders
LEGAL AND TAX OPINIONS	• Market-standard opinions from legal counsels and tax advisor to JGC on the legality and validity of the securities being offered – Comfort on the adequacy of information in the Prospectus / IOC (10b-5 Opinion) – Comfort on no need to register the offering in the US (No-Registration Opinion) – Comfort on the tax treatment of the securities offered (Tax Opinion) • Executed at filing and upon closing	• Lead: IC, UC • Key parties: JGC
COMFORT LETTERS	• Auditors provide JGC with an auditor's comfort letter – Market-standard opinion provided by Company's independent auditors to the JGC in relation to financial information contained in the Prospectus / IOC and verifying that no material adverse changes in Company's financial position have taken place since the date of the latest accounts – SAS 72 comfort letters – No more than 135 days must pass since the date of the latest financials, otherwise numbers are considered 'stale' • Auditors or business consultants to provide comfort on relevant KPIs included in the offering documentation • Executed at filing and upon closing	• Lead: A • Key parties: Company, IC, UC, JGC
LOCK-UP AGREEMENTS	• Commitment to the JGC not to sell Company's shares within an agreed period of time (market standard [180/365] days) • Commitment sought from the issuer, shareholder and top management (if they own shares)	• Lead: UC • Key parties: Shareholders, Company, IC, JGC

JGC: Joint Global Coordinator; A: Auditor; UC: Underwriters' Counsel; IC: Issuers' Counsel

Early marketing (July – October 2019)

The second workstream, related to the marketing of the transaction, starts shortly after the management presentation. During the early stages of the process, it is in fact common to have some limited interaction with selected investors. This is the first point of contact with investors to introduce them to the Sanlorenzo equity story and immediately gauge potential interest towards the transaction and initial key questions. It is important to understand what might be the concerns and points of attention from a market perspective to be properly addressed during the marketing phase, while giving the management of the company the opportunity to test themselves in front of investors ahead of the bookbuilding phase.

The meetings are usually 60 minutes long, with a Q&A session at the end. This is the first checkpoint in assessing the good health of the transaction. The preliminary feedback that can be gathered from investors provides a huge hint on the potential market interest. At this stage, all the communications with the market are carried out following the acceptance of a Non-Disclosure Agreement ("NDA") and (potentially) under the Market Abuse Regulation ("MAR"), if applicable, leaving the transaction on a private level. If no interest is shown towards the company, the JGCs, after consulting with the shareholders, can decide to pull the transaction and avoid any unnecessary bad public reputation.

Usually, the pre-IPO investor approach is driven by the importance of building a strong personal relationship with key anchor investors ahead of the actual offer. The four main categories of investors involved in the Sanlorenzo transaction were the following:

I. **Long-Only/Institutional investors:** These are the ideal investors at IPO with potential for large anchor orders. The investment decision is taken by various PMs for each managed fund and demand is aggregated by the Capital Markets desk.
II. **Hedge Funds:** Important investors in terms of order size potential, feedback pro-activeness, and generation of momentum during bookbuilding. Investment decision taken by senior PMs and, in some cases, demand is aggregated by the Capital Markets desk.
III. **Italian Investors:** Italian investors important to demonstrate local buy-in in the Sanlorenzo story but tend to be market followers on valuation. Proximity to the story makes them ideal candidates for site visits.
IV. **UHNWI/PWM networks:** Ability to participate in IPO with sizeable and often price insensitive demand, but unlikely to provide market-leading valuation feedback. Investment decision taken by ultimate wealth owner and aggregated as a single order under each institution/network.

Given the preliminary stage of the process, the document that is presented to the selected audience of investors is usually not very detailed. Market regulations require that only public information should be shared with investors, especially from a financial standpoint.
A first round of meetings was held in July, across Europe and the US. Specifically, the management met with around 40 high-quality accounts with a fundamental-driven approach in 1-on-1s across 7 days in London, Milan, Paris, and New York. A second round was held in early October in London. The Fort Lauderdale boat show, taking place at the end of the October, presented the perfect opportunity to assess the US-based demand, taking advantage of the display of Sanlorenzo's fleet. Across all the interactions, around sixty 1-on-1s were held resulting in interesting and constructive feedback and concerns.

Figure 5 **Early look presentation cover page**

Figure 6 **Early look itinerary**

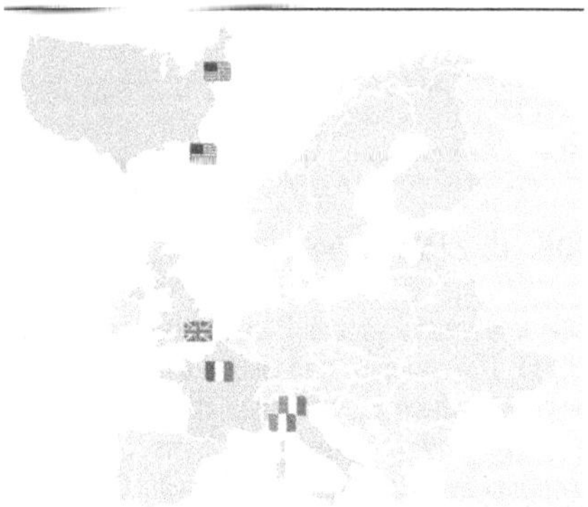

Analyst presentation and preparation of research reports (10 September 2019)

A crucial step towards the success of the Initial Public Offering is the publication of the research reports. These are equity reports written by equity research analysts, working for the investment banks mandated on the deal, with independence and unbiased views. The analysts prepare their work only with the available public information, which is then circulated to and discussed with potential investors during the Pre-Deal Investor Education phase. This is an additional important instrument, alongside the 1-on-1 meeting with the management during the roadshow, that an investor can use when assessing potential interest and work on the valuation. The research report

in fact contains sections containing the analysts' estimates of the future financials and a valuation section that contains the recommendation on the company's estimated value (that cannot be disclosed to the team working on the other side of the Chinese wall, i.e. ECM or IBD/Corporate finance, to preserve the independent nature of the valuation).
In order to give to the research analysts all the information they need to correctly assess the future evolution of the financial profile, the valuation of the company, and its selling points, the Joint Global Coordinators (helped by the company and its advisors) prepare a presentation that is discussed in an ad hoc meeting called the analyst presentation. Sanlorenzo decided to hold the analyst presentation during the Cannes boat show, on 10 September, profiting from the presence of the yacht exhibition and giving analysts the opportunity to experience in first person its fleet and the customer experience.
This presentation, compared to the management presentation and to the one used during the early marketing activities, was improved thanks to the feedback from investors, and contained a section dedicated to the offer structure with some details on, for example, expected free float, split between primary and secondary offer, selling restrictions, lock-up, etc.

Figure 7 **Analyst presentation agenda**

Figure 8 **Indicative offer structure slide**

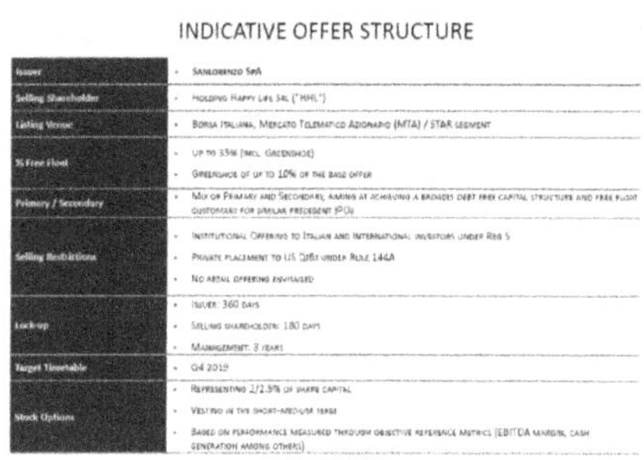

PDIE (12-22 November 2019)

This is a crucial moment for the transaction because at this stage the deal enters into the public phase. The company had issued a press release on 23 September (the so-called "intention to float" or "ITF") where it announced that "*it has filed the application with Borsa Italiana for the admission to listing of its ordinary shares on the Mercato Telematico Azionario organized and managed by Borsa Italiana. In connection with the Listing, the Company has prepared the Prospectus which has been filed with Consob for approval.*" This press release also gave some preliminary details regarding company overview and offer structure. Final terms and the structure of the offering would be determined and announced immediately before the commencement of the offering, once the prospectus was approved by Consob.
Following the publication of the ITF, we entered the pre-deal investor education stage of the transaction. The analysts that published the research reports started to take meetings and calls with various investors, educating them on the transaction details and potential valuation of the company. During the 2 week-long PDIE exercise, the analysts held c. 200 meetings across Europe and the US to discuss their research reports with mainly long-only accounts, that given their long-term investment view are a crucial component of the final demand during the bookbuilding stage.

Figure 9 **PDIE detailed itinerary**

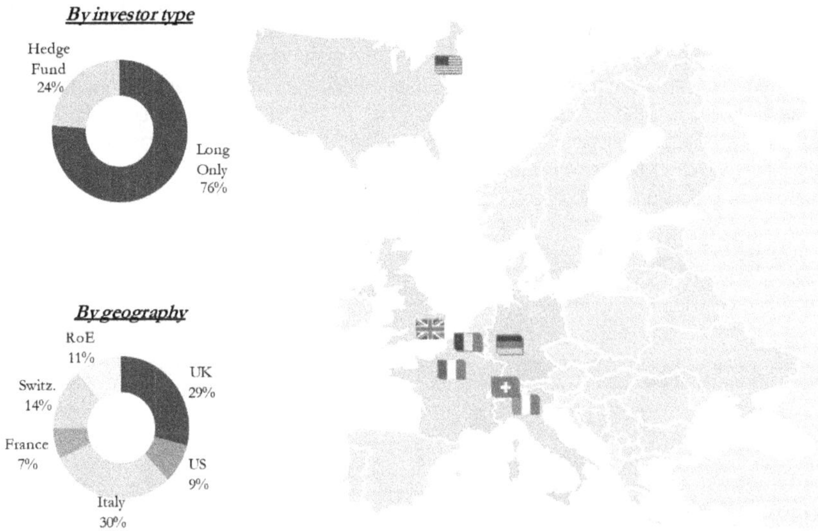

The Joint Global Coordinators were able to collect 355 lines of feedback that were presented to the company and its advisors on dedicated evening calls from 12 November to 22 November. There are usually two types of information that the sales force tries to gather from investors when asking for feedback during the PDIE exercise. On the one hand, there are qualitative information that are usually split into: general comments on the company, attractions, and concerns. From this info the JGCs can understand what are the key selling points that will have to be stressed and the biggest concerns that will have to be addressed during the roadshow meetings between investors and management. In this case, most of the investors appreciated the high quality and unique business, the management team, the resiliency over the cycle, and the business model based on a mono-brand approach, with direct distribution and a high-quality customer base. On the other hand, there is valuation feedback, that will be used for the price range setting. Usually, when evaluating equity investments for IPOs, investors tend to use the market multiples methodology, supported by fundamental approach cross-check, unless there is a specific business model that requires other methods. In the valuation feedback collected in Pre-Deal Investor Education, there is usually an indication regarding the kind of multiples, the reference year, and the peer group considered. For Sanlorenzo, the majority of investors were looking at EV/EBITDA on 2020 numbers (1 year forward looking multiples thanks to a high visibility provided by the solid and resilient backlog), with P/E 2020 used as cross-check, while very few were using the DCF methodology. Given the lack of listed peers in the yachting sector, most investors were looking at a mix of boat, industrials, and luxury goods peers, while some were referencing the failed Ferretti IPO. The valuation indications were at a premium to boat peers (given the higher quality) and at a discount to luxury peers (due to structural differences between business models, i.e. higher cyclicality/capex and lower margins). Another common aspect when evaluating a company that is trying to list, is to consider an IPO discount towards peers, that is mainly related to the fact that investors are taking a risk in terms of liquidity and lack of historical performance. Market conditions at launch have a huge impact on valuation and need to be factored in.

This is a second checkpoint for the transaction. If there is not as much interest in the company as expected or if the valuation indications are too far from the client's expectations, the JGCs, along with the selling shareholder, can decide to pull the deal or postpone it to another market window, on the basis of improved market conditions.

Price range setting (26 November 2019)

From the feedback gathered by the sales force after the investor meeting with the analyst, the banks were able to gather c. 60 valuation data points. Having a brief indication of the valuation and potential order size from investors met by the analyst is crucial for the price range setting stage, because with those data the banks are able to understand where investors are positioning the company and test if the client's expectations could be met. The output produced starting from the investors' valuation feedback is called the "waterfall," that indicates at the various levels of the share price, which investors would be available to enter the transaction. This is an efficient and visual way to understand what price could be a good starting point for the range.

Figure 10 Valuation waterfall

Share price

14.00	14.50	15.00	15.50	16.00	16.50	17.00	17.50	18.00	18.50	19.00
Investor 1	Investor 1	Investor 1	Investor 1	Investor 1	Investor 1	Investor 1	Investor 1	Investor 1	Investor 1	
Investor 2	Investor 2	Investor 2	Investor 2	Investor 2	Investor 2	Investor 2	Investor 2	Investor 2	Investor 2	
Investor 3	Investor 3	Investor 3	Investor 3	Investor 3	Investor 3	Investor 3	Investor 3	Investor 3	Investor 3	
Investor 4	Investor 4	Investor 4	Investor 4	Investor 4	Investor 4	Investor 4	Investor 4	Investor 4	Investor 4	
Investor 5	Investor 5	Investor 5	Investor 5	Investor 5	Investor 5	Investor 5	Investor 5	Investor 5	Investor 5	
Investor 6	Investor 6	Investor 6	Investor 6	Investor 6	Investor 6	Investor 6	Investor 6	Investor 6	Investor 6	
Investor 7	Investor 7	Investor 7	Investor 7	Investor 7	Investor 7	Investor 7	Investor 7	Investor 7	Investor 7	
Investor 8	Investor 8	Investor 8	Investor 8	Investor 8	Investor 8	Investor 8	Investor 8	Investor 8	Investor 8	
Investor 9	Investor 9	Investor 9	Investor 9	Investor 9	Investor 9	Investor 9	Investor 9	Investor 9	Investor 9	
Investor 10	Investor 10	Investor 10	Investor 10	Investor 10	Investor 10	Investor 10	Investor 10	Investor 10	Investor 10	
Investor 11	Investor 11	Investor 11	Investor 11	Investor 11	Investor 11	Investor 11	Investor 11			
Investor 12	Investor 12	Investor 12	Investor 12	Investor 12	Investor 12	Investor 12	Investor 12			
Investor 13	Investor 13	Investor 13	Investor 13	Investor 13	Investor 13	Investor 13	Investor 13			
Investor 14	Investor 14	Investor 14	Investor 14	Investor 14	Investor 14	Investor 14	Investor 14			
Investor 15	Investor 15	Investor 15	Investor 15	Investor 15	Investor 15	Investor 15	Investor 15			
Investor 16	Investor 16	Investor 16	Investor 16	Investor 16	Investor 16	Investor 16	Investor 16			
Investor 17	Investor 17	Investor 17	Investor 17	Investor 17	Investor 17	Investor 17	Investor 17			
Investor 18	Investor 18	Investor 18	Investor 18	Investor 18	Investor 18	Investor 18	Investor 18			
Investor 19	Investor 19	Investor 19	Investor 19	Investor 19	Investor 19	Investor 19	Investor 19			
Investor 20	Investor 20	Investor 20	Investor 20	Investor 20	Investor 20	Investor 20	Investor 20			
Investor 21	Investor 21	Investor 21	Investor 21	Investor 21	Investor 21	Investor 21	Investor 21			
Investor 22	Investor 22	Investor 22	Investor 22	Investor 22	Investor 22	Investor 22	Investor 22			
Investor 23	Investor 23	Investor 23	Investor 23	Investor 23	Investor 23					
Investor 24	Investor 24	Investor 24	Investor 24	Investor 24						
Investor 25	Investor 25	Investor 25	Investor 25	Investor 25						
Investor 26	Investor 26	Investor 26	Investor 26	Investor 26						
Investor 27	Investor 27	Investor 27	Investor 27	Investor 27						
Investor 28	Investor 28	Investor 28	Investor 28	Investor 28						
Investor 29	Investor 29	Investor 29	Investor 29	Investor 29						
Investor 30	Investor 30	Investor 30	Investor 30	Investor 30						
Investor 31	Investor 31	Investor 31	Investor 31	Investor 31						
Investor 32	Investor 32	Investor 32	Investor 32	Investor 32						
Investor 33	Investor 33	Investor 33	Investor 33	Investor 33						
Investor 34	Investor 34	Investor 34	Investor 34	Investor 34						
Investor 35	Investor 35	Investor 35	Investor 35	Investor 35						
Investor 36	Investor 36	Investor 36	Investor 36	Investor 36						
Investor 37	Investor 37	Investor 37	Investor 37	Investor 37						
Investor 38	Investor 38	Investor 38	Investor 38	Investor 38						
Investor 39	Investor 39	Investor 39	Investor 39	Investor 39						
Investor 40	Investor 40	Investor 40	Investor 40	Investor 40						
Investor 41	Investor 41	Investor 41	Investor 41	Investor 41						
Investor 42	Investor 42	Investor 42	Investor 42	Investor 42						
Investor 43	Investor 43	Investor 43	Investor 43	Investor 43						
Investor 44	Investor 44	Investor 44	Investor 44	Investor 44						
Investor 45	Investor 45	Investor 45	Investor 45	Investor 45						
Investor 46	Investor 46	Investor 46	Investor 46	Investor 46						
Investor 47	Investor 47	Investor 47	Investor 47	Investor 47						
Investor 48	Investor 48	Investor 48	Investor 48	Investor 48						
Investor 49	Investor 49	Investor 49	Investor 49	Investor 49						
Investor 50	Investor 50	Investor 50	Investor 50	Investor 50						
Investor 51	Investor 51	Investor 51	Investor 51	Investor 51						
Investor 52	Investor 52	Investor 52	Investor 52	Investor 52						
Investor 53	Investor 53	Investor 53	Investor 53	Investor 53						
Investor 54	Investor 54	Investor 54	Investor 54	Investor 54						
Investor 55	Investor 55									
Investor 56	Investor 56									
Investor 57										

Setting the 'right' price range is of critical importance for the success of the IPO and the trading of shares in the aftermarket. The width of the price range should leave scope to exploit bookbuilding momentum (a significant aspect in a difficult market environment) and give adequate 'price guidance' to investors. It is market practice to leave a ±10-12.5% from the mid-point of the range. Setting the bottom end of the price range is of particular importance because it obviously needs to be set at an attractive level, which will act as a 'hook' to generate significant investor interest and early orders. The main objective is the creation of momentum to push investors with limit orders up into the upper half of the price range. The top end of the range is important as well, because it should be set at a level that is demanding but achievable if all external factors are favourable. Setting the top end too high will encourage investors to disregard it and focus on the bottom number. Given the challenging market environment, the company decided to set the price range from EUR 16 to EUR 19 per share. The overall offer structure resulting from this price range is the following:

Figure 11 Analysis at various prices (AVP)

Share Price (€)	14.0	14.5	15.0	15.5	16.0	16.5	17.0	17.5	18.0	18.5	19.0	19.5	20.0
# Shares Pre-money (m)							30.0						
Equity Value Pre-money (€m)	420	435	450	465	480	495	510	525	540	555	570	585	600
# Newly Issued Shares (m)							4.5						
Primary Component (€m)	63	65	68	70	72	74	77	79	81	83	86	88	90
Equity Value Post-money (€m)	483	500	518	535	552	569	587	604	621	638	656	673	690
Free Float Post Greenshoe (%)[1]	*35.1%*	*35.1%*	*35.1%*	*35.1%*	*35.1%*	*35.1%*	*35.1%*	*35.1%*	*35.1%*	*35.1%*	*35.1%*	*35.1%*	*35.1%*
Enterprise Value (€m)	509	524	539	554	569	584	599	614	629	644	659	674	689

On 26 November, the company published a press release announcing to the market that "*The price range has been set at between €16.00 and €19.00 per share, corresponding to a capitalisation following the capital increase of between €552 million and approximately €656 million.*"

Nulla Osta from Consob (28 November 2019)

Before being able to open the books and start taking orders, the company needs to obtain approval from the Consob ("*nulla osta*") on the Italian prospectus. The standard IPO authorization process in Italy takes between 8-10 weeks. The Italian Prospectus is usually drafted by the Issuer's counsel in accordance with the schemes provided by the European Regulation.
The nulla osta was received on November 28th and a press release was issued on the same day. From that moment, the Italian prospectus was printed and circulated to Italian institutional investors.

Roadshow/Bookbuilding (27 November – 5 December)

Following the early publication of the International Offering Circular, on Monday, 25 November, the management of the Company had a preliminary 1-on-1 meeting with an important investor in London. Other meetings, following the first one, took place in Paris, Brussels, Milan, New York, and Frankfurt. During the last day in Milan, both physical meetings and conference calls with international investors were held. During these eight days of travelling, the company managed to meet more than 90 institutions across the globe. A good commitment was shown by the accounts met in the early marketing stage, with a hit ratio (accounts met during early marketing who also took a roadshow meeting) of c. 52%, despite the difficult market environment.

Figure 12 Detailed roadshow itinerary

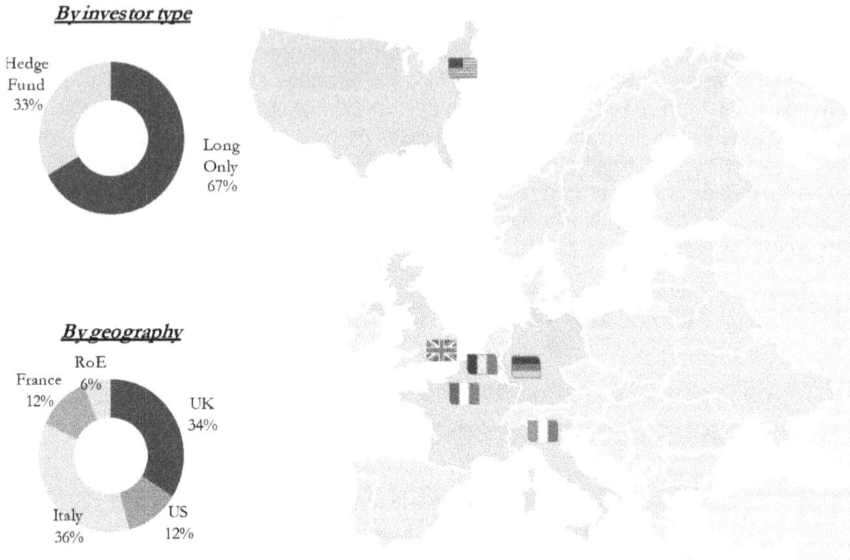

Most of the meetings conducted in London on the first day of the roadshow went positively, with some very constructive feedback and interest from a broad panel of investors. The market environment was tough, with 11 IPOs postponed or cancelled amid increasing investor selectivity and price sensitivity due to a volatile geopolitical scenario and lower appetite for less liquid SMEs approaching year end.

With measured but constant progress in the demand evolution, on the second-to-last day the anticipated order from a key UK/US investor materialized and fuelled strong momentum that made it possible to disseminate the book covered message to the market. Sending messages to the market is a way to provide public reassurances on the positive outcome of the transaction. One of the most important messages is the one that communicates that the book is officially covered, hence there is enough demand for the deal to close.

Source: Used with permission of Bloomberg Finance L.P.

The book covered message reassured the market on the very likely success of the transaction and brought total demand to c. EUR 290mn. The following message was disseminated to the market ahead of the book closing deadline:

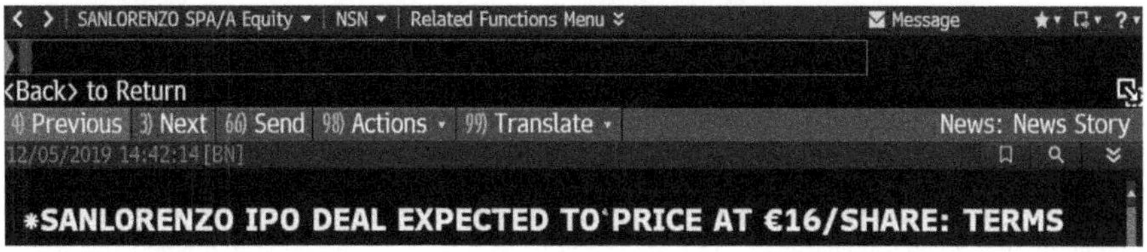

Source: Used with permission of Bloomberg Finance L.P.

Pricing (6 December 2019)

The IPO is a best effort transaction; in fact, the syndicate of banks typically does not underwrite/purchase the securities that might remain unsold (such as in an underwritten transaction, i.e. a rights issue). If there is not as much demand from the market compared to the number of shares offered in the transaction, the IPO will not be priced and the company will stay private. In the context of an IPO, a book should be well oversubscribed in order to be allocable (and therefore for the transaction to be priceable). Oversubscribed is a term used when the demand for the shares is greater than the number of securities offered. Achieving a simple 1x coverage of the offer size does not guarantee the success of the deal. It is common practice for investors to inflate their order in order to be allocated at the desired amount. It is uncommon for investors to have their orders 100% allocated. It is also positive to have the possibility to choose among investors, preferring the non-opportunistic ones with more of a long-term investment horizon.

In a normal market context, a successful transaction will have more than one level of price with a book coverage ratio greater than 1x. In these cases, the role of the JGCs is to maximise the value of the company while leaving investors happy with the price level they will have to pay. The order is not binding and a too aggressive move on pricing might create a negative reaction from investors, that can either cancel the order or sell the shares on the first day of trading (taking advantage of the Greenshoe as a "stop-loss" mechanism) and drive the performance towards negative territory. In the complex market environment where Sanlorenzo was priced, the price choice was pretty straightforward at EUR 16 per share, where coverage was strong and investors were confident at that valuation.

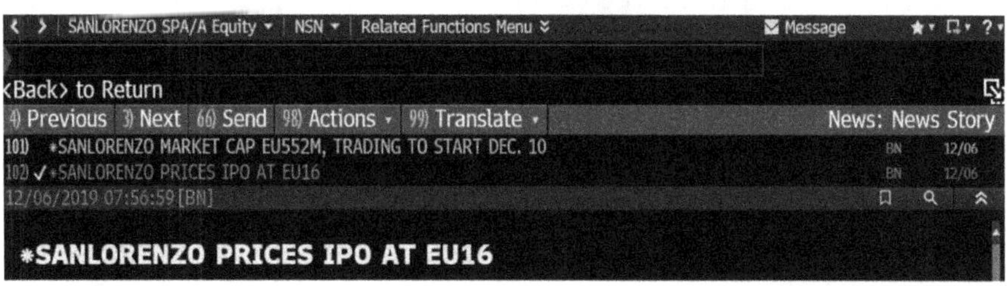

Source: Used with permission of Bloomberg Finance L.P.

The following step is to allocate the shares offered to the demand expressed by investors, filling their orders in a totally discretional way. The role of the Joint Global Coordinators is to provide an allocation proposal (that will maximise the quality of the book and the stock performance in the aftermarket) that the company and its advisors can then evaluate and work on.

The allocation objectives are to maximise the valuation achieved at IPO, taking into consideration the prevailing market conditions and investor demand, while creating a sustainable, long-term shareholder base for the company. The goal is to seek a positive aftermarket performance for the shares post-IPO and sufficient liquidity for the stock. The recommendation tends to be to allocate to investors that have done the necessary work to fully understand the investment case and that will be supportive in the immediate aftermarket as well as over the longer term. This requires demonstrable knowledge and understanding of the sector, the company's strategy, and the financial return prospects. The allocation should moreover reflect the individual counterparty risk and provide approximately for a sufficient degree of aftermarket liquidity. Among the factors to be considered when deciding the allocation are: the overall subscription levels, the investor's price sensitivity, whether the investor's order is consistent with the investment strategy and objectives, participation in the marketing stages, quality of feedback provided during the marketing process, behaviour in previous IPOs and potential order inflation, timing of the investor's interest, and geographical presence. Given that hedge funds are seeking more of a short-term capital gain, it is less likely for them to support the aftermarket of the stock and therefore less is allocated to them compared to long-only or private wealth accounts.

SANLORENZO IPO: SUCCESSFUL CONCLUSION OF THE INSTITUTIONAL PLACEMENT OFFERING
The offering price was set at € 16.00 per Share. The Offering comprises (i) 4,500,000 newly-issued shares resulting from a capital increase with exclusion of pre-emption rights, and (ii) 7,600,000 shares offered for sale by Holding Happy Life S.r.l. (the "Selling Shareholder"), the Company's majority shareholder controlled by Massimo Perotti, Executive Chairman of Sanlorenzo, including 1,100,000 Over Allotment option Shares subject to the exercise of the greenshoe option.
Based on the Offering Price, the total value of the transaction, including the Greenshoe Option, amounts to € 193.6 million and the resulting capitalization of Sanlorenzo is € 552 million, including the € 72 million capital increase. The Offering encountered strong interest from the Italian and international investor community, with demand at the Offer Price for approximately € 290 million by leading qualified investors and particularly by long-only ones. Approximately two-thirds of the demand come from international investors and about one- third from Italian investors.
The date of commencement of trading of the ordinary shares of the Company, subject to verification by Borsa Italiana of the existence of the requirements for distribution to the public, was scheduled for Tuesday 10 December 2019.

First day of trading (Tuesday, 10 December)

On 10 December the Sanlorenzo stock began to trade on the Milan stock exchange. Before the start of trading, as is common on these important occasions, an event was hosted by Borsa Italiana at Piazza Affari to celebrate the effort and ring the famous bell at the market opening.

Figure 13 **First day of trading ceremony**

The stock opened at EUR 16.25 p.s. before going back down to its IPO price at 9:41 a.m. and touching a low of EUR 15.95 p.s. at 10:28 a.m.

Source: Used with permission of Bloomberg Finance L.P.

The security traded for the rest of the day above the IPO price with a small spike in the afternoon, before closing at EUR 16.00 p.s.

Source: Used with permission of Bloomberg Finance L.P.

Greenshoe (10 December 2019 – 9 January 2020)

The "greenshoe" or "over-allotment" option is an option granting underwriters in an Initial Public Offering the ability to sell additional shares to investors compared to the number of shares initially sold in the IPO, usually in an amount up to 15% of the initial offer size, at the original offer price. In the context of an IPO, the greenshoe option is contained in the underwriting agreement and is granted to the Underwriters either by the Issuer or by a Selling Shareholder. In addition, it is common to also grant a lending option in an IPO whereby the Underwriters are given an option to borrow the same amount of existing shares from an Issuer (if it has treasury shares) or from a Shareholder prior to the greenshoe option being exercised in full. The lending option and greenshoe option may be exercised within 30 days of the IPO closing.

A greenshoe option provides additional price stability to a security issuance because the Underwriters can increase supply and smooth out price fluctuations. In particular, the greenshoe option is usually exercised if the market demand for shares in the IPO exceeds demand and the price of the shares rises too quickly: placing additional shares in the market is aimed at helping satisfy demand and stabilising the price of the shares. Conversely, if demand for the shares is weak or if the price of the shares is not performing as expected, the Underwriters may determine not to exercise the greenshoe option, thereby limiting the number of shares in the market to the original IPO amount.

The lending option allows the Underwriters to manage these scenarios prior to deciding to place the additional shares on the market permanently. By exercising the lending option, the Underwriters can place the additional shares in the market for stabilisation purposes and then buy them back as required (returning them to the Issuer or the Shareholder) without then confirming the final additional sale through exercise of the greenshoe option.
Sanlorenzo's greenshoe options allowed the Joint Global Coordinators to sell up to 10% more shares than the original amount set by the Issuer for up to 30 days after the IPO if demand conditions warranted such action. In particular, the offering comprised 4,500,000 newly-issued shares (primary component) and 7,600,000 shares offered for sale by the reference shareholder (secondary component), including 1,100,000 overallotment option Shares subject to the exercise of the greenshoe option. As indicated above, Underwriters usually use the greenshoe option in one of two ways.
First, if the IPO is a success and the share price surges, the underwriters, having previously exercised the lending option, may exercise the greenshoe option in full, buy the extra stock from the Issuer or Shareholders at the predetermined price, and issue those shares to their clients. Conversely, if the price starts to fall, they buy back the shares from the market instead of the Issuer or the Shareholder to cover their short position, supporting the stock to stabilize its price; in this case they will return any borrowed shares to the Issuer or a Shareholder and not exercise the greenshoe.
The Issuer and the stabilisation manager are required to disclose any purchase made in connection with the greenshoe option. Below are the details of the movements related to the utilization of the overallotment option:

Date	# of shares purchased	# of transactions	Price range (EUR p.s.)
10 December	483,120	298	15.95-16.00
11 December	259,554	89	15.53-16.00
12 December	11,024	8	15.30-15.50
13 December	9,470	52	15.20-15.32
17 December	206	1	15.99
18 December	18,871	19	15.85-15.95
19 December	10,000	5	15.70-15.72
23 December	10,000	3	15.65-15.75
7 January	28,139	45	15.874
8 January	84,331	96	15.80-15.88
9 January	27,308	32	15.802-15.904
Total	942,023		

At the end of the 30-day period, the overallotment option was exercised for 157,977 shares by the JGCs, leading to a final offer size of 11,157,977 ordinary shares, corresponding to c. 32.3% of the company's share capital.

Fee

An IPO is a complex and expensive process for the company. The fees and expenses to be considered include, but are not limited to, the following: sponsor's fees (in the case of an IPO on the STAR segment), Issuer's and Banks' legal counsels, Auditor's fees, tax consultants, MIS consultants, non-accounting data consultants, advertising expenses, printer, roadshow manager and travel expenses, PR manager, newspaper legal notices, and Borsa Italiana and Consob fees.
The commission for the banks consisted of a fee of up to 3.25% of the offer size (including the greenshoe option, if exercised), divided into a base fee (a fixed amount to be paid if the deal is priced) and an incentive component (which can be paid at the selling shareholder's total discretion as addi-

tional remuneration to the banks). The underwriting fee does not include the operational expenses (i.e. travel) sustained by the JGCs during the IPO process that are reimbursed by the company.
In addition, according to market practice, in the event an IPO does not conclude successfully, and the transaction is postponed or cancelled, the banks usually have no right to any remuneration except for the reimbursement of the expenses incurred during the process.

Questions and answers

1. *What are the main objectives of being listed on an exchange for a firm and its shareholders?*
   From the firm's perspective, listing on an exchange has four main objectives:

   1. financial structure;
   2. acquisition currency;
   3. reputation;
   4. management compensation and discipline.

   From the point of view of the shareholders, the decision to get listed is basically related to cash; we can identify the following three main reasons:

   1. disinvestment;
   2. privatization;
   3. agency problems with the management.

2. *What are the main risks and costs of going public?*
   IPOs do not come without drawbacks. Typically, we can identify the following four main risks and limitations:

   1. increased formalisation of the decision-making process;
   2. burden of disclosure requirements and compliance costs;
   3. pressure on short-term performance;
   4. exposure to takeover risk.

   In terms of costs, we need to consider both direct and indirect costs. Direct costs include "one-off" costs related to the IPO process and recurring costs related to being listed, while indirect costs stem from the fact that IPOs are usually underpriced (i.e. money is "left on the table").

3. *What do we mean by a "Rule 144a equity offering"?*
   A Rule 144A equity offering is an unregistered offer and sale of equity securities issued by a US or foreign company, the shares of which are neither listed on a US exchange nor quoted in the US. A 144A offering allows the Company to access US demand without the additional burden of the US registration process under SEC requirements.
   There are minimal additional costs or time for the Company, but it is possible to

target Qualified Institutional Buyers in the US, which make up the bulk of the target US institutional investment community.

4. *What is an ADR?*
   American Depositary Receipts (ADRs) are US dollar-denominated negotiable instruments issued by a depositary bank, representing ownership of the underlying ordinary shares of a non-US issuer. Trading in ADRs permits US investors to trade in non-US companies directly in the US equity markets.

5. *Describe the Pre-Deal Investor Education within the IPO process.*
   After the publication of the research report and the IPO announcement, the syndicate research analysts will independently educate fund managers on the issuer investment case. This is the so-called Pre-Deal Investor Education (PDIE), an important element in disseminating the equity story to investors. It will be the first time the investor community hears the overall issuer story; therefore, credibility of research will be key for the success of the issuer's offering. The main focus of the PDIE should be to obtain quality feedback in order to establish the price range for bookbuilding and to prepare the management for the roadshow.

6. *What is the typical syndicate structure in an IPO process?*
   The typical syndicate is composed of three parts (in order of importance), and the first two are called "the underwriting group."

   1. **The managing group:** Global Coordinator(s), bookrunner and joint book-runner(s). These banks manage the syndicate and have responsibility for the deal origination. Moreover, they underwrite the issuance and also have placement functions. The Global Coordinator(s), which gets the largest portion of fees, is responsible for: (1) due diligence, (2) roadshow, (3) book-building, (4) allocation, and (5) aftermarket. It is common to see multiple bookrunners, in particular for the largest IPOs.
   2. **The non-managing underwriters**: the group of banks, called co-lead managers, that underwrite part of the shares, the proportion of which is determined by the managing group under the "underwriting agreement," and execute the placement activity.
   3. **The selling group:** the banks that just put their best effort in selling the shares, without underwriting them. In other words, they do not guarantee the allocation (typically they are present only in the retail tranche).

7. *What is the typical fee structure in an equity offering?*
   Usually, fees applied in an equity offering have three components: management fee (20%), underwriting fee (20%), and selling concession (60%).

   - **The management fees** compensate the global coordinator(s) for structuring the offering, drafting the prospectus, organizing the syndicate, managing the roadshow, dealing with regulators, overseeing the due diligence, etc.

- **The underwriting fee** is meant to compensate the underwriting group for the underwriting risks.
- **The selling concession** is split among the syndicate members, based on the number of shares underwritten by each single bank. In practice, the selling concession is paid to the bank under pre-agreed economics.

8. *What is the stabilization process? Name the main stabilisation techniques*
The US Securities and Exchange Commission (SEC) defines stabilization as "the buying of a security for the limited purpose of preventing or retarding a decline in its open market price in order to facilitate its distribution to the public." The main stabilisation techniques include (i) pricing stabilisation via overallotment and the greenshoe option, and (ii) lock-up and bonus share.

9. *What is overallotment and the greenshoe option?*
Overallotment is the allocation of extra shares on top of the base IPO size, generally capped at 15% of the IPO size and technically implemented via stock lending: the issuer and/or the selling shareholder(s) lend the overallotment shares to the stabilization agent, with a maturity of up to 30 days.
The greenshoe option, also referred to as an overallotment option, is a call option sold by the issuer and/or selling shareholder(s) to the stabilization agent for an amount of shares up to the overallotment at a price equal to the IPO price.

10. *What is a lock-up clause?*
A lock-up clause is a provision which regulates and limits the ability to offer additional equity of the company shortly after the IPO, in order to avoid the share price disruption which would be generated by such an event. Lock-ups are generally comprised between 180 and 365 days and, the longer the period, the more the clause might be seen by the market as a sign of confidence in the future of the company. The overall lock-up clause can involve one or more of the following: Issuer lock-up, Management lock-up, and Shareholder lock-up.

11. *In a bookbuilding pricing approach, how is the final IPO price determined?*
In the bookbuilding process, the banking syndicate builds an order book with all the orders collected from the investors via the sales & trading franchise; such orders result in a demand function which links different levels of demand to different levels of the IPO prices The final IPO price will then be determined by the bookrunners and the issuer and/or selling shareholder(s), starting from this function and also considering the potential allocation outcomes at different price levels.

7 The Equity Capital Market: Secondary Offerings

by Andrea Tortoroglio and Matteo Scalfi

7.1 Introduction to Seasoned Equity Offerings (SEOs)

In the previous chapter, we looked at Initial Public Offerings (IPOs). IPOs are, in a way, the culmination of a growth path which takes the company from its founding (or from a transformational deal) to the public market. At the same time, the interaction between a company and the market does not end with the IPO process: once a company is listed, there are various potential transactions which can take place, called Seasoned Equity Offerings (SEOs), or follow-on offerings.

An SEO is a transaction through which the equity of an already-listed company is offered to the market. Unlike IPOs, where the process is the same, regardless of the IPO rationale (primary vs secondary, new listing vs re-listing, etc.), there are two main structures to implement an SEO: Rights Offering and Accelerated Bookbuilding (ABB).

Rights offering and ABB differ in various aspects, and their differences explain which one is the best option given the actual scenario in which the specific SEO is to take place.

In a rights offering (often also referred to as rights issue), a company issues subscription rights to existing shareholders through which they can buy newly-issued shares. It is already evident that in a rights issue, the company has an active role in the transaction, since it distributes rights to existing shareholders, with the purpose of raising new capital.

In an ABB, a company and/or one or more relevant investors offer shares to the market, selling them to institutional investors via a rapid transaction (generally lasting one day); the offered shares may or may not be newly-issued shares.

As happens in IPOs, SEOs are generally performed via a banking syndicate; similarly, the offering can be fully or partially underwritten by the syndicate in the event the company considers this to be the best solution, generally for a higher fee.

Apart from the structure of the transaction, an SEO can also be analysed from different fundamental perspectives which explain the peculiarities of each approach and are useful to identify the best solution given the specific needs:

1. Direct vs indirect offering;
2. Dilutive vs non-dilutive impact;
3. Primary vs secondary nature;
4. With or without discount.

A first difference between rights offering and ABB is the process through which participating investors obtain the offered shares. ABB are direct offerings, meaning that investors directly purchase the offered shares from the company and/or one or more relevant investors. On the other side, a rights offering is an indirect offering: existing shareholders are entitled to rights to purchase offered shares from the company (as a sort of "dividend in kind") and can decide either to exercise such rights, or to sell them to new investors that can purchase such rights, and consequently, participate in the offering.

The impact of the transaction refers to the offering from the point of view of an existing shareholder in the company. If the offering involves, in whole or in part, the issuance of new shares and the existing shareholder is not able to participate pro-rata in the underwriting, the transaction is dilutive for the existing shareholder, since the shareholder ought to participate in the transaction to retain the same proportion of capital and/or voting rights held before the transaction. On the contrary, if the offering involves already-issued shares, the transaction is clearly non-dilutive: it counts as if it were a sale on the secondary market.

- Rights issues are generally considered non-dilutive, since the existing shareholder is able to maintain the status quo by fully exercising the rights (s)he is entitled to; however, this means fresh money will have to be allocated to the investment, hence a cash-neutral participation in the rights issue is implicitly dilutive.
- ABB are potentially dilutive, depending on their nature: since in an ABB the offered shares are reserved to one or more institutional investors, in the case of a primary ABB an existing shareholder might not be able to participate pro-rata in the new issuance.

The nature of the transaction considers the offering from the point of view of the company. If the offering involves the issuance of new shares, it is a primary transaction and results in fresh equity and additional capital for the company. On the other side, if the offering involves only already-issued shares, it is a purely secondary transaction. A rights offering is always a primary transaction, while an ABB can be primary, secondary, or a mix of the two. Here lies a second difference between rights issue and ABB: a rights issue does not entail a pre-set limit for the new equity which can be issued, while primary issuance within an ABB is generally limited (e.g. max 10% of existing equity capital). Also, it is important to note that rights issues and secondary ABBs represent two extremes in terms of involvement for the company: in a rights offering the company is the main active player, while in a secondary ABB it is a purely passive subject (with various indirect impacts: e.g. change in shareholders' base, impact on share price, etc.).

The transaction discount refers to the difference between the price at which the shares are offered and the prevailing market price when the offering is announced. The majority of SEOs generally take place at a price which offers a discount to the market price, and the depth of the potential discount is a function of different variables, including one or more of the following:

- General market conditions (e.g. positive market with strong demand for risky assets vs distressed market with significant risk premium applied to risky assets);
- Investor appetite for the company's shares;
- Size of the SEO;
- Use of proceeds in the case of a primary offering (e.g. expected and appreciated growth-enhancing acquisitions vs emergency measure to raise liquidity and capital);
- Details on the seller(s) profile (e.g. following a lock-up expiration already known and expected by the market vs well regarded investor(s) unexpectedly disposing of its stake);
- Details on anchor investor(s), if any (e.g. well regarded investor(s) committing to the offering).

Generally, rights offerings have a deeper discount than ABB, since they tend to be larger in size and have a higher impact for the company.

7.2 Rights offerings

Rights offerings (often also referred to as rights issues) are the transactions most similar to a primary IPO, as the company taps the capital markets to increase its equity. However, while an IPO is generally a growth story (in terms of expanding sources of funding, raising fresh capital for new investments, widening the investor base, increasing the company's visibility, etc.), rights issues are most often a transformational story (e.g. company restructuring, M&A activity, reshaping the capital structure, etc.).

A company generally announces a rights offering when it wants to raise a significant amount of fresh capital, without excluding existing shareholders from the offering and with the purpose of maximising the potential size of the transaction.

A rights offering has the purpose of raising capital via the issue of rights to participate in a capital increase, with the aim of offering all shareholders in the company the ability to participate in the capital increase via the issuance of rights attached to the existing shares. Two key features of such transactions are therefore already clear from what we just stated: the purpose (a significant capital increase, often with a transformational rationale) and the target (all shareholders in the company, not only a portion).

Depending on the rationale of the offering, the market might have a very different reaction: to think about two extremes, consider (a) a rights issue to fund a takeover with considerable synergies and a tangible increase in value for the company, versus (b) a rights issue to restore a proper level of equity capital after an unexpected and significant loss.

Given their deep transformational nature, rights offerings generally include a lengthy roadshow process, with the management of the company meeting both existing important investors, as well as new potential anchor investors. This is another similarity with the IPO process and in practical terms means an intensive (and time-consuming) effort by the whole management team in securing the required additional capital. To justify such an effort, the amount of capital to be raised has to be significant: typically much more than what can be raised with a simple ABB.

The banking syndicate is generally quite broad, often including more than one bank; the bigger the offering, the more complex the banking syndicate. For example, the UniCredit 2017 rights issue had the following structure (see **Figure 7.1**): UniCredit CIB acted as Structuring Advisor and Joint Global Coordinator alongside Morgan Stanley, UBS, BofA Merrill Lynch, J.P. Morgan, and Mediobanca, with the syndicate also including:

- five Co-Global Coordinators (Citigroup, Credit Suisse, Deutsche Bank, Goldman Sachs, and HSBC);
- nine Joint Bookrunners (Banca IMI, Banco Santander, Barclays, BBVA, BNP Paribas, Commerzbank, Crédit Agricole CIB, Natixis, and Société Générale).

Three Co-bookrunners, one Co-Lead Manager, and seven Co-Managers. In this case, which will be analysed in detail through a dedicated case study, the main activities of the syndicate were: (i) structuring of the transaction, (ii) equity story prepara-

Figure 7.1 UniCredit 2017 capital increase: the syndicate structure

The Syndicate structure		
6	**Joint Global Coordinators**	UniCredit Corporate & Investment Banking, UBS, J.P. Morgan, Morgan Stanley, Mediobanca, Bank of America Merrill Lynch
5	**Co-Global Coordinators**	HSBC, Goldman Sachs, Citi, Deutsche Bank, Credit Suisse
9	**Joint Bookrunners**	Banca IMI, Santander, Crédit Agricole, Societe Generale, BNP Paribas, Commerzbank, BBVA, Natixis, Barclays
3	**Co-Bookrunners**	**Senior Role**: Macquarie, ABN AMRO; **Junior Role**: Banca Akros
1	**Co-Lead Manager**	Danske
7	**Co-Managers**	CaixaBank, SMBC Nikko, RBC, Jefferies, Equita, KBW; **Junior Role**: Haitong

Source: UniCredit

tion, (iii) roadshow preparation, (iv) pre-underwriting agreement, and (v) underwriting agreement. All banks in the consortium committed to subscribe separately and without joint and several liability any shares which had not been exercised at the end of the market offering, up to a total of EUR 13bn.

In terms of quantitative details, the offering is characterised by one known parameter, two implicit values, and two unknown variables:

1. The known parameter is the subscription price, which is set when the rights issue is announced and is often indicated also in terms of discount to the theoretical ex-right price (TERP).
2. The implicit values are the theoretical ex-right price (TERP) and the right's theoretical value.
3. The unknown variables are the amount of rights which the shareholders will collectively exercise, and as a result, the amount of fresh capital which will be raised (unless the offering is fully underwritten by the banking syndicate when announced; in this case, only the amount of rights exercised is an unknown variable).

The subscription price is the price per share at which shareholders can buy the new shares within the capital increase. In other words, it is the price the shareholders will have to pay for each new share when deciding to exercise their rights. The subscription price is always at a discount to the market price when the offer is announced. Moreover, for shareholders to have an interest in participating in the capital increase, it will have to be below the market price of the share when the offering expires (otherwise interested investors could simply increase their participation via secondary market purchases at a price below the subscription price). The subscription price is generally indicated in terms of a discount on the previous market price and/or the TERP.

A key feature of rights issues is that, in the majority of cases, the share price performs poorly when the offering is announced. There is a direct relationship between the negative performance of the shares, the discount size, and the amount of capital to be raised: the more capital has to be raised, the deeper the discount, and the deeper the discount, the larger the drop in the market price of the share when the offering is announced.

7.2.1 Theoretical Ex-Right Price (TERP)

Starting from the market price and the subscription price, we can calculate two implicit values which have a key role during the offering period: the value of a right and the theoretical ex-right price (TERP).

The value of a right is linked to the relationship between share price, subscription price, and the amount of rights required to buy one new share. Normally you need multiple rights for one share, because the number of new shares issued is generally lower than the number of shares outstanding. The TERP is the theoretical market value of one share when the right(s) have been granted to the entitled shareholder (hence, detached from the share).

To understand the role of TERP and how it works, the easiest way is to look at the right as if it were a "dividend in kind," disregarding for the moment any technicalities associated with the capital increase and the issuance of new shares.

As a result of the rights issue, an existing shareholder will be granted right(s) (let's say one right for each share). However, what does it take to be an "existing shareholder"?

- As happens with dividend payments, to be entitled to the right (the dividend) it is necessary to be a shareholder in the company on the record date.
- Similarly to dividends, the ex-right date (the day on which the share price no longer incorporates the value of the right) occurs before the record date (since the trades executed on the ex-date will settle the day after the record date).
- The cum-right date is the latest day in which the share incorporates the right's value because (again, similarly to dividends) a trade executed on the cum-right date will settle on the record date, and as a result, entitle the holder to receive the right on the distribution date.

On the ex-right date, *ceteris paribus*, the share should have a price which excludes the value of the right: this is called TERP, and conceptually, it is the same as the share price adjusted for the dividend when the share trades ex-dividend. However, while dividends have an explicit monetary value, this is not the case for rights; in fact, rights have a market price when they start to trade separately from existing shares on the ex-date, but no explicit monetary value before then. This is why TERP is so important in a rights issue. In particular:

1. It indicates where the share should trade once the right is detached, *ceteris paribus.*
2. It helps in calculating the theoretical value of a right, being the difference between the cum-right price and the theoretical ex-right price.
3. It provides a practical indicator of how the market is reacting to the rights issue.

Specifically with reference to point (3), rights issues generally take place at a discounted price; hence, the shares will generally trade below where they were trading before the issue was announced. However, the share price above TERP on the ex-date and the market price of rights above their theoretical value implicitly signal a positive market reaction to the offering, despite the shares trading below where they were trading before the rights offering was announced.

How is TERP calculated? The standard formula to calculate TERP is the following:

$$\text{TERP} = \frac{[(\text{Cum-Right Price}) \times (\text{Outstanding Shares}) + (\text{Subscriptions Price}) \times (\text{New Shares})}{(\text{Outstanding Shares} + \text{New Shares})}$$

Example – TERP

- Cum right price: EUR 30/share
- Outstanding shares: 100mn
- Subscription price: EUR 20/share
- New shares: 50mn

TERP = [(30 × 100mn) + (20 × 50mn)]/(100mn + 50mn) = EUR 26.67

Once TERP is calculated, we can easily obtain the Theoretical Value of a Right (TVR) as the difference between the cum-right price (practically, the closing price on the last cum-right day) and the theoretical ex-right price

$$\text{TVR} = \text{Cum-Right Price} - \text{TERP}$$

Example – TVR

- Cum right price: EUR 30/share
- TERP = EUR 26.67/share

TVR = EUR 30 – EUR 26.67 = EUR 3.33

Once rights are assigned, an existing shareholder can do one of the following:

1. Exercise all rights and fully participate in the capital increase: this is the case if the investor does not want any dilution in terms of % of the company owned. Clearly it means fresh money will have to be committed from the investor.
2. Implement a cash-neutral strategy: sell part of the rights in order to purchase shares with the sale proceeds, with a partial dilution but avoiding the need to invest extra capital. This strategy is referred to as "tail swallowing."
3. Sell all the rights (or anyway, more rights than needed in the cash-neutral scenario): the investor will convert the "dividend in kind" into a cash proceed, but will face a larger dilution in the capital.
4. Do nothing and let the rights expire: this probably means you are doing either so well or so bad with your other investments that you forgot to do something.

Example – Subscription strategies

- Cum right price: EUR 30/share
- Outstanding shares: 100mn
- Subscription price: EUR 20/share
- New shares: 50mn

- TERP = EUR 26.67/share
- TVR = EUR 3.33/right
- Subscription ratio: 1 new share for every 2 shares held
- Shares held by investor xyz: 100

Case 1: exercise 100 rights with a 1:2 subscription ratio. The investor receives 50 new shares in the company at a price of EUR 20/share, for EUR 1,000 of fresh capital invested in the company. The investor owns 150 shares in the company after the capital increase.
Case 2: exercise an amount x of rights with a 1:2 subscription ratio and sell an amount (1-x) of rights in the market, such that the fresh capital invested = proceeds from the rights' sale. By selling 76 rights in the market @ EUR 3.33/right, the investor receives EUR 253; the remaining 24 rights can be exercised to partially subscribe the capital increase, receiving 12 shares at EUR 20/share for a total disbursement of EUR 240 (the exact proportion of rights to be sold would be 75.0186%, we then have to round it for practical reasons).
Case 3: sell 100 rights in the market for a total proceed of EUR 333, the investor still owns 100 shares in the company after the capital increase, however with a larger amount of outstanding shares.

An interesting feature arises with reference to the secondary rights market. As happens with TERP vs share price, the theoretical value of a right is not necessarily (actually, almost never) exactly the same as the market price of a right.

Why is that the case? For a very simple reason: the actual market price of a right and the actual market price of the share ex-right are represented by the equilibrium between demand and supply in the market (i.e. the equilibrium price between sellers and buyers), whereas TERP and TVR are quantitative parameters purely defined by the offering terms, whether directly or indirectly.

If the market price of the right is higher than the theoretical value of the right, an existing shareholder would be better off selling the right in the market and buying shares directly in the secondary market instead of keeping the right and exercising it. If the market price of the right is lower than the theoretical value, the existing shareholder is better off selling the shares and buying rights in the market.

It is rather typical for hedge funds to arbitrage market discrepancies between the price of a right, its theoretical value, and the share price ex-right with long/short strategies involving the trading of both rights and shares. As a result of this arbitrage activity, it is relatively common to see volatility spikes in both the share as well as the right price; the closer the end of the subscription period, the more pronounced such spikes are.

Example – Arbitrage around a rights offering

- Cum right price: EUR 30/share
- Outstanding shares: 100mn
- Subscription price: EUR 20/share
- New shares: 50mn

- TERP = EUR 26.67/share
- TVR = EUR 3.33/right
- Subscription ratio: 1 new share for every 2 shares held
- Shares held by investor xyz: 100

Case 1: market price of a right @ EUR 4. The investor sells two rights in the market for EUR 8 in total and buys one share for EUR 26.67, for a net outflow of EUR 18.67 (EUR 1.33 less than the subscription price)
Case 2: market price of a right @ EUR 2. The investor sells one share in the market for EUR 26.67, buys two rights for EUR 4 in total and exercises such rights at the subscription price, for a net gain of EUR 2.67

When the subscription period ends, the company will know the exact amount of rights exercised: this is a key parameter if the offer does not have any underwriting agreement in place with a banking syndicate, while it is only a qualitative indicator for the company in case of a full underwriting agreement. Why would a company take the risk and not enter into a full underwriting agreement with a banking syndicate? Because such guarantee clearly comes at a (relevant) cost, hence the company

Figure 7.2 **Rights issue recap**

Pre-rights issue		
Share price (€)	30	P
Shares outstanding (mn)	100	n
Market Cap (€ mn)	3,000	C = n × P
Rights issue		
Subscription ratio (shares for one right)	0.50	E
Subscription price (€)	20	S
New shares (mn)	50	N = n x E
Capital increase (€ mn)	1,000	A = S x N
TERP (€)	26.67	T = (C+A)/Z
Discount vs previous mkt price	33%	F = (P-S)/P
Discount vs TERP	25%	D = (T-S)/T
Theoretical Value of a Right (€)	3.33	R = (T-S) x E
Post-rights issue		
Shares outstanding (mn)	150	Z = n + N
Market Cap (€ mn)	4,000	Y = T x Z

might prefer to avoid paying such cost if it is confident that the offer will be well received by the existing shareholders and the market.

When the rights offering is over, the process is completed: the company will have a new total amount of shares outstanding, a new market price for its share and hence a new market cap. The shareholders' breakdown will most likely be different, since each shareholder could have a different level of participation in the capital increase.

Under normal conditions, the market cap of the company and the number of shares outstanding will be higher than before the capital increase, while the price will be lower (most likely between the price pre rights issue and the subscription price, with TERP as the ideal equilibrium value).

Case study **UniCredit Rights Issue, by Jean Pierre Mustier, Chief Executive Officer UniCredit Group (from July 2016 to February 2021)**

UniCredit: a successful Rights Issue

At the beginning of 2017, UniCredit successfully launched and completed a 13 billion euro Rights Issue, the largest Rights Issue in Italy and one of the largest in Europe. This case study explains the rationale behind the strategy chosen by the bank, how it was structured, and its outcomes.

Rationale

In 2016, when I was appointed Chief Executive Officer of UniCredit, the share price was underperforming both the Italian market and the European banking sector, with a Price to Book Value (P/BV) below par[1]. A comprehensive assessment of the reasons behind the bank's underperformance was then initiated.

The aim of the analysis was to understand if there was a need for capital and what was the amount needed.

The two main dimensions evaluated were:

a. Quality of the loan book;
b. Capital position.

Taking risk is at the core of the banking business, in particular when it comes to giving loans to clients. Statistically a certain portion of the loans will default, and even small numbers – on a total loan base that for UniCredit is more than 400 billion euros – can make a difference. It is therefore important that once the loans become Non-Performing, they be correctly marked in the Balance Sheet, by allocating the right amount of provisions.

The most transparent way to assess if Non-Performing Exposure ("NPE") is correctly marked is to ask a third party to carry out a valuation. This is what we did by executing what then was the largest NPE portfolio disposal in Europe.[2] We sold on the market a portfolio of 17 billion euros of Gross Book Value made up of different asset classes, and then we aligned the valuation of the portfolio on our books to those that we sold. This adjustment alone resulted in more than 8 billion in provisions.

Capital ratio is the main measure of a bank's solidity as it expresses the bank's capacity to sustain losses with its own funds and it is one of the indexes that regulators look at to measure the "health" of a financial institution. Banks all over the world use a measure called CET1 ratio,[3] which takes into account the capital of highest quality versus the total assets of the bank weighted for their risk. It is not sufficient to simply comply with the regulatory requirements, but it is also important to have a sufficient buffer above the minimum set by the Regulator to have leeway in the case of adverse events. In July 2016, UniCredit had a CET1 ratio of 10.3%, 30bps above its minimum requirement. The management decision was to have a buffer over the minimum required of c. 250bps, hence an overall capital level of 12.5%.

The combination of these two assessments, together with other minor adjustments, resulted in the need to increase the capital by more than 500 CET1 basis points.[4]

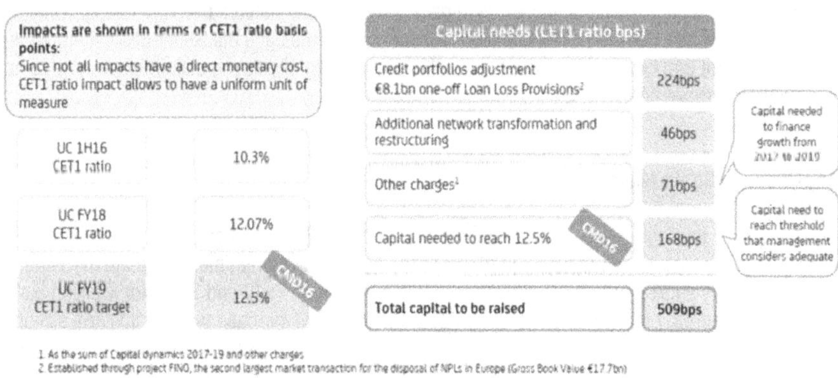

Unicredit's strategy to address the Capital need

Once the magnitude of the capital need was addressed, the next question became how to raise the capital. A series of different possibilities were considered and ultimately the management decided on a mix of two strategies:

- c. 350bps through a rights issue of 13 billion euros;
- more than 150bps from disposals of assets.

Selecting disposals of company assets as a source of funds is an option that allows for not altering the shareholding structure, but generally entails the sale of profitable businesses to attract potential buyers and to allow the company to adequately benefit from the deal. Among the other elements that must be taken into account in the assessment phase, there is the time required to conduct the negotiations and to close the deal, and the limited size of the existing portfolio of activities as a constraint.

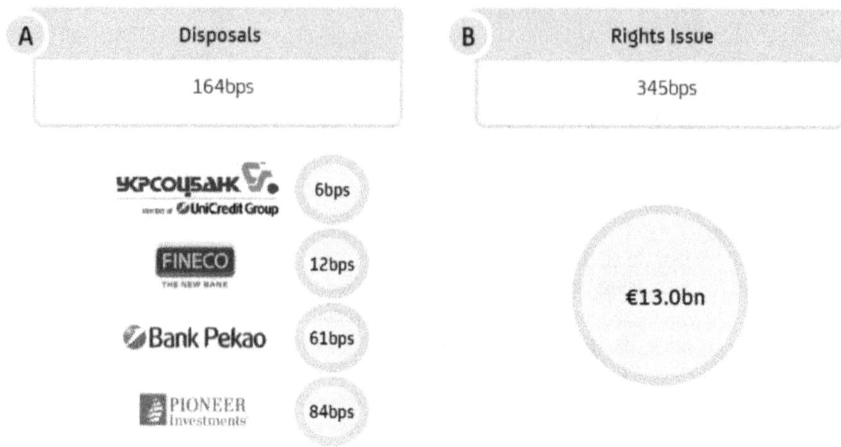

Most of the capital needs were addressed via Rights Issue – a capital increase where existing shareholders have pre-emptive rights to buy tradable shares proportionally to their ownership in the company.
The main advantages of such a transaction are (i) flexibility on size – which can be tailored to company needs, and (ii) not having an industrial impact. The cons are instead given by the high volatility in the FIG market, the risks of not having a full subscription in the case the issuer overestimated the amount of capital that could be absorbed, as well as the dilution of existing stakeholders who do not exercise their pre-emptive rights.

Deep-dive on Rights Issue

Once the size of the Rights Issue was determined, the time for execution came.
Before going into that, let me remind you of where the bank was at that time. It was the third capital call in a relatively short timeframe, with two issuances already in 2010 and 2012, for 4 billion euros and 7.5 billion euros, respectively. The magnitude of the capital increase was particularly sizeable – c. 85% – when compared to the market capitalisation at that time.[5] In absolute terms, it was the largest Rights Issue ever carried out in Italy and one of the largest in Europe.

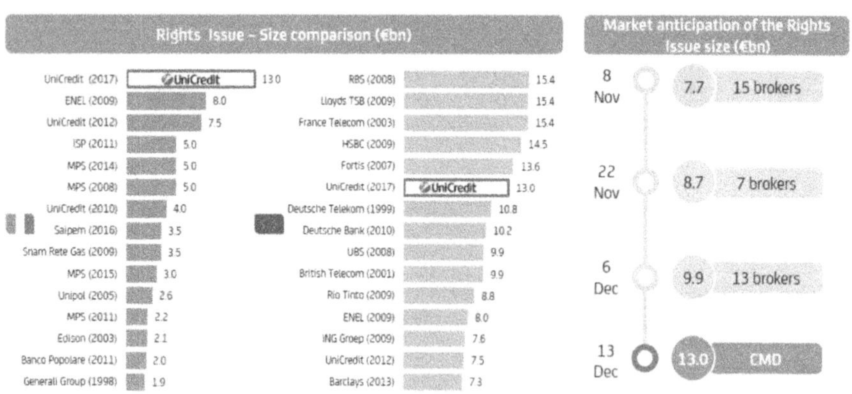

From an execution point of view the main decision to make is the discount to offer on the new share issuance. The decision needs to balance the need for it to be appealing for new investors – that will proportionally have a higher shareholding post-rights issue – and not too penalising for existing shareholders. UniCredit's 13 billion euros right issue was priced at a 38% discount over TERP.[6]
In the weeks before the Rights Issue, the bank market capitalization was at c. 16 billion euros, with 618m outstanding shares at the price of 26.6[7] euros. The discount ratio on the TERP resulted in an exchange ratio of 5 to 13, i.e. the possibility for existing shareholders to buy 13 additional shares for every 5 they owned at the discounted price, with a consequent dilution of 72% for existing shareholders. The new share price became 8.09 euros per share, with c. 2.2 billion of shares outstanding and a market capitalization of 29 billion euros.
One of the key elements for the success of the Rights Issue was the underwriting agreement with Investment Banks. A consortium of 31 banks committed to subscribing separately and without joint liability the new shares not exercised at the end of the market offering. This subscription of a pro-quota portion of capital increase covered UniCredit against the risk of a non-full subscription of the shares, and gave certainty to investors on the success of the transaction. On top of the underwriting agreement, banks also provided support in a plethora of activities, including the preparation of appropriate market communications, a convincing storyline, and a worldwide roadshow with investors.

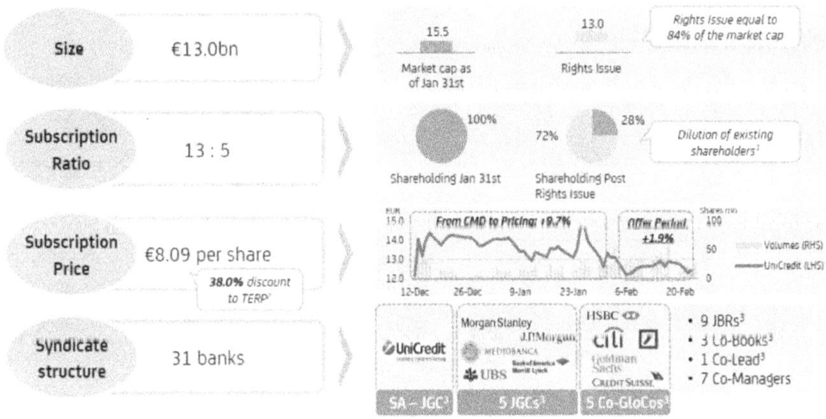

The last step to guarantee the success of the Rights Issue was the communication to the financial markets. We needed to transparently tell our stakeholders (investors, financial analysts, media, colleagues) why we needed the Rights Issue, how the proceeds would be used and how they would be remunerated for them to place their trust in us. To this end, we organised a Capital Markets Day on 13 December 2016, where we gathered more than 200 attendees among investors, analysts, and media, to announce the details of the right issues as well as the unveiling of the new business plan, Transform 2019. The whole management team presented the plan, clearly communicating the actions already taken to improve the capital position of the bank and the value creation underlying Transform 2019 thanks to its credible deliverables.
Together with the business plan, we also presented a new remuneration plan whereby a sizeable amount of management compensation is linked to long-term value creation for shareholders, to ensure that there is alignment in the interests of managers and shareholders.

Right after the disclosure to the market, a one-month roadshow to meet the main investors (with more than 750 meetings with investors in 26 different cities in North America, Europe, the Middle East, and Asia) took place.

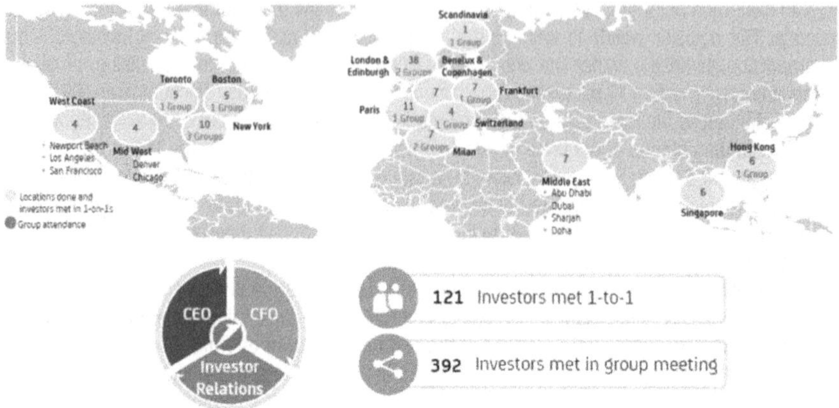

Finally, after the approval of the terms by the UniCredit Board of Directors, on 6 February 2017, the Rights Issue was launched.

Outcomes and Lesson Learnt

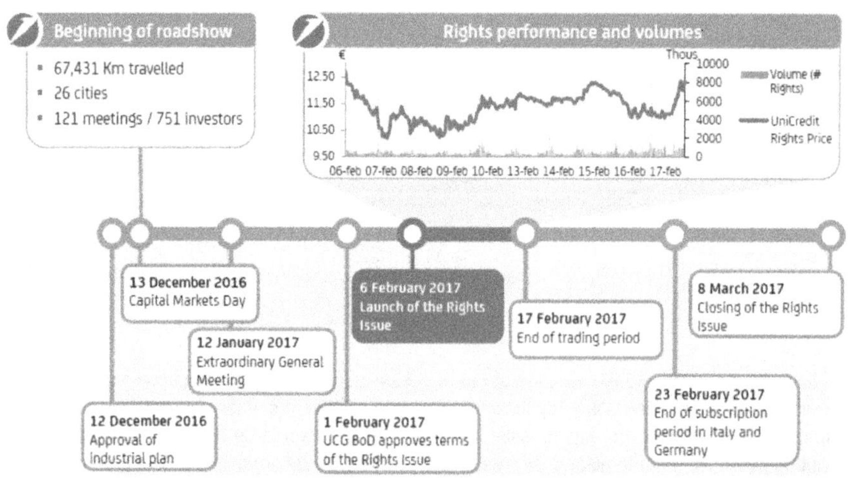

At the end of the trading period, within one month after the launch of the market offering, 99.8% of the subscription rate was achieved, demonstrating the great success of the operation. Moreover, the capital increase was subscribed mainly by institutional investors, bringing the institutional shareholder base to 90%, compared to 80% prior to the new Rights Issue, and signalling the appreciation of the quality of the transaction by the most professional investors. As a matter of fact, analysts' recommendations went from 36% in June 2016 to 65% advice to buy in March 2017. The appreciation of the market was immediately reflected also in the share price, which increased 16% the day after the CMD and was sustained over time, with +18.5% 4 days later, and constantly outperforming the banking sector.

What can be inferred from this story is that there are a few elements for a successful Rights Issue. First of all, the strategic plan linked to the increase in equity needs to be strongly credible, with

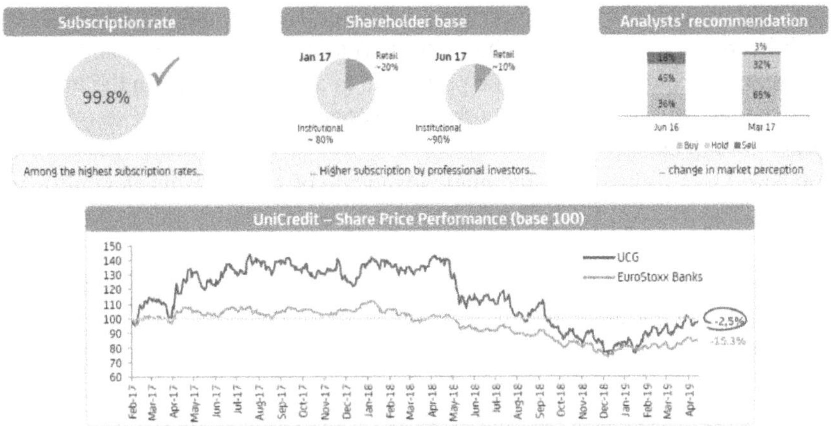

challenging, but at the same time, achievable targets. Secondly, communication needs to be fully transparent and discipline is key ("We say what we do, and we do what we say").

[1] P/BV was equal to 0.7061 as of 1/7/2019.
[2] Established through project FINO ("Failure Is Not an Option"), the second largest market transaction for the disposal of NPLs in Europe (Gross Book Value 17.7 billion euros).
[3] Common Equity Tier 1 (CET1) is a capital measure introduced in 2014 by the Basel Committee as a precautionary means to protect the economy from a financial crisis. Specifically, it is the "strictest" requirement for banks to absorb Unexpected Losses, and it comprises a minimum bank's core capital in proportion to its Risk Weighted Assets (RWA).

$$CET1\ \text{ratio} = \frac{\textit{Bank's Core Capital}}{\textit{Bank's RWA}} \times 100$$

The eligible "core capital" includes common shares, stock surpluses resulting from the issue of common shares, retained earnings, common shares issued by subsidiaries and held by third parties, and Accumulated Other Comprehensive Income (AOCI).
[4] Impacts are shown in terms of CET1 ratio basis points since not all impacts have a direct monetary cost. CET1 ratio impact makes it possible to have a uniform unit of measure.
[5] 15.5 billion euros as of 31/12/2016.
[6] Theoretical Ex-Rights Price.
[7] Pro forma.

7.3 Accelerated Bookbuilding (ABB)

As we have seen in the previous section, rights offerings are a complex and lengthy process given a variety of features intrinsic in the process itself, and coherent with a transformational moment for a listed company. A complementary process to a rights issue, with different pros and cons, is the accelerated bookbuilding process.

An accelerated bookbuilding is a transaction through which the company and/or one or more significant investors sell existing and/or newly-issued shares to institutional investors that may or may not be existing shareholders in the company.

An accelerated bookbuilding is generally implemented to place a significant amount of shares in a time-efficient way. ABB is a flexible transaction with certain similarities to a standard market sale, which (i) allows both primary and secondary share placement, and/or (ii) might be preferable to an outright sale in the market (e.g. to minimise negative market impact from prolonged selling activity, to optimise the execution period, etc.).

Compared to a rights issue, the main advantage of a ABB is its flexibility, which includes:

- Selling entity: in an ABB, the selling entity can be the company itself and/or one or more significant investors;
- Nature of the offering: an ABB can be used to place primary and/or secondary shares;
- Time to market: an ABB can take as little as one day to complete the selling process;
- Price: investor demand can be taken into account when deciding the ABB price;
- Backstop: the banking syndicate can guarantee a minimum price to the seller(s) in exchange for an extra fee;
- Fee: generally cheaper commission rate from the banking syndicate;
- Effort: no need to tie down the management in a lengthy roadshow process.

In case of a primary ABB, all the above points represent an advantage for the company. At the same time, rights offerings have various advantages over ABBs: the point is not which one is the best (in fact, there isn't one per se), but to weight the different peculiarities, on the basis of which a company might prefer one or the other given a specific situation.

Example – Primary transaction
You are the CEO of a listed company with a EUR 20bn market cap and you need to raise capital for an acquisition.
Case 1: big transformational deal. Takeover of a major competitor for EUR 10bn, 100% cash, 50/50 between new equity and debt: a rights offering will most likely be the best way to raise the EUR 5bn of fresh capital required.
Case 2: bolt-on acquisition. Acquisition of a niche tech player in your supply chain in order to exploit potential synergies and acquire their technology, for EUR 500mn, 100% new equity: an ABB will most likely be the best way to rapidly raise the necessary capital.

In the case of a secondary ABB, the trade-off is between the block sale or a sale in the market: an ABB is best suited when the overall combination between market impact, desired time to execute it, and execution costs of a block sale leaves the selling shareholder in a better position than an outright sale in the market.

Example – Secondary transaction

Your fund has a 1.5% stake in a company with a EUR 10bn market cap and very liquid shares (EUR 50mn average daily traded value)

Case 1: you need to sell a EUR 5mn stake. Your stake is 10% of the average value traded in a single day: an outright sale in the market will be more efficient, more rapid, and cheaper than a block sale.

Case 2: you need to fully dispose of your EUR 150mn stake, which is equivalent to the overall volume traded in three trading days:

- a full sale in the market over a single day will have a strong negative impact on the price;
- assuming a 20% volume cap to reduce the market impact, it will take you 15 trading days (i.e. 3 weeks) to sell down the whole stake;
- the market impact will be reduced, but not eliminated;
- you are exposed to market volatility over those 3 weeks.

An ABB, on the other hand, will allow you to dispose of your stake in one day, with potentially even lower market impact and surely with zero residual market volatility.

Perhaps the easiest way to understand the main advantages of an ABB is to look at the practical process typically implemented, with a special focus on the efficiency and rapidity through which:

- A company can raise the required fresh capital (primary ABB);
- An existing shareholder can dispose of its stake in whole or in part (secondary ABB).

During the morning, the seller(s) and the banking syndicate decide whether to proceed or not with the transaction; if the "go/no-go" decision is positive, the key offer-

Figure 7.3 ABB – Launch Timeline

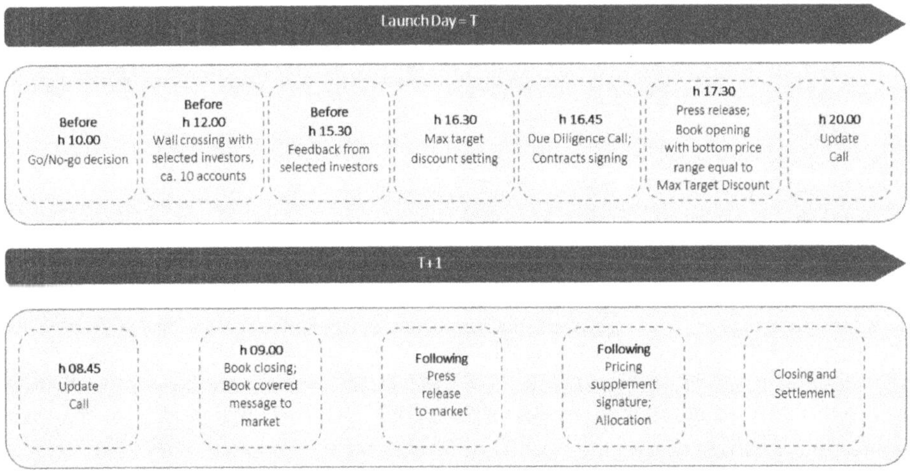

ing features are determined before the market closes (e.g. maximum target discount, amount to be placed, wall-crossed investors) and contracts between seller(s) and syndicate are signed accordingly.

When the market closes for the day, the ABB transaction is announced by the banking syndicate to institutional investors via their coverage on the public side (i.e. the sales force on the trading floor), detailing all key features of the ABB (size, indicative price range, who is selling, primary/secondary shares, transaction purpose, use of proceeds, etc.).

Real-life example: Renault 2017 ABB – Bloomberg message from Deutsche Bank trading desk

Announcement & details

```
***RENAULT SA*** ABB OF UP TO 14M SHARES ***
SALES RESTRICTIONS:
SALES TO US QIBS ONLY (WITH TWO-WAY INVESTOR LETTER)
NO SALES TO AUSTRALIA, CANADA OR JAPAN
REG S ELSEWHERE
NUMBER OF SHARES: UP TO 14M SECONDARY SHARES/REPRESENTING
C.4.73% OF SHARES OUTSTANDING
RENAULT HAS IRREVOCABLY COMMITTED TO TAKE UP 1.4M SHARES IN
THE PLACING (10% OF THE DEAL)
PRICE: EUR 86.21 WITH REFERENCE TO MARKET
BUYBACK: RENAULT SA WILL BUYBACK 1.4M SHARES FROM THE FRENCH
STATE AT THE OFFER PRICE
SELLING SHAREHOLDER: APE (FRENCH STATE)
SHAREHOLDING POST PROPOSED TRADE: C. 15.0%
LOCK UP: 180 DAYS
LAUNCH DATE: 02 NOVEMBER 2017
EXPECTED SETTLEMENT DATE: 07 NOVEMBER 2017
STOCK DETAILS:
STOCK: RENAULT SA
SECTOR: AUTOMOBILES
COUNTRY: FRANCE
BLOOMBERG TICKER: RNO FP
REUTERS TICKER: RENA.PA
ISIN: FR0000131906
BOOKS ARE NOW OPEN AND MAY CLOSE WITH MINIMAL NOTICE
SECONDARY COMMISSIONS AND MARKET CHARGES AS APPLICABLE
```

Institutional investors communicate their interest in the transaction, if any, placing an order (either in number of shares or in monetary terms) which may or may not have a price limit.

The banking syndicate rapidly starts to build an order book with all the various orders (the source of the name "accelerated bookbuilding"), assessing the overall interest in terms of (i) aggregated size and (ii) price. The banking syndicate also updates investors throughout the bookbuilding process (see example below), until the book is closed and no additional orders can be accepted. Generally, the whole bookbuilding process only lasts a few hours.

Real-life example: Renault 2017 ABB – Bloomberg message from Deutsche Bank trading desk

Books updates (different messages)

```
(02/11/2017 18:32 CET) BOOKS COVERED
(02/11/2017 18:51 CET) BOOKS ARE COVERED THROUGHOUT THE RANGE
(AT EUR 86.60)
(02/11/2017 19:24 CET) ORDERS BELOW EUR 86.60 RISK MISSING THE
DEAL. BOOK TO CLOSE AT 18:35 UK
```

Once the book is closed, the syndicate allocates the offered shares to the various investors that placed an order. Each investor's allocation (with respect to its order amount) will depend on a variety of factors, the main ones being (i) overall demand and (ii) profile of the investor (e.g. in the case of a primary ABB multiple times oversubscribed, the company might prefer a relatively higher allocation to stable investors such as pension funds and "real money" long-only mutual funds vs a relatively lower allocation to speculative investors such as "fast money" hedge funds).

The following morning, before the market opens, the banking syndicate communicates the final offering price and informs each investor of its allocated amount.

Real-life example: Renault 2017 ABB – Bloomberg message from Deutsche Bank trading desk

Pricing and allocation

```
***RENAULT SA***ABB - PRICING AND ALLOCATIONS
ISSUE PRICE: EUR 86.60 PER SHARE
TOTAL DEAL SIZE: 14M SECONDARY SHARES/C. EUR 1.2 BILLION
ALLOCATION TO [CLIENT ABC]: XX SHARES
TRADE DATE: 03 NOVEMBER 2017
EXPECTED SETTLEMENT DATE: 07 NOVEMBER 2017
```

From the process described above, it is easily understandable why a company might opt for a primary ABB: its flexibility, efficiency, and speed of execution allow for a rapid sale of newly-issued shares to an institutional base, raising fresh money in just a few hours.

In a similar way, it is straightforward to appreciate why a significant existing shareholder (e.g. a Private Equity Fund which has a 5% stake in the company) might opt for a secondary ABB to dispose in whole or in part of its position, instead of selling such stake outright in the secondary market during standard market hours. In such case, an ABB transaction will allow the seller to:

- dispose of the whole desired amount in one single transaction: no need to allocate time and effort to executing the selling activity in the market;
- optimise the time required to execute the sale: only a few hours instead of several trading days;
- minimise the market impact: prolonged selling activity in the market might adversely impact the share price, resulting in a de facto deeper discount;
- take advantage of strong demand: investors might react positively to the offering, while the market would simply passively absorb the selling flow.

There is an important point to be highlighted with reference to the selling price. Generally, ABB transactions are announced with an indicative price range based on the latest market price. The price range can be at an explicit discount (e.g. closing price € 75, pricing range €68 – €72), at a potential discount (e.g. pricing range € 73 to market) or at no explicit discount (i.e. "with reference to market"). While ABBs are normally priced at a discount, sometimes the transaction is priced at the closing price; most often in the case of very strong demand and no explicit discount.

Also, the market reaction following an ABB can be positive: this typically happens when the market has widely anticipated the sale and/or the transaction is seen by the market as a positive indicator. The placement of 4.73% of Renault by the French Government in November 2017 mentioned above provides a clear example (please see the case study at the end of the chapter for more details on the overall process).

Case study **ABB FinecoBank, by Paolo Garzarelli, Managing Director, Head of ECM Italy, UniCredit Bank AG.**

Introduction

The purpose of this section is to provide a tangible overview of the preparatory activities and then of the subsequent execution steps in the context of an accelerated bookbuilding trade, from origination to execution. Hence, the following pages will describe the process related to the FinecoBank (hereinafter referred to as Fineco) clean-up trade executed by UniCredit S.p.A. (hereinafter referred to as UniCredit) in July 2019, which represents the last step of the exit strategy that begun in 2014 with the Fineco IPO.

Fineco at a glance and UniCredit exit Strategy Milestones

Fineco is a multi-channel bank offering banking, credit, trading, and investment services from a single account. It is a brokerage leader in Europe with one of the largest networks of financial advisers and a capillary network of Fineco centres throughout Italy.

Below are the key milestones of the Fineco sell-downs executed by UniCredit since the Fineco IPO:

- In July 2014, Fineco was listed on the Mercato Telematico Azionario organised and managed by Borsa Italiana. Including shares purchased in the exercise of the over-allotment option, a total of 209.2mn Fineco shares were sold by UniCredit (that held 100% of the company), equal to 34.5% of the share capital, for aggregate proceeds of approximately EUR 774mn. UniCredit CIB acted as Joint Global Coordinator in the stock market listing alongside Mediobanca and UBS.
- In July 2016, UniCredit sold 10% of Fineco via an ABB (60.7 mn of secondary shares for a total amount of EUR 328mn), reducing its controlling stake from 65% to 55%, at an offer price of EUR 5.4 p.s. with a discount of -6.1%. UniCredit CIB acted as Joint Bookrunner alongside UBS.
- In October 2016, UniCredit sold an additional 20% of its stake (121mn shares for a total amount of EUR 552mn) via an ABB, further reducing its controlling stake from 55% to 35% at an offer price of EUR 4.55 p.s. implying a 4.97% discount. UniCredit CIB acted as Joint Bookrunner alongside UBS.
- In May 2019, UniCredit and Fineco announced that their respective Boards of Directors approved certain actions and procedures to be respectively implemented in order to allow Fineco to operate as a fully independent entity from a regulatory, liquidity and operational standpoint. On the same day, UniCredit sold an additional 17% stake via an ABB (103.5mn shares for a total amount of EUR 1,014mn), further reducing its controlling stake from 34% to c. 18% at an offer price of EUR 9.80 p.s. implying a 4.85% discount. UniCredit CIB acted as Joint Bookrunner alongside JPM and UBS.
- In July 2019, UniCredit completed its exit strategy by selling the final c. 18% stake via an ABB at an offer price of EUR 9.85 p.s. implying a 4.42% discount. UniCredit CIB acted as Joint Bookrunner alongside JPM and UBS.

Here is a summary of the path that UniCredit followed as an exit strategy from Fineco:

Accelerated Bookbuild

An accelerated bookbuild (abbreviated as "ABB") is a transaction that allows for placing on the market large stakes of a listed company in a short time period (usually within one day). Sellers can either be existing shareholders (secondary shares where proceeds go to selling shareholders) or the company (primary shares, usually max 10% of outstanding shares given its non-pre-emptive nature, where proceeds are cashed in by the company). The deal is launched after market close in order to avoid the impact of the transaction in the stock price. Due to the absence of a prospectus and the short execution timeframe, buyers are exclusively qualified institutional investors. The deal could be backstopped when a certain minimum price for the shares is granted by the banks to the selling shareholders or best effort in the case of pure selling effort without any guarantee of a minimum price to selling shareholders.

Usually, it is addressed to shareholders with significant holdings in a company, or companies that wish to raise equity in a short period of time without a prospectus (max. up to 10% of the subscribed capital in Italy).

Origination Phase

On 8 July 2019, UniCredit completed the sale of its remaining stake in Fineco via ABB, as part of a series of measures jointly announced with Fineco on 7 May 2019, providing a smooth transition of its Fintech subsidiary into a fully independent entity. The proceeds from the last two ABBs achieved a total 51bps of CET1, contributing to the Bank's strategy of achieving the upper end of the 200-250bps CET1 ratio buffer over regulatory requirements by 2019YE.
Following the successful completion of the ABB executed in May, UniCredit held a minority stake which has been classified as a financial asset, increasing the Fineco free float to c. 82%. So with the last trade, UniCredit sold its final 18% stake in Fineco.
The ABB was launched after a substantial re-rating of Fineco shares (+10.8% L1M), benefitting from improved investor sentiment towards Italy (as demonstrated in the tightened BTP-Bund spread of around 200bp also thanks to the withdrawal of the Excessive Deficit Procedure against the country). The transaction represented the last step of UniCredit's exit strategy from Fineco, selling its stake with an attractive implied P/E of 22.6x, well above its main peers (11.1X) – Banca Mediolanum, Banca Generali, Azimut Holding, and Anima Holding.
Despite the negative close of European equity markets (Stoxx50 down 0.12%) in part driven by the banking sector (-1%), UniCredit decided to launch the transaction also on the back of the strong stock performance, allowing books to be covered within c. 35 minutes of launch.

Execution Phase

Legal Documentation and Bring Down Due Diligence Call
The accelerated bookbuilding trade is a quick and flexible option to go into the market. Indeed, it is fully undocumented, so no prospectus is needed.
Even if no prospectus is required, a number of legal documents must be prepared by the legal advisors. Here below is a standard list that can differ depending on the transaction peculiarities:

- **Press Release**: to announce the launch and the pricing of the deal to the entire market.
- **Block Trade Agreement**: a legal agreement between the banks and the client that defines their relationship from a legal perspective including, *inter alia*: purchase and sales obligations, commissions, expenses that can be reimbursed to the banks, representations, warranties and undertakings of the client and of the underwriting banks, potential lock-up, and banks' indemnity.
- **Term of Sales**: a final document that summarizes the number of shares sold and the final price.
- **Legal Opinions**: these documents are written by banks' legal counsels in order to give the banks assurance that the agreements have been properly executed by counterparties with the power to undertake obligations, that the documents are legally binding and enforceable, and that the offer and sale of the shares by the banks are not required to be registered under the US Securities Act of 1933.

On top of the documents above, banks' legal teams prepare a list of questions to be submitted to the company during the Bring Down Due Diligence call ahead of the launch of the transaction.

Go/No-Go Call and Deal Announcement

Syndicate banks organize several calls during the day in order to give market update to the client. Crucial for the launch of the transaction is the Go/No-Go call where on the base of the market conditions, the client decides whether to launch the transaction also based on the recommendation received by the syndicate banks. The Go/No-Go call usually is set at 5:00pm CET in order to have enough time to launch the deal right after market close.

During the launch day of the last Fineco trade, the banks and client organized several market updates from 11 am CET to 5 pm CET in which banks updated the seller on market conditions in order to understand the feasibility of the transaction. As already mentioned above, despite a negative close of European equity markets (Stoxx50 down 0.12%) in part driven by the banking sector (-1%), UniCredit decided to launch the transaction.

At market close, the syndicate banks and client communicated the launch of the transaction via a press release on the client website, detailed press wires of the transaction via financial info providers (such as Bloomberg, Reuters, and so on) and bilateral messages from sales to potential investors.

In the case of the last Fineco trade, a press release was published right after European markets closed.

Press release example:

UniCredit launches accelerated bookbuilding of its residual stake in FinecoBank

08 July 2019 - h 17:41 | PRICE SENSITIVE   Financial

NOT FOR RELEASE, PUBLICATION OR DISTRIBUTION, IN WHOLE OR IN PART, DIRECTLY OR INDIRECTLY, IN, INTO OR FROM THE UNITED STATES, CANADA, AUSTRALIA, JAPAN, SOUTH AFRICA OR ANY OTHER JURISDICTION WHERE TO DO SO WOULD CONSTITUTE A VIOLATION OF THE RELEVANT LAWS OF THAT JURISDICTION

As part of the financial measures announced on 7 May 2019, including targeting to be at the upper end of the 200 [illegible] buffer over regulatory requirements by year end 2019 through the disposal of certain assets, UniCredit S.p.A. ("**UniCredit**" or "the Group"), following the accelerated bookbuilding process closed on 10 May 2019 which resulted in the deconsolidation of FinecoBank S.p.A. ("**Fineco**" or the "**Company**") from its financial statements (the "**First Placement**"), today announces the launch of a placement of ordinary shares in Fineco, representing ca. 18.3 per cent of the Company's existing share capital, equivalent to the entire shareholdings held in the Company (the "**Placement**"). The Placement will be made to certain institutional investors by way of an accelerated bookbuilding process.

Bookbuilding will commence immediately. UniCredit reserves the right to change the terms or timing of the Placement at any time. The Placement will further increase the free float of Fineco shares on the Milan Stock Exchange.

In connection with the Placement, J.P. Morgan and UBS Investment Bank, in consultation with UniCredit Corporate & Investment Banking, - as Joint Bookrunners of the UniCredit's First Placement - waived the lock-up provisions agreed by UniCredit in the context of such transaction.

J.P. Morgan, UBS Investment Bank and UniCredit Corporate & Investment Banking have been appointed by UniCredit to act as Joint Bookrunners of the Placement.

Bloomberg message example:

Source: Used with permission of Bloomberg Finance L.P.

Bilateral message example:

*** STRICTLY NOT FOR DISTRIBUTION INTO THE UNITED STATES (EXCEPT TO QIBS), CANADA, JAPAN, AUSTRALIA, SOUTH AFRICA OR ANY OTHER JURISDICTION WHERE TO DO SO WOULD CONSTITUTE A VIOLATION OF THE RELEVANT LAWS OF THAT JURISDICTION***
*** STRICTLY ONLY TO QUALIFIED INSTITUTIONAL BUYERS IN THE UNITED STATES***

THIS IS NOT A REGISTERED OFFERING UNDER THE US SECURITIES ACT OF 1933, AS AMENDED (THE "SECURITIES ACT"). OFFERING INTERNATIONALLY PURSUANT TO REGULATION S OF THE SECURITIES ACT AND INTO THE US TO QIBS ONLY (AS DEFINED UNDER RULE 144A OF THE SECURITIES ACT)

FinecoBank (FBK IM) placement of c. 111.6m shares via accelerated bookbuild.
Placement of secondary shares offered by UniCredit S.p.A..
UniCredit / Kepler Cheuvreux role: Joint Bookrunner

Company:	FinecoBank S.p.A. ("Fineco")
Listing:	Borsa Italiana
Ticker / ISIN:	FBK IM / IT0000072170
Syndicate:	UniCredit, in cooperation with Kepler Cheuvreux, is acting as Joint Bookrunner, alongside JPM and UBS
Selling Shareholder:	UniCredit S.p.A.
Offering Type:	Accelerated Bookbuilt Offering (100% Secondary)
Securities Offered:	Secondary shares owned by UniCredit S.p.A.
Offering Size:	c. 111.6m shares / c.18.3% of issued share capital – clean-up trade
Offer price:	Reference to market

Bookbuilding and Updates to the market

Once the message is out, syndicate bank Sales teams start to contact the investor community in order to gather orders and build the book of demand. This execution phase is called bookbuilding. Basically, investors provide orders in terms of number of shares and price with banks building up the orderbook into a dedicated system shared by all the banks' syndicate teams.

Investors place the order with a limit, linking the buy order to certain price, or at strike, meaning without any price limit.

During this phase, ad hoc calls are set up in order to update the client on the book development and to decide what messages to deliver to the market. The info that banks share with the client are related to order flow monitoring, detailed order specific information, and order book analysis in terms of breakdown by investor type (Long-Only vs Hedge Fund) and by geography.

When the deal is well-subscribed, the syndicate banks, in agreement with the client, send a book covered message in order to update the market on the deal status.

In the last Fineco trade, books were covered within c. 35 minutes. The ABB was launched with no discount guidance (reference to market).

Book covered message example:

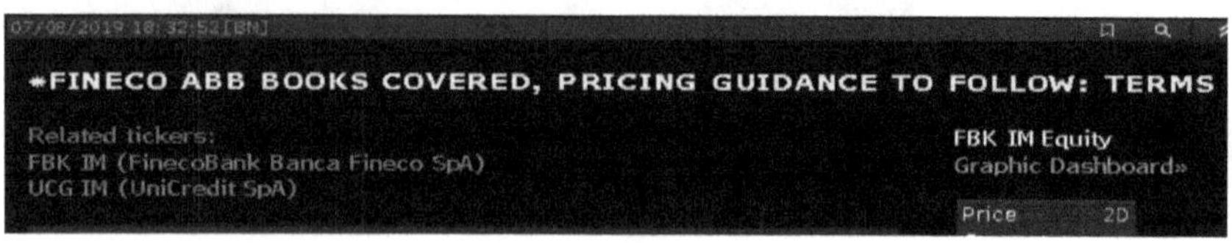

Source: Used with permission of Bloomberg Finance L.P.

Following the book covered message, price guidances are sent out to the market in order to guide investors toward the final price depending on the order evolution and the analysis of the book of demand. This message is crucial for the successful pricing of the transaction.

Usually there is an initial guidance to guide investors around a price range in the event an initial reference to the market message was delivered without any indication of the discount (as happened with Fineco), followed by a final guidance to set the final price with a message such as "Orders below X price risk missing."

Price guidance message example:

Final guidance message example:

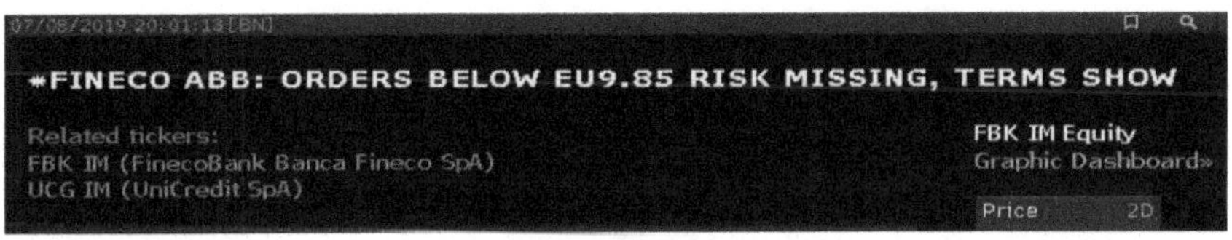

Source: Used with permission of Bloomberg Finance L.P.

Final Price and Allocation
Once the book is closed, the syndicate banks organize an ad hoc call with the client in order to set up the final price and then coordinate allocation to investors of the offering.
The final price is set up in order to balance client and investor price expectations and is set at a level where investor demand is strong, and the level is agreed on by the client.
Fineco's final price was set at EUR 9.85 p.s., translating into a c. 4.42% discount on the previous closing price. The book was more than 3 times covered with approx. 150 lines at final offer price showing strong interest from the investor community.
Allocations are needed because, in a successful offering, demand received is higher than the shares offered to the market, translating into an oversubscribed transaction.
Allocations are usually skewed towards long-only investors in order to gather relative stability to the shareholder base after the sell-down. Most of the orders are allocated pro-rata with quality accounts reserved for a higher allocation.
The allocation process follows strict requirements that are part of the Mifid 2 regime guidance (**Commission Delegated Regulation (EU) 2017/565 and ESMA Technical Standards**) with standard principles usually along the following lines:

- Prioritisation of long-only and fundamental institutions especially where there is a history of interest in the stock;
- Prioritise investors that showed price leadership and early demand.

In any case, ahead of the transaction launch, the syndicate banks share the allocation policies with the client via email for MIFID purposes.
Once the allocations are agreed among the banks, the syndicate organizes a call with the client to share the allocation proposal and agrees with the client on a final allocation proposal. This phase usually starts around 9:00 p.m. and could last until late at night because the banks and client could have different views on the allocation and finding a balance between parties takes time.

Pricing and Allocation Announcement

When the allocations are agreed on between the banks and client, the final price and the closing of the transaction (excluding the allocation) are communicated to the market via press release and financial info providers.

Pricing press release example:

UniCredit successfully completes the sale of its remaining stake in FinecoBank

08 July 2019 - h 23:45 | **PRICE SENSITIVE** Financial

NOT FOR RELEASE, PUBLICATION OR DISTRIBUTION, IN WHOLE OR IN PART, DIRECTLY OR INDIRECTLY, IN, INTO OR FROM THE UNITED STATES, CANADA, AUSTRALIA, JAPAN, SOUTH AFRICA OR ANY OTHER JURISDICTION WHERE TO DO SO WOULD CONSTITUTE A VIOLATION OF THE RELEVANT LAWS OF THAT JURISDICTION

The gross proceeds amount to approximately €1.099 million, deriving from the sale of approximately 111.6 million ordinary shares of FinecoBank, at a price of €9.85 per share

In line with the previously communicated financial measures which will underpin UniCredit's 2020-23 business strategy and further to the press release published on 8 July 2019, UniCredit S.p.A. ("**UniCredit**") announces the successful completion of the accelerated bookbuild offering to institutional investors of approximately 111.6 million existing ordinary shares in FinecoBank S.p.A. ("**Fineco**" or the "**Company**"), equal to approximately 18.3 per cent of the Company's issued share capital, at a price of €9.85 per share (the "**Placement**"). The settlement of the Placement will take place on 11 July 2019.

The price represents a discount of approximately 4.4 per cent to the pre-announcement last closing price of Fineco.

The overall capital impact is estimated to be an increase of approximately 30 basis points in the UniCredit Group CET1 capital ratio in 3Q 2019.

J.P. Morgan, UBS Investment Bank and UniCredit Corporate & Investment Banking acted as Joint Bookrunners of the Placement.

Bloomberg pricing message example:

Source: Used with permission of Bloomberg Finance L.P.

Before the pricing is communicated to the market, legal documents must be finalized and signed by the counterparties.

Usually, allocations are communicated to the investors around 8:00 a.m. CET on the day after the launch of the transaction, before market open.

Allocations are communicated by the syndicate banks to their sales teams that subsequently inform the investors.

Settlement

The settlement represents the last phase of the transaction.

In a standard accelerated transaction, settlement is set at T+2, meaning two days after the pricing of the transaction. With the settlement the funds and stocks are effectively transferred from investors to client and vice versa.

7.4 Equity-linked – Convertibles

Regardless of any potential differences, the secondary offerings described so far have a common trait: they involve an equity instrument, be it an existing share, a new share, or rights to acquire new shares. Not all secondary offerings involve only equity instruments though, as it is also possible to raise capital via a more hybrid approach, using a specific feature of equity-linked instruments.

In general terms, an equity-linked instrument is easily explainable with its literal meaning: it is an instrument whose value and performance is, in one way or another, linked to the value and performance of an equity instrument. Most often, in practical jargon, the term "equity-linked" is used to indicate an equity-linked note.

An equity-linked note is a type of structured note, i.e. it is a debt instrument (a note) which includes, in its structure, a bond and an option component.

The plain vanilla example of such a note (assuming a world of non-negative interest rates) is a capital-protected note which at maturity pays back 100% of the capital invested + the performance of an underlying equity instruments (e.g. S&P 500), if positive. It is nothing more and nothing less than the combination of a zero-coupon bond and an at-the-money call option in a single instrument, to provide the payoff just described above.

Equity-linked notes have a wide application in the investment world and can take a huge variety of forms; one format which plays a very relevant role in the secondary equity offering is the convertible bond.

A convertible bond is a bond which, at maturity, can be converted into a pre-defined amount of shares of a reference entity, at a pre-defined strike price (at a premium versus the current price level) and at the underwriter's discretion. It is straightforward to notice that a convertible bond is a combination of (a) a plain vanilla bond and (b) an out of the money call option.

The main actors involved in a convertible bond issuance are:

- the issuer, i.e. the company which issues the bond (hence, the bond will be a debt instrument of such company);
- the reference entity, i.e. shares in the company into which the bond can be converted;
- the underwriter(s), i.e. the initial "buyer(s)" of the bond;
- the banking syndicate, i.e. the pool of banks implementing the issuance process.

The easiest way to understand why both the issuer and the underwriter might have an interest in such an instrument is to look at how it works. The main steps are:

1. At inception, the underwriter lends €100 to the issuer and receives a €100 nominal amount of the convertible bond (let's assume issuance at par for simplicity).
2. During its life, the convertible bond pays a coupon to the bondholder.
3. At maturity, the bondholder has the right to decide whether to receive back €100 of principal or to convert such principal into shares of the reference entity at a pre-defined conversion price. In practice:
   a) If the share is trading below the conversion price, the underwriter will decide to receive €100.
   b) If the share is trading above the conversion price, the underwriter will decide

to receive the stocks (since the overall monetary value will clearly be above €100).

Why would an investor buy such an instrument? Because it offers the opportunity to participate in the potential upside of the reference entity's share above the conversion price, while at the same time earning interest (the stream of coupons) and limiting the downside to the issuer's credit risk . In other words, a convertible bond allows for an asymmetric payoff where the bondholder is entitled to an extra-return in a favourable scenario, while retaining all features of a fixed-income security in the case of less optimistic outcomes.

Why would the issuer issue such an instrument? Because it makes it possible to reduce the cost of financing thanks to the implicit sale of an out of the money call to the underwriter, while at the same time (i) expanding the sources of funding by reaching all potential investors (i.e. not only pure bond/pure equity investors) and (ii) avoiding the negative price reaction and/or dilutive impact of an outright equity offering.

So far, we have been referring to "the issuer" and "the reference entity" as if they were, potentially, two different actors; this is indeed the case, as in a convertible bond issuance the issuer may or may not be the same as the reference entity. To understand this point, we need to go back to the "primary vs secondary" nature of an ABB transaction and look at the convertible bond with the same reasoning approach. In other words:

i. If the issuer and the reference entity of the convertible bond are the same entity, the convertible bond is most likely issued with the same rationale as a primary transaction – i.e. to raise funding to support the issuer's operations.
ii. If the issuer and the reference entity are two different entities, the convertible bond is most likely issued with the same rationale as a secondary transaction – i.e. monetising the stake in the reference entity.

A final point can be made on the secondary market impact of a convertible issuance:

- A solid primary transaction, e.g. convertible issued with a significant conversion premium and underwritten in size by a well-regarded investor, can be taken very positively by the market, as it signals confidence in the future potential performance of the company both from the management team as well as from the investor.
- A weak secondary transaction, e.g. convertible issued by the vehicle holding the relative majority of the company with a small conversion premium and weak investor demand, can have a negative impact as it may signal (i) low confidence in future share performance, (ii) low appetite from investors, and (iii) potential selling ahead by one of the main shareholders.

Example – Convertible bond

- Issue price: EUR 100 (i.e. at par)
- Denomination: EUR 100,000
- Maturity: 7 years
- Coupon: 1.75% p.a.
- Reference share price: EUR 12.98
- Conversion premium: 50%
- Convertible market price: EUR 121
- Share market price: EUR 17.41

Conversion price = (reference share price) × (1+conversion premium) = EUR 19.47

Conversion ratio = (denomination)/(conversion price) = 1 bond for 5,136 shares

Theoretical share price = [(bond mkt price) × (denomination/100) × (conversion ratio)] = 121 × (100,000/100) × (1/5,136) = EUR 23.56

Premium or discount: [(theoretical share price)/(share market price)] -1 = 35.32% premium

Case study **Nexi Convertible Bond, by Francesco Papa, Managing Director ECM, Goldman Sachs**

1. Background and rationale for the issuance of a Convertible Bond by Nexi

On 19 December 2019, Nexi SpA ("Nexi") announced the acquisition of Intesa Sanpaolo Merchant Acquiring activities, a significant transaction to strengthen the industrial partnership between the two companies to provide Payment Technology solutions. The consideration for the purchase was €1 billion to be paid at the time of closing, expected c. 6 months after the announcement. In order to have certainty of funding, Nexi arranged a bridge financing facility at the time of announcement of the acquisition with the intention to access the capital markets over the subsequent months in order to set-up a "permanent" financing structure for the consideration to be paid to Intesa Sanpaolo.
Following the escalation of the Covid-19 crisis in Europe and the US and the sharp market sell-off in March, both Nexi's share price and credit spreads came under significant dislocation:

- Nexi shares dropped from the €16-16.50 area to below €9 and then started recovering towards the €13-13.50 level over the course of April;
- Nexi credit spreads widened significantly and remained elevated throughout April, around 4-4.5%.

On the back of the initial signs of improvement in the general market backdrop, Nexi started evaluating the opportunity to access the financing markets as a first step to finance the acquisition of Intesa Sanpaolo Merchant Acquiring activities. The convertible bond instrument appeared to provide a number of advantages:

[1] **Implied attractive valuation of the call options embedded in the convertible instrument**, reducing the cost of funding;
[2] **Setting of an "aspirational" conversion price as a function of the achievable conversion premium, following the share price rebound** during early April, thus **limiting the perception of a "ceiling"** being set on the shares;

[2] **Setting of an "aspirational" conversion price as a function of the achievable conversion premium, following the share price rebound** during early April, thus **limiting the perception of a "ceiling"** being set on the shares;

[3] Tap into the strength of the Convertible Bond Market: as a matter of fact, the **Convertible Bond market had been one of the first to re-open following the Covid market crisis and had seen increasing momentum over the course of April, particularly in the US but also in Europe and with a marked preference for Technology/high growth issuers.** On the other end, the debt financing market had reopened at attractive terms for Investment Grade-type of issuers, but activity in High Yield had remained subdued.

After carefully evaluating and comparing the embedded cost of capital for different financing alternatives (straight vs convertible debt), Nexi decided to access the market with a €500m convertible bond in order to raise financing at i) attractive cost levels, ii) long maturity, and iii) with an ambitious conversion price and thus limited equity dilution attached to the instrument.

Goldman Sachs alongside JP Morgan and Bank of America were appointed as Joint Global Coordinators to execute the Convertible Bond offering of Nexi.

2. Structuring and execution features for the Nexi Convertible Bond

2.1 Convertible Bond structuring features

Nexi issued a €500m senior unsecured convertible bond due 2027 with a coupon of 1.75% per annum, payable semi-annually in arrear and a conversion price of €19.47, a premium of 50% above the price of the stock at the close prior to the launch of the bookbuilding.

- The bond was the largest equity-linked placement on the Italian market since 2017.

The table below includes the key highlights from the termsheet of the Nexi Convertible Bond

Exhibit 1: Convertible Bond Termsheet

Launch/Pricing Date	16-April-2020, post market-close
Issuer	Nexi S.p.A.
Ranking	Senior, unsecured
Issuer Rating	BB- at S&P's/Ba3 at Moody's/BB at Fitch
Bond Rating	Not rated
Issue Size	**€500m** *(25.7m shares/4.1% TSO*/4.5x 6m ADTV[1])*
Maturity Date	24-Apr-2027 (7 years)
Issuer Soft Call	Callable from 16-May-2025 (5 years) subject to 130% trigger
Issue/Redemption Price	100.00%
Coupon/YTM	**1.75% p.a.** *(vs marketing range of 1.00 – 1.75%)*
Conversion Premium	**50.0%** *(vs marketing range of 45.0 – 50.0%)*
Reference Price	€12.98 *(placing price of concurrent delta placing)*

Conversion Price	€19.47
Dividend Protection	Full dividend protection
Settlement	Physical only (subject to subsequent shareholder approval)
Listing	Vienna MTF of the Vienna Stock Exchange (*Dritter Markt*)
Distribution	Reg S (Cat 1)
Use of Proceeds	Finance a portion of the acquisition of Banca Intesa Sanpaolo's merchant acquiring activities and/or general corporate purposes
Concurrent Equity Placement	€43m *(3.3m shares)* delta placed on behalf of investors looking to hedge their positions in the Bonds flat to closing price

* *TSO*: Total shares outstanding.
ADTV: Average daily traded volume
Source: Goldman Sachs

2.2 Execution Hurdles
Based on the structure and mechanics of a convertible bond, a shareholders' authorization is required for the issuance of the shares underlying the instrument, in the case the share price is above the conversion price at maturity.

Nexi did not have any shareholders' authorization in place at the time of launch of the deal and did not want to wait for a shareholders' meeting to be convened given the risk of missing the right window to access the market.
In order to solve the issue, the instrument was placed to investors on a cash-settled basis and conditional on approval by the shareholders. This feature is relatively common in Italy for the issuance of convertible bonds, as it allows the issuer to access the market without waiting for the organisation of the shareholders' meeting (at least 30 days after the session is called) and the investor to be repaid at par (plus a small premium) in case the shareholders' meeting votes against the resolution.

Nexi decided to access the market in April, therefore ahead of the publication of Q1 20 results that were due on 12 May. In order to provide visibility to the market on the evolution of the business amid the ongoing Covid-19 lockdown and facilitate the company's ability to access the market, Nexi released a business update on 15 April, outlining the series of initiatives put in place to safeguard employees, as well as an update on the evolution in transaction volumes and preliminary visibility on Q1 20 results.

The business update was issued independently on the convertible bond issuance, but allowed for removing the information asymmetry with the market and the share price to seasonbefore starting the investor outreach.

Exhibit 2: First Page of Nexi Business Update Press Release

Nexi, update in relation to Covid-19 impacts

- *Ensured full business continuity and highest efficiency of service, while safeguarding health and safety of all employees*
- *Increase in transaction volumes in January-February compared to the same period last year, followed by a progressive decline starting from March and the beginning of April, as a consequence of the lockdown measures in Italy*
- *Preliminary results in 1Q2020 expected to be broadly in line with 1Q2019; Revenues expected in excess of €220 million and EBITDA expected in excess of €110 million, despite the deterioration in the final part of the quarter due to the lockdown*
- *Given the high level of uncertainty on the evolution of the health emergency, financial guidance conservatively suspended*
- *Solid underlying business fundamentals, with strong cash position*

Milan, April 15 2020 – Nexi S.p.A. ("Nexi" or the "Company") is closely monitoring on a daily basis the development of the Covid-19 pandemic and has swiftly implemented effective business continuity plans to ensure the normal functioning of its business, safeguarding the health and safety of its employees and guaranteeing the highest efficiency of service for partner Banks and end customers.

Since the first day of emergency Nexi has implemented numerous initiatives, in line with the directives provided by the competent Authorities and those dictated by the internal continuity plans, which immediately ensured safety of all operations, with more than 95% of staff, including the call centre activities, transitioned in a few days to working remotely and the implementation of precautionary measures for the limited number of employees still working in the operational centres.

Italy was the first European country to impose severe restrictive measures in early March, with a generalized lockdown nationwide. In this emergency context, in which electronic payment solutions are increasingly fundamental for the normal functioning of the whole country's economy, Nexi remains focused on providing and ensuring its services to partner Banks and end customers with the usual standards of quality and safety.

Moreover, Nexi has launched several initiatives to support merchants and professionals in order to facilitate their businesses activities. In addition to the XPay platform for accepting online payments, Nexi has made available to its clients Pay By Link, a service which allows customers to cash-in remotely even without having their own e-commerce website, Nexi Welcome, a zero-fee Mobile Pos; and the refund of commissions for payments lower than 10 euros from the first of March until the end of the year to support small merchants.

Trading Update

During the 1Q2020, in the market context described above, overall Nexi managed more than 1 billion issuing and acquiring transactions in the period January-February, up by 13.2% Y/Y, with value of managed transactions totalling €72.5 billion (+5.4% Y/Y); in March, given the implementation of the lockdown measures nationwide, managed issuing and acquiring transactions were 338.1 million, down by 31.1% Y/Y, with value of managed transactions totalling €24.9 billion (-33.0% Y/Y).

After an initial -8% drop upon announcement, Nexi shares rebounded on the following day, bouncing back to the €13 level, thus enabling the Company to kick off the execution of the Convertible Bond.

An additional execution hurdle that needed to be addressed as part of the preparatory phase was related to the ban that Consob had imposed on short selling of shares in the Italian market. By way of background, multiple investors that purchase a convertible bond (namely hedge funds) typically undertake delta-hedging activity on the call option embedded in the instrument in order to build a synthetic neutral position on the underlying stock. In order to do so, those investors borrow shares in the market and sell them over the course of the session when the bookbuilding occurs for the convertible bond.

The restrictions imposed by Consob on short selling activities pre-empted hedge funds from executing such operations, thus significantly reducing the addressable universe of potential buyers for the Nexi convertible bond.

Following consultation with the Consob, Nexi and the syndicate banks agreed to launch and execute the bookbuilding of the convertible bond overnight, following the market close, in order to allow for the delta-hedging activity to be executed via the Joint Global Coordinators, in charge of aggregating all the sales orders by hedge funds and placing them via an Accelerated Bookbuilt Offering alongside the convertible bond.

As a result, the transaction had two books, the main one gathering the orders for the convertible bond instrument and a second one aggregating the indications of interest to buy into the placement of shares from the delta-hedging activity by hedge fund investors participating into the convertible bond placement.

Exhibit 3: Detailed Timetable of Execution

	Timing (UKT)	Action
16 April	09:20 a.m.	• Start of investors' wall-crossing process
	From 5:05 p.m.	• Announcement – **Launch Press Release** • Launch and Start of Bookbuilding • (Launch Termsheet)
	6:30 p.m.	• ***Convertible Bond and Delta books covered message***
	7:50 p.m.	• ***Book Close message*** • Pricing expected at 50% premium with 1.75% coupon • ***Delta update*** • Indication on Delta placement coming at last close €12.98 with expected size of €20-40m
17 April (T) (Pre Mkt Open)	6:47 a.m.	• **Pricing Press Release** and release of **Allocations** • (Pricing Termsheet)
29 Jun		• **EGM Approval of underlying shares issuance**

3. Wall-crossing of Investors

As part of the investor engagement strategy to maximise demand and price tension, 12 investors were approached via a wall-crossing exercise that kicked-off in the morning of the launch of the Convertible Bond on Thursday, 16 April 2020. Target investors included convertible focused funds (both long-only investors and hedge funds) as well as few long-term investors in Nexi.

The wall-crossing procedure is strictly regulated and allows an investor to be "brought inside the Chinese Wall," i.e. to receive restricted confidential information ahead of market public disclosure in exchange for a trading restriction in all the related securities. The restriction is removed only when a pre-determined "*cleansing event*" occurs, i.e. the announcement/launch of the transaction or the passage of time or any other events pre-agreed among the parties.
In this case, the investors that accepted being restricted on Nexi were updated on the intention of the company to issue a convertible bond over the following days and briefed on the structure and indicative valuation inputs of the proposed instrument.

Investors reverted with feedback on their intention to participate, size, and indicative levels prior to launch of the deal, providing visibility on enough demand to cover the size of the issuance.

The wall-crossing is an optional step as part of the execution tactics, but in the case of the Nexi issue, given the post-Covid market volatility, it proved to be a helpful tool to provide visibility on sources of demand and increase bookbuilding momentum post-announcement with investors made aware that the size of the issuance was already "covered by indications gathered during the wall-crossing process," and therefore those additional investors that wanted to participate had to come into the book soon and with an attractive indication.

4. Transaction launch and Bloomberg message

Following the indications of feedback gathered from investors during the wall-crossing, the convertible bond bookbuilding phase was launched at around 17:00 Italian time, with a range of coupons – 1% to 1.75% – and conversion premiums – 45% to 50% as guidance for the investors in the bookbuilding.

Given the combination of two metrics – coupon and conversion premium – the "bottom" of the bookbuilding range corresponded to the combination of higher coupon and lower premium (1.75%/45%), while the "top" of the range was the lower coupon and higher premium (1%/50%).

The relevant valuation parameters for investors underlying the instrument were the EUR Swap Rate at -0.18%, Nexi credit spread at 375bps, and Volatility for pricing the call options at 35%. Such valuation parameters were adopted by investors to assess their interest in buying the instrument and at what valuation level within the marketing range.

We have included below a the Bloomberg message that was distributed to the broad institutional investor community at the time of launch and opening of the books as a first outreach to investors, supported by the effort by the sales forces of the Joint Global Coordinators to contact all potential buyers and convert orders into the book.

Exhibit 4: Bloomberg Launch Message

Offering of EUR 500 Million Senior Unsecured Equity-linked Bonds due 2027 Convertible into Ordinary Shares of Nexi S.p.A.

Not for distribution in or into the United States, Australia, Japan, South Africa or any other jurisdiction in which such distribution would be prohibited by applicable law

Target market/ PRIIPs: Manufacturer target market (MIFID II product governance) is eligible counterparties and professional clients only (all distribution channels). No PRIIPs/no KID has been prepared as not available to retail in EEA or UK

This communication is being distributed solely to investment professionals outside the United States in reliance on Regulation S under the US Securities Act of 1933 as amended (the "Securities Act"). If you are not an investment professional, any investment or investment activity to which this communication relates is not available to you, and will not be engaged in with you, and you may not rely on this communication.

This material is confidential and for your information only, is not intended to be used by anyone other than you and may not be forwarded to any other person. This information is subject to change and does not purport to be a complete description of these securities or the offering. Please refer to the Terms of the Bonds for a complete description.

Goldman Sachs International is Joint Global Coordinator and Joint Bookrunner together with BofA Securities and J.P. Morgan on a **Regulation S (Category 1)** convertible bond offering with the following indicative terms:

Issuer:	Nexi S.p.A. (the "Issuer")
Underlying Shares:	Ordinary shares of the Issuer (the "Shares")
Securities Offered:	Euro-denominated senior unsecured equity-linked bonds due 2027 (the "Bonds")
Issuer Rating:	Ba3 (stable) by Moody's/BB (negative) by Fitch/BB- (stable) by S&P
Bond Rating:	The Bonds are not expected to be rated
Status of the Bonds:	Direct, unconditional, unsubordinated and (subject to the Negative Pledge) unsecured
Currency:	EUR
Issue Size:	EUR 500 million
Form:	Registered
Maturity Date:	24 April 2027 (7 years)
Principal Amount:	EUR 100,000 (the "Principal Amount")
Issue Price:	100% of Principal Amount
Redemption Price:	100% of Principal Amount
Coupon/Yield to Maturity Range:	1.00 – 1.75% per annum, payable semi-annually
Conversion Premium Range:	45.00 – 50.00% above the Reference Share Price
Initial Conversion Price:	EUR [•] per Share
Reference Share Price:	EUR [•] per Share, being the placing price of a Share in the Concurrent Accelerated Bookbuilding

Dividend Protection:	Downward adjustment of the Conversion Price for any distributions paid or made in respect of the Shares
Anti-Dilution Provisions:	Euro-market standard anti-dilution provisions dealing with, *inter alia*, share consolidations, share splits, share distributions, spin-off events and rights issues
Shareholder Approvals:	The Issuer will convene a general meeting of the shareholders to be held not later than 31 December 2020 (the "Long-Stop Date") to seek shareholders' approval in respect of the increase in share capital of the Issuer and disapplication (for the purposes of the relevant capital increase) of preferential subscription rights pursuant to article 2441(5) of the Italian Civil Code to enable the issue of Shares on conversion and the delivery of the physical settlement notice (the "Shareholder Resolutions")
Fair Market Call:	If the Shareholder Resolutions are not passed by the Long-Stop Date, the Issuer may elect to redeem all but not some only of the Bonds at the greater of (i) 102% of the principal amount of the Bonds, together with accrued interest and (ii) 102% of the fair bond value of the Bonds together with accrued interest
Settlement upon Conversion:	Cash settlement only until Shareholder Resolutions are passed and Issuer enables physical settlement of the Bonds; thereafter physical settlement only
Settlement upon Redemption:	Cash settlement only
Issuer Soft Call:	Callable on or after 16 May 2025, subject to a 130% share price trigger
Clean-up Call:	Clean-up call at any time if 85% or more of the Bonds have been redeemed, exercised, converted or purchased and cancelled
Bondholder Put:	Yes, upon the occurrence of a Change of Control or Free Float Event at the Redemption Price together with accrued but unpaid interest
Take-Over Protection	Standard temporary Conversion Price adjustment upon Change of Control and Free Float Event alongside Bondholder Put
Event of Default:	Yes, substantially in line with the Issuer's 1.75% Senior Notes due 2024 (the "2024 Notes")
Cross Acceleration:	Yes, in respect of the Issuer and its Subsidiaries, subject to an aggregate threshold of the greater of (i) €100 million and (ii) 22% of Consolidated Pro Forma EBITDA
Negative Pledge:	Yes, in respect of the Issuer and its Subsidiaries in respect of Relevant Indebtedness
Issuer Tax Call/Gross-up:	Yes, subject to Bondholders' right not to be so redeemed and receive, thereafter, net payments of interest/Yes, subject to customary Italian exceptions
Lock-Up:	90 days from Issue Date applicable to the Issuer and its Subsidiaries, subject to customary exceptions and waiver by the Joint Global Coordinators
Use of Proceeds:	Finance a portion of the price for the acquisition of Banca Intesa San Paolo S.p.A.'s merchant acquiring activities as communicated to the market on 19 December 2019 (with a corresponding reduction in the amount committed under the bridge facility made

	available to the Issuer by certain of the Joint Bookrunners or their affiliates in connection with such acquisition) and/or general corporate purposes
Governing Law:	English Law
Launch Date:	16 April 2020
Pricing Date:	Expected to be on 17 April 2020
Issue/Closing Date:	Expected to be on 24 April 2020
ISIN Code of Bonds:	[•]
Listing of the Bonds:	Application will be made to admit the Bonds to trading on the Vienna MTF of the Vienna Stock Exchange no later than 90 days after the Issue Date
Selling Restrictions:	Institutional private placement pursuant to Regulation S (Cat. 1) only, No Rule 144A, TEFRA Rules do not apply. No offers or sales into the United States, Japan, Australia or South Africa or in any other jurisdiction in which offers or sales would be prohibited by applicable law Offers and sales only to Qualified Investors in the EEA and UK Offers and sales only to institutional investors who are both an accredited investor and a Canadian permitted client in Ontario, Quebec, British Columbia or Alberta
MiFID II Target Market:	MiFID II product governance: Professional clients/Eligible Counterparties only/No PRIIPS KID/No sales to retail investors in the EEA, the United Kingdom or elsewhere
Concurrent Delta Placement:	The Managers may organise a simultaneous placement of existing Shares in short sales, at a placement price to be determined via an accelerated bookbuilding process (the "Concurrent Accelerated Bookbuilding") to purchasers procured by the Managers, on behalf of certain subscribers of the Bonds. The Issuer will not receive any proceeds from any sale of Shares in connection with the Concurrent Accelerated Bookbuiding. Any offer or sale of Shares in any Concurrent Accelerated Bookbuilding will be made (i) outside the United States in offshore transactions in reliance on Rule 903 of Regulation S under the US Securities Act of 1933 (the "US Securities Act") or (ii) inside the United States to qualified institutional buyers (as defined in Rule 144A under the US Securities Act) pursuant to an exemption from, or in a transaction not subject to, the registration requirements of the Securities Act.
Joint Global Coordinators and Bookrunners:	Banca IMI, BofA Securities, Goldman Sachs International and J.P. Morgan
Joint Bookrunners/Managers:	Banca IMI, BofA Securities, Goldman Sachs International, HSBC, J.P. Morgan, Banco Akros S.p.A. Gruppo Banco BPM, Mediobanca – Banca di Credito Finanziario S.p.A and UBI Banca

Communications that a transaction is covered (i.e., aggregate demand indications exceed the amount of the security offered) are not an assurance that the transaction will be fully distributed.

We will notify the market when we have received orders in an amount equal to the deal size (i.e., covered). However, this is not an assurance that the deal will be fully distributed.
This communication does not constitute an offer to sell or the solicitation of an offer to buy any securities in any jurisdiction to any person to whom it is unlawful to make such offer or solicitation in such jurisdiction. Prepared by Sales/Trading personnel of Goldman Sachs International from generally available information believed to be reliable but no representation is made that it is accurate or complete. Not a product of Goldman Sachs Investment Research. These securities are being offered by the issuer and represent a new financing. These securities have not been and will not be registered under the Securities Act, and are subject to United States tax law requirements. These securities may not be offered, sold or delivered within the United States. Price/availability subject to change without notice. Past performance is not indicative of future results. Goldman Sachs International and its affiliates may, for its own account, place an order in the book and previously may have accumulated a long or short position in any subject investment. Not for distribution in the United Kingdom to private customers (as defined under Financial Services Authority's rules). If you are located outside the United States, you may not forward this material into the United States.

5. Demand Bookbuilding and Pricing

The bookbuilding progressed with healthy momentum, with coverage on the full offer size achieved in less than one hour of launch and good price tension within the bookbuilding range.

In particular, the transaction benefited from the participation of a diverse group of investors, not only convertible bond specialists but also accounts that had followed Nexi shares since the IPO and used the convertible bond to add additional exposure to the company in their portfolio.
Given the appetite shown by investors, the Joint Global Coordinators were able to push the price above the wider end of the range and in particular with respect to the conversion premium that was set at a compelling +50% vs the prior closing price.
Books closed around 21:00 Italian time, several times oversubscribed.

As mentioned above, in parallel to the convertible book, an equity placement was run in order to identify demand indications for the placement of the delta. The book for the equity placement was several times oversubscribed too, a testament of the very strong interest also from pure equity investors, that made it possible to price the delta with no discount to the previous market close of Nexi shares.

Exhibit 5: Breakdown of Convertible Bond Demand by Geography and Type of Investors

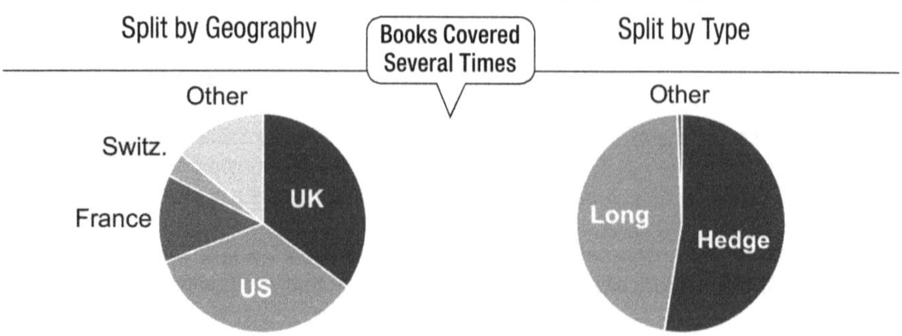

Source: Goldman Sachs

Exhibit 6: Breakdown of Equity Placement Demand by Geography and Type of Investors

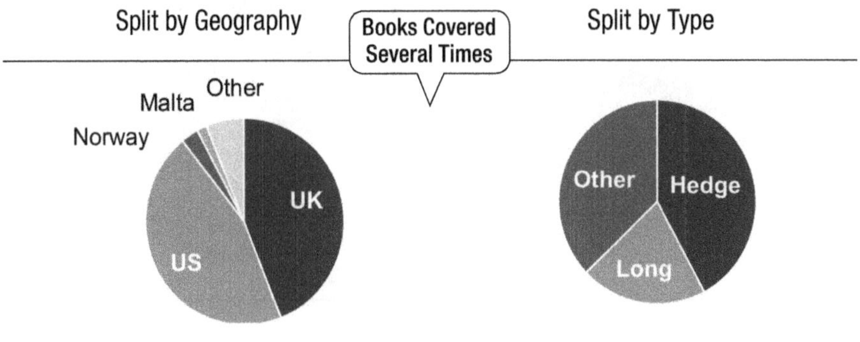

Source: Goldman Sachs

6. Allocations

The allocation process for the convertible bond was aimed at supporting healthy trading in the aftermarket and also at rewarding those investors who have been historically supportive of Nexi.

Approximately 70% of the deal was allocated to long-only investors and the final allocated book included several of the top institutional shareholders of Nexi who decided to buy into the convertible bond as well, in order to gain additional exposure to the stock and leverage the expected upside potential.

Participation from UK and US investors was very high, accounting for c. 70% of the total demand/65% of the allocation.

Exhibit 7: Breakdown of Convertible Bond Allocation by Geography and Type of Investors

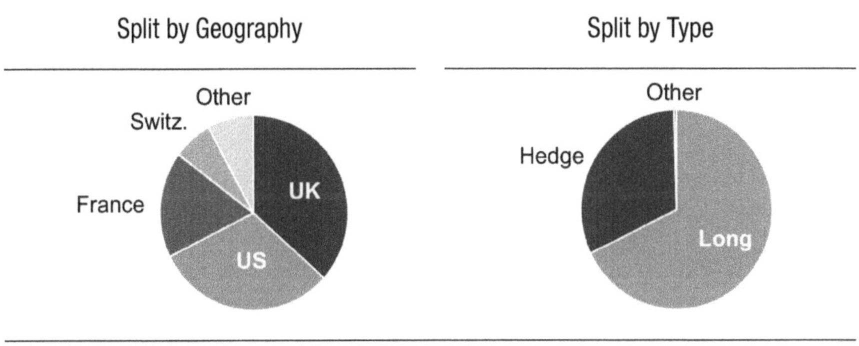

Source: Goldman Sachs

Exhibit 8: Breakdown of Equity Placement Allocation by Geography and Type of Investors

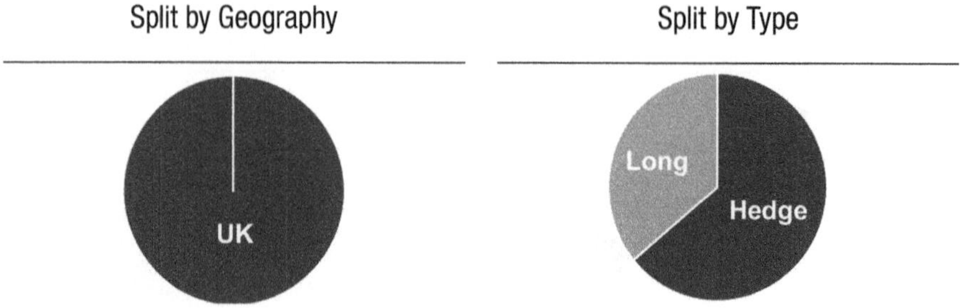

Source: Goldman Sachs

7. Aftermarket Performance

With a turnover of ~€60m, Nexi's inaugural convertible bond closed its first trading day at a quotation of 101.85-102.35% above par, with the underlying stock closing up at €13.50 (c. +4% vs previous close).

The strong aftermarket performance of the convertible was supported by both a positive share price evolution and strong demand across both the long-only and multi-strategy investor community that was satisfied by some hedge funds, taking some profits on their existing exposure.

In terms of relative value, the conversion option embedded in the instrument gained by c. 1% volatility point, only due to the aforementioned pent-up demand of certain investors topping up their position. That trading level indicates that the convertible pricing was set at the appropriate level, with no value left on the table.

Exhibit 9: Nexi Share Price Performance on the CB First Trading Day

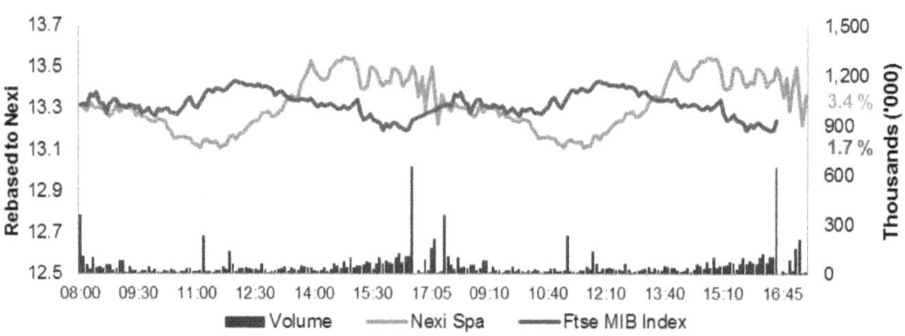

CB price chart over the first day of trading not available as convertibles are traded on OTC platforms from pricing until settlement and data are usually not available in this timeframe.

Source: Bloomberg

7.5 Strategic Equity Transactions

Alongside the various secondary offering transactions described above, investment banks have the ability to offer more complex, tailored solutions to clients wishing to achieve liquidity on a company's stake, generally by way of a desk called "Strategic Equity Transactions," which among other things, is able to structure complex equity-related financing solutions.

Such solutions can be thought of as a sort of synthetic secondary offering, where the client is able to use its stake for liquidity purposes without having to sell it. The ability not to sell (i.e. to retain ownership rights and to preserve the percentage of voting rights owned) is a key benefit of such solutions.

There are two main strategic equity financing tools which can be helpful in raising liquidity versus a stake: put-based financing and collar financing.

In put-based financing, the investor buys a put option on a certain amount of shares at a strike price generally below the spot price, and at inception, receives the present value of the overall notional at strike (i.e. PV[strike price x total number of shares]), net of the option premium. At maturity, assuming the client wants to retain the initial stake, the overall notional at strike will be reimbursed; any positive gain on the option will be cash-settled. Put-based financing is an efficient way to provide non-recourse financing without capping the upside potential for the client on the underlying position, but clearly comes at a cost (the option premium) which is higher the higher the required loan to value (LTV) is, since in put-based financing, LTV = PV[strike price]/spot price.

Example – Put-based financing
An Investor has a stake in a listed company (EUR 100mn) and wants to raise financing against it on a 2-year horizon:

- Share price: EUR 10
- Stake: 10mn shares
- Value of stake: EUR 100mn
- Put strike: 85%
- Volatility: 25%
- Risk-free rate: 0.25%
- Dividend yield: 3.00%

Given the above parameters, using the Black and Scholes option model, a 2-year put option with strike @ 85% should have a premium of around 8.31%. The actual premium will be higher, to account for the size: let's assume 0.50% is enough to compensate for that, for a total premium of 8.81%. The put-financing agreement works as follows:

1. At T+0, the client receives EUR 75.77mn (EUR 84.58mn PV of strike, net of EUR 8.81mn premium).
2. At T+2 years, the client will reimburse EUR 85mn.
3. The actual annual financing rate for the client is (EUR 8.81mn/2 years)/EUR 75.77mn = 5.81% p.a.

As a result, for an annual rate of 5.81%, the client has been able to generate liquidity from its stake while (i) retaining its ownership rights, and (ii) being entitled to compensation in the case of a reduction in the share's value below 85% of the strike price.

In collar financing, a collar is implemented on the shares (for a notional amount equal to the stake) instead of a simple put option. This way, the cost of the structure is reduced by the sale of a call option while retaining the ability to receive non-recourse financing; at the same time, though, any upside potential in the share price above the call strike price is foregone by the client.

Example – Collar financing
An investor has a stake in a listed company (EUR 100mn) and wants to raise financing against it on a 2-year horizon:

- Share price: EUR 10
- Stake: 10mn shares
- Value of stake: EUR 100mn
- Put strike: 85%
- Call strike: 115%
- Volatility: 25%
- Risk-free rate: 0.25%
- Dividend yield: 3.00%

Given the above parameters, using the Black and Scholes option model, a 2-year put option with strike @ 85% should have a premium of around 8.31%, whereas a 2-year call option with strike @ 115% should have a premium of around 6.65%. Let's assume 0.50% adjustment for the size on both the put and call option premiums, which become 8.81% and 6.15%, respectively (investor buys put and sells call). The collar financing agreement works as follows:

1. At T+0, the client receives EUR 81.92mn (EUR 84.58mn PV of the put strike, net of EUR 2.66mn given (i) EUR 8.81mn put premium to pay and (ii) EUR 6.15mn call premium to receive).
2. At T+2 year, the client will reimburse EUR 85mn, be compensated for any decrement in the stock value below 85%, and forego any gain above 115%.
3. The actual annual financing rate for the client is (EUR 2.66mn/2 years)/EUR 81.92mn = 1.62% p.a.

As a result, for an annual rate of 1.62%, the client is able to generate liquidity from its stake. The cost is significantly lower than put-based financing, but the investor will have to forego any increment in the share's value above 115%.

A very famous type of collar financing structure is the "zero cost collar": in such a structure, the put strike and call strike (and, hence, the premiums) are set at such a level that the two premiums offset in value. The main advantage for the client is, clearly, the ability to generate liquidity at zero cost (apart from the opportunity cost of the potential upside which will be missed).

Example – "zero cost" collar
An investor has a stake in a listed company (EUR 100mn) and wants to raise financing against it on a 2-year horizon:

- Share price: EUR 10
- Stake: 10mn shares
- Value of stake: EUR 100mn
- Put strike: 85%
- Call strike: TBD%
- Volatility: 25%
- Risk-free rate: 0.25%
- Dividend yield: 3.00%
- Put premium: 8.31%
- Size adjustment to premium: 0.50%

The zero-cost collar requires a call strike such that the call premium = 9.31% (so that the call premium adjusted for size = 8.81% = put premium adjusted for size). Back-solving for the call strike using the Black and Scholes option model, we can see that the strike @ 105.2% gives a call option premium of 9.31%. A zero-cost collar structure can be implemented with rounded strikes of 85%/105%.

In both put-based financing and collar financing more complex mechanics than the ones we just described can be implemented behind the scenes (e.g. the stake can be used as collateral for the exposure and borrowed by the bank to hedge its delta exposure), but the crucial point is not the mechanics per se: when a key shareholder needs both liquidity as well as retaining ownership and voting rights, banks have the ability to structure tailored solutions to fulfil such needs.

As can be imagined, Strategic Equity Transactions are not limited to the financing side. Similarly, there are various solutions through which Investment Banks can help a client build a strategic position in a company. One of those is the Accelerated Stake Building, through which Investment Banks can help the client to rapidly build a stake in a specific company (as the name suggests), or to increase the existing stake with a similarly rapid pace.

Case study — On the accelerated stake building and subsequent placement by the French State (APE) in Renault, by Deutsche Bank Corporate Finance Team

Renault – Accelerated Stake Building (2015) and subsequent Accelerated Bookbuilding (2017) by APE (Agence des participations de L'État – i.e. the French State)
The following case study describes an accelerated stake building in 2015 and an accelerated bookbuilding in 2017, implemented by Deutsche Bank on Renault shares, on behalf of APE. The original transaction, an accelerated stake building in 2015, was implemented with the unique objective for the French State to be in a position to block a resolution at the Annual General Meeting (AGM). The second transaction in 2017 was the ABB in Renault through which APE disposed of the same stake when the dispute came to an end.

Accelerated Stake Building (2015)

On 7 April 2015, Deutsche Bank structured a stake building and 6-month hedging transaction for APE on shares of Renault representing 4.7% of the company's share capital, c. 11 ADTVs (average daily trading volume). Deutsche Bank was able to sell at inception 9.6m Renault shares in a single block transaction with an additional 4.4m purchased via on-market transactions over the following 9 trading days. This transaction was structured and signed over 4 calendar days, demonstrating Deutsche Bank's structured solutions expertise and its ability to deliver bespoke alternatives to its clients under tight deadlines.
Transaction summary:

1. APE increased its holding in the French car manufacturer Renault SA ("Renault") to 19.7% from 15.0% in order to support the adoption of double voting rights by Renault, which was being opposed by the management and would be voted on at the next AGM held on 30 April 2015.
2. APE entered into an option contract over 14.0m ordinary shares of Renault, representing about 4.7% of the company's share capital, with Deutsche Bank selling its initial hedge ("Initial delta") of 9.6m Renault shares to APE as a single block at inception.
3. Deutsche Bank subsequently purchased for APE 4.4m Renault shares (1 – Initial delta) from the equity market.
4. APE obtained downside protection on its additional Renault stake by buying put options from Deutsche Bank and subsidised the associated options cost by selling some upside by way of call options also to Deutsche Bank.

Transaction highlights

APE
AGENCE DES PARTICIPATIONS DE L'ETAT

RENAULT

Trade date:	7 April 2015
Underlying:	Renault SA
Notional:	EUR 1,193.6m
Underlying shares:	14.0m
As of outstanding shares:	4.7% (c.11 ADTVs)
Initial delta sale:	9.6m shares, EUR 814.8m (c.68% of Notional)

Deutsche Bank

Sole Counterparty on the option contract
Sole Counterparty for the brokerage mandate

"This transaction demonstrates the willingness and ability of the State to use all the weapons now available to investors, but to promote a capitalism of progress, long-term, serving the employees and the development of companies. This shows that the State is both a savvy investor and defender of the general interest."
Emmanuel Macron, French Economy minister
8 April 2015, press release from the French government

Source: Bloomberg, 8 April 2015.

Transaction structure

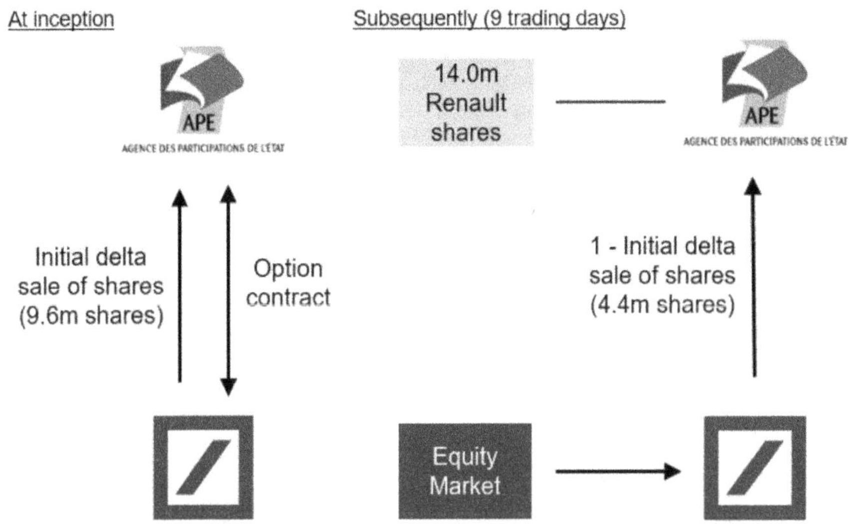

Source: Deutsche Bank, press releases from the French government, 8 April 2015 and 22 April 2015.

Accelerated Bookbuilding (2017)

On 2 November 2017, Deutsche Bank successfully priced a EUR 1.2bn ABB of Renault on behalf of APE acting as Joint Bookrunner. After the stake building in Renault and the related hedging transaction implemented for APE in April 2015 to secure double voting rights, Deutsche Bank was mandated as Sole Advisor on the unwinding of that position via an ABB.

Transaction summary, ABB Renault 2017

Pricing date	2 November 2017
Issuer	Renault SA
Selling shareholder	French State (through APE)
Deal size	€1,212mn
Offer price	€86.60
Discount to last close	0.0%
Offer shares	14.0m (incl. 1.4m buyback by the company)
% share capital	4.3%
% free float	7.4%
Days trading (3m ADTV)	10.5x
Lock-up	180 days
Deutsche Bank role	Joint Bookrunner

Source: Deutsche Bank, Company press releases, 2 November 2017.

Transaction summary:
Below are the transaction highlights, the source is Deutsche Bank syndicate.

- Strong early momentum gained with books covered within 20 minutes post-launch, then covered throughout the price guidance in under an hour.
- Simultaneous share buy-back by Renault putting an order at strike representing 10% of the book.
- Pricing at €86.60, i.e. at no discount to last close, with the book multiple times covered.
- Tightest pricing for a European secondary ABB over €1bn since 2014.
- Allocations skewed towards long-only investors and concentrated with the top 20 accounts taking c. 70% of the shares on offer.
- Successful pricing despite a challenging equity market backdrop with European and US indices trading in the red, as investors digested mixed earnings reports and details of the draft tax bill in the US.

by Geography

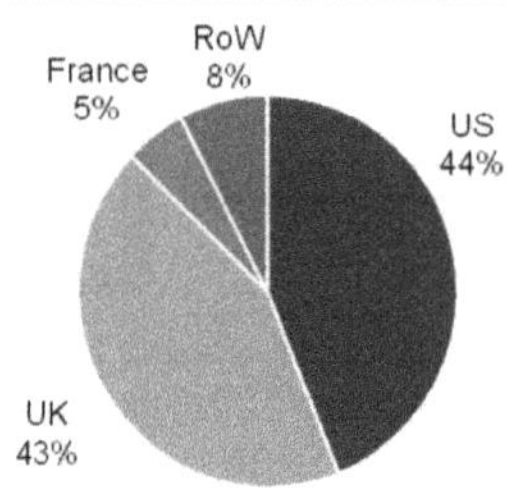

by Type

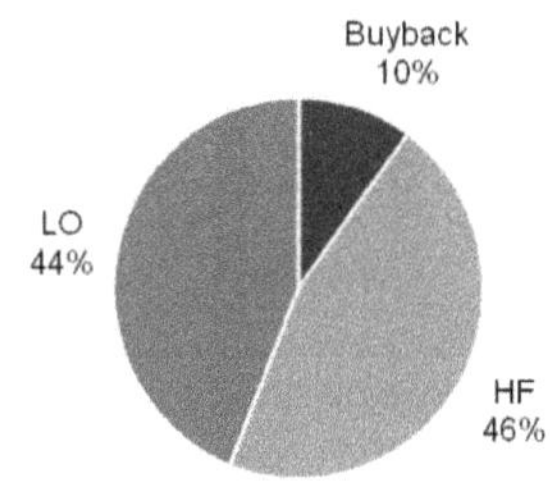

Source: Deutsche Bank syndicate

Finally, as you can see in the following figure, the transaction was launched close to the highs of the previous twelve months.

Renault share price

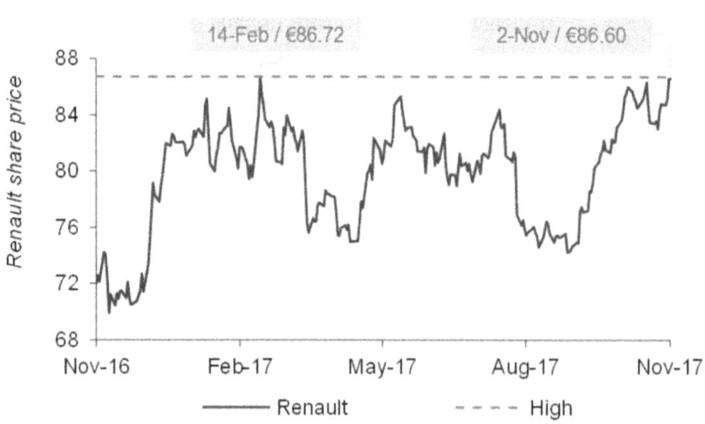

Source: Deutsche Bank syndicate

Questions and answers

1. *What is a Seasoned Equity Offering (SEO) and what are the two main SEO structures?*
   A seasoned equity offering (SEO) is a transaction through which the equity of an already-listed company is offered to the market. The two main structures to implement a SEO are rights offerings and accelerated book building (ABB).

2. *When is a SEO dilutive?*
   A SEO is deemed dilutive if the offering involves the issuance of new shares, in whole or in part, and if an existing shareholder is not able to participate pro-rata in the issuance, since the shareholder would have to participate in the transaction in order to retain the same proportion of capital and/or voting rights held before the transaction.

3. *Are rights issues generally dilutive?*
   Rights issues are generally considered non-dilutive, since the existing shareholder is able to maintain the "status quo" by fully exercising the rights (s)he is entitled to. However, this means fresh money will have to be allocated to the investment; consequently, cash-neutral participation in the rights issue is implicitly dilutive.

4. *What is the difference between a primary and a secondary SEO?*
   A primary offering involves the issuance of new shares and results in fresh equity and additional capital for the company. On the other side, a secondary offering involves only already-issued shares and simply results in the sale of an already-existing block of shares from one or more shareholders.

5. *Explain what a "transaction discount" is, and name at least three variables which help determine its depth.*
   A transaction discount refers to the price at which the shares are offered, with reference to the market price when the offering is announced. The majority of SEOs generally take place at a price which offers a discount to the market, and the depth of the potential discount is a function of different variables, including one or more of the following: general market conditions, investor appetite for the company's shares, size of the SEO, use of proceeds in the case of primary offering, details on the investors' profile, and details on anchor investor(s), if any.

6. *What is the purpose of a rights offering?*
   A rights offering has the purpose of raising capital via the issue of rights to participate in a capital increase, with the aim of offering all shareholders in the company the ability to participate in the capital increase via the issuance of rights attached to the existing shares.

7. *In a rights offering, what is the "subscription price" and how is it generally indicated?*
The subscription price is the price per share at which existing shareholders can buy new shares within the capital increase. In other words, it is the price they will have to pay for each new share acquired when deciding to exercise their rights. The subscription price is generally indicated in terms of a discount over the previous market price and/or the TERP.

8. *In a rights offering, what is the "TERP" and how is it calculated?*
The TERP is the theoretical ex-right price and represents the theoretical market value of one share when the rights have been granted to the entitled shareholders (hence, detached from the share). The standard formula to calculate the TERP is:

TERP = [(cum-right price)*(outstanding shares) + (subscription price)*(new shares)]

(outstanding shares + new shares)

9. *How can an existing shareholder take advantage of discrepancies between the market price and the theoretical value of a right?*
If the market price is higher than the theoretical value of the right, an existing shareholder can sell the right in the market and directly buy shares in the secondary market, instead of keeping the right and exercising it. If the market price of the right is lower than the theoretical value, the existing shareholder can sell the shares, buy rights in the market, and exercise them.

10. *What is an Accelerated Bookbuilding and why is it generally implemented?*
An accelerated book building is a transaction through which the company and/or one or more significant investors sell existing and/or newly-issued shares to institutional investors that may or may not be existing shareholders in the company. An accelerated bookbuilding is generally implemented to place a significant amount of shares in a time-efficient way.

11. *Rank, by time, the different communications from the trading desk to the clients during an ABB.*

    1. Announcement and details as soon as the market closes ("books are now open").
    2. Books update during the bookbuilding process ("books are covered" and/or "books are covered multiple times" and/or "books are covered throughout the range" and/or "orders below €xx risk missing the deal").
    3. Books closing once the bookbuilding process is completed ("book to close at xx:yy" and/or "books are now closed").
    4. Pricing and allocation generally the morning after before the market opens.

12. *How does price guidance work in an ABB?*
Generally, ABB transactions are announced with an indicative price range with reference to the latest market price. The price range can be at an explicit discount, at a potential discount, or at no explicit discount. While ABBs are normally priced at a discount, sometimes the transaction is priced at the closing price, most often in the case of very strong demand and no explicit discount.

13. *What is a convertible bond and how does its structure work?*
A convertible bond is a bond which, at maturity, can be converted into a pre-defined amount of shares of a reference entity, at a pre-defined strike price (at a premium versus the current price level), and at the underwriter's discretion. Its structure is a combination of (a) a plain vanilla bond and (b) an out of the money call option.

14. *How does a convertible bond work from inception to maturity (assuming it is issued at par)?*
At inception, the underwriter lends €100 to the issuer and receives a €100 nominal amount of the convertible bond. During its life, the convertible bond pays a coupon to the bondholder. At maturity, the bondholder has the right to decide whether to receive €100 of principal or to convert such principal into shares of the reference entity at a pre-defined conversion price:

- if the share is trading below the conversion price, the underwriter will decide to receive €100;
- if the share is trading above the conversion price, the underwriter will decide to receive the stocks (since the overall monetary value will clearly be above €100).

15. *Why would an issuer issue a convertible bond and why would an investor buy it?*
An issuer would issue a convertible bond because it allows for reducing the cost of financing thanks to the implicit sale of an out of the money call option to the underwriter, while at the same time (i) expanding the sources of funding by reaching all potential investors, and (ii) avoiding the negative price reaction and/or dilutive impact of an outright equity offering. An investor would buy such an instrument because it offers the opportunity to participate in the upside of the reference entity's share above the conversion price, while at the same time earning a stream of coupons and limiting the downside to the issuer's credit risk.

16. *In a convertible bond, are the issuer and the reference entity the same?*
In a convertible bond, the issuer may or may not be the same as the reference entity. If the issuer and the reference entity are the same entity, the convertible bond is most likely issued with the same rationale as a primary transaction; if they are two different entities, the convertible bond is most likely issued with the same rationale as a secondary transaction.

17. *What is an equity-related financing solution within the "strategic equity transactions" perimeter, and what is a key advantage of such a solution?*
    In strategic equity transactions, an equity-related financing solution is a financing solution through which an investor is able to use its stake in a company for liquidity purposes without having to sell it; the ability not to sell (i.e. to retain ownership rights and to preserve the % of voting rights owned) is a key benefits of such solutions, which works as a sort of synthetic secondary offering.

8 Private Equity Deals

by Stefano Caselli and Giulia Negri

8.1 Private equity: Definitions and main mechanisms

The term "**private equity**" refers to investments made in unlisted, i.e. private, companies that may find themselves at any stage of their life cycle, from being newly-founded companies to bankrupt companies. In the event the investee company finds itself in a development stage and in the first years of business activity, the investment is referred to as "venture capital."

The first element that characterizes the private equity business is the fact that **private equity investors** (i.e. private equity managers or private equity firms) invest money that is not theirs and that is aggregated in a **fund**. In this sense, it can be said that the private equity operator acts as a fund manager, deciding on the money allocation on behalf of the **investors**. Investors own the money that is being invested by a private equity operator. Regardless of whether the investee company is young or mature, whenever a private investor becomes one of its shareholders, it will be called a Venture Backed-Company (VBC). **Figure 8.1** shows how VBC are related to private equity and their investors.

Typical investors are, among others, pension funds, insurance funds, family offices, and sovereign wealth funds. When investors commit their money to the hands of private equity, they waive every right to decide on the allocation of these flows as they acknowledge the competence and expertise of the private equity manager.

The tasks of private equity consist of raising the money that makes up the total value of the fund: the larger the size of the fund, the larger the investment possibilities for the private equity investor and the fund. Once the total value of the fund is

Figure 8.1 Private Equity investment structure

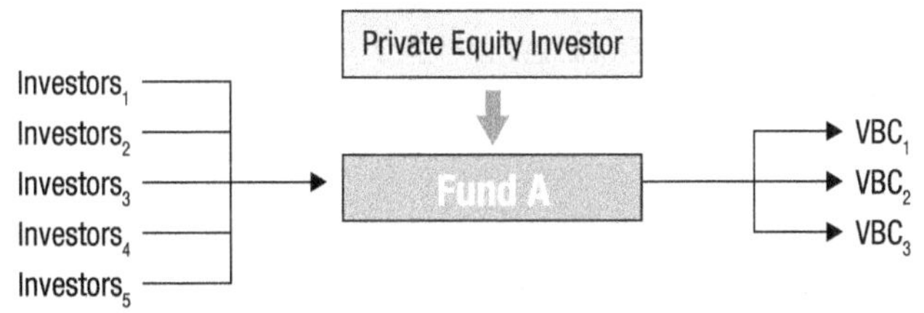

reached, the fund is operative and can be "launched." From that moment until the end of the fund's life, the fund will make investments in VBCs, the private equity fund will implement actions to generate further value from them and exit from them, re-investing the money. In this sense, it can be said that the day-by-day business of a private equity fund consists of raising funds, investing, managing and monitoring the investments, and exiting them.

Within the private equity business, investment banks can play one of the following roles:

- they can act as the private equity investor;
- they can act as pure investors;
- they can act as advisors or "financial sponsors," liaising VBCs and the private equity investor.

With reference to each of the roles that can be played by the bank, it is important to stress that the third one is the one that is most frequently played. In fact, if banks wanted to act as fund managers or pure investors, they would have to set aside a large amount of regulatory capital, in light of the high risk represented by investment in unlisted equities.

8.2 Private equity investment clusters

VBCs can be either mature companies or expanding ones. The approach of a private equity investor will evolve and change depending on the stage of life a VBC finds itself in. There are six stages of life for a company:

1. Development,
2. Start-up,
3. Early Growth,
4. Expansion,
5. Maturity,
6. Crisis.

Each of these stages presents a specific trend at the investment level: profitability, cash flow generation, and sales growth are different. These trends are shown in **Table 8.1**.

Each stage of life of a company generates a different private equity investment "cluster," classified by:

- risk-return profile,
- critical issues,
- stake owned by the private equity fund, that can be either a minority or a majority stake.

Table 8.1 The characteristics of the four drivers of a firm's different stages

	Investment	Profitability	Cash flow	Sales Growth
Development	Concentrated on developing the idea	Negative	Negative	n.a.
Start-up	Concentrated on buying productive factors	Strongly negative	Strongly negative	Starting
Early Growth	Limited to inventory	Negative but decreasing	Negative but decreasing	Positive and increasing
Expansion	Inventory and replacement	End of increasing	End of increasing	Close to zero
Mature Age	Limited to inventory	Positive and increasing	Positive and increasing	Positive and increasing
Crisis or decline	Not possible to identify	Plummeting	Plummeting	Negative

Every stage of the life of the company has risk, measured as total or partial loss of invested sources, delays in project implementation, lower profits, etc., and an expected return usually measured as the **internal rate of return** (IRR). In addition, there are critical issues to be managed at every stage in a company's growth. **Figure 8.2** shows the matching between the different stages of life of a company and the private equity investment cluster.

Figure 8.2 Stage of life of a company and private equity deals

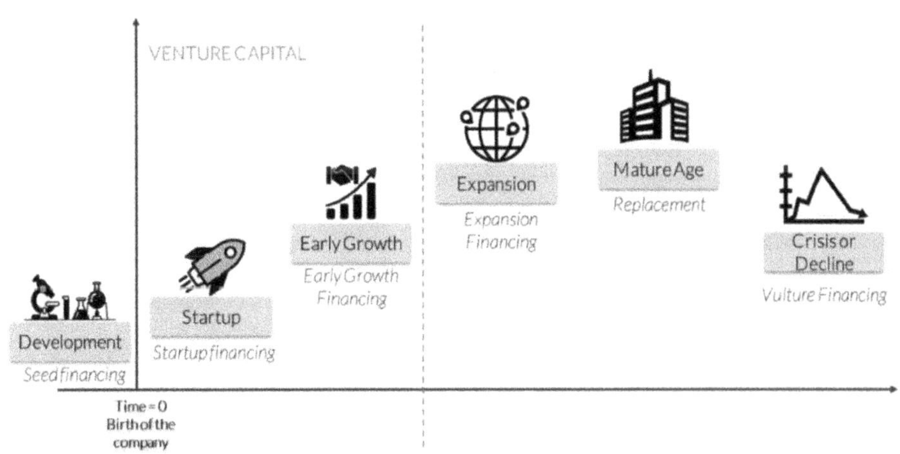

8.2.1 Seed financing

Seed financing is necessary for the development of a new firm. Development indicates that the business idea or the development plan of a product has not been created yet. During this type of financing, funded firms do not have an actual product or an output to sell and are unable to earn revenue. This is also called the first round or initial financing. The purpose of seed financing is to transform R&D projects into successful business companies or start-ups. Therefore, the financing is used to create new ventures. The risk–return profile is very difficult to define, because the risk is very high, while expected returns are impossible to calculate due to the uncertainty of R&D results and the difficulties of transforming R&D into business. Also, the huge risk and uncertainty derive from the fact that once the product is being produced it may not have a market, or worse, be marketable. This is particularly true for biotech and high-technology projects, which generate products that have a market but do not have marketability due to their complexity or high costs.

Seed financing investors do not ask financiers to be managers, because the project has just taken off. However, the role played by investors is not passive; on the contrary, they support research activities and translate the business idea into a production process. They support research activities, translate the business idea into a patent and production process, build the company team, and manage any sudden death risk. The most important elements financiers provide are business plan preparation, analysis, and validation. Typically, a minority stake is owned.

8.2.2 Start-up financing

Seed financing transforms R&D into a business idea, and start-up financing converts the business idea into a real operating company. The financing collected in this phase is used to set up projects and launch production.

During seed financing, financiers are expected to be experienced in the relevant technical and engineering fields. In start-up financing, because the R&D stage has already been completed, financiers are expected to support the business plan, have an in-depth understanding of its nature and its assumptions, value the management team, and define the strategy used to implement proposals.

For this reason, private equity operators are very involved in a firm's management and own a large number of shares, even if it is very rare for them to own a controlling stake in the VBC.

8.2.3 Early stage financing

Early stage financing is essential when moving from the start-up phase to the real business life cycle. In this phase, sales and firm growth begin. The objective of early stage financing is to create a stable and permanent organization.

During this phase, all problems related to project, design, test, and launch have been resolved. Financial resources are used to fund a little developed company that needs equity to boost its growth. For financiers, this is the stage where financing really begins.

The risk–return profile at this stage is similar to earlier phases: there is more uncertainty within the market rather than on technical items or feasibility questions. Because of this, financing during this phase is opened to investors new to the sector or the market. The activities carried out and required range from assistance to strategic decisions to business plan certification to marketing and financial advice. Typically, a minority stake is owned.

8.2.4 Expansion financing

Expansion financing is for companies that need or want to expand their business activity. If the market conditions are right, it can be a great move; some businesses find they need expansion financing when fast business growth is possible.

Equity or debt is provided to support growing debt and inventories. The company is growing but may not be showing profits at this stage. Funds may be provided for the major expansion of a company that has increasing sales volume and is reaching break-even or has achieved initial profitability. They are utilized for further plant expansion, marketing, and working capital or for development of an improved product, a newer technology, or an expanded product line. In addition to an organic growth scenario, there is the possibility for the company to grow through acquisitions and mergers externally.

For the investor, the risk in expansion financing is moderate and depends on the sector. Money is used to finance sales growth or to improve projects in known fields, so there is no risk due to uncertainty. Returns should be lower at this stage.

Although firms are already operating, financial institutions also play a fundamental role during this phase. At this point they are asked to develop effective growth plans. Because of the size of a firm and the financier's need to diversify its portfolio, the percentage of shares depends on the specific deal. Typically, a minority stake is owned, but in some deals a majority stake can be owned.

8.2.5 Replacement financing

After the growth phase (whether rapid and slow), the size of the firm becomes more stable and the company enters a mature age. Although profitability and cash flows are stable, private equity financing still plays an important role. During the mature age entrepreneurs modify their needs, and while almost all priorities have been driven by sales development and increase in size, in this period problems may arise from governance or corporate finance decisions. Replacement financing funds companies looking for strategic decisions associated with the governance system and the firm's status, rather than the firm's approach to finance.

Replacement financing is never used to boost sales growth or to realize investment in plants. Instead it is used for strategic or acquisition processes. Replacement capital is the proper solution to fund spin-off projects, equity restructuring, shareholder substitution, IPOs, family buy-in or family buyout, etc.

For investors, the risk profile of these deals is moderate because:

- the firm's business model is successful;
- the firm's governance is settled even though it is in a shifting phase;
- entrepreneurs usually remain and work for the company development.

The actual risk also depends on the whole sector/market risk and the quality of the process to be put in place.

In this case, private equity operators buy a large number of shares issued by the firm they are working with. This makes the whole plan easier to be implemented, and very often the private equity operators turn into the controlling shareholder. However, even though the investors hold the majority of the company's shares, they do not participate in the current management, allowing the entrepreneur to retain the top management role.

Typically, a majority stake is owned, but in some deals a minority stake can be owned. In the event a majority stake is owned, it is possible to talk about a Buy-Out. In cases where a large portion of leverage is used to finance the deal, this is called a Leveraged Buy-Out (LBO).

8.2.6 Vulture financing

Even when firms are facing a decline or a crisis, private equity operators may be suitable partners. When a firm is financially distressed, private equity operators can offer what is called vulture financing. This is used to restructure companies to enable them to improve their financial performance, exploit new strategic opportunities, and regain credibility. In extreme situations, restructuring can represent the difference between a company surviving or filing for bankruptcy.

For investors, vulture financing is very risky; there is no guarantee that the business will be revitalized by the survival plan. The risk is linked to the "nature" of the crisis: a business crisis is different from an audit fraud crisis because it is due to macroeconomic factors and not mismanagement of funds.

Vulture investors frequently gain control by purchasing senior securities, and they often become board members or managers of the target company. From this position they can propose a survival plan, implement it, and monitor the growth of the firm. Vulture financing serves to impose discipline on managers of companies in financial distress. Typically, a majority stake is owned.

Many skills are required of financial institutions operating in this environment, because their intervention forces them to act as an advisor and consultant, or, more often, as an entrepreneur. The fundamental role of the private equity operator is to support managerial strategic decisions and the implementation of the entire design of the deal. This requires deep industrial knowledge or the ability to manage corporate governance issues and corporate finance deals.

8.3 Private equity in Europe

In the European Union (EU), private equity is considered as a financial service, and as such, it is supervised by a dedicated authority. Because it is supervised, private equity financing is perceived as safer, more stable, and easier to control than unsupervised financing. Unfortunately, safety and regulations are put in place in exchange for higher costs and more specific constraints.

According to the EU rules, private equity is considered as a financial activity and must be supervised. Private equity firms must comply with rules that regulate the entire European financial system. The organizational structure of investments in equity is regulated by the following acts:

- Banking Act (1988–1993);
- Financial Services Act (1998);
- AIFM Directive (Alternative Investment Fund Managers) (2011);
- MiFID (Markets in Financial Instruments Directive) active until January 2018, and MiFID II (active from January 2018).

As a Union of 27 Member States, the EU issues directives that must be implemented on a local level with ad hoc laws. In Europe, these are the players allowed to carry out private equity operations:

- banks;
- investment firms;
- closed-end funds (based on the UK or US models).

Banks and investment firms deal in credit intermediation, so investment in equity is only one of the activities they can undertake; we will explain later why they rarely undertake it. On the other hand, investment in equity is the core activity of a closed-end fund. The rest of this section explains how closed-end funds and investment banks invest in private equity.

8.3.1 Understanding funds schemes

According to the definition of financial services proposed by the EU, there are some activities that cannot be offered by banks directly but can be managed by specialized organizations such as funds, special investment firms, and other structures accepted by single country regulations.

In the private equity business, the most important non-banking activity is asset management, because it assumes a direct or indirect investment in firms. Generally speaking, there are two main structures used to manage investment in private companies:

- limited partnership, used in the US and in the UK (Anglo-Saxon market), and presented later;
- funds and AMCs, used in the European Union.

Funds are financial institutions where a separate manager or firm (AMC) manages a specific amount of money that does not necessarily belong to them. The operating structure of a fund in the PE context is seen in **Figure 8.3**. Funds are by far the most widespread vehicle in continental Europe to conduct private equity operations.

Because European legislation requires supervision of financial institutions, control of the responsible managers becomes inevitable. Managers create a separate entity, the so-called AMC, in countries where the fund system is adopted, the AMC is one of the financial institutions included and defined by acts providing for financial services management.

Generally speaking, there are three main groups of funds:

- open-end funds;
- closed-end funds;
- hedge funds.

An **open-end fund** is defined as a floating-sized fund; investors are able to enter and exit without specific time limits. The most important features of this fund are:

Figure 8.3 The organizational structure of funds

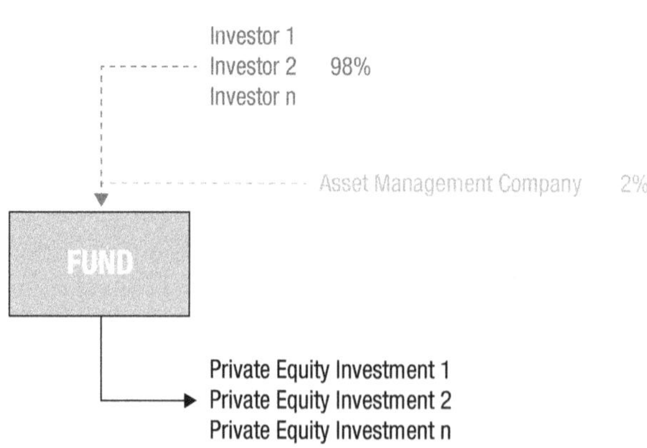

- Liquidity. It should be able to manage its liquidity at any time, which is the reason it invests mainly in listed securities.
- It is principally dedicated to the retail market.
- It cannot invest in private equity.
- It cannot leverage.

A **closed-end fund** includes non-floating size funds; investor are able to invest only at the initial phase of the fund and exit only at the end of life of the fund. This fund can invest in private equity because the private equity business needs resources and liquidity without any kind of exit pressure from the investor side. Closed-end funds are separate entities that invest money for a group of investors. The relationship between the parties involved is mainly based on mutual trust. Investors invest their own money in a specific fund because they trust the manager's ability to successfully manage this money. Like the open-end fund, it cannot leverage. This means that the capital collected among the investors is the only (and maximum) monetary basis that can be used to undertake the investments. If the PE fund wants to use leverage, the AMC has to create an external Special Purpose Vehicle (SPV) that will take on the leverage.

A **hedge fund** is a fund that is allowed to leverage, unlike the other two types of funds described above. It can be either an open- or closed-end fund depending on its purpose. The fund supervisor decides who invests in the fund (i.e., according to EU regulations, retail investors cannot invest in these funds due to the high risk).

The scheme used to invest in private equity is a double-level system made up of the:

- AMC;
- closed-end fund.

8.3.2 AMC in private equity

An AMC is a financial institution that hosts funds (both closed- and open-end) and manages financial services as defined by the Banking Acts (i.e., an AMC may supply personal management of savings, dealing, brokerage, or advisory services). Rules concerning AMCs are the same throughout Europe. The set of rules for closed-end funds is very short, with regulatory activity delegated to the country's supervisor, and governed by the internal code of activity of each fund created. Generally speaking, AMCs can manage only one type of fund, either an open- or closed-end fund. This country-specific rule is in place to better regulate the typical relationship between companies and the financial system. In the context of a private equity investment, the private equity firm plays the role of the AMC. Table 8.2 shows the private equity firms most active in Europe. They are ranked based on the capital raised in the last decade in Europe-focused funds. The most represented country is the UK with eight firms out of 20. In the list, we can see three

Table 8.2 Largest Fund Managers by Capital Raised for Europe-Focused Funds as of July 2020

Rank	Firm	Headquarters	Total Capital Raised in Past 10 Years (€bn)
1	CVC	London, UK	59.5
2	Ardian	Paris, France	58.2
3	EQT	Stockholm, Sweden	26.2
4	Permira	London, UK	25.3
5	Cinven	London, UK	22.3
6	Advent International	Boston, US	20.0
7	Apax Partners	London, UK	15.1
8	Carlyle Group	Washington, US	14.0
9	BC Partners	London, UK	13.7
10	Partners Group	Zug, Switzerland	12.0
11	Bridgepoint	London, UK	11.0
=	Coller Capital	London, UK	11.0
13	LGT Capital Partners	Pfäffikon, Switzerland	10.3
=	Nordic Capital	St Helier, Jersey	10.3
15	Russian Direct Investment Fund	Moscow, Russia	9.6
16	KKR	New York, US	9.1
=	Triton	St Helier, Jersey	9.1
18	PAI Partners	Paris, France	8.7
19	Bain Capital	Boston, US	8.1
=	Hg	London, UK	8.1

Source: Authors' elaboration based on data from PreqinPro.

US private equity firms that have great interest in European unlisted companies. France and Switzerland are also very active countries in terms of private investments, with Ardian, a Paris-based fund, being one of the biggest firms at the global level as well.

8.3.3 Closed-end funds

Closed-end funds have a fixed maturity and a fixed amount of money to invest, and thanks to these two features are allowed to invest in private equity.

The rules for closed-end funds reported in the funds' Internal Code of Activity include:

- General framework:
  - maturity;
  - disinvestment process;
  - certificate;
  - loans;
  - amount of investments;
- Investment policy;
- Relationships with the market:
  - presence of public offering;
  - absence of public offering.

In Europe, according to the AMC funds system the internal code of activity is not a contract but an act that must be submitted and approved by the supervisor, that defines the relationship between the AMC and the fund investors. It is a set of managerial rules supervised by authorities to be used during the life of the fund; it is a strong expression of the freedom and limitations of an AMC.

The relationship between the AMC and a closed-end fund is quite complex both economically and financially (see **Figure 8.4**). Groups with a significant role in this relationship include:

Figure 8.4 **The relationship between the AMC, the closed-end fund, and the main groups involved**

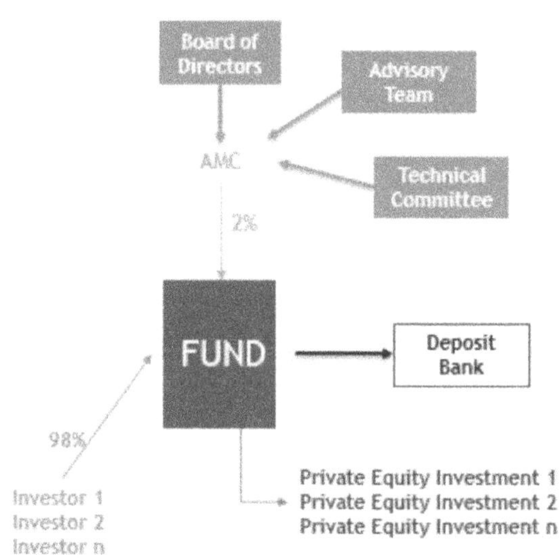

- AMCs,
- AMC's boards of directors,
- closed-end fund(s),
- investors,
- custodian or deposit bank,
- advisory team (or company),
- technical committee,
- anchor investor.

The AMC is composed of:

1. Board of Directors: oftentimes agrees on with the shareholders who decide to launch the AMC;
2. Advisory company: external company that by law must be completely separate from the AMC;
3. Technical committee.

Tasks and duties for all groups involved are quite clear and stated:

- The AMC has the responsibility to manage the closed-end fund, even though the assets coming from investors are separate from AMC assets. AMC is responsible towards the investors.
- The AMC's Board of Directors is responsible for managing the AMC.
- Closed-end fund(s) are owned and managed by the AMC.
- Investors purchase certificates issued by the closed-end fund.
- The custodian bank receives the money raised in the fundraising process by the fund.
- Advisory team (or company). If it exists, it is a company chosen by the AMC to analyse potential investment, develop due diligence, and evaluate exit strategy.
- The technical committee is a team of technicians operating inside the AMC. It supports the Board of Directors to define strategies, monitor the market, and share the recommendations coming from the advisory company.
- The anchor investor, if any, is the investor holding a particularly significant stake in the fund (minimum 20%). As the main investor, he has a very active role in attracting other investors to the fund. For this reason, it finds himself in a very strong position with respect to the private equity investor that launched the fund: it is aware of the fact that the fund would not be launched without its name or brand attracting other investors' capital. This is why the private equity fund launching the investment usually agrees on some benefits; for instance, it gives the anchor investor the right of co-investing.
- Each private equity firm may start multiple funds. **Table 8.3** shows the largest Europe-focus funds closed in 2020. Consistent with the league table presented before, the role of the UK is confirmed in this table as well, where three out of ten funds are English. French firms were also very active, with two mega-funds

Table 8.3 Largest Europe-Focused Private Equity Funds Closed as of July 2020

Rank	Fund	Firm	Headquarters	Fund Size (mn)
1	CVC Capital Partners Fund VIII	CVC	UK	21,300 EUR
2	ASF VIII	Ardian	France	19,000 USD
3	IK IX Fund	IK Investment Partners	UK	2,850 EUR
4	EMK Capital Partners II	EMK Capital	UK	1,500 EUR
5	Francisco Partners Agility II	Francisco Partners	US	1,500 USD
6	Gilde Buyout Fund VI	Gilde Buy-Out Partners	Netherlands	1,346 EUR
7	Deutsche Beteiligungs AG VIII Deutsche Beteiligungs	Deutsche Beteiligungs AG	Germany	1,109 EUR
8	Five Arrows Secondary Opportunities V	Five Arrows Secondary Opportunities	France	1,000 EUR
9	Summit Partners Europe Growth Equity Fund III	Summit Partners US	US	1,089 USD
10	Stirling Square Capital Partners Fourth Fund	Stirling Square Capital Partners	Jersey	950 EUR

Source: Authors' elaboration based on data from PreqinPro.

closed in 2020: one raised by Ardian, and one raised by the French firm FASO (Five Arrows Secondary Opportunities).

8.4 Banks as Private Equity Managers

In the aftermath of the insolvencies in 2007 and 2008, supervisors harshened regulations in terms of capital requirements. While the previous version of the Basel Framework proposed specific rules with reference to "investment in private equity and venture capital"[1] in art. 80 of Part 2, this article was completely changed in Basel III when that section was revised. In the new version, this article mentions "Equity investments in funds" and is supposed to include investment in VBCs, as investment in venture capital or private equity typically occurs via a fund.[2] However, the new format provoked an on-going debate between Invest Europe, the European Association of Private Equity and Venture Capital, and the Basel Committee. Accord-

[1] *Basel I – Part 2: The First Pillar – Minimum Capital Requirements*, art. 80.

[2] "Response to European Commission Consultation on implementing the final Basel III reforms in the EU", *Invest Europe*, 20 December 2019.

ing to the new version of the article, equity investments in funds must be treated in a manner consistent with one or more of the following three approaches, which vary in their risk sensitivity and conservatism: the "look-through approach" (LTA), the "mandate-based approach" (MBA), and the "fall-back approach" (FBA).[3]

The LTA, as the name itself suggests, requires a bank to risk-weight the underlying exposures of a fund as if the exposures were held directly by the bank. This is the most granular and risk-sensitive approach. It must be used when:

- there is sufficient and frequent information provided to the bank regarding the underlying exposures of the fund, and
- such information is verified by an independent third party.

To satisfy the first condition above, the frequency of the fund's financial reporting must be the same as, or more frequent than, that of the bank, and the granularity of the financial information must be sufficient to calculate the corresponding risk weights. To satisfy the second condition above, there must be verification of the underlying exposures by an independent third party, such as the depository or the custodian bank, or where applicable, the management company. Under the LTA, banks must risk-weight all underlying exposures of the fund as if those exposures were directly held. So the same applies, theoretically, for private equity investments, that are typically held via funds. According to the LTA, the percentage that could be set aside could correspond to 150%. The second approach, the MBA, provides a method for calculating regulatory capital that can be used when the conditions for applying the LTA are not met and information is not available. In this case, banks may use the information contained in a fund's mandate or in the national regulations governing such investment funds. Where neither the LTA nor the MBA is feasible, banks are required to apply the FBA. The FBA applies a 1250% risk weight to the bank's equity investment in the fund.

Although it may be inferred that private equity investments are grouped within equity investments via funds, in an issue of December 2017, the Basel Committee explains that banks must assign a risk weight of 400% to "speculative unlisted equity exposures" and a risk weight of 250% to all other equity holdings. This issue describes "speculative unlisted equity exposures" as investments with a short-term perspective or with resale purposes or that are considered venture capital or similar instruments, and that are acquired in anticipation of significant future capital gains.[4] Bodies such as Invest Europe dread the possibility that such high-risk weights may discourage banks from supporting private equity deals as direct investors.

[3] *CRE Calculation of RWA for credit risk – CRE60 Equity investments in funds*, issued on December 2019 and effective from January 2022.

[4] *Basel III: Finalising post-crisis reforms.*

8.5 Investment Banks sponsoring Private Equity Deals

In light of the constraints indicated above, banks very rarely invest directly in private companies; rather, they set up their own AMC if they want to engage in this business. Still, their vast involvement in the private equity business derives from the advisory work done for private equity firms when they have to invest in the equity of VBCs. **Table 8.4** and **Table 8.5** present the league tables of the investment banks advising private equity deals in the US and in Europe, respectively.

From a theoretical point of view, investment banks can sponsor every type of private equity deal. However, there are two in particular where investment banks are most active:

- M&A,
- Leveraged Buy-Outs.

Table 8.4 **League table by PE deal location: US**

Rank	Investment banks by PE deal location: US
1	Houlihan Lokey
2	Lincoln International
3	Jefferies Financial Group
4	William Blair & Company
5	Piper Sandler Companies
6	Robert W. Baird & Co.
7	Raymond James Financial
	Harris Williams
9	The Goldman Sachs Group
10	Stifel Financial
11	KeyBanc Capital Markets
	Evercore Group
13	Bank of America
14	Morgan Stanley
	Capstone Headwaters
	Lazard

Source: Authors' elaboration based on data from PitchBook.

Table 8.5 League table by PE deal location: Europe

Rank	Investment banks by PE deal location: Europe
1	KPMG Corporate Finance LLC
2	Lincoln International
3	GCA Corporation
4	Houlihan Lokey
5	Jefferies Financial Group
6	The Goldman Sachs Group
7	Corporate Finance International
8	Lazard
	William Blair & Company
10	Benchmark International
11	Fineurop Soditic
12	Raymond James Financial
13	Livingstone
	ABG Sundal Collier

Source: Authors' elaboration based on data from PitchBook.

8.5.1 M&A

Following the taxonomy presented before, it can be said that private equity is involved in M&A campaigns when a VBC finds itself in the so-called "Expansion" phase. An expanding VBC turns to a private equity firm seeking help in selecting the right target and to negotiate the fair price. When a PE-backed company acquires another company, it is possible to talk about an "**add-on.**" In the case the fund manager buys the equities of a company that has a strong position in the market and uses it as a "platform" to buy smaller companies, it is possible to talk about a "**bolt-on**." In both cases, the VBC becomes the bidder company of an M&A operation and banks can provide advisory for these kinds of deals in different ways. In the case of add-ons or bolt-ons, the process followed by the VBC and the private equity firm is the following:

- **Deal origination.** In this step, fund managers scout the market to find the right target that will generate synergies after the merger.
- **Due Diligence and Valuation.** In this step, the VBC has to appraise the fair price of the target company. To do so, proper due diligence will be conducted by the private equity along with the investment bank.

- **Funding**. In the event that the VBC does not have the liquidity necessary to take over the target, it may be necessary to get a financial loan. In this phase, the bank plays the role of the lender and thanks to the strong network of the private equity firm, it will be easier for the VBC to obtain financing.
- **Post-merger Integration.** For the private equity manager, this is the most delicate phase and will determine the creation of synergies for the VBC.

The M&A operation can be deployed in two different ways, depending on the leverage necessary for the VBC and on the strategic importance of the target.

The first way in which the M&A can be carried out is with a "direct investment": the fund manager invests in the equity of a venture-backed company in exchange for shares. Thanks to the money injection and to the potential further debt raised within the banking system, the company has enough liquidity to carry out the M&A and buy the target company.

The second way in which a VBC can carry out an M&A is with an "indirect investment," which is done by creating a separate entity, a Special-Purpose Vehicle (SPV). The SPV is controlled by the VBC and will play the role of the bidder in the M&A operation for acquiring the target company. The SPV is an "empty box" built with the only purpose of a specific extraordinary operation. This company does not have any assets or liabilities and equity before the operation takes place. This is done when the acquiring company needs a very large portion of debt to finalize the acquisition and it does not want to change the solvency profile of its balance sheet for reporting reasons. The process develops in three separate steps, as indicated in **Figure 8.5**:

1. The private equity investor sets up a Special Purpose Vehicle (SPV).
2. Once the SPV is set up, the acquiring company, with the help of the private equity

Figure 8.5 Indirect investment to carry out an M&A by a PE-backed company

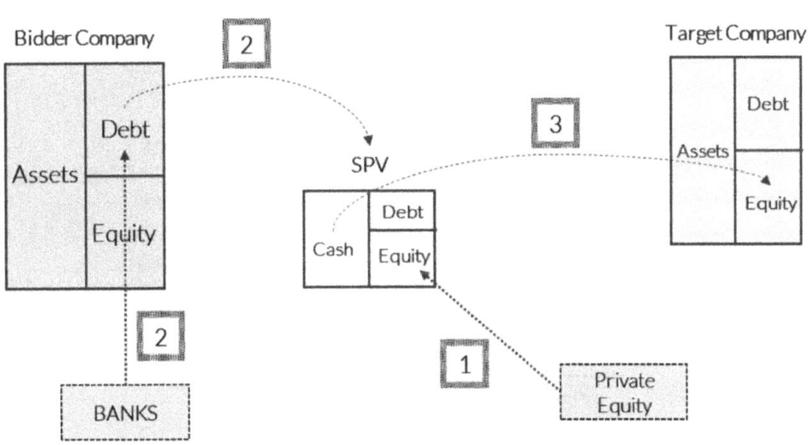

investor, collects money from the banking system and transfers the funds collected to the balance sheet of the SPV.
3. The SPV buys the target company.

8.5.2 LBO

As explained in Section 8.2, LBO deals involve a majority stake in the VBC. The equity stake is bought by the private equity investor thanks to a large component of debt. The LBO functioning is represented in **Figure 8.6**.

This operation takes place in the following steps:

1. **Target identification.** The first step is common to every private equity deal. Due to the large presence of financial leverage that makes the deal very risky, the company subject to the LBO deal has to have specific features (presented in the next paragraph).
2. **Set-up of an SPV.** After the target company has been identified, the investor sets up an SPV and it becomes its sole owner.
3. **Debt Raising.** In this moment, the private equity firm collects financial debt in order to carry out the deal. Through this cash injection, the SPV is able to Buy-Out the target company, and with the cash flow generated by the target, it will settle the payment of the financial loans.
4. **Value creation.** During the holding period, the private investors work to increase marginality and cash flow in order to enlarge the enterprise value of the target company.

Figure 8.6 LBO set-up in PE deals

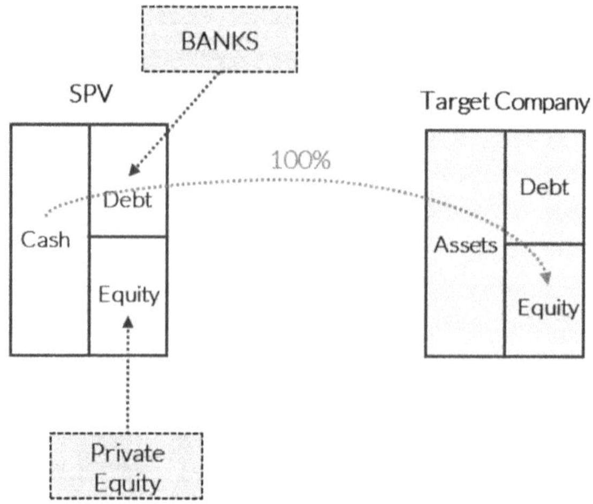

5. **Exit**. After the deal is finalised, the investor may exit the investment as it owns the whole company. The fact that the private equity firm owns 100% of the company will make the sale less difficult. As a matter of fact, when the private investor owns all of the equity, it is easier to find a counterparty interested in taking over as a 100% shareholder.

Typical candidates for a Leveraged Buy-Out

In a LBO, it is not possible to refer literally to a VBC, as the target company is acquired by the SPV, and typically it is the investor that scouts for companies to take over and not the other way around, as happens for all other private equity deals. The private equity firm buys the target to enhance its performance and be able to sell it at a much higher price at the end of the holding period. Due to the peculiar nature of the deal, the target company should show some specific characteristics:

1. **Stable cash flows**. The company that is bought out has to pay off high leverage debt. For that, it should be able to generate stable and predictable operating cash flows.
2. **High Coverage Ratio**. The company's EBIT should be larger that Net Financial Expenses.
3. **Consolidated market position**. The fact that a company is in the maturity stage reduces the spectrum of investments and therefore makes it easier to monitor.
4. **Valuable Assets**. The target company should have assets that can be pledged as collateral for lenders.

In addition to all the aforementioned features, the target has to have growth potential and relatively high margins.

It is important to stress that firms operating in markets with intense levels of growth and offering high-tech products may be unsuitable for a Buy-Out because of the huge funds needed to support the increase in commercial credits, stocks, and marketing expenses as well as the resources necessary to enlarge the production structure. There is always a risk of high-tech products becoming obsolete, which not only causes enormous costs from a research and development standpoint, but it is impossible for these products to be used as collateral for fund providers.

The risks of a Leveraged Buy-Out

In an LBO transaction, the biggest role is played by the private equity investor who decides to buy a significant or total participation in the target firm. The role of the investor is key in the management of the company in terms of control and strategic decisions: the larger the value added generated during the holding period, the larger the exit price and the return on the specific investment. Despite showing some positive economic and financial indicators, it is critical to understand how and if a change in the debt-to-equity ratio can impact the value creation of a company. Discussing debt definition, the benefits and costs of the debt, and tools used for assessing the leverage level can help understand how the debt equity ratio can impact a company's value.

- **Debt definition:** Debit is classified using three criteria:
  - Debt imposes contractual obligations that have to be complied with by the target company in both periods of recession and expansion.
  - Contractual payments (i.e. interest expenses) on the debt are treated favourably by tax policies.
  - Any breach of the contractual agreements may lead to loss of control of the firm, or lead banks to waive the loan.
- **Benefits and costs of debt:** One benefit is that interest is tax deductible. On the other side, the presence of debt entails three disadvantages:
  - Increasing leverage increases the possibility of default. The direct costs of bankruptcy include legal fees and court costs as well as indirect costs. High levels of debt signal a company is in financial trouble. If this feeling is widespread among stakeholders, employees, customers, and suppliers, it can easily lead to default and bankruptcy.
  - The need for debt caps the future debt capacity, which can mean future and profitable business opportunities are out of reach for the firm.
  - Agency costs represented by the divergence of interest between equity investors and fund providers cannot be ignored. This type of conflict causes parties to protect their respective rights by adding covenants, reducing financing, and modifying dividend policies.

There are specific indicators that can help identify the company's optimum level of debt. The first KPI to be monitored is the EBIT/Net Financial Expenses ratio, that is typically used to compute the credit spread under the "synthetic approach."[5] The second tool is the cost of a capital approach, which helps understand the debt-to-equity ratio that minimizes the company's cost of capital and maximizes its value. This approach is easy to use but does not include agency and bankruptcy costs. These are included when the optimal leverage structure generates a combination between cash flow and cost of capital to maximize the firm's value. The last tool is the adjusted present value method (APV). The APV adopts the same standpoint as the DCF: the current value of the company corresponds to the future cash flow that it will be able to generate. With the APV, great importance is given to the tax benefits generated by the large presence of debt that may change over the period of forecast.[6]

---

[5] "Estimating a synthetic rating and cost of debt" by Aswath Damodaran (http://pages.stern.nyu.edu/).

[6] Under the DCF approach, the leverage ratio is assumed to stay unvaried in the forecast period.

8.6 Private equity in the Anglo-Saxon context: Venture capital funds

Venture capital funds (VCFs) are not based on the European system of closed-end funds; it was in fact the European legislator that tried to implement a successful way of investing in private equity in Europe after the vast experience of the US. The first thing that should be remarked is that VCFs are the vehicle investing in the private company, but the legal entity behind such vehicle is the limited partnership (LP). The name refers to the limited liability of the providers of capital (limited partners), that is limited only to the extent of the investment made. This means that equity investment is considered simply as a business and not a financial activity, unlike in the European framework.

Despite there not being any such indications in US or UK law, most VCFs have a maturity of 10 years, as the maximum maturity of 10 years is one of the conditions to benefit from the tax exemption. The shareholding structure of the LP is made up of two different categories of partners (shareholders) (see **Figure 8.7**):

- Limited Partners (LPs);
- General Partners (GPs).

In an LP, GPs are the investment manager and LPs are providers of capital. The partnership is governed by an LPA (Limited Partnership Agreement) negotiated and signed by the parties involved. This agreement is similar to the EU internal code of activity introduced in the previous section.

Limited partners are investors of funds; they do not manage the company and their liability is limited to the extent of their investment. However, their participation in the company's equity is considerably high (99% of the stake).

GPs are managers of the company and they are fully liable for business debt. General partners control the company and manage investments. The investment of general partners is about 1% of invested funds. Due to the high-risk exposure of GPs, they

Figure 8.7 Shareholding structure of an LP

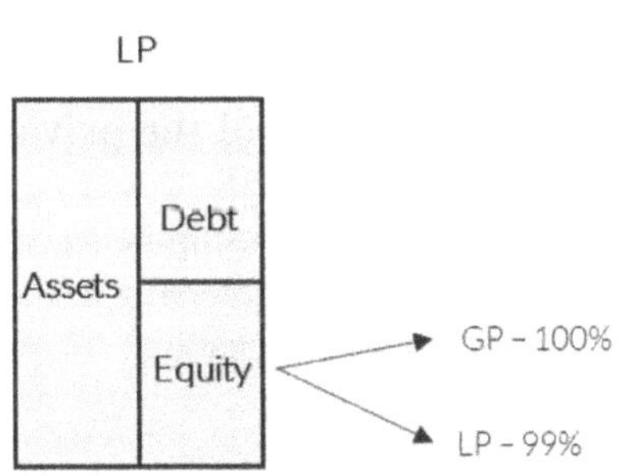

Figure 8.8 Organizational structure of venture capital funds

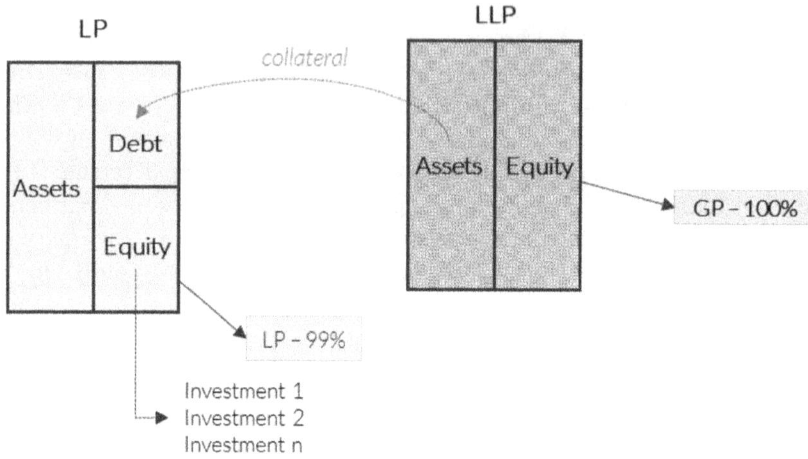

operate as LPs of an advisory company that is set up as a limited liability partnership (LLP) to reduce their risk. In a LLP, the liability of partners is limited to the extent of their investments; nevertheless, the partnership is fully liable for business debt. For this reason, the assets of the LLP are used as collateral of the LP. General partners cover their risk exposure by signing insurance contracts with insurance companies. These rarely-used contracts considerably reduce risk but they are very expensive[7] and negatively affect the final IRR of the overall investment portfolio (see **Figure 8.8**).

The great success of limited partnerships is due to two main reasons: they are simple to manage and they can benefit from tax exemptions on the proceeds of the investment, provided that some conditions are met. There is full flexibility regarding earnings distributed and the allocation of capital gains and losses to the limited partners. Therefore, each limited partner keeps its specific fiscal profile with no exemption applied. LPs typically attract investors such as banks, insurance companies, pensions funds, private investors, etc. VCFs, unlike closed-end funds, are allowed to leverage.

8.7 The remuneration mechanisms of the private equity industry

This section illustrates the economic relationship between the fund, the managers, and the investors. In this section, the terms referring to the European or to the Anglo-Saxon framework may be used interchangeably.

[7] Generally, the total cost is around 2% of the overall fund managed.

8.7.1 General overview of costs and revenues

The closed-end fund represents the source of the costs and revenues for all the groups. Its revenues include:

- capital gains from investments,
- dividends and interest from investments,
- interest from the deposit bank.

Its costs include:

- losses from investments,
- interest due for loans,
- management fees to the AMC,
- carried interest to the AMC.

The AMC distributes costs and revenues created from the closed-end fund and receives as revenues:

- entrance fee from investors,
- management fee from the closed-end fund,
- carried interest from the closed-end fund.

The costs it bears are:

- operating costs,
- deposit bank fee,
- percentage of management fee for the advisor,
- percentage of carried interest to the advisory company for its efforts with helping to identify the best possible opportunities in the market.

8.7.2 Management fee

The management fee[8] is due annually[9] and is calculated as a percentage of the net asset value (NAV)[10] of the closed-end fund. However, the higher the management fee, the lower the amount of money left for investment activities. The percentage of the management fee is negotiated between the LPs and GPs, since it is in the best interest of the investor to pay a lower percentage of fixed costs, while the opposite is true for

[8] The average amount could range between 2 and 3.5%.

[9] It can be computed at the initial phase at time 0.

[10] Net asset value is the total value of the portfolio of investments less any liabilities. But, as mentioned previously, closed-end funds cannot leverage.

Case study Remuneration in a Closed-End Fund

Here follows the information of a closed-end fund active for 10 years and for 1 extra year of extension, with an initial size (Committed Capital) of € 700 million, for which the AMC put in 2% at the beginning of the life of the fund (i.e. € 14 million). The table shows the following elements:

- **Draw-downs**. This is the capital committed by the investors and eventually injected into the fund: the biggest part is injected at the beginning of the period in order to allow the AMC to proceed with the investments. In this case, 98% of Committed Capital is injected by LPs and 2% by GPs. It can be said that PE acts as an investor at 2%.
- **Investments**. This is the amount of money that is invested in VBCs. It can be seen that most investing activity is done mainly in the first half of the life of the fund, while after year 7 the investment size decreases, as it is time to exit from the investments.
- **Divestments**. These correspond to exits from the VBC. We see that most divestments occur in the second half of the life of the funds, as the expiry date approaches.
- **Management fees**. In this example, it is assumed that management fees are 2% of Committed Capital. They are paid yearly, even in the extra-time year.
- **Cash of the period**. This is the cashflow generated in the period for the fund, and it is calculated as:

$$\textit{Cash of period}_{(t)} = \text{Drawdowns}_{(t)} - \text{Investments}_{(t)} + \text{Divestments}_{(t)} - \text{Management fees}_{(t)}$$

- **Total Cash (Fund Size)**. This is the size of the fund, and it fluctuates during the period of activity. In the first year, in light of the huge amount of investments made, the size of the fund is very small, but eventually at the end of the period the size is around € 2.5 billion. Total cash is calculated as:

$$\textit{Fund size}_{(t)} = \textit{Cash of period}_{(t-1)} + \textit{Drawdowns}_{(t)} - \textit{Investments}_{(t)} + \textit{Divestments}_{(t)} - \textit{Management fees}_{(t)}$$

Table Cash flow of a Closed-End Fund

Years	1	2	3	4	5	6	7	8	9	10	11	Total
Draw-downs	400	200	100	–	–	–	–	–	–	–		700
Investment	350	200	140	170	370	470	120	100	100	–		2,020
Divestment	–	50	60	270	390	430	410	270	690	650	750	3,970
Management Fee	14	14	14	14	14	14	14	14	14	14	14	154.0
Cash of the period	36	36	6	86	6	–54	276	156	576	636	736	2,496
Total Cash (Fund Size)	36	72	78	164	170	116	392	548	1,124	1,760	2,496	

In order to compute the remuneration for managers, namely the AMC, and for the investors, it is necessary to introduce other data: the Hurdle Rate, 8%, and the Carried Interest, 25%.
There are two ways to compute the remuneration: the first is called Global IRR and the second is called Yearly IRR.

A. Global IRR

Global IRR, as the name itself says, does not take into account the passing of time and roughly computes by how much the fund has grown or shrunk over the years. Once the global IRR has been computed (Step A.1), the Hurdle Rate needs to be deducted to calculate the Net Global IRR (Step A.2) that is multiplied by the Input Carried Interest, in order to find the Carried Interest with which the AMC is remunerated (Step A.3). This is multiplied by the Committed Capital (Step A.4), and the difference between the final fund size and the AMC remuneration is dedicated to "pure" investors (Step A.5).

- Step A.1: Computation of the Global IRR of the fund

$$Global\ IRR\ (\%) = \frac{Final\ Amount - Committed\ Capital}{Committed\ Capital} = \frac{2{,}496 - 700}{700} = \mathbf{256.57\%}$$

- Step A.2: Calculation of the Net Global IRR

$$Net\ Global\ IRR\ (\%) = Global\ IRR\ (\%) - Hurdle\ Rate\ (\%) = 256.57\,\% - 8\% = \mathbf{248.6\%}$$

- Step A.3: Computation of the Carried Interest (C.I.) as a percentage of the Net Global IRR

$$Carried\ Interest\ (\%) = Net\ Global\ IRR\ (\%) \times Input\ Carried\ Interest\ (\%) = 248.6\% \times 25\% = \mathbf{62.1\%}$$

- Step A.4: Remuneration for Managers (PE firm)

$$PE\ remuneration\ (€) = Carried\ Interest\ (\%) \times Committed\ Capital = 62.1\% \times 700 = \mathbf{€\ 435\ million}$$

- Step A.5: Remuneration for pure investors

$$Investors\ Remuneration\ (€) = Final\ Size\ of\ the\ Fund - PE\ Remuneration = 2{,}496 - 435 = \mathbf{€\ 2{,}061\ million}$$

IRR for Private Equity

Once the remuneration is computed in absolute terms, it is possible to convert it into a percentage and compute the IRR. For this purpose, the IRR will be the discount rate that makes the Net Present Value of the cash flows related to the initial contribution and the PE final remuneration equal to zero:

$$0 = NPV = -\frac{Management\ initial\ contribution}{(1 + IRR)^1} + \frac{Management\ Remuneration}{(1 + IRR)^T}$$

where:
T = end of the fund's life.

$$0 = NPV = +\frac{-14}{(1 + IRR)^1} + \frac{435}{(1 + IRR)^{11}} = \mathbf{41.01\%}$$

The formula above can be simplified in the following way:

$$IRR\ for\ PE\ (\%) = \left(\frac{Management\ Remuneration}{Management\ Initial\ Contribution}\right)^{T-1}$$

IRR for Investors

When it comes to the computation of the IRR for investors, it is important to take into account the fact that different portions of the draw-downs may occur at different moments in time. Thus, the IRR will be the discount rate that makes the Net Present Value of the cash flows related to capital injections and investors' remuneration equal to zero:

IRR for Investors

When it comes to the computation of the IRR for investors, it is important to take into account the fact that different portions of the draw-downs may occur at different moments in time. Thus, the IRR will be the discount rate that makes the Net Present Value of the cash flows related to capital injections and investors' remuneration equal to zero:

$$0 = NPV = -\left(\sum_{t=1}^{n} \frac{DDowns_t}{(1+IRR)^t}\right) + \frac{Investors'\ Remuneration}{(1+IRR)^T}$$

where:
DDowns = Draw-downs
n = last year of capital call
T = end of the fund's life.

$$0 = NPV = \frac{-400}{(1+IRR)^1} + \frac{-200}{(1+IRR)^2} + \frac{-100}{(1+IRR)^3} + \frac{2061}{(1+IRR)^{11}} = \mathbf{12.09\%}$$

B. Yearly IRR

The yearly IRR, as the name itself says, takes into account the passing of time. Once the yearly IRR has been computed (Step B.1), the Hurdle Rate needs to be deducted (Step B.2). If under the computation of the Global IRR the deduction of the Hurdle Rate was not particularly significant in light of the large size of the Rate of Return, under the yearly scenario, the choice of deducting or leaving the hurdle rate may considerably affect the Net Yearly IRR. The Net Yearly IRR is multiplied by the Carried Interest Input, in order to find the Carried Interest at which the AMC will be remunerated (Step B.3). Since in this scenario the passing of time is relevant to the computation, in this case the Carried Interest is used as a rate to capitalize the Committed Capital, as if it were the growth rate at which it grew over the years of the fund's activity (Step B.4). The difference between the final fund size and the AMC remuneration is dedicated to the "pure" investors (Step B.5).

- Step B.1: Computation of the yearly IRR of the fund

$$0 = NPV = -\frac{Committed\ Capital}{(1+IRR)^1} + \frac{Final\ Size\ of\ the\ Fund}{(1+IRR)^T}$$

where:
T = end of the fund's life.

$$0 = NPV = +\frac{-700}{(1+IRR)^1} + \frac{2{,}496}{(1+IRR)^{11}} = \mathbf{13.56\%}$$

The formula above can be simplified as follows:

$$Fund\ Yearly\ IRR\ (\%) = \left(\frac{Final\ Size\ of\ the\ Fund}{Committed\ Capital}\right)^{T-1}$$

where:
T = end of the fund's life.

- Step B.2: Calculation of the Net Global IRR

$$Net\ Yearly\ IRR\ (\%) = Yearly\ IRR\ (\%) - Hurdle\ Rate\ (\%) = 13.56\% - 8\% = \mathbf{5.56\%}$$

- Step B.3: Computation of the Carried Interest (C.I.) as a percentage of the Net Yearly IRR

$$Carried\ Interest\ (\%) = Net\ Global\ IRR\ (\%) \times Input\ Carried\ Interest\ (\%) = 5.56\% \times 25\% = \mathbf{1.39\%}$$

- Step B.4: Remuneration for Managers (PE firm)

$$PE\ Remuneration\ (€) = CC \times (1 + Carried\ Interest\ \%)^{T} - CC$$

where:
CC = Committed Capital
T = end of the fund's life.

$$PE\ Remuneration\ (€) = 700 \times (1 + 1.39\%)^{11} - 700 = \textbf{€ 114.73 million}$$

- Step B.5: Remuneration for pure investors

$$Investors\ Remuneration = Final\ Size\ of\ the\ Fund - PE\ Remuneration =$$
$$= 2{,}496 - 114.73 = \textbf{€ 2,381.27 million}$$

As for the Global IRR, once the remuneration is computed in absolute terms, it is possible to convert it into a percentage and compute the IRR with the same process.

IRR for Private Equity

$$0 = NPV = -\frac{Management\ initial\ contribution}{(1 + IRR)^{1}} + \frac{Management\ Remuneration}{(1 + IRR)^{T}}$$

where:
T = end of the fund's life.

$$0 = NPV = +\frac{-14}{(1 + IRR)^{1}} + \frac{114.73}{(1 + IRR)^{11}} = \textbf{23.41\%}$$

The formula above can be simplified as follows:

$$IRR\ for\ PE\ (\%) = \left(\frac{Management\ Remuneration}{Management\ Initial\ Contribution}\right)^{T-1}$$

IRR for Investors

$$0 = NPV = -\left(\sum_{t=1}^{n} \frac{DDowns_t}{(1 + IRR)^{t}}\right) + \frac{Investors'\ Remuneration}{(1 + IRR)^{T}}$$

where:
$DDowns$ = Draw-downs
n = last year of capital call
T = end of the fund's life.

$$0 = NPV = \frac{-400}{(1 + IRR)^{1}} + \frac{-200}{(1 + IRR)^{2}} + \frac{-100}{(1 + IRR)^{3}} + \frac{2381}{(1 + IRR)^{11}} = \textit{\textbf{13.81\%}}$$

In the example above, the waterfall mechanism was used. It means that the Hurdle Rate was deducted to calculate the Net IRR. This approach is also called "without catch-up." In the event the Hurdle Rate is not deducted, the approach is called "with catch-up" and the Net IRR and Fund IRR are the same.

GPs. This fee cannot be too low, because it is supposed to cover all operating costs incurred by the AMC. The management fee is a gross fee, since it covers operating expenses, pays the Advisory Company and the Technical Committee and fixed costs, and ultimately the remuneration[11] for the AMC director.

8.7.3 Carried interest

Carried interest is due only at the closing of the closed-end fund and is a percentage[12] of the difference between the Fund IRR of the closed-end fund and a fixed interest rate ("hurdle rate" or "floor IRR") as defined at the starting date of the closed-end fund. It is computed as follows:

$$Carried\ Interest = \%[Final\ IRR - Hurdle\ Rate]$$

It is the percentage of profits the AMC receives from investors in the form of capital gains and it goes to the fund managers. Carried interest and the floor rate are set at the beginning of the fund's life and they are specified in the internal code of activity of each fund. They are determined through long negotiations between investors and the AMC.

Sometimes, by using a private agreement, a pre-determined percentage of both the management fee and the carried interest are transferred by the AMC to the advisory company. There is a strong link between the reputation of the advisory company and the percentage it can obtain by the end of the disinvestment phase as a capital gain.

8.8 The four pillars of private equity investment

Vehicles dedicated to equity investment have a specific value chain with phases and organizational functions that can be classified worldwide. The typical phases of the managerial process of the investments are four: fundraising, investing, managing and monitoring, and exit.

8.8.1 Launching a fund: Fundraising

Fundraising is the promotion of a new equity investment vehicle within the business community; the purpose is to find money and create a commitment. The main motivation, considered by investors during the selection of the funds, is based on obtain-

[11] Salaries, but not the capital gain.

[12] Typically ranging between 15 and 40%.

ing returns higher than those offered by the financial market. Private equity investors normally want a market premium of about 5%. This extra performance covers the extra risk connected with the lesser liquidity of the fund and the higher risk connected with private companies. The track record of the investment managers, based on factors such as their competencies, reputation, and previous performance, can also make a difference in the fundraising phase. Fundraising is a tough step for all funds, especially for those without a track record, because many investors are reluctant to invest in an unproven team even if the partners have successful individual track records. Fundraising activity is directly influenced and determined both by the supply of private equity (the relative desire of institutional investors to allocate capital in the sector), and by the demand for private equity (the number of entrepreneurs with good ideas who want to be financed). Some theories argue that fundraising activity depends on the status of the public equity market: during expansion phases, the market allows new firms to issue shares and entrepreneurs to achieve liquidity and monetize the value of their companies.

8.8.2 Selecting private equity firms: Investing

Depending on the specific phases of the life cycle of the target firm, investments can be classified under the six clusters presented at the beginning of this chapter. Investors of risk capital must focus on the origination activity, which consists of a steady flow of investment opportunity. This is the key factor for starting the investment process. The origination phase includes the selection of an investment opportunity carried out through appropriate professional resources and information. This phase requires a lot of time due to the extremely selective nature of the investment decision through risk capital, especially if early stage expansion or the buyout of a small to medium-size family firm with a high level of innovation is selected. The selection is based on the industry and the position inside the industry of the target firm, the validity and reliability of the business plan, the entry price, the quality and skills of the entrepreneur and/or management of the target firm, and the exit strategy. During investment activity, the PE is supposed to have a clear entry and exit strategy as well as a set of rules about transparency, involvement in the Board of Directors, and a general overview of company management. It is critical to define the timing and the privacy of the investment deal, to be fully engaged in the negotiation process, and to ignore the rumours and deal in the financial market and with other equity investors.

8.8.3 The term-sheet: Monitoring the investment

As the goal of the private equity is to generate IRR, managers should define covenants in order to protect the value of the VBC. For this reason, it is possible to say that the PE firm is not a silent shareholder. On the contrary, the governance and management of the VBC requires rules to reduce conflicts and mitigate agency problems between the investor and management. This strategy is realized by using the best practice rules adopted by the firms through contractual schemes such as covenants and ratchets. Covenants are rules settled and defined in order to regulate the relationship among investors and managers. These rules specify duties and rights while minimizing opportunism, moral hazard, and conflicts of interest. The covenants are presented in the Internal Code of Activity or in the LPA and they can be positive or negative.

Positive covenants are the list of things the company agrees to do including producing audited reports, holding regular board meetings, and paying taxes on time. **Negative covenants** are included to forbid an action. The most common are:

1. Lock-up — An agreement between the investor, existing shareholders, and/or the management that prohibits them from exiting by selling their stakes to third parties.
2. Permitted transfer clause — A provision between the investor and existing shareholders that prohibits both existing shareholders and private equity investors from selling their shares without the approval of the other party.
3. Staging technique — This ensures that financial resources are invested in the firm in multiple instalments. Investment of these instalments is carried out after specific business targets are met.
4. Earn-out agreement — A payment system consisting of a postponed payment of a part of the original acquisition price. This is executed upon realization of defined performance indicators fixed a priori by mutual agreement between the seller and the venture capitalist. The indicators are checked within a year or two of acquisition of the shares. This tool reduces the financial investor's economic risk.
5. Stock options — This allows the shareholder (typically the entrepreneur) the right to buy or sell at a pre-determined price and a specific date. These stock options can be assigned both to the management and to the entrepreneur to motivate and increase their desire to maximize the company's value.
6. Puttable securities — These are part of the financial agreement in which the private equity investor has the right to sell the stocks to the existing shareholders. The option agreement can be executed with or without a specific date on which to be exercised. In underwriting a puttable security, the investors assume that the entrepreneur will have enough liquidity to buyback the stake. This can be provided by setting up an escrow account or by transforming the payment in cash into a payment in kind whereby the entrepreneur will give the PE firm his stake in the case of a lack of liquidity.
7. Tag-along right — In the event the majority entrepreneur decides to sell, this allows the minority PE firm the right to join the deal so it can sell its stake in the venture-backed company at the same terms and conditions to the same buyer.
8. Drag-along rights or anti-dilution clause — If the private equity firm wants to sell its stocks, this mechanism provides the right to ask to all other shareholders to sell their stake at the same conditions and to the same buyer.
9. Right of first refusal — If the entrepreneur wants to sell his stakes, this provision

allows the PE firm to avoid undesired new shareholders in the company. The investor has the right to refuse the new shareholders' entrance, but he must acquire the stake of the selling shareholders at the same conditions offered by the potential buyer.

10. Exit ratchet — This is a motivation method for both the entrepreneur and the private equity firm. It provides an exit when the company's shares are re-allocated between the entrepreneur or the private equity firm. The exiting party pays the counterparty a portion of the capital gain realized at the exit.
11. Covenants on Asset Sales, Asset Purchase, M&A — Restrictions set to prevent the entrepreneur from eroding the value of the VBC without checking with the Private Equity firm in advance.

8.8.4 Exit

These are typical exit strategies relevant to today's market:

- Trade sale;
- Buyback;
- Sale to other private equity investors;
- Write-off;
- IPO or sale post IPO.

Concerning the presence of the investment bank industry, it is worth mentioning that the exit where banks can play the role of the advisor is the IPO.

Trade sale

A trade sale exit occurs when the private equity investor sells the stake to a corporation, or, for example, to an industrial shareholder. This exit strategy it is often used in European markets. It is based on industrial relationships among the private equity investor, the buyer, and the venture-backed company.

Buyback

A buyback exit occurs when the private equity investor sells its stake to existing shareholders in the corporation or their representatives. The buyback alternative is an opportunity to support and develop a business when shareholders do not want to leave the company.

An exit through a buyback most likely will occur when:

- shareholders have initiated a venture capital operation to collect funds for development of the business idea (seed financing), the business development (start-up financing), or the company's growth (development financing);

- shareholders manage a governance turnaround;
- shareholders transfer ownership to other people.

A profitable buyback can be accomplished when other remaining shareholders want to own the business, have the money to buy back the shares, and have a clear problem of turnaround or inheritance. This exit option assumes that the entrepreneur has the liquidity necessary to buy the stake, which may not always be the case.

Sale to other private equity investors/Secondary Buy-Out

This type of exit consists of selling the stakes to another private equity or venture capital fund.

Typical sales between private equity investors include:

- Seed financer sells the stake to a start-up financer to "start the engine";
- Start-up financer sells its stake to an expansion financer to sustain growth;
- Expansion financer sells its stake to a replacement financer to develop acquisition, turnaround, or IPO;
- Vulture financer (rare) sells its stake to a replacement financer to end the work of restructuring.

In the event the majority stake (if not the total control) of the company passes from one institutional investor to another, it is possible to talk about a Secondary Buy-Out (SBO). This type of divestment is similar to a trade sale; the only difference is that the buyer is a financial investor, not an industrial partner. This strategy is utilized when there is no debt and the target company is mature.

The main drawback of this kind of exit is that the goal of the buyer (i.e. the private equity investor) is the inverse of that of the seller (i.e. another private equity investor). In this sense, the buyer will want the lowest possible price, in order to maximize the capital gain, and at the same time the seller will want to the highest possible price in order to maximize the capital gain.

Write-off

A write-off is usually included during disinvestment, as well as total or partial devaluation of the stake as a consequence of money loss unrelated to a transfer of property. Investors decide to write off a deal when the stake and the company are unable to produce value in the future. The write-off process is used when no economic return is generated from the stake.

IPO or sale post IPO

When the private equity investor sells the stake through the stock exchange, the exit strategy is called an IPO. This type of divestment is attractive in terms of reputa-

Table 8.6 League Table of Investment Banks advising PE&VC-backed IPOs

Rank	Investment banks by PE-exit: PE- & VC-backed IPOs
1	The Goldman Sachs Group
2	J.P. Morgan
3	Morgan Stanley
4	Bank of America
5	Credit Suisse
6	Cowen Group
7	Barclays
	William Blair & Company
9	Stifel Financial
10	Canaccord Genuity
11	RBC Capital Markets
12	Raymond James Financial
13	SVB Leerink
	Piper Sandler Companies
	Evercore Group

Source: Authors' elaboration based on data from PitchBook.

tion and economic return even if the realization is very difficult. The exit is complex, especially for small or medium companies, and is considered in a long-term strategy after the target firm has reached an adequate level of development and seniority. There are advantages and disadvantages to the IPO exit strategy. Advantages include the opportunity to sell the stake at a higher price, satisfying management, and increase potential gains for the institutional investor. On the other side, it is difficult to exit via IPO and monetize as expected, as IPO performance will depend on other factors that are out of the Private Investor's direct control. Table 8.6 presents the list of investment banks that sponsored the largest number of PE-backed IPOs in the world in 2019. It is evident that US banks lead the ranking, occupying four of the top five positions.

8.9 Corporate valuation applied to private equity investments

While Section 8.7 presented how to assess the performance of a fund, it is equally important to understand how to measure the performance of single investments undertaken during the fund's life.

8.9.1 Private equity method

The private equity method is used to calculate the IRR of a single investment. It can be implemented when it is possible to estimate future cash flows with a high level of certainty. When this estimation is not possible, the investment profitability is valued through the Venture Capital Method, presented in the next section.

The private equity method computes the target exit price, i.e. the future value of the stake of the Equity Market Value bought by the investor, and benchmarks it with the entry price, i.e. the value of the investment. An example is provided here:

Expected EBITDA at exit	€ 9,000,000
Expected holding period	3 years
Expected NFP at exit	€ 4,000,000
Expected EBITDA multiple at exit	4x
Investment	€ 6,500,000
Post money share percentage	25%
where:	
EBITDA = earnings before interest, taxes, depreciation, and amortization	
NFP = Net Financial Position.	

Step 1: Computation of the future Enterprise Value (EV)

$$EV_{(n)} = EBITDAmultiple \times EBITDA_{(n)} = 4 \times 9{,}000 = \textbf{€ 36 million}$$

where n = the end of the holding period.

Step 2: Equity Market Value

$$Equity\ Market\ Value = EV - NFP = 36{,}000 - 4{,}000 = \textbf{€ 32 million}$$

Step 3: Private Equity's Market Value of the Equity Stake (i.e. expected Exit Price)

$$\%\ PE\ Stake = Post\ money\ share\ percentage \times Equity\ Market\ Value = \\ = 25\% \times 32 = \textbf{€ 8 million}$$

Step 4: IRR of the investment

$$IRR = \left(\frac{Exit\ Price}{Entry\ Price}\right)^{1/n} - 1 = \left(\frac{8{,}000}{6{,}500}\right)^{1/3} - 1 = \textbf{7.17\%}$$

where n = the end of the holding period.

8.9.2 Venture capital method

The venture capital method focuses on the relationship between the expected IRR, the growth of the firm, and the percentage of shares to buy. Its use depends on the definition of the participation price and the return required for the single investment. This approach is typically used when the price setting is dominant and during seed or start-up deals where there are negative cash flows and earnings with high uncertainty but potentially substantial future rewards. According to this approach IRR is treated as an input, as there is not enough data to compute future cash flow information or future EBITDA. Therefore, typically, the only target that is estimated is Perspective Net Income. Net income serves as the basis to compute Equity Market value with the help of a target Equity Multiple.

The key steps to the venture capital method are

- Step 1: Terminal value calculation;
- Step 2: Future value of the investment;
- Step 3: Percentage of shares to subscribe;
- Step 4: Amount of shares to issue;
- Step 5: Value of newly issued shares.

Step 1: Terminal value calculation
The expected holding period and the calculation of the terminal value are addressed. The terminal value is usually calculated with comparables, typically the P/E and DCF approaches. *For example*: If the expected holding period is 4 years and the expected net income at year 4 is €6 million, a terminal value calculated through a P/E comparable of 5 would be €30 million.

Step 2: Future value of the investment
Calculation of the future value of the investment taking into account the expected holding period and the expected IRR, which is defined by the constraints of the investor. *For example*: If the investment is €2 million, the holding period is 4 years, and the expected IRR is 55%, the future value is €11.54 million, obtained by capitalising the investment of €2 million by 55% for 4 years.

Step 3: Percentage of shares to subscribe
Calculation of the shares the investor has to buy to acquire the expected IRR. The number of shares is found by dividing the future value of the investment by the terminal value of the firm. *For example*: If the future value of the investment is €11.54 million and the terminal value is €30 million, the percentage of shares for the investor is 38.46%.

Step 4: Amount of shares to issue
Calculation of the number of new shares that the venture-backed company has to issue to ensure a particular percentage of capital for the investor. This calculation derives from the proportion inferred from the formula below:

$$\%\ PE\ Shares = \frac{New\ Shares}{New\ Shares + Pre - existing\ Shares}$$

$$New\ shares = \frac{PreExisting\ Shares\ x\ (\%\ PE\ Shares)}{(1 - \%\ PE\ Shares)}$$

For example: If the percentage of shares the investor must have is 38.46% and the shares existing before the PE investment are 300,000, the number of new shares available to issue is 187,488, where:

$$187{,}488 = \frac{300{,}000 \times 38.46\%}{1 - 38.46\%}$$

Step 5: Value of newly-issued shares

The calculation of the price of newly-issued shares for the investor is executed by dividing the amount of the investment by the number of new shares. *For example*: if the investment is €2 million and the number of new shares is 187,488, the price per new share is €10,67. The implied pre-money valuation is 10.67, so the value of 300,000 shares equals €3.201 million and the post-money value of all 487,488 shares equals €5.201 million.

Questions and answers

1. *Consider the investment made in a "Company Alpha" that has just filed for bankruptcy, in which a Fund has invested in a "vulture financing" deal. As a PE, would you want to have the majority or the minority stake in this company?*
   In the event a PE buys a stake in a bankrupt company, it would be better to have majority control of the equity. This is to ensure that the PE controls the bankruptcy procedure. In addition, in negotiations with other stakeholders (i.e. creditors, employees, trade unions), it is crucial to be recognized as the controlling equity holders to be a key player in negotiations.

2. *What are the PE deals that mostly involve investment banks?*
   Investment banks are mostly involved in M&A and LBOs. In the first case, deals belong to so-called "Expansion Financing." The role of the investment bank is to advise the VBC in order to carry out the M&A. LBOs are included in so-called "replacement financing" deals. The role of the bank is to sponsor the deal by injecting huge financial debt into the SPV in order to buy the target company.

3. *According to you, why may it be convenient for a PE firm to recover a distressed firm?*
   The convenience can be explained with three activities:
   1. the opportunity to rationalize the existing structure of the target company;
   2. asset divestment;
   3. extraordinary financial operations focused on specific strategic business units.

4. *Consider the Fund Delta, a ten-year European private equity fund with the following information:*
   - *management fee 2.0%*
   - *hurdle rate 7.5%*
   - *carried interest 30%*
   - *committed capital (mn.) 650*
   - *managers' percentage (GPs) 2%*

   The cash flow statement is the following:

Years	1	2	3	4	5	6	7	8	9	10	11	Total
Draw-downs	400.00	150.00	100.00	–	–	–	–	–	–	–	–	
Investment	350.00	200.00	140.00	170.00	370.00	470.00	120.00	300.00	100.00	–	–	
Divestment	–	50.00	60.00	270.00	390.00	430.00	410.00	270.00	690.00	650.00	750.00	
Management fee												
FINAL Cash												

What are the yearly management fees, the yearly final cash, the final size of the fund, and the remuneration received by GPs and LPs, with and without catch-up?

SUBTRACTING HURDLE RATE

Fund Global IRR	247.23%
Net Global IRR	239.7%
Carried interest	71.9%
For managers (GPs)	467,475
For investors (LPs)	1,789,525
Gross return for managers (GPs)	3,596.0%
Gross return for investors (LPs)	275.3%

NOT SUBTRACTING THE HURDLE RATE

Fund Global IRR = Net Global IRR	247.23%
Carried interest	74.2%
For managers (GPs)	482,100
For investors (LPs)	1,774,900
Gross return for managers (GPs)	3,708.5%
Gross return for investors (LPs)	273.1%

5. *What are the most common ways to exit from a private equity investment? Can you imagine the pros and cons of each exit?*
   1. **Buyback.** The PE sells its stake to an existing shareholder or to a buyer chosen by the existing shareholders.
      –PRO – this is a safety net for the PE, as it knows in advance it will have the possibility to exit;

–CON – there may be the case where the entrepreneur may not have the necessary liquidity to buy back the stake.

2. **Sale to another PE.** The PE sells its stake to another private equity investor. This kind of exit is not that easy due to the fact that different PE investors have different goals: the first one wants to maximize the capital gain, whereas the second one wants to buy the stake at the lowest possible price (in order to maximize the capital gain in the future).
   –PRO – the company can be granted further development by an investor investing in the following stage of life;
   –CON – the negotiation may be particularly tricky.
3. **IPO**. With this exit, the VBC is listed on the Stock Exchange. This way, the PE can maximize the capital gain. Through an IPO, the investor sells its stake in the stock exchange.
   –PRO – the most remunerative exit;
   –CON – it is very long and complicated. In addition, the market may not be in a good place or it may not be able to understand the company's product or business.
4. **Trade Sale**: the private equity investor sells its stake to another corporation or to another entrepreneur.
   –PRO – assuming that the industrial buyer has a strong interest in the VBS, it may be very remunerative;
   –CON – the entrepreneur may not want to sell to another player in the industry. In this case, the "right of first refusal" or the "drag-along" right may be applied.
5. **Write-off:** the private equity investor cancels the stake from its balance sheet.
   –PRO – no pro in this exit;
   –CON – the worst possible exit, the PE just cashes out without selling or selling it back to the entrepreneur but at a very low price.

6. *What is the term-sheet? Why is it important in your view?*
   The term-sheet reports all the covenants that a VBC must or must not meet. Covenants can be positive (what a company must do) or negative (what a company must not do). This document regulates the relationship between the VBC and the private equity firm, hence it must be drawn up carefully as it contains the tools through which the private equity firm monitors the value generated with the investment.

7. *Considering this data referring to a private equity investment in a mature company:*

- *Expected EBITDA at exit (€)* *7,000,000.00*
- *Expected holding period* *4*
- *Expected NFP at exit (€)* *2,500,000.00*
- *Expected EBITDA multiple at exit* *7.5*
- *PE Investment (€)* *9,800,000*
- *Post-money share percentage* *40%*

What is the IRR of the investment?

$EV_{(n)}$ = EBITDA multiple x $EBITDA_{(n)}$ = **€ 52.5 million**
Equity Market Value = EV – NFP = **€ 50 million**
% PE Stake = Post-money share percentage × Equity Market Value = **€ 20 million**

$$IRR = \left(\frac{Exit\ Price}{Entry\ Price}\right)^{1/n} - 1 = 19.52\%$$

8. *Referring to an M&A deal, what are the activities that involve the investment bank, in detail?*
   In the M&A deal, the investment bank acts as an advisor, hence its role is concentrated on activities such as:

   - Deal origination. The investment bank may help the PE in scouting the market.
   - Due Diligence and Valuation. The investment bank is in charge of the company valuation.
   - Funding. In case it is necessary, the VBC may borrow some liquidity in order to take over the target company.

9. *Referring to LBOs, what are the indicators that can help identify the optimal cost of debt?*
   LBOs are very complex deals due to the large financial leverage that is used in order to take over the target company. There are three indicators useful to identify the company's optimum level of debt:

   1. EBIT/Net Financial Expenses: this is used to compute the credit spread under the "synthetic approach";
   2. the cost of a capital approach: this helps understand the debt-to-equity ratio that minimizes the company's cost of capital and maximizes its value;
   3. the APV: like the DCF, this is a cash-based valuation model, but in the APV, great importance is given to the tax benefits generated by the large presence of debt that may change over the period of the forecast.

10. *What is the earn-out? Can you imagine the drawback of such covenant?*
    An investment system consisting of a postponed payment of a part of the original acquisition price. This is executed upon the realization of defined performance indicators fixed a priori by mutual agreement between the seller and the venture capitalist. Despite obliging the company to implement concrete actions and achieve results, some VBCs may need immediate liquidity, hence a postponed payment may not be a suitable option for capital intensive businesses.

9 M&A Transactions

by Gimede Gigante[1]

9.1 M&A: Introduction

Mergers and Acquisitions, also known as "M&A," can be considered as any process in which the ultimate beneficial ownership and the respective control of a firm (in the case of a majority deal in which the acquirer ultimately owns more than 51% of the merged/combined entity) are transferred from one subject (or group of subjects) to another. In an M&A transaction, a *seller*, a party which is willing to sell its assets, subsidiaries, or the entity as a whole, gives up control in exchange for a certain compensation: either cash, stock, or a mix of the two. On the other side of the transaction, the party which acquires/takes the ownership of those assets is called the *bidder*.

As the definition implies, M&A encompasses "all transactions resulting in a transfer of ownership." Therefore, even though the name "M&A" can be misleading, it is central to remember that M&A incorporates not only the most common type of corporate finance transactions such as acquisitions and mergers, but also other types of deals such as divestitures, restructurings, or joint ventures. This is very important to understand, as including divestitures and restructuring transactions among M&A deals explains why, despite its cyclicality, the M&A market remains active not only in *healthy* economic conditions, but also in *weaker ones*.

Indeed, during economic booms, companies experience *stronger profits* and *higher stock prices* which incentivize them to take advantage of this prosperity to acquire new products, technologies, production facilities, and/or entire companies in order to boost their growth and develop faster than their competitors.

However, in economic downturns, the M&A market remains active for many different reasons. First, financial difficulties force companies to refocus on their core business and divest "non-core assets" in order to increase their cash reserves. Second, the expansionary monetary policies often undertaken by central banks during periods of economic recession lead to lower interest rates, and companies frequently take advantage of those relatively low interest rates to cost-effectively utilize debt to finance their acquisition-based growth strategies. Finally, lower stock price valuations also play an important role in difficult economic times as they result in *lower*

[1] A special thanks to Maria Teresa Iardella, Baptiste Gilliot and Rodolfo Pambianco for the contribution and the precious support and for all the suggestions provided during the review of the chapter.

acquisition prices, giving strong/cash-rich companies the opportunity to begin bargain shopping, picking off distressed and downtrodden competitors at a fraction of their market value compared to expectations just a short twelve to eighteen months earlier.

Overall, we can clearly see that at least from a corporate point of view, M&A is a major component of corporate strategy as it enables firms to pursue their growth objectives while adapting to the fast-changing economic conditions. As a matter of fact, Google (Alphabet), whose growth has been driven by an acquisition strategy (e.g. YouTube for $1.7bn in 2006, Motorola Mobility for $ 12.5bn in 2012, Waze for $1.2bn in 2013, and Fitbit for $2.1bn in 2020), highlights how important M&A is for companies; since its inception, Google has bought over 200 technology firms related to its core business.

In the next section, we will see how the increasing pressure to grow turned the spotlight on the opportunity to achieve growth through acquisitions and how this strategy became the primary way companies provide returns to their owners and investors. Then, still within the context of M&A, we will focus on (i) evidence of historical M&A effects for the bidder and the target, (ii) the differences among M&A transactions, (iii) how companies are valued in order to determine their price and how the latter might be affected by premiums and discounts, and (iv) the M&A Process, and finally the Risk management activity behind M&A deals, that will be investigated in Chapter 10. To sum up, M&A transactions will be analyzed along various dimensions as reported in **Table 9.1**.

Table 9.1 M&A Analysis

Objectives	• **Strategic bidder**: bidder is a corporate which executes the M&A transaction to accomplish its own **corporate objectives** • **Financial bidder**: bidder is a Financial Investor (PEs, HFs, the management etc.) looking for a targeted **financial return**
Type	• **Statutory Merger:** target is merged into the bidder and ceases to exist • **Acquisition of Target:** target continues to exists as a subsidiary of the bidder • **Acquisition of Assets:** target's Assets transferred to the bidder
Consideration	• **Cash:** bidder pays seller(s) in cash • **Equity:** bidder pays seller(s) with its own shares, in exchange for the shares of the target • **Mixed:** bidder pays seller(s) with a mix of cash and its own shares
Financing	• **Debt Financing:** consideration is financed through debt • **Equity Financing:** consideration is financed through the raising of equity
Status of the Target	• **Private:** target is sold through a private transaction, between bidder and seller(s) • **Public/Tender Offer:** a public offer to buy shares is made by the bidder to the target's shareholders

9.2 The use of M&A in corporate strategy

As we highlighted in the introduction, operating businesses see M&A as one means to accomplish strategic goals. In fact, as mentioned earlier, in economic booms, companies tend to pursue M&A in order to benefit from the economic conditions and follow expansionary strategies, acquiring complementary assets (to correct an asset weakness) or supplementary assets (to reinforce an asset strength). To the contrary, during periods of economic contraction/stagnation, companies tend to focus more on restructuring strategies aiming at streamlining operations and refocusing on core activities.

However, no board of directors should take for granted that those strategies should be implemented based on the above-mentioned economic outlooks. Indeed, they tend to be used by managers in such a way (expansionary strategies in a bull market and restructuring strategies in a bearish market) simply because they are the strategies that, most of the time, create value for their shareholders. Nonetheless, a firm's corporate strategy should be determined by identifying *where* to create value (attractive market spaces to enter or maintain and defend) and *how* to create value in the spaces selected. In other words, corporations need to investigate the possible value creation options that are available to them and opt for the strategy that would maximize the Net Present Value of Cash Flows to the equity.

For example, let us suppose that at a given instant "t," a manager has a variety of options and needs to choose whether to:

a) keep the firm size constant, thus working on the business model;
b) divest non-core assets, preferably at a premium to market value;
c) develop internal activities, known as organic growth;
d) seek external growth via acquisitions, mergers, and joint ventures.

The manager will therefore have to access the feasibility of each option and estimate which one is expected to generate a higher return on equity, in order to decide how and where to allocate the firm's resources to create the highest value for shareholders.

As can be seen in the list above, managers not only need to identify and access new external/internal growth projects to invest in (**Figure 9.1**), but also to weigh what they are doing (1st option) against what they could be doing with their resources. If the potential is greater in new areas of opportunity, the old lines of business should be converted into cash by selling them off to a firm where they fit, possibly at a premium, and the cash should be redeployed to new lines through internal or external development. Controlling this continuous redeployment process is what strategic planning is all about.

However, if a firm decides that an expansionary strategy, either through organic or external growth, will create more value for shareholders than any other alternative, then the company should solve the "Buy or Make Dilemma": are we better off buying a new capability, market entry, customer base, earnings opportunity, and so on, or attempting to build it ourselves?

Figure 9.1 Corporates' growth strategies

Organic (internal) growth	External growth
• Increase production capacity • Expand distribution platforms • Innovation/Product mix • Commercial strategy/Marketing	• M&A transactions – Mergers – Acquisition – Joint Ventures

Later on in this Chapter, we will see more in detail that this dilemma can be solved using the "Asset Valuation methods," which entail a cost-benefit analysis that gives firms the possibility to decide whether to undertake a "make" strategy (organic growth) or a "buy" strategy (external).

Nonetheless, it is essential to take into account other peculiarities of "making" strategies that may lead a company to opt for an external growth strategy rather than an internal growth strategy even though the latter is more profitable (from an NPV perspective):

a) **Speed of Execution**: sometimes, achieving objectives through organic growth may require a high level of patience and may result in some lost opportunities. Therefore, even if the company's standalone NPV is higher, it might be essential to merge with/acquire an external entity in order to speed up the process to reach to the desired objective. For instance, it is much more complex to enter a foreign market independently than to partner with or acquire a local player that has an existing business model, infrastructure, and customer base.
b) **Resource availability**: M&As may be driven by scarcity of critical resources (Rhodes-Kropf and Robinson, 2008). In fact, sometimes companies cannot access some resources or produce in-house as they may not have access to the needed technology, raw materials, etc. Therefore, the only solution would be to integrate the supply chain (acquiring a supplier) in order to have greater control over key raw materials and other essential inputs.
c) **Ego/Hubris**: Even though this is not a good reason for pursuing external growth instead of growing internally, managers, especially when close to retirement age, might be motivated to pursue M&A in order to boost their compensation (Zhang and Guo, 2007). In fact, as growing internally requires much more time than growing externally, managers will tend to prefer the latter option in order to be rewarded earlier.
d) **Strategic realignment:**
   - **Market Consolidation**: Companies decide to pursue external growth to increase their size, as usually happens, in the pharmaceutical industry, for instance;
   - **Adaptation/Reaction to abrupt and disrupting market changes**: Industrial and technological changes usually lead to merger waves (Quiry et al., 2017). In fact, the threat of industry or technological disruption in a specific indus-

try fosters M&A activity as it constrains managers to urgently develop their arsenal in order to reinvent themselves or simply survive within the industry. The speed at which those disruptors can enter and unsettle the industry forces old-fashioned companies to acquire new assets that can enable them to quickly update and improve their products and/or services so that they can still compete with other substitutes.[2]

e) **Synergies**: Corporations may opt for acquisitions due to the implementation of potential synergies that will create long-term value for their shareholders. Synergies can be defined as "the expected cost savings, growth opportunities, and other financial benefits that occur as a result of the combination of two businesses." There are several types of synergies falling into two main categories:
   - **Operating synergies** are linked to cash flow improvement. They can be cost synergies (i.e. reduction in operating expenses and capital expenditures), asset synergies (one-off increases in cash flows coming from extraordinary disposal of redundancies), tax synergies (net operating losses transferred from the target to the bidder), and revenue synergies (cross-selling, lower competition, distribution, access to distribution networks, brands, complementarity in products, pricing power, etc.);
   - **Financial synergies** derive either from lower pro-forma cost of capital, or from an improved or optimised capital structure.[3]

To sum up, in many instances, growth through an acquisition represents not only a *cheaper way* (higher NPV), but also a *faster* and *less risky* option than building a business from scratch. Green-fielding a new facility, expanding into a new geographic region, and/or moving into a new product line or distribution channel is typically more risky, costly, and time-consuming than buying an existing company with an existing business model, infrastructure, and customer base. This can explain why corporations tend to prefer external means of growth in their pursuit of growth and enhanced profitability. More precisely, corporations are often guided by a variety of acquisition strategies that belong to two broad categories of strategies:

a) **Horizontal integration**: Acquisition of a company at the same level of the value chain as the acquirer;
b) **Vertical integration**: A company either expands upstream in the supply chain by acquiring an existing or potential supplier, or downstream by acquiring an existing or potential customer.

---

[2] A noticeable example of industry disruption is the emergence of internet in the 2000s, which reorganized the newspaper industry as customers rapidly subsidized physical newspapers through digital news ("BuzzFeed") but also through social media like Facebook and Twitter.

[3] "For Financial Institutions you could also have "regulatory synergies," such as, for example, in banking mergers the application of buyers' internal rating models for Risk-Weighted-Assets (RWA) calculation in the case the target was using the standard rating models." (R. Pambianco, 2020).

Alternatively, even though this type of acquisition strategy is not very common nowadays, some companies still make acquisitions in relatively unrelated business areas, an acquisition strategy known as *conglomeration.*

9.2.1 Horizontal growth strategy

As just mentioned, a horizontal deal is a transaction involving two or more business entities operating at the same level within the same industry. Such a combination generally aims at potentially:

a) Increasing the market share of a business in that particular industry by expanding the acquirer's geographic reach, product lines, services, and/or distribution channels, and;
b) Achieving both economies of scale and scope by leveraging the fixed cost base and know-how for greater production efficiencies.

Horizontal deals can usually be easily recognized, as due to the strategic fit of the combined entities, they often result in significant *cost* and *revenue synergies.*

On the one hand, the so-called *cost synergies* (reduction of costs due to the combination of two entities) arise from the elimination of redundancies and from leveraging the acquirer's existing infrastructure and overheads.

On the other hand, *revenue synergies* are achieved thanks not only to the acquirer's increased size, which typically affords greater leverage with suppliers and customers (with the former providing greater purchasing power and the latter providing greater pricing power), but also due to leveraging each respective company's distribution network, customer base, and technologies.

Nonetheless, despite all the benefits that come from this type of transaction, horizontal integration deals tend to be risky, as they are often subject to the scrutiny of antitrust authorities, which ensure that the combination of companies' strengths does not distort the competitive dynamics of a particular industry.

9.2.2 Vertical growth strategy

A vertical transaction is a deal between business entities operating at different levels within an industry's supply chain. Vertical integration seeks to provide a company with cost efficiencies and potential growth opportunities by affording control over key components of the supply chain. When companies move upstream to purchase their suppliers, it is known as *backward integration*; conversely, when they move downstream to purchase their customers, it is known as *forward integration.*

Overall, vertical integration is often motivated by multiple of potential advantag-

Figure 9.2 **Vertical Growth Strategy**

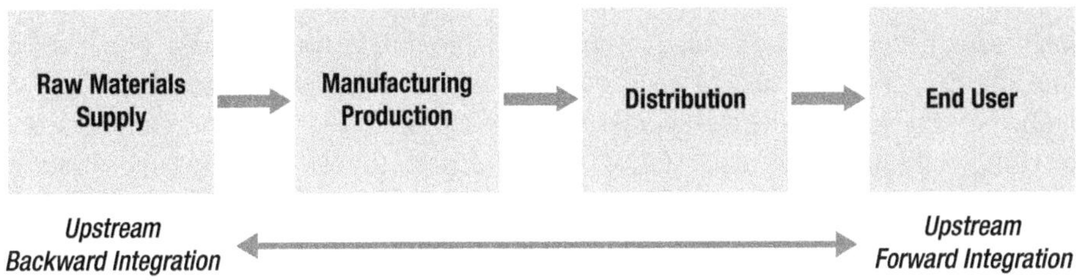

es, including increased control over key raw materials and other essential inputs, the ability to capture upstream or downstream profit margins, improved supply chain coordination, and moving closer to the end user to own the customer relationship. Owning the means of production or distribution potentially enables a company to serve its customers faster and more efficiently while affording greater control over the finished product and its delivery, which helps ensure high standards and customer satisfaction (**Figure 9.2**).

At the same time, vertical integration can pose business and financial risks to those moving up and down the value chain. By moving the supply chain in house, for example, companies risk losing the benefits of choosing from a broad group of suppliers, which may limit product variety, innovation, and the ability to source competitively as possible on price. Furthermore, the financial return and profitability metrics for upstream and downstream businesses tend to differ, which may create pressure to separate them over time. However, the greatest challenge for successfully implementing a vertical integration growth strategy is that the core competencies for upstream and downstream activities tend to be fundamentally different. As companies broaden their scope, it becomes increasingly difficult to remain a "best-in-class" operator in multiple areas of competence.

9.2.3 Conglomerates' growth strategy

A conglomerate transaction is a deal between two or more *unrelated business entities* – entities that basically have no business activity in common. That kind of deal is usually undertaken either by conglomerates such as 3M, General Electric, and Siemens, or so-called "Holdings" such as Exor and Wendel that invest in different sectors and hold a diversified portfolio of companies. The rationale behind those "conglomerate transactions" is to:

a) bring different businesses under a common corporate umbrella and leverage not only the use of best practices, but also a common management team, infrastructure, and balance sheet.

b) diversify operations, leading to more stable cash flows while affording managers the flexibility to opportunistically invest in a higher growth segment.

Nonetheless, there are two major types of conglomerate transactions, which differ quite significantly from one another: *pure* and *mixed* conglomerate deals.

On the one hand, *pure conglomerate* transactions involve business entities that are completely unrelated (e.g. AOL – Time Warner[4]). In that case, the incentive for the deal is to *diversify the portfolio of businesses* in order to achieve a risk-neutral position. As portfolio managers do in Asset Management, corporate executives of firms operating in cyclical businesses often try to diversify their operations in order to achieve greater stability of their cash flows, which will reduce business risk, result in better credit ratings, lower the firm's cost of capital, and thus create significant value for shareholders.

On the other hand, *mixed conglomerate* transactions involve firms that are looking for *product extensions or market extensions* (e.g. Pepsi/Pizza Hut[5]). In that case, even though the companies are not operating in the same industry, there is a strategic rationale behind the deal. The assets combined are somewhat "complementary" and often result in the creation of additional value not only for shareholders, but for stakeholders as a whole (customers, suppliers, shareholders, etc.). **Figure 9.3** presents an overall picture of different possible expansion solutions.

9.2.4 Wrap up: 3 main growth strategies

Those different types of M&A strategies – Horizontal, Vertical and Conglomerates – are the three main strategies behind M&A deals. However, those transactions are motivated by more precise and thoughtful reasons. In fact, pursuing a horizontal integration per se is not a reason for engaging in M&A. Yet the willingness to lower costs and improve competitiveness throughout economies of scale is, and this can be achieved through a horizontal integration strategy.

Therefore, before advising corporations, investment banks need to clearly understand the needs of their clients and the different reasons behind their willingness to pursue external growth strategies. Over time, those financial advisors have divided the different reasons underlying M&A into two broad categories:

[4] In 2000, America Online agreed to purchase Time Warner for $165 billion, in what would be the biggest merger in history at that time. The company was renamed AOL Time Warner. Unfortunately, in 2009, Time Warner decided to spin off AOL, unwinding one of the most ill-fated marriages in the history of the media and technology business.

[5] In 1977, Pizza Hut merged with PepsiCo, becoming a division of the global soft drink and food conglomerate. Sales that year reached $436 million.

Figure 9.3 Summary of different possible growth strategies

Direction	Explanation
Vertical + forward	• Acquiring businesses downstream in the supply chain – customers. • Goals: – Capture downstream profit margins – Improve coordination to serve customers faster and more efficiently – Move closer to the end user to own the customer relationship
Vertical + backward	• Acquiring businesses upstream in the supply chain – suppliers. • Goals – Capture upstream profit margins – Gain control over key raw materials and other essential inputs – Improve coordination between the suppliers and the acquiring entity
Horizontal	• Acquiring a business at the same stage of the supply chain – competitors. • Goals: – Increase market share – Achieve economies of scale and scope (eliminating redundancies, and spreading fixed costs to a greater number of units produced) – Obtain cost and revenue synergies (pricing and purchase power, leveraging distribution channels, etc.)
Conglomerate	• Pure conglomerate: Acquiring totally unrelated businesses • Goals – Diversify operations in order to stabilize cash flows • Mixed conglomerate: Acquire companies in order to extend product offering and geographic presence • Goal: – Complement existing assets to create additional value

a) "**Sensitive reasons**" which are rational objectives behind such important transactions, and;
b) "**Dubious objectives**" that are considered as "not good enough reasons" to pursue an M&A strategies.

9.2.5 Reasons behind M&A deals

a. Sensitive Reasons for M&A

First and foremost, the most common reason behind an M&A transaction is the bidder's willingness to achieve greater economies of scale and/or increase its market share in order to better compete with prominent players operating in its industry. The bidder can achieve such objectives by pursuing a horizontal strategy that will broaden the size of the acquirer's firm, and therefore, with regard to "economies of scale," will enable it to reduce its per-unit cost by using excess capacity or by spreading the fixed costs to a greater number of units.

Secondly, another reason which in this case supports a vertical integration growth strategy is the firm's willingness to integrate its supply chain in order to achieve greater "economies of vertical integration." Economies of vertical integration include not only greater control over suppliers, which may reduce the firm's input costs, but also an enhancement of supply production efficiency. In addition, acquirers may pursue vertical integration strategies in order to be more protected against potential new entrants increasing current market power and entry barriers. Generally, firms pursuing vertical integration strategies are large companies that would like to gain as much control and coordination as possible over the production process by expanding back toward the output of the raw material and forward to the end consumer. However, vertical integration has fallen out of fashion recently as many companies are finding it more efficient to outsource many of their activities.

Thirdly, another sensitive reason for pursuing mergers and acquisitions is to acquire the "missing piece of the puzzle." In fact, small firms may have a unique product but may lack the engineering and sales organization necessary to produce and market it on a large scale. Therefore, the firm may develop engineering and sales talent from scratch, but it may be quicker and cheaper to merge with a firm that already has ample talent. The two firms have what is called "complementary resources."

Fourthly, if a firm in a mature industry has few, if any positive NPV projects available, acquisitions may be the best way to use its funds. Indeed, firms with a surplus of cash and a shortage of profitable investment opportunities can turn to cash-financed acquisitions in order to redeploy their capital. Often, energetic managers opt for this strategy when they have excesses of cash on their balance sheet, as they try to avoid being passive and simply redistributing cash to shareholders through stock buybacks and exceptional dividend payments.

Fifthly, another common reason for engaging in M&A, which is popular in Private Equity M&A deals, is the elimination of inefficiencies. In fact, strategic buyers such as corporations with strong management teams or financial buyers may pursue opportunistic M&A transactions in order to enhance the performance of a defined target: cutting its costs or increasing its sales.[6]

Finally, industries with too many firms/competitors and too much capacity usually trigger waves of M&As. In fact, in order to survive in an over-competitive industry, corporations tend to acquire each other, which reduces the competitive dynamics and improves the overall profitability of the industry. This process is called "industry consolidation."

b. Dubious reasons for mergers and acquisitions.

Not every transaction is motivated by the aforementioned "sensitive reasons." In fact, sometimes managers pursue M&A for reasons that are not always in the best interest of their shareholders (**Box 9.1**). However, even though some reasons are

[6] "In addition, private equity-owned companies tend to pursue a series of M&A transactions in order to quickly grow their size. This will allow the companies to reach a "critical mass" in a short time frame that could maximize exit options for the financial investor (i.e. sell the company, but also, for example, list the company on the public market)." (R. Pambianco, 2020)

Box 9.1 Accretion/Dilution Analysis

ACCRETIVE BAD DEALS AND DILUTIVE GOOD DEALS

Accretion/dilution analysis only considers the impact of the deal on the Buyer's eps. It does not indicate whether the deal has a positive NPV and thus creates value for shareholders. There are accretive bad deals and dilutive good deals!

Accretive bad deals are those in which the Target's P-E ratio is low for a good reason—because it's risky or in a market with no growth. If this type of Target is fairly valued and a Buyer with a high P-E pays a premium to buy it, the Buyer's eps will go up, showing a nice growth trend. But the growth is illusory—the deal will actually destroy value, because the company was fairly valued in the first place.

Companies that take this route get trapped in a vicious cycle. To satisfy the eps growth expectations of the market, they have to keep doing ever-bigger deals. But the companies they buy are typically pretty mediocre (they had low P-Es for a reason). Over time, the portfolio of mediocre companies gets larger and larger. At some point, the market figures out what's going on and the stock price drops. If the managers were dishonest, accounting irregularities and other sins may be uncovered at this time. This is basically the story of Tyco and World.com, companies whose former CEOs are now in jail.

However, even good companies with honest managers can find themselves trapped on the so-called eps treadmill. Such companies cannot hide their sins by getting acquired—their P-E ratios are high, so they have to be the Buyer in an accretive deal. The best they can do is to structure deals that will "share the pain" with the Target's shareholders. But—by definition—these high-flying shares are overvalued; thus, honest managers must be careful not to commit securities fraud. When the bubble bursts, the shareholders of recently-acquired companies will feel defrauded, and will file lawsuits to pursue their case. This is basically the story behind AOL's acquisition of Time Warner, and the University of California's subsequent lawsuit against that company and its managers.

Dilutive good deals are those in which the Target's P-E is high for a good reason—because it is experiencing a temporary crisis or because it is in a market with very high growth. These acquisitions will dilute the Buyer's eps in the short run, but will enhance it in the long run.

If a large company uses stock to purchase companies with promising growth prospects but low earnings, those deals will be dilutive. Large companies that pursue this strategy prefer to keep their acquisitions small, so that the growth in their core business can mask the dilution caused by their M&A activity. In this fashion, a serial acquirer can do a set of dilutive good deals and still "deliver" earnings-per-share growth to the market. Cisco is well known for having executed this strategy.

Let us assume that an acquiring company has a higher price per share than the target company – at the same earnings per share and number of shares. When the acquirer issues shares to buy the target's shares, the proportion of shares is not 1:1 (as priced higher, the acquirer can issue a number of shares lower than the number of shares of the target; if the $P_{acquiring} = 2P_{target}$ the acquirer will issue half of the shares of the target). Hence, after the transaction the number of shares of the two merged companies is lower than the sum of the shares of the two separate companies and therefore the earnings per share increase in the short-term after the transaction only because the total number of shares decreased.

With this accounting trick we didn't create any value for shareholders: in fact, the new market value is equal to the sum of the market value of the two companies standing alone (we didn't add any value). Hence, shareholders will not pay any premium for the transaction, also because the Price-Earnings Ratio goes down: we are exchanging higher earnings today for lower earnings per share in the future (the market is going to value the merged company less).

	Acquirer before	Target before	Acquirer after transaction
No. of shares (same)	150	150	225,000 = 150,000 + (0.5*150,000)
EPS (same)	2	2	2.67= 600,000/225,000
Price per share (acq>target)	60	30	60 (same of acquirer before)
Price/Earnings ratio	30 (60/2)	15 (30/2)	22.5 = 60/2.67
Total earnings	300,000	300,000	600,000
Total mkt value	9,000,000 (60*150,000)	4,500,000 (30*150,000)	13,500,000
Earning per dollar invested	0.033 (2/60)	0.67 (2/30)	0.045 = 2.67/60
(EPS/Price per share)			

If the target is undervalued: so far we have assumed that the target was not undervalued. However, a possible viable justification for an M&A is that the market is currently undervaluing the target, assigning it a lower price, and the management of the acquirer expects that the value will increase in the future.

1. Determine the exchange ratio; $ER=P_{target}/P_{acquirer} = 30/60=0.5$ (acquirer needs to give target's shareholders only half of its own shares to acquire the totality of target's shares).
2. Determine the total amount of shares after the transaction:

$$N.\ Shares_{after} = N.\ shares\ target(100\%)+(ER*N.shares\ acquirer) = 150{,}000 + (0.5*150{,}000)=225{,}000.$$

3. Determine the P/E ratio = Total mkt value/Total earnings = 13,500,000/600,000 = 22.5
4. Determine the EPS = Total Earnings/N. $Shares_{after}$ = 600,000/225,000 = 2.67
5. Determine the current earnings per dollar invested, as: EPS/Price = 2.67/60=0.045

clearly categorized as "dubious reasons," some managers continue to justify their willingness to grow externally under the pretext of (i) "diversification" or (ii) "immediate accretion of Earnings per Share," which are considered dubious reasons because they do not create additional value for shareholders, and most of the time they even destroy value.

First and foremost, the willingness to diversify a shareholder's portfolio is considered "dubious" as shareholders do not need diversification at a corporate level; some shareholders can diversify their own portfolio by investing in the stock market itself. In fact, instead of pursuing M&A deals in which shareholders often need to pay a premium to market price in order to take over the target, the latter can simply acquire shares on the open market at the current market price. Therefore, as some shareholders can diversify their portfolio themselves at a cheaper cost and with more flexibility, diversification at a corporate level in some cases cannot justify managers' willingness to pursue mergers and acquisitions.

Furthermore, the second dubious reason behind M&As which is often quoted in press releases is the immediate accretion of Earnings Per Share, which, even though it can sometimes create long-term value for shareholders, it can also simply be an illusionary trap. In fact, sometimes investors do not take the time to understand the reasons behind the accretion of EPS post-transaction, and therefore, may fall into the so-called "Bootstrap Game" trap. This trap arises when an acquirer purchases a target that has a lower P/E ratio than the bidder, and even without any synergies, post-merger, the acquiring company experiences a short-term EPS accretive impact.

This is due to the fact that if a high P/E ratio company acquires another firm (which has a lower P/E ratio) using its stock as a purchase consideration, then there will be fewer combined shares outstanding post-merger. However, since earnings remain the same but there are fewer shares of stock, the earnings per share ratio increases favourably. Yet, instead of coming to know the underlying reason behind the sudden surge, investors may believe the earnings per share increased because of the synergy created through the merger, resulting in the increase in the value of the post-merger stock. However, this accretive impact on the acquirer's EPS is just a short-term effect that would not be repeated over the medium to long-term, unless managers continue to expand through M&A at the same compound rate. Obviously, this strategy cannot persist forever, as one day expansion will slow down or even stop, causing earnings growth to cease, and the "house of cards" to fall.

To sum up, we can keep in mind that different reasons can adequately justify managers' willingness to pursue M&A transactions. In fact, the bidder may undertake horizontal/vertical integration strategies in order to achieve specific objectives such as lowering costs of production, improving the efficiency of the supply chain, etc.

However, some managers still justify their willingness to pursue M&A deals using "dubious reasons." They usually tend to do so when they pursue external growth strategies for the wrong reasons such as for their personal ego. In that case, a principal/agent issue arises as managers may undertake actions that are not always in the best interests of their shareholders.

Therefore, as M&A can sometime be detrimental to shareholders, we can ask ourselves: do M&A pay?

9.3 Does M&A pay? Empirical evidence from past transactions

In an M&A transaction, as the final objective of the entire process turns out to be the transfer of control in exchange for compensation, it all comes down to the identification of the right price to be paid. What is meant by "right" is the price that brings together the (sometimes) conflicting objectives of the bidder and of the seller (respectively, price minimization versus price maximization), trying to find fertile and common ground for the deal to take place. Specifically, this price shall reflect several considerations that will guide the negotiations and determine the final purchase price, among which:

a) the minimum price at which the seller is willing to take the deal;
b) the fair price of the target as defined by the buyer;
c) the bargaining power of the parties;
d) market competitive forces (Massari, Gianfrate and Zanetti, 2016);
e) accretion/dilution analysis.

Ideally, as M&A deals should result in the creation of synergies, the bidder should acquire the target for its fair value plus part of the synergies created. In that way, both parties will benefit from the transaction, since:

a) The seller will be able to sell its assets at a premium to market price, capturing part of synergies;
b) The bidder will also be able to capture some of the synergies resulting from the merger.

However, even though finding the right price seems to be a relatively easy task (fair value + part of synergies), it is in reality a very difficult task as this is to be considered more an art than a science. In fact, the bidder should estimate not only the fair value of the target, which is relatively difficult per se, but also the expected synergies. Therefore, from this point, we can already imagine two sources of errors that may result in the bidder overpaying for the target:

a) First, the bidder could overvalue the target's fair value;
b) Second, the bidder could be over-optimistic with regards to the creation of synergies and therefore, pay the target's shareholders a price which accounts for synergies that the bidder will never be able to implement.

Therefore, as the success of M&A deals is heavily sensitive to the price paid, it would be interesting to see how much and to whom M&As have proven to be value accretive up to now.

Starting from literature research, there are a variety of studies that are mostly concerned with M&A value creation and that have empirically assessed the performance of historical M&A transactions. Those studies can be grouped into four main areas according to the methodology chosen to conduct the analysis:

a) Event studies;
b) Accounting studies;
c) Clinical studies; and
d) Surveys of executives.

In the next sections we will discuss the results of those four types of studies in order to answer the following question:

> "Is there any empirical evidence that M&A creates value for shareholders?"

9.3.1 Event studies

Event studies (*Market-based returns to shareholders*) conducted to analyse M&A value creation are a direct measure of value created for investors and consist of an observation of the market price (that represents, in theory, the present value of expected future cash flows) of the stocks of the bidder, target, and of the combined entity before, during, and after the transaction announcement date. The assumption underlying such kind of studies is that the cumulative abnormal stock returns (CARs) defined as the sum of subsequent abnormal returns (Dallocchio et al., 2017) shall be considered as an index of the value creation or destruction caused by the transaction (Andrade et al., 2001). In other words, if CARs are positive, then M&A can be considered to create value for the shareholders in question; conversely, if CARs are negative, then it can be taken for granted that M&A tend to destroy value for shareholders.

From the wealth of event studies that have been conducted, we can retain three main points.

First, the different studies in the literature have found that CARs for target shareholders are systematically positive regardless of the transaction's success (Eckbo, 1983) and of the type of consideration paid (Andrade et al., 2001). This finding has also been confirmed by multiple authors such as Asquith, Bruner and Mullins (1990) and by the comprehensive research of Weston et al. (2004). Put succinctly, this empirical evidence has important implications as it demonstrates that target shareholders always benefit from M&A deals.

Second, to complement the previous point, academics have researched which type of deals have tended to create more value for target shareholders. In this research, they found that stock deals seemed to bring less value to target shareholders, because as explained by Andrade et al. (2001), raising equity (i.e. paying via stock) entails information asymmetry between investors and the issuer, thus confirming the possibility that firms are more likely to issue equity when they believe their stock to be overvalued. Consequently, cash only deals are seen as being more transparent and fairly valued, and therefore generate superior returns that accrue to target shareholders.

Third, in line with the wrong market signalling hypothesis in the case of stock transactions, on the other side of the deal, bidder shareholders seem to earn low to no abnormal returns (Andrade et al., 2001). However, the effect of M&As on bidder shareholders is not entirely clear, as the literature provides conflicting results. In conclusion, the vast literature on the topic seems to generally agree on the fact that M&A generates positive returns for target shareholders, break-even values for bidders, and on the aggregate, positive returns for the shareholders of the combined entity (Healy, Palepu and Ruback, 1992; Mulherin and Boone, 2000; Andrade et al., 2001; Bruner, 2002; Weston et al., 2004).

This type of analysis requires significant assumptions about the functioning of the stock markets (such as efficiency, absence of arbitrage, rationality).

9.3.2 Accounting studies

Right after the event studies, accounting studies (returns estimated from reported financial statements) are the second most common kind of analysis implemented to assess M&A value creation (Laabs, 2009). Specifically, instead of detecting anomalous changes in stock prices, those studies focus on analysing, from an accounting standpoint, signs of outperformance of the acquirer entity vis-à-vis its market comparables.

Examples of financial performance indicators that are usually benchmarked against peers are profitability measures such as return on equity (ROE), return on assets (ROA), EBITDA margin, Net Income, earning per shares (EPS), etc.

However, while event studies have shown similar results across different research, accounting studies show contrasting results. In fact, among the results of the many studies conducted over time, some highlight the value destructive post-transaction effects of M&As. To the contrary, others show, respectively, cash flow enhancements, profitability improvements, and synergies that accrue to acquirer companies. Many other studies lie in the middle ground, showing no striking evidence of any neat effect of M&A on value.

Nonetheless, by focusing on profitability enhancements, we can find similar results across studies. Indeed, most studies agree on the fact that some of the key M&A drivers profoundly and positively impact pro-forma profitability (Bruner, 2002). Starting from the most optimistic findings, the present value of expected synergies is believed to strongly drive value creation, and this is mostly true for cost synergies thanks to their easier achievability and traceability. Additionally, low book-to-value ratios, all cash deals, and tender offers are all value accretive features.

However, the backward looking nature of those studies, their sensitiveness to inflation and deflation due to the historic cost approach, and the fact they ignore the value of intangibles assets together with their inhomogeneity in terms of accounting standards of the observations (i.e. cross-border comparison is difficult) and the years chosen to conduct the study, are all reasons that motivated papers such as Bruner (2002) and Laabs (2009) to resort to alternative analyses such as clinical studies and surveys of executives.

9.3.3 Clinical studies

Clinical studies (inductive research) consist of an in-depth analysis of certain past transactions, in order to assess on a case-by-case basis the drivers that led a specific deal to create or destroy value for shareholders. More generally, they belong to the broader category of case studies that are concerned with understanding the dynamics of a specific setting which may involve one or multiple observations at a time. Bruner (2002) brings together a vast literature of case studies of past M&A transactions, and eventually, some value creation and destruction patterns emerge:

a) **Value creation**: in the cases assessed, its drivers are difficult to trace. However, Kaplan (1989) points at possible candidates, such as cost efficiency enhancements, tax synergies and sale of non-core/non-strategic or unused assets;
b) **Value destruction**: here the drivers are much neater and confirmed by many authors (e.g. Bruner and Eades, 1992; Kaplan, Mitchell and Wruck, 1997). Indeed, value erosion seems to be associated with incentives misalignment between management and capital providers, hubris, loss of control, leverage, and difficult achievability or distrust in achievability of synergic benefits.

These analyses are objective and are ideal for discovering new patterns and behaviours, but at the same time the fact that the research reports are necessarily based on small number of observations makes it difficult for readers to generalize from the case(s).

9.3.4 Executive surveys

The last identified type of analysis is the use of executive surveys. Out of the 12 studies collected by Bruner (2002) using sample observations in time intervals within the period of 1955-1998, 6 studies led to a negative result (among which those of McKinsey & Co., PA Consulting, and Bahree), while the others seemed to be inclined towards a neutral or positive position.

The studies cited above were performed by practitioners, and have limited capability of being replicated, as opposed to those surveys conducted by scholars on wider sample bases. Furthermore, the results of the latter studies show that more than two-thirds of the managers interviewed believe that the positive profitability impact of M&As on firms has a long-lasting effect (Ingham, Kran and Lovestam, 1992).

In conclusion, as a result of the online survey conducted by Bruner (2002) and extended to 50 executives, two findings emerged:

a) "According to those who had the greatest knowledge about deals, M&A pays;"
b) "When talking about external deals (i.e. not involving their own firms), executives show a strongly negative sentiment about M&A value creation; most likely, this may be caused by hubris, leading executives to look at their own deals with rose-coloured lenses and to disregard others' effects on value and profitability."

Surveys of managers present benefits due to the insights on the value creation process that could be not known in the stock market, but at the same time suffer from giving the perspective of managers whose estimates of value creation may not be focused on economic value.

9.3.5 Wrap-up: Does M&A pay?

To sum up and integrate the findings gathered from the four different approaches analysed up to now, the picture emerging of M&A impact is fragmented and not extremely clear. However, what seems not to be challenged is the fact that M&A does pay both for target shareholders and at an aggregate level (for the pro-forma entity shareholders), while in the words of Jensen and Ruback (1983), bidding shareholders simply do not lose.

Therefore, evidence demonstrating the benefits arising from M&A transactions explains why M&A transactions are still pursued by managers. In fact, if it were proven that M&A did not pay, it would have been very difficult to understand why managers undertake such long and exhaustive processes that we will describe in the next section.

9.4 M&A: The M&A process

As we just saw in the previous section, the sale or acquisition of a company, division, subsidiary, or collection of assets is a life-changing and lucrative event for its owners, management, employees, and other stakeholders. However, it is also a process which is very complex, expensive, and which requires a significant amount of information, money, and time; usually spanning several months.

As companies do not necessarily have the competencies, resources and time to handle the transaction, most of the time they hire several external advisors including M&A advisors or investment bankers, corporate lawyers, and strategic consultants to ensure that key objectives are met and a favourable result is achieved. In this instance, a company, either for a buy-side or a sell-side mandate, will turn to its investment bank for a comprehensive financial analysis of the various strategic alternatives available to it. For example, in the case of a sell-side mandate, the investment bank will evaluate all the different alternatives available to the seller:

a) sell all or only a part of the business (majority vs minority deals);
b) launch an Initial Public Offering;
c) continue with the status quo, etc.

Each M&A transaction has its own set of unique attributes and nuances, to which skilled investment bankers constantly need to adapt. In fact, in addition to the single client's needs, several external factors, such as legal and regulatory requirements, will dictate some aspects of the deal structure and process. However, due to the complexity of the transaction, investment banks tend to follow a codified M&A process (**Figure 9.4**) which is adapted to the specific structure of the Sale/Purchase. For instance, the timeline of a transaction structured as a "Negotiated Deal" will usually be shorter and more flexible than a "Broad Auction." Therefore, in the following sections we will clearly distinguish the two above-mentioned process:

a) **Auctions**, which are usually used in sell-side mandates and are very frequent in Private Equity exits;
b) **Negotiated deals**, which can be used either in sell-side mandates or buy-side mandates.

9.4.1 The investment bank's role

The role of an investment bank begins from the moment a buyer and/or seller "tests the waters" to see if there is a deal to be done, and follows every step of the process from the signing of the letter of intent to the due diligence, valuation, structuring, and completion of the transaction. A key issue in M&A is quantifying the deal's

Figure 9.4 The M&A Process Timeline (Auction Bid)

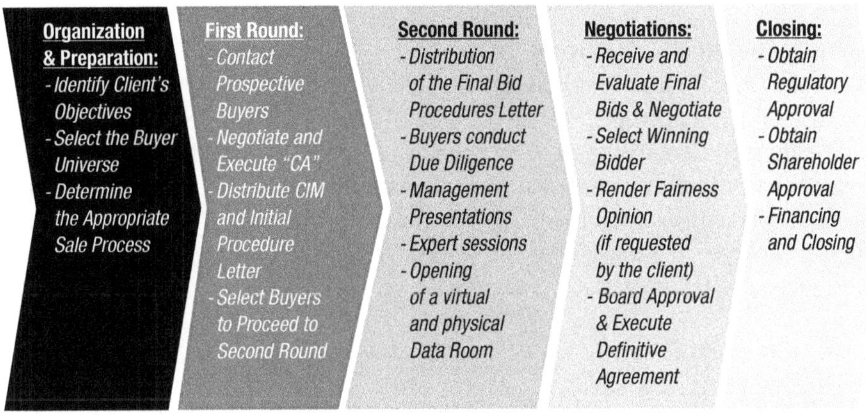

potential value. The complexity of valuing the target explains why many buyers and nearly all publicly-listed sellers in an M&A transaction rely on the advisory services of investment banks or M&A advisory boutiques, not only for deal brokering, but also for deal valuation services. These valuation analyses are used to frame both buyers' and seller's price expectations, select the "potential buyers" for the next rounds, set guidelines for the range of acceptable bids, evaluate offers received, and ultimately guide negotiations on the final purchase price; therefore, valuation impacts many stages of an M&A transaction, which explains why conducting an accurate and thorough valuation is truly essential.

Due to the importance of valuation and the significant amount of time investment banks dedicate to corporate valuation, we could surmise that the advisors on the sell-side and the buy-side will arrive at very similar intrinsic valuations of the target. However, in reality, the advisors might have very different valuations of the same target because the valuations of each side will tend to defend their own/clients' interests: while the seller wants to sell its asset for the most attractive price (and so will tend to be over-optimistic with regard to the projected financials), the buyer will be willing to acquire the company at the lowest price and so will be cautious on its financial projections. Notwithstanding the fact that the two opposite parties may have very different "target prices," those valuation models will be used for negotiations, bridging these opposing motivations to arrive at an acceptable outcome for both parties.

Nonetheless, it is important to mention that price may not be the buyer or seller's priority, and that clients do not hire investment banks only for their valuation services. In fact, the seller may be more concerned about confidentiality, speed of execution, and certainty of completion. Therefore, in any transaction, the main role of dealmakers is to identify the buyer or seller's priorities from the onset and craft a tailored sale/acquisition process.

9.4.2 Auctions (sell-side mandate)

9.4.2.1 Organization & Preparation

a. Identify the client's objectives

At the very beginning of the transaction, the advisor works closely with its client in order to identify its objectives, determine the appropriate sale process to conduct, and develop a process roadmap. To efficiently structure and conduct the transaction, it is central that the investment bank spend a significant amount of time investigating and understanding the underlying plans of their client. As a perfect example, investment bankers should avoid taking for granted vague and general objectives and should seek specific aspirations such as:

a) increasing market share;
b) expanding geographically;
c) acquiring new products or technologies;
d) achieving a certain amount of operational synergies, etc.

b. Select the Buyer Universe

After having identified the client's objectives, the mandated investment bank should identify potential buyers that might be interested in the transaction. The success of this step depends on whether the investment bank has set out the client's business objectives and growth strategy in a clear, rational, and data-oriented way. For example, if the client's goal is to sell part of its business in order to invest in other more lucrative activities, but without losing control of its core business, understanding this point is essential, as the investment bank will have to look for acquirers that might be interested in investing in minority positions. In this example, if the advisors do not recognize the full intent behind the transaction, they might not approach those investors that usually pay lower multiples (do not pay for control) and the transaction might fail.

We can clearly see that the selection of an appropriate group of prospective buyers is a critical part of the preparation stage. The omission or inclusion of a potential buyer can lead to the failure of the transaction. Therefore, when looking for potential candidates, the investment bank need at the same time to be cautious (not contact buyers that are not interested in acquiring the company but that may benefit from the information disclosed during the process) but also to think outside the box (do not omit candidates). Based on the client's needs, the investment bank will approach not only "Strategic Buyers" including competitors, conglomerates, companies operating along the supply chain, etc., but also "Financial Sponsors" such as Sovereign Wealth Funds, Family Offices, Hedge Funds, and Private Equity Funds.[7]

However, it is not possible to assess the likelihood and ability to acquire the tar-

---

[7] "Depending on the client's objectives, a sale process could be limited only to strategic buyers or only to financial sponsors. However, common practice in broader auctions is to have a mix of the two categories." (R. Pambianco, 2020)

get of thousands of potential buyers. As a consequence, investment bankers will do a first "rough screening," by applying an unequivocal knockout criterion to quickly reduce the number of companies to a manageable amount. Usually, for reasons of simplicity the criteria should be capable of simple application on the basis of readily available data. For Strategic Buyers, the Investment Bank will usually investigate and apply a threshold on the following elements:

a) **Strategic fit**: A company that has a strong strategic fit with the target will be more likely to be interested in the transaction;
b) **Potential synergies**: A company that can create some synergies with the target will be more likely to be interested in the transaction and can afford to pay a price above its fair value;
c) **Accretive/dilutive impact**: If the transaction is accretive for the "Pro-Forma" acquirer, the buyer might be interested. To the contrary, dilutive transactions are usually not appreciated by the market, which may impact the buyer's willingness to submit a bid;
d) **Ability to pay**: A company with low leverage, a strong balance sheet, significant size, and which has access to capital in financial markets will be more likely to seriously participate in the auction (especially for large transactions);
e) **M&A track record**: Companies that have a strong M&A track record, which have successfully completed multiple M&A transactions, will be more likely to continue to seek external growth (momentum effect).

c. Choose the type of M&A process

As mentioned previously, the principal role of an investment bank in an M&A transaction is to work closely with the seller to identify its objectives in order to determine the appropriate sale process. As a consequence, the advisor must first gain a clear understanding of the seller's priorities so as to tailor the process accordingly.

Then, based on their client's considerations, investment banks will decide to opt for one of the two common auction processes and tailor the chosen process to the client's needs: "Broad Auction" and "Targeted Auction."

i) Broad Auction

The Investment Bank will usually consider running a "Broad Auction," reaching out to many potential interested parties, if the client is concerned about value maximization and is largely indifferent toward:

a) confidentiality;
b) timing;
c) potential business disruption.

As a matter of fact, a broad auction is designed to maximize competitive dynamics and heighten the probability of finding one buyer willing to offer the best value. By including as many strategic and financial sponsors as possible, the advisor encourages bidders to put forth their best offer both in terms of price and conditions.

However, as the target is marketed to a vast number of prospective buyers, this auction process may have potential drawbacks including information leakage. In addition, certain prospective buyers may decide not to participate in a broad auction given their reluctance to commit serious time and resources to a situation where they may have a relatively low likelihood of winning.[8]

ii) Targeted Auction

If the seller is still willing to maximize the value of its asset but is somewhat concerned about confidentiality, the investment bank may opt for a "targeted auction" in which only a select group of potential buyers are approached. Generally, in this type of auction, the investment bank tends to focus on a few clearly-defined buyers that have been identified as having a strong strategic fit and/or desire, as well as the financial capacity to purchase the target. In this case, the information is divulged to a limited number of individuals and the client can decide whom to select for the bid, excluding, for example, a specific category of potential acquirers such as direct competitors, that could benefit from the divulged information.[9]

9.4.2.2 First Round

a. Contact Prospective Buyers/Sellers

The first round begins when the advisor contacts the potential buyers in order to launch the M&A process. Remember that in an auction process, the advisor will contact multiple parties that might be interested in the transaction, while in a targeted auction, the advisor will only approach a limited number of clearly-identified counterparties. At this stage, the advisor distributes two essential documents to all the parties it has approached:

a) the Teaser;
b) the Confidentiality Agreement.

i) The Teaser

The "Teaser" is a marketing material which is the first formal introduction of the target to prospective acquirers. This document that presents publicly available information about the target is essential for sparking the interest of the counterparties and creating a favourable first impression (**Figure 9.5**). An effective teaser is generally a

[8] "Having to deal with multiple buyers will also occupy a significant amount of the seller's management team, distracting them from the day-to-day management of the company." (R. Pambianco, 2020)

[9] "However, the two structures are not self-excluding. The Investment Bank, in agreement with the seller, could decide to start bilateral discussions with a selected group of potentially interested buyers (i.e. a targeted process). These discussions could be limited in time with the objective of reaching the desired sale price following a quick interaction. If this objective is not met, the Investment Bank could always decide to open up the process to other parties, moving towards a broader auction-style process." (R. Pambianco, 2020)

Figure 9.5 Example of an M&A Teaser

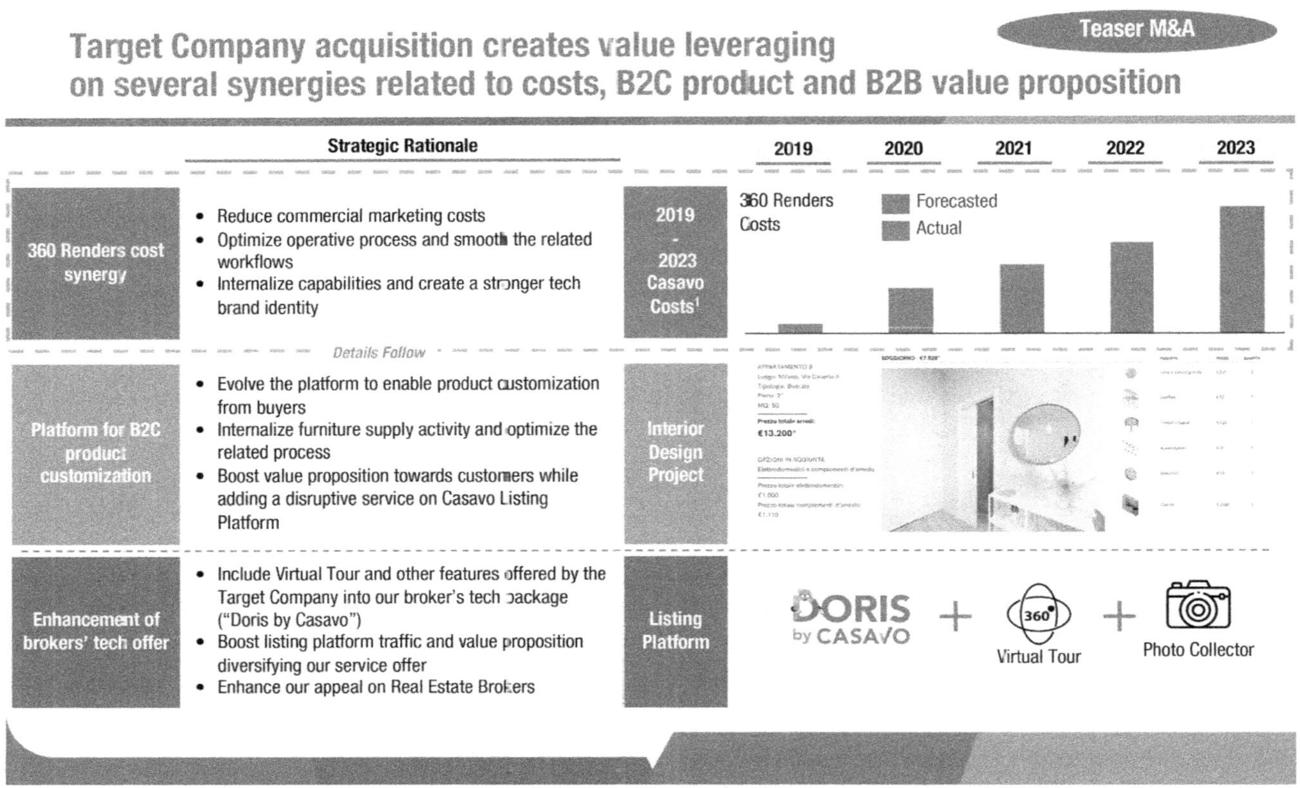

Source: Casavo S.p.a

brief one or two pages on the target designed not only to inform buyers, but also to generate sufficient interest for them to submit a bid.[10]

ii) The Confidentiality Agreement

The Confidentiality Agreement is a legally-binding contract between the seller and the buyer(s) that governs the sharing of confidential information. This contract is typically drafted by the seller's counsel. If the party disagrees with the Confidentiality Agreement, it will not be allowed to move forward, as the receipt of more detailed information is conditional on execution of this agreement. In general, the Confidentiality Agreement governs the following provisions:

a) **Use of information**: all the information furnished by the seller, whether oral or written, is considered proprietary information and should be treated as confidential and used solely to make a decision regarding the prospective transaction;
b) **Terms**: the time period during which the confidentiality restrictions remain in effect;
c) **Permitted Disclosures**: the circumstances under which the counterparty is allowed to disclose the confidential information provided;
d) **Return of confidential information**: the return or destruction of all documents once the counterparty exits the process;
e) **Standstill agreement**: prohibits prospective buyers from making unsolicited offers to the target's management, board of directors, etc.;
f) **Restrictions on "clubbing"**: preventing prospective buyers from collaborating without the prior consent of the target.

Note that when the parties agree to sign the Confidentiality Agreement, they must keep the information confidential or they may be criminally liable.

b. Negotiate and Execute a Confidentiality Agreement with Interested Parties & Distribute the Confidential Information Memorandum (CIM) and Initial Bid Procedure Letter

After contacting the potential counterparties, distributing the Teaser and the Confidentiality Agreement, the buyer's and the seller's counsels negotiate the Confidentiality Agreement based on the input from their respective clients. Often, the buyer(s) and the seller do not directly agree on the terms and provisions drafted in the agreement. For example, knowing that the agreement is legally binding, buyers might not be willing to be governed by very strict provisions, as they may incur severe punishment in case of breach. Therefore, they often negotiate to agree on some terms and move forward with the execution.

[10] "It is not uncommon to have a teaser in an anonymized format so not to disclose the name of the company up for sale in this very preliminary phase of the process." (R. Pambianco, 2020)

Afterwards, following the execution of the Confidentiality Agreement, the sell-side advisor is legally able to distribute the:

a) Confidential Information Memorandum (CIM);
b) Initial Bid Procedure Letter (or also referred to as the "Phase I Process Letter").

i) Confidential Information Memorandum (CIM)
The Confidential Information Memorandum (CIM) or Preliminary Information Memorandum (PIM) is a detailed written description of the target, often more than 50 pages long, that serves as the primary marketing document. The CIM typically contains:

a) An Executive Summary;
b) Investment Considerations;
c) An Overview of the Market in which the Target operates;
d) A Business History and Detailed Description of the Target;
e) A Review of the Financial Projections (not always) and the Historical Financials;
f) A Presentation of the Management Team of the Target;
g) Process Considerations.

The most important section of the CIM is the detailed financial section presenting historical and projected financial information. The past and expected future performance is associated with a narrative explanation commenting on and defending the different figures and assumptions presented. Prospective buyers are typically given several weeks to review the CIM, study the target and its sector, and conduct preliminary financial analysis prior to submitting their initial non-binding bids.

In possession of the CIM, the buy-side advisor helps its client assess the target from a valuation perspective and determine a competitive initial bid price. The trick for the buy-side advisor is to propose a bid that has to be credible (neither too low nor too high) and which is approved by its clients (potential acquirer).

ii) The Initial Bid Procedure Letter
The Initial Bid Procedure Letter (or "Phase I Process Letter") states the date and time by which interested parties must submit their written, non-binding preliminary indications of interest. It also defines the exact information that should be included in the bid, such as:

a) purchase price and the form of consideration (cash, stock or mix);
b) key assumptions to arrive at the stated purchase price;
c) structural and other considerations;
d) information on financing sources;
e) treatment of management and employees of the Target;
f) timing for completing a deal and diligence that must be performed;
g) key conditions for signing and closing;

h) required approvals;
i) contact details of the advisors hired;
j) contract information (draft of the Share Purchase Agreement (SPA).

c. Receive and Evaluate Initial Bids & Select Buyers to Proceed to Second Round

On the "first-round bid date" which is mentioned on the Initial Bid Procedure Letter, the sell-side advisor receives the initial non-binding bids from prospective buyers. At this stage, the sell-side advisor's role is to conduct a thorough analysis of the bids received. The advisor should prepare a summary of the bids received and present them to the seller along with a recommendation on which buyers to invite to the Second Round.

As the bids are non-binding, the investment bank should assess the likelihood that the potential buyer will agree on those terms and that it would be able to pay the stated purchase price. A bid that is irrationally too high may be viewed as suspicious by the sell-side advisor. However, the investment judgment will be based not only on the proposed purchase price, but also the considerations offered (cash, stock, mix), the key deal terms, and other stated conditions.

9.4.2.3 Second Round

a. Due Diligence

The second-round centres on facilitating the prospective buyers' ability to conduct detailed due diligence so that they can submit strong, final binding bids by the set due date. The seller gives access to key information only after the first round, and at the end of the round, the seller selects only few candidates that, according to the sell-side advisor, are truly interested in participating in the transaction and not benefiting from sharing the seller's confidential information.

b. Distribute Final Bid Procedures Letter

Similarly to the "initial bid procedure letter" in the first round, the seller will distribute to the selected potential bidders the "Final Bid Procedure Letter" (or "Phase 2 Process Letter") which outlines the exact date and guidelines for submitting a final, legally-binding bid. This typically marks the formal kick-off of the Second Round. Compared to the "Initial Bid Procedure Letter," the requirements for the final bid are more stringent. They include:

a) Purchase Price details and form of purchase consideration;
b) mark-up of the Share Purchase Agreement;
c) evidence of committed financing and information on financing sources;
d) attestation to completion of due diligence;
e) required regulatory approvals;
f) Board of Directors' approvals.

c. Due Diligence

The diligence process is meant to be exhaustive, typically spanning several weeks. However, the length and nature of the due diligence often differ based on the buyer's profile. On the one hand, a strategic buyer directly competing with the target may already have in-depth knowledge of the business, and will therefore only focus on firm-specific information. On the other hand, a financial sponsor that is unfamiliar with the target and its sector will take more time for the due diligence and will usually hire consultants, strategic advisors, and industry experts to assist its due diligence.

During the due diligence stage, the buyers' advisor needs to understand the target from a *financial, operational, legal, tax, accounting, environmental, cultural, strategic*, and *risk perspective*. Generally, the advisors performing due diligence explore the following areas:

a) **Market**: How large is the target's market? How fast are specific segments growing? Are there threats from substitute technologies or products? To what extent is the market influenced or controlled by governments?
b) **Customers**: Who are the target's major customers? What are their purchase criteria: Price, Quality, Reliability? Do buyers of product X also buy product Y, and do they buy both through similar channels? Are there unmet needs? Are changes in buying behaviour to be expected? What is the Customers' concentration?
c) **Competitors**: Who are the target's major competitors? What is the degree of rivalry? What are the competitors' strengths and weaknesses? What barriers to entry exist for new competitors? How will the competitors try to exploit the merger or integration issues to their own advantage?
d) **Culture and human resources**: Which key people must be kept, which core areas of competence should be retained, and how possible is it to do either? Are there major cultural discrepancies with the target? If they could cause major defections or other losses of productivity, is the organization willing to resolve them? If so, at what cost?

This due diligence work is particularly important as that research will form the basis for the valuation work that will be performed by prospective buyers, but also identify the potential risks that are key for preparing the contract negotiations, declarations and guarantees.

c. Conduct Management Presentations

Management presentations are generally held a few weeks after the beginning of the Second Round. In this way, the potential buyers have already had the chance to review additional documentation and have likely received access to the data room.

A management presentation provides the perspective buyers with the opportunity to meet with the top management of the target (generally in person). During the management presentations, key executives including the CEO, CFO, and heads of key divisions make presentations about the company and answer questions from potential buyers. These presentations are usually the buyer's first meeting with the management, and so, they represent a unique opportunity to supplement the due diligence and gain a deeper understanding of the business directly from the individuals who know the company best.

d. Conduct Expert Sessions & Q&A

In conjunction with the management presentations, "Expert Sessions" are also usually organised. Expert Sessions are meetings organised on specific topics such as HR, Legal, Tax, Finance, etc. These sessions usually tend to be more technical and the speakers are generally the Head of HR, Head of Legal, etc. Expert Sessions provide an opportunity for the buyers to meet with the Business/Function Heads of the target to discuss more detailed topics that will not be discussed during the main Management Presentations given the different level of executives attending (CEO, CFO, etc.).

At the same time, it is common during the entire period of the Second Round for the financial advisors to coordinate a "Q&A Process" during which the potential buyers will have the chance to ask a (usually) limited number of questions of the target's management. The Q&A process follows stricter rules than are usually outlined in the Phase 2 Process Letter. Generally, the Q&A are raised in the data room, that in most cases has tools available to allow potential buyers to ask questions online and the seller to answer.

e. Provide data room access

In the initial phase of the Second Round and potentially slightly ahead of the management presentation, the seller gives potential buyers access to the so-called data room: a location, or most often an online platform, where comprehensive detailed information about the target is stored. Among all the information shared, the buyers can find detailed financial reports, industry reports, consulting studies, customer and supplier lists, labour contracts, purchase contracts, description, and terms of outstanding debt and lease and pension contracts, which will help buyers in making an informed investment decision.

Having access to the data room, buyers will spend a significant amount of time exploring the data in order to adjust their financial models, and thus, the purchase price considered. Due to the amount of information to be analysed, the buyers typically enlist a full team of accountants, attorneys, consultants, and other financial specialists to conduct a comprehensive investigation of the company's data.

However, not all bidders have access to the same information! The access to the data room is often tailored to individuals in order to restrict the sharing of information from which the other party may benefit. For example, strategic buyers that compete directly with the target may be restricted from viewing very sensitive information, at least until the latter stages.

In addition, in the Second Round a copy of the Share Purchase Agreement (SPA) will generally made available to the selling party in a form that the seller is willing to accept. Potential buyers will review the SPA and provide comments. Usually, the submission of the final bid also includes the submission of a copy of the SPA that includes the buyer's comments. The amount of comments/changes provided by the buyers to the originally uploaded SPA will also be taken into consideration by the selling party when deciding on the successful bidder.

9.4.2.4 Negotiation phase

a. Reception and Evaluation of Final bids

On the "second-round bid date" which is mentioned in the final bid procedure letter, prospective buyers submit their final bid offers. The sell-side advisor works together with the seller and its legal counsel to conduct a thorough analysis of the price, structure, and conditions of the different final bids. Even though the sell-side might be concerned about price maximization, the price is not the only element taken into consideration when evaluating offers. For instance, a bid with a higher offer price but significant conditions may be deemed weaker than a firmer bid at a lower price. Once this analysis is completed, based on its advisor's recommendations, the seller selects a preferred party or parties (generally 2 to 3) with whom to negotiate a definitive agreement. Those final negotiations are aimed at pushing bids a bit further, until a "winning bidder" is identified.

b. Selecting the Winning Bidder

After the negotiations, the seller should have identified the auction winner, with whom the sell-side advisor and the legal counsel negotiate the final definitive SPA. This agreement is a legally binding contract which details not only the terms and conditions of the sale transaction, but also how disputes will be resolved, if they arise. A definitive M&A SPA usually contains the following terms and provisions:

a) An overview of the transaction price, deal currency and deal structure;
b) Representations and warranties and a related disclosure schedule in which parties provide information and allocate risk;
c) Pre-closing agreements such as covenants which are promises about what actions the buyer will take in order to complete the deal, and how they will be restricted until the deal is completed;
d) Closing conditions which are events that must occur before the two companies are obliged or permitted to complete the deal;
e) "Go-Shopping" provisions that prevent the target from actively seeking or assisting potential topping bidders.
f) Termination/walkaway provisions;
g) Earnouts provisions that guarantee the seller will obtain additional compensation in the future if the business achieves certain financial goals, which are usually stated as a percentage of gross sales or earnings;
h) Indemnities in case of adverse changes:
   - De minimis: "when the value of the indemnification arising from every single liability is equal or less than [EUR]";

- Absolute exemption: "no indemnification is due until the total sum due (without considering the de minimis), reaches [EUR], considering that when the exemption threshold is passed, the seller is obliged to reimburse only the difference";
- Relative exemption: "when the exemption threshold is passed, the seller is obliged to reimburse the entire amount of the loss incurred";
- Cap: "the total amount due from the Seller will not be greater than [%] of the selling price."

When the contract is fully negotiated, the deal is presented to the target's board of directors for approval.

c. Fairness Opinion, Acceptance of Board Approval, and Execution of the Definitive Agreement

In response to a proposed offer, the target's board of directors typically requires a fairness opinion to be rendered before making a recommendation on whether to accept the offer and approve the execution of a definitive agreement. As its name implies, a fairness opinion is simply an opinion from an external party (usually from another investment bank or M&A advisory boutique) on the "fairness" of the consideration offered in a transaction.

If the seller's board of directors votes and approves the deal, the deal is announced publicly, and the definitive agreement is executed by the buyer and seller. In order to close the deal, the buyer and the seller still need to accomplish a variety of tasks such as getting shareholder approval (if needed), regulatory clearance, and potential financing. (If minorities are represented on the Board, then an independent fairness opinion is also required to protect their position.)

9.4.2.5 Closing

As mentioned above, the closing of an M&A transaction is governed by the definitive SPA that sets forth the parties' obligations and commitments between the signing of the contract and the closing of the deal. For example, it clearly defines which party is responsible for seeking regulatory approval and addresses possible antitrust problems. At this point, the two parties need to:

a) obtain regulatory approval;
b) obtain shareholder approval;
c) obtain financing.

a. Obtain Regulatory Approval

The need to obtain regulatory approvals depends on the size of the transaction. However, the definition of "size" differs among countries. In the United States, the "size" of the transaction refers to the pro-forma market share of the combined companies. If the deal is sizable, the U.S. corporations will have to file respective notifications and report forms with the Federal Trade Commission (FTC) and Antitrust Division of the Department of Justice (DOJ). This system based on market shares is also applied in Spain, but in France and Italy, the size of the transaction is established by looking at the pro-forma revenues (the sum of the merged companies' revenues). In Italy, every merger requires the approval of the antitrust regulators if both the following conditions are fulfilled:[11]

a) aggregate turnover in Italy of all undertakings involved is above **€ 504 million**, and
b) individual aggregate turnover in Italy of at least one of the two parties involved in the transaction is above **€ 31 million.**

An important point to mention is that even for a local M&A transaction (merger between two companies in the same country), the parties may require the approval of foreign regulatory authorities such as the European Commission (Europe) if the latter have significant operations in foreign markets. Therefore, depending on the international nature and the size of the transaction, obtaining the necessary approvals may span for several months, and in some cases regulators may require the divestiture of some operations (**Box 9.2**).

Box 9.2 Regulatory Approval of Anheuser-Busch InBev's Acquisition of SABMiller

In 2015, Anheuser-Busch InBev decided to acquire SABMiller for more than $100bn, creating a combined entity that would hold 30% of worldwide beer sales. When the deal was announced, the companies made it clear that they intended to engage in sufficient divestitures to obtain clearance from the numerous national regulatory bodies that oversee antitrust rules in their markets. The companies revealed plans in which SABMiller would sell not only its participation in MillerCoors to the market, but also SABMiller's 49% stake in the joint venture with China's best-selling brand of beer "Snow" to the state-backed China Resources Beer Company for $1.6bn. However, because of regulatory uncertainties, it was unclear upon the announcement whether the transaction would close. The complex clearance process meant that the deal would take at least nine months after signing to complete – significantly longer than the typical M&A process – and during this time economic or political events could have affected the individual companies' respective valuations or the combined company's overall strategy.

Due to the antitrust uncertainty, SABMiller negotiated to include a provision in the definitive agreement in which in case Anheuser-Busch InBev failed to obtain regulatory approval, it would have to pay $3bn in cash to SABMiller.

[11] With effect from 23 March 2020, the Italian Competition Authority has approved the new turnover thresholds beyond which prior notification of mergers becomes mandatory (Section 16(1) of Law No. 287 of 10 October 1990).

b. Obtain Shareholder Approval

In addition to obtaining regulatory approval, in some cases the seller and/or buyer need to obtain the approval of their own shareholders. To do so, a formal shareholders' meeting is organized in which shareholders will vote on whether to approve or reject the proposed transaction. Prior to this meeting, for listed companies, a "proxy statement" is distributed to shareholders. The proxy statement contains:

a) a summary of the terms of the transaction;
b) some background information;
c) the recommendation of the Board;
d) the fairness opinion statement(s);
e) a summary of the financials and pro-forma data;
f) the definitive SPA.

Note that the buyer may also need to obtain shareholder approval if and only if stock is being offered as a form of consideration. For example NYSE and NASDAQ rules in the US require a buyer shareholder vote if the deal will result in the issuance (actual or potential) of shares constituting 20% or more of the pre-deal outstanding shares or voting power.

c. Financing & Closing

Along with obtaining all the necessary approvals and consents as defined in the definitive agreement, the buyer proceeds to source the necessary capital to fund and close the transaction. The timing of this financing process can be fast if a group of underwriting banks is involved; in case of take-out in the debt or equity market, the banks provide a bridge so that the company does not need to wait for the right market window.

When funds are obtained, the buyer will channel those funds to the seller in accordance with the process mentioned in the definitive SPA (deferred payment bullet) and the deal is finally closed.

9.4.3 Negotiated deals

Even though auctions have become increasingly prevalent with the surge of Private Equity Funds that seek to maximize their return on investment and therefore run broad auctions to maximize the exit multiple of their assets, a substantial number of mergers and acquisitions are conducted throughout "negotiated transactions," especially among strategic buyers. Although "negotiated transactions" are often initiated in the case of a buy-side mandate (a buyer looking for targets in order to grow its business), the process can also be initiated by a seller.

In that case, in contrast to auctions, in a negotiated deal the seller will focus its efforts on discussing and negotiating with a single (or few) prospective buyer(s). Even though the seller might have less leverage compared to a broad auction due to the absence of a competitive environment, negotiated sales are still particularly compel-

Figure 9.6 The M&A Process Timeline (Negotiated Deal)

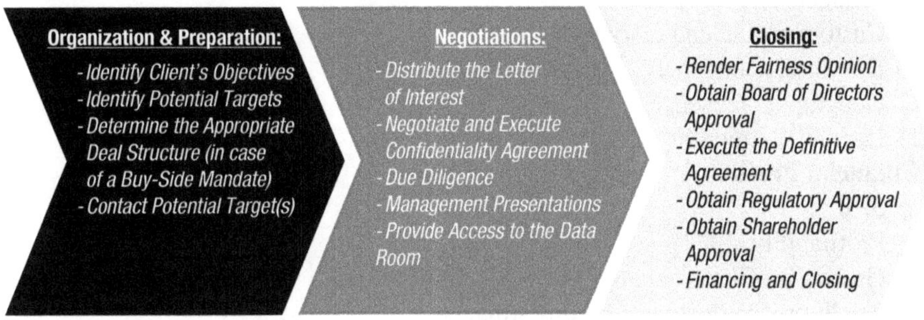

ling in situations involving a natural strategic buyer that fits strategically and could achieve clear synergies. Ideally, the seller could sell the target at a premium to market by capturing some of the estimated synergies while avoiding all the potential risks and disadvantages of an auction (business disruption, confidentiality breaches...). Furthermore, negotiated transactions are usually more flexible than auctions and can be customized, as there is only a single or limited number of buyers. However, depending on the nature of the buyer and seller, the size of the transaction, as well as the intensity of negotiations between the two parties, a negotiated deal can be just as intense and lengthy as an auction. During negotiations, opposite parties have to agree on key terms but before reaching an agreement; the buy-side and sell-side usually contest the provisions and terms proposed by the other party, which may require multiple interactions over an extended period of time.

However, as mentioned earlier, negotiated sales are most often initiated by buyers looking for external growth.

As you may notice from the timeline above (**Figure 9.6**), the negotiated sale process is fairly similar to that of an auction, but with a more compressed timetable. Therefore, in the following sections we will only discuss the steps that are unique to a Negotiated Sale:

a) identification of Potential Targets;
b) the distribution of the Letter of Intent.

a. Identify Potential Targets

After having identified its client's objectives, as the advisor does when identifying the buyers' universe, the mandated investment bank should identify potential targets (in the case of a buy-side mandate). To the same extent, the identification of targets essentially depends on whether the investment bank has set out the client's business objectives and growth strategy in a clear, rational, and data-oriented way. If the investment bank has a crystal-clear understanding of its client's objectives, it can start profiling the ideal candidate by defining the following criteria:

1. **Business Profile**
   a) Industry or industry segment in which the target operates
   b) Products and services
   c) Customers and end markets
   d) Distribution channels
   e) Geographic presence
   f) Particular strengths
2. **Financial Profile**
   a) Size
   b) Profitability
   c) Growth profile
   d) Credit profile (leverage, credit rating, etc.)
3. **Transaction Considerations**
   a) Preferred consideration (cash, stock or mix)
   b) Approximate value/market price.

Admittedly, it is very unlikely that a single dream candidate will be clearly identified after having met all the following criteria. First of all, it might be possible that the ideal candidate does not exist, i.e., that no candidate satisfies all the above-mentioned criteria. Second, even though the ideal candidate might exist, it is very unlikely that its shareholders would be willing to sell at an affordable price.

In Negotiated Deals, the Client and the investment bank tend to focus on a limited number of counterparties (both for a sale and for an acquisition). In most of the cases, this is done for confidentiality reasons or because given the sector in which the company operates and its size, there are a limited number of potential buyers/targets. In other cases, the company might have already received offers for the sale.

Therefore, based on the client's strategy, investment bankers will have to weigh the importance of each of the above-mentioned characteristics in order to rank different candidates by attractiveness. However, it is not possible to assess the attractiveness of many potential targets. As a consequence, investment bankers will do a first "rough screening," by applying an unequivocal knockout criterion such as sector, size, or location to quickly reduce the number of companies to a manageable number. Usually, for simplicity of application, the criterion should be based on readily available data. On a buy-side mandate, such criteria could be, for example:

a) a price/earnings ratio not more than "x %" higher than ours (so that the deal can be accretive for the buyer);
b) a growth rate for the last five years of "y" per cent per annum, compounded annually;

This first screening will, of course, let through some bad deals and is also likely to eliminate some desirable deals, but when there is a large number of choices, an arbitrary method of elimination is better than none at all.

b. Determine the Appropriate Deal Structure

After having determined potential targets, the investment bank should decide on how to structure the transaction in order to fit with the client's objectives. In fact, how the transaction will be structured will impact:

a) the target shareholder's post-merger incentive in the success of the merger;
b) the liabilities assumed by the acquirer;
c) leverage;
d) the target's post-transaction existence.

In choosing the deal structure, the buyer has the choice between three common deal structures, that we will explore further later on in this chapter:

a) Sale of share: the acquirer takes control of the target by acquiring the stock held by the firm's shareholders;
b) Merger: the sellers tender their shares to the bidder and receive shares of the bidder in exchange;[12]
c) Asset Contribution: the acquirer purchases only a part of the target's assets with either cash or stock.

c. Distribute the Letter of Intent (LOI)

In a negotiated deal, after the "organisation & preparation" phase, the buyer may draft a letter of intent which describes the desired objectives and gives an overview of the proposed financial and operational aspects of the transaction. The LOI is an important step because it lays out the basics of the final deal:

1. Essential elements of the transaction
   - Transaction structure
   - Valuation range
   - Procedure (due diligence)
   - Potential exclusivity
   - Transaction timing
   - Conditions
2. Binding terms and provisions
   - Confidential obligations
   - Exclusivity obligation
   - Stand-still obligation if the target is listed: Provisions that govern how a bidder for a company can purchase, dispose of, or vote stock of the target company
   - Length
   - Penalty if the obligations are not met.

[12] For listed companies.

However, in negotiated deals, the letter of intent is not always issued. In fact, whether a letter of intent is issued or not depends on the type of negotiated deal. While in a transaction involving a public company an LOI is a required document, in transactions involving private companies, it is considered optional and is not always used in the deal process. However, most of the time dealmakers do draft a letter of intent, as they believe that the letter of intent plays a pivotal role in the early stages of deal negotiations. A letter of intent can be especially valuable in complex transactions where it is important for the parties to determine early in the negotiations whether they agree on the transaction's price and fundamental structure so that time and effort is not wasted in drafting lengthy documents. The exercise of drafting the letter can serve as a benchmark to assess whether the buyer and seller are working in the same direction and with the same end-goal in mind.

9.5 Structuring an M&A transaction

If you read financial newspapers such as The Wall Street Journal, Financial Times, etc., you may have already realized that there is virtually an infinite number of ways in which a corporate merger or acquisition may be structured. Investment bankers always innovate not to create the most complex structure, but rather to create a structure that fairly reflects the goals and objectives of the buyer and the seller. Naturally, not all of the objectives of each party will be met each time, as there will almost always be a degree of negotiation and compromise.

Moreover, despite their willingness to tailor a deal that would perfectly fit their clients' needs, investment bankers may be limited from a creative point of view because of different variables that impact the structure of deals, among which we can find:

a) **the nature of the bidder**; Strategic Buyers vs Financial Buyers;
b) **consideration paid to target's shareholders**: Cash, Stock or Mixed;
c) **the status of the target**: Public or Private;
d) **the approach**: Friendly or Hostile.

Nonetheless, to keep it simple, lecturers and practitioners often refers to three broad types of M&A structures, which can be subdivided into three very common subcategories known as:

1. Acquisitions:
   a) Acquisition of Assets;
   b) Stock Purchase;
   c) 338(h)(10)Elections (US deals);
2. Mergers;
3. Consolidations.

Figure 9.7 Acquisition of Assets

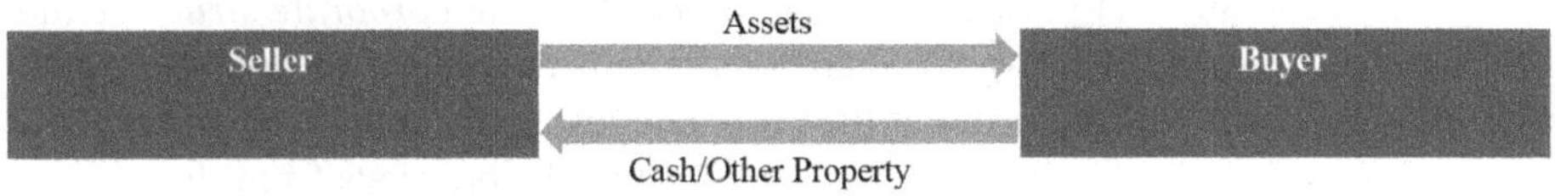

9.5.1 Acquisitions

An acquisition is the purchase of a majority or minority stake or of specific assets (Figure 9.7). Although often used interchangeably, an acquisition differs from a merger in that the acquiring company is typically significantly larger than the asset or entity being purchased. Acquisitions can take several forms:

a) Acquisition of Assets;
b) Acquisition of Equity, known as Stock Purchases;
c) 338(h)(10)Elections.

9.5.1.1 Acquisition of Assets

In an asset acquisition, the buyer purchases either all the assets or only a selection of the business's assets (in the case of a contribution of assets) and takes on only the liabilities directly associated with the assets selected. Under this structure, the target legally remains in existence post-transaction even if the acquirer acquires all the assets linked to the firm.

This structure has some advantages.

First, it can help alleviate the buyer's risk, especially when there may be substantial unknown contingent liabilities. In fact, as the bidder will only assume some of the target's liabilities, it will not be responsible for any liabilities not assumed by the acquirer (e.g. scandals, fraud, etc.).

Second, asset purchases provide *tax benefits* in the event that they can "step up" the tax basis of the target's acquired assets to fair market value, as reflected in the purchase price. In other words, the acquirer will be allowed to increase the value of the asset to its purchase price ("step up/write up") and deduct the tax expense that comes from the depreciation and amortisation of the stepped-up portion.

Finally, contrary to purchase of stock, the purchase of assets enables the acquirer to avoid the potential problem of having to *deal with minority shareholders*. Indeed, the acquirer will only purchase the assets and not the liabilities of the target, and so, the asset acquired will belong 100% to the acquirer.

Nonetheless, despite the fact that this acquisition is particularly advantageous for the bidder, it also has drawbacks especially for the target's shareholders.

First, one drawback for the bidder is that asset purchases tend to have higher transaction costs and longer processes than other type of acquisitions because the parties need to identify and transfer the assets and liabilities that are legally transferred to the acquirer.

Second, as in an asset purchase, the *selling entity is the corporate structure* (not the shareholders), and the target's shareholders will be subject to double taxation (**Box 9.3**); first, they will be taxed at the corporate level, and subsequently, they will be taxed on their capital gains once they will receive the proceeds from the transaction (**Figure 9.8**).

In the case of a minority stake acquisition, the buyer typically has limited governance powers (although with presence on the Board and some veto rights) so it relies on the management team and the experience of the majority shareholder. The purchase of minority stocks is often accompanied by a put/call option with the possibility to increase over time the percentage in the target at pre-agreed prices. In the case of minorities, the buyer does not consolidate the target.

Box 9.3 The double taxation issue in an Asset Acquisition deal

Suppose that Company A has agreed to acquire a specific division of Company B for 1,000 EUR. Currently, the book value of the asset acquired is 800 EUR. Therefore, a gain on the sale of 200 EUR is reported on the seller's income statement. However, as the selling entity is Company B (and not its shareholders) the sale of the asset is subject to taxation at the corporate level (e.g. 40% tax rate). Therefore, post-corporate tax the proceed received by the seller is: 200 EUR – (40% × 200) = 200 EUR – 80 EUR = 120 EUR. However, when the proceeds are distributed to the seller's shareholders, the latter will also be subject to taxation: shareholder taxes. In our example, 120 EUR will be distributed to shareholders and therefore, assuming a 20% tax rate at the shareholder level, the proceed net of taxes will be: 120 EUR – (20% × 120) = 120 EUR – 24 EUR = 96 EUR.

Figure 9.8 Example of double taxation issue in an Acquisition of Asset Deal

Purchase Price	**$ 1,000.00**
Asset Basis	**$ 800.00**
Gain on Sale	**$ 200.00**
Corporate Taxes (40%)	**$ 80.00**
Proceed After Corp. Taxes	**$ 120.00**
Shareholder Taxes (20%)	**$ 24.00**
Net Proceed	**$ 96.00**

9.5.1.2 Acquisition of Equity/Stock Purchase

An acquisition of equity is the purchase of an equity interest in a business entity. As its name implies, the main difference between an acquisition of assets and an acquisition of equity is that as the acquirer purchases the equity (or portion of it) of the target, it will not have the opportunity to acquire only some assets of the target, and therefore, it will have to acquire the entire business entity or minority stake, including the related assets and liabilities (**Figure 9.9**). Generally, academics consider stock purchases less favourable to bidders for two different reasons.

First, in the case the acquirer purchases all the equity of the target, post-transaction, the target will become a wholly-owned subsidiary of the acquirer and the target's shareholder will no longer have an interest in the firm. This exposes the bidder to:

a) "**Success Risk**": as post-transaction, the sellers will have no stake in the target, they will have a very low incentive for the transaction's success, and facilitating post-deal integration;
b) "**Liability Risk**": as the acquirer will have to assume all the target's past, present and future, known and unknown liabilities.

However, in order reduce those risk exposures, the acquirer can negotiate representations, warranties, indemnifications, and earnouts. For example, in order to incentivize shareholders to participate in the deal's success, the acquirer may negotiate some guarantees such as contingent variable payments linked to the future performance of the target and/or an earnout clause. Those guarantees will link the purchase price to the transaction and post-integration success, and therefore, the target's shareholders will give their heart and soul to contribute to its success in order to maximize the value of their investment.

Second, stock purchases are less appreciated by bidders, because compared to asset purchases they are less advantageous in fiscal terms. Indeed, while in an asset purchase the D&A expense linked to the write-up portion is tax deductible, in a stock acquisition, the difference needs to be further scrutinized. Here, the difference between the purchase price paid and the value of the entity as per its balance sheet cannot all be attributed to a "stepped up" asset, and may be attributed to other items, such as intangible assets or goodwill. While intangible assets can still be amortised,

Figure 9.9 Example of an Acquisition of Equity, also known as a Stock Purchase transaction

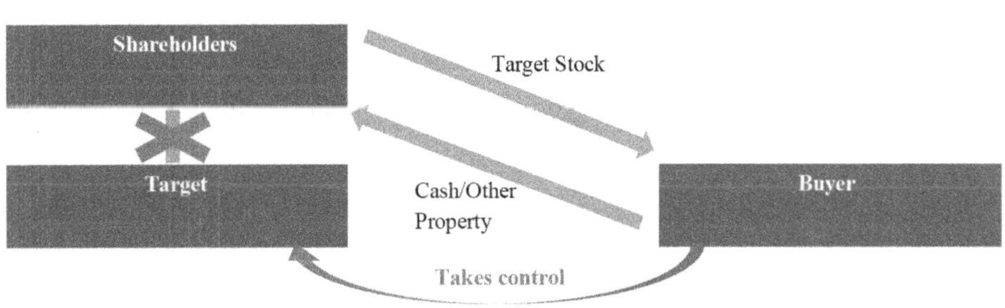

goodwill cannot, at least under US GAAP rules. Because goodwill cannot be amortised, it will not receive the same tax benefits as amortisable assets. Therefore, the main disadvantage of this transaction structure is that the bidder cannot benefit from the tax deduction linked to an asset write-up. However, this particular structure will be more beneficial than an asset contribution for the target's shareholders, as they will not be subject to the double taxation mentioned earlier. In fact, in that case the legal seller(s) are directly the shareholders, and not the corporation (**Box 9.4**). Therefore, shareholders will only be subject to taxation at the shareholder level (**Figure 9.10**).

Box 9.4 Taxation in a Stock Purchase deal

Take the same example indicated in the previous section. Just for reference, the key figures of the example were:

- Purchase Price: 1,000 EUR
- Asset Book Value: 800 EUR
- Equity Value: 800 EUR
- Corporate Tax Rate: 40%
- Shareholders Tax Rate: 20%

In the case of a stock purchase, the sellers will themselves be shareholders. Therefore, as the proceeds do not transit through the corporation, they will not be taxed at the corporate level. The only taxes paid would be those paid directly at shareholder level when the latter record their gains (immediately in the case of a cash deal or when the bidder's shares are sold on the market in the case of a stock deal).

Figure 9.10 Example of simple taxation in an Acquisition of Equity

Purchase Price	**$ 1,000.00**
Asset Basis	**$ 800.00**
Gain on Sale	**$ 200.00**
Corporate Taxes (40%)	
Proceed After Corp. Taxes	**$ 200.00**
Shareholder Taxes (20%)	**$ 40.00**
Net Proceed	**$ 160.00**

9.5.1.3 338(h)(10) Elections (US deals)[13]

To sum up, for a *buyer*, an *acquisition of assets* is generally preferred for several reasons. First, the buyer will not be subject to additional liabilities beyond those directly associated with the assets, and second, the buyer can receive the tax benefits of an asset "step-up."

However, for a seller, an acquisition of 100% of the equity is generally preferred, as the entire business, including all its liabilities, is sold and its shareholders can avoid the double-taxation they face in asset purchases.

Therefore, the "338(h)(10) election" can be considered as a "best of both worlds" scenario, allowing the buyer to record a stock purchase as an asset acquisition in which the buyer can still record the asset "step-up." Section 338(h)(10) election has historically been available to buyers of subsidiaries only, but is now permitted in acquisitions of S corporations (corporations in which earnings are passed on directly to shareholders and therefore not taxed at a corporate level). Thus, an S corporation acquisition can be set up as a stock purchase, but it can be treated as an asset purchase followed by a liquidation of the S corporation for tax purposes.

9.5.2 Mergers

A merger is the combination of two or more business entities that are typically similar in size and in which only one entity remains. In other words, if Company A merges with Company B, then Company A will cease to exist, and all its asset and liabilities would be transferred to Company B (**Figure 9.11**).

Figure 9.11 Example of a "Merger" transaction (e.g., Uniorcdit and Hvb Bank acquisition of Hypovereinsbank, now member of Unicredit)

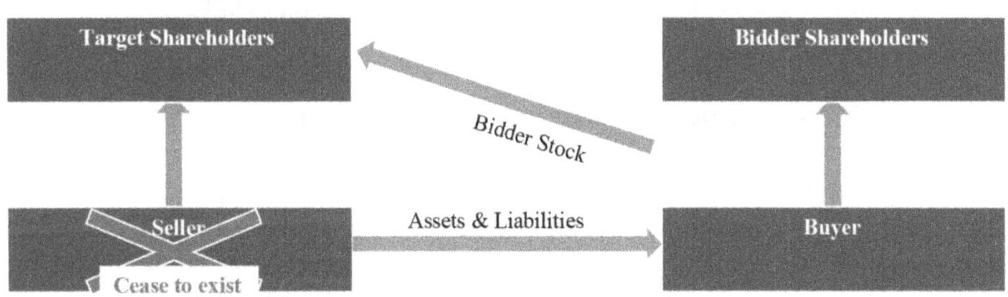

[13] "Section 338(h)(10) Election is an election to treat a stock acquisition of the target corporation generally as an asset acquisition for US federal income tax purposes. A buyer may want to make this election if it would receive a stepped-up basis in the target corporation's assets (i.e., if the buyer's cost basis in target's assets would exceed the carryover basis it would otherwise take in a stock acquisition)," Thomson Reuters Glossary.

This type of M&A structure requires the approval of both the bidder's and the seller's shareholders' as the target's shareholders will need to approve the extinction of their legal entity and the bidder's shareholders will need to approve the issuance of additional shares that will be issued to the target's shareholders at the time of the combination. Those shares will be issued to the target's shareholders in exchange for the target's shares and the number of shares received by the target's shareholders for every share held will depend on the so-called "exchange ratio," which itself depends on the "relative weight" and the number of shares of the bidder and the seller.

$$\textit{Exchange Ratio} = \textit{Relative Weight} \times \textit{Bidder/Target shares ratio} = \\ = \frac{\textit{Target Equity Value}}{\textit{Bidder Equity Value}} \times \frac{\#\ \textit{Bidder shares}}{\#\ \textit{Target shares}}$$

The main advantage of this deal structure is that it is relatively safer than any other M&A structure. In fact, as the target's shares are exchanged against the bidder's shares, and thus no debt is raised to afford the purchase price, the financial risk is minimized, the operational risk is shared by the bidder and seller, and the shareholders still own part of the broader company and therefore may benefit from the potential upsides, such as the impact of synergies generated by the merger.[14]

9.5.3 Consolidations

Similarly to mergers, consolidations are combinations of more than one business entity. However, what differentiates combinations from mergers is that in combinations the business entities are merged into an entirely new entity. As a consequence, the former entities transfer all their assets and liabilities to the new entity, and they cease to exist legally. The new entity will then issue newly-created shares to shareholders of the combined entities. As all entities cease to exist, combinations require the approval of a majority (usually two-thirds) of the shareholders of every entity (**Figure 9.12**).

9.5.4 The different elements impacting deal structuring

As already introduced earlier, a number of variables limit the possibility of how M&A deals may be structured. In fact, depending on (i) the nature of the bidder (strategic buyer vs financial sponsor), (ii) the consideration that can be offered by the acquirer (cash vs stock), (iii) the status of the bidder and the target (private vs public), and (iv) the way the bidder has approached the target, investment bankers will try to tailor a deal structure that would satisfy the clients' needs and expectations as much as possible while dealing with the restrictions imposed by those variables.

---

[14] In certain cases, however, debt is still required to back up existing lines (in the case of change of control clauses or breach of covenants that need to be waived) or to refinance the debt.

Figure 9.12 Example of a "Consolidation" transaction (E.G. Bpu Banca, Banca Lombarda)

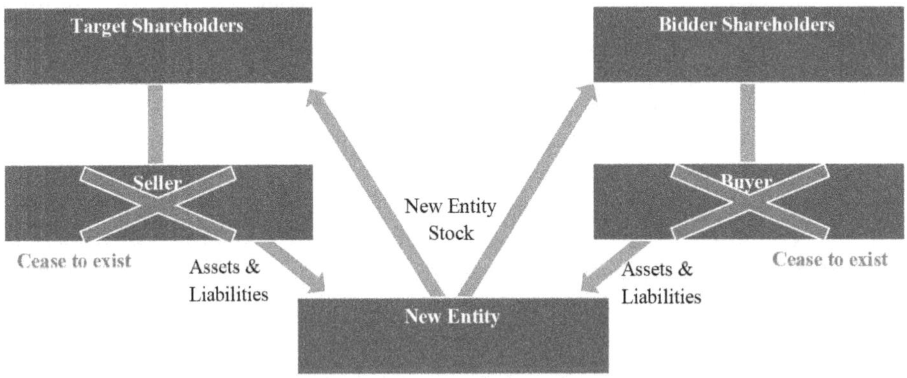

9.5.4.1 *The Impact Of The Bidder's Nature On The Deal Structure*

First of all, in M&A deals, investment bankers may be restricted to a limited number of deal structures because the buyer is a financial sponsor. In fact, in M&A deals, bidders are identified as either Strategic Buyers or Financial Buyers. Those two categories of bidders are clearly distinguished, as their reasons for acquiring companies usually differ significantly, as do the financing, structure, and target prices of their acquisitions.

On the one hand, Strategic Buyers are more often companies that operate in the same industry as the target (or perhaps a related or adjacent one) and are interested in acquiring a company that would fit in their long-term business plans and corporate strategy. Their interest may include a vertical expansion (toward customers or suppliers), horizontal expansion (expansion into new geographies, markets, product lines), elimination of competition (acquiring a competitor), development of economies of scale and scope, and/or an enhancement of some of its own weaknesses (technology, marketing, distribution, research and development, etc.). Strategic buyers are often able to pay relatively high multiples for a particular target because they can implement synergies that will make the combined enterprise more valuable than the sum of the two companies alone. In other words, as opposed to financial buyers, strategic buyers are often willing to pay a price higher than the current market value, as they can consider part of the estimated synergies.

Strategic Buyer Acquisition Price = Market Value of the Target + Part of the Estimated Synergies

On the other hand, Financial Buyers such as private equity firms and hedge funds are generally classified as investors interested in the return they can achieve from buying and subsequently selling a business. They usually target returns greater than 20% and try to achieve such returns by acquiring businesses with strong cash flows, maximizing leverage and realistic future exit opportunities, growing their acquisitions' cash flows through different ways such as revenue enhancement, expense reductions, or by creating economies of scale. Their goal is to improve the financial performance of the company in a relatively short period of time (usually 3 to 5 years) and re-sell the company at a price that is higher than the one at which they acquired it. The different options for selling the companies in their portfolios are known as exit opportunities. The most common exit opportunities are:

a) **IPOs** (**Initial Public Offerings**) where businesses are "taken public," hopefully at a higher earnings multiple than paid at acquisition.
b) **Selling to a Strategic Buyer** such as corporates, competitors, conglomerates, etc. This is the preferred option, as the latter are often able to afford higher prices due to the implementation of synergies.
c) **Secondary Buyouts** in which the exited companies are sold to other Financial Buyers.

From this brief introduction on how Financial Sponsors operate, it is obvious that the number of ways those financial actors can structure their transactions is limited.

9.5.4.2 The Impact Of Financing On Deal Structures

Secondly, after having identified the nature of the bidder, the investment bank should determine how the financing may be able to impact the deal structure.

For reference, M&A transactions can usually be financed in three different ways:

a) **Cash on hand**: the acquisition is financed by using the acquirer's excess of available cash;
b) **Debt Financing**: the acquisition is financed by raising additional debt such as loans, bonds, etc.;
c) **Equity Financing**: the acquisition is financed by raising equity (e.g. Rights issue) or by distributing outstanding shares directly to the target's shareholders.

The choice between those financing solutions or a combination of them will depend not only on the availability of sufficient funds (cash on hand), the state of capital markets, and the macroeconomic environment, but also on the preferences of both the bidder and the target's shareholders. In fact, the form of financing will determine the form of consideration that will be paid to the target's shareholders, and therefore, it is important that both parties agree on the type of consideration before raising the necessary financing. However, the parties may have conflicting interests with regards to the financing solutions.

On the one hand, the bidder will try to negotiate with the target's shareholders in order to opt for the form of financing that would have the most positive impact on

M&A consequences, such as the accretion (or lower dilution) of pro-forma Earnings Per Shares (EPS), and on pro-forma credit statistics (impacting the cost of financing). As we will see later on, cash on hand and debt are less expensive and therefore result in more accretive transactions, but they also reduce the firms' flexibility and might negatively impact the rating assessment and thus the cost of financing.

On the other hand, the target's shareholders will prefer one form of financing to another depending on whether they want to retain an interest (some ownership) in the combined entity. In fact, if the target's shareholders are worried about the performance of the firm post-transaction and therefore do not want to be exposed to the acquirer's stock price, they will negotiate with the bidder in order to structure the transaction as an all-cash deal in which they will exchange their shares for cash. However, if they want to benefit from the potential upside of the acquirer's stock price (e.g. the implementation of synergies), they will try to retain a certain stake in the new entity by demanding a stock-for-stock transaction (exchange their shares against shares of the acquirer). In some cases, deals can be executed as a mix of cash and stock (mainly for listed companies).

a. Cash on Hand Financing

The use of cash on hand pertains only to strategic buyers that employ excess cash on their balance sheet to fund acquisitions, such as when financial sponsors issuing debt as part of their strategy to foster a return on investment. Nominally, cash on hand is the cheaper form of financing for strategic buyers, as its cost is simply the foregone interest income earned on cash, which is minimal in a low-interest rate environment. However, in practice, companies tend to view use of cash on hand in terms of the opportunity cost of raising external debt, as cash can theoretically be used to repay existing debt or to fund working capital/capex needs. Moreover, having sufficient cash reserves has become a condition sine qua non for both debt and equity markets. From a credit perspective, we can therefore consider that raising new debt and using excess cash are equivalent, although contracting new debt increases the firm's leverage as well as its interest expenses. Typically, companies tend to use a portion of excess cash if available (leaving a buffer) and finance the rest with debt, trying to keep total leverage under control.

b. Debt Financing

Debt financing refers to the issuance of new debt such as term loans or bonds to partially or fully fund an M&A transaction. The cost of debt for a particular strategic or financial buyer depends on the party's credit profile, which includes many elements such as the firms' leverage ratio, credit track record, sector, size, etc. The strong advantage of debt is that interest payments are tax deductible, which effectively reduces the real cost of debt. However, while debt is cheaper than equity, acquirers are constrained with regard to the amount of debt they can contract. In fact, debt reduces the firm's flexibility, as in some cases (mainly bank financing) there is an amortisation schedule and financial covenants. Moreover, credit rating agencies also limit the amount of debt that each firm can contract; if they find that the leverage risk of a particular firm is too high, they will downgrade the firm's credit rating, increasing the latter's cost of debt.[15] Therefore, companies with public ratings, as well as those without credit ratings, put a lot of emphasis on trying to maintain their credit standing, in order to minimize their cost of financing.

c. Equity Financing

Equity financing refers to a company's use of its stock as acquisition currency. An acquirer can either offer its own stock directly to target shareholders, and the selling shareholders join the purchasing shareholders as owners of the acquiring company, or it can offer the cash proceeds from an equity offering. Even though equity is much more expensive than debt financing, it is a mainstay of M&A financing particularly for large-scale public transactions. In fact, the strong advantage of equity financing is that it provides issuers with greater flexibility. However, using equity as a form of financing is expensive and for shareholders it may add uncertainty and time before the deal closes; for example, when the acquiring company issues more than a certain percentage of its outstanding shares, it will need to obtain the approval from its own shareholders. Therefore, determining the right financing structure (% of debt vs % of equity) is essential not only to optimize the firm's capital structure, leverage ratio, etc., but also to obtain approval from the shareholders. If they vote against the capital increase, the deal will not move forward unless the firm is able to opt for another financing structure which requires more time and effort. In the even of needing to raise equity, a bridge with banks should be established to accelerate the timing of the execution. In such a case, the banks assess the feasibility of the transaction and have an equity commitment letter as a backup (either from the existing shareholders or the consortium of banks that will be involved in the equity – typically the banks are the same as the ones providing the bridge).

Coming back to our initial point, it is again fairly straightforward to understand how financing constraints may impact an M&A deal structure. On the one hand, despite the greater flexibility, shareholders often (but not always) prefer to avoid issuing additional shares because of the dilutive impact of issuing new equity. On the other hand, lenders also limit the amount of debt that can be raised by a specific company in order to keep the leverage ratio below certain thresholds to avoid the risk of default in the future. This clearly explains why managers need to plainly define the optimal financing structure before moving forward with the deal execution.

9.5.4.3 How The Consideration Offered Can Impact M&A Structures

In line with the two above-mentioned variables that may impact the structuring of an M&A transaction, the consideration that can be offered to the target's shareholders also certainly impacts the deal structure. In fact, if a bidder is unwilling to co-exist with the target's shareholders or simply does not want to issue shares, then it will

[15] The same occurs for unrated companies, since banks have internal scoring systems based also on leverage ratios.

opt for a cash transaction, eliminating the possibility to structure the deal as a merger, a consolidation, or any type of stock deal. Similarly, if the seller is willing to secure the economic consideration, it will negotiate for a cash deal, which again eliminates the possibility to structure the deal as a merger, a consolidation, or any type of stock deal. Note that obviously, the consideration offered to the target's shareholders in an M&A deal also depends on the type of financing chosen by the acquirer, which itself already impacts the structuring of a deal.

However, as the structuring of a deal depends on the bidder's and target's willingness to distribute/receive a certain consideration, it is important to understand the different types of considerations that can be used in M&A deals and the different advantages and drawbacks of each option.

In that context, we can simply state that the consideration that can be offered to the target's shareholders are:

a) **Cash**: in an all-cash deal the bidder pays the seller(s) in cash;
b) **Equity**: in a stock-swap or a merger, the bidder pays the seller(s) with its own shares, in exchange for the target's shares;
c) **Mixed**: in some deals, the bidder may decide to pay the seller(s) with a mix of cash and its own shares.

All-cash deals are the most common type of consideration offered in M&A deals, with the exception of large-caps, that are very difficult to finance with cash. The popularity of this consideration is mainly due to three different reasons.

First, debt and cash on hand are cheaper than equity, and therefore, result in more accretive transactions.

Second, even though the use of cash reserves decreases financial flexibility, it allows the acquiring shareholders to expel target shareholders from the structure, and therefore results in a governance advantage. The acquirer will be able to implement a defined strategy without having to deal with the opinions of the minority shareholders.

Finally, even though we can clearly see from the two points above that cash transactions benefit acquirers, it is also the type of consideration that is most often preferred by the target's shareholders, as it eliminates the economic risk linked to the deal's value. Indeed, in an all-cash transaction, the economic consideration that shareholders will receive is fixed and certain. Upon the deal's conclusion, the target's shareholders know that they will receive $X in exchange for each share tendered to the bidder.

This is not the case in stock transactions, in which the seller is exposed to the performance of the bidder's share price. If that price decreases after the transaction, the target's shareholder will still own the same amount of the acquirer's stock, but it will have lost part of its value.

However, the strong advantage of stock transactions is that they offer the seller certain tax benefits that cash transactions do not provide; they enable shareholders to defer the capital gain, and thus defer the tax payments.

Furthermore, as we mentioned previously, the target's shareholders may sometimes find stock compensation more attractive than cash offers provided that the acquirer's shares are perceived to have upside potential (potentially thanks to the implementation of the deal's estimated synergies). However, most of the time, the selling shareholders are suspicious about stock transactions, as according to the signalling theory, they imply that the bidder's stock is overvalued. In fact, in most stock transactions, the seller requests extra compensation in order to bear the risk of accepting the bidder's stock as consideration.

Nonetheless, remember that many transactions are executed with a mixed method of payment (e.g. Facebook and WhatsApp[16]) that allow for mitigating the pros and cons of all-cash and all-stock payments.

In a nutshell, the main points to retain from this paragraph on M&A consideration are the three essential factors that influence the chosen methods of payment, and subsequently the deal's structure:

a) Sharing of risk among the acquirer and target shareholders;
b) Signalling by the acquiring firm;
c) Governance.

9.5.4.4 How The Status Of The Target/Bidder May Impact Deal Structure

Another element that contributes to the diversity of M&A transactions while restricting the flexibility of deal structuring is the status of the target and the bidder prior to the deal announcement. There are two different possible types of status:

a) **Private**: the target/bidder is private, not listed on the public markets, and
b) **Public**: the target/bidder is publicly listed on stock markets and their shares can be purchased in the open market.

In the case of a private target, the status of the target adds additional risk for the bidder, and thus not only impacts how the deal may be structured, but more broadly, the overall feasibility of the deal. In fact, the main difference between M&A deals involving either a private or a public target is that private companies have less pressure to publish and disclose their financial information to the market. As a consequence, the bidder will bear the risk of acquiring a company that could overstate its performance in order to sell its assets at a higher value. However, in reality, bidders do not really bear the risk, as they tend to discount the target's value in order to take into account this very specific risk. Therefore, depending on how far in advance

[16] "Facebook Inc will buy fast-growing mobile-messaging startup WhatsApp for $19 billion in cash and stock, as the world's largest social network looks for ways to boost its popularity, especially among a younger crowd," Reuters, 19 February 2014.

the seller is planning, if it really wants to structure the deal properly, having an audit by a reputable accounting firm can be of enormous benefit. An audit by a third party can reduce the perceived risk of the financial results for an acquirer, presenting them as part of the process; by lowering the perceived risk, the seller maximizes its valuation.

However, differences in M&A deals are not only due to the target's status, but also the bidder's, which in this case has a tremendous impact on the deal's structure. Indeed, the main differences between deals involving either a public or a private bidder will concern the consideration offered. In fact, it is most often a losing battle to try to convince a seller to take stock in another private company as consideration for the transaction; it overlooks a common key driver of the sale process: liquidity. Therefore, if the bidder is private, then it has very little chance of concluding a stock transaction such as a merger, consolidation, etc.

9.5.4.5 How The Acquisition Approach May Impact Deal Structure

Finally, the last variable that impacts the structure of M&A transactions is the way the target has been approached by the bidder and whether the target's management team is receptive to the transaction or not.

If an acquisition is accomplished in agreement with the target company's management and board of directors, or if the management seeks the acquisition, the transaction is what practitioners refer to as a "Friendly Acquisition." In that case, a public offer of stock or cash is made by the acquiring firm, and the board of the target firm will publicly approve the terms.

However, sometimes acquisitions are accomplished without the agreement of the target company's management or board of directors, or even against their will. In that case, the acquisition is a Hostile Takeover and is conducted through other means to obtain acquisition approval, such as dealing directly with the company's shareholders. This type of approach is very risky from the bidder's perspective, as the latter will not have access to inside information, therefore rendering the valuation stage much more difficult and imprecise. In fact, being in conflict with the target, the bidder will not have the opportunity to conduct due diligence and therefore will take substantial risks to conclude the transaction. Target companies can also put up preventative antitakeover measures, which are sort of "walls" to discourage raiders from making hostile bids, and active takeover defences, which come into play once the hostile bid is made and are designed to prevent the bid from being successful.[17]

[17] Examples of preventative antitakeover measures are poison pills and corporate charter amendments. Poison pills often come in two forms: the flip-in and flip-over strategies. Flip-in strategies work by flooding the market with new shares of the target company's stock in order to dilute the equity interest of the hostile acquirer and make it harder to pursue the takeover. A flip-over poison pill strategy allows stockholders of the target company to purchase the shares of the acquiring company at a deeply discounted price if the hostile takeover attempt is successful. Corporate charter amendments make it more difficult for the acquirer to complete the acquisition, for example requiring a substantial majority

The most common ways to solicit support from shareholders of public corporations without direct approval from the company management are:

a) Tender offer: the bidder makes a public offer at a fixed price above the current market price directly to the target's shareholders;
b) Proxy fight: the bidder tries to persuade enough shareholders, usually a simple majority, to replace the management with new management which will approve the takeover;
c) "Creeping tender offer": Quietly purchasing enough stock on the open market to effect a change in management.

9.6 M&A valuation

9.6.1 What does it take to make M&A pay?

A variety of studies have focused on what are empirically identified as being the key success factors for M&As. In particular, Leaman et al. (2004) and Calipha, Tarba and Brock (2010), conducted comprehensive research on the topic by bringing together the most relevant studies up to that time and identified two of the most significant drivers of M&A success: price and strategic fit (Calipha et al., 2010).

In terms of price, it is essential to have a clear understanding of the fair value of the target in order to maximize the value coming from the transaction (Severson, 1989; Calipha et al., 2010). On the other side, certain studies such as Kusewitt (1985) put to question the real effect of such factors on deal success, finding no empirical link between the two elements. In favour of Calipha et al. (2010), Leaman et al., 2004 studied how much variable valuations affect the success rate of deals. According to their results, targets that have a higher valuation (indicated by a higher multiple) show higher performance, even if this is only applicable to a longer-term horizon.

As for the second factor, i.e. the strategic fit, Leaman et al. (2004) empirically tested how pivotal relatedness in diversification is to M&A success. This was also confirmed by Walker (2000), Wansley, Lane and Young (1983), and many other studies that found a positive relationship between related diversification and returns. In DeLong (2001), transaction relatedness between the two parties in terms of business and geographical area accounted for 2-3% value accretion compared to other types of M&As. With respect to geographical relatedness, Harris and Ravenscraft (1991) conducted a study on US targets purchased by foreign bidders, with the evidence

(i.e. 90%) of the shares to vote to approve for the merger (a so-called "***supermajority amendment***") or by implementing changes in the corporate governance rules of the target that therefore decrease the likelihood of a hostile takeover. There is also a third measure that is often used, called a golden parachute, which can be embedded in the employment contract of the target's top management and that provides for large benefits to be paid to them if a hostile takeover succeeds and the target management is removed.

indicating that cross-border deals led to statistically significant higher gains (cross border M&A pays more).

In conclusion, it seems clear that even if M&A is a complex exercise whose outcomes are difficult to predict exactly, parties may and should take into account the factors described above when targeting a firm in order to improve the chances of success of the transaction. Moreover, financial performance and geographical location might affect the price determination dynamics. In the next section, we will see how to accurately evaluate a target and the different pitfalls to avoid when conducting such a difficult task.

The ultimate rationale of a merger or an acquisition should be to bring together two or more companies in order to create further value for shareholders with respect to the previous situation (Box 9.5). Therefore, it is very important to evaluate both companies as single entities, but especially to assess the value of the combined firm and the synergies achievable.

Box 9.5 Does M&A create value?

BOX: WHEN DO M&As CREATE VALUE?

Many deals that are supposed to create great value for a firm end up destroying value. Why?

Acquisitions are complex and difficult to execute and manage successfully. In addition, in mergers and acquisitions, the buyer always pays a premium to the shareholders of the target company. It is precisely because this premium is usually too high (overpaid) that subsequent mergers and acquisitions will destroy value.

Valuation plays a key role in explaining whether the merger will create value. The value of a company depends not only on the cash flows it provides to investors, but also on the timing and risks of these cash flows. Creating value for the buyer means that at least some of the proceeds from the transaction have to be retained by the shareholders of the acquiring company.

Value (A+B) > V(A) + V(B)

- **Value (A+B)** → value of the combined firms
- **V (A)** → stand-alone value of A
- **V (B)** → stand-alone value of firm B

The process of valuation in the context of M&As can be very complicated because it is subject to high levels of information asymmetry (between the bidder, the target, and the market) and uncertainty over the future concretization of the forecasted plans. In fact, before the completion of the deal, the bidder and the target firms pursue different interests and this situation gives rise to a certain degree of information asymmetry. With regard to the valuation of the target company, the two parties naturally have conflicting views: on the one hand, the selling company will push for a high valuation so as to maximize the price it will get, while on the other hand, the acquiring company will try to keep the acquisition price as low as possible in order to make a good buy and not to overpay. Moreover, since there are no observable market prices for the combined entity yet, the valuation has to rely heavily on accurate assumptions and forecasts. Given the critical nature of the situation, in most cases investment banks or external specialists step in and assist the acquiring firm's management, either by conducting the valuation or providing a fairness opinion concerning the terms of the deal so as to increase the odds of reaching a fair valuation for both parties.

Concerning the actual valuation, Damodaran (2001) proposes splitting the process into three different steps:

a) first, the valuation of the target as a separate entity at the status quo;
b) second, the valuation of the target's corporate control;
c) and third, the valuation of the achievable synergies.

In the first step, the target company is valued "as is," or rather with the current financial structure, investment strategy, dividend policy, and all the other variables under management's control. Then, in the second step, the value of corporate control should be estimated. This sum represents the difference between the target's value under better management and the target's value under the current management (that is the value obtained in the previous valuation step). In the third and last step, the value of the potential synergies from the combination of the firms should be estimated. This value can be calculated in different ways according to the specific characteristics of the potential synergies identified.

9.6.2 The value of the target "as is"

Beyond the issues regarding information asymmetry and uncertainty, the valuation of a target company is further complicated by the fact that each entity is one of a kind. Consequently, no standard recipe or method for valuation can exist. Among the various valuation methods that will be considered below, the appraiser has to carefully select the most appropriate ones in relation to the nature of the target. Well-conducted due diligence can guide this choice.

Below we provide a brief list of the most cited and used valuation methods in M&As and their relative characteristics. In each of these methods, it is important to consider non-operating assets (i.e. cash and marketable securities, and portfolio investments in other companies' shares) separately from operating assets.

a. Book value method
The valuation of a company based on its accounting book values reflects the actual values of the assets (and liabilities) shown on its balance sheet. By its very nature, this method is focused on the past, as it considers what a company has accumulated so far and ignores future prospects and potential (Bruner, 2004). Moreover, it fails to consider intangible assets (i.e. brands, know-how) that most of the time represent a significant portion of a firm's value. For this reason, valuations based on book val-

ues are rarely used as the main method. Notable exceptions are cases involving holding and real estate companies; the assets of these types of firms are usually valued at market prices. Moreover, they do not possess significant intangible assets and their activities are fairly stable. Despite its flaws, the book value method represents a good way to investigate the balance sheet of a target company and assess the value of the single assets, which leads to even deeper knowledge about the target.

b. Liquidation value method

The liquidation value of a company represents the amount obtainable by its "assets sold separately less its liabilities and expenses incurred in liquidating the firm" (DePamphilis, 2011). This method is very seldom used, but it provides an indication of the minimum floor of the target company's enterprise value (Marren, 1993) and could be appropriate in the valuation of distressed firms (Bruner, 2004; DePamphilis, 2011).

c. Replacement costs method

In practical terms, the decision to undertake a merger or an acquisition can be the result of a "make-or-buy" decision for the acquiring firm. The replacement costs method estimates the investments that the target would incur to replace its assets, resources and capabilities. In other words this method estimates the cost of beginning the business from scratch. The main weakness of this method lies in the fact that it is very difficult for outsiders (but for insiders as well) to evaluate the replacement cost of intangible assets (Bruner, 2004). However, the calculation of the target's replacement costs can be a component of the fulfilment of due diligence requirements (Reed et al., 1999).

d. Market value method

In the case a target company's shares are publicly traded on a stock exchange, the target's equity value can be estimated at market prices by multiplying the number of shares by the share price. Then the market value of the net debt should be added to obtain the enterprise value. The firm value resulting from this method is usually used as a starting point to set the ultimate acquisition price, which will contain a premium over the current market price (Bruner, 2004). In fact, traded market prices reflect information available to the public, not private information which is known only to insiders or potential acquirers. Since this valuation method is based on public market prices, it can be adopted only in the event the target is listed on a stock exchange. Moreover, the reliability of this method is higher in the case the target's shares are actively traded on an efficient market in terms of public information availability (Bruner, 2004).

e. Comparables method: trading multiples

Comparable valuation methods are based on the assumption that multiples of comparable companies reflect the general market outlook and appeal of the specific industry and therefore also the target itself. Multiples of comparable companies can be inferred from the financial and business data of comparable listed companies. Multiples are usually ratios with the enterprise or the equity value (both at market prices) in the numerator and an income or business indicator as the denominator. The characteristics of the target firm and its related industry (i.e. cyclicality, value drivers, profitability) determine which multiples are to be applied.

Both valuation practitioners and researchers have repeatedly insisted on the fact that the choice of the comparable companies on which to base this valuation is of fundamental importance for a reliable and useful valuation benchmark (Marren, 1993; Bhojraj and Lee, 2002; Bruner, 2004; PwC, 2012). Beyond belonging to the same industry, it is indeed essential for the selected comparables and the target companies to share analogous value drivers and characteristics: growth, investment policy, geographic presence, financial structure, profitability, and so on. Obviously, it is impossible to find comparable firms that correspond to the target in every aspect. However, it is better to restrict the pool of comparable companies to few, but good elements (**Table 9.2**).

An advantage of this method is the possibility of applying it both with historical multiples (based on past data) and with prospective data (based on market forecasts). On the other hand, valuations based on comparable transactions have to face some (potential) limits: first, this method can be properly applied only in the presence of true comparables; second, it can be heavily influenced by differences in accounting practices (Marren, 1993; Bruner, 2004); and third, it can be distorted by temporary stock market over- or undervaluation, since it relies entirely on public market judgements and expectations (Reed et al., 1999; DePamphilis, 2011).

Table 9.2 Trading Multiples – Strengths and Weaknesses

Multiples	Strengths	Weaknesses
P/E Ratio between the market price of a company's stock and earnings per share. It is known as Price/Earnings per share (P/E).	– Simple to calculate, intuitive, linked to the actual return for shareholders; – Really represents the point of view of the equity investor.	– Profits can be volatile or negative in some cases; – Influenced by the management, and the company's financial and accounting policy.
EV/EBITDA Market multiple given by the ratio between the value of a company and the gross operating margin (EBITDA, Earnings before interest, taxes, depreciation and amortisation.	– Takes into account the profitability of the company; – Not affected by the company's budget policy; – Approximates the generation of cash flow (prior to the dynamics of working capital).	– Does not consider the underlying elements of EBITDA that could steal money and be recurring (e.g. Taxes).
EV/Sales Market multiple given by the ratio between the value of a company and its turnover.	– Sales cannot be negative, applicable in case of negative profitability.	– Does not take into account profitability; – Does not take into account the capital structure.

Source: Author's adaptation from "Evaluation Guide; Borsa Italiana S.p.A."

f. Comparables method: transaction multiples

Multiples of peer companies can also be found in past comparable transactions. The possibility of using this method depends on the existence of past comparable mergers or acquisitions. Indeed, the comment regarding the importance of the choice of comparables for trading multiples is valid also for transaction multiples (Table 9.3).

Differently from trading multiples, transaction multiples include a control premium and synergies, as they reflect prices that were paid in the context of change of control transactions (Marren, 1993; Bruner, 2004; DePamphilis, 2011). Another issue that has to be taken into account is that past acquisition prices were the result of a specific situation and period of time (Reed et al., 1999).

Table 9.3 **Industry-specific transaction multiples**

Sectors	Multiples	Rationale
Insurance	– Embedded Value (sum of the value of the income flow and the adjusted net equity of the company at market values) and Goodwill.	– Represents the *Appraisal* value and allows you to distinguish between profits from existing activities (Embedded Value) and future profits (Goodwill).
Airline Companies	– EV/EBITDAR.	– EBITDAR represents the gross operating margin before leasing fees for aircraft and allows a uniform representation between the various companies, regardless of the decision regarding the ownership/leasing of their own fleet (the "R" represents the costs incurred for the leasing); allows comparability between companies that own and lease fleets of airplanes.
Real Estate Finance Company	– NAV (Net Asset Value).	– Requires the identification of a sample of comparable companies and the calculation of the relative average discount compared to the NAV.
Power & Energy	– Multiple of physical drivers (EV/MWH, RAB, etc.).	– Multiples that place the value in relation to physical variables: for electricity companies, the installed capacity and the quantity of energy produced (measured respectively in MW, MWh or KW) are considered, while to evaluate electricity transmission or gas distribution companies the so-called RAB (Regulatory Asset Base) model is used, which represents the value of the corporate assets defined by the Authority.
TMT	– Multiple of users/clicks.	– Due to the high expected growth and negative profitability of start-ups, it makes it possible to consider the possibility of generating future income based on the company's subscribers/customers/users. Not tested on performance.

Source: Author's adaptation from "Evaluation Guide; Borsa Italiana S.p.A."

g. Discounted Cash Flow method

The discounted cash flow (DCF) method estimates the value of a company by discounting its forecasted future cash flows using the related cost of capital, which should approximate the risk involved. The DCF is a key tool for valuation purposes in M&A settings because it delivers a valuation reflecting the intrinsic value of the company in prospective (forward-looking) terms, which is exactly the focus of a potential acquirer. Furthermore, given the analytical insights this model requires regarding the company's fundamentals, the DCF is considered as the most robust valuation method in general. However, some weaknesses are present as well. First, this method is characterized by a considerably high level of difficulty in terms of both execution and comprehension. Second, a notable issue is represented by the assumptions that have to be made in the act of forecasting future cash flows. As a consequence, it is important to perform a number of sensitivity analyses on relevant value drivers that are able to significantly influence future cash flows and therefore the resulting value of the company (i.e. growth, terminal value, reinvestment rate, cost of capital). The value obtained through this valuation approach can sometimes diverge from external market valuations.[18]

Table 9.4 Comparison among DCF, Trading, and Transaction Multiples

Valuation Methodology	Description	Strengths	Weakness
DCF	– Present Value of future cash flows; – Equity Value vs Enterprise Value.	– Detailed and prospective analysis of the drivers of a company's value.	– Many Assumptions; – Requires extensive data analysis and simulation work.
Trading Multiples	– Based on multiples calculated as the ratio between stock market values and economic, equity, and financial performance of a selected sample of comparable companies.	– Among the simplest and most commonly used methodologies; – Easy to be presented; – Based on the market.	– Assumes the full efficiency of the financial market.
Transaction Multiples	– Based on multiples paid in similar M&A transactions carried out in the past.	– Easy to be presented. – Incorporates synergies and control premium.	– Potentially incompatible among transactions that have to be compared; – Subject to the cyclical nature of multiples paid in different market conditions.

Source: Author's adaptation from "Evaluation Guide; Borsa Italiana S.p.A."

[18] "For financial services/capital regulated businesses, the Dividend Discount Model ("DDM") is used." (R. Pambianco, 2020).

According to literature, the DCF and comparables methods are the most used for valuation in mergers and acquisition transactions (Bruner, 2004; DePamphilis, 2011). DCF is probably the most reliable approach to objectively value a target company and to obtain better insight on its future prospects, but it lacks simplicity and consideration of an external market perspective. The popularity of valuation methods based on trading and transaction comparables is given by two main factors: first, by their relative simplicity, and second, by the fact that they should reflect the external market valuation of the target firm, which is the natural complement of the internal valuation obtained through the DCF method.

Since the valuation process in the context of M&As is particularly complex, the two methods cited above, together with others, should be used to complement each other. The use of several approaches allows the appraiser to see the valuation process from different perspectives and to reach a final valuation which is comprehensive of all relevant factors.

9.6.3 The value of control

The value of control of a firm is generated by the belief by the acquirer's management that it would be able to run the target firm better than its current management. This value of control should, therefore, be inversely proportional to the perceived quality of that management and its capacity to maximize firm value. In other words, the value of control will be much greater for a poorly managed firm that operates at below optimum capacity than it will be for a well-managed firm. As a formula:

(I) Value of Control = Value of firm with restructuring (-) Value of firm with no-restructuring

This incremental value needs to be clearly distinguished from any form of synergies between the companies involved in the deal.[19] This is because this specific value represents the economic gains from potential changes to the way the target company is currently operating as a single entity; therefore, it is completely independent from the coupling of the two firms' resources and capabilities. As previously noted in the section concerning the reasons for M&As, the hubris hypothesis by Hambrick and Phyllis (1984) states that sometimes M&As are motivated by this precise belief. However, since it represents an ex-ante judgement, the acquirer's management's opinion can prove to

[19] Example: consider the target firm B with the following characteristics:

- Value of firm B (status quo) = USD 2 million
- Value of control = USD 1 million
- Value of synergies = USD 1.5 million (created with the acquisition)

The Value of B with synergies and restructuring is given by the sum of the three figures above: USD (2 + 1 + 1.5) million. The result, USD 4.5 million, represents the maximum price that has to be paid in order to get the control of the target.

be wrong. Therefore, when speaking about the value of control, it is more appropriate to define it as the *expected* value of control (Damodaran, 2005b). In fact, this value is not only influenced by possible improvements, but more importantly by the probability that these improvements may be implemented. Indeed, the possibility that the current management is not underperforming and that the planned improvements are not feasible cannot be ignored. In this respect, Damodaran (2005b) argues that "the control premium should vary depending upon why a firm is performing badly," that is, the control premium should be higher when a certain firm is underperforming because of poor management than when the firm's difficulties are due to external market factors. In the former case, the change of control (that would bring a change in management) is likely to generate value through performance improvements, while in the latter case, bad performance drivers would remain out of even the best management's control.

Nevertheless, it is worth examining the principal ways through which a new management may increase the value of the target firm. Damodaran (2005b) suggests considering the ways management can influence the basic drivers of a company's value from the perspective of a DCF valuation. As already seen before, it is worth considering this valuation method because it is the most suited to determine the intrinsic value of a firm in prospective terms (indeed, this is the case of the control premium), since it considers forecasted future cash flows. There are three basic factors that determine the DCF value of a firm: cash flows, firm growth, and the cost of capital. A new management can succeed in increasing the company's cash flows in many ways. For instance, it can redeploy assets from low- to high-performing investments, it can improve the efficiency of processes and investments in place, or it can better manage inventories and working capital. Regarding the increase of expected growth, the management also has a number of moves potentially available: it can decide to devote funds to investments with higher ROIC, to increase the reinvestment rate, or it can lead the company to gain a significant competitive advantage that will extend the high-growth period. As for the reduction of the cost of capital, the new management could potentially change the company's financial structure so as to minimize its cost of capital, or it could also try to better match the duration of liabilities with the duration of assets, so as to ensure a higher coincidence of the cash flows.

After analysing which of the above drivers could be influenced by a change of control, and to what extent, the target firm should be evaluated again with the potentially improved value driver(s), according to the DCF method. Then, from this new value of the company "with better management" the appraiser should subtract the value of the company "as is" which was obtained before. The resulting difference will represent the value of control over the specific target company.

9.6.4 The value of synergies

This final step regarding the valuation of expected synergies is of fundamental importance. Misvaluation of synergies is in fact one of the factors most cited as responsible for M&A failures (KPMG, 1999; Christofferson, McNish and Sias, 2004; Chatterjee, 2007; Kummer and Steger, 2008; and KPMG, 2011). The quantification of the economic value coming from future potential synergies is of course a very difficult task. For this same reason, a deep understanding of the characteristics of each source of synergy can be of substantial help in this valuation process.

In practice, while there has been a mixed degree of success across companies and sectors in terms of successful realization of synergies, certain patterns have emerged. For example, synergies tend to be greater, and the degree of success higher, when acquirers buy targets in the same or closely related businesses. In these cases, the likelihood of overlap and redundancies is greater and acquirers can leverage their knowledge of the business and market dynamics to achieve greater success.

Moreover, it is also assumed that so-called cost synergies, which are more easily quantifiable, tend to have a higher likelihood of success than revenue synergies.

Those operating synergies come from different sources such as economies of scale/scope, increasing pricing power, higher growth potential, etc., that greatly affect the operations of the combined firm. They generally show up as higher expected cash flows and can provide higher margins, and higher returns and growth. The most common type of cost synergies come from easily identifiable sources such as:

a) **Economies of Scale**, which refers to the notion that larger companies are able to produce and sell more units at a lower cost per unit than smaller competitors. Therefore, by combining two firms operating in the same industry (horizontal M&A), the consolidated entity will become more cost-efficient and profitable;
b) **Economies of Scope**, which allow for the allocation of common resources across multiple products and geographies. They enhance a company's ability to leverage its fixed cost base (e.g. administrative overhead, marketing and advertising expenses, manufacturing and sales facilities, and sales force) across existing products;
c) **Combination of Different Functional Strengths**, which leads to the adoption of best practices whereby either the acquirer or target's systems and processes are implemented globally by the combined company;
d) **Headcount reduction and consolidation of overlapping facilities**: following the combination of two companies, there is no need for two CEOs, CFOs, accounting departments, etc., and therefore, the combined entity may be able to close redundant corporate, manufacturing, distribution, and sales facilities.
e) **Greater Pricing Power**, which comes from reduced competition and higher market share, which may result in the intention to obtain better terms from suppliers.

On the other hand, revenue synergies refer to the enhanced sales growth opportunities, tax benefits, effects of diversification, use of excess cash, and impact of higher debt capacity that arise from the combination of businesses. Like cost synergies, they sometimes show up as higher cash flows, but sometimes, they can also take the form of lower discount rates. The principal sources of revenue synergies are:

a) **Excess cash (or cash slack)**: A company with limited project opportunities (and large cash balances) and a firm with high-return projects (and limited cash) can yield a payoff in terms of higher value for the combined firm. In fact, the cash-rich company will transfer funds to the firms with abundant opportunities in order to invest the funds and generate a return on investment. This synergy is likely to show up most often when large firms acquire smaller firms, or when publicly-traded firms acquire private businesses. Usually, the former businesses have large amount of cash to invest but few opportunities, while the latter have lot of potential growth projects but very limited funds to invest in those projects;
b) **Debt Capacity**: Debt capacity can increase, because when two firms combine, their earnings and cash flows may become more stable and predictable. This, in turn, allows them to borrow more than they could have as individual entities, which creates a tax benefit for the combined firm. This tax benefit usually manifests itself as a lower cost of capital for the combined firm;
c) **Tax Benefits**: Tax benefits can arise either from the acquisition taking advantage of tax laws to write up the target company's assets or from the use of net operating losses to shelter income;
d) **Diversification**: Diversification is the most controversial source of financial synergy, since in most publicly-traded firms, investors can diversify at far lower cost and with more ease than the firm itself. For private businesses or closely-held firms, there can be potential benefits from diversification.

As suggested by Damodaran (2005b), in order to avoid the double counting of the control premium, it is better to assume the value of the target company with an optimal management as the starting point of the synergy appraisal process. This way it is possible to identify the value which can be created by bringing the specific companies involved together under common ownership.

In order to properly consider the different characteristics of synergy sources in the challenging process of assigning them an economic value, it can be sensible to adopt the categorization into two classes proposed by Bruner (2004): synergies from assets or activities in place, and real option synergies.

a. Valuation of synergies from assets or activities in place

These synergies potentially arise from the coupling and sharing of the current companies' resources and capabilities. Since in this case the sources of potential synergies can be directly observed and controlled by the respective management groups, their payoff can be reasonably predicted, and modelled into differentials in cash flow streams. Therefore, in this case, the most suitable valuation approach is discounted cash flow (Bruner, 2004; Damodaran, 2005a). However, it is very important to apply this method with the necessary prudence. It is important for the choice of the discount rate to be consistent with the risk connected to the specific synergy (Bruner, 2004), which can differ from the discount rate used to value the target company as a whole. In fact, as already mentioned before, a study conducted by McKinsey (Christofferson, McNish and Sias, 2004) proves that certain types of synergies (cost reduction) are easier to achieve than others (revenue enhancement). Considering proper levels of risk in the valuation process is certainly one way to avoid misvaluation of synergies. Bruner (2004) proposes choosing discount factors in the following way:

a) the firm's cost of debt for synergies bearing risk in terms of EBIT (e.g. asset and cost reduction synergies),
b) the firm's WACC for synergies bearing risk similar to that of the enterprise (financial synergies),
c) the firm's cost of equity for synergies bearing risk in terms of residual cash flows (e.g. revenue enhancement synergies)
d) and a venture capital rate of return (about 30%) for synergies bearing risk in terms of very speculative projects.

Another critical passage of the synergy valuation process is to reasonably estimate their duration, so as to capture their entire expected life, and if necessary, to consider a terminal value (Bruner, 2004), Damodaran, 2005a).

Valuation of real option synergies

It is often recognized that the DCF model is not always suitable to capture the entire potential of some synergies (Smith and Triantis, 1995; Bruner, 2004; Damodaran, 2005a; Kinnunen, 2010). This is the case when real option strategies are to be valued. The combination of different companies can create strategic options that go beyond the reciprocal exploitation of resources and capabilities already possessed. Since the realization of this type of synergies lies completely within the purview of management decisions on whether to exploit the option or not, it is more appropriate to value them according to an option framework (Bruner, 2004; Damodaran, 2005a; Kinnunen, 2010). Researchers suggest that, as for real options in general, real option synergies can also be reasonably evaluated as if they were financial options, either through the Black-Scholes model (Black and Scholes, 1973) or through the binomial method (Cox, Ross and Rubinstein, 1979). Interestingly, Kinnunen (2010) proposes the view of real option synergies as being in-the-money real options only for the acquirer (or for the combined entity), because it is the coupling of the *specific* companies involved in the deal that can potentially create these options.

9.6.5 Common errors in valuing synergies

Certain common errors made even by practitioners must be avoided when valuating synergies. In fact, it should always be kept in mind that synergies come from the combination of two entities and therefore cannot be attributed to either the target or the bidder. Therefore, they must be shared between the target's and the bidder's shareholders and the discount rate must reflect the risk linked to the achievement of those synergies.

The three common errors made are the following.

a. Not sharing synergies

As mentioned, a common error when valuating synergies is to provide the target shareholders premiums for items or strengths that these shareholders had no role in creating. For example, synergies are created by neither the bidder's nor the target's shareholders and thus they must be split between them based on a contribution analysis.

b. Mixing control and synergies

Another error to avoid is mixing premiums for control and synergies. While synergies are used as a reason for many mergers, the other oft-stated rationale in acquisitions is control.

In many acquisition valuations, the value of control and synergies are assessed together, and it is difficult to determine where one ends and the other begins.

The value of control is very different from the value of synergies:

Synergies require the existence and combination of two entities (firms, businesses, projects) to be carried out.

Control, on the other hand, resides entirely in the target firm and does not require an analysis of the acquiring firm (or its valuation).

If both control and synergies are motives in the same acquisition, it is best to assess their values separately. In fact, the value of control should be estimated first by valuing the target firm twice, once on a status quo basis (with existing management) and once with the changes that are intended in how the company is run.

Once the value of control has been estimated, the value of synergies can be estimated.

c. Applying the wrong discount rate

Last but not least, synergies must be discounted at the appropriate discount rate, which is neither the target's nor the bidder's. Using the wrong discount rate on synergy cash flows would result in synergies being misvalued.

The general principle that governs the estimation of discount rates, which is that they should reflect the non-diversifiable risk in the cash flows, continues to hold when it comes to cash flows from synergies. Notwithstanding this principle, there are some common errors that continue to be made when it comes to valuing synergy.

In fact, cash flows generated by synergies accrue to the combined firm and not to the target or acquiring firm separately. Therefore, we should be using the combined firm's cost of equity and/or capital to discount these cash flows. Moreover, analysts often discount tax savings that arise as a consequence of acquisitions at the riskless rate. However, cash flows generated by synergies are never riskless, and using the riskless rate to discount cash flows is inappropriate. What if in the subsequent years the firm generates losses? There is always a certain degree of risk that a firm or a country is facing. What about deductions? It is a matter of country laws.

Finally, if the synergy involves entering new businesses with very different risk characteristics than those in which either the acquiring or target firms are involved at the time of the merger, the discount rate used for the cash flows should be different from both the acquiring and target firms' costs of capital.

9.6.6 The acquisition premium

In essence, during the determination of the acquisition premium, the acquiring company has to decide how much of the potential gain coming from the transaction it is willing to share with the target company. This premium that the acquiring company will offer to pay over the target's market value will be composed by a portion of (or the whole) value of control and the value of the synergies achievable through the transaction. In fact, after assessing the value of control, the acquiring company should decide how much of this value to insert in the premium they will offer to pay over the target's market price (**Figure 9.13**). The same reasoning will be applied after assessing the value of achievable synergies. The more of this combined value the acquirer will pay for the acquisition, the more it will transfer in terms of wealth to the target firm's shareholders, and the smaller the potential gain from the transaction will be. Therefore, the decision concerning what portion of the premium to pay is a purely strategic one. Like in every bidding process, competition among acquirers is likely to increase the premium price that the target's shareholders eventually receive (Haunschild, 1994; Varaiya and Ferris, 1987). According to research, in recent decades, acquiring companies have paid on average premiums in the range of 40% to 50% over the target's market price (Haunschild, 1994; Hayward and Hambrick, 1997; Krishnan et al., 2007).

Nevertheless, an acquiring company should be careful to avoid paying an excessive premium. In fact, research widely suggests that there is a significant negative relationship between the amount of the premium paid and the return to the acquirer's shareholders (Varaiya and Ferris, 1987; Datta et al., 1992; Haunschild, 1994; Hay-

Figure 9.13 Visual interpretation of the Acquisition Premium

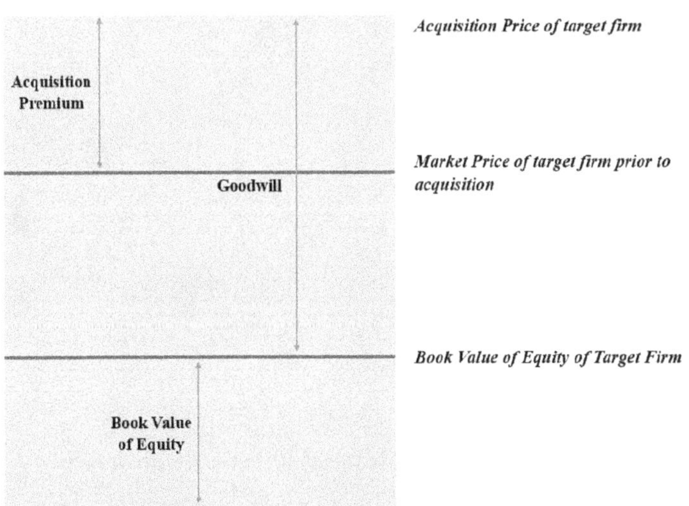

ward and Hambrick, 1997). This negative relationship seems to be caused partially by the fact that large premiums are often paid by acquirers with a management group characterized by exaggerated self-confidence, that wrongly believes it is able to create huge amounts of value (Hayward and Hambrick, 1997). An alternative reason could be that the payment of a large acquisition premium puts pressure on the management of the acquiring (or of the combined) firm to realize the improvements and the synergies expected, which should lead to shareholder returns (O'Shaughnessy and Flanagan, 1998; Krishnan et al., 2007). Under this pressure, the management is likely to focus only on actions that will create short-term returns (i.e. asset liquidation, workforce reduction, etc.) overlooking or even jeopardizing more long-term aspects, which represent the real rationale behind many mergers and acquisitions (Gigante G., 2020).

9.7 Accretion/Dilution Analysis and merger gains/costs

9.7.1 Value creation analysis

EPS Accretion/Dilution indicates the positive (negative) effect of the deal on the EPS of the combined entity. This analysis provides useful insights to evaluate the financial viability of a transaction (**Box 9.6**).

Box 9.6 EPS calculation

BOX: THE ALGEBRA OF ACCRETION/DILUTION

Since value addition and dilution are important to managers, below we present the algebra behind value-added transactions. Taking into account the issue of equity, every share of the buyer's company becomes a share of the new company (NewCo). Therefore, the accretion/dilution analysis compares the buyer's pre-transaction earnings per share with the NewCo's post-transaction earnings per share. Let us start with the following assumptions:

EpsB = the earnings per share of the Buyer (pre-deal);
EpsT = the earnings per share of the Target (pre-deal);
EpsN = the earnings per share of the NewCo (post-deal);
X = the exchange ratio (NewCo shares per Target share).
By definition if epsN > epsB , the deal is accretive; otherwise, it is dilutive.

To keep things simple, let us ignore synergies. The Target and the Buyer just want to aggregate their revenues and then distribute them based on the percentage implied in the exchange ratio agreed on for the deal. Therefore, each Target share will be converted into "X" NewCo shares.
Intuitively, the earnings per share of one Target stock will be spread over "X" shares of the NewCo. Thereby:

If EpsT/X > EpsB, then EpsN > EpsB, and the deal is accretive.
Therefore, if you simply divide the Target's earnings per share by the exchange ratio and compare the result with the Buyer's earnings per share, you will immediately know whether the transaction is accretive or dilutive.
We now consider the exchange ratio that makes the deal accretive. If X < Xmax = EpsT/EpsB , then the deal is accretive.
The Buyer then may be reluctant to provide an exchange ratio above Xmax because doing so will make the deal dilutive, and the Buyer's Eps performance will be affected in the short term.

The type of consideration (cash vs stock) may impact this analysis.

The starting point of this analysis is the fact that shareholders enjoy stand-alone earnings. These numbers come from the consensus in the market place. If the transaction is executed, what will happen to earnings?

Stand-Alone Earnings
(+) *Stand-Alone Earnings (Target)*
(–) *Restructuring Cost*
(–) *Interest Paid on Debt to buy the Company (net of taxes)*
(+) *Synergies Achieved*
= *New Combination Earnings*

This accretion/dilution analysis is conducted on a per share basis. Then, we need to make some adjustments:

- Stand-Alone Earnings of the acquirer and new combination earnings are calculated on a different number of shares
  - Extra care should be dedicated if the consideration is (partly) provided in shares.

How will investors look at these earnings? It is natural that at the beginning restructuring costs will dilute the new earnings base → investors can neglect the first year, and they can be neutral after two years, but starting in the third year they want to see accretion.

From this analysis, some potential issues may arise:

- Timing
  - For example, more time to realize synergies → more dilution;
- If the company is not listed, the consensus basis is questionable;
- Restructuring costs can be much higher (on average, 120 – 150% of the synergies);
- Interest paid: maturity, currency of funding, refinancing, management of the mismatch between assets and liabilities, and other key terms of the financing agreement can be criticized;
- Dis-synergies;
- Different scenarios can be included → measure the solidity of numbers through sensitivity analysis.

How can we make the numbers credible/solid? They can be validated by external entities + management credibility.

The extra care required for different types of consideration is described below:

100% Cash	**% Cash/% Stock**	**100% Stock**
	Debt Adjustments	
Cost of interest payments (or foregone interest income on cash used each year)	*Cost of interest payments (or foregone interest income on cash used each year)*	*No interest*
	New Shares Adjustments	
No new shares issued	*Shares issued for portion that is stock. Can be any combination of cash and stock*	*Shares issued to pay equity consideration*

Other key facts to consider are:

- **P/E** multiples are a measure of relative valuation in **all-stock transactions:** higher P/E = higher acquisition currency (investors are willing to pay more per dollar of earnings) vs lower P/E:
  - Buyer's P/E > target's P/E: deal will tend to be accretive, since the buyer's currency is more valuable than that of the seller;
  - Buyer's P/E < target's P/E: deal will tend to be dilutive, since the buyer's currency is less valuable than that of the seller;
- With **all cash transactions**, the target's P/E should be compared with the **implied P/E** of the "cash," or better, of the additional debt used for the acquisition:
  - Implied "cash" P/E can be calculated as follows:

$$\textit{Implied P/E} = \\ = \frac{1}{[(\textit{cost of additional debt for the acquisition}) \cdot (1 - \textit{corporate tax rate})]}$$

  - Implied "cash" P/E is greater > target P/E: transaction is accretive

To reconcile the (relatively) S-T vision of the investors with L-T strategies of a corporate (i.e. value creation), the value creation analysis is performed as follows:

Stand-Alone Value (Buyer), i.e. Market Cap
(+) *Stand-Alone Earnings (Target)*
(+) *Synergies*
(-) *Interest Paid on Debt to buy the Company (net of taxes) (-) Restructuring Costs*
(-) *Value of Debt*
= *New Combination Earnings*

Through this process, we can see how the value of a company is evolving during a transaction. In the accretion/dilution case, instead, we get the trajectory of earnings.

In this process, the key assumption to be made is **stability of trading multiples**. For example, if the cost of equity goes up because the new combined entity is perceived as being riskier, the P/E ratio will decrease.

Value creation is the key to make the decision. Usually, accretion/dilution and value creation reach the same conclusion, but in transitional times they might lead to different results (e.g. acquisition of FinTech).

9.7.2 Cost and gain assessment

If a financial manager of firm A needs to analyse the possible acquisition of firm B, the first thing that should be taken into account is the possible economic gain from the transaction. As seen above, there is an economic gain only if the two firms are worth more together than apart. Let us consider the following example.

The value of the combined firms A and B is the present value PV_{AB}.

The value of the two firms separately is the sum of the two present values: PV_A, PV_B.

So, if the difference between the present value afterwards and the present value before is positive, we have a gain. So, if:

$$\Delta PV = (PV_{AB} - (PV_A + PV_B) > 0, \quad \text{if} \quad PV_{AB} > PV_A + PV_B.$$

This gain (ΔPV) is obtained in synergies.

It means that the value of the two firms together is higher than the sum of the two values of the firms standing alone, as the result of one or more of the sensitive reasons; note that for dubious reasons, the gain in terms of added present value is equal to 0.

The cost of thc acquisition is the difference between the cash paid and the stand-

Box 9.7 The NPV analysis of the Acquisition

PV_A=400 PV_B=100 PV_{AB} = 550. Cash Paid = 130.
Gain = 550 – (400 + 100) = 50. Cost = 130 – 100 = 30.

NPV = 50 – 30 = 20.
NPV = wealth with merger – wealth without merger = (PV_{AB} – CashPaid) – PV_A = (550-130) – 400=20

Target's stock price changes in anticipation of the merger. We have two cases:

1) The market reflects only the stand-alone value of the target:

	Acquirer A	Target B (case 1)
Price per share	400	200
N shares	1 mn	0,5 mn
Mkt value of firm	400 mn	100 mn

If cash paid = 130, the cost is again (130-100) = 30 and the NPV is again 20.

2) If the news of the acquisition leaks to the market, the shares of the target appreciate ($P_B\uparrow$); for example, the price rises by 24. The intrinsic market value of the target before the transaction is overestimated by (24*0.5)=12 mn. This can happen only to listed firms.

So, the PV_B = 100 – 12 = 88 mn, as 12 have already been attached by the market to the target.
The cost is now (130 – 88) = 42, due to the fact that the target shares were overvalued when the news of the acquisition spread on the market. This is why the acquisition premium must be determined the day of the acquisition itself, as the acquisition premium is implicitly included in the higher PV_B.
So, the correct evaluation is the one which starts from PV_B as a stand-alone business, as if the merger were not going to happen. On the other hand, the evaluation is wrong if the market anticipates the merge.

alone value of the target company, so: Cost = cash paid – PV_B. This formula can be used only in the case of cash payment, not in the case of equity payments. Note that the additional cost for the acquiring shareholders is an additional gain for the shareholders of the target company. The cost equals the premium that the bidder is willing to pay as an extra in cash above the PV_B. The NPV of the acquisition is the difference between the gain and the cost (**Box 9.7**).

9.8 Overview of M&A activities in 2019 and outlook for 2020 after the impact of the COVID-19 crisis

Transaction volumes in 2019 remained almost unchanged compared to 2018 (**Figure 9.14**), even as the value per transaction decreased. M&A deals in excess of $250 million fell by 9% globally compared to 2018. From a regional perspective, a 13% and 6% decrease in volumes in the EMEA region and Asia Pacific, respectively, was offset by a 10% increase in North America driven mainly by "megadeals." This growing trend of megadeals manifested itself in the first half of 2019 and was then offset by a much less intense activity in the second half of the year. The opposite happened in Europe and Asia: the year started slowly and subsequently there was a marked improvement.

9.8.1 Main sectoral trends

Over the past 5 years, two main trends have been identified in the context of M&A:

- the TMT sectors, the energy sector, and the manufacturing sector as the main drivers of M&A activity;
- a change in the nature of deal-making.

Figure 9.14 Activities of the M&A sector by value from 2006 to 2019 (billions of USD)

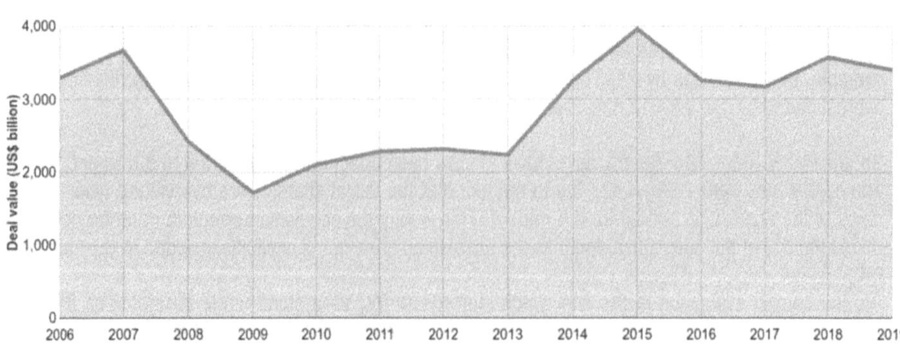

Source: Author's elaboration based on data from White & Case.

Figure 9.15 2015-2019 M&A activity by sector

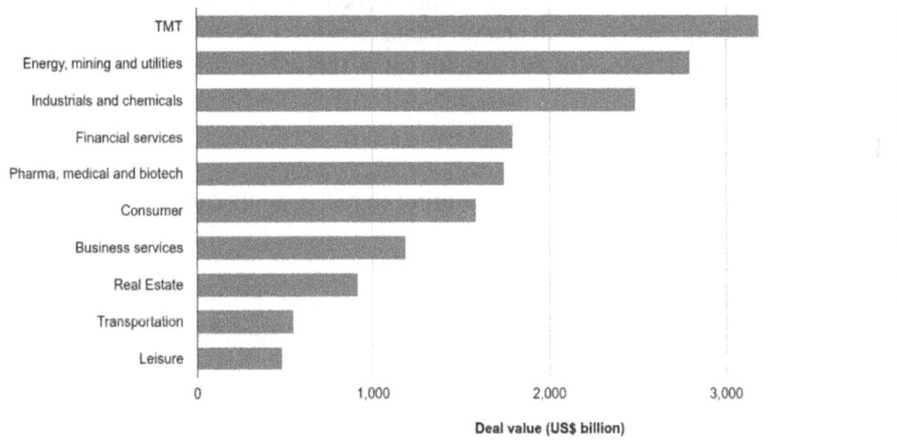

Source: Author's elaboration based on data from White & Case.

In **Figure 9.15** it clearly emerges that, in the last 5 years, the TMT sector holds the record in terms of relative value of M&A transactions, that is equal to 18.92% of the total value in the market, followed by the energy sector with a value equivalent to 16.1% of the total.

The nature of deal making continues to change. In the past, most transactions had economies of scale as their main goal, reducing costs or leveraging common customers and thus becoming larger players in the market. However, in the last two years this situation has shifted in favour of "scope deals" (i.e. those transactions that focus mainly on the development of growing business lines or on the acquisition of new "capabilities").

9.8.2 Impact of COVID-19 on M&A activity

The impact of COVID-19 on the M&A market is evident in the short term: many deals have been cancelled or delayed due to financial difficulties, with a general disruption of business plans and negotiation problems created by the crisis. However, the future may not be as dark as it seems. Indeed, event-driven downturns such as the current one generally lead to faster recovery than a structural cyclical crisis. The empirical evidence for this claim is provided by three major down-cycles over the past three decades. The one recorded in 1990-1991 was an event-driven crisis, with a 41% decline in total M&A activity in 22 months, and the recovery took nearly three years. The 2001-2002 crisis, defined as a structural down-cycle, led to a 65% decline in 32 months, and it took almost four years to return to the original value of M&A activity. Finally, the cyclical-structural crisis of 2008-2009 led to a total decrease of 52% in activity in 27 months, and the recovery did not take place until after six years. Confirming this general perspective, it should be stressed that companies in most sectors, financial sponsors, and capital providers (including banks) are in good shape and may be able to react quickly as soon as the market recovers, especially in a situation of high liquidity coming from central banks. However, given the uncertain and constantly evolving context, a careful assessment of individual cases is more critical than ever in this perspective.

9.8.3 Ranking of Financial Advisors relating to M&A deals concluded in Italy in 2019

In 2019, those who participated in the megadeal between FCA and PSA excelled among financial advisors.[20] In Italy, Mediobanca is at the top of the list, as can be seen from **Table 9.5** here.

9.9 The Art of M&A: Summary

M&A can be considered any process where the ultimate beneficial ownership, and potentially the control of a firm, are transferred from one subject (or group of subjects) to another.

M&As involve two different actors:

- the acquiring company (that acquires the control or a stake in the target): referred to as the bidder or buyer or acquirer;
- the target company (that is to be bought): seller/target.

The main objectives of M&A transactions are:

- Strategic Objectives: Bidder is a corporate which executes the M&A transaction to accomplish its own corporate objectives;
- Financial Objectives: Bidder is a financial investor (PEs, HFs, the management, etc.) looking for a targeted financial return.

What about the future of the target (or its assets) after the transaction? It depends on how the deal is shaped:

- Statutory Merger: Target is merged into bidder and ceases to exist;
- Acquisition of Target: Target continues to exist as a subsidiary of the bidder;
- Acquisition of Assets: Target's assets are transferred to the bidder.

---

[20] On 18 December 2019, Groupe PSA ("PSA"), the listed automotive company headquartered in France, and Fiat Chrysler Automobiles NV ("FCA"), a listed company in Italy and the United States, announced their merger to the market, to create one of the world's leading automotive groups.

Table 9.5 The top 20 advisors by value of deals in Italy – 2019.

Posizione	Advisor	Valore (EUR M)	Numero di Deals
1	Mediobanca S.p.A.	17174	37
2	KPMG	11515	57
3	Goldman Sachs & Co. LLC	10673	7
4	Banca IMI/Intesa Sanpaolo	9460	16
5	Bank of America	8284	9
6	UBS Investment Bank	8269	10
7	EQUITA S.I.M. S.p.A	7453	10
8	PwC	6098	55
9	Rothschild & Co	5371	27
10	JPMorgan	5307	9
11	Lazard	4345	16
12	Morgan Stanley	3804	3
13	Barclays	3228	9
14	UniCredit Group	3098	39
15	BNP Paribas SA	3044	12
16	HSBC	2966	2
17	Moelis & Company LLC	2841	1
18	Societe Generale	2835	7
19	Natixis SA	2701	4
20	Deloitte	2497	60

Source: Author's elaboration based on data from Mergermarket.

How is the bidder going to pay the seller(s)?

- Cash: bidder pays seller(s) in cash (available on balance sheet or raising debt);
- Equity: bidder pays seller(s) with its own shares, in exchange for the shares of the target;
- Mixed: bidder pays seller(s) with a mix of cash and its own shares.

Financing could be of two different types:

- Debt Financing: acquisition is financed through cash on balance sheet or raising debt;
- Equity Financing: acquisition is financed by raising equity (e.g. Rights issue).

The status of the Target could be:

- Private: target is sold through a private transaction, between the bidder and the seller;
- Public (Tender Offer): a public offer to buy shares is made by the bidder directly to Target's shareholders.

An M&A transaction can be shaped in various forms, with different characteristics, depending on the combination of the above options. The ultimate goal has to be the creation of value for the acquiring shareholders, and in order to do that, it is important to properly evaluate the final acquisition price paid to the target shareholders. The final price paid by the acquirer is composed by two different "elements": the stand-alone value of the Target, and the so-called Acquisition Premium (Synergies plus Premium for Control).

The stand-alone value is the value of the Target company in the market as is. This valuation is the starting point for all of the Buyer's strategies and considerations. There are several methods used to calculate the stand-alone value:

- DCF, probably the most commonly used and popular method. Depending on what type of value the Buyer is interested in (Enterprise Value or Equity Value), two kinds of cash flows are calculated: "Free Cash Flow to the Firm" and "Net Cash Flow," respectively;
- Trading Multiples. In this case the valuation is based on multiples of key financial indicators of a group of comparable companies. The most common multiples used to calculate the Enterprise Value are: EV/EBITDA, EV/EBIT, and EV/Sales. To the contrary, to calculate the Equity Value, the following are used: P/E, P/BV, etc. This kind of valuation is quicker than the DCF method and also easier to understand and interpret. On the other hand, the pool of comparable companies used must be really similar to the Target firm under consideration; otherwise, the results would not be consistent.

To calculate the Acquisition Premium, two main methods can be applied:

1. Estimate the amount of value that can be created by restructuring the Target company (Premium for Control) and then sum the estimated amount of the possible future synergies that the two companies can exploit (Synergies) and discount this value at time 0;
2. Use Transaction Multiples. In this case, the acquisition premium is calculated as the difference between Transaction and Trading Multiples.

The calculation of the Acquisition Premium is fundamental for the Buyer. The sum of the stand-alone value and the estimated premium indicates the maximum price that the Buyer is willing to pay for the Target. If the price paid is too high, the bidder is paying this extra value with a portion of its own stand-alone value, or in other words, the company is destroying value for its own shareholders. This is why the first reaction of the market to an M&A announcement is a drop in the acquirer's price (if the acquisition price is perceived to be too high). The market needs time to factor in possible synergies.

An important tool that tells us something about the convenience of the transaction is the accretive/dilutive analysis. The critical indicator we should look at is Earnings Per Share (EPS) post-merger. If this ratio is greater than the acquirer's EPS, it means that the deal has been accretive (at least from an accounting perspective). To the contrary, if the post-merger EPS is lower, then the deal has been dilutive and the acquirer has destroyed value. The calculation of the post-merger EPS is different depending on how the transaction has been paid, in cash or shares.

Useful consideration: when the acquirer negotiates a stock deal, it should never agree on a fixed price, because if the price on the market decreases, the company is forced to issue more shares, increasing the ownership dilution for the existing shareholders and giving a negative signal to the market that could lead to a further drop in the price.

Questions and answers

1. *Give a definition of M&A*

   M&As are corporate finance deals used by companies to implement their strategies. The strategies that a corporate can implement are:

   - Growth Strategies;
   - Divestiture Strategies.

   Both are considered M&A transactions. As for Growth Strategies, the goal is to increase the Net Present Value of Cash Flows to equity, so as to maximize the value for shareholders. To create value, a firm should generate higher returns than the market. The two available options are organic (internal) growth and external growth.

Organic (internal) growth	External growth
• Increase production capacity • Expand distribution platforms • Innovation/ Product mix • Commercial strategy/ Marketing	**M&A transactions (Mergers, Acquisitions and JVs):** • Quick result = CEOs have a limited time frame and M&A may be a good solution to reach results faster. Generally, when the board is about to be renewed, transactions diminish. Once the renewal comes, there are waves of M&A • Allow for Overcoming Entry barriers (e.g. regulatory, technological, markets, geographies) = Cross-border activity • Make "scarce" resources available (e.g. technologies, brands, IP) = the aim to buy a company is based on it being a scarce resource • Faster gain in market shares/market positioning • Efficiency enhancement • Financial and tax benefits (US regulators dedicate considerable attention to this topic, as the aim is to avoid conflicts on tax advantages) • Adapt/react to changes in the "rules of the game"

M&A is an alternative form of investment to fuel the growth of a company with respect to organic/internal development. Selection between the two alternatives should be based on cost-benefit analysis and execution risks assessment ("Make or Buy" decisions).

2. *Why would a company want to acquire another company?*
   There are several possible reasons:
   - The buyer wants to gain market share by buying a competitor.
   - The buyer needs to grow more quickly and sees an acquisition as a way to do that.
   - The buyer believes the seller is undervalued.
   - The buyer wants to acquire the seller's customers so it can up-sell and cross-sell to them.
   - The buyer thinks the seller has a critical technology, intellectual property, or some other "secret sauce" it can use to significantly enhance its business.
   - The buyer believes it can achieve significant synergies and therefore make the deal accretive for its shareholders.

3. *Why would an acquisition be dilutive?*
   An acquisition is dilutive if the additional amount of Net Income the seller contributes is not enough to offset the buyer's foregone interest on cash, the additional interest paid on debt, or the effects of issuing additional shares.

4. *Is there a rule of thumb for calculating whether an acquisition will be accretive or dilutive?*
   In general, no – you have to go in and calculate the effects. However, if it's an all-stock deal you can use a shortcut to assess whether it is accretive (see questions #5 and #6).

5. *A company with a higher P/E acquires one with a lower P/E; is this accretive or dilutive?*
   Trick question. You can't tell unless you also know that it's an all-stock deal. If it's an all-cash or all-debt deal, the P/E multiples of the buyer and seller don't matter because no stock is being issued.
   Sure, in general getting more earnings for less is good and is more likely to be accretive, but there's no hard-and-fast rule unless it's an all-stock deal.

6. *What is the rule of thumb for assessing whether an M&A deal will be accretive or dilutive?*
   In an all-stock deal, if the buyer has a higher P/E than the seller, it will be accretive; if the buyer has a lower P/E, it will be dilutive. On an intuitive level, if you're paying more for earnings than what the market values your own earnings at, you can guess that it will be dilutive; and likewise, if you're paying less for

earnings than what the market values your own earnings at, you can guess that it would be accretive.

7. *Why do Goodwill/Intangibles get created in an acquisition?*
These represent the value over the seller's "fair market value" that the buyer has paid. You calculate the number by subtracting the book value of a company from its equity purchase price.
More specifically, Goodwill and Intangibles represent things like the value of customer relationships, brand names, and intellectual property – valuable assets, but not true financial assets that show up on the Balance Sheet.

8. *What are synergies, and can you provide a few examples?*
Synergies refer to cases where 2 + 2 = 5 (or 6, or 7...) in an acquisition. Basically, the buyer gets more value out of an acquisition than what the financials would predict.

   There are 2 types of operating synergies: revenue synergies and cost (or expense) synergies.

   - Revenue Synergies: the combined company can cross-sell products to new customers or up-sell new products to existing customers. It might also be able to expand into new geographies as a result of the deal.
   - Cost Synergies: the combined company can consolidate buildings and administrative staff and can lay off redundant employees. It might also be able to shut down redundant stores or locations.

9. *How are synergies used in merger models?*
Revenue Synergies: Normally, you add these to the Revenue figure for the combined company and then assume a certain margin on the Revenue; this additional Revenue then flows through the rest of the combined Income Statement.
Cost Synergies: Normally, you reduce the combined COGS or Operating Expenses by this amount, which in turn boosts the combined Pre-Tax Income and thus Net Income, raising the EPS and making the deal more accretive.

10. *Are revenue or cost synergies more important?*
No one in M&A takes revenue synergies seriously because they are so hard to predict. Cost synergies are taken a bit more seriously because it's more straightforward to see how buildings and locations might be consolidated and how many redundant employees might be eliminated.

11. *All else being equal, which method would a company prefer to use when acquiring another company; cash, stock, or debt?*
Assuming the Buyer had high reserves (cash on balance sheet), it would always prefer to use cash when buying another company. Why?

- Cash is "cheaper" than debt because interest rates on cash are usually under 5% whereas debt interest rates are almost always higher than that. Thus, foregone interest on cash is almost always less than additional interest paid on debt for the same amount of cash/debt.
- Cash is also less "risky" than debt because there's no chance the buyer might fail to raise sufficient funds from the banking system and/or from the debt capital/market.
- It's hard to compare the "cost" directly to stock, but in general, stock is the most "expensive" way to finance a transaction; remember how the Cost of Equity is almost always higher than the Cost of Debt? That same principle applies here.
- Cash is also less risky than stock because the buyer's share price could change dramatically once the acquisition is announced.

12. *How do you determine the Acquisition Price for the target company in an acquisition?*
    You use the same Valuation methodologies we already discussed. If the seller is a public company, you would pay more attention to the premium paid over the current share price to make sure it is "sufficient" to win shareholder approval (generally in the 15-30% range).
    For private sellers, more weight is placed on the traditional methodologies.

13. *A Buyer pays $100 million for the seller in an all-stock deal, but one day later the market decides it is only worth $50 million. What happens?*
    The buyer's share price would be cut in half, and it would instantly lose half of its market capitalization. Depending on how the deal was structured, the seller would effectively only be receiving half of what it had originally negotiated.
    This illustrates one of the major risks of all-stock deals: sudden changes in share price could dramatically impact valuation.

14. *Why do most mergers and acquisitions fail?*
    Like so many things, M&A is "easier said than done." In practice, it is very difficult to acquire and integrate a different company, actually realize synergies, and also turn the acquired company into a profitable division.
    Many deals are also done for the wrong reasons, such as CEO ego or pressure for short-term results from shareholders. Any deal done without both parties' best interests in mind is likely to fail.

10 Risk Management in M&A Transactions

by Gimede Gigante[1]

10.1 Introduction

Mergers and acquisitions are complex transactions that are very risky due to a number of uncertainties around not only the future of macro and micro economic environments impacting the target's cash flows, but also the value of the bidder's stock price in the short/medium-term, that may impact the deal terms in stock transactions.

The academic literature has clearly identified three distinct types of risk in traditional M&A transactions:

a) post-closing risk arising after the deal closure, during the integration phase;
b) pre-closing risk arising between the definitive agreement and the deal closure;
c) market risk linked to the transaction (currency, interest rates fluctuations, etc.).

First, post-closing risk refers to the uncertainty around the future performance of the target as well as wrong estimates of the specific M&A parameters (integration costs and synergies, above all). It entails the possible failure of the target company to perform up to the bidder's expectations, which results in overpayment for the target.

In an M&A deal, the acquisition price of the target is computed by estimating its future cash flows and discounting them to the present value. However, free cash flows cannot be predicted with certainty, as they are subject to a number of unpredictable variables including economic and political conditions, trends in customer demand, etc.

Therefore, when valuing the target, the bidder bears the risk of overestimating the target's expected cash flows, which will result in overpayment for the target, and which in turn, will destroy value since the market will negatively react to the announcement of the deal;[2] the bidder price will decrease.

This type of risk (post-closing risk) is more important in M&A deals involving a target that has no track record and/or belongs to a relatively unknown industry (e.g. a private fast-growing tech firm), as this kind of firm usually does not have a stable track record of financials that could be used to estimate its future performance and

[1] With the precious contribution and the collaboration of Maria Teresa Iardella, Baptiste Gilliot and Rodolfo Pambianco.

[2] "If the market believes in an overestimation of the cash flows since the day of the announcement." (R. Pambianco, 2020).

since its cash flows are very sensitive to the expected growth rate (being heavily dependant on one variable).

Therefore, to limit this risk linked to the estimation of the target's future cash flows – paying today for something that will probably generate cash flows in the future – the bidder might propose to pay part of the purchase price in the future, contingent on the achievement of a given result by the target. The bidder will therefore pay a certain percentage of the acquisition upfront (at the closing date) and the rest in the future (generally 3 to 5 years) based on the financial performance achieved by the target, which will be measured using metrics that companies cannot manipulate such as sales or EBITDA. This particular deal structure enabling the acquirer to defer payment and link it to the target's performance is called an "earnout agreement"[3] and is a common instrument used in order to reduce so-called "post-closing risk" exposure.

However, M&A deals are not only subject to the aforementioned "post-closing risk," but also to "pre-closing risks" in the case of stock transactions. This "pre-closing risk" is mainly due to the possibility that fluctuations of bidder share prices between the Definitive Agreement and the closing date will influence the terms of the deal, and reduce the likelihood that the deal closes.

To clarify, when parties reach an agreement (price, exchange ratio, consideration, clauses, etc.), advisors draft what is called the "Definitive Agreement" listing all the deal terms. However, the definitive agreement does not imply that the deal is closed; before closing the deal, parties need to seek not only approval from the authorities and shareholders (when required), but also financing (in the case of a cash deal), which generally takes a few months but can be quicker in the case of underwriting by one or more banks. Since stock market prices may change during such a long period of time (reacting to new information), the bidder stock price may have significantly deviated from its level at the time of the Definitive Agreement, and this may have materially impacted the proposed deal terms, potentially reducing the parties' incentive to close the deal (whether the bidder or the target).[4]

For example, suppose that the two parties agreed that the bidder will distribute X number of its own shares in exchange for the target's shares, and that they announce the deal to the market. Before closing the deal, some time passes as parties may need the shareholders' approval, the antitrust go-ahead, etc. However, if the bidder's share price surges, the bidder may be willing to jump out of the deal as it will overpay for the target; there will be the same number of shares issued to the target's shareholders, but then each share of the bidder's stock will be worth more. To the contrary, if the bidder's share price decreases, the seller may be willing to jump out of the deal in

[3] The earnout agreement is then basically an option on the target company's future performance. An earnout is a plan that involves triggering payment to the seller. The trigger is based on a specific agreement to measure progress and takes the form of a legal contract. This allows the buyer to pay a fixed amount today, and then, when certain performance indicators are reached in the future, additional payments are made to the seller.

[4] For stock deals.

order to seek a better offer. In any case, either the bidder or the target has an incentive to renegotiate or even try to abandon the deal.

In order to avoid that, the two parties might decide to include a "collar agreement"[5] in the definitive agreement, which will limit the impact of extreme price fluctuations in the equity prices of the bidder.

Last but not least, in an M&A transaction, the bidder and the target are also subject to actual market risk, such as currency fluctuation. For example, in a cross-border deal, the bidder may have to exchange its local currency for a foreign currency in order to pay for the target. If the foreign currency appreciates against the domestic currency, then the acquisition price will be more expensive for the bidder, and so may not be attractive anymore. To reduce this type of risk exposure, "deal-contingent derivatives"[6] are used.

In the following sections we will explore further how earnouts, collars, and deal-contingent derivatives – three different M&A risk management instruments – are used in transactions in order to mitigate the risks associated with M&A deals (market, post and pre-closing).

10.2 Earnouts

10.2.1 Literature review of earnouts

This section aims to provide an overview of existing literature related to earnout structuring in M&A deals, as well as the main effects resulting from the inclusion of such clauses in purchase agreements. Datar et al. (2001)[7] provide evidence that whenever the bidder and the seller agree that a portion of the payment will be made contingent on the performance of the target company, the parties are able to reach an agreement and close the deal even when there is substantial divergence in terms

[5] The share exchange ratio ("Collar") is allowed to fluctuate within certain limits so as to compensate for the uncertain value of the deal in the future. There are *fixed share exchange agreements* that fix the share exchange ratio between the signing and the closing of the transaction and there are *fixed value (offer price) agreements* that fix the value of the offer price per share by allowing the share exchange ratio to fluctuate.

[6] A "deal-contingent derivative" is essentially a derivative financial instrument signed before the completion of the transaction. The financing cost and/or forward exchange rate are locked in from the beginning and, if the M&A is not completed, the corporate will not pay any penalties.

[7] "[The Authors] examine the effects of adverse selection and agency costs on the structure of the consideration offered in an acquisition. Specifically, they investigate factors affecting the benefits arising from use of earnouts. They find that when targets have greater private information, consideration is more likely to be based on the future performance of the target. They also find an earnout is more likely to be used in an acquisition if the target is a smaller, private company in a different industry than the acquirer. In addition, earnouts are more likely to be used when fewer acquisitions take place within an industry and when targets are service companies or companies with more unrecorded assets. Finally, they compare the use of earnouts with the use of stock and find that financing considerations are a more important factor in the use of stock." © Oxford University Press, 2001.

of valuation, because part of the uncertainty will be resolved in the future at the time when the payment is due. Thus, the authors describe an earnout as a risk-hedging mechanism against information asymmetry. In particular, they state that earnout contracts are mainly used in cases where the target is a private company, for which no market price is available and disclosure requirements are limited, or if the target belongs to the service or high-tech industries, both well-known as being significantly affected by uncertainties due to the high amount of intangible assets reported on the balance sheet.

Frankel (2005)[8] reports that when predicting the performance of a target company, sellers and bidders will naturally adopt optimistic and pessimistic views, respectively, which leads to deviations in forecast results and ultimately to substantial valuation gaps. Bidders expect that synergies generated by the integration can make up this gap, and sometimes this gap will be narrowed through compromise between the two parties. However, differences in valuation opinions may be difficult to overcome. In this case, earnouts can help the parties reach a deal by delaying the final valuation.

Reuer, Shenkar and Ragozzino (2004)[9] suggest that a direct relationship exists between the likelihood of the use of an earnout and the uncertainty related to the acquiring firm. Adverse selection and moral hazard problems may be aggravated in cross-border acquisitions due to the bidder's unfamiliarity with the target firm's legal and regulatory environment, domestic accounting information, infrastructure to carry out extensive due diligence, etc.

By reducing the risk of misevaluation and of target non-performance, Ragozzino and Reuer (2009)[10] report that earnouts mitigate the adverse selection problem in acquisitions, while any earnout premium paid after the closing date would only reflect the target company outperforming the bidder's expectations.

Quinn (2012)[11] focuses on the fact that earnouts enable sellers to convey unobservable information to potential bidders, and by deferring valuation until after the

[8] "The author explains how to construct earn-outs that minimize the risk of future disagreement and litigation." © 2005 Wiley Periodicals, Inc.

[9] "[The Authors] study "how monitoring and verification of accounting-based performance benchmarks influences the design and efficiency of earnout contracts. Earnouts are commonly used to resolve agency conflicts arising in mergers and acquisitions, but these contracts create measurement and other agency problems when contingent payments are tied to future accounting-based performance." https://doi.org/10.1057/palgrave.jibs.8400053

[10] "This study of acquisitions examines the incidence and determinants of contingent earnouts [...]. The evidence indicates that the usage of such contracts increases with information asymmetries surrounding mergers and acquisitions, in particular when privately held targets are young or possess knowledge bases that are dissimilar from those of the acquirers." https://ssrn.com/abstract=2422306

[11] "[The Author] seeks to answer the question whether earnouts really serve to respond to adverse selection, as commonly believed, or if alternatively, do they better address problems created by symmetric uncertainty. [...] I do not find significant differences in the fair value disclosures at the time of acquisition and during the post-closing period, which suggests that parties rely on earnouts primarily to resolve the problem of uncertainty rather than adverse selection." https://ssrn.com/abstract=1958617

transaction is completed, sellers can create reliable information signals, thereby resolving potential adverse selection problems.

Viarengo et al. (2016) describe the earnout as a self-selection mechanism: only sellers who have a high degree of confidence in their company's quality and ability to generate revenues throughout the forecasted period can accept a performance-based payment structure. High-quality sellers are then willing to include an earnout provision in the purchase agreement, and those sellers that reject contingent payment clauses implicitly convey private information to buyers.

Beard (2004)[12] highlights that whenever the seller accepts a part of the purchase price to be paid contingent on future performance, this reveals confidence regarding the company's ability to meet pre-specified performance benchmarks. For low-quality companies, this signal is too costly to replicate since they are not confident of reaching the demanded performance goals of the earnout.

Regarding the structure and design of the earnout clause, Cain et al. (2011)[13] pointed out that the choice of the earnout metric is very important because it is a means of tracking the value of the target company and the efforts made to improve its performance. In addition, the length of the measurement horizon increases with the importance of R&D and intangible assets, and decreases with the fluctuation of the target company's industry return.

10.2.2 Structuring earnouts

Following a brief introduction to earnouts and a review of the main findings in scholarship, this section will now focus on defining the key parameters that should be properly considered and managed when arranging contingent consideration, as well as providing tools to understand how to properly structure earnouts in M&A deals. There is a potentially infinite number of earnout structures that can be implemented: terms and conditions are usually tailored on each the characteristics of each deal and are often shaped by intensive negotiations between the parties. Each structure will result in different economic and strategic effects that both the bidder and the seller should accurately analyse. Ideally, earnouts should be structured in order to align the two parties' interests towards a positive development of the target company. We shall start by presenting the main earnout parameters, as well as theoretical considerations

[12] "The purpose of this dissertation is to study the ability of earnouts to mitigate problems associated with asymmetric information and problem of agency." https://digitalcommons.lsu.edu/gradschool_dissertations/2387

[13] The authors "empirically examine earnout contracts," and the analysis "reveals considerable heterogeneity in the potential size of the earnout, the performance measure on which the contingent payment is based, the period over which performance is measured, the form of payment for the earnout, and the overall sensitivity of earnout payment to target performance. Our tests of the determinants of contract terms yield support for the view that earnouts are structured to minimize the costs of valuation uncertainty and moral hazard in acquisition negotiations." https://doi.org/10.1016/j.jacceco.2010.05.001

and practical evidence on the main variables affecting the choice and determinants of such parameters.

10.2.3 The earnout parameters

Based on the definition given to earnouts, that can be simply reported here as those deferred variable payments contingent on the target company's ability to meet pre-determined performance objectives within a certain time window following the deal closing date,[14] we can now analyse the key parameters that jointly constitute an earnout mechanism:

a) **Earnout payment**. The size of the earnout consideration to be paid to the seller contingent on the target's performance. Such parameter is also defined as an earnout premium or an earnout pay-out.
b) **Earnout ratio**. The earnout payment as a proportion of the overall acquisition price (inclusive of both the fixed upfront consideration at the acquisition date and the earnout payment).
c) **Performance measurement period**. The specified time interval over which the target's performance is measured to determine whether the earnout clause has been triggered.
d) **Performance measure**. The specified parameter on which the earnout payment is based.
e) **Performance target**. The specified performance level to be achieved in order to trigger the earnout payment.

The pay-out structure

The relationship between the actual outcome of the performance target and the corresponding earnout payment may be linear or non-linear. A linear pay-out structure implies a constant relationship between the target performance and the earnout payment. In the vast majority of cases, however, the parties agree to arrange more complex non-linear pay-out structure in order to better capture target performance effect on bidder's wealth. Often, the earnout payment profile is similar to a financial call option pay-off, with the target shareholders receiving additional payments based on a function of the performance measure only once a minimum threshold has been reached and nothing below such level (see **Box 10.1**).

Option-like earnout structure often comes with caps to the maximum additional payment, reducing the degree to which the seller participates in the target company upside potential and protecting the bidder from outstanding performance of the acquired business. Furthermore, evidence suggests that is common for the

[14] Reuer, Shenkar & Ragozzino (2004, p. 20).

Box 10.1 Earnout as part of the purchase price

The following is a hypothetical example of the earnout as part of the purchase price:

1. Lump-sum payment at closing: the Seller receives $100 million at the closing;
2. Earnout payment: the Seller receives four times the excess of the actual average annual net operating cash flow over the baseline projection three years after closing, not to exceed $80 million.

Below is an analysis that explains the total earnout payment made to the seller after three years ($76.6 million)

Figure 10.1 Earnout example

	Base Year		
First Full Year of Ownership	**year 1**	**year 2**	**year 3**
Baseline Projection (Net Cash Flow) from the Business Plan	$20	$24	$30
Actual Performance (Net Cash Flow)	$30	$40	$50
Earnout at the end of the years [($30 – $20) + ($40 – $24) + ($50 – $30)] / 3 × 4 = $61.34			

parties to agree on a binary pay-out structure, where earnout is paid as a predetermined lump-sum payment as soon as the acquired company reaches the performance target.

Professional practice suggests that earnouts represent complex contracts whose structure should be carefully addressed based on specific deal peculiarities, considering the effects that earnout structures might have on valuation and accounting treatment, which will be discussed in the following sections.

The earnout payment

As seen, earnouts serve as self-selection mechanisms which allow target shareholders to convey private information about the value of their company. Indeed, only sellers that have high confidence in the value of their company, as well as its capacity to achieve specific performance targets, will be willing to accept bids in which a large part of the purchase price is tied to future performance. Thus, we expect earnouts to play a significant role in acquisitions characterised by a high level of uncertainty related to the target company's fair value and, as a consequence, we expect the earnout payment and ratio to be higher.

Furthermore, considering that earnouts reduce moral hazard risk in a principal-agent context where target managers are also shareholders and incentives are needed to tie shareholders' payoffs to target performance, the earnout ratio should be positively related to the importance of the managerial team within the target company.

The performance measure

The choice of the performance measure to be used as a proxy is a crucial step when designing an earnout provision. The importance of such a choice is twofold: on the one side, the performance measure should match the bidder's expectations by adequately reflecting the target company's performance and profitability (Frankel, 2005); on the other side, a clear definition of the metric used, how calculation will be implemented, and where data will be retrieved, enhances accounting transparency, thus reducing the risk of managerial discretion as well as the possibility of future lawsuits (Caselli, Gatti, Visconti, 2006).[15]

Furthermore, potential performance measures to be included in earnout provisions include both financial and non-financial metrics. Financial metrics are represented by accounting figures such as revenues; earnings before interest, taxes, depreciation and amortisation (EBITDA); earnings before interest and taxes (EBIT); net income; cash flow; and various valuation multiples based on the cited accounting items. Usually, earnouts are linked to the original acquisition price and multiples are applied to the financial metric calculated. It is uncommon to pay a portion of the financial metric, since the common practice is to pay a multiple of the financial metric. Non-financial metrics, instead, refer to a wide range of milestones related to product development (e.g. successful launch of a new product, R&D activity, FDA approvals, patents and licenses) or to the achievement of specific, large customer contracts (e.g. public tenders).

The vast majority of earnout provisions are based on financial measures, and in particular, cash flows and sales represent the most commonly used metrics given that such figures can be computed and monitored more easily with respect to profitability measures.

The earnout measurement period

The length of the time window over which the target company's performance is valued and earnout payment might be triggered has a crucial role in designing an effective earnout structure. Usually, earnout provisions come with a stated duration, which usually covers a 2 to 3-year period. However, there is debate among scholars on which are the main determinants in the choice of the earnout period, as well as whether a short duration generates benefits or not.

Lukas and Heimann (2014) believe that extending the earnout period leads to a higher probability of manipulating the target's operating and financial performance

[15] "It is not uncommon to detail in the Definitive Agreements the exact steps to be followed in calculating the identified performance measure." (R. Pambianco, 2020)

to avoid triggering the earnout payment. As a result, long-term earnouts often lead to disputes and litigation, independent of the successful post-closing performance of the target company, which may harm the target company and bring additional costs to bidders.

On the contrary, Barbopoulos and Sudarsanam (2012),[16] by analysing a sample of acquisitions of UK firms from 1986 to 2008, point out that the earnout measurement period, contrary to the earnout ratio, has no power in explaining bidders' gain.

Finally, Cain et al. (2011) report that, when the target value is highly influenced by uncertainty and depends on the success of time-critical R&D projects, the earnout period tends to be longer.

However, where high uncertainty also indicates the target company's industry, this positive effect is usually offset. In fact, the higher the volatility of the target industry, the shorter the earnout measurement period seems.

Overall, existing literature does not provide a clear and comprehensive answer to the determinants of the earnout period, and empirical results are inconsistent, leaving room for further research.

The issue of control

As a matter of fact, we expect the bidder to obtain full control of the target company's operations following the closing date, with the seller becoming dependent upon the bidder's management and control of the company. In the first instance, this results in an adverse incentive problem, since the buyer might refrain from boosting target company performance in order to avoid triggering the earnout payments, especially in cases of significant earnout ratios. Alternatively, the buyer might be incentivized to artificially manipulate operations, and consequently financials, with the aim of voluntarily missing performance targets (e.g. increasing R&D expenditures in a significant way in order to reduce net income).

Potentially, two solutions might be adopted by the parties to mitigate the adverse incentive problem. First, the parties might decide to set specific parameters, guidelines, and constraints under which the target company should be run, in order to reduce the buyer's managerial discretion and favour the seller's monitoring activities. Second, the buyer might allow the seller to retain minor control over the target company. Despite leading to concerns related to the governance structure, the solution just mentioned also provides the buyer with a tool to retain key managers after the acquisition of companies that strongly depend on their managerial team.

---

[16] They examine "the wealth effects of a comprehensive sample of UK bidders offering contingent payment, or earnout, as consideration for their acquisitions." They show that "bidders using earnout generate significantly higher announcement and post-acquisition value gains than bidders using non-earnout currencies (such as cash, stock exchange, or mixed payments)." https://doi.org/10.1016/j.jbankfin.2011.10.007

Valuing earnouts

The ASC 805 and IFRS 3R requirement to measure earnouts at fair value comes with challenges.[17] For valuation purposes, bidders are required to accurately consider terms and conditions regulating the contingent consideration in order to opt for the most appropriate valuation technique.

Two alternative approaches may be considered:

a) **Deterministic approach**: focuses on calculating the present value of cash flows related to a single potential scenario which is deemed to be the most probable future outcome;
b) **Probabilistic approach**: based on a probability distribution analysis aimed at considering the likelihood of any potential scenario and its associated pay-out.

While the two approaches lead to the same result in the case of linear pay-out structures, this is not the case when non-linear structures are adopted in arranging earnouts within deal terms. For non-linear pay-out structures, the cash flow related to what is deemed to be the most probable scenario does not correspond to the expected cash flow calculated through a probability distribution analysis (**Box 10.2**).

Box 10.2 Non-linear pay-out analysis

Consider an exemplary earnout agreement that obliges the bidder to pay contingent consideration equal to 50% of year-end EBITDA. No payment is required if the EBITDA is lower than €100m. Assume that there is a 30% probability for the EBITDA to reach €90m at year-end and a 70% probability of reaching €110m, and that no further outcomes are possible:

Figure 10.2 Two different approaches to value Earnouts: Deterministic vs Probabilistic

Deterministic approach	Probabilistic approach
50% [(\$90m × 30%) + (\$110m × 70%)] = = \$52m	(0 × 30%) + [(50% × \$110m) × 70%)] = = 0 + \$38.5m = \$38.5m

The above example is based on a simplified binary choice and illustrates how, under non-linear pay-out structures, the two approaches lead to different estimates of

[17] "ASC 805 and IFRS 3R define contingent consideration as usually being an obligation of the acquirer to transfer additional assets or equity interests to the former owners of the acquiree as part of the exchange for control of the acquiree if specified future events occur or conditions are met (an "earnout"). However, contingent consideration also may give the acquirer the right to claw back previously transferred consideration if specified conditions are met (a "clawback")," VFR Valuation Advisory #4 Valuation of Contingent Consideration, by the appraisal foundation, February 2019.

earnout fair value, since the deterministic approach does not adequately reflect cash flows from each potential scenario. Thus, the relevance of conducting a detailed analysis of the deal terms and conditions governing contingent consideration, with particular attention to the pay-out structure, is highlighted.

An overview of prevailing earnout valuation techniques is presented below. Commonly implemented methods to estimate fair value for contingent consideration include: (i) discounted cash flow analysis, (ii) probability weighted scenario analysis, (iii) the Monte Carlo simulation model, and (iv) the real option-pricing model.

Discounted cash flow analysis

The traditional DCF can discount the most likely cash flow from contingent consideration into the present value through a risk-adjusted discount rate (**Box 10.3**).

Box 10.3 Dcf analysis for Earnout

Consider an illustrative earnout agreement that obliges the bidder to pay a €40m earnout in 2019 and €50m in 2020 contingent on the target company achieving predetermined targets each respective year. Payments will be due on 30 June in the following reporting period. Assuming a valuation date of 31/12/2017 and a discount rate of 10%, the present value of the contingent consideration will be equal to:

Figure 10.3 Valuing Earnouts using a Discount Cash Flow Analysis

Payment date	June 30, 2019	June 30, 2020
Earnout payment	€ 40m	€ 50m
N° of discounting periods	1.5	2.5
Discounted flows	€ 34.68m	€ 39.40m

As shown above, this type of analysis is applicable to what are deemed to be the most probable future cash flow, and no deterministic approach is performed. The discount rate plays a key role in DCF analysis and is responsible for embedding all the uncertainties related to the achievement of performance targets, and therefore, the possibility of effectively paying the earnout. Based on these observations, the DCF analysis is confirmed to be a rough and simple method to estimate the fair value of the earnout that depends on the proper determination of the discount rate.

Probability-weighted scenario analysis

Probability-weighted scenario analysis aims to assess earnouts by associating, at each potential scenario, and thus at each potential payoff, a specific weight based on the probability of each event to occur. As a result, compared with the DCF method, this method has a greater ability to capture the highly differentiated range of possible future scenarios, thereby performing more powerful and comprehensive analysis (**Box 10.4**).

Box 10.4 Scenario analysis for Earnout

Consider an earnout agreement designed as a linear function that binds the bidder to pay an earnout equal to 6x EBIT in 2019. Payment will be due on June 30, 2020. Assuming a valuation date of 31/12/2017 and a discount rate of 10%, the present value of the contingent consideration will be equal to:

Figure 10.4 Valuing Earnouts using a Probability weighted scenario analysis

Future scenario	EBIT 2019 (€m)	Earnout payment	Probability	Probability weighted earnout payment
Upside case	66.67	400	40%	160
Base case	50	300	50%	150
Downside case	33.34	200	10%	20
Expected earnout payment				€ 330m
PV factor (10%, 2.5 yrs)				0.7879
Fair value of the earnout liability				**€ 260.04m**

However, the probability-weighted scenario analysis requires the bidder to precisely forecast timing, occurrence, and probability of future events, as well as cash flows related to specific outcomes.

Monte Carlo simulation model

The Monte Carlo simulation[18] is a model which artificially generates random scenarios to observe results originating from a wide range of potential outcomes. This

[18] "The Monte Carlo method was invented by scientists working on the atomic bomb in the 1940s, who named it for the city in Monaco famed for its casinos and games of chance. Its core idea is to use random samples of parameters or inputs to explore the behavior of a complex system or process. The scientists faced physics problems, such as models of neutron diffusion, that were too complex for an analytical solution – so they had to be evaluated numerically. They had access to one of the earliest computers – MANIAC – but their models involved so many dimensions that exhaustive numerical evaluation was prohibitively slow. Monte Carlo simulation proved to be surprisingly effective at finding solutions to these problems. Since that time, Monte Carlo methods have been applied to an incredibly diverse range of problems in science, engineering, and finance – and business applications in virtually every industry." https://www.solver.com/monte-carlo-simulation-overview

method allows the bidder to analyse a much higher number of scenarios related to the target company performance by making assumptions about future growth rates and margins, together with inputs related to the minimum and maximum earnout payment. Based on both historical data and future projections, the model generates a probability distribution as a result of multiple simulations. Despite the ability to capture risk and uncertainty with reference to future outcomes and related earnout payments, the Monte Carlo simulation model comes with increased complexity. The model is based on assumptions which are provided by the management and are not observable on the market, creating material challenges in relation to the auditing procedure.

Real option pricing model

An earnout provision might be seen as a call option on the target company's future performance, with the seller holding a long position in the call option and receiving an earnout premium at the end of the measurement period in the case performance targets are achieved. Therefore, earnouts might be considered as real options and valuation can be conducted based on the option pricing model developed by Black-Scholes.

Comparing earnouts to call options also makes it possible to derive some conclusions about specific earnout parameters which are expected to ultimately affect the fair value of the option-like earnout. According to option pricing theory, the probability of an option to end up in the money is positively dependent upon the uncertainty of the target's future performance and the length of the earnout measurement period, while it is inversely dependent upon the amount of performance increase which is required to trigger the earnout payment. Moreover, it is intuitive that higher probability of receiving the earnout payment results in a lower incentive for the target managers-shareholders. Thus, the only way for bidders to increase target managers' efforts in boosting performance is to increase the earnout ratio, i.e. the contingent part of the purchase price.

10.3 Collars

As mentioned in the introduction, stock price volatility has always been a problem in M&A deals, particularly those involving two listed companies that are structured as stock-for-stock swaps. In fact, in stock M&A transactions the parties are exposed to the so-called "pre-closing risk" which is caused by fluctuations of the bidder's stock prices between the definitive agreement (listing the deal terms such as the price, exchange ratio, etc.) and the closing date at which the transaction is concluded.

Notice that this "pre-closure risk" is unique to stock exchange transaction, as in an all-cash deal the consideration is independent of any changes in the bidder's share price.

It is also very important to mention that in a stock transaction, both the target and the bidder are exposed to fluctuations of the bidder's stock price and that based on the type of deal structure (fixed-exchange ratio vs floating exchange ratio), the parties bear different kind of risks.

In fact, in a *fixed-exchange ratio deal*, the two parties bear an "economic risk": risk of significant changes in the overall deal value.

On the other hand, in a *floating-exchange ratio*, the parties bear a "governance/control risk": risk of changes in the shareholder structure in terms of percentage of ownership.

a) Risk Exposure in a Fixed-Exchange Ratio Stock Deal

In a fixed-exchange ratio deal, the parties define the exchange ratio: the number of shares of the bidder's stock to be exchange for each share of the target's stock. For example, the parties may agree on a "2:1" exchange ratio, meaning that the target's shareholders will receive two of the bidder's shares for each of the target's share. Therefore, as the amount of the bidder's shares received is constant, the respective pro-forma ownership percentages for the acquirer and the target remain fixed regardless of share price movements between the execution of the definitive agreement and the deal closing.

However, as the number of shares issued to the target is fixed, the offer price per share (constituting the value of the target) moves in line with the underlying share price of the acquirer.

If the price decreases, the overall value of the transaction decreases; the number of shares distributed to the target's shareholder remains fixed, but the bidder's shares are worth less than at the time of the definitive agreement.

Inversely, if the price increases, the overall value of the transaction will surge as the number of shares distributed to target's shareholder will still be fixed, but each of the bidder's shares distributed will be worth more.

Those two examples clearly highlight why, in a fixed exchange ratio structure, the parties are not exposed to "governance risks" (as the ownership percentages are fixed), but are exposed to an "economic risk" as the value paid for the target depends on the bidder's share price. In public market transactions, if the market believes the transaction will go through, it will automatically adjust any deviation from the fixed-exchange ratio to avoid market arbitrage.[19]

To illustrate this a little bit better, let us provide a very simple example (see **Box 10.5**).

[19] "I.e. buying stocks of the target in the market for a value of €X and exchanging them for the stocks of the buyer based on the fixed exchange rate, receiving an amount equal to €X+€1)." (R. Pambianco, 2020)

Box 10.5 Fixed-Exchange Ratio Deals

Let us suppose that the bidder and the target both have 1,000 shares outstanding and that they have agreed to merge with a 1:1 exchange ratio, meaning that the target's shareholders will receive 1 share of the bidder for each share of the target. In other words, upon the closing date, the bidder will distribute 1,000 of its shares to the target's shareholders.

Also suppose that when the definitive agreement was drafted, the bidder's stock price was $10, valuing the target's share at $10 per share or $10,000 overall.

Since in a fixed-exchange ratio the number of shares distributed to the target shareholder is fixed, the parties do not face any "governance/control" risk, as the structure is pre-defined. The bidder will own 50% of the firm (1,000 shares) while the target's shareholder will own the other 50% (1,000 shares) no matter what.

However, if at the closing date the price of the bidder surges to $15 per share, the bidder will overpay for the target; it will distribute the same amount of shares that are worth $5 more. In fact, the bidder will still distribute 1,000 shares, but they are now worth $15 per share, valuing the target at $15,000 instead of $10,000. Subsequently, the bidder may have fewer incentives to move forward and might be willing to exit the deal.

On the contrary, if at the closing date the price of the bidder decreases to $5 per share, the target's shareholders will receive economic consideration worth half of what they were supposed to receive months earlier. Again, they will still receive 1,000 of the bidder's shares, but the latter are worth $5, valuing the target at $5,000 instead of $10,000.

As we can clearly see in both the example above and the chart below, the parties do not bear any "governance or control risk" in a fixed-exchange ratio stock deal, but they both bear an economic risk.

Figure 10.5 Illustration of the Economic Risk in a Fixed-Exchange Ratio M&A deal

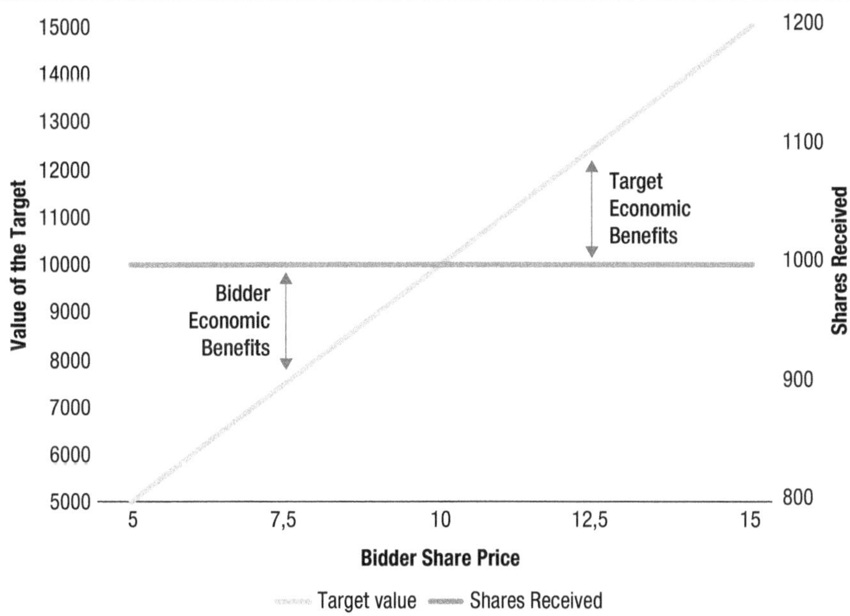

b) Risk Exposure in a Floating-Exchange Ratio Stock Deal

A floating-exchange ratio represents the *set dollar amount per share* that the acquirer has agreed to pay for each share of the target's stock in the form of shares of the bidder stock. As opposed to a fixed-exchange ratio, in a floating-exchange ratio structure, the dollar offer per share (value of the target) is set, and the number of shares exchanged fluctuates in accordance with the movement of the acquirer's share price.

This structure presents both the bidder and target's shareholders with greater certainty in terms of value paid/received, as the acquirer/seller assumes the full risk of an increase/decline in the bidder's share price. However, in this kind of transaction, the target and the bidder both bear "governance/control risk" since the number of shares distributed, defining the post-deal structure, depends on the bidder's share price.

Again, to illustrate this fact, let us provide a very simple example (see **Box 10.6**).

10.3.1 Fixed-exchange ratio and floating exchange ratio collars

In order to deal with the above-mentioned risks – both economic and governance/control risks – M&A advisors have developed a particular kind of contingent offer, called a "collar offer," that limits counterparties' risks in a stock-for-stock deal in the event that:

a) the bidder's stock price falls below or above a certain level in a fixed-collar offer;
b) the ratio of the bidder's to the target's stock price, also known as the exchange ratio, moves outside a pre-specified range in a floating-collar offer.

Those "collars" are instruments that fix risk boundaries thanks to a careful combination of a "floor" and a "cap."

The floor eliminates the risks borne by the target's shareholders in both a fixed-exchange ratio or a floating-exchange ratio deal. In fact, the floor will limit the impact caused if the bidder's stock price falls below \$X (in a fixed-exchange ratio deal) or increase above \$Y (in a floating-exchange ratio deal) between the signing and the closing of the deal, and protects the target company's shareholders from the effect of a reduction of the bidder's share price in a fixed-exchange ratio deal (economic risk), and from the target's risk of a reduction of its ownership stake in the combined entity in floating-exchange ratio offers (governance risk).

On the contrary, the cap protects the bidder from a surge of its stock price (fixed-exchange ratio) or the exchange ratio (floating-exchange ratio) by limiting the target's upside. This upper bound protects the bidder company's shareholders from overpayment in fixed-exchange ratio offers, or against the risk of control dilution in floating-exchange ratio deals.

Box 10.6 Floating-Exchange Ratio Deals

Let us assume that instead of structuring the deal as a fixed-exchange ratio, the bidder and the target mentioned in our previous example opt for a floating-exchange ratio structure. In that case, they will agree in the Definitive Agreement to fix the price of the target's stock at $10 per share, or $10,000 overall. If at the closing date the bidder's price is still $10 per share, the latter will issue 1,000 shares to the target's shareholders ($10,000/$10 = 1,000). Pro-forma, both the bidder and the target will own 1,000 shares, or 50% of the company.

However, if the bidder's share price surges to $15 dollars per share, the bidder will issue c. 667 shares to the target's shareholders ($10,000/$15 = 666.67). Note that even though the target's shareholders will still receive economic consideration worth $10,000 (667 shares worth $15), they will experience a governance/control dilution as they will own c. 40% of the firm pro-forma instead of 50%. Therefore, if the target's shareholders are more interested in the ownership than the economic consideration, they might be willing to exit the deal.

On the contrary, if the bidder's price plummets to $5 per share, the bidder will issue 2,000 shares to the target's shareholders ($10,000/$5 = 2,000). As a consequence, pro-forma, the target's shareholders will own 66.67% of the firm to the detriment of the bidder's shareholders, that will be diluted to 33.33%, and thus might have fewer incentives to close the deal.

As we can clearly see both in the example above and the chart below, in floating-exchange ratio deals, the parties do not bear any "economic risk" but "governance or control risks" (risk of ownership dilution).

Figure 10.6 Illustration of the Dilution Risk in a Fixed Exchange Ratio M&A deal

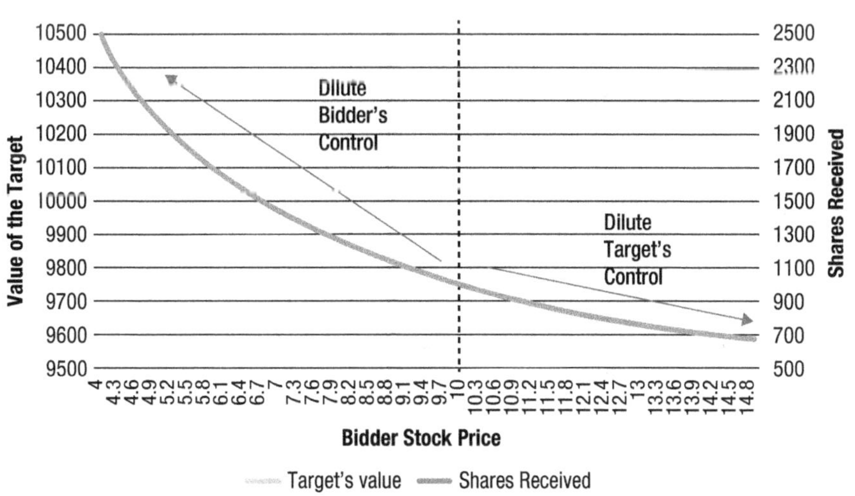

However, as the two different deal structures (fixed-exchange ratio and floating-exchange ratio) imply different risk (economic vs governance), two main types of collars exist:

a) Fixed-Exchange Ratio Collars, also called "Egyptian";
b) Floating-Exchange Rate Collars, also called "Travolta."

a) Fixed-Exchange Rate Collars

As we mentioned earlier, in a fixed-exchange ratio stock deal, the target's shareholders receive a certain amount of the bidder's shares in exchange for the target's stock. As the amount of shares distributed to the target's shareholders is fixed, the parties do not bear any "governance/control risk," but do bear an "economic risk" as the deal value moves in line with the bidder's stock price. If the latter plummets, the target's shareholders will receive the set amount of the bidder's shares, but the economic consideration will be lower than expected as each share is worth less. To the contrary, if the bidder's stock price surges, the bidder will overpay for the target; the target's shareholders will received the set amount of the bidder's shares, but the economic consideration will be greater than expected as each share is worth more than at the time of the Definitive Agreement. In either case, one party has lower incentives to conclude the deal, which may jeopardize the transaction.

In order to reduce those economic risks, M&A practitioners have created a particular instrument called "Fixed-Exchange Ratio Collars" (see **Box 10.7**), which specify a constant exchange ratio over a range of bidder stock prices, with adjustments outside that range. In other words, the bidder guarantees a fixed number of shares for the target stock price ratios if the bidder's share price falls within the "width of the collar," and if the bidder price falls below/above the lower/upper bound, the consideration is a fixed price.

Box 10.7 Fixed-Exchange Ratio Collars

In this example, we will need to make three assumptions:
First, let us suppose that the bidder and the target both have 1,000 shares outstanding and that they have agreed to merge with a 1:1 exchange ratio, meaning that the target's shareholders will receive 1 share of the bidder for each share of the target. This means that overall, the bidder will distribute 1,000 of its shares to the target's shareholders.
Second, suppose that when the definitive agreement was drafted, the bidder's stock price was $10, valuing the target's shares at $10 per share, or $10,000 overall.
Finally, assume that both the bidder and the target want to reduce the economic risk linked to the volatility of the bidder's share price in a fixed-exchange ratio transaction, and thus agreed to include a Fixed-Exchange Ratio Collar in the definitive agreement. This agreement specifies that:

- The acceptable range of values for the bidder price is [$7-$13]; meaning that if the bidder's stock price is within the acceptable range of values at the time of the deal's closure, the deal will be concluded with a 1:1 exchange ratio, and 1,000 shares of the bidder will be distributed to the target's shareholders;
- If the bidder's stock price is below $7, the number of shares will be adjusted to keep the value to the target constant: $7 per share, or $7,000 overall;
- If the bidder's stock price is above $13, the number of shares will be adjusted to keep the value to the target constant: $13 per share, or $13,000 overall.

While without a collar agreement the price for the target could theoretically go from $0 to +∞, with the collar agreement the target's value can only fluctuate between $7,000 and $13,000 – the range

which is defined as acceptable for both the bidder and the seller. This demonstrates that the boundaries fixed by the collar significantly reduce the volatility of the acquisition price.
However, let us give some examples to illustrate this point and see how the deal terms would change if, instead of remaining at $10 per share, the bidder stock price were $5, $8, $12, or $20 at the time of closing.

- If at the closing date the bidder price were $5 per share (which is outside the collar width), under the collar agreement, the bidder would have to issue 1,400 shares ($7,000/$5 = 1,400) to the target's shareholders in order to pay the agreed-upon consideration: $7,000 (lower bound consideration). Without the collar, the target's shareholders would receive significantly lower economic consideration: 1,000 shares × $5 = $5,000. However, since with a collar agreement the bidder would have to issue 1,400 instead of the 1,000 that it would issue under a no-collar fixed-exchange ratio structure, its percentages of ownership would be diluted. In fact, instead of owning 50% of the pro-forma firm, the bidder would only own c. 41.67%. Nonetheless, the use of a collar would result in a lower governance dilution than would be the case if the deal were structured as a pure "Floating-Exchange Ratio" deal. In that case, the bidder would not have to issue 1,400 shares, but 2,000 ($10,000/$5 = 2,000), which obviously would be more dilutive; the bidder's ownership would be c. 33.33%.
- If at the closing date the bidder stock price were $8, which would fall within the acceptable value range, the bidder would issue 1,000 shares (50% of the firm) worth $8 dollars each, valuing the target at $8,000. While this $8,000 value of the target would be well below the initial $10,000 valuation, it would still be acceptable for the seller.
- Similarly, if at the closing date the bidder price were $12, which again, would fall in the acceptable range of values, the bidder would issue 1,000 shares worth $12 dollars each, valuing the target at $12,000. This $12,000 valuation would make the target much more expensive for the bidder, but again, it would belong to the range which would be acceptable for the bidder.
- However, if at the closing date the bidder price were $15 per share, under the collar agreement, the bidder would issue 867 shares ($13,000/$15 = 867) to the target's shareholders in order to pay the defined consideration: $13,000 (upper bound consideration). Without a collar, the acquisition price would be significantly higher for the bidder: 1,000 × $15 = $15,000. Moreover, as the bidder would issue only 867 shares instead of the 1,000 it would have to issue if the deal didn't included any collar agreement, the transaction would be more accretive for the bidder. In fact, instead of owning 50% of the company, with the collar the bidder would own 53.56% of the combined firm.

As in the example above, the graphs below clearly demonstrate the impact of the "Fixed-Exchange Ratio Collar" on economic and governance risks.
More thoroughly, we can clearly see in the chart on the left that the value of the target remains between $7,000 and $13,000 no matter the price of the bidder's stock, which definitely reduces the economic risk of the initial Fixed-Exchange Ratio deal.
However, in the chart on the right, we notice that under the collar provision, the parties bear a government/control risk, since if the bidder's share price does not fall within the range of acceptable values, the bidder will issue more shares (if the bidder's stock decreases below the lower bound) or fewer shares (if the bidder's price increases above the upper bound) to the target's shareholders. In other words, the fixed-exchange collar will add a governance/control risk if the bidder's price is outside of the collar width, as the number of shares will fluctuate depending on the bidder's stock price. Therefore, despite reducing the economic risk, a fixed-exchange ratio collar exposes the parties to the risk of governance/control dilution.

Figure 10.7 The use of Fixed-Exchange Ratio Collars to reduce Economic risks (increasing Dilution risk)

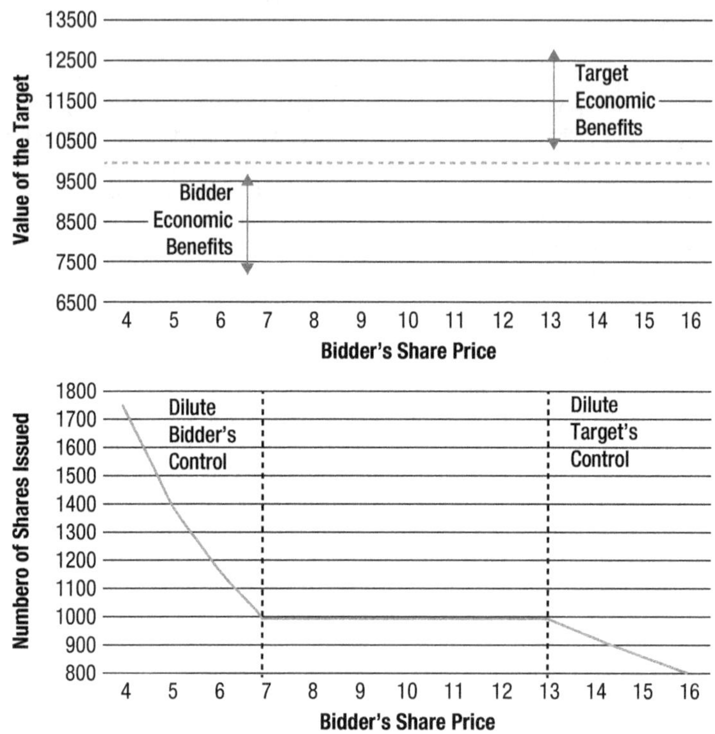

b) Floating-Exchange Ratio Collar (Fixed-Price Collar)

Instead of using fixed-exchange ratio structures which define the number of shares that the bidder will distribute to the target's shareholders, some M&A transactions are structured as "floating-exchange ratio" deals (see **Box 10.8**) in which the exchange ratio is free to float, but the target's acquisition price is set and paid in the form of shares of the bidder's stock. In other words, in "floating-exchange ratio deals," the acquisition price of the target is fixed, and the number of shares issued will be adjusted to afford the acquisition price. The advantage of this kind of deal structure is that whatever the bidder stock price at closing, the value to the target shareholders is certain. However, the ownership structure is uncertain, as the number of shares is adjusted according to the bidder's stock price. If the bidder's share price increases, the bidder will have to distribute fewer shares to the target's shareholders in order to afford the acquisition price, resulting in a dilution of the controlling power for the target's shareholders. On the contrary, if the bidder's share price decreases, it will have to issue more shares to acquire the target, resulting in a dilution of the bidder's percentages of ownership pro-forma.

Box 10.8 Floating-Exchange Ratio Collars

Consider the example discussed in the previous section with two additional assumptions.
First, let us assume that the bidder and the target have decided to fix the value of the target by using a floating- exchange ratio. In this case, the bidder will adjust the amount of shares issued in order to maintain the value of the target at $10,000, or $10 per share.
Second, let us take for granted that both the bidder and the target are worried about the post-transaction ownership structure, and they want to limit the governance and control risk associated with the deal. Thus, they will include a "Floating-Exchange Ratio Collar" which will allow the exchange ratio to float as low as 0.77 (but no lower) and as high as 1.43 (but not higher). Provided the ratio stays within the bounds [0.77: 1.43], the target company's shareholders are guaranteed a constant dollar price per share ($10 in our case), but if the ratio moves above or below those boundaries, the price per share paid will become a linear function of the bidder company's share price.
As can be seen in the figure below, the upper bound allows the bidding company's shareholders to avoid a material dilution if the bidder company's share price falls sharply in the period between when the board sets the cash amount for each target company's share and when the transaction is actually closed.
In fact, if the exchange ratio goes above 1.43 (corresponding to a bidder price lower than $7 if the target price is fixed at $10 per share), the bidder will issue c. 1,428.57 shares ($10,000/$7 = 1,428.57) to the target's shareholders independently of the value of its stock. In other words, the bidder will reduce its governance risk (risk of control dilution) as it is protected from having to issue more than 1,429 shares to afford the acquisition price.
On the contrary, the lower bound will guarantee that the target company's shareholders will receive at least a pre-determined percentage of the combined entity. If the exchange ratio is lower than 0.77 (corresponding to a bidder price higher than $13 if the target price is fixed at $10 per share), the bidder will issue c. 769.23 shares ($10,000/$13 = 769.23) to the target's shareholders independently of the value of its stock. In other words, it guarantees that the target's shareholder will receive at least 769 shares of the bidder's stock no matter what.
To clarify the above points, we provide some illustrative examples.

- If the bidder's price decreases to 5$ per share, the deal exchange ratio would be 2:1, which is outside of the acceptable range of values. As a consequence, the bidder would have to issue the number of shares pre-determined in the collar agreement (upper bound). In our example, we already mentioned that if the exchange ratio goes above 1.43, the bidder would have to issue 1,428.57 shares to target's shareholders. This reduces the bidder's control dilution risk as without the collar, the bidder would have to issue 2,000 shares to the target's shareholders ($10,000/$5 = 2,000). However, as the number of shares is fixed, the economic consideration received by the target is lower than expected. In fact, instead of receiving consideration worth $10,000, the target will receive c. 1,428.57 shares worth $5 each, which corresponds to c. $7,143 overall. However, this economic consideration is greater than what it would be if the deal were structured as a pure "Fixed-Exchange Ratio" deal; in that case, the target would receive 1,000 shares worth $5, or $5,000 overall.
- If the exchange ratio is 0.8, which is within the acceptable range of values, the bidder would have to issue enough shares worth $12.5 each ($10/0.8 = $12.5) in order to afford the fixed $10,000 acquisition price. In that case, the bidder would have to issue 800 shares ($10,000/$12.5 = 800), which is less than what the bidder would have to issue if its share price were $10 per share (share price at the time of the Definitive Agreement). Even though these deal terms are more dilutive in terms of governance and control for the target's shareholders, they are still in the range of values which are "acceptable" for the target's shareholders. Pro-forma, the target's shareholders would receive economic consideration of $10,000, corresponding to c. 44.44% of the firm.

Figure 10.8 The use of Floating-Exchange Ratio Collars to reduce Dilution risks (increasing Economic risk)

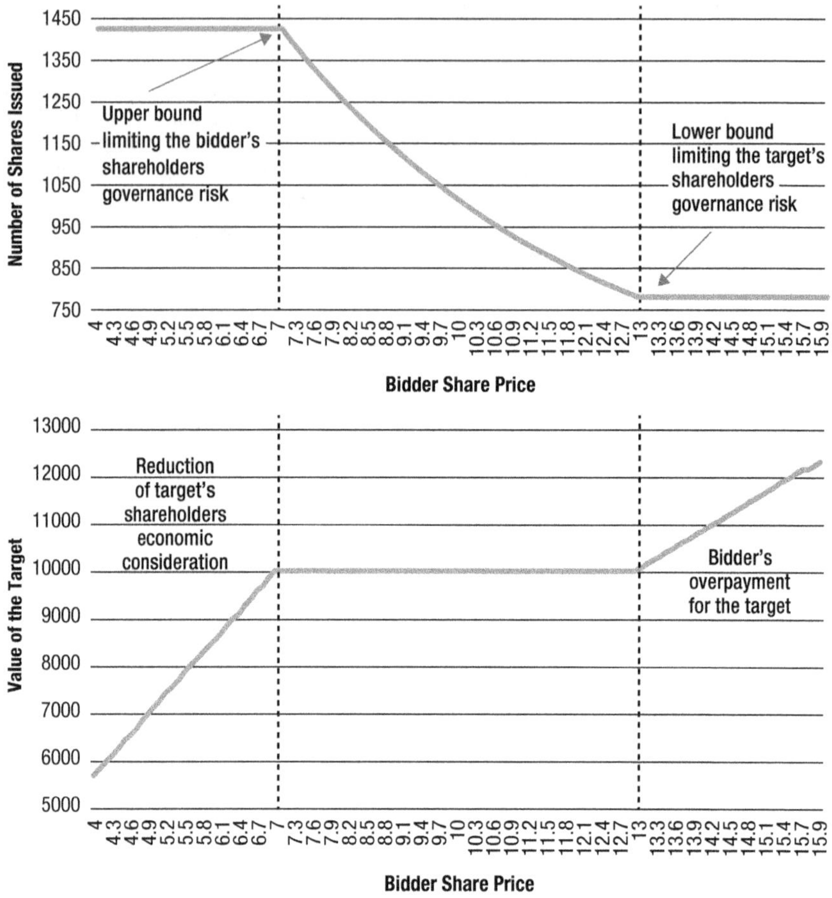

- If the exchange ratio were 1.2, which belongs to the acceptable range of values, the bidder would have to issue enough shares worth c. \$8.33 each (\$10/1.2 = \$8.33) in order to afford the fixed \$10,000 acquisition price. Indeed, the bidder would have to issue 1,200.48 shares, which is more than what the bidder would have to issue if its share price were \$10 per share (share price at the time of the Definitive Agreement). Even though these deal terms would be more dilutive in terms of governance and control for the bidder's shareholders, they are still in the acceptable range. Pro-forma, the bidder would pay \$10,000 to acquire the target and it would own c. 45.45% of the firm.
- If the exchange ratio were 0.5, meaning that the bidder's share price would be \$20, the bidder would have to issue the number of shares pre-determined in the collar agreement (lower bound). In our example, we already mentioned that if the exchange ratio were below 0.77, the bidder would have to issue c. 769.23 shares to the target's shareholders. This would reduce the target's control dilution risk, as without the collar it would only have received 500 shares of the bidder's stock (\$10,000/\$20 = 500). However, as the number of shares would be fixed, the amount paid for the target would move in line with the bidder's stock price. Therefore, instead

of paying $10,000, the bidder would issue c. 699.79 shares each worth $20, which corresponds to c. $14,000 overall. Although in that specific case the bidder will overpay for the target, the economic risk is tighter than what it would be if the deal were structured as a pure "Fixed-Exchange Ratio" deal, as in the latter case, it would issue 1,000 shares worth $20, or $20,000 overall.

To sum up, Fixed-Price collars are used in order to reduce the governance and control risks borne by both the bidder and the target in Floating-Exchange ratio deals. By fixing a lower and an upper bound, the collar limits the fluctuations of ownership percentages. In our example, both the target and bidder's shareholders would not hold less than 45% of the firm. Note that without collars the ownership percentages could theoretically fluctuate between 0% and 100%. Therefore, even though the floating-exchange rate collar adds economic risk for both the bidder and the target, it significantly reduces governance/control risk.

Therefore, to limit the uncertainty on the ownership structure, the two parties might negotiate a floating-exchange ratio collar, also known as fixed-payment collar, which guarantees the target's shareholders a fixed value ($10,000 for example) as long as the exchange ratio stays within a given range (for example [0.77:1.43]), and a fixed number of shares if the exchange ratio breaks out of the bounds. Notice that outside those bounds, as the number of shares is fixed, the value is uncertain and depends on the bidder stock price.

10.3.2 The economic rationale for collars

The main economic rationale for including collars is to minimize the costs of re-negotiation that will arise if the deal terms materially change between the definitive agreement and the closing date.

As we saw earlier, in classic stock deals (either floating-exchange ratio or fixed-exchange ratio deals) the parties are exposed to the volatility of the bidder price, which may significantly impact the deal terms: either the economic consideration or the post-transaction ownership structure.

If, due to volatility of the bidder's share price, the deals terms change to a great extent, the parties will bear huge renegotiation costs, as both the bidder's and the target's boards of directors have an ex-post incentive (and a fiduciary duty) to demand renegotiation of the proposed merger terms in order to act to the benefit of their shareholders. Therefore, even though the use of a collar may increase the initial pre-bid costs of contracting, it could significantly reduce the ex-ante expected costs of renegotiation, which are usually more expensive that those pre-agreement. The academic literature supports this point, as it has demonstrated that the inclusion of a collar in a merger bid significantly reduces the probability (by half) that the bid price will require renegotiation prior to resolution.

Therefore, this explains why collars are often used in M&A transactions involving firms that face very different economic shocks, or have very different market value sensitivities to the same shocks (i.e., are not positively correlated). In this type of stock deal, an economic event will impact the bidder and the target stock price to different extents, and so, it is likely to require ex-post renegotiation.

10.3.3 Merger arbitrage

Merger arbitrage (also known as risk arbitrage) is an important segment of the fast-growing "event-driven strategies" in the hedge fund industry. In very simple terms, merger arbitrage is a strategy that consists of betting on whether an M&A transaction will be successful or not. It involves buying the target firm (and sometimes shorting the bidder) on the announcement of a takeover bid in the hope that the bidder will succeed in acquiring the target and benefitting from the changes in the bidder's and target's price caused by the event.

It should be remembered that historically in M&A deals, post-announcement, the target's stock price tends to go up while the bidder stock price tends to depreciate. According to the literature, this is due to the fact that as the bidder will pay a premium to market in order to take over the target, the target's stock price will converge towards the offered price, while the bidder's stock will decrease as it will take into account the risk of overpaying and unsuccessfully integrating the target after the transaction.

As a result, a typical merger arbitrage aims at benefiting from the surge of the target stock price, purchasing the target stock on announcement of the takeover, and holding it until the end of the offer period. If the bid is successful, the target stock is sold to the bidder and the full "premium spread" will be gained.

However, in reality, merger arbitrage strategies are a little bit more difficult, as they differ depending on whether the M&A deal is a cash deal or a stock deal.

In a cash offer, an arbitrageur will simply take long positions in the target company – buy stock – and bet that the deal will be successful. The arbitrageur's profit is in that case the "arbitrage spread" between the stock price at the time of announcement and the offer price (which is often at a premium to the market price) if the deal goes through.

However, in stock offers, the acquiring company does not offer cash, but rather its own shares in exchange for target shares. As a consequence, an arbitrageur will buy target stock as in a cash offer, but he will also have a short position – borrowing to sell – in the acquirer stock. An arbitrageur does this because if the deal is successful, in return for the target's shares he will receive the promised number of the acquirer's shares. As event-driven hedge funds are not interested in owning the acquirer stock but in monetizing their investment, they will short the acquirer's stock. Therefore, the profit for the arbitrageur will be the combination of the increasing target price (long the target's stock) and the possibly falling acquirer price (short the acquirer's stock).

a) Merger Arbitrage Return in a Cash Deal

The expected return for purchasing one share of a target firm at the announcement of a cash bid with an offer price $P^{Target}_{Bid\ Success}$, and holding it until the conclusion of the bid period, can be written as follows:

$$E\left(R^{Target}_{Cash}\right) = \pi R^{Target}_{Bid\ Success} + (1-\pi)E\left(R^{Target}_{Bid\ Failure}\right)$$

Where:

$$R^{Target}_{Success} = \frac{P^{Target}_{Bid\ Success} - P^{Target}_{Pre\text{-}Announcement}}{P^{Target}_{Pre\text{-}Announcement}} \text{ and } E\left(R^{Target}_{Bid\ Failure}\right) = \frac{E\left(P^{Target}_{Bid\ Failure}\right) - P^{Target}_{Pre\text{-}Announcement}}{P^{Target}_{Pre\text{-}Annoucement}}$$

$\pi R^{Target}_{Bid\ Success}$ is the known bid period return that will accrue to holders of the target stock if the bid succeeds $\left(R^{Target}_{Bid\ Success}\right)$, multiplied by the probability that it will succeed (π). $R^{Target}_{Bid\ Success}$ is known and not expected as $P^{Target}_{Bid\ Success}$ is fixed upon the deal's announcement: it is the price the acquirer offered the target's shareholders.

On the other hand, $(1-\pi)E\left(R^{Target}_{Bid\ Failure}\right)$ is the expected bid period return that will accrue to holders of the target stock if the bid fails $\left(R^{Target}_{Bid\ Failure}\right)$, multiplied by the probability that it will fail ($1-\pi$). In this case, the return is estimated and not known as the return will depend on how the market reacts to the announcement of the deal's failure. In any case, the target's share price will tend to decrease, as the acquirer will not pay the premium to market price offered in order to takeover the target. However, to what extent the target's price may fluctuate post-failure announcement is unknown. For example, the target's stock price could simply go back to its level before the M&A announcement $\left(P^{Target}_{Pre\text{-}Announcement}\right)$. However, it may go below or above the pre-announcement price as the media coverage around the transaction may have incentivized analysts to investigate the company and assess its fair value.

b) Merger Arbitrage Return in Stock Deal

In a stock-swap bid, the offer price for the target company is the bidder's expected price at the conclusion of the bid period, $E\left(P^{Bidder}_{Bid\ Success}\right)$, multiplied by the exchange ratio, ω. In this case, the expected return for purchasing one share of the target at the announcement of the bid and holding it until the conclusion of the bid period is as follows:

$$E\left(R^{Target}_{Stock}\right) = \pi E\left(R^{Target}_{Bid\ Success}\right) + (1-\pi)E\left(R^{Target}_{Bid\ Failure}\right)$$

Where:

$E\left(R^{Target}_{Bid\ Failure}\right)$ is as above, but the expected return on the target stock if the bid is sucessful becomes:

$$E\left(R^{Target}_{Bid\ Success}\right) = \frac{\omega E\left(P^{Bidder}_{Bid\ Success}\right) - P^{Target}_{Pre\text{-}Announcement}}{P^{Target}_{Pre\text{-}Announcement}}$$

As in a stock-swap takeover, the merger arbitrage position is established by buying the target at the start of the offer period and at the same time short-selling ω shares of the bidder's stock; the arbitrageur will benefit from both the increase in the target's share price and the decrease in the acquirer's share price. However, if the deal does not complete or is withdrawn, the negative returns will also come from the positions of both the target (long position) and the acquirer (short position).

If the takeover succeeds, the trader sells the target shares to the bidder at $\omega P^{Bidder}_{Bid\ Success}$ per share as soon as the outcome is known, and at the same time buys back the bidder's shares at $P^{Bidder}_{Bid\ Success}$. If the takeover fails, the trader sells the target shares at $P^{Target}_{Bid\ Failure}$ and buys back the bidder's shares at $P^{Bidder}_{Bid\ Failure}$. The expected return of this merger arbitrage strategy (ignoring transaction costs for simplicity) is $E(R^{MA}_{Stock})$, and can be written as follows:

$$E\left(R^{MA}_{Stock}\right) = E\left(R^{Target}_{Stock}\right) - E\left(R^{Bidder}\right) = \pi\left(\frac{\omega E\left(P^{Bidder}_{Bidder\ Success}\right) - P^{Target}_{Pre-Announcement}}{P^{Target}_{Pre-Announcement}}\right) +$$

$$(1-\pi)\left(\frac{E\left(P^{Bidder}_{Bid\ Failure}\right) - P^{Target}_{Pre-Annoucement}}{P^{Target}_{Pre-Annoucement}}\right) - \pi\left(\frac{E\left(P^{Bidder}_{Bid\ Success}\right) - P^{Bidder}_{Pre-Announcement}}{P^{Bidder}_{Pre-Announcement}}\right) -$$

$$-(1-\pi)\left(\frac{E\left(P^{Bidder}_{Bid\ Failure}\right) - P^{Bidder}_{Pre-Annoucement}}{P^{Bidder}_{Pre-Annoucemeny}}\right)$$

However, accepting this fact does not necessarily compromise the fundamental theory of efficient financial markets. Merger arbitrage returns are obtained by the arbitrageur taking large risks, which the average investor does not want to bear. A large portion of the returns gained by the arbitrageurs can be explained by their role in merger and acquisitions transactions.[20]

10.3.4 The arbitrage spread

Merger arbitrage is an investment strategy that takes advantage of the difference between the share price and the offer price of a target after the announcement of a merger or an acquisition bid.

In fact, upon the deal announcement, the target's share price will react to a takeover bid by nearing the bid offer, but because of deal completion risk, there remains a small premium in the share price which is called the "arbitrage spread." In other words, when an announcement is made, the target shares will instantly jump to a lev-

[20] "In common financial practice, a signal to assess market perception on the likelihood of a deal (i.e. successful or not) when there is a fixed-Exchange Ratio ("ER") is to monitor the ratio of the target share price and the bidder share price. If this ratio is in line with the announced ER, the market believes the deal will go through at the proposed conditions." (R. Pambianco, 2020)

el close to, but usually not exactly equal to, the offer price due to uncertainty regarding the ultimate success of the takeover. The difference between what the stock price jumps to, the post-announcement share price, and what the acquirer has proposed to pay for the target stock is called the arbitrage spread. The size of this spread depends on the probability of success for the deal: it tends to diminish with the time left to complete the deal and with positive signals from shareholders and regulators.

The practitioners of this trade are the arbitrageurs who take positions after a takeover announcement to harvest the arbitrage spread. Merger arbitrage is not like classical arbitrage in the sense of the absolute risk-free trading of similar assets at different prices; it does entail the risk of the merger failing and the share price falling to pre-announcement levels. In reality, there are many risk factors that can cause an M&A deal to fail:

a) **Shareholder problems**: Any merger or acquisition is dependent on the shareholders of the target company approving the offer by the acquirer. When an offer announcement is made, it is up to the majority of the shareholders to approve the offer in a vote. If they approve of selling their shares to the bidder, they "tender" their shares successfully. If the offer bid is too low in the minds of the shareholders, the merger will be unsuccessful. It is easier for shareholders to oppose mergers than tender offers. A merger has a long time frame, giving activists a better opportunity to convince shareholders to vote against it. In a tender offer, with a much shorter time frame, shareholders may have tendered their shares already by the time they receive word of opposition. In addition, they will receive the consideration from the tender offer much sooner than any better deal in the future.
b) **Regulatory problems**: In many instances, a merger will need approval from certain government agencies in order to be completed. These are often agencies that are tasked with monitoring and regulating market competition in a country. The Federal Trade Commission and the U.S. Department of Justice Antitrust Division are the main regulatory agencies in charge of ensuring fair competition and consumer protection in the US. If one of these agencies sees a merger between two companies as "anticompetitive," and fears that the result of the merger will be monopolistic power, unfair competitive advantages, and increased consumer prices, they might step in and stop the merger. In fact, all mergers between listed public companies in the U.S. require the explicit consent of the Federal Trade Commission to be valid.
c) **Funding problems**: Funding risk is the risk that the necessary funding required to complete a transaction will not be available. Due to changing factors such as market and deal conditions, the acquirer might lose the financing required to complete a deal. Overall market conditions might change, making what once seemed a profitable investment unprofitable. Elements such as changing interest rates can sometimes reduce the net present value of merger projects.
d) **Internal target resistance**: Not all mergers are "happy marriages" between consenting parties. If the merger is in fact a hostile takeover, the acquirer might face resistance from within the target company. There are several defences against hostile takeovers, such as "poison pills" that can stand in the way of a merger.

Figure 10.9 Illustration of the Arbitrage Spread

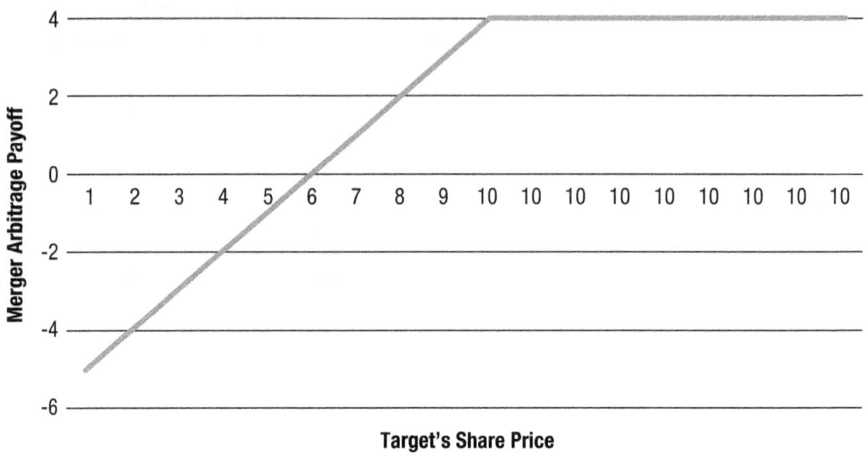

e) **Material Adverse Change (MAC)**: There is a contingency found in most M&A contracts stipulating the conditions in which the acquirer may legally terminate the deal in the event of certain occurrences in the deal process. The clauses usually regard the surfacing of aspects of the target company during the due diligence that drastically change the valuation of the company.[21] The rationale for these kinds of contracts is the protection of the acquiring firm from shady business practices. In general, judicial expertise is a necessity for arbitrageurs to understand the highly sophisticated deal terms of tender offers.

10.3.5 The interpretation of the arbitrage spread

The arbitrage spread is an indicator of the likelihood of deal completion. Indeed, the current target stock price can be seen as the probability-weighted average of two outcomes:

a) the deal is consummated and the Target's shareholders receive the bid price; or
b) the merger fails and the Target price is at its stand-alone level:

$$P^{Target}_{Current} = Pr.P^{Target}_{Bid\ Succces} + \left(1 - Pr.\right) P^{Target}_{Bid\ Failure}$$

---

[21] "Or changes to the macroeconomic conditions/scenario in which the merger has been announced. For example, a drop in financial markets by more than X% between the announcement date and the closing. Companies and their advisors tend to extensively negotiate MAC clauses in the transaction documents." (R. Pambianco, 2020)

Therefore, if there are significant risks that the deal may not close, the arbitrage spread will be larger, while on the contrary, if the deal is very likely to close, the spread will be very tight. The spread tends to diminish with the time left to complete the deal and with positive signals from shareholders and regulators.

10.4 Deal-contingent derivatives transactions

Deal-contingent derivatives are instruments used by Corporates, Financial Sponsors and other entities to hedge the market risk present in M&A deals. In fact, M&A transactions are also subject to a number of external variables that may impact the acquisition price. Let us take the example of a cross-border deal: an Italian corporation looking to acquire a target in the United States. In order to pay the acquisition price (denominated in US Dollars), the buyer may enter into a FX Forward Agreement ("FX Forward") to buy the USD amount required versus EUR on a forward basis. However, if the M&A does not complete for any reason, the FX Forward is cancelled, so the client would have the issue of having to settle the FX Forward, or dealing with a mark-to-market which could be positive or negative, in the case where they no longer need the USD to complete the M&A. In order to avoid that kind of situation, banks have created "Deal-Contingent Derivatives" which allow the parties to hedge a specific market risk, and in case the deal does not go through, cancel the hedge at zero mark-to-market leaving the bank with a sudden loss (or profit) equal to the value of the contingent contract. This potential loss can be mitigated by hedging with options. The underlying hedge is normally an FX Forward, but could also be an interest rate or currency swap.

Therefore, as the bank will take on the risk that the deal may fail, at the point of agreeing on the DC Forward with the client, it will typically immediately enter into a vanilla back-to-back Forward ("BtB Hedge") with the market. The risk of the M&A not materializing can be mitigated by the bank using hedging that can be expensive. Given its characteristics and risks, not all banks are able to offer these products. It is easier for banks that are part of the advisory group, that have more insight on the likelihood of success of the M&A.

10.4.1 Deal timeline/approach

Typically, clients enter into Deal-Contingent Hedges at or shortly after the time the M&A is announced, and the Shareholder Purchase Agreement or equivalent (the "SPA") is signed.

The period of the Contingency Risk is from that point up until the earliest of the dates on which the M&A completes, the Long Stop Date of the SPA is reached, or the Shareholder Purchase Agreement terminates because it has become clear that the deal contingency cannot be satisfied before the Long Stop Date ("Contingency Risk Period"). Normally, the Contingency Period can vary from a few months up to a year. The main risk is the potential failure of the underlying M&A Deal.

Figure 10.10 Deal Timeline of Contingent Derivatives

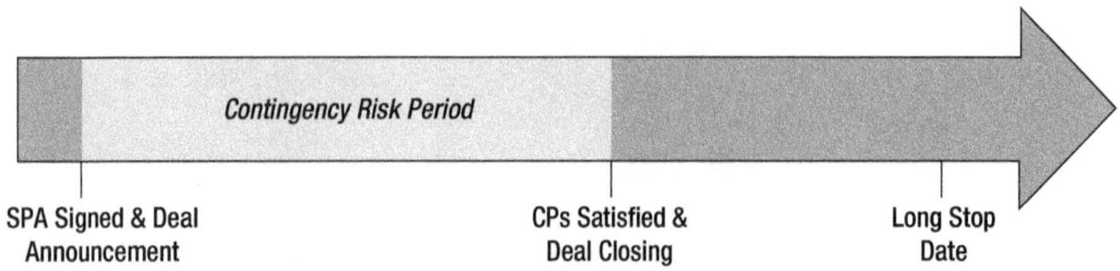

Banks charge a premium for the DC Risk, over and above the cost of the vanilla FX Forward ("DC Premium"). The DC Premium is a % that reflects the probability of deal failure (the market requests a percentage between 20 and 30% for highly probable transactions).

10.5 Conclusions

To sum up, we should keep in mind that M&A transactions are important steps for corporates and financial sponsors, but they are also very risky transactions. When acquiring a target, the bidder is exposed to two distinct type of risks:

a) the post-closing risk occurring after the deal closure, during the integration phase;
b) the pre-closing risk occurring between the definitive agreement and the deal closure.

First, post-closing risk is the risk that is related to the uncertainty around the future performance of the target. Remember that a fundamental theory of finance is that the price of an asset should be equal to the present value of the future cash flows that the asset is expected to generate. However, depending on the target, the estimation of the future cash flows could be difficult to assess. In fact, cash flows can be impacted by many unpredictable factors and variables such as customer demand/trends, macroeconomic conditions, regulations, etc. Therefore, due to the impossibility to predict with certainty the target cash flows (in most cases), the bidder bears the risk of overpaying for the target: overestimating the future cash flows. On the other hand, the seller also bears the risk of undervaluing its assets due to the impossibility to accurately predict the asset's cash flows. Therefore, in order to hedge this specific risk, Investment Bankers have created an instrument called "Earnouts" which enables parties to defer part of the acquisition price and adjust the acquisition price depending on the target performance (Sales, EBITDA, etc.). Moreover, according to the literature, earnouts are not only a useful instrument to hedge post-closing risk, but also an instrument that reduces the information asymmetry in M&A. In fact, this view affirms that earnouts provisions are accepted only by sellers that have a high level of confidence in the quality of their company, as well as in the company's ability to generate earnings across the forecasting period. Therefore, more than acting as hedging instruments, earnouts can also enable bidders to identify "healthy" targets.

Second, both the bidder and target are subject to another type of risk entitled "pre-closing risk." This risk is mainly due to the fact that, between the Definitive Agreement listing all the key deal terms including the acquisition price and the actual deal's conclusion, some time is required, and fluctuations of bidder share prices may influence the terms of the deal, and consequently reduce the likelihood that the deal closes. Note that this "pre-closure risk" is unique to public M&A transactions, as in an all-cash deal the consideration is independent of any changes in bidder share price. It is also very important to mention that in a stock transaction both the target and the bidder are exposed to fluctuations of the bidder's stock price and that, based on the type of deal structure (fixed-exchange ratio vs floating-exchange ratio), the parties bear different kind of risks. In fact, in a fixed-exchange ratio deal, the two parties bear an "economic risk"; the risk of significant changes in the overall deal value. This is due to the fact that in a fixed-exchange ratio deal, the number of the bidder's shares distributed to the target is fixed and therefore, if the price fluctuates, so does the consideration paid to the target. On the other hand, in a floating-exchange ratio, the parties bear a "governance/control risk"; the risk of changes in the shareholder structure in terms of percentage of ownership. Here, as the acquisition price is fixed, the number of shares issued to the target is variable and fluctuates depending on the acquirer's stock price. If its stock price increases, then the bidder will have to issue fewer new shares to afford the acquisition price, and therefore, the bidder's shareholders will own a greater percentage of the company than estimated before. On the contrary, if the bidder's stock price decreases, then it will have to issue more shares, and thus its control of the pro-forma firm would be more diluted. Therefore, in order to limit to what extend the bidder and the target are subject to the bidder's stock price volatility, Investment Bankers have invented "collars." More specifically, in a fixed-exchange ratio deal, as the target and the bidder are exposed to economic risk, the parties may decide to include a collar provision stating that the exchange ratio will remain fixed if the bidder's stock price belongs to the range [x:y] upon completion, and otherwise (outside of the boundaries) a floating-exchange ratio will be implemented in order to fix the floor and ceiling acquisition price. On the other side, in a Floating-Exchange Ratio deal, the parties are exposed to Dilution risk, and thus they may decide to include a Floating-Exchange Ratio Collar in order to limit this risk. In that case, the exchange ratio will be floating if upon completion the bidder's price is within the interval [x:y]. That way, the acquisition price will be fixed if the bidder's stock price varies slightly; otherwise, the acquisition price will fluctuate but it would not impact the post-deal shareholder structure (dilution).

Finally, to mitigate FX and interest/currency risks in a future M&A deal, corporates can use Contingent-Hedging Instruments.

10.6 Summary

When there is a difference between the bid and ask in a negotiation, one way for companies to find common ground is to agree on a variety of deferred/value-bridging payment structures. One solution is to do an earnout, meaning that the Buyer and the Seller agree on deferred payment based on Target performance post-acquisition in addition to the Buyer's initial payment to the Seller. An earnout structure may meet the Seller's desire to continue upside participation in the company's stand-alone prospects. When doing an earnout, it is important to consider the period of the earnout, the parties involved, the measurement of performance, or the form of compensation.

Earnouts on the Target's performance can be divided in two categories.

- Strictly-performance based: if the buyer and the seller disagree on the future performance of the company, they may want to stipulate an earnout deal where a payment is made upfront, and potential additional payments will be made if the company generates high earnings.
- Event-based: for example, if the target company's future performance depends largely on the registration of a new patent, there may be an earnout depending on the outcome of this event.

For Sellers, the main advantage of earnouts is allowing the Seller's shareholders to lock in a base value for the company while retaining participation in further upside. Meanwhile, the main disadvantage is the risk of shifting the risk entirely onto the seller's side.

For Buyers, the main advantage is to close the gap and possibly decrease the overall price demanded for the acquisition from the Target company. The disadvantage is that this structure may lead to ongoing operational, financial, and management conflicts.

Questions and answers

1. *What are the three different risks in M&A transactions?*
   a) The post-closing risk occurring after the deal closure, during the integration phase;
   b) the pre-closing risk occurring between the definitive agreement and the deal closure;
   c) the market risk linked to the transaction (currency, interest rates fluctuations, etc.).

2. *What are the three different instruments that corporates and financial sponsors can use to mitigate those risks?*

   a) Earnouts;
   b) Collars;
   c) Deal-Contingent Derivatives.

3. *According to the literature, what is the signal that earnouts send to the market?*
   According to the literature, Earnouts reduce the information asymmetry in an M&A transaction as the target's shareholders would only accept an earnout clause if they are confident that the business will perform up to expectations in the future. In other words, Earnouts prove that the management of the target is optimistic about the target's future performance and health.

4. *Name the two types of stock exchange ratios in stock-for-stock transactions. How do they differ?*
   a) Fixed-Exchange Ratio Deals: the number of shares issued by the bidder to the target is fixed and the economic consideration depends on the bidder stock price;
   b) Floating-Exchange Ratio Deals: the acquisition price is fixed and the number of shares issued to the target depends on the bidder stock price. The bidder should issue enough shares in order to afford the acquisition.

5. *In the case of a Fixed-Exchange Ratio Deal, what is the risk borne by the parties? How can they limit the risk?*
   In the case of a Fixed-Exchange Ratio Deal, the risk borne is an Economic Risk, as the post-deal ownership structure is fixed but the consideration will depend on the bidder's stock price. To reduce that risk, the parties may agree to include a Collar agreement limiting the economic risk by setting a minimum and maximum acquisition price (floating-exchange ratio outside of the collars bounds).

6. *In the case of a Floating-Exchange Ratio Deal, what is the risk borne by the parties? How can they limit the risk?*
   In the case of a Floating-Exchange Ratio Deal, the risk borne is a Dilution Risk, as the acquisition price is fixed but the number of shares issued by the bidder depends on its stock price. To reduce that risk, the parties may agree to include a Collar agreement limiting the economic risk by setting a minimum and maximum number of shares issued (fixed-exchange ratio outside of the collar bounds).

7. *How can the market risks linked to an M&A deal be reduced? What is the specificity of this kind of derivative?*
   In order to hedge market risks, corporates can acquire Deal-Contingent Derivatives. The main advantage of this instrument is that in the case the M&A fails, the hedge can be cancelled with zero mark-to-market.

11 Corporate Restructuring

by Gimede Gigante and Luigi Caprotti[1]

11.1 Introduction. Market trends and evolution of restructuring

With the outbreak of the 2008 crisis, the number of refinancing deals as well as the number of defaults and restructurings increased astonishingly. In the previous decade, capital markets and corporate structures were heavily affected by the new private equity activities and "*modus operandi*" of raising debts to run large-scale acquisitions worldwide. The huge amount of debt raised and circulated in several countries and several currencies, the related collateralized instruments (CDOs, CLOs, and other derivatives) and the increasing appetite for leveraged buyouts, made the global capital markets highly interconnected and interdependent and corporate capital structures extremely complex and risky. Eventually, this situation started to collapse, with the fall of Lehman Brothers and the global financial crisis. The new market conditions revealed companies' difficulties, inefficiencies, and wrong strategies, which ultimately resulted in unsustainable asset and liability structures, unprofitable P&Ls, and a shortage of cash flows. This is why companies started hiring financial advisors to help them get out of trouble and fix their financial structures and business models. This resulted in a dramatic rise of restructuring deals, and in the worst cases, of defaults.

However, even though the amount of debt rapidly decreased right after 2008, companies again raised their level of indebtedness in recent years, becoming an element of concern for the market, especially under the light of the current global pandemic, which is exposing more companies to the risk of default everyday. As a matter of fact, restructuring and refinancing deals have again gained a lot of traction among financial institutions.

Figure 11.1 shows how the share of refinancing deals spiked after 2008. In 2009, refinancing accounted for more than 60% of all the deals run in Europe. The share in volume terms eventually went down, but it remained significantly higher than in the pre-financial crisis period.

The number of defaults and restructurings followed a trend similar to that of refinancing.

[1] With the precious support of Maria Teresa Iardella and Andrea Cerri.

Figure 11.1 Deal Purpose Diversification (based on volume)

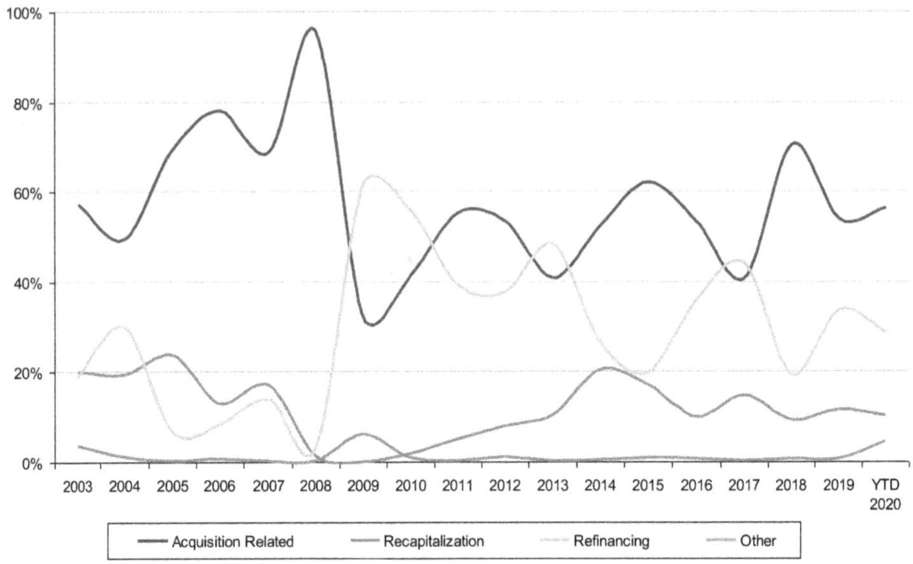

Source: Authors' elaboration based on data from S&P Global, Market Intelligence. 2020 Observations: 82 deals with €37.2bn equivalent volume

Although they have never gone back to the 2009 level, defaults and restructurings have risen significantly since the Covid-19 pandemic outbreak, as shown in **Figure 11.2**.

Figure 11.3 points out that, after 2007, European companies started deleveraging, as suggested by the average Net Debt/EBITDA ratio reduction between 2007 and the last part of the decade (from approximately 6.0x to 4.0x in only three years). Moreover, in this period, Second Lien indebtedness became almost null as a result of its high cost for the debtor side, and the high risk for the creditor side. Second Lien Debt eventually become fashionable again, as the overall Net Debt/EBITDA ratio resumed growing. As also mentioned previously, Covid-19 affected the market significantly. The overall EBITDA contraction across several industries since the outbreak of the pandemic has made the overall ratio increase again significantly, to approximately 5.5x.

The **Figure 11.4** below points out how sources of debt have changed over time in Europe. Right after the 2008 crisis senior debt was the main source of financing, given its much lower risk profile, and the market consistently reduced the usage of bonds as source of financing. It is interesting to notice though that after the crisis, borrowers started looking for alternative hybrid solutions such as mix of senior debt and bonds or senior debt and Second Lien financings, which became increasingly fashionable after 2010.

Figure 11.2 Number of Defaults vs Restructuring

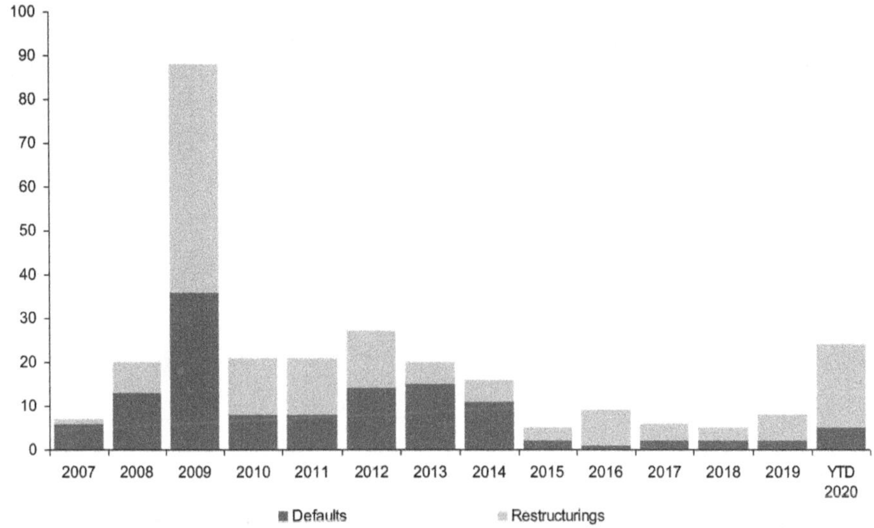

Source: S&P Global, Market Intelligence. Distressed credits are issues rated D or restructuring. Volume by Sr. Par Issue reflects only total amounts of senior loan debt issued as tracked by LCD's analysis.

Figure 11.3 Annual Pro Forma Debt/EBITDA Ratios

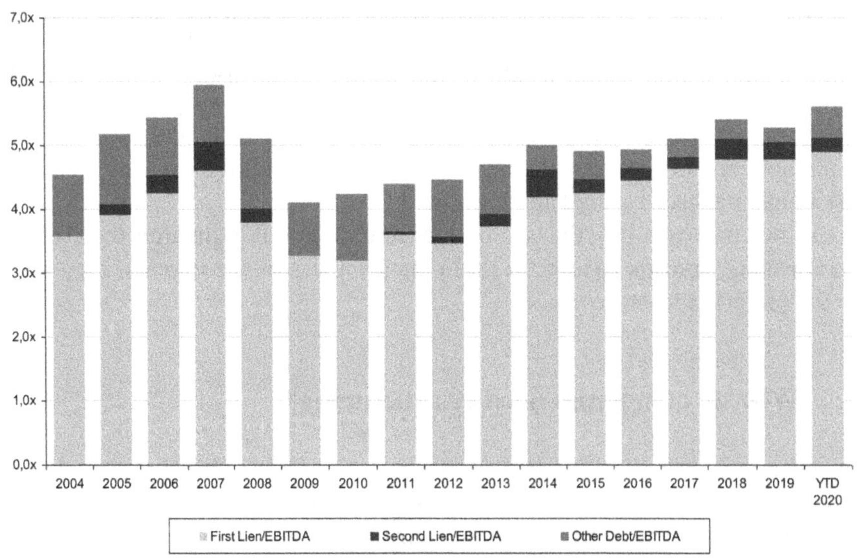

Source: S&P Global, Market Intelligence. Excludes Broadcasting, Cable & Telecom loans prior to 2002.

Figure 11.4 European borrowers' sources of funding

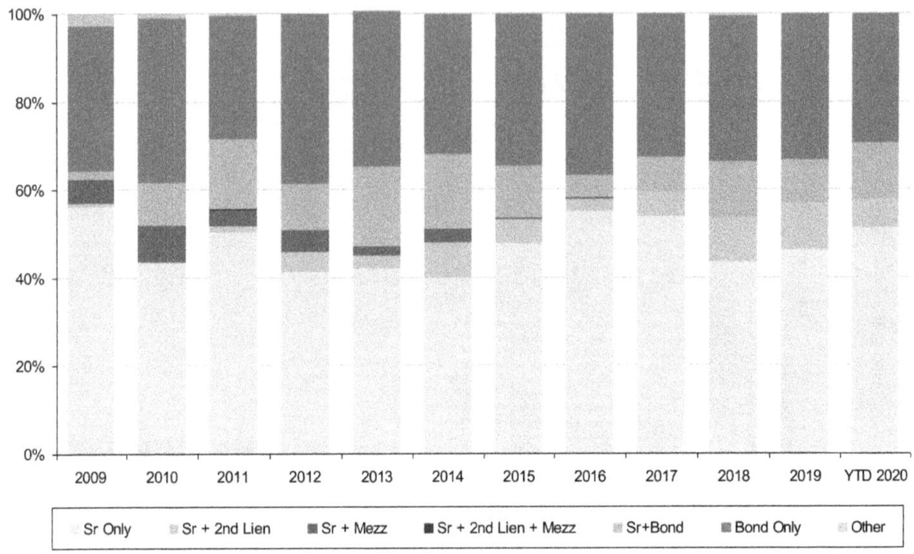

Source: S&P Global, Market Intelligence. The chart shows sources of funding used by European borrowers in the leveraged finance space. LCD looks at all leveraged loans, HY bonds, and mezzanine transactions and calculates the share based on transaction count. For example, in 1H15, 48% of all European borrowers in the lev fin space relied solely on the leveraged loan market while 35% relied solely on the HY bond market.

As indicated in **Figure 11.5**, just one year after the 2008 contraction due to the global financial crisis, high-yield bonds went back to their pre-crisis levels, but with a more prudent configuration, as subordinated bonds almost disappeared and secured bonds increased their weight up to almost 50% in 2010. The overall amount of high-yield bonds kept growing especially in 2013 and 2017, but with a relatively stable weight between secured and unsecured.

As shown in **Figure 11.6**, the cost of debt rose massively right after the crisis. Although average spreads have been declining for the past three years, they are far from the pre-crisis level.

11.2 Why do companies need restructuring?

Companies need restructuring when they enter a crisis and fall into financial distress.

The number one reason why a business goes into distress is its inability to generate profits and cash and ultimately to meet its obligations. Denis & Denis (1990) define distress as three consecutive years of net losses, however, we need to go a little deeper to understand the real drivers behind such a situation.

Figure 11.5 European High-Yield Bond Volume

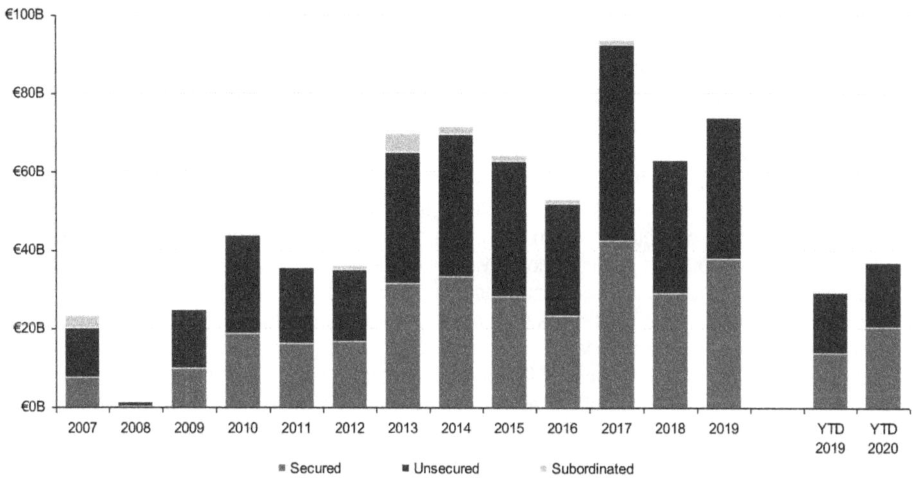

Source: S&P Global, Market Intelligence. Includes fixed and floating rate notes.

Figure 11.6 Distribution of Spreads Based Upon Facilities

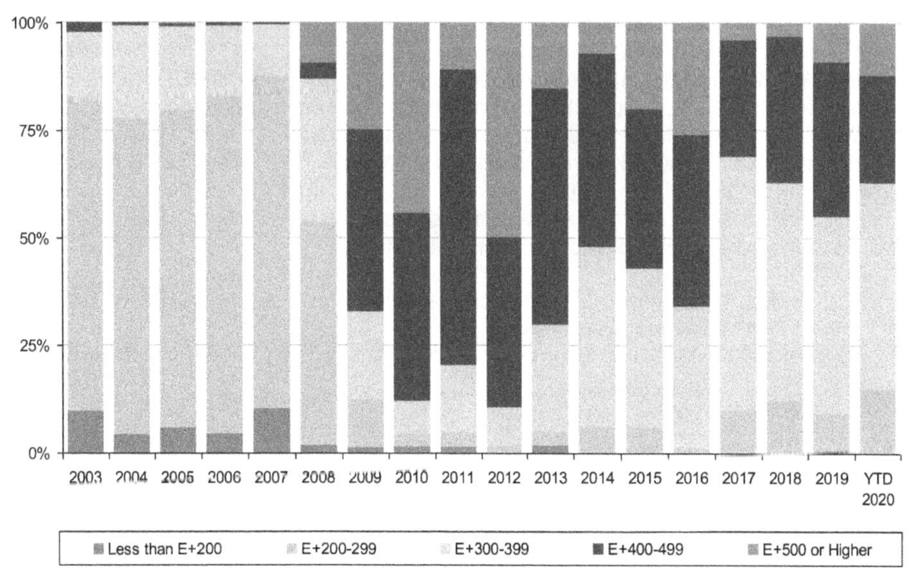

Source: S&P Global, Market Intelligence. Based only upon First Lien tranches. Shares are based upon facility count.

Box 11.1 Examples of business crises

Blockbuster

On 1 September 2010, Blockbuster, the long-lasting video rental leader from the 1990s, filed for bankruptcy protection under Chapter 11 after over a decade of crisis, characterized by cumulative losses, unsustainable capital structure, and failed attempts to regain profitability.
Founded in 1985, in Dallas, Texas, Blockbuster quickly grew in the video rental business through its brick and mortar stores strategy and established a dominant position in the US, but also abroad, being present in over 16 countries with more than 2,000 physical stores. While trying to maximize the profitability of its core business with its famous "late fees" model, in the early 2000s Blockbuster pursued an expansion strategy into the videogame rental market also via acquisitions, which ultimately led to an increasing level of indebtedness and to an expensive capital and asset structure. On the other side, new competitors were making their entry into the video rental market with innovative offerings. One of those new players was Netflix.
Ultimately, what led Blockbuster out of the market was the combination of the multiple factors: increasing competition in the media entertainment industry, that Blockbuster initially disregarded (confident of its dominant position, the company did not feel any threat to its core business and did not realize that competitors, mainly Netflix, had started eating into its consumer base); new consumer preferences that the company was not able to spot (i.e. mailing and delivery preferred to physical presence at stores); technological innovation and digital expansion, for which it was not sufficiently prepared (i.e. the rise of Netflix and digital platforms); the high level of debt contracted in periods of expansion and "soft competition"; and finally, the 2008 global economic crisis, which made the operating environment much more complex.[1]

Kodak

In 2012, Kodak filed for bankruptcy (Chapter 11) after recording net losses for five straight years and with assets worth $5.1bn versus $6.8bn of debt. Ultimately, the long-lasting crisis was a result of the lack of innovation and late entrance of Kodak into the digital camera market. For three years, starting in 1993, the company pursued a cost cutting strategy, to make its products more accessible and competitive against the successful rise of low cost films such as Fujifilm. However, during those years, Kodak was not able to keep up with digital innovation. It made its debut into the digital segment only in 1996, with the DC20 line, when the market was already crowded with many players (HP, Sony, Canon, etc.). Furthermore, even if Kodak was investing in digital cameras, it was not able to shift its core competences from film manufacturing.[2]

[1] Source: Davis T., Higgins J., (2013) "A Blockbuster Failure: How an Outdated Business Model Destroyed a Giant." The University of Tennessee.
[2] Source: Raffaelli R., Snively C., "The Reinvention of Kodak." (24 August 2020). Harvard Business School.

Companies usually go into a financial crisis for one or more of the following reasons:

- Wrong strategy and business model, which result in non-competitiveness in the market, lack of topline growth, operational inefficiencies, and lower EBITDA margin than competitors. Poor business performance also indirectly affects the

Table 11.1 Nature of Risk and Reasons for the Crisis - conceptual table

Nature of the Risk	Reasons for the Crisis
Strategic Risks	Wrong Strategy and Business Model; Managerial Overconfidence; Product/Service Obsolence; Lack of Innovation
Financial Risks	Unsustainable Capital Structure; High Leverage; Expensive Asset Structure
Operational Risks	Employee Misconduct; Fraud
Legal Risks	Fraud; Changes in Market Regulations; New Patenting Legislation
Other Risks	External Macroeconomics Factors; High Public Debt; Political Turmoil; Global Pandemic; Natural Disasters

cost of indebtedness, as creditors ask for a higher return given the company results, which further reduces profitability.[2]

- Managerial overconfidence ("hubris"). CEOs and managers might take risky decisions which ultimately turn out to be very detrimental for the company. For example, expanding into a new market with a lot of up-front investments, or placing all bets on the wrong product.
- Product/Service obsolescence and lack of innovation. The source of a company's competitive advantage (a product or a service) becomes obsolete as new and better solutions become available in the market, and the company is not able to innovate and change the business model (i.e. Blockbuster or Kodak, as examples).
- Expensive Asset structure. Fixed investments (tangible and intangible) and CAPEX are too high and it is hard for the company to deliver an acceptable ROA and ROI above the cost of capital, benefit from economies of scale, and cover for depreciation and amortization. This problem becomes even bigger in the case of a drop in demand which leads to excess capacity and thus the inability to sustain fixed overheads.
- Unsustainable capital structure. When working capital is too positive and the company is not able to finance its current operations (i.e. disproportionate ratio between receivables and payables, or too high inventory), or when the company is under-capitalized or the level of debt is simply too high versus equity (D/E ratio).
- External Macro factors. New regulations which make the company no longer competitive and expel it from the market, new legislation over patenting rules and protection, high public debt and political turmoil, a national or global financial crisis, and pandemics and natural disasters.
- Fraud. For example, the Enron and Parmalat cases.

[2] This vicious loop of poor performance, higher cost of debt, and higher probability of default is interconnected with credit ratings. The worse the credit rating, the higher the risk, the higher the cost of debt and the higher the probability that the company will not be able to cover interest and principal payments. This is why numerous studies stress the importance of managing credit ratings (Ayers et. al 2010; Graham & Harvey 2001).

All these reasons for a crisis can be grouped into 5 different types of risks according to Miles (2010) and illustrated in **Table 11.1**:

1. Strategic Risks;
2. Financial Risks;
3. Operational Risks;
4. Legal Risks;
5. Other risks.

However, most of these problems could be veiled until some disruptive event occurs or the financial situation becomes unbearable and it becomes clear to the board of directors that the company is in a situation of distress. For example, when long-lasting inefficiencies are ignored or not properly tackled, sooner or later they will translate into shrinking margin and operating losses, equity decline and debt increase, and ultimately into a shortage of cash and thus into a financial crisis. Unfortunately, most of the times, a sense of urgency arises only when it's too late and the probability of recovery is very limited.

A financial crisis, rather than a cause, is the effect of these factors and can be identified with two main elements:

- Dramatic reduction of available cash;
- Losses, Equity reduction, and increase in Debt/Equity ratio.

The magnitude of financial distress can vary considerably. Tutino & Ranciaro (2015) divide the stages of crisis into three main blocks:

a) Underperforming Business. In this situation, the company has not necessarily breached covenants in financial agreements but is suffering from a credit downgrade as a result of poor performance. The management still has control over the business.
b) Restructuring Business. In this case, a breached of a covenant has taken place, the company is experiencing an Equity Value decrease, and the creditors start having more influence on the business.
c) Insolvent Business. This is the extreme case where the company is in deep financial troubles. The court must intervene to appoint an administrator and assets are disposed of in the attempt to minimize losses.

When the crisis is clear, the company hires a financial advisor, to seek all the possible solutions that could help improve its business model, profitability and liquidity, and to put it on a sound financial footing.

There are several actions that the company needs to take while the crisis is announced. Some of them are short-term oriented and aim at preserving the going concern, such as:

- appointment of advisers;
- if asked by banks, appointment of a chief restructuring officer (CRO);

- definition of new operational priorities;
- short-term analysis of resources needed and liquidity future estimates;
- facilities management (e.g. new short-term financing);
- working capital management;
- press management and internal communication management across all stakeholders.

Others are more long-term oriented and aim to radically change the business model and the capital structure of the company:

- business model and route-to-market review (this can be done together with a strategic consultant);
- performance, margin, and profitability improvement plan;
- overhead, blueprint, and footprint rationalization;
- assessment of liquidation scenario (to evaluate the extreme case of insolvency);
- financial restructuring;
- sale of non-core assets.

The overall process of solving a financial distress situation is called Restructuring. Agarwal & Helfat (2009) define restructuring as the series of action taken by the company to prevent bankruptcy and to improve its profitability, solidity, and liquidity.

The restructuring can be decided by the management team, or the shareholders, when they fear for the return of their investment or for the future of the company, and also by the creditors when they feel their open position is at risk. The nature of the stakeholder who actually initiates the process is fundamental for the overall restructuring. Originally, financial advisers were appointed by the borrower ("borrower-side mandates") with the aim of orchestrating the process in the interest of the company and its going concern status. Now, the financial creditors are usually the ones who initiate the process and hire the advisers ("creditor-side mandates"), given the situation initially described of highly-complex financial structure, layers of debt, a high number of creditors, and geographical and business differentiation.

Depending on the actions taken to save the company from bankruptcy, there are two types of restructuring:

- **Asset restructuring.** This consists of an extensive analysis of the company's business model to really understand which businesses, branches, assets, and products create value, and which actually drain resources or do not have any strategic relevance. The goal is, on the one hand, to get rid of whatever assets require resources and management attention and are not important for the survival and future of the company, or if they are too expensive to restructure, and on the other hand, to fix and reorganize the core strategic activities. The ultimate goal is to better strategically reposition the company and reset the basis for future growth.
- **Financial restructuring (or liabilities restructuring).** This is a deep dive on the company's capital structure, its solidity and debt sustainability, and the conse-

quent actions to take in order to fix it, protect the creditors, and preserve the status of going concern. This chapter will focus mostly on the financial restructuring side from both the standpoint of a private turnaround, and from a legal standpoint.

11.3 Assessing a distressed company

11.3.1 When does distress begin?

Before starting to dig into financial restructuring, it is important to understand what being in default means from a financial and accounting point of view.

A company is defined as in default when the value of its assets is not sufficient enough to cover its obligations and thus it is not able to meet lenders' terms. This means that total Assets are lower than Liabilities, hence equity is null or even negative. In other words, when the Recovery Ratio (RR), defined as the ratio between the value of assets and the value of existing liabilities, is lower than 1.

$$RR = (Value\ of\ Assets)\ /\ (Value\ of\ Liabilities)$$

Let us take into consideration the following example. In the second half of 2008, Company A showed the following financial figures:

- Total Assets \$1000m
- Total Liabilities \$900m
- Senior Debt \$850m
- Subordinated Loans \$50m
- Total Equity \$100m
- EBITDA \$90m

The implied Net Debt/EBITDA ratio was 10.0x and the Debt/Equity leverage 9x. Given the situation at that time, in the middle of the financial turmoil, analysts estimated that the market value of Company A's assets was \$500m (50% of the Book value), implying an EV valuation of 5.6x EBITDA (versus the initial 11.1x). With the Enterprise Value far below the Liabilities Value the company was in financial distress. **Figures 11.7** and **11.8** summarize the balance sheet composition (asset and liability sides) before and after the outbreak of the crisis.

As we can see in the table below, the Book Value moves from \$1000m to \$500m, making the Recovery Rate (RR) smaller than 1:

$$RR = 500/900 = 56\% < 1$$

The company is in default, equity gets cancelled, and only a portion of Senior Debt can be repaid while the rest of debt is either written off or converted into equity.

Usually, before a company goes into default, there are some important financial and non-financial KPIs to be noted, as they may be indicators of an unhealthy business:

Figure 11.7 Company A Balance Sheet before financial distress

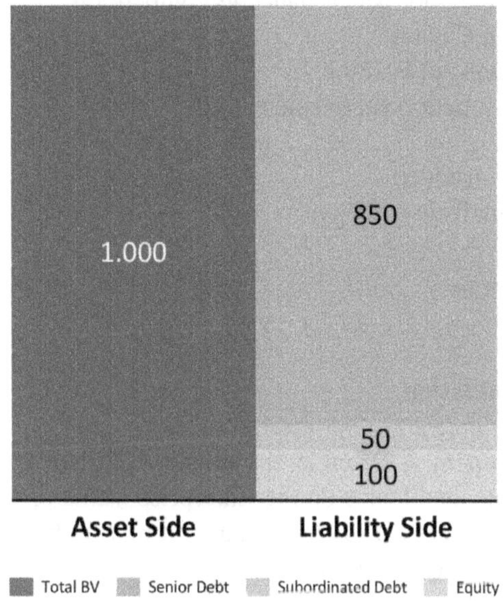

Figure 11.8 Company A Balance Sheet during financial distress

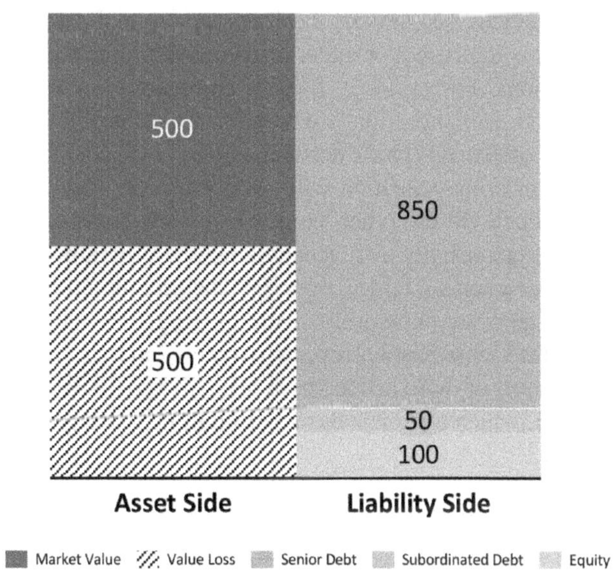

- decline of revenues and profitability;
- results far below business plan targets;
- market share loss and poor performance vs competition;
- worsening Working Capital;
- increase of Net Financial Position;
- capex cut and investment postponement;
- scarce cash flow;
- high management turnover;
- unclear and/or unrealistic strategy;
- poor innovation;
- no liquidity headroom.

11.3.2 Distressed valuation

As we saw in the Company A example, the situation of distress depends on the Market Value of the Assets, and hence on the Enterprise Value of the company. For this reason, valuation is crucial in a restructuring, and market benchmarks, like trading or transaction multiples, represent only one possible indicator.

Valuation is far more complex for distressed businesses than for healthy ones. While the methodologies remain the same (trading multiples, transaction multiples, discounted cash flows, etc.), the results and the interpretation need to be adjusted given the distress situation and the possibility for the shareholders to liquidate the business.

Trading Multiples and Transaction Multiples valuation is based on the underlying assumption that in Capital Markets the profit generated by one company is valued in the same manner as profits made by similar companies (similarity in terms of industry, products, services, risk profile, business model, and capital structure etc.). When it comes to firms in distress or under restructuring, such a methodology could give distorted valuations. For example, when a company is in the initial phase of a restructuring process, it is more likely to deliver higher profits in the future than comparable healthy companies (profit defined as EBITDA, EBIT, EBIAT, etc.). By using the same multiples, the valuation will not capture the extra growth generated by the restructuring deal. On the other hand, when using transaction multiples, the value of past transactions usually also accounts for the premium price the acquirer paid to get control over a certain target company. The premium reflects the possibility for the acquirer to generate more profits from the target by improving its business model, capital structure, cost profile, revenue streams, and so on. If a company is under restructuring, most of these actions have been already undertaken. Thus, using a transaction multiple, which also includes a premium price, might lead to overvaluation of the company.[3]

[3] See Gilson, S.C., "Valuing Companies in Corporate Restructurings: Technical Note." Harvard Business School Technical Note 201-073, December 2000.

Discounted Cash Flow methodology measures the Enterprise Value over the preset discounted value of the future cash flows generated by the company. In a distress valuation there are some alternative DCF methodologies that can be applied: the Adjusted Present Value method and the Capital Cash Flow method.[4]

The Adjusted Present Value (APV) and the Capital Cash Flow (CCF) methods differentiate the cash flows into three clusters, each one discounted with different discount rates (in APV) or with the same discount rate (in CCF): cash flows from operations (starting from EBIAT, Earnings Before Interest After Taxes), cash flow generated by tax shields (from deduction of interest expenses) and cash flows generated by NOLs (Net Operating Losses) carried over. The first bucket allows for evaluating the company's profit as it operated without any debt. The second cluster allows for evaluating the tax benefits from interest deduction. Given a fixed tax rate, any changes in cash flows due to a tax shield are due to the variation of interest expenses. By separating these cash flows, the valuation is able to capture the right level of risk related to interest expenses. Moreover distressed companies usually have a very high level of Net Operating Losses, which are carried over and generate large tax savings. The third bucket separates these savings from the first two. During restructuring, companies have a constantly-changing level of indebtedness which might distort the cash flow evaluation. By taking into account these three different cash flows, the APV method allows for more correctly estimating Enterprise Value under a changing level of debt.

On top of the consideration presented above, there are also other common adjustments to make when valuing a distressed company, that include:

a) Weighted Average Cost of Capital (WACC): in the classical methodology, WACC already captures the tax savings from interest expense deductions, with the (1-t) factor applied to the D/E ratio, which needs to be adjusted;
b) working capital (distressed companies usually have difficult relationships with suppliers and unreliable inventory);
c) non-recurring expenses/restructuring costs (turnaround costs could be significant and have a material impact on deliverable cash flows across the plan);
d) need for considerable investment/capex (which could have been deferred for a long while because of cash shortage);
e) restricted cash (cash which is unavailable for certain reasons, like duties towards minority shareholders);
f) higher risk-return profile, which needs to be included in the cost of capital (the Capital Asset Pricing Model-based cost of equity has to be adjusted accordingly).

Research has demonstrated another interesting difference versus the classical valuation methodologies: that equity returns in financially distressed companies are lower

[4] Gilson, 2000.

than in those firms that are not in financial trouble.[5] This goes in the opposite direction of the Fama and French convention that higher risk leads to higher returns.[6] The explanations of this phenomenon are the following:

- by solving the financial distress and saving the company from bankruptcy, shareholders will fully or partially recover their investment, which would anyway be better than in case of insolvency (Garlappi L. and Yan H., 2011);
- a distressed company's information, once circulated, negatively affects the equity returns due to the high risk of default (Opp C.C.G., 2011);
- there is difference between actual default probability and risk neutral default probability (Ozdagli A. K., 2010).

When valuing distressed companies, it is important to apply a risk premium to the CAPM formula. Cost of equity would then be calculated as follows:

$$Ke = Rf + \beta \times MRP + DP$$

Where:

Ke = cost of equity
Rf = risk-free rate
β = company's beta
MRP = long-term market risk premium
DP = distress premium.

The distress premium refers to the opportunity cost of investing in a company with very high risk as well as bankruptcy costs.

Duff and Phelps (2010) calculated the distress premium using the Altman's z-score.[7] This methodology envisaged a comparison between groups of companies. It selected financially distressed companies with very high leverage, that were in bankruptcy or in liquidation or that in the past five years showed a negative net income available for common shareholders. Then it further divided these companies into three areas: "Safe Area," "Grey Area," and "Distress Area." Each cluster was

---

[5] Dichev, I.D., "Is the risk of bankruptcy a systematic risk?," *Journal of Finance*, 53, 1998; Griffin, J.M. and Lemmon, M.L., "Book-to-market equity, distress risk and stock returns," *Journal of Finance*, 57, 2002; Campbell, J.Y., Hilscher, J., and Szilagyi, J., "In search of distress risk," *Journal of Finance*, 63, 2008.

[6] Fama, E.F., and French, K.R., "Multifactor explanations of asset pricing anomalies," *Journal of Finance*, 51, 1996.

[7] Altman, E.I., "Financial ratios, discriminant analysis and the prediction of corporate bankruptcy," *Journal of Finance*, 23, 1968; Altman, E.I., *Predicting Financial Distress of Companies: Revisiting the Z-Score and ZETA® Models*, Stern School of Business, New York University, July 2000; Altman, E.I., *Revisiting Credit Scoring Models in a Basel 2 Environment*, Stern School of Business, New York University, May 2002.

then assigned a specific z-score with an associated premium for distress to add to the CAPM formula.

However, there is not a unique method to calculate distress premiums, which are usually the results of quantitative and qualitative considerations. This is why financial advisor expertise in a distress situation is a critical factor for a correct valuation.

11.3.3 Debt sustainability

When a company gets into default, there are some financial metrics that become fundamental and need to be constantly tracked and monitored in order to assess Debt Sustainability. This practice aims to analyse the company from a profitability, liquidity, and solidity point of view in light of the company's ability to meet its obligations.

The most important metrics are the following:

a) **Net Debt/EBITDA**. Ideally, this ratio should not exceed 3x in order for a company not to be considered at risk of default. However, the acceptable level can vary depending on the industry in which the company operates, and on the stability of cash flows. Cyclical industries, for example, usually show very limited (if not zero) debt, while companies in the infrastructure business can operate at a 7x or 8x Net/EBITDA ratio and still be in the investment grade span. A high Net/EBITDA ratio can also be reached in the case of shrinking EBITDA (decreasing denominator), which can be a temporary effect and does not necessarily mean that the company is running a risk of default.
b) **Net Debt/Equity**. Companies which are highly leveraged tend to be much more vulnerable in the case of a market shock or external factors. Lehman had a Net Debt/Equity leverage of 19.7x, which left very little space between the assets' book value and the value of liabilities.
c) **Debt Service Coverage Ratio (DSCR)**: the ratio between the cash available to meet annual debt interest and principal payments and interest and principal. If DSCR is less than 1, it means that the company does not have enough cash to face all the payments of interest and principal due in the year. Ideally, an acceptable level should be around 1.2x.

$$DSCR = UFCF \,/\, (Interest + Principal)$$

$$UFCF = FCFE + Interest + Principal$$

d) **Interest Coverage Ratio (EBITDA/Interest)**. This metric shows how easy it is for the company to pay interest on its outstanding debt thanks to the profitability of its current operations. Ideally, the ratio should be above 4x.
e) **Level of Cash and availability of committed lines.**

11.3.4 Distress and leveraged buyouts

As we saw in the Company A example, one of the main reasons why a company goes into a distress situation is leverage. A disproportionate amount of Net Debt over Equity leaves a very narrow safety net for the company in the case that assets (and the Enterprise Value) lose value.[8] Research also shows that around 20% of defaults are attributable to high leverage (Asquith, 1994). We saw that the big wave of defaults and restructurings in 2009 followed an ex-ante increase of the Net Debt/EBITDA ratio worldwide and the hype around Leveraged Buyouts and leveraged acquisitions in the early 2000s. This section aims to highlight the fact that defaults are a possible outcome of risky leveraged buyouts.

11.3.4.1 Definition of Leveraged Buyouts

Leveraged Buyouts are acquisitions of a target company, a business, a division, or a group of assets, conducted by using a large amount of money sourced mostly with debt. The remaining part of the financing is provided via equity mainly by Private Equity firms, which aim to achieve adequate returns with a potential future IPO or by selling their investment to other Private Equity Firms or to industrial investors. The investor usually tries to maximize the leverage used (and thus minimize its equity investment) with debt below investment grade rate. This debt is then secured with the target company's shares and assets and remains in the target company's post-acquisition balance sheet. The future cash flows that the company will generate after the acquisition are used to pay back the outstanding debt. In a way, it is like saying that the target company pays for its own acquisition. From a practical point of view, in an LBO deal sources of financing (debt & equity) are collected into a Special Purpose Vehicle (SPV), which is then merged into the target company after the acquisition. In this case, the SPV will benefit from the proximity to the entity actually generating cash flows. The debt in the SPV will then become part of the target company's balance sheet.[9] The new owners of the company are the equity providers, which, by investing a relatively small amount of money, are able to acquire control and shares of much more valuable assets thanks to the assistance of leverage (we can recall the famous quote from Archimedes: "give me a lever long enough [...] and I shall move the world"). In the US, for example, in the first decade of the 2000s (before the outbreak of the financial crisis) the average debt used to run LBOs reached a level of 6.2x the target EBITDA and more than 70% the total source of financing.[10]

---

[8] We saw that value breaks when assets are worth less than net debt and so equity is null. This usually happens when the market value of the assets varies considerably from their current book value, due to market shocks or any other negative events.

[9] However, this practice in not allowed in all jurisdictions. In this case, debt remains in the Hold. Co. and thus become even riskier.

[10] Source: S&P Capital IQ Leveraged Commentary & Data. Retrieved from: Note on LBO Capital Structure, Harvard Business School, 11 October 2013.

To sum up, LBOs are M&A deals that differ from traditional acquisitions based on three main elements:

- the large usage of debt to finance the deal (LBOs belong to so-called Highly Leveraged Transactions – HLT);
- the number of investors is relatively small, thanks to the leverage effect;
- the cash flow generated by the future company is used to pay back the debt raised to acquire the target company.

Depending on the goal, players, and investors, LBOs can have different forms: Management Buyouts (MBOs), Management Buy-ins (MBIs); Buy-in Management Buyouts (BIMBO), Family Buyouts (FBO), Employee Buyouts, Institutional buyouts (IBO), and Reverse Leveraged Buyout (RLBO).

There are multiple reasons for conducting an LBO. Among the most common, it is worthwhile to mention the following:

- to support generational change;
- to make a private company public;
- to privatize a public company;
- to reorganize and restructure an underperforming company.

There are several mechanisms to design Leveraged Buyouts. The most commonly used method is the KKR method.[11] Figure 11.9 summarizes the main steps for a Leveraged Buyout:

1. **Step 1**. Equity is collected by the Private Equity investor (usually with a majority stake) and by other sponsors of the acquisition (the management team, industrial investors, other financial investors etc. depending on the nature and motives of the deal).
2. **Step 2**. Debt is raised from the banking system. The role of the Private Equity investor is extremely important in leveraging its network to raise debt (the presence of an equity anchor investor can facilitate the process even more). Debt can be raised in several forms with different maturity, seniority, and nature, which will be briefly explained later on.
3. **Step 3**. The financing is collected in a Special Purpose vehicle (New Co) which has only cash assets.
4. **Step 4**. The SPV's cash is generally used to pay out the existing shareholders and thus for the equity investor to acquire control of the target company.
5. **Step 5**. The Target company is then merged into the SPV. Its balance sheet will have an asset structure composed of its existing assets and goodwill from the acquisition (if any), and a liability side consisting of its existing debt plus the SPV

[11] Named after the Private Equity firm Kohlberg Kravis Roberts & Co. (KKR).

Figure 11.9 Example of LBO transaction steps (KKR Method)

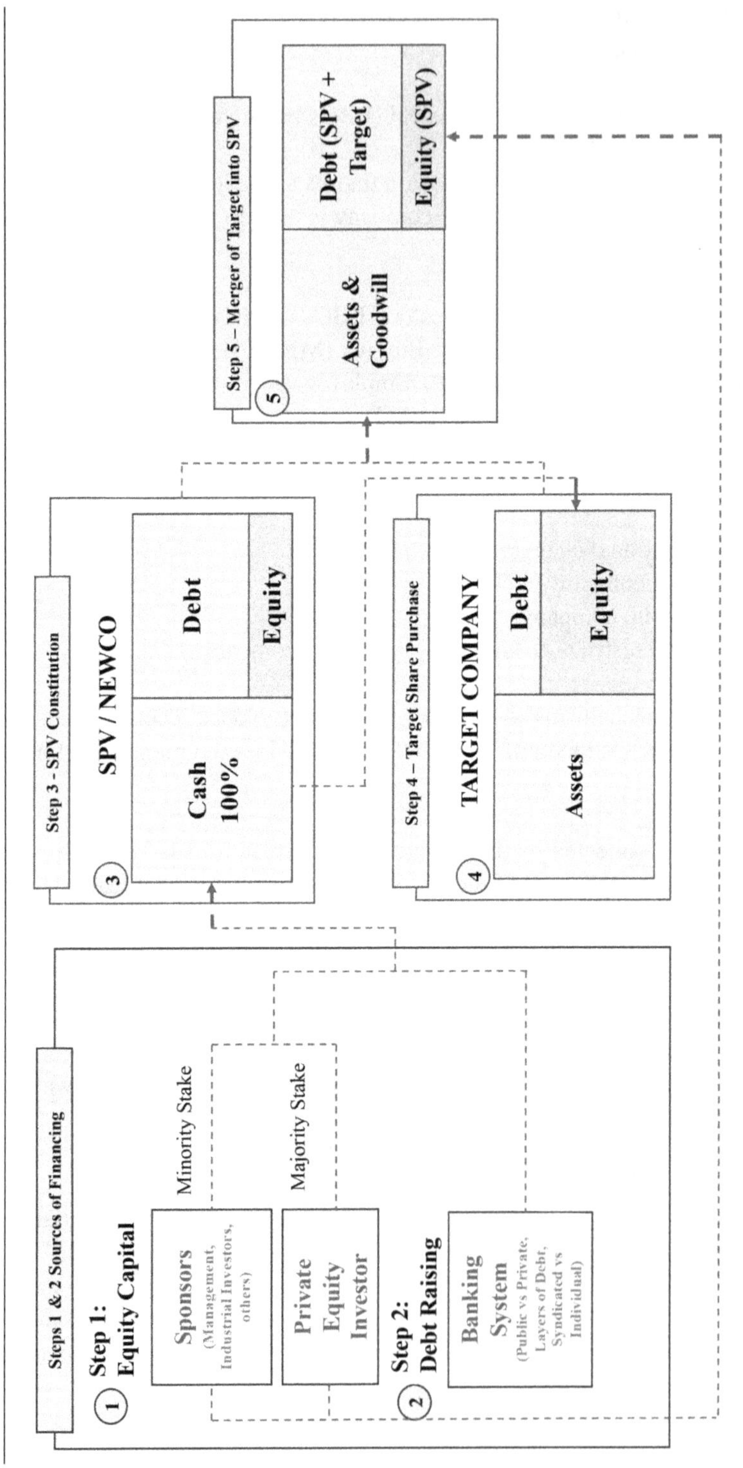

debt (collected to run the deal). As a matter of fact, the equity will be the sum of the remaining target company's shareholders' position (if any) and the new shareholders' stakes.

11.3.4.2 Leveraged Buyout Capital Structure

Not only is the debt raised for a LBO very large, but it usually has a high level of sophistication and differentiation, in terms of seniority, nature, risk profile, etc. Debt can be first of all be differentiated between Senior Secured Debt and Junior Debt. The main difference between the two is the fact that Senior Debt holders have priority over claims from the company's junior debt holders, which is extremely important when it comes to restructuring and liquidation.

Senior Debt can be further divided into:

- **Asset-Backed Loan (ABL)**, which is the most senior loan in a liability structure of a company. Its main characteristics is the fact that it is secured by the value of underlying collateral such as real estate, accounts receivable, productive assets (i.e. machinery), and so on. ABLs usually do not have very strict covenant structures.
- **Leveraged Loan**, very similar to an ABL except for the fact that it is not backed by the value of underlying collateral, but by the cash flows generated by the debtor. For this reason, leveraged loans are usually provided by private institutions and have a very strict covenant structure (most covenants usually require the respect for specific financial KPIs). However, thanks to the high concentration of debt, covenants can be easily renegotiated, while with other instruments such as bonds, renegotiation is much harder.

Junior Debt, on the other hand, lays in between Senior Debt and Equity and also includes quasi-equity instruments. Given its nature, junior debt is usually unsecured and has a much riskier profile than senior debt. The most common Junior Debt instruments are: High-Yield Bonds and Mezzanine Loans. High-Yield Bonds (also called "junk bonds") are a public debt fixed-income instrument. Bonds usually have a longer maturity than Senior Debt, and given their public nature, do not foresee any particular information requirements (contrary to Leveraged Loans, where the private investors benefit from a very extensive level of information from the debtor). The covenants scheme usually includes typical bond indentures that become effective only when the debtor undertakes some specific extraordinary actions (for example, pursuing an acquisition, starting a Joint Venture, issuing new debt etc.). Mezzanine financing, on the other hand, is a private, highly illiquid source of financing, which can include Payment in Kind (PIK) instead of typical cash payments and also equity kickers with a trigger event.

The choice between the different types of debt depends heavily on the market and the region in which the deal is carried out. In the US, for example, LBOs are usually financed with Leveraged Loans and public High-Yield Bonds, while in Europe, most of the debt is raised privately from a very limited number of banks.[12] One of the reasons behind this geographical difference is linked to restructuring regulations in the US and Europe, as will be discussed later on in section 11.6. In the US, Chapter 11 guarantees extensive protection also for minority bondholders, while in Europe, the restructuring process is usually run privately out-of-court. For this reason, in both restructuring and liquidation procedures, junior lenders or bondholders do not have much control over the process and are indeed very exposed.[13]

11.3.4.3 Leveraged Buyouts: ex-post effects and general considerations

LBOs have been proven to be extremely effective in private equity deals, generational changes, reorganizations, and also M&As, and offer a very appetizing and unique mechanism for investors, who can achieve high returns in a relatively short period of time. Exit is usually foreseen after 3 to 4 years via IPO or sale of the company to another investor (mostly a Private Equity firm, but not necessarily). The higher the target company exit valuation is compared to the entry valuation, the higher the return for the investor is. This is why we can observe that in the US market, for example, leveraged buyouts skyrocketed in the first decade of the millennium not only in terms of amounts, but also in average size. LBOs jumped from a volume of around $50bn in 2004 up to approximately $420bn in 2007.[14] Moreover, in 2007, the average size of LBOs in the US was around $1.9bn, versus less than $0.4bn in 2004. As the financial crisis spread, LBO volume fell massively again in 2008 and 2009, but resumed growing in recent years, up to around $100bn each year, with average size in line with the level right before the crisis.

On the other side of the coin, LBOs are extremely risky, and not all companies are suitable to be targets. After a leveraged buyout, the target company suffers from a clear worsening of the Net Debt/Equity ratio, Net Debt/EBITDA ratio, Debt Service Coverage Ratio, and Interest Coverage Ratio. Not to mention that the high level of debt generates high interest per se, which eats into the bottom line every year.

In fact, problems arise when, after the acquisition, the target company underperforms versus expectations, and is not able to deliver the promised cash flows to pay the outstanding debt. Delivering modest (if not null or negative) growth and margin deterioration creates a lot of problems for the target company. In the event there are also external headwinds, or adverse market circumstances (i.e. the 2008 financial crisis), the company is in even more trouble.

When a firm is loaded with debt and suffers from revenue and margin declines, it gradually starts approaching a crisis, and eventually a distress situation. This is why the amount of defaults and restructuring deals rose drastically following 2008.

[12] This is why mezzanine loans are usually preferred over bonds as junior debt.

[13] Source: Note on LBO capital Structure, Harvard Business School, 13 October 2013.

[14] Source: SDC Platinum, Mergers & Acquisitions Database. Data provided by Thomson Reuters.

The outbreak of the 2008 financial crisis ultimately unveiled the real weaknesses of companies which were already struggling after leveraged buyouts, and gave them the final kick towards distress and default. As a matter of fact, in the US (and elsewhere) leveraged buyouts market cooled down compared to the previous years, as can be seen in **Figures 11.10** and **11.11**.

Given the above considerations, the selection of the target company is indeed extremely important for the success of an LBO. The most important characteristics to consider are the following:

- The industry in which the target company operates should be mature, non-cyclical, characterized by stable revenues streams and cash generation, and should not require a high level of investments.
- The target company should have an initial low level of debt.
- The target should be able to generate abundant and stable cash flows.
- The target should have assets to provide as collateral, but also that could be sold independently.
- The management team should be experienced and able to manage highly-stressed situations.
- There should be an efficient market for corporate control.

Figure 11.10 S&P/LSTA Index: Par Amount of Leveraged Loans in Payment Default or Bankruptcy

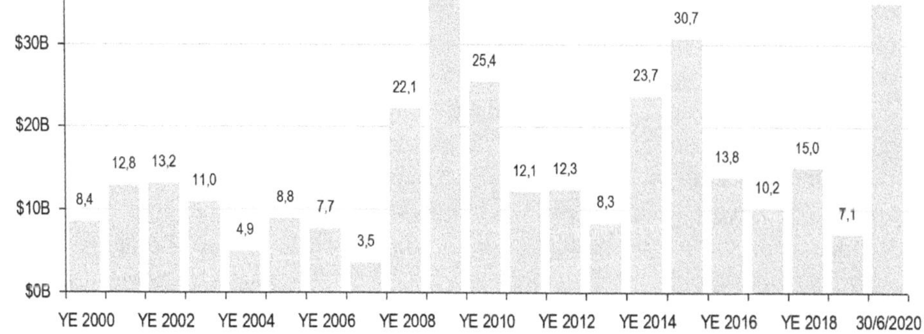

Source: S&P Global. Market Intelligence. Includes all loans, including those not included in the LSTA/TRLPC mark-to-market service. Primarily institutional tranches.

Figure 11.11 S&P/LSTA Index: Par Amount of Leveraged Loans in Payment Default or Bankruptcy

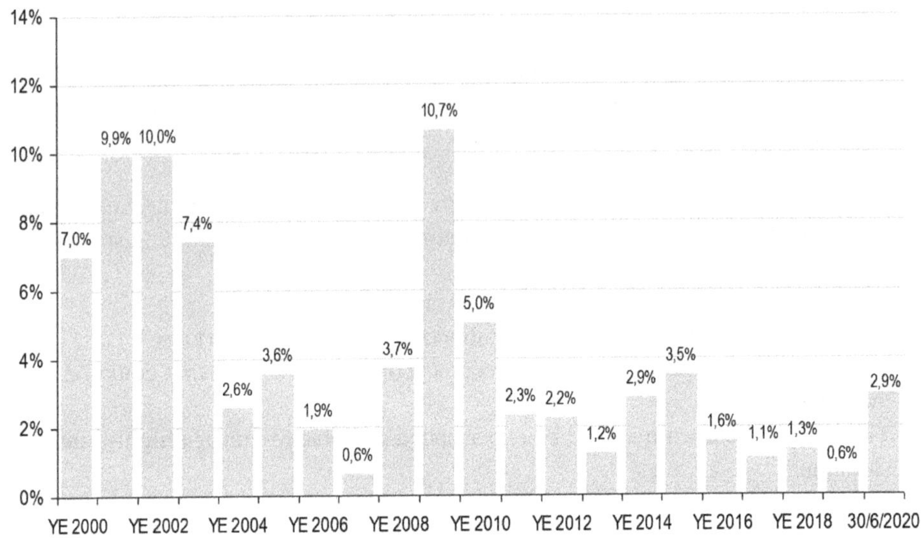

Source: S&P Global. Market Intelligence. Includes all loans, including those not included in the LSTA/TRLPC mark-to-market service. Primarily institutional tranches.

11.4 Private workouts vs in-court procedures

When talking about Financial Restructuring, there are two legal options in the hands of the company:

1. **Private Workouts**. A restructuring Plan is put in place by the company together with the shareholders and the creditors. The company takes control of the process and no legal authority is involved. Private workouts usually guarantee higher recovery rates, flexibility for the parties, and protect its reputation. However, in order to successfully implement a private workout, a high consensus (if not unanimity) is needed across lenders and the company cannot prevent holdouts (the creation of a minority category of creditors which might block the process).
2. **In-Court Procedures**. The process is driven by an authority in court (usually a judge) and guarantees fair and equal treatment of all creditors, and can either lead to a restructuring procedure, or, in case of failure, to a liquidation procedure, which will put an end to the company's existence. The main advantages of the in-court procedures are: the presence of a third party who supervises and coordinates the process and protects creditors' rights, and the possibility to "cram down" dissenting creditors (enforce specific solutions on minority lenders who do not agree with the terms). However, in-court procedures are usually very time-con-

Figure 11.12 Private Workouts vs In-Court Procedures

	Private Workouts	In-Court Procedures
Average Recovery Rate	High	Low
Duration	Relatively Short	Can be very long
Flexibility	High	Low
Reputational Damage	Low	High
Protection of creditors' rights	Low	High
Cram-Down possibility	No	Yes
Information Asymmetries	High	Low
Possibility for new Financial Facilities	Low	High
Losses are Tax deductable	No	Frequently

suming, with much lower recovery rates, highly impact the company's reputation, and damage the company's intangible assets.

The choice between the two options depends on the nature of the restructuring (whether it is hostile or consensual) and of course on the legal framework of the country where the company is registered. Figure 11.12 illustrates the main differences between private workouts and in-court procedures.

11.5 Private workouts

11.5.1 Players involved and due process

The first step in a financial restructuring is to understand the key stakeholders involved in the process from the beginning to the end.

The company and its management team is of course the first of these. Usually, the Board of Directors is one of the parties who in the first place declares the crisis and decides that the company needs restructuring. During a private workout, the company controls and coordinates the process with the aim of minimizing the restructuring costs, guaranteeing the commercial operations and business continuity, focusing management attention on fixing the structure, sticking to the business plan and achieving milestones and targets, and of course, gradually deleveraging the balance sheet. The company (and sometimes the lenders themselves) can also hire a Chief Restructuring Officer (CRO) in the event that there is a lack of experienced and skilled managers that could put the process at risk.

Majority Shareholders also might initiate the process. Majority shareholders play a key role in supervising the work of the board of directors by influencing the governance decisions and maintaining ownership. They manage the relationship with the most important lenders and can also become a source of liquidity for the company itself with money injections (which will be discussed later on). They will ultimately benefit from any equity upside in the case of successful restructuring.

Minority Shareholders play a less important role in the restructuring process: they aim to minimize the dilution of their position and benefit from future equity upside as majority shareholders do, at the same terms and conditions.

Senior Lenders/Bondholders are among the most important players in the process. Their main interest is to protect their position and minimize (if not avoid) debt write-offs. Of course, they also seek to de-lever the balance sheet so as to be in a much safer zone.

Junior Lenders/Bondholders. Given the possibilities of holdouts and the inability for the company to cram down dissenting lenders, junior creditors become extremely important in private workouts. They of course aim to minimize their write-offs and to swap their debt into equity where possible at reasonable terms. In order to protect their interests, they can form a blocking position to better control the outcome of the process.

Financial Advisors. Last but not least, the financial advisors (hired by the company or by the lenders/bondholders) are probably the most important stakeholders in the process. In the absence of a legal authority (i.e. a judge), the financial advisors play a pivotal (technical and managerial) role in coordinating and supervising the restructuring. Their most important responsibilities are: to perform the proper credit analysis and assess the company's Debt Capacity; to guide the valuation in the case of M&A; to manage the relationship with the company, the shareholders, and the creditors; to coordinate the due diligence and the drafting of documentation; to negotiate the terms and conditions of the restructuring agreements; and to look for funds. The advisors are also crucial to manage the relationship between senior and junior lenders/bondholders, which is key to delivering a successful restructuring. Finally, the financial advisors supervise the financial plan drafted by the company together with a strategic advisor/consultant. The ultimate goal for the advisors is to maximize the Recovery Rates for the lenders/bondholders and to achieve the best agreement to help the company overcome the crisis.

The role of the advisors and the senior lenders/bondholders varies a lot depending on the size of the to-be-restructured company and on the fragmentation of the corporate debt, as shown in **Figure 11.13**.

The advisor's role becomes crucial in the case of highly fragmented debt, with numerous creditors with different seniorities and positions. They in fact need a third-party player who can coordinate and guide them and who can find satisfactory terms and conditions for all parties. On the other hand, when debt is concentrated, the main lender (i.e. the main bank) takes a leading role in the process. However, if the restructured company is a large corporation, with a high level of complexity, then one sole lender cannot coordinate the whole process by itself, but needs the help of the financial advisors instead.

As discussed at the beginning, the restructuring actually starts when the insolven-

Figure 11.13 Role of Financial Advisor

Debt Composition	Size of restructured company: Large	Size of restructured company: Small/Medium
Concentrated	COOPERATION BETWEEN LENDERS/BONDHOLDERS AND ADVISOR	MAIN LENDER LEADS THE PROCESS
Fragmented	ADVISOR LEADS THE PROCESS	ADVISOR LEADS THE PROCESS

cy/default is declared. From that moment on, the Board of Directors (or the lenders) will look for and hire the financial advisors. What follows is a typical timetable of a private workout:

1. **Business Plan definition**. The company, together with the Financial Advisors (with the help of a Legal Advisor and sometimes of a Consultant), drafts a business and financial plan to "fix" the profitability and the capital structure, with a major focus on Cash flow.
2. **Restructuring proposal**. Based on the business plan defined in point 1. The company defines a restructuring proposal to bring to the lenders/bondholders.
3. **Presentation of the proposal**.
4. **Coordination Committee**. The lenders form a committee with the role of steering the proposal, managing the relationship with the company, asking for information, and putting pressure on the management team. Usually, when the company is small-sized or when the debt is concentrated in the hands of one major lender, the committee is led by the single player, or can even be absent. Each class of creditors usually forms its own committee with a dedicated advisor.
5. **Standstill Request**. The company presents a request for a Standstill Agreement between itself and the lenders. The standstill agreement is a contract which prevents the lenders from demanding payment, claiming rights, suing the company, or starting legal actions for a specific time frame. The purpose of the agreement

Figure 11.14 Restructuring Flow Chart

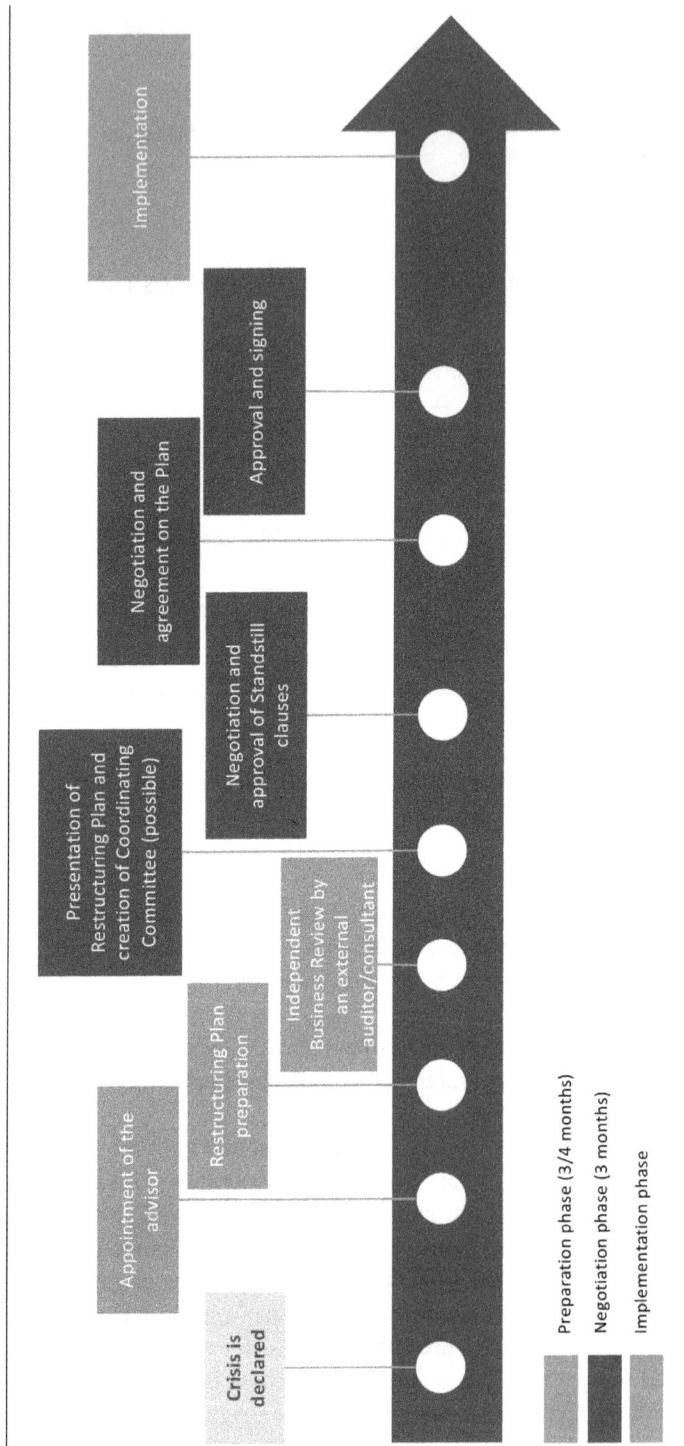

is to give the company sufficient time to reorganize and focus on the restructuring proposal and to avoid individual actions from lenders that could jeopardize the process.

6. **Independent Business Review**. While the company presents the Restructuring Plan, creditors conduct an Independent Business Review (IBR), usually performed by a third party auditor to test the solidity of the business plan and challenge it where necessary.
7. **Negotiation, approval, and signing**. The final approval usually comes after considerable back-and-forth between the parties. The more fragmented the debt is, the higher the number of consensual lenders will be needed. After an agreement is reached, the company starts implementing the plan.

The steps presented above are a simplified description of the process, which is summarized in Figure 11.14 below. From the time of appointment of the advisor, the overall restructuring can last more than seven months. The first two to three months are usually dedicated to hiring the advisor and preparing the plan to present to the lenders. An extra two to three months are then needed for the creditors to get organized, form committees, conduct the Independent Business Review, and negotiate and approve the restructuring.

11.5.2 Types of debt and lenders

As mentioned in the previous paragraphs, the complexity of restructuring and the overall process itself depend heavily on the debt structure of the company. We have seen in the first section that in the past decade, companies sourced a huge amount of debt with increasing levels of sophistication. It is important then to bring some clarity to the different classes of debt, which ultimately define the different classes of lenders.

We can define debt according to the following segmentation:

- **Short-term vs Long-Term**. The maturity of the debt varies from shorter types of indebtedness, usually of a more commercial nature, such as factoring, to longer-term financial loans or bonds. Debt collected to carry out leveraged buyouts, for example, is usually long-term.
- **Senior vs Junior**. Lenders/bondholders might have different seniorities and thus different priorities in terms of rights satisfaction. Senior creditors have the right to be paid before junior (subordinated) creditors, and of course have a much less risky profile. Junior debt lies somewhere between debt and equity, has a higher cost for the company, and can include special features, such as PIK (Payment in Kind).[15]

[15] Payment in Kind is a type of financial instrument which foresees payment of interest at maturity with equity or additional debt, instead of cash.

- **Secured vs Unsecured**. Security packages give the creditors rights over certain company assets or shares, and reduce the risk profile of the creditor. Senior debt is typically secured, but such security packages can also be granted to junior lenders on a subordinated basis.
- **Private vs Public**. Bank loans vs bonds which are publicly traded in the market. Private lenders usually have much more information compared to public ones, who can in fact rely only on publicly available data.

When it comes to restructuring, different types of debt show different Recovery Rates. According to Moody's Default Risk Service, Senior Secured Debt showed an average recovery rate of 56.4%, while Senior Unsecured only 36.5%. Junior subordinated also had a RR level much lower than the average of the sample (27.1%), and so did preferred stocks, of course, with just 10.1%.[16]

11.5.4 Restructuring options. From renegotiation to refinancing and M&A

After a thorough analysis of the restructuring process, players, stakeholders, and dynamics, it is time to focus on the practical side of the deal.

There are many options at the borrower's disposal to go through a financial restructuring. The first solution, of course, would be for the management to actually **ignore** the distressed situation and try to solve it without involving the creditors and other parties. This practice would save the company a lot of time and resources, but it is extremely dangerous, especially if the problem is underestimated, and it is not possible in the case a covenant in a finance agreement is breached.

The company can undertake one or a combination of the following strategic initiatives:

1. renegotiate terms and conditions of its debt;
2. refinance:
3. debt write-off and/or debt-to-equity-swap;
4. M&A activity (i.e. asset divestiture).

When liquidity is very scarce and the financial structure becomes unbearable for the company, or also when a covenant is breached, one solution for the company is to **renegotiate** the terms and conditions of its debt. Renegotiation tools depend on the nature of the debt, whether it is private or public.

In the case of **private debt**, there are two main solutions the borrower can pursue:

- **Covenant reset**: modification of the conditions for financial covenants in order to make them lighter, based on the company's recent financial troubles. A covenant

[16] The analysis was run on the market value of defaulted debt as percentage of par, 30 days after default, between 1970 and 2008. Source: Moddy's Default Risk Service.

reset usually comes with a fee adhere (called "amendment fees") and/or a spread increase granted to the creditors. The approval of a covenant reset agreement typically happens with the assent of a 51% majority of creditors. In some cases of declining or even negative EBITDA (like the ones experienced during the Covid-19 pandemic), companies may ask for "Covenant Holidays," which is a de facto suspension of the terms for a specific period of time.
- **Amend-to-extend**: extension of the maturity of the debt. Given its more invasive nature, an amend-to-extend agreement needs to be approved by all the creditors.

When it comes to **public debt**, the borrower can pursue one of the following actions in the market:

- **Tender Offer**: buying back bonds from the holders at a pre-defined price (usually lower than the par value but higher than the current market value). It is hard to see high participation in a tender offer unless the terms of the buyback are very appealing;
- **Exchange Offer**: exchanging a debt security with another instrument under approval of all creditors;
- **Open-market Deal**: basically a tender offer, but with the possibility to buy back only part of the securities and not all of them;
- **Consent Solicitation:** bondholder meeting to amend the terms of the covenants.

Other than renegotiating debt terms and conditions, the borrower might want to seek to **refinance**. However, most of the times, refinancing is just an instrument to gain time and postpone the problem. Moreover, the feasibility of such operations is not great, as it is very hard for the company to find investors and sources of financing when it is in financial trouble.

Debt refinancing can also be very useful in the case of positive market conditions with low interest rates (or at least lower than the ones currently paid). By doing so, the borrower can at the same time extend the maturity and reduce the cost of its indebtedness. Finally, the borrower might want to simplify its current liability structure and get rid of excess layers of debt, or vice versa, to diversify its indebtedness and add new layers with different seniorities and security packages. These techniques of course apply also in normal situations where the company is not in financial distress and under restructuring.

Commercial investors (such as banks) prefer to avoid providing cash, especially if outside a formal restructuring process and without a super seniority grade. Some other investors (especially hedge funds), are specialized in lending new money to the company in a difficult situation with the aim of gaining control of it over time.

A separate section on refinancing should be dedicated to existing shareholders' new money. Even though it is not a debt restructuring practice per se, injection of additional resources by the existing shareholders might be very useful for the company to get through the period of crisis. As we saw previously, in a restructuring framework, shareholders' number one concern is to avoid dilution of their position and to keep control and governance over the company. Shareholders' attitudes towards restructuring can vary significantly depending on the nature of the shareholders (industrial vs financial) and on the connection they have with the company. Shareholders might be asked by creditors to re-capitalize the firm or they might want to do it themselves in order to avoid equity dilution, or to go for an in-court procedure and protect their reputation.

If the restructuring and the consequent business plan is successfully achieved, shareholders' new money can deliver very positive returns. Let's imagine that Company A has €400 million net debt and €50 million EBITDA (8x Debt/EBITDA Ratio). Comparable companies show a 6x EV/EBITDA multiple, which would lead to a €300 million enterprise value. This means that €100 million of debt is left uncovered and the equity is worth 0. Company A is in distress. Based on the restructuring plan approved by the Board of Directors, €250 million is the maximum financial indebtedness the company must have (5x EBITDA), and €50 million is the new money injection required from the shareholders to support the company's current operations and fixing costs. In this case, the debt write-off is €150 million. Let us now suppose that the restructuring plan foresees the company reducing its net debt from €250 million to €125 million within three years thanks to organic growth of revenues, cost management, and working capital adjustments to maximize cash flows and repay part of the outstanding debt. After three years, keeping the borrower EV constant (€300 million), the new Equity Value for the company would account for €175 million, implying a return for the shareholders of 350% (i.e. 3.5x Money on Money: the ratio between the final equity value and money initially injected, €175 million/€50 million). **Table 11.2** below offers a synthetic view of the main Company A figures.

This example is very simplified. Normally, restructuring agreements also envis-

Table 11.2 Example of Shareholders' money injection

	Company A
EBITDA	50,0
Trading Multiple	6.0x
Enterprise Value	**300,0**
Net Debt	400,0
Net Debt / EBITDA	8.0x
Net Debt After Restructuring	**250,0**
Shareholders' new money	**50,0**
Write-off	150,0
Net Debt after 3Y	125,0
Equity Value 3Y	175,0
Shareholders' return	**3.5x**

age debt-to-equity-swaps in combination with other measures, which dilute equity and hence reduce the shareholders' return on their new money.

Debt-to-Equity-Swap is another viable option for the company. With this transaction lenders can convert their debt position into equity, becoming shareholders of the company. A debt-to-equity-swap is a very effective tool for the company to quickly reduce its leverage (Debt/Equity). This instrument can also be combined with debt refinancing, giving the company the possibility to substitute the just-converted debt with fresher and cheaper debt. On the creditor side, shares represent a form of payment and remuneration and give lenders all the rights held by shareholders (voting and governance participation above all), which can be very interesting for those who want to pursue a loan-to-own strategy, but also reduce their priority in receiving cash from the debtor. On this topic, negotiation can be tough, as shareholders will of course fight against the possible dilution of their current position.

Stand-Alone Debt-to-Equity Swap is an alternative to the classic swap. In this operation, the lender can decide to convert its debt into convertible bonds, instead of common shares.

Divestitures are typical asset restructuring deals. The sale of a non-core business creates a significant appetite for the creditors, as it is a relatively quick measure to de-leverage the business and inject a good amount of cash into the company's coffers. However, the risk of rushing into these solutions is very high and might be detrimental for the recovery rates and the overall restructuring. The choice of whether and what to divest must be taken very carefully. A company should divest or liquidate a certain business or asset in the case of the following circumstances:

- poor integration and connection with the core business;
- poor performance of a division or product line and disproportionately high costs required to fix it;
- Inverse Synergies: when a company under-utilizes a certain business line that could be better off if separated from the parent company;
- better access to capital markets for the company post-divestiture thanks to a simpler structure;
- immediate proceeds and cash injections from the divestiture.

Divestitures are not the only **M&A** option a company can undertake under restructuring. Other instruments at the debtor's disposal are:

- equity carve-outs;
- spin-offs;
- sell-offs.

Equity carve-outs consist of the public offering of a stake in a subsidiary. This implies a number of nuances, one of which is that the divested subsidiary must become a separate legal entity, with its own Board of Directors. Moreover, the parent company must decide how much of the subsidiary should be sold: the sale rarely exceeds

20%, since this way, many legal frameworks, such as that of the US, allow for the full tax and accounting consolidation of the subsidiary. This can create a conflict due to the discrepancy between ownership of the firm and its actual management structure. The effect of the announcement of equity carve-outs on stock prices, although predominantly positive, is not substantiated by empirical findings regarding the long-term return of stocks, which show contradicting results. It is possible to observe, however, that subsidiaries' long-term performance is superior to that of parents. Similarly, studies regarding the post-transaction performance of parents show ambiguous results, while subsidiaries still tend to improve at a higher rate than their parent companies.

Spin-offs are a divestiture mode in which the parent company distributes the shares of the divested company to existing shareholders on a pro-rata basis (e.g. a person holding 30% of the parent will own 30% of the divested company). Just like equity carve-outs, this transaction involves the creation of an independent company, however, unlike the previous mode, it does not involve any sort of cash transaction, and as such they are often tax exempt. Since all the shares are given out, the new entity has no formal link with the parent, except for having the same shareholders, so it enjoys complete independence and freedom to reach its own goals. Spin-offs' market reception is observed to be much better than for equity carve-outs: findings show a strongly positive effect on stock prices, which is then reinforced by an abnormal return on the outstanding stock price for the subsidiaries and mild positive impact on the parent's stock price. Operating-wise, parents have shown little to no improvement after the transaction, with some studies highlighting worsened performance, whereas subsidiaries show positive or null effects.

Sell-offs are the simplest transaction of the three: they are the sale of assets, part of or whole subsidiaries, in exchange for consideration which can be cash or other securities. Unlike the previous two, there is no creation of third entities, since what is sold only changes ownership. A sell-off is different from liquidation in the sense that it does not involve the closure of the entity; however, it shares the possibility of being either voluntary, when it is a conscious choice for corporate portfolio management, or involuntary, when it is a divestiture coerced by an authority, such as in the case of antitrust issues or Chapter 11 reorganizations. Sell-off announcements have been shown to have a mildly positive effect on the stock price of the parent company, which is contradicted by ambiguous long-term stock performance. Operating performance, however, is shown to improve by almost all empirical studies, especially for focus improving transactions.

When a company is under restructuring, there are of course some clauses that limit its freedom to a certain extent. Out of the several clauses, the most common ones can be grouped as follow:

- To-do clauses: mandatory actions that need to be taken as indicated by the Debt Restructuring Agreement;
- Not-to-do clauses. The company is usually forbidden from conducting extraordi-

Figure 11.15 Company A Balance Sheet after Financial Distress

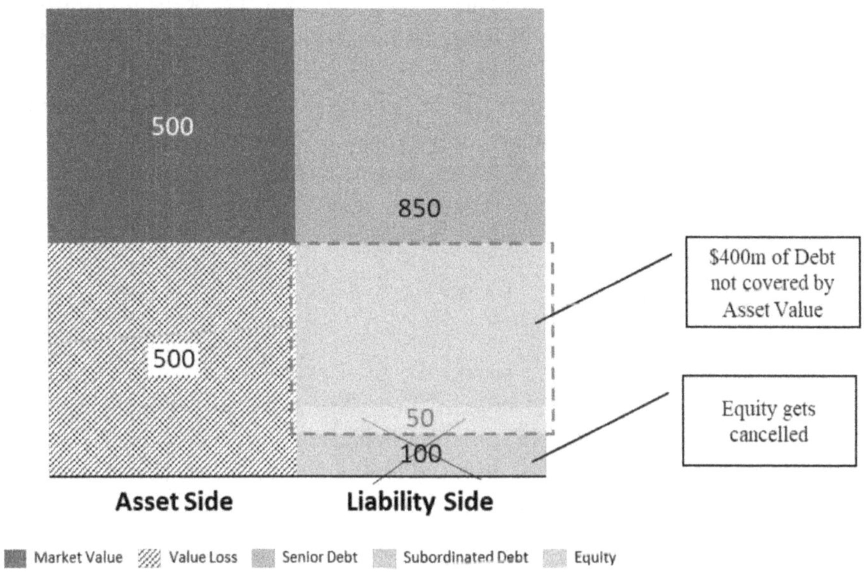

nary operations (such as M&As or Joint Ventures) or raising additional debt over the permitted indebtedness level and outside predefined time windows;

- Information and Communication. It is mandatory for the company to provide the creditors all the relevant qualitative and quantitative information and communications.
- Financial covenants. The company has to respect pre-defined levels of Debt Sustainability Ratios (i.e. Debt/Equity, Debt/EBITDA, Interest Coverage ratio etc.);
- Other provisions, such as earn-out structures, cash waterfalls etc.

Let us now recall our initial Company A example. In the second half of 2008, the firm went into distress as shown in the table below. The imbalance between the asset side and liability side after default is clear and equity is worth 0, as shown in **Figure 11.15**.

The first option would be to cancel all the debt not covered by the assets' value and repay only $500m to Senior Debt owners, guaranteeing them the following Recovery Rate:

$$RR\ Senior\ Lenders = 500/850 = 59\%$$

However, we saw that a plurality of creditors might create obstacles in the workout procedures and subordinated/junior lenders might themselves oppose this solution. This is why it is important to also grant them a portion of repayment instead of imposing a 100% write-off. Company A is to guarantee satisfaction to the senior secured creditors and to convert the rest of the debt into equity.

Let us suppose that the advisors then define the maximum debt capacity the company can afford as $270m (3x EBITDA). This means that Company A will have to reduce its level of indebtedness by $630m. By converting 21% of the remaining debt ($130m) into equity and writing off the remaining $500m,[17] Company A will be able to reset its level of indebtedness to an acceptable level with a leverage of 1.2x. The debt owners (both senior and junior) will have the possibility to become shareholders of the company. On the other side, of course, shareholders will "suffer" from the dilution of their position. **Figure 11.16** shows the debt restructuring breakdown and the consequent balance sheet composition after the deal is completed.

11.6 In-court procedures

In the previous sections, we have provided a brief overview of the main differences between private workouts and in-court procedures. Private workouts are usually the preferred choice to follow in the case of consensual restructurings. They guarantee higher recovery rates and much more flexibility. They also happen to be less time-consuming and less expensive, and protect the company from reputational damage, which tends to be inevitable when the parties go to court. However, it is not always possible to pursue a consensual private restructuring deal, for example when minority lenders form a blocking position. In this and other cases, an in-court procedure represents the only possible (or the best) solution. Out-of-court procedures also show limitations due to free-riding and opportunistic behaviour by some classes of creditors and a high level of information asymmetry for lenders, which might not have a full and clear picture of the real status of the company.

In-court procedures vary across countries and jurisdictions, of course; however, the common legal solutions for the company can be divided into two groups:

a) business continuity and preservation of going concern status, to allow the company to take the actions and implement a restructuring;
b) liquidation/insolvency/bankruptcy to put an end to the company's existence.

It has been observed that there has been an increasing tendency by legal authorities worldwide to facilitate the protection of going concern and business continuity. Financial institutions have recognized in recent decades that collaborating through a restructuring process is more likely to bring more value to all the parties than forcing liquidation and bankruptcy.[18] This means that in in-court procedures as well, both the judge and the creditors may be inclined to look for possible turnarounds.

---

[17] In this example, let us assume that the senior creditors will convert 14% of their Debt ($850m) into Equity, while subordinated creditors convert 20% of $50m. The write-off will then amount to 55% and 70%, respectively.

[18] INSOL International, "Statement of Principles for a global approach to multi-creditor workouts": "During the last thirty years there has been a growing recognition amongst the world's fi-

Figure 11.16 Company A Debt Restructuring and ex-post Balance Sheet

			€m
CURRENT NET DEBT			**900**
	DEBT CAPACITY	*3x EBITDA*	*270*
	DEBT REDUCTION		*630*
DEBT-TO-EQUITY SWAP			**130**
	SENIOR	*14%*	*120*
	SUBORDINATED	*20%*	*10*
DEBT WRITE-OFF			**500**
	SENIOR	*55%*	*465*
	SUBORDINATED	*70%*	*35*
DEBT POST-RESTRUCTURING			**270**
	SENIOR		*265*
	SUBORDINATED		*5*
RECOVERED DEBT			**30%**
	SENIOR		*31%*
	SUBORDINATED		*10%*
D/E Leverage			**1,2**
NET DEBT/EBITDA			**3,0**

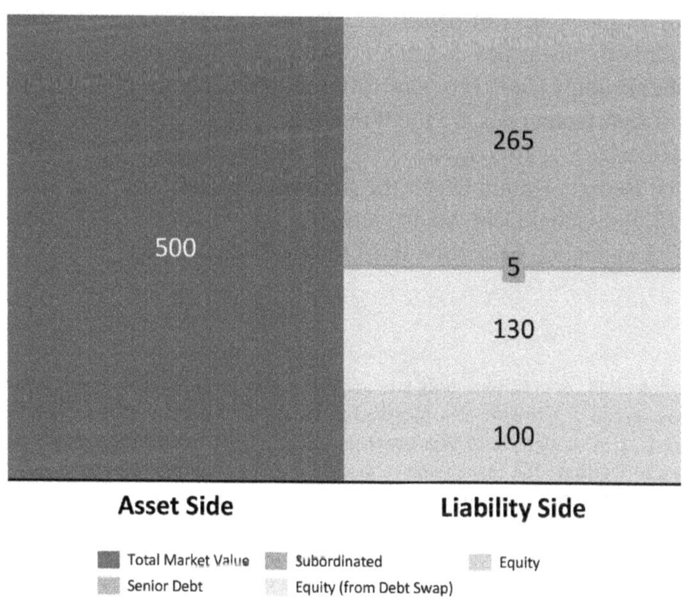

In Europe, some jurisdictions tend to be much more debtor-friendly, such as Italy, France, or Spain, where the system tends to incentivize the debtor to re-establish its financial health. In these countries, the legal authorities guarantee debtor protection (i.e. standstill periods) of from one to four months; cram-down for dissenting lenders is usually foreseen (upon hitting a specific majority, typically 2/3); and the management remains in charge.

Other countries, such as the UK or Germany, tend to favour creditors, giving them a lot of power and control over the process. Management teams can be replaced with new appointments suggested by creditor committees; senior and secured creditors may have unlimited power to claim their rights; and debt-to-equity swaps are foreseen even without agreement of the shareholders.

One of the biggest problems in Europe is the presence of many different jurisdictions and regimes which make cross-border restructuring deals very complicated.

For the sake of time and simplicity, we will analyse two legal frameworks, the US and the Italian ones, to offer a comparison between the Anglo-Saxon and the European approaches.

11.6.1 US legal framework[19]

In the US, all bankruptcy cases are handled in federal courts under rules outlined in the U.S. Bankruptcy Code. The US Congress is empowered by the US Constitution to enact laws on the subject of bankruptcy.[20] The US Bankruptcy Code governs the procedures for both businesses and individuals.

The US Bankruptcy Code provides different protocols for company filings; however, the most significant ones are the following:

- Chapter 11. Reorganization Under the Bankruptcy Code;
- Chapter 13. Individual Debt Adjustment;
- Chapter 7. Liquidation Under the Bankruptcy Code.

nancial institutions that, as creditors, they can achieve better returns through supporting an orderly and expeditious rescue or workout of a business in financial difficulty than by forcing it into formal insolvency [...]. Although there is a growing international trend in the development of local insolvency laws to facilitate the rescue and rehabilitation of companies and businesses in financial difficulty (as opposed merely to closing them down through liquidation), it is a truism that, no matter how debtor-friendly and "rescue"-orientated local insolvency regimes may be, there are often material advantages for both creditors and debtors in the expeditious implementation of informal or contract-based rescues or workouts (particularly in cases of debtors having cross-border businesses or complex capital structures), compared with the unpredictable costs and uncertainties of a formal insolvency."

[19] Thanks to Andrea Cerri (academic fellow at Bocconi) for contributing to this section 11.6.

[20] Legislators have passed several laws on the subject of bankruptcy, the most recent and organic has been the Bankruptcy Reform Act of 1978, which largely governs current US bankruptcy laws.

Chapter 11. This is the most common procedure adopted worldwide. Chapter 11 allows the company to continue its operations while preparing a restructuring plan to be presented to all creditors. Filing for Chapter 11 can be voluntary, if the company proactively starts the action, or involuntary, in the case the creditors/bondholders take the action. Chapter 11 protection is characterized by the following elements:

- The restructuring plan must be presented within 120 days from the filing.
- During this period the management remains in charge and the company is granted a standstill period (lenders cannot ask for payment for their obligations). This provision is extremely important in order to relieve pressure on the company and allow it to focus on the improvement of its business model and operations.
- Chapter 11 also gives the company the possibility to receive new senior money (so-called "Debtor-in-Possession" or "DIP"). Debtor-in-Possession means that the company maintains ownership of the assets on which creditors have rights and has the possibility to receive funds to carry on its current operations. Thanks to the protection granted by Chapter 11, those creditors that provide DIP financing enjoy a super senior status (even more senior than senior secured creditors).[21] Finally, the debtor can also receive "exit financing" (an extra debt injection after Chapter 11 protection).
  - The restructuring plan needs to be approved by the majority of each class of creditors (and not unanimously). More precisely, Chapter 11 establishes that approval must be given by half of the creditors representing at least two-thirds of the value for each class of lender. Once approved, the debtor can proceed in carrying out the Restructuring Agreement.
  - One big advantage of Chapter 11 is the possibility for the judge to "cram down" dissenting creditors and force a specific solution.
  - On the other side, the legal authority guarantees protection for junior lenders, and enough power is also reserved to the subordinated creditors committee (and bondholders committees), which can actively participate in the negotiation of the plan.

In the event that the out-of-court procedure or the Chapter 11 restructuring plan fails, the company must follow the insolvency protocol and file for bankruptcy.[22]

It is important to mention that under Chapter 11, shareholders only risk the value of their investment in the company: the restructuring plan cannot touch any of

[21] Elayan and Meyer (2001) showed a positive correlation between the usage of DIP financing and the success of restructuring.

[22] In some cases, especially if there is a particular public interest or in the case of bad management, considered not able to carry out and successfully implement the restructuring plan, the court can appoint a temporary trustee. A trustee manager can also be appointed when Chapter 11 is dismissed or converted into Chapter 7. The court is responsible for the appointment and it can choose the trustee during the period ranging from the bankruptcy filing date and the date when the bankruptcy plan is confirmed. Under Chapter 11, the appointed trustee has extensive powers over the company.

the shareholders' personal belongings and assets. However, a sole proprietorship does not have an identity separate and distinct from its owner(s), and in this case the bankruptcy procedure affects both the business and the personal assets of the owners-debtors. Finally, in a partnership bankruptcy, in some cases the partners' personal assets may be used to pay creditors and the partners may be forced to file for bankruptcy protection themselves.

Chapter 13. This is an extreme liquidation procedure, which obliges the company to pay the creditors in several instalments (usually in three to five years) by the sale of its assets.

Chapter 7. Similar to Chapter 13, but it allows the debtor to separate its personal assets from the corporate assets and use only the latter to repay the creditors.

Chapter 7 foresees the liquidation (i.e. the sale) of a debtor's non-exempt property and the distribution of the proceeds to creditors. This liquidation procedure is common for individuals who cannot make regular payments to their creditors, but also for businesses that choose to terminate their operations, instead of trying to preserve the going concern through a restructuring plan (like with Chapter 11).

In the last decade, a secondary, hybrid mechanism has received considerable appreciation from companies in distress: **pre-packaged bankruptcy**. Under a pre-packaged bankruptcy, the company prepares the restructuring plan as in an out-of-court procedure, but the plan needs to be approved under supervision of the court. This dual way of operating offers, on the one hand, the speed and flexibility that characterize a private workout, and on the other, protection from holdouts and opportunistic creditors. However, this method might not be as effective as it seems, if the debtor has very complex and fragmented liabilities.

11.6.2 The Italian legal framework

The primary legislation governing insolvency and restructuring procedures in Italy is set out in the Bankruptcy Law (*Regio Decreto n. 267/1942*) called also "Legge Fallimentare."

Italy has recently replaced its Bankruptcy Act of 1942 with a comprehensive reform that started on 19 October 2017, when the Parliament passed Law No. 155 of 2017, which included a comprehensive reform of the rules governing financial crises and insolvency procedures. On 10 January 2019, the Government approved Legislative Decree No. 14 of 2019, entitled "Code for Distress and Insolvency" (*Codice della Crisi d'Impresa e dell'Insolvenza* – the "Code"). The new Code was supposed to take effect on 14 August 2020, but has been moved to 1 September 2021 due to the Covid-19 pandemic emergency.

The Italian insolvency law procedures are extremely formal and require the involvement of the court, as well as public and private authorities regardless the size of the bankruptcy estate. These procedures are very often lengthy and costly, less dynamic when compared with American procedures, and the average duration is more than five years.

In the Italian system, there are different types of claim and creditor sub-classes. As defined by the priority rule set out in Article 111 of the Bankruptcy Law (Royal Decree 267/1942), senior classes of creditors must be paid in full before junior classes, as follows:

- **Super-senior claims** (*"prededuzione"*) that include the costs and expenses incurred by the trustee and the court during the bankruptcy (e.g. trustee expenses, professional fees, and other costs relating to the liquidation or continuation of the business) and other claims originating from previous restructuring proceedings.
- **Secured claims**, that include claims originating before the bankruptcy petition was filed and are secured by mortgages, pledges, or liens. The proceeds derived from the assets must be used to pay the secured claims (and a portion of the preferential claims) before any other claims. If the proceeds are insufficient to repay the secured claims in full, the same procedure will apply to the unsecured creditors for the remaining portion.
- **General unsecured claims** are those incurred before the bankruptcy petition is filed, for which the holder does not benefit from a lien, a mortgage, or a pledge. Holders of these claims generally receive a pro-rata share of the distributed funds and rights after all senior claims are satisfied.
- **Subordinated unsecured claims** are claims subordinated either by pre-bankruptcy agreement or by the bankruptcy court's order under the principles of equitable subordination.
- **Shareholders** do not generally receive distributions.

In recent years, in order to optimize the procedures, alternative "in-court" and "out-of-court" arrangements have been introduced.

Currently, under Italian legislation, the insolvency procedures (also called "Procedure Concorsuali") are:

- **Bankruptcy ("Fallimento")**. This is a liquidation procedure which stops the company[23] from operating and foresees the sale of company's assets to repay the creditors according to the principle of equal treatment. The procedure can be initiated by the company, the creditors, and also by the court. The Bankruptcy procedures follow the "par condicio creditorum" principle, according to which lenders and bondholders cannot claim their rights individually, but need to follow the court-led process along with all the other creditors. Liquidation of assets is the

[23] The bankruptcy can affect businesses organized in the form of a company but also run by individuals. With the exception of state entities and small businesses such as farmers and a few other categories, Italian Bankruptcy Law applies to all entrepreneurs.

main outcome of "Fallimento," but this can also be avoided in the event creditors agree to be only partially satisfied by the company. This provision is called bankruptcy composition ("Concordato Fallimentare").
In general, bankruptcy can be defined as a liquidation (not a workout) procedure. This procedure requires that the company is in a state of insolvency, even if not yet in default. The debtor company, the creditors, and the bankruptcy court are authorized to request the start of the procedure.
During the procedure, the debtor is deprived of the authority to manage the company and has to dispose of its assets (except for a few assets necessary for daily activities in the case of individual bankruptcy). The powers are delegated to a bankruptcy administrator, the trustee manager ("*Curatore Fallimentare*"), under the direction and supervision of the bankruptcy judge ("*Giudice Delegato*") to whom she/he refers. In some circumstances, the trustee manager could decide to run the business also with the support of the former administrator(s) for a period of time ("*Esercizio Provvisorio*"), in order not to impoverish the value of the assets (especially the intangible ones), that could be sold as a whole rather than in a piecemeal sale.
It is worth mentioning that the procedure can also be transformed into a composition in bankruptcy (*Concordato Fallimentare*) in order to avoid the liquidation of the assets, if there is a new entrepreneur or financial investor that would purchase the whole firm with a restructuring plan that guarantees better satisfaction of the creditors than the liquidation.
In some situations, a **Compulsory Liquidation** (or receivership) can take place. This kind of liquidation is a special procedure applicable in certain supervised markets of public interest (e.g. banks, financial intermediaries, and insurance companies).

- ***Liquidazione Coatta Amministrativa* (Administrative Compulsory Liquidation)**. This is a procedure similar to Bankruptcy, but where the insolvency is controlled by an administrative authority instead of a legal one. Receivership applies for a company that is outside of the bankruptcy perimeter, such as banks, insurance companies and cooperative companies. Compulsory liquidation is activated in cases of insolvency or material irregularities in the management of the company. The court appoints an administrator who performs a role similar to the trustee in the classic bankruptcy procedure.

- ***Concordato Preventivo* (Pre-Bankruptcy Composition Procedure)**. This is a court-controlled agreement which aims at guaranteeing the going concern. The agreement must be approved by the majority of creditors by amount and in each class, and is binding also on dissenting creditors. The debtor can also file for a "*concordato preventivo*" without having a restructuring plan ready yet, with the obligation to present one within 120 days. If the company fails to deliver the plan, or if the agreement it is not approved, the court then proceeds with a bankruptcy procedure.

In order to strengthen the position of the unsecured creditors, Article 160 of Italian Bankruptcy Law establishes that the "*Concordato*" proposal should grant the payment of at least 20% of the unsecured creditors' claims; if this provision is not reached, the pre-bankruptcy procedure will be converted into a bankruptcy liquidation. The plan must be approved by creditors holding at least 50% plus one of the unsecured claims. Once creditors are divided into classes, the favourable vote of the majority of the voting creditors of each class is required. Votes are counted according to the amount of the claims.

- ***Amministrazione Controllata* (Extraordinary Administration).** Introduced with the Insolvency Proceedings Reform in 2006, this is a procedure similar to "*concordato preventivo,*" but designed for large, strategic corporations. In this case as well, the goal is to protect the company's status as a going concern. The main difference is that the definition and implementation of the restructuring plan is usually run by an expert appointed by the court or by the government, given the high strategic relevance the corporation has for the nation (more on this in section 11.6.3).

- **Debt restructuring Agreements.** Bankruptcy Law regulates not only the in-court procedures, but also restructuring agreements during private workouts, with a wide range of provisions (also illustrated in **Table 11.3** below).
  - **Restructuring Plan – Art. 67 (para. 3 I. d).** The Restructuring Plan is prepared by the company and evaluated by an expert from the standpoint of feasibility and truthfulness . The plan must be adequate to guarantee the restructuring of the indebtedness and the rebalancing of the financial structure, but apart from this, it is not subject to any other procedures. Art. 67 guarantees an exemption from "Revocatory Bankruptcy" as well as from bankruptcy crime charges for the payments and actions foreseen for the implementation of the

Table 11.3 Italian Bankruptcy Law Protocols

Characteristics	Restructuring Plan – Art. 67	Restructuring Agreement – Art. 182-bis	Composition in Continuity – Art. 186-bis
Flexibility	High	Low	Very Low
Duration	Low	High	Very High
Publication of the information and Bad Publicity	None	Yes	Yes
Fiscal Benefit for the Debtor	High	Very High	Very High
Fiscal Benefit for the Creditors	None	Very High	Very High
Standstill Period	None	Yes	Yes
Cram-Down Possibility	None	None	Yes

restructuring agreement. Finally, Art. 67 grants a tax deduction for income derived from debt reduction.

- **Restructuring Agreement – Art. 182-*bis*.** The content of the plan is the result of the agreement between the company and the creditors/bondholders. The agreement must be approved by creditors representing at least 60% of the debt value. The agreement must also be homologated by the court, which is responsible for verifying the truthfulness of the information and the appropriateness of the agreement. The court also guarantees the regular payment of the dissenting creditors within 120 days from the homologation (if the debt is already overdue, otherwise within 120 days from the due date). The effects of a restructuring agreement pursuant to Art. 182-*bis* only apply to the assenting creditors and include:
  - standstill period for the creditors (for 60 days from the homologation date);
  - tax deductibility for the loans (including bridge financing) received under the restructuring agreement (only if foreseen by the agreement);
  - exemption from "Revocatory Bankruptcy" and bankruptcy crimes for the actions and payments foreseen in the Restructuring Agreement.

Art. 182-*bis* guarantees greater supervision and protection for both the debtor and the creditors. However, it is not easy to reach 60% approval, dissenting creditors must be paid in full, and the court's intervention and homologation represent bad publicity for the company.[24]

- **Pre-Composition ("*Pre-Concordato*") – Art. 161, para. 6.** Pre-Composition was introduced in 2012 by Decree Law 83/2012 (called the "Development Decree"). The company can file for pre-composition simply by providing the balance sheets for the past three years even without a restructuring proposal. From the moment of filing, the debtor has up to 120 days to provide all the missing documentation, but can already benefit from the court's protection (i.e. a standstill period). During this period the company is allowed to carry out ordinary operations and extraordinary operations (upon Court's approval). After the pre-composition period is over, the debtor usually moves to the Composition in Continuity procedure pursuant to Art. 186-*bis*.
- **Composition in Continuity – Art. 186-*bis*.** According to this provision, the company can preserve its status as a going concern with the following conditions:
  - the restructuring plan must contain a detailed financial and business plan for the subsequent years;

[24] It is worth pointing out that Decree No. 83/2015 introduced Article 182-*septies* creating a special procedure as regards debt restructuring agreements involving mainly financial intermediaries, if the agreement is more convenient for the bank than bankruptcy liquidation. Article 182-*septies* states that the effects of a debt restructuring agreement, concluded with other creditors belonging to the same class and representing 75% of the value of the class, can be extended to dissenting financial creditors if, inter alia, under the terms of the agreement they are paid no less than they would receive according to "feasible alternatives" and the debtor's indebtedness is mainly towards banks and other financial creditors.

- the feasibility of the plan needs to be evaluated by a third-party expert;
- the payment of privileged and strategic creditors (e.g. suppliers, banks, and senior secured creditors) can be postponed up to 12 months from the homologation;
- strategic creditors can be satisfied with debt or equity instruments such as PIK, Participative Financial Instruments, debt-to-equity swaps, etc.;
- the composition must be approved by creditors representing more than 50% of the debt value in the majority of classes of creditors;
- the implications also apply to non-voting creditors.

The effects of Composition in Continuity are very similar to the Restructuring Agreement pursuant to Art, 182-*bis*, but offer more flexibility and the possibility to cram down dissenting creditors. However, like the Restructuring Agreement, the procedure can be very lengthy and generates bad publicity.

11.6.3 Italian insolvency procedures for large corporations

Italian law also provides special procedures for large corporations. There are two main procedures for large firm insolvencies.

The Prodi extraordinary administration procedure

The first example of a special law for large companies is the decree adopted in January 1979 on "urgent rules for the administration of large enterprises in crisis," which became known as the "Prodi Law."

The law was primarily aiming at protecting large enterprises (and consequently, employment) through the continuity of business activities. In practice, many of the enterprises subject to extraordinary administration ended up being liquidated, and the main effect of the procedure was to cushion the impact of insolvency on workers by delaying layoffs.

From an operative point of view, according to the "Prodi Law," a company is eligible for the procedure when it has i) more than 200 employees, and ii) a total indebtedness of no less than two-thirds of the aggregate of the total assets and the revenues in the preceding financial year.

The process starts with the court declaring the company's insolvency and appointing a judge and up to three judicial administrators to supervise the company's management and to assess whether the conditions for the extraordinary administrative procedure are present. In a second step, the Ministry of Economic Development appoints up to three extraordinary administrators in charge of the company's management and administration to be responsible for the preparation and implementation of the plan, and an oversight committee as well (which includes creditors' representatives).

The restructuring agreement needs to be approved by the Ministry of Economic Development and include both a liquidation and restructuring plan. Creditors are paid pro-rata and in accordance with the ranking of their credits on the basis of the proceeds deriving from the sale of the business (in the case of a divestment plan) or on the basis of the terms provided under the restructuring plan (in the case of a restructuring plan).

The Prodi Law was amended in 1999 (called the Prodi-*bis* Law) after it was found to be incompatible with European law.

The Marzano extraordinary administration procedure

The insolvency of the Parmalat group in 2003 prompted the authorities to enact special legislation to address the complex issues raised by the case. A new special regime for very large enterprises was then enacted by the minister Antonio Marzano, and thus called the Marzano law.

The new procedure is based on the Prodi-*bis* Law, but with special rules for very large enterprises by allowing for more flexible and less cumbersome procedures, reducing the possibility of liquidation, and assigning more powers to the administration at the expense of the judiciary authorities.

To be eligible for the Marzano law procedure, a company must have i) more than 500 employees and ii) a total indebtedness of more than €300 million.

The main characteristics of this procedure are roughly equivalent to those of the Prodi extraordinary administration procedure. This procedure is based on debt restructuring and the sale of those assets considered not strategic or not part of the company's core business.

An innovative aspect of the Marzano Decree is that the Minister, rather than the bankruptcy court, has the responsibility to supervise the procedure; the bankruptcy court is required only to confirm the company's insolvency status and to verify the lawfulness of the process.

The Marzano Law was subsequently amended with the Special Procedure for Large Insolvent Companies, prompted by the urgent situation involving the Alitalia airline company's insolvency. The amendment of the Marzano Law was enacted by Decree Law No. 134 of 28 August 2008, converted into Law No. 166 of 27 October 27 2008 (the Amended Marzano Law).

11.6.4 The Italian insolvency law reform

A new insolvency code was passed in 2019 (the "New Insolvency Code"), which was scheduled to take effect on 14 August 2020. Due to the Covid-19 pandemic emergency, the entry into force of the new Code of Crisis and Insolvency has been postponed to 1 September 2021.

The reform, in line with the newly enacted European "Harmonization Directive" No. 2019/1023, has the aim to promote "preventive and early" restructuring of economically sustainable companies in crisis (understood as a state of economic and financial difficulty that makes insolvency likely), to safeguard the company's going concern (called "rescue culture"), and to make restructuring, insolvency, and debt discharge procedures more effective and less time-consuming.

The New Insolvency Code will provide new rules encouraging new and interim loans from both lenders and equity holders whose claims can be satisfied with priority over both secured and unsecured claims in the case of subsequent insolvency, new tools providing for the repayment in full of dissenting creditors, and the possibility to satisfy a claim by equivalent means and to extend any stay of individual actions or maturity extensions to dissenting creditors.

Case study **Ferroli***

Ferroli S.p.A. was founded by Dante Ferroli in San Bonifacio (Verona) and is one of the global leaders active in the design, production, and installation of heating and air conditioning systems for residential and industrial use. Over the years, Ferroli has established a strong position in more than 15 countries in several continents with a portfolio of 12 different brands. Its industrial footprint consists of 13 production facilities in several countries (6 in Italy).
In 2014, Ferroli recorded the following figures, also shown in the following tables:

- Net Revenue: €430m (approx.)
- EBITDA: €8m (approx.)
- Net Financial Position: €337m
- Long-Term Bank Debt: €249m
- Short-Term Bank Debt: €91m
- Number of employees: 3,000 (1,000 in Italy)

Ferroli Group Income Statement

Income Statement - Ferroli Group (€m)	2012	2013	2014
Net Sales	**537,6**	**509,7**	**428,3**
YoY growth (%)		(5,2%)	(16,0%)
Cost of goods sold	(351,6)	(338,6)	(285,2)
Gross Margin	**186,0**	**171,1**	**143,1**
% on Net Sales	*34,6%*	*33,6%*	*33,4%*
Fixed production costs	(9,3)	(7,5)	(7,1)
Freight out	(14,5)	(12,6)	(11,5)
Variable commercial costs	(24,7)	(22,7)	(18,2)
Fixed commercial costs	(62,3)	(61,1)	(58,6)
R&D costs	(4,8)	(5,2)	(4,9)
SG&A & other costs	(37,0)	(37,5)	(34,6)
EBITDA	**33,4**	**24,6**	**8,2**
% on Net Sales	*6,2%*	*4,8%*	*1,9%*
D&A & Leasing costs	(24,4)	(24,7)	(24,7)
EBIT	**9,1**	**(0,2)**	**(16,5)**
% on Net Sales	*1,7%*	*(0,0%)*	*(3,9%)*
Financial income / (costs)	(11,7)	(8,3)	(9,7)

Income Statement - Ferroli Group (€m)	2012	2013	2014
Other income / (costs)	0,1	(12,1)	(5,8)
Extraordinary income / (costs)	(1,5)	(2,9)	(134,5)
EBT	**(4,0)**	**(23,5)**	**(166,4)**
% on Net Sales	*(0,7%)*	*(4,6%)*	*(38,9%)*
Taxes	(3,3)	(0,5)	(4,8)
Net Income / (Loss)	**(7,4)**	**(24,0)**	**(171,2)**
% on Net Sales	*(1,4%)*	*(4,7%)*	*(40,0%)*

Ferroli Group Balance Sheet

Balance Sheet - Ferroli Group (€m)	2014	*% Capital Employed* 2014
Fixed Assets	**199.7**	**88.0%**
Inventory	84.9	
Trade receivables	149.4	
Trade payables	(120.2)	
Other receivables/(payables)	7,7	
Net Working Capital	**126.3**	**55.6%**
Provisions & other long-term payables	**(98.9)**	**-43.6%**
Total Capital Invested	**227.1**	**100%**
Shareholders' Equity	**(109.8)**	**-48%**
Short-term financial debt	91.1	
Long-term financial debt	259.4	
(Cash)	(13.6)	
Net Financial Position	**336.9**	**148%**
Total Sources	**227.1**	**100%**

As shown in the tables above, Ferroli was far from being a healthy and profitable company. Since 2012, Net Sales have been declining by 11%, compounded as a result of the prolonged crisis in the real estate sector, that affected markets with high strategic relevance for Ferroli (such as Italy and Spain), and of fierce competition. EBITDA margin kept shrinking during these years due to the expensive overhead structure (especially on commercial costs and SG&A costs), losing 4.3p.p. in three years. Depreciation and amortization remained steady at a relatively high level (approximately €24.7m) due to the high amount of fixed assets, making EBIT fall into negative territory already in 2013 (it accounted for -€16.5m in 2014). Costs were mainly related to the on-going restructuring and business reorganization process (e.g. tangible and intangible asset write-downs, personnel restructuring, closure of production sites, and advisory costs) that made Ferroli record a yearly net loss of -€171.2M (the third year in a row of cumulative losses).

The 2014 Ferroli balance sheet clearly shows that the company was having problems financing its own operations given the high level of Net Working Capital. Debt, especially the long-term financial debt, was disproportionately high with respect to the asset side, available cash, and EBITDA (the Net Debt/EBITDA ratio was 41.3x in 2014). The value finally broke when the cumulative losses made the equity worth nothing (technically negative), bringing the company into financial distress.

In June 2015, Ferroli filed for protection as granted by Italian Bankruptcy Law under "Concordato Preventivo con Riserva" (Art. 161, paragraph 6) in order to start a debt restructuring procedure.

The reasons for the Ferroli crisis can be grouped as follows:

- **External Market Conditions.** Strong competition and the prolonged crisis of the real estate sector in some of the most important markets for Ferroli (Italy and Spain above all).
- **Strategy and Internal Organization:**
  - wide and expensive international presence not in line with the financial structure;
  - margin and profitability reduction;
  - wide product range and sub-optimized product mix, which contributed to low profitability;
  - expensive fixed structure: very high depreciation and amortization and ROI below cost of capital.
- Extraordinary Factors

Mediobanca was hired as the sole financial advisor for the transaction.
The debt restructuring process was divided into the following steps (as indicated in the table below).

- After filing for "Concordato Preventivo con Riserva," the company worked to prepare a restructuring agreement to be presented to banks, investors, and shareholders.
- As a first step, Ferroli obtained a bridge loan from investors and banks of €35m (provided in three tranches in four months), authorized by the court (pursuant to Art. 182-*quinques* B.L.), before the homologation of the Debt Restructuring Agreement.
- A competitive M&A deal was orchestrated by Mediobanca, where Oxy Capital and Attestor Capital combined bought 60% of Ferroli shares from the family. As new majority shareholders, they appointed a new management team and radically changed the governance.
- A super-senior loan (DIP) of €63m with a 5-year bullet maturity was underwritten by the equity investor Attestor Capital; this loan was also crucial to refinance the bridge financing obtained while drafting the Debt Restructuring Agreement.
- The restructuring involved approximately €270m of outstanding bank debt (5-year bullet maturity), with the banks committing to convert up to a maximum amount of €160m of debt into quasi-equity instruments during the business plan period agreed between the parties, with the aim to cover losses and equity reductions.
- Banks also committed an extra €60m short-term loan with automatic renewal for 5 years in the case of successful achievement of the business plan targets.
- A cash waterfall mechanism was implemented in order to distribute any excess cash and proceeds generated from the investor exit, extraordinary operations, and over-delivery of the business plan.

Ferroli Transaction Timetable

Main transaction events / steps	2014	2015											
	Dec	Jan	Feb	Mar	Apr	May	Jun	Jul	Aug	Sep	Oct	Nov	Dec
Selection of the Investor as the most suitable counterparty for the relaunch of the Group & negotiation with the existing shareholders													
Negotiation and signing of an MoU between the parties													
Filing for the protection granted by Art. 161, comma 6 of the Italian Bankruptcy Law ("Concordato Preventivo con Riserva")													
Finalization of the Financial Plan and negotiations between all the parties on the terms of the Transaction													
Bridge financing granted by the Banks and the Investor (new financing facility ex Art. 182-quinquies B.L.)							Tranche 1	Tranche 2		Tranche 3			
Finalization and signing of Debt Restructuring Agreements ex Art 182-bis B.L.													
Homologation of the DRA by the relevant Court													

The Debt Restructuring Agreement was accompanied also by a strong Asset Restructuring Plan and a business plan to support Ferroli in driving revenue growth, margin optimization, and profitability improvement over the next 5+ years.

The financials in the tables below show the post-restructuring results of the group.

The year **2015** was one of transition, when the restructuring started. In that period the company suffered from a drop in Net Sales of -29%, which made EBITDA fall into negative territory at -€4.0m, despite the actions taken in overhead cuts (e.g. Freight Out costs went down by 32% and Commercial Costs by €9.2m) and in structure rationalization (Depreciation & Amortization moved from -€24.7m to -€16.6m).

In **2016** Ferroli was able to deliver positive EBITDA and Net Income (€10.4m and €26.7m, respectively) thanks mainly to the following drivers:

- Margin Improvement. Gross Margin jumped from 35.5% in 2015 to 37.9% of Net Sales in 2016, thanks to strong savings in Cost of Goods Sold, which allowed Ferroli to grow absolute Gross Margin, despite a negative Net Sales trend YoY (-4.0%)
- Fixed Costs Rationalization especially in fixed production costs, commercial costs, and SG&A (+€11.9m savings in all overhead combined).
- Extraordinary income was mainly related to the effects of the Debt Restructuring Agreement (i.e. release of provisions, non-recurring income related to contingent assets & liabilities)

After 2016, with a much leaner structure, the company started to grow Net Revenues again, which fuelled new investments especially in Variable Commercial Costs and at the same time improved EBITDA margin (coming in at 5.6%, not far from pre-crisis profitability levels).

Ferroli Group Income Statement after Restructuring

Income Statement - Ferroli Group (€m)	2014	2015	2016	2017	2018
Net Sales	**428.3**	**303.9**	**291.3**	**319.4**	**336.0**
YoY growth (%)	(16.0%)	(29.0%)	(4.2%)	9.6%	5.2%
Cost of goods sold	(285.2)	(196.0)	(180.9)	(201.3)	(216.3)
Gross Margin	**143.1**	**107.9**	**110.4**	**118.1**	**119.7**
% on Net Sales	*33.4%*	*35.5%*	*37.9%*	*37.0%*	*35.6%*
Fixed production costs	(7.1)	(6.4)	(5.5)	(5.7)	(5.9)
Freight out	(11.5)	(7.8)	(7.0)	(7.5)	(8.0)
Variable commercial costs	(18.2)	(13.0)	(13.7)	(17.5)	(18.5)
Fixed commercial costs	(58.6)	(49.4)	(40.6)	(39.5)	(40.7)
R&D costs	(4.9)	(5.2)	(5.0)	(3.8)	(3.7)
SG&A & other costs	(34.6)	(30.1)	(28.1)	(25.9)	(24.1)
EBITDA	**8.2**	**(4.0)**	**10.4**	**18.0**	**18.8**
% on Net Sales	*1.9%*	*(1.3%)*	*3.6%*	*5.6%*	*5.6%*
D&A & Leasing costs	(24.7)	(16.6)	(13.7)	(13.7)	(13.7)
EBIT	**(16.5)**	**(20.6)**	**(3.3)**	**4.3**	**5.1**
% on Net Sales	*(3.9%)*	*(6.8%)*	*(1.1%)*	*1.4%*	*1.5%*
Financial income / (costs)	(9.7)	(8.0)	(13.0)	(15.8)	(16.4)
Other income / (costs)	(5.8)	(6.8)	52.1	11.7	(7.7)
Extraordinary income / (costs)	(134.5)	9.3	(7.1)	(1.7)	(0.4)

Income Statement - Ferroli Group (€m)	2014	2015	2016	2017	2018
EBT	**(166.4)**	**(26.1)**	**28.8**	**(1.5)**	**(19.5)**
% on Net Sales	*(38.9%)*	*(8.6%)*	*9.9%*	*(0.5%)*	*(5.8%)*
Taxes	(4.8)	(0.3)	(2.1)	(1.8)	(0.9)
Net Income / (Loss)	**(171.2)**	**(26.5)**	**26.7**	**(3.4)**	**(20.4)**
% on Net Sales	*(40.0%)*	*(8.7%)*	*9.2%*	*(1.1%)*	*(6.1%)*

Ferroli Group Income Statement Org Variances YoY (abs & %)

Income Statement - Ferroli Group (€m)	15 vs 14 abs	15 vs 14 org %	16 vs 15 abs	16 vs 15 org %	17 vs 16 abs	17 vs 16 org %	18 vs 17 abs	18 vs 17 org %
Net Sales	**(124.4)**	**-29%**	**(12.7)**	**-4%**	**28.1**	**10%**	**16.6**	**5%**
YoY growth (%)								
Cost of goods sold	89.2	31%	15.1	8%	(20.4)	-11%	(15.0)	-7%
Gross Margin	**(35.2)**	**-25%**	**2.5**	**2%**	**7.7**	**7%**	**1.7**	**1%**
% on Net Sales								
Fixed production costs	0.6	9%	0.9	14%	(0.2)	-3%	(0.2)	-3%
Freight out	3.7	32%	0.8	10%	(0.5)	-7%	(0.5)	-7%
Variable commercial costs	5.3	29%	(0.8)	-6%	(3.8)	-27%	(1.0)	-6%
Fixed commercial costs	9.2	16%	8.8	18%	1.0	3%	(1.2)	-3%
R&D costs	(0.3)	-5%	0.2	4%	1.1	23%	0.2	5%
SG&A & other costs	4.6	13%	1.9	6%	2.2	8%	1.8	7%
EBITDA	**(12.1)**	**-149%**	**14.4**	**361%**	**7.6**	**73%**	**0.8**	**4%**
% on Net Sales								
D&A & Leasing costs	8.0	32%	3.0	18%	(0.0)	0%	(0.0)	0%
EBIT	**(4.1)**	**-25%**	**17.4**	**84%**	**7.6**	**233%**	**0.8**	**18%**
% on Net Sales								
Financial income / (costs)	1.7	17%	(4.9)	-62%	(2.8)	-22%	(0.7)	-4%
Other income / (costs)	(1.0)	-17%	58.9	870%	(40.4)	-78%	(19.4)	-166%
Extraordinary income / (costs)	143.8	107%	(16.4)	-177%	5.4	75%	1.3	76%
EBT	**140.3**	**84%**	**55.0**	**210%**	**(30.3)**	**-105%**	**(18.0)**	**-1192%**
% on Net Sales								
Taxes	4.4	93%	(1.8)	-511%	0.3	13%	0.9	49%
Net Income / (Loss)	**144.7**	**85%**	**53.2**	**201%**	**(30.1)**	**-113%**	**(17.1)**	**-508%**

Ferroli Group Balance Sheet after Restructuring

Balance Sheet - Ferroli Group (€m)	2018	*% Capital Employed* 2018
Fixed Assets	**140.2**	**64.4%**
Inventory	84.9	
Trade receivables	93.2	
Trade payables	(62.9)	
Other receivables/(payables)	1.9	
Net Working Capital	**117.0**	**53.8%**
Provisions & other long-term payables	**(39.5)**	**-18.2%**
Total Capital Invested	**217.6**	**100%**
Shareholders' Equity	**(8.2)**	**-4%**
Short-term financial debt	21.2	
Long-term financial debt	220.7	
(Cash)	(16.1)	
Net Financial Position	**225.8**	**104%**
Total Sources	**217.6**	**100%**

The Ferroli debt restructuring was considered extremely critical due to the following aspects:

- It was the first deal implemented in Italy with the DIP financing Technique.
- It also involved a generational transition from the founder.
- It involved many parties (investor, multiple banks, shareholders, and other creditors).
- The turnaround relied on strong cooperation between creditors and equity investors.
- The equity investor played a pivotal role acting as a lender on the behalf of the banks (for example, by providing DIP financing).

* Thanks to Mediobanca investment bank for the data and all the support.

Case study C.M.C. di Ravenna*

Cooperativa Muratori & Cementisti (CMC) di Ravenna is a cooperative organization founded in 1901 in the northeast area of Italy. CMC is one of the largest and most important construction companies, operating in infrastructure projects such as roads, tunnels, dams, and (high speed) railways both in Italy and in foreign markets.
CMC's international expansion started in the mid-1970s with projects in Iran. From that moment on, CMC kept expanding in foreign markets, which now account for more than 70% of the total turnover generated. It is present in over 40 countries on 4 continents with 24 offices around the globe.
As of December 2017, CMC recorded the following figures:

- Turnover €1.1bn
- EBITDA €170m
- Backlog €3.7bn (80% of which consists of public contracts for infrastructure, hydroelectric, and building works both in Italy and abroad).
- Total Debt €2.0bn
- Unsecured Debt €1.9bn

In December 2018, CMC filed for a Composition with Creditors Procedure on a going concern basis under the terms of Art. 161 of the Italian Bankruptcy law (the so-called "Concordato Preventivo in continuità").
The reasons for the crisis that led CMC di Ravenna to file for "Concordato Preventivo" were the following:

- the long-lasting downturn of the Italian construction sector in the past years, which mainly affected companies that were cooperating with the public sector. The lasting business contraction made the company very vulnerable from a financial standpoint.
- high immobilization of work in progress, also as a consequence of the industry slowdown, especially in the public sector. This became a problem mainly when work in progress was growing faster than receivables collection.
- High level of indebtedness. Based on the cited metrics, CMC had a Total Debt/EBITDA ratio of 11.8x, higher than the average amount for the infrastructure industry of 7x/8x. However, one of the biggest problems was the large amount of unsecured debt (95% of total debt).
- Problems in generating cash and profitability in certain projects in the portfolio.

The transaction had three main criticalities:

- As a cooperative company, CMC did not have an "entrepreneur figure."
- The number of counterparties was astonishingly high. There were over 11,000 creditors and over 50 financial institutions (30 banks and 20 insurance companies), which made the negotiations very complicated.
- CMC also had listed bonds. The tensions around the bond market price and the information required represented an additional element of complexity.

Under the protection of "Concordato Preventivo con Continuità," with the support of its advisors, the company prepared an economic and financial plan with the goal of preserving the going concern (the "Composition Plan"). The final objective of the plan was to maximize the satisfaction of a plurality of creditors. In order to do so, the plan contained a dual approach: 1) Direct Business Continuity and 2) Disposal of Non-Core Assets.

- In line with the preservation of the going concern, Direct Business Continuity was implemented by:
  - selecting only part of existing projects in Italy and abroad, in order to focus attention only on those works that could generate better cash flow and be profit accretive;
  - signing new contracts over the period of the business plan.
- Furthermore, non-strategic assets were sold in order to inject new cash into the company and increase creditor satisfaction. This included construction claims, receivables, real estate assets, and other assets related to terminated projects that were no longer considered strategic for the company and its business continuity.

CMC's proposal was to distribute the expected cash flows generated by the economic and financial plan to the creditors in compliance with the pre-emptive rights.
This meant first fully satisfying the **secured and preferential creditors** within 12 months of court homologation of the "Composition Plan," as well as the **strategic suppliers** (that are technically unsecured creditors, but considered of high strategic importance for business continuity) within 12 to 24 months of the homologation.
After fully satisfying secured and strategic creditors, the company granted partial or non-monetary satisfaction to the **unsecured creditors** with the subscription of PFIs (Participatory Financial Instruments) convertible into bonds with the following characteristics:

- The Participatory Financial Instruments (PFIs) granted the creditors the right to receive excess cash until June 2031 (if not converted into bonds upon request from the creditors). A floor amount was foreseen to be paid by maturity.
- The bonds gave the holders the right to receive excess cash until December 2026, with a fixed amount to be paid by maturity.

The "Composition Plan" was approved at the beginning of 2020 and received the homologation from the Court of Ravenna, which allowed the company to avoid bankruptcy and implement its plan to preserve going concern status.
Given the highly fragmented debt and the need to enhance profitability and cash generation, the role of the advisors was extremely important, mainly for two reasons: *i*) they supported the structuring and development of the economic and financial plan, and; *ii*) they coordinated the process, mediated between the parties and created the condition for a high consensus among the relevant creditors.
The table offers an overview of the deal process and key steps.

CMC Transaction Timeline

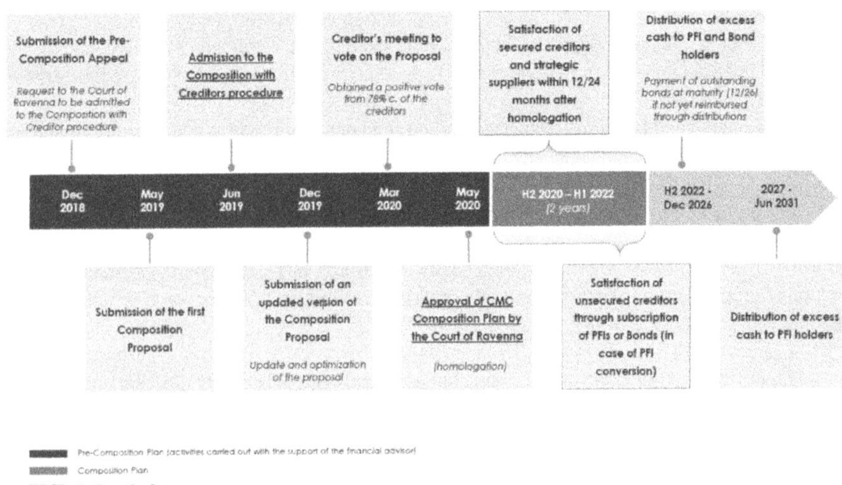

*Thanks to Mediobanca investment bank for the data and all the support provided.

Questions and answers

1. *Illustrate and present the arguments for why a company needs restructuring.*
   Companies usually go into a financial crisis for one or more of the following reasons:

   - Wrong strategy and business model, which results in non-competitiveness in the market, lack of topline growth, operational inefficiencies, and lower EBITDA margin than competitors. Poor business performance also indirectly affects the cost of indebtedness, as creditors request a higher return given the company's results, which further reduce profitability.

- Managerial overconfidence ("hubris"). CEOs and managers might take risky decisions which ultimately turn out to be very detrimental for the company. For example, expanding into a new market with a lot of up-front investment, or placing all their bets on the wrong product.
- Product/service obsolescence and lack of innovation. The source of competitive advantage of a company (a product or a service) becomes obsolete as new and better solutions become available on the market, and the company is unable to innovate and change the business model (i.e. Blockbuster or Kodak).
- Expensive asset structure. Fixed investments (tangible and intangible) and CAPEX are too high and it is hard for the company to deliver an acceptable ROA and ROI above the cost of capital, benefit from economies of scale, and cover for depreciation and amortization. This problem becomes even bigger in the case of drop in demand which leads to excess capacity and thus inability to sustain the fixed overheads.
- Unsustainable capital structure. When working capital is too positive and the company is not able to finance its current operations (i.e. disproportionate ratio between receivables and payables, or too high inventory), or when the company is under-capitalized or the level of debt is simply too high versus equity (D/E ratio).
- External Macro factors. New regulations which make the company no longer competitive anymore and expel it from the market, new legislation over patenting rules and protection, high public debt and political turmoil, a national or global financial crisis, and pandemics and natural disasters.
- Fraud. For example, the Enron and Parmalat cases.

2. *What are the key financial and non-financial indicators of a company crisis?*
   Usually, before a company goes into default, there are some financial and non-financial metrics that are important to note as they could be indicators of an unhealthy business:

   - decline or revenues and profitability;
   - results far below business plan targets;
   - market share loss and poor performance vs competition;
   - worsening Working Capital;
   - increase of Net Financial Position;
   - capex cut and investment postponement;
   - scarce cash flow;
   - high management turnover;
   - unclear and/or unrealistic strategy;
   - poor innovation;
   - no liquidity headroom.

3. *Illustrate the main adjustments that need to be applied in the case of valuation of a distressed company.*
   Typical adjustments to be made when valuing a distressed company include:
   - working capital (distressed companies usually have difficult relationships with suppliers and unreliable inventory);
   - non-recurring expenses/restructuring costs (turnaround costs could be significant and have a material impact on deliverable cash flows across the plan);
   - need for considerable investments/capex (which could have been deferred for a long while because of cash shortage);
   - restricted cash (cash which is unavailable for certain reasons, like duties towards minority shareholders)
   - higher risk-return profile, which needs to be included in the cost of capital (the Capital Asset Pricing Model-based cost of equity has to be adjusted accordingly).

4. *List and describe the most important Debt Sustainability KPIs.*
   The most important metrics are the followings:

   Net Debt/EBITDA. Ideally this ratio should not exceed 3x in order for a company not to be considered at risk of default. However, the acceptable level can vary depending on the industry in which the company operates, and on the stability of cash flows. Cyclical industries, for example, usually show very limited (if not zero) debt, while companies in the infrastructure business can operate at a 7x or 8x Net/EBITDA ratio and still be in the investment grade span. A high Net/EBITDA ratio can also be reached in case of shrinking EBITDA (decreasing denominator), which can be a temporary effect and does not necessarily mean that the company is running a risk of default.

   Net Debt/Equity. Companies which are highly leveraged tend to be much more vulnerable in case of a market shock or external factor. Lehman had a Net Debt/Equity leverage of 19.7x, which left very little space between the assets' book value and the value of liabilities.

   Debt Service Coverage Ratio (DSCR): the ratio between the cash available to meet annual debt interest and principal payments and interest and principal. If DSCR is less than 1, it means that the company does not have enough cash to face all the payments of interest and principal due in the year. Ideally, an acceptable level should be around 1.2x.

   Interest Coverage Ratio (EBITDA/Interest). This metric shows how easy for the company is to pay interests on its outstanding debt thanks to the profitability of its current operations. Ideally, the ratio should be above 4x.

   Level of Cash and availability of committed lines.

5. *Let us consider the balance sheets of companies A and B:*

€m	Company A	Company B
Operating Assets	1,000	–
Accounts Receivable	100	500
Cash and Equivalents	1,000	–
Total Assets	**2,100**	**500**
Accounts Payable	200	200
Financial Debt	10,000	1,500
Total Liabilities	**10,200**	**1,700**

Calculate the Recovery Rate for Company A and Company B.

€m		Company A	Company B
Operating Assets	A	1,000	0
Accounts Receivable	B	100	500
Cash and Equivalents	C	1,000	0
Total Assets	F	**2,100**	**500**
Accounts Payable	D	200	200
Financial Debt	E	10,000	1,500
Total Liabilities	G	**10,200**	**1,700**
Recovery Rate	**F/G**	**20,6%**	**29,4%**

6. *What is a leveraged buyout and why is it connected to corporate restructuring and defaults?*
Leveraged Buyouts are acquisitions of a target company, a business, a division, or a group of assets, run by using a large amount of money sourced mostly with debt. The remaining part of the financing is provided via equity by mainly Private firms. The investor usually tries to maximize the leverage used (and thus minimize its equity investment) with debt below investment grade rate. This debt is then secured with the target company's shares and assets and remains in the target company's post-acquisition balance sheet. The future cash flows that the company will generate after the acquisition are used to pay back the outstanding debt. In a way, it is like saying that the target company pays for its own acquisition. The new owners of the company are the equity providers, which, by investing a relatively small amount of money, are able to acquire control and shares of much more valuable assets thanks to the assistance of leverage.
LBOs are extremely risky and not all the companies are suitable to be targets. After a leveraged buyout, the target company suffers from clear worsening of the Net Debt/Equity ratio, Net Debt/EBITDA ratio, Debt Service Coverage Ratio,

and Interest Coverage Ratio. Not to mention that the high level of debt generates high interest per se, which eats into the bottom line every year.
In fact, problems arise when, after the acquisition, the target company underperforms versus the expectations, and is not able to deliver the promised cash flow to pay the outstanding debt. Delivering modest (if not null or negative) growth and margin deterioration creates a lot of problems for the target company. In case there are also external headwinds, or adverse market circumstances (i.e. the 2008 financial crises), the company is even more in trouble. When a firm is loaded with debt and suffers from revenue and margins decline, it gradually starts approaching a crisis and eventually a distress situation.

7. *Let us assume that Company A has total liabilities of $900m and assets with total book value of $1,200m, of which $400m is goodwill from past acquisitions which is subject to yearly evaluation. After an auditing review, at Year 0, the goodwill is fully impaired and so worth 0. What is the value of the equity before and after Year 0? What is the Recovery Rate of company A?*

€m		**Before YO**	**After YO**
Operating Assets	A	800	800
Goodwill	B	400	0
Total Assets	**C = A + B**	**1,200**	**800**
Total Liabilities	**D**	**900**	**900**
Equity	**E**	**300**	**-100**
Recovery Rate	**C/D**	**133.3%**	**88.9%**

8. *List the main differences between private workouts and in-court procedures. What are the main advantages and disadvantages of the two procedures?*
Private Workouts. A restructuring Plan is put in place by the company together with the shareholders and the creditors. The company takes control of the process and no legal authority is involved. Private workouts usually guarantee higher recovery rates, flexibility for the parties, and protect its reputation. However, in order to successfully implement a private workout, a high consensus (if not unanimity) is needed across lenders and the company cannot prevent holdouts (the creation of a minority category of creditors which might block the process).
In-Court Procedures. The process is driven by an authority in court (usually a judge) and guarantees fair and equal treatment of all creditors, and can either lead to a restructuring Procedure, or, in case of failure, to a liquidation procedure, which will put an end to the company's existence. The main advantages of the in-court procedures are: the presence of a third party who supervises and coordinates the process and protects creditors' rights, and the possibility to "cram down" dissenting creditors (enforce specific solutions on minority lenders who did not agree with the terms). However in-court procedures are usually very

time-consuming, with much lower recovery rates, highly impact the company's reputation, and damage company's intangible assets.

9. *Describe the role of financial advisors in restructuring deals.*
The financial advisors (hired by the company or by the lenders/bondholders) are probably the most important stakeholders in the process. In the absence of a legal authority (i.e. a judge), the financial advisors play a pivotal (technical and managerial) role in coordinating and supervising the restructuring. Their most important responsibilities are: to perform the proper credit analysis and assess the company's Debt Capacity; to guide the valuation in the case of M&A; to manage the relationship with the company, the shareholders, and the creditors; to coordinate the due diligence and the drafting of documentation; to negotiate the terms and conditions of the restructuring agreements; and to look for funds. The advisors are also crucial to manage the relationship between senior and junior lenders/bondholders, which is key to delivering a successful restructuring. Finally, the financial advisors supervises the financial plan drafted by the company together with a strategic advisor/consultant. The ultimate goal for the advisors is to maximize the Recovery Rates for the lenders/bondholders and to achieve the best agreement to help the company overcome the crisis.
The role of the advisors and the senior lenders/bondholders varies a lot depending on the size of the to-be-restructured company and on the fragmentation of the corporate debt. The advisor's role becomes crucial in case of highly fragmented debt, with numerous creditors with different seniorities and positions. They in fact need a third-party player who can coordinate and guide them and who can find satisfactory terms and conditions for all parties. On the other hand, when debt is concentrated, the main lender (i.e. the main bank) takes a leading role in the process. However, if the restructured company is a large corporation, with a high level of complexity, than one sole lender cannot coordinate the whole process by itself but needs the help of the financial advisors instead.

10. *What types of actions can the company take in order to* ***renegotiate*** *its indebtedness in case of private and public debt?*
When liquidity is very scarce and the financial structure becomes unbearable for the company, or also when a covenant is breached, one solution for the company is to renegotiate the terms and conditions of its debt. Renegotiation tools depend on the nature of the debt, whether it is private or public.
In the case of private debt, there are two main solutions the borrower can pursue:

- Covenant reset: modification of the conditions for financial covenants in order to make them lighter based on the company's recent financial troubles. A covenant reset usually comes with a fee adhere (the so-called "amendment-fees") and/or a spread increase granted to the creditors. The approval of a covenant reset agreement typically happens with the assent of a 51% majority of creditors. In some cases of declining or even negative EBITDA (like the ones ex-

perienced during the covid-19 pandemic), companies may ask for "Covenant Holidays", which is a de facto suspension of the terms for a specific period of time.
- Amend-to-extend: extension of the maturity of the debt. Given its more invasive nature, an amend-to-extend agreement needs to be approved by all the creditors.

When it comes to public debt, the borrower can pursue one of the following actions in the market:

- Tender Offer: buying back bonds from the holders at a pre-defined price (usually lower than the par value but higher than the current market value). It is hard to see high participation in a tender offer unless the terms of the buyback are very appealing.
- Exchange Offer: exchanging a debt security with another instrument under approval of all creditors.
- Open-market Deal: basically a tender offer but with the possibility to buy back only part of securities and not all of them.
- Consent Solicitation: bondholder meeting to amend the terms of the covenants.

11. *Describe a debt-to-equity swap transaction and how it impacts the company, the shareholders, and the creditors/bondholders.*
Debt-to-Equity-Swap is another viable option for the company. With this transaction lenders can convert their debt position into equity, becoming shareholders of the company. A debt-to-equity-swap is a very effective tool for the company to quickly reduce its leverage (Debt/Equity). This instrument can also be combined with debt refinancing, giving the company the possibility to substitute the just-converted debt with fresher and cheaper debt. On the creditor side, shares represent a form of payment and remuneration and give lenders all the rights held by shareholders (voting and governance participation above all), which can be very interesting for those who want to pursue a loan-to-own strategy, but also reduce their priority in receiving cash from the debtor. On this topic, negotiation can be tough, as shareholders will of course fight against the possible dilution of their current position.

12. *What types of M&A transactions can the company undertake in restructuring deals?*
Divestitures are typical asset restructuring deals. The sale of a non-core business creates a significant appetite for the creditors as it is a relatively quick measure to de-leverage the business and inject a good amount of cash into the company's coffers. However, the risk of rushing into these solutions is very high and might be detrimental for the recovery rates and the overall restructuring. The choice of whether and what to divest must be taken very carefully.

Equity carve-outs consist of the public offering of a stake in a subsidiary. This implies a number of nuances, one of which is that the divested subsidiary must become a separate legal entity, with its own Board of Directors. Moreover, the parent company must decide how much of the subsidiary should be sold: the sale rarely exceeds 20%, since this way, many legal frameworks, such as that of the US, allow for the full tax and accounting consolidation of the subsidiary. This can create a conflict due to the discrepancy between ownership of the firm and its actual management structure. The effect of the announcement of equity carve-outs on stock prices, although predominantly positive, is not substantiated by empirical findings regarding the long-term return of stocks, which show contradicting results. It is possible to observe however, that subsidiaries' long-term performance is superior to that of parents. Similarly, studies regarding the post-transaction performance of parents show ambiguous results, while subsidiaries still tend to improve at a higher rate than their parent companies.

Spin-offs are a divestiture mode in which the parent company distributes the shares of the divested company to existing shareholders on a pro-rata basis (e.g. a person holding 30% of the parent will own 30% of the divested company). Just like equity carve-outs, this transaction involves the creation of an independent company, however, unlike the previous mode, it does not involve any sort of cash transaction, and as such they are often tax exempt. Since all the shares are given out, the new entity has no formal link with the parent, except for having the same shareholders, so it enjoys complete independence and freedom to reach its own goals. Spin-offs' market reception is observed to be much better than for equity carve-outs: findings show a strongly positive effect on stock prices, which is then reinforced by an abnormal return on the outstanding stock price for the subsidiaries and mild positive impact on the parent's stock price. Operating-wise, parents have shown little to no improvement after the transaction, with some studies highlighting worsened performance, whereas subsidiaries show positive or null effects.

Sell-offs are the simplest transaction of the three: they are the sale of assets, part of or whole subsidiaries, in exchange for consideration which can be cash or other securities. Unlike the previous two, there is no creation of third entities, since what is sold only changes ownership. A sell-off is different from liquidation in the sense that it does not involve the closure of the entity; however, it shares the possibility of being either voluntary, when it is a conscious choice for corporate portfolio management, or involuntary, when it is a divestiture coerced by an authority, such as in the case of antitrust issues or Chapter 11 reorganizations. Sell-off announcements have been shown to have a mildly positive effect on the stock price of the parent company, which is contradicted by ambiguous long-term stock performance. Operating performance, however, is shown to improve by almost all empirical studies, especially for focus improving transactions.

13. *When should a company consider a divestiture/sale of a business/assets in a restructuring transaction?*
A company should divest or liquidate a certain business or asset in case of the following circumstances:

- poor integration and connection with the core business;
- poor performance of a division or product line and disproportionately high costs required to fix it;
- Inverse Synergies: when a company under-utilizes a certain business line that could be better off if separated from the parent company;
- better access to capital markets for the company post-divestiture thanks to a more simple structure;
- immediate proceeds and cash injection from the divestiture.

14. *Suppose that Company A at Y0 shows the financials indicated below:*

€m	Y0
EBITDA	30.0
Implied EV	150.0
Net Debt	330.0

Let us assume that Company A starts a restructuring deal that foresees a debt write-off of €80m. According to the Debt Restructuring Plan approved by the board, the company has to reduce its level of indebtedness by another €19m within 3 years (to land at a net debt level of 2x EBITDA). The existing shareholders are unsure as to whether to invest €50m of new money into the company or not.
Assuming that EBITDA and EV will remain unchanged in Year 3, evaluate the shareholders' possibility of refinancing and calculate the return on their investment (Money on Money) after 3 Years.

€m		Y0	Y1	Y2	Y3
EBITDA	A	30.0	30.0	30.0	30.0
Implied EV	B	150.0	150.0	150.0	150.0
Net Debt	C = C (Y – 1) – (D + E)	330.0	250.0	130.0	60.0
Debt Write-Off	D		80.0		
Pay-back of Outstanding Debt	E			120.0	70.0
Shareholders Refinance	F		50.0		
EQUITY VALUE	G = B – C	180.0		20.0	90.0
Shareholders Return (MoM)	H = G/F				**1.8**

15. *Illustrate Chapter 11 and its main characteristics.*
Chapter 11. This is the most common procedure adopted worldwide. Chapter 11 allows the company to continue its operations while preparing a restructuring plan to be presented to all creditors. Filing for Chapter 11 can be voluntary, if the company proactively starts the action, or involuntary, in the case the creditors/ bondholders take the action. Chapter 11 protection is characterized by the following elements:

- The restructuring plan must be presented within 120 days from the filing.
- During this period the management remains in charge and the company is granted with a standstill period (lenders cannot ask for payment for their obligations). This provision is extremely important in order to relieve pressure on the company and allows it to focus on the improvement of its business model and operations.
- Chapter 11 also gives the possibility to the company to receive new senior money (so-called "Debtor-in-Possession" or "DIP"). Debtor-in-possession means that the company maintains ownership of the assets on which creditors have rights and has the possibility to receive funds to carry on its current operations. Thanks to the protection granted by Chapter 11, those creditors that provide DIP financing enjoy a super senior status (even more senior than senior secured creditors).[25] Finally the debtor can also receive an "exit financing" (an extra debt injection after Chapter 11 protection).
- The restructuring plan needs to be approved by the majority of each class of creditors (and not unanimously). More precisely, Chapter 11 establishes that approval must be given by half of the creditors representing at least two-thirds of the value for each class of lender. Once approved, the debtor can proceed in carrying out the Restructuring Agreement.
- One big advantage of Chapter 11 is the possibility for the judge to "cram down" dissenting creditors and force a specific solution.
- On the other side, the legal authority guarantees protection for junior lenders, and enough power is also reserved to the subordinated creditors committee (and bondholders committees), which can actively participate in the negotiation of the plan.

16. *What are the main restructuring procedures regulated by Italian Bankruptcy Law for private workouts?*
Restructuring Plan – Art. 67 (para. 3 I. d)
Restructuring Agreement – Art. 182-*bis*
Pre-Composition ("*Pre-Concordato*") – Art. 161, para. 6
Composition in Continuity – Art. 186-*bis*

[25] Elayan and Meyer (2001) demonstrated a positive correlation between the usage of DIP financing and the success of the restructuring.

17. *Describe the Composition in Continuity procedure (pursuant to Art. 186-bis, Bankruptcy law) and its main pros and cons.*
    Composition in Continuity – Art. 186-bis. According to this provision the company can preserve its going concern with the following consideration:

    - the restructuring plan must contain a detailed financial and business plan for the subsequent years;
    - the feasibility of the plan needs to be evaluated by a third-party expert;
    - the payment of privileged and strategic creditors (e.g. suppliers, banks, and senior secured creditors) can be postponed up to 12 months from the homologation;
    - strategic creditors can be satisfied with debt or equity instruments such as PIK, Participative Financial Instruments, debt-to-equity swaps, etc.;
    - the composition must be approved by creditors representing at least more than 50% of the debt value in the majority of classes of creditors;
    - the implications apply also for the non-voting creditors.

    The effect of Composition in Continuity are very similar to the Restructuring Agreement ex. Art 182-*bis* but offer more flexibility and the possibility to cram down dissenting creditors. However, like the Restructuring Agreement, the procedure can be very lengthy and generates bad publicity.

12 Inside M&A Transactions[1]

by Gimede Gigante

12.1 Case study: Merger between Banco Popolare and Banca Popolare di Milano

12.1.1 Introduction

On Wednesday 23 March 2016, **Banco Popolare** – Società Cooperativa ("Banco Popolare") and **Banca Popolare di Milano S.c.a.r.l.** ("BPM") signed a Memorandum of Understanding for a **merger** to be carried out through the incorporation of a new bank holding company in the form of joint-stock company. Under this deal structure, Banco Popolare's and BPM's shareholders tendered their shares to the NewCo ("Banco BPM") and received a pre-defined number of new shares issued by the freshly-created corporation. With the exception of the treasury shares that were held by both banks and were cancelled with no share exchange, the shares of the merging companies were swapped with the following exchange ratios:

a) 1 Banco BPM share for every Banco Popolare share;
b) 1 Banco BPM share for every 6.386 BPM shares (or 0.15659 Banco BPM share for every BPM share), with cash settlement of any residual fractions resulting from the stock swap by the intermediaries with whom the BPM shares were deposited.

Based on the share swap, the deal saw **Banco Popolare (BP) effectively leading the deal with 54.6% of the capital and BPM making up 45.4%**. Furthermore, this exchange ratio valued BPM at EUR 0.3351 based on the BP closing share price of EUR 2.14 as of 30 June 2016, one day prior to the announcement of the exchange ratio, or EUR 0.84564 based on the BP share price of EUR 5.4 one day prior to the announcement on 23 March 2016.

Banco BPM actually started trading on the Mercato Telematico Azionario ("MTA") on 2 January 2017, opening at EUR 2.25 and closing at EUR 2.50, with a daily trading volume of 27,636,170 shares exchanged.

This deal represented a **historical milestone within the Italian financial institu-**

[1] In collaboration and with the contribution of Baptiste Gilliot, authors would like to thank Mediobanca investment bank for the data and all the support provided.

tions sector, since it was the first merger between two leading banking groups in almost a decade and was the **first step towards the expected consolidation among "Popolari banks"** following the 2015 reform under the Italian government's Decree Law No. 3/2015 converted into Law No. 33/2015.

The merger of one of Italy's stronger leaders, BPM, and one of Italy's weakest banks in terms of exposure to bad loans, Banco Popolare, created the third largest Italian Banking Group in the wealthiest area of the country. The combined entity has a network of ~2,500 branches with a **market share above 8%, a leading position in the North of Italy, more than 4 million clients across Italy**, and a presence in private banking, bancassurance, asset management, unsecured consumer credit, and leasing and factoring, creating significant value for both Banco Popolare and BPM shareholders. Both banks reported that pre-tax run-rate synergies in costs, funding, and revenues arising from the merger would amount to **€365 million per year**, which would help bringing the combined cost-to-income ratio below 60% and increase return on equity from 5.5% to 9% over the following three years. Moreover, Giuseppe Castagna, Chief Executive Officer of the newly created bank, Banco BPM, said that the merger would also be an impetus for a more concerted asset quality push and that they would take advantage of this event to **reduce their exposure to one of the most problematic issues in the Italian banking system: Non-Performing Exposures, also known as "NPEs."** Mr. Castagna published a 2016-2019 Strategic Plan (entitled "The New Leading Bank: Building Our Future") in which he affirmed that Banco BPM would aim to reduce NPEs by EUR 8 billion by 2019 in order to bring the coverage ratio of NPEs in line with Italian market best practices.

In the subsequent sections we will i) describe the parties involved in the transaction (Banco Popolare and BPM), ii) analyse the rationale behind the transaction, iii) discuss the transaction's structure, and finally iv) present the particularities of Financial Institution Group ("FIG") deals.

12.1.2 The parties

Banco Popolare

Listed on the Milan Stock Exchange, Banco Popolare Società Cooperativa, also known as Banco Popolare, was a large commercial and retail franchise mainly operating in the wealthiest regions of Northern Italy such as Piedmont, Veneto, and Lombardy, where its market share exceeded 8%. The Group principally provided a full range of financial products and services to households, SMEs, and corporates, which together represented approximately 85% of its total customer base.

In 2016, **Banco Popolare was ranked as Italy's fourth largest bank by total assets** and the largest cooperative banking group by number of branches; it had about EUR 123 billion in total assets, 1,815 branches across Italy and ~17,000 full-time employees.

Originally, the Group was formed in 2007 following the merger of Banca Popolare di Verona e Novara and Banca Popolare Italiana. In 2009, Banco Popolare acquired the troubled bank Banca Italease, active in real estate leasing, but this acquisition together with Italy's worsening economic environment led to a significant deterioration in the Group's balance sheet. Therefore, **Banco Popolare went through a restructuring process with the aim of strengthening its balance sheet**, as well as streamlining the Group's organization. As part of this process, Banco Popolare (i) rationalized its operations with the disposal of non-strategic businesses and the merger of local banks into a centralized holding company; (ii) optimized its distribution network through the closure of more than 300 branches, the reduction of ~2,700 FTEs, and the implementation of the "Hub & Spoke model"; (iii) strengthened its capital position with two capital increases for a total of EUR 3.5 billion and disposal of assets; and (iv) strengthened risk management, including an increase in provisioning levels and the run-off of Banca Italease.

In 2016, after four years of consecutive losses, the bank was expected to return to profit. In fact, although Banco Popolare's cost of credit risk remained high in the view of the rating agencies, it was reduced significantly, helping the bank to report net profit of EUR 350 million for 9M 2015, compared to a loss of EUR 122 million for 9M 2014. Further **improvement in commission income, as well as in cost efficiency, was needed to offset on-going pressure on net interest margin deriving from the low interest rate environment and increased market competition**. Moreover, in October 2015, the bank disposed of a portfolio of unsecured bad loans for a gross book value ("GBV") of ~ EUR 950 million.

Banca Popolare di Milano

Banca Popolare di Milano S.c.a.r.l., also known as "BPM," was an Italian cooperative bank, established in 1865 by Luigi Luzzatti, which offered banking products and services to households, individuals, businesses, traders, professionals, artisans, and SMEs, institutions and associations based in the local areas where the bank was operating. Since the 1950s, BPM has grown considerably by acquiring equity interests in other banks such as Banca Popolare di Roma, Banca Briantea, Banca Agricola Milanese, Banca Popolare Cooperativa Vogherese, Banca Popolare di Bologna e Ferrara, Banca Popolare di Apricena, INA Banca, Cassa di Risparmio di Alessandria, Banca di Legnano, and Banca Popolare di Mantova. All of those acquisitions fuelled its continuous growth and enabled BPM to provide its clients a wide range of products and services including retail banking, corporate banking, and treasury and investment banking. The retail banking segment catered to individual customers and to the private banking business. The corporate banking segment dealt with middle, upper, and large corporate customers. The treasury and investment banking segment engaged in the bank's own securities portfolio, trading on its own account in securities, and in foreign exchange and treasury activities.

In 2017, before merging with Banco Popolare, **BPM was the 13th largest bank in Italy** in terms of total assets (approximately EUR 45 billion in total assets). The bank was listed on Borsa Italiana (the Milan Stock Exchange), employed 4,791 employees in 656 different branches across Italy, and generated a net income of EUR 41.31 million. Nonetheless, like Banco Popolare, BPM's operations were mainly concentrated in the northern and central regions of Italy, with a strong presence in Lombardy, Lazio, and Apulia.

12.1.3 The rationale behind the transaction

This merger between the two cooperative banks was motivated by a number of different factors including i) **political and regulatory pressure from the Italian government regarding consolidation in the banking sector**, ii) **the difficult economic and financial environment**, and iii) **the willingness to scale the business to improve efficiency and competitiveness.**

i) Regulatory and political pressure: the 2015 "Popolari" bank reform

The first reason behind the transaction was that, as both banks had more than EUR 8 billion in consolidated total assets, they were subject to the aforementioned **2015 Popolari Bank reform** which required "*popolari*" banks, commonly translated with the term "cooperative banks" and to be distinguished from "*banche di credito cooperativo*" or "cooperative credit banks,"[2] to transform themselves into joint-stock companies.

This measure undertaken by Italian government led by Prime Minister Matteo Renzi aimed at reducing the fragmentation of the sector and moving beyond the structural weaknesses resulting from the business model (heavily exposed to economic trends in the core reference market), organizational structures, and the small size of individual banks, paving the way for consolidation among Italy's cooperative banks which would enable them to cut costs and boost their capital levels. In fact, Banco Popolare declared that this legal shift was likely to promote further improvements in corporate governance and efficiency, as well as strengthen the Bank's ability to raise capital and/or participate in a possible consolidation. Therefore, **this deal was seen as a direct consequence of the reform**, and since it was the first deal among leading Italian banks, it was expected to foster significant consolidation in the Italian banking system.

---

[2] *Banche di credito cooperativo* or cooperative credit banks (also known under the acronym of "BCCs") are local cooperative or mutual non-profit banking institutions acting in specific geographic areas and characterized by strong links with local communities and institutions. Unlike *popolari banks*, BCCs were subject to the *Riforma del Credito Cooperativo* under Law No. 49/2016 requiring i) each BCC to join a cooperative banking group or become a joint-stock company, ii) each cooperative banking group to have a parent company regulated and authorized to carry out banking activities and have a share capital of at least EUR 1 billion, and iii) the parent company of the cooperative banking group to be incorporated as a joint-stock company with the majority of shares held by the BCCs.

ii) Difficult economic and financial environment

Second, another factor that incentivized banks to merge was the **difficult economic environment** (**low GDP growth and high amount of NPEs**) and **financial environment** (**low interest rates**), that, in a relatively fragmented and competitive market, led to a significant contraction in revenues.

a) Difficult economic conditions: low GDP growth and high amounts of NPEs.

At the time of the merger, the Italian economy was experiencing lackluster GDP growth for more than 15 years and it was not expected to see a growth renaissance anytime soon. Indeed, as highlighted in the Banco BPM 2016–2019 Strategic Plan, in 2015, the Italian real GDP growth rate was 0.6%, and it was widely expected to stay around 1% until 2019 (see **Figure 12.1**). This **low growth environment, combined with the struggles of Italian businesses since Italy joined the Eurozone in 1999, worsened the amount of NPEs on Italian banks' balance sheets**. Since 1999 Italian banks have incurred a huge amount of bad debt, a lot more than most European banks.

For instance, from 2009 to 2015 (the peak of the outstanding stock of NPEs in the Italian market), the amount of so-called non-performing exposures ("NPEs") in Italy increased by 92%, reaching close to ~20% of total loans or GBV ~ EUR 282 billion for the Italian banking system as a whole. As of 2016, the year in which the merger took place, there was a GBV of EUR 271 billion in outstanding NPEs in the Italian Banking system (of which ~62% bad loans and ~36% UTPs) (see **Figure 12.2**). Just for contrast, German banks' NPE ratio stood at circa 2.5%. This huge amount of **NPEs impacted bank's revenues as the increase in NPEs led to an increase in Loan Loss Provisions (LLPs) which reduced the bank's ability to lend, and therefore lowered the inflows from performing loans**. As a result, on an aggregate basis, the net result for Italian banks declined by 69% year-on-year (YoY) to EUR 1.9 billion as of September 2016.

Figure 12.1 Italian GDP and Inflation

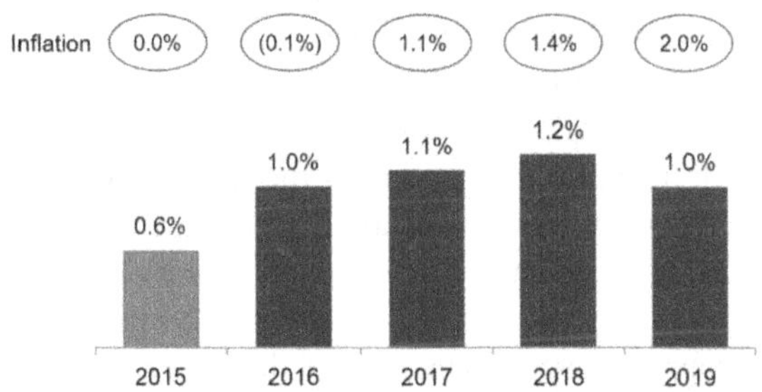

Source: Banco BPM Presentation – "The New Leading Bank Building – Our Future Strategic Plan 2016 – 2019." 9 June 2016.

Figure 12.2 Evolution in Gross NPLs (in EUR billions)

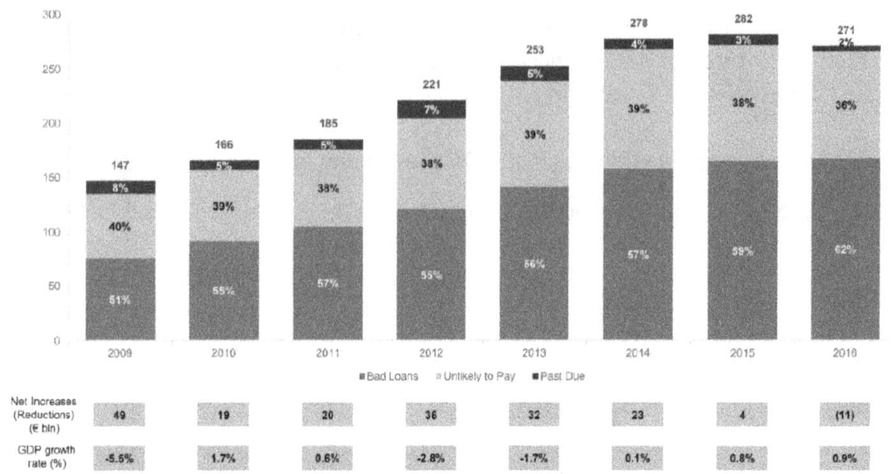

Source: Dominion Bond Rating Service (DBRS) Morningstar. May 2nd, 2017.

Addressing the higher level of NPEs in a low-growth environment became a key priority not only for banks, but also for the Italian Government, as well as the ECB, which pressured banks to accelerate the balance sheet clean-up. **NPEs were viewed as constraints on banks' ability to lend**, which was a key driver of the Italian economy. If banks were not able to lend to corporations, SMEs, etc., those companies would not be able to finance their projects and that would result in lower economic growth, which, in turn, would lead to higher NPEs.

Therefore, another reason behind the Banco Popolare and BPM merger was the **willingness to consolidate and scale up the size of the business in order to deal with the competitive pressure of the industry, the low growth rate environment, and the pressure from regulators to clean up their balance sheets (reduce NPEs).** Mr. Castagna, the CEO of the combined entity Banco BPM, announced in the 2016-2019 Strategic Plan that **better efficiency and profit through synergies would help the banks afford a write-off of billions of euros of bad debts** in order to bring the bank's NPE coverage ratio in line with Italian market best practices. Note that due to Banco Popolare's relatively high NPE ratio of around 25% (one of the highest in the country), Banco BPM ended up having one of the highest NPE levels in the sector. However, BPM's management was well aware of that issue and had clearly stated that a lower NPE ratio was the most important strategic priority for the group.

The merger enabled both banks to combine their assets in order to build a stronger and more efficient group that would be able to make the capital intensive effort to reduce NPEs, which was further motivated by i) **the introduction of IFRS 9** in 2018, and ii) **the implementation of the public guarantee scheme on bad loan securitization called "Garanzia Cartolarizzazione Sofferenze" or "GACS."**

In the following section, we will briefly discuss the two factors mentioned above that helped the combined entity to clean up its balance sheet. Notice that even though the implementation of IFRS 9 and the GACS would have enabled each bank to individually reduce its exposure to NPEs, the process of securitizing bad loans was very costly and capital intensive, and it was very difficult to implement such structural changes without a merger.

1) IFRS 9

In 2018, the introduction of the IFRS 9 accounting standard **incentivized banks to reduce the stock of NPEs by requiring banks to account for "expected losses" on loans as realized losses** (see Figure 12.3). This regulation, through the adoption of the principles of "expected loss" and "forward looking" (evaluation tools aimed at measuring the probability of default of the loans disbursed), produced significant effects on the banks' financial statements. It changed the way banks classified and measured financial liabilities, introducing a three-stage model for impairment (stage 3 being non-performing).

As IFRS 9 introduced a **forward-looking view on expected losses, banks had to review their portfolio strategy at a much more granular level than they did before**. In fact, in order to forecast expected losses, banks had to analyse different factors and variables that were supposed to impact the probability of default. For example, banks had to take into account:

a) **The economic sector**. The forward-looking nature of credit provision under IFRS 9 means that banks need to reconsider their allocation of lending to economic sectors with greater sensitivity to the economic cycle. Industries that are highly cyclical and dependent on economic conditions are considered riskier, which required banks to report higher expected losses (less profitable).
b) **Transaction duration**. The more distant the redemption, the higher the probability that the counterparty will default. Under IFRS 9, stage 2 impairments were based on lifetime expected credit losses – all possible default events over the expected life of the financial instrument – and, therefore, required higher loan-loss provisions.

Figure 12.3 Schematic presentation of IFRS 9

	Stage 1	Stage 2	Stage 3
Introduced by IFRS 9	Yes		No
Financial instrument quality	Performing	Deteriorated	Non performing
Credit risk increase	Not significant	Significant	Objective evidence of impairment
Impairment recognition	12-month expected credit losses	Lifetime expected credit losses	
Effective interest		Gross book value	Net book value

Source: BNP Paribas Report on "the impact of IFRS 9 first-time adoption on southern European banks." 8 November 2018.

c) **Collateral.** Unsecured exposures were hit harder under the new standard, as collateral guarantees helped mitigate the increase in provisions for losses.
d) **Counterparty ratings**. IFRS 9 imposed heavier average provision "penalties" on exposure to higher-risk clients, so counterparty ratings had a direct impact on profitability.

Moreover, in addition to this forward-looking principle, the new standard required banks **to record provisions for impairment as soon as a loan was made**, or a debt security was purchased. Subsequently, any significant increase in credit risk on this asset required the recognition (at each reporting date) of additional provisions for impairment, even in the absence of a credit event. This represented a fundamental shift from the previous standard, IAS 39, in which the impairment model only recognized incurred credit losses (losses with evidence of impairment such as a default, for example).

These new accounting standards incentivized southern European banks to reduce their amount of NPEs, as the forward looking estimations of expected losses would dramatically impact their P&Ls, and the recognition of non-performing assets at their fair-market value would depreciate their balance sheet. This element was also a strong point behind the Banco Popolare and BPM merger, as even though securitizing bad loans would facilitate profitability, the process of bad loan securitization remains very costly and capital intensive. Nonetheless, cleaning the balance sheet was one of the main reasons behind the merger and explains why Banco BPM had already reached several important agreements to sell its non-performing exposures, including the so-called Rainbow Deal consisting of secured loans backed by real estate, even before the conclusion of the merger.

2) The "GACS" state guarantee scheme, or "Garanzia Cartolarizzazione Sofferenze"

Both banks also aimed to take advantage of the GACS guarantee scheme enacted by the Italian Government to reduce their exposure to NPEs. This guarantee on securitisation of bad loans (GACS) was an instrument that the Treasury made available to banks and other financial institutions so as to facilitate the dismantling of non-performing exposures.

As the figure below highlights, in order to securitize bad loans, banks had to create a Special Purpose Vehicle ("SPV") that would issue different tranches of notes in order to acquire the bad loans portfolio (see **Figure 12.4**). To facilitate the sale of bad loans, the Italian Government proposed guaranteeing the most senior tranches issued by the SPV, which led to a lower cost of financing.

This securitization process was a key point behind the merger, as both banks knew that **by combining their assets they would benefit from cost, revenue, and financing synergies that would enable them to reduce their bad debt exposure, securitizing an amount between EUR 3 and 5 billion of bad loans.**

Figure 12.4 Structure of a GACS securitization of NPLs

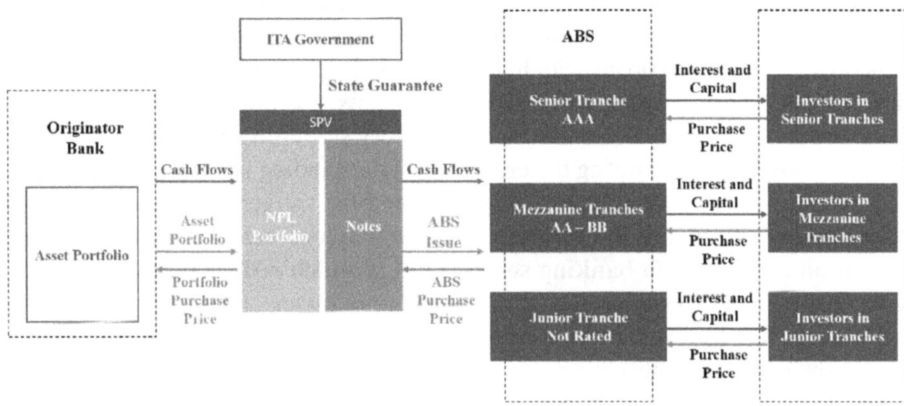

Source: Authors' elaboration.

b) Difficult financial environment

In addition to this challenging economic environment characterized by a fierce and competitive banking industry operating in a low-growth environment with substantial exposure to NPEs, banks also had to deal with the challenges of the **low interest rate environment** (see Figure 12.5).

Historically, the banking sector's profitability has in fact increased along with interest rates, as banks earn interest on the cash deposited by their customers. More precisely, banks benefit from the difference between the yield at which they invest and the interest they pay out to their customers. Therefore, when interest rates rise, banks generate more income, as the spread between the yield they pay to their customers and the yield at which they invest gets wider. On the contrary, in a low interest rate environment the spread the banks earn is lower as the interest rate they can

Figure 12.5 Euribor 3 months

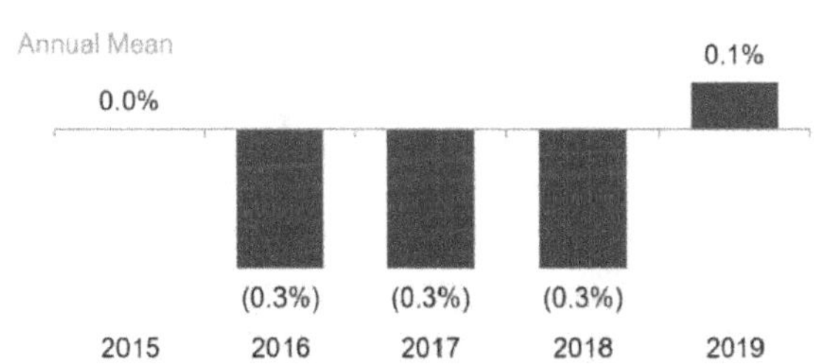

Source: Banco BPM Presentation: "The New Leading Bank Building – Our Future Strategic Plan 2016 – 2019." 9 June 2016.

earn on the market gets substantially lower and becomes closer to the interest rate paid by the bank to its customers.

Moreover, the academic literature has demonstrated that when short-term interest rates are low, the spread earned by banks is lower, but banks also relax their lending standards and grant new loans with higher credit risk. This suggests that **low interest rates increase banks' appetite for risk**. Nonetheless, it is important to mention that low interest rates also reduce credit risk in the very short run since they reduce refinancing costs, thereby lowering the credit risk of outstanding bank loans.

These elements provide further reasons behind the merger of the two important Italian banks. Indeed, this **low interest rate environment, combined with the fragmentation of the Italian banking sector, both of which reduce industry profitability, encouraged consolidation in the banking industry** and thus partly explains why Banco Popolare and BPM merged; by combining their strengths and market shares, the combined entity aimed to reduce competition and thus improve profitability.

iii) Synergies

In addition to the reasons mentioned above, the merger between the Italian financial institutions was also motivated by the **great complementarity of their assets and the strong strategic fit** that was expected to lead to significant **synergies**. Indeed,

Figure 12.6 Branch Networks by Region

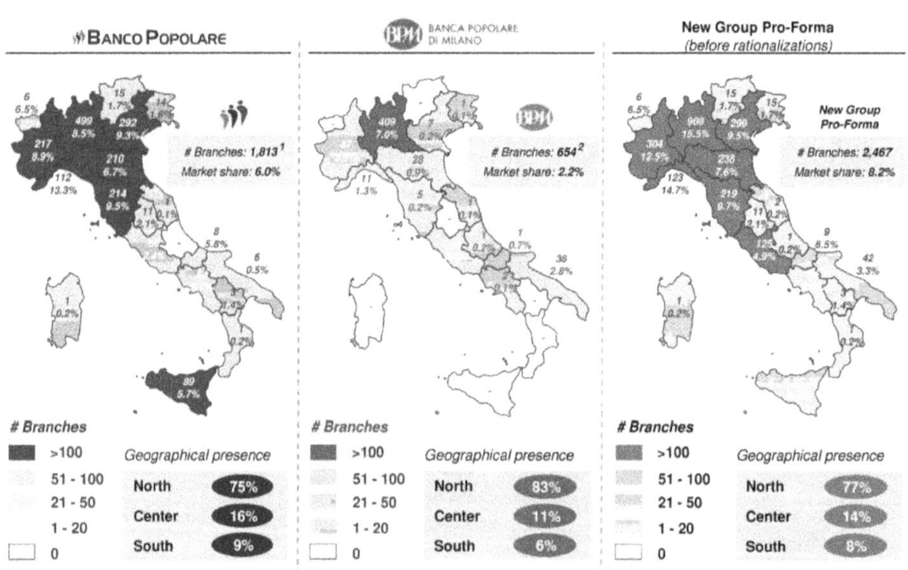

Source: Banco BPM Presentation: "The New Leading Bank Building – Our Future Strategic Plan 2016 – 2019." 9 June 2016.

Mr. Castagna said that despite its relatively high NPE ratio (around 25%), "Banco Popolare was the best in terms of industrial fit, from the beginning." "It's a sort of wider BPM, because they are very present in Lombardy, they have a strong presence in other regions of Northern Italy, and a few branches also in the centre or south of Italy" (see **Figure 12.6**).

This strategic fit and geographic overlap offered the *Popolari* banks the opportunity to rationalize their branch network, broaden their range of products, and improve their distribution, leading to significant cost savings and greater revenue diversification. Indeed, pro-forma, the estimated synergies in costs, funding, and revenues from the merger amounted to EUR 365 million per year, bringing the combined cost-to-income ratio below 60% and increasing the return on equity from 5.5% to 9% over the following three years (see **Figure 12.7**).

The cost savings were expected mainly from **workforce reduction and rationalization of administrative costs**, whereas revenue synergies were expected to arise from the expansion of product offering and enhanced distribution capabilities, especially across the Corporate segment. In fact, geographical overlaps would allow the merged entity to close 350 branches, with a similar number slated for closure as part of the shift to digital channels (see **Figure 12.8**).

Moreover, Banco BPM expected to reduce its headcount by almost 10%, even though it was well-known that domestic legislation in Italy favours employees, and it is very difficult to cut staff in the country (see **Figure 12.9**). However, Banco BPM said it had already reached a layoff agreement with unions.

Nonetheless, despite the banks' geographic strengths being very complementary, in particular in Lombardy where it aimed to have a dominant position after the merg-

Figure 12.7 Fully phased Synergies Gross of Tax (in EUR millions)

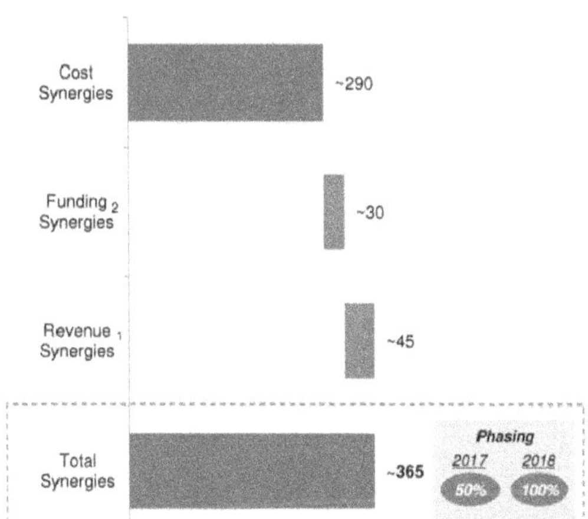

Source: Banco BPM Presentation: "The New Leading Bank Building – Our Future Strategic Plan 2016 – 2019." 9 June 2016.

Figure 12.8 Branch evolution

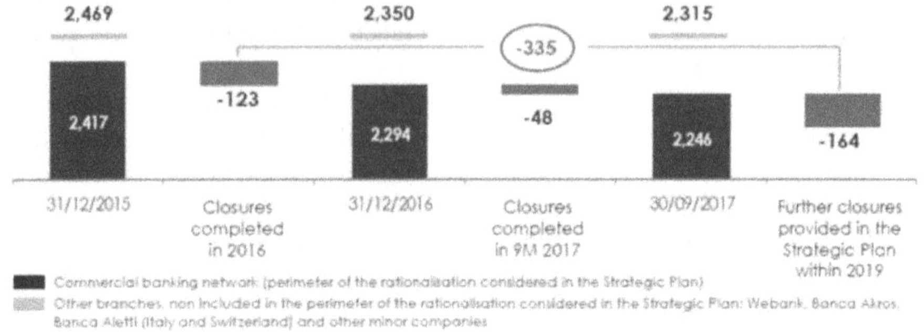

Source: Banco BPM Presentation: "The New Leading Bank Building – Our Future Strategic Plan 2016 – 2019." 9 June 2016.

Figure 12.9 Headcount evolution

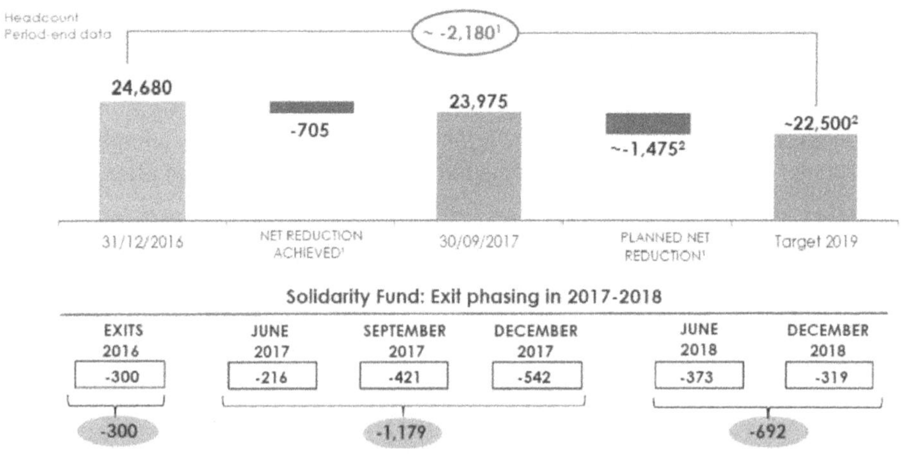

Source: Banco BPM Presentation: "The New Leading Bank Building – Our Future Strategic Plan 2016 – 2019." 9 June 2016.

er, Mr. Castagna said that there was **very little overlap of clients**, with overall numbers set to grow to 4 million in the merger.

The key strength of the merged entity was its strong market position in the North of Italy and more importantly, in Lombardy (14.7%), which accounts for **more than 20% of Italy's total gross domestic product**. Being the leader in this region was central as, despite the low growth at the national level, Lombardy was still the second-largest region in the European Union by total gross domestic product. It was widely viewed as one of the wealthiest areas not only in Italy, but in Europe as well, along with Upper Bavaria, Ile-de-France, and Catalonia. For comparison, GDP per capita in Lombardy was twice as high as in southern regions of Italy, such as Calabria, Apulia, Basilicata, and Sicily, and based on GDP per capita, Lombardy was even richer than many regions of the United Kingdom, Austria, Germany and the Benelux countries, which are among the wealthiest in the European Union (see **Figure 12.10**).

In addition, Banco BPM has a Top-3 market position in other northern regions of Italy, particularly in Veneto and Piedmont, which are also significant contributors to Italian GDP; together, the three account for almost 40% of the country's gross national product (see **Figure 12.11**).

Moreover, banks were also looking to benefit from **financing synergies** that the management identified as one of the group's key strategic goals: **to improve its funding mix in order to reduce its financing costs**. In fact, pre-merger, the main challenge for BPM was to reduce its financing costs, which were among the highest among Italian banks on issued bonds. As the chart below shows, while BPM's share of bonds in total liabilities had significantly decreased over a few quarters, this funding source still represented around 20% of the group's liabilities (see **Figure 12.12**). Pro forma, the new entity would have total assets of EUR 171 billion, direct funding of EUR 120 billion, customers loans of EUR 113 billion, and indirect funding of EUR 105 billion, of which approximately EUR 56 billion would be assets under management.

Figure 12.10 ISTAT: "GDP Per Capita at Market Prices by Region," 2016

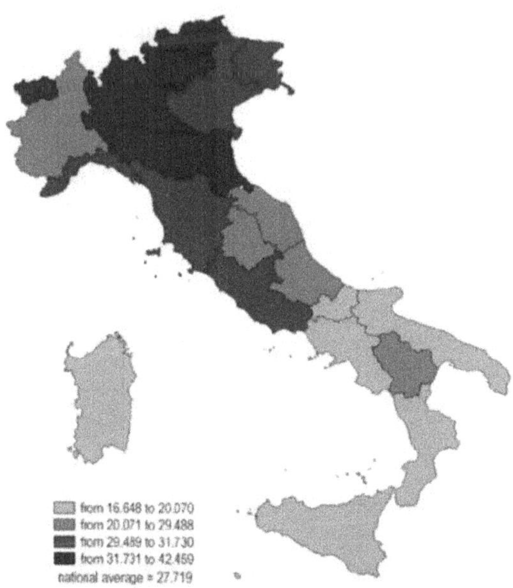

Source: ISTAT, "Regional Accounts - Years 2015-2016," 20 December 2017.

Figure 12.11 Banco BPM and Renaissance Research: "Banco BPM: Regional market share," 2017

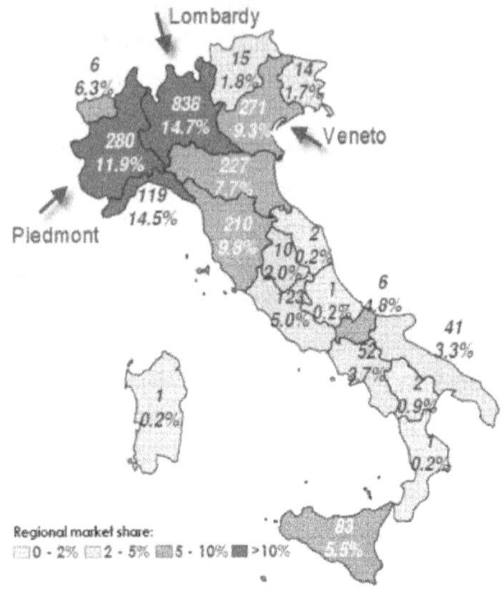

Source: Company data, Renaissance Research

Figure 12.12 Fundings

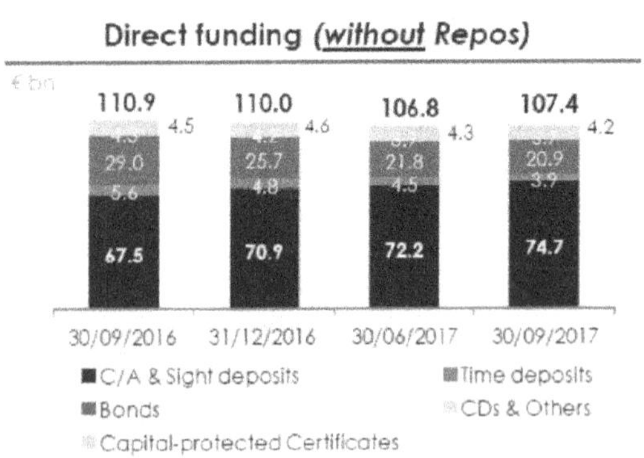

Source: Company data

12.1.4 Terms of the transaction

As mentioned in the introduction, the merger between BPM and Banco Popolare was structured as a merger to be carried out through the incorporation of a new bank holding company in the form of joint-stock company. Under this deal structure, the shareholders of Banco Popolare and BPM tendered their shares to the NewCo ("Banco BPM") and received a pre-defined number of new shares issued by the freshly-created corporation. With the exception of the shares that were held by both banks and were cancelled with no share exchange, the shares of the merging companies were swapped on the basis of the following ratios:

a) 1 Banco BPM share for every Banco Popolare share;
b) 1 Banco BPM share for every 6.386 BPM shares (or 0.15659 Banco BPM share for every BPM share), with cash settlement of any residual fractions resulting from the stock swap by the intermediaries with whom the BPM shares were deposited.

Based on the share swap, the deal saw **Banco Popolare effectively leading the deal with 54.6% of the capital and BPM making up 45.4%**.

The transaction also envisaged the spin-off of the retail banking operations in the provinces of Milan, Monza e Brianza, Como, Lecco, and Varese into a BPM S.p.A. bank network, subject to coordination and direction by the NewCo.

However, the peculiarity of this deal was that despite all the fanfare when the merger was announced in March, the ECB immediately threw cold water on any excitement by **demanding a EUR 1 billion capital increase by Banco Popolare as well as imposing a strict timetable for reducing NPEs as part of its conditions for approving the merger**. This was hardly an encouraging sign for Italian bank consolidation hopes, given that this was the first merger the ECB oversaw in the context of the **Single Supervisory Mechanism**. However, the bankers involved in the process suggested the ECB's thinking was that a more systemically-important bank needed a higher capital ratio. As a consequence, the extra capital would allow Banco Popolare to increase provisions on NPEs (increasing the bad debt coverage ratio from 37% to 41%), and the merged entity to converge towards capital ratios that were closer/in line with the Italian and EU banking sector standards (e.g. CET1 ratio, leverage ratio, RWA density etc.).

Therefore, in June 2016, the share capital increase transaction of EUR 1 billion was successfully concluded, approved by the Extraordinary Shareholders' Meeting of 7 May. More specifically, on 2 June, the Board of Directors approved the final conditions for the share capital increase, resolving to issue a maximum of 465,581,304 new shares, to be offered under option to shareholders at a **ratio of 9 Banco Popolare shares for every 7 shares held, at a price of EUR 2.14 each**. This subscription price represented a **discount of 29.3% with respect to the Theoretical Ex Right Price** ("**TERP**"), calculated on the basis of the closing price on 1 June 2016. During the offer under option period, which started on 6 June and ended on 22 June, 359,863,966 option rights were exercised for the subscription of 462,682,242 shares, corresponding to **99.377% of the total shares offered**, for a total equivalent value of around EUR 990 million. The option rights that were not exercised were offered on the stock market, and in the first two sessions of 24 and 27 June, were all sold.

Visual Interpretation of the merger

i) Pre-Transaction

Banco Popolare (2015YE)				**BPM (2015YE)**			
Assets (€m)		**Liabilities (€m)**		**Assets (€m)**		**Liabilities (€m)**	
Financial assets	25,207	Customer deposits	58,672	Financial assets	11,270	Customer deposits	30,688
Loans to customers	75,840	Financial liabilities	29,921	Loans to customers	34,771	Financial liabilities	7,051
Intangible assets	1,752	Other liabilities	21,173	Intangible assets	82	Other liabilities	8,453
Goodwill	1,110	Equity (pre capital increase)	7,645	Goodwill	-	Equity	4,938
Other assets	14,612	BP shareholders	7,575	Other assets	5,008	BPM shareholders	4,937
Total assets	117,411	Total liabilities & Equity	117,411	Total assets	51,131	Total liabilities & Equity	51,131
Net income			**430**	**Net income**			**289**
# of Shares (post capital increase) (#m)[1]			**828**	**# of Shares (#m)[1]**			**4,390**
Earnings per share			**0.52**	**Earnings per share**			**0.07**

[1] Net of treasury shares.

ii) Contribution analysis

Figures as of 2015YE – €bn[1]	**Banco Popolare**	**BPM**	**Combined**	**B. Popolare %**	**Banco BPM %**
Balance sheet					
Total assets	120.5	50.2	**170.7**	71%	29%
Gross loans to customers	85.3	36.7	**122.1**	70%	30%
- o/w gross NPE	*20.6*	*6.0*	**26.6**	*77%*	*23%*
Net loans to customers	78.4	34.2	**112.6**	70%	30%
- o/w net NPE	*14.1*	*3.6*	**17.7**	*80%*	*20%*
Direct funding	82.1	37.6	**119.7**	69%	31%
Indirect funding	71.1	34.1	**105.2**	68%	32%
- o/w asset under management	*35.4*	*20.9*	**56.3**	*63%*	*37%*
Book value	8.5	4.5	**13.0**	65%	35%
Tangible book value	6.5	4.5	**10.9**	59%	41%
Capital increase	1.0	-	**1.0**	100%	0%
Tangible book value pro-forma	7.5	4.5	**11.9**	62%	38%

Figures as of 2015YE – €bn[1]	Banco Popolare	BPM	Combined	B. Popolare %	Banco BPM %
Income statement					
Operating income	3.7	1.7	**5.3**	69%	31%
Operating costs	(2.4)	(1.0)	**(3.4)**	71%	29%
- o/w asset under management	*(1.4)*	*(0.6)*	**(2.0)**	*70%*	*30%*
- o/w asset under management	*(0.8)*	*(0.3)*	**(1.1)**	*73%*	*27%*
Net income	0.4	0.3	**0.7**	57%	43%
KPIs					
Cost/income ratio adjusted (%)[2]	58.6%	57.2%	**58.2%**		
Return on Equity (%)	5.1%	6.2%	**5.5%**		
Cost of risk (bps)	103	100	**102**		
Gross NPE ratio (excl. write-offs)	24.2%	16.3%	**21.8%**		
NPE coverage (excl. write-offs)	31.9%	39.6%	**33.6%**		
Net NPE ratio (excl. write-offs)	17.9%	10.6%	**15.7%**		
CET1 FL ratio (%)	12.4%	12.2%	**12.3%**		
Key operational data					
Branches in Italy (#)	1,813	654	**2,467**	73%	27%
FTEs (#)	17,337	7,743	**25,080**	69%	31%

[1] Restated reclassified data as of 31 December 2015 as per semi-annual financial report as of 30 June 2016.
[2] Cost/income ratio adjusted excludes charges for redundancy incentives and solidarity fund and ordinary and extraordinary systemic contributions (DGS and SRF).

iii) Focus on Asset Quality

Banco Popolare (2015YE – €m)[1]	GBV	LLP	NBV	% GBV	Coverage %	% NBV
Bad Loans (NPL)	10,471	(4,012)	6,458	12.3%	38.3%	8.2%
Unlikely to Pay (UtP)	9,911	(2,521)	7,390	11.6%	25.4%	9.4%
Past due (PD)	263	(54)	209	0.3%	20.7%	0.3%
NPE	**20,645**	**(6,588)**	**14,057**	**24.2%**	**31.9%**	**17.9%**
Performing	64,692	(328)	64,365	75.8%	0.5%	82.1%
Loans to customers	**85,338**	**(6,916)**	**78,422**	**100.0%**	**8.1%**	**100.0%**

BPM (2015YE – €m)[1]	GBV	LLP	NBV	% GBV	Coverage %	% NBV
Bad Loans (NPL)	3,276	(1,785)	1,491	8.9%	54.5%	4.4%
Unlikely to Pay (UtP)	2,622	(578)	2,043	7.1%	22.1%	6.0%
Past due (PD)	100	(9)	90	0.3%	9.3%	0.3%
NPE	**5,997**	**(2,373)**	**3,624**	**16.3%**	**39.6%**	**10.6%**
Performing	30,748	(185)	30,563	83.7%	0.6%	89.4%
Loans to customers	**36,745**	**(2,558)**	**34,187**	**100.0%**	**7.0%**	**100.0%**

Combined (2015YE – €m)	GBV	LLP	NBV	% GBV	Coverage %	% NBV
Bad Loans (NPL)	13,747	(5,798)	7,949	11.3%	42.2%	7.1%
Unlikely to Pay (UtP)	12,533	(3,100)	9,433	10.3%	24.7%	8.4%
Past due (PD)	363	(64)	299	0.3%	17.6%	0.3%
NPE	**26,642**	**(8,961)**	**17,681**	**21.8%**	**33.6%**	**15.7%**
Performing	95,440	(513)	94,927	78.2%	0.5%	84.3%
Loans to customers	**122,083**	**(9,474)**	**112,608**	**100.0%**	**7.8%**	**100.0%**

[1] Figures excluding write-offs.
Source: annual reports as of 31 December 2015.

iv) EPS Accretion / Dilution

The following table is an illustrative analysis of the impact of the transaction on the earnings per share of Banco Popolare (after the €1.0bn capital increase) and BPM as per financial year 2015 from a pre and post synergies perspective. EPS accretion/dilution analysis is commonly performed on expected net income for the subsequent fiscal years, that is not available in this case. For the same reason, post synergies computation is based on announced annual run rate post-tax synergies.

Figures as of 2015YE	#	Ref.	Banco Popolare	BPM	Combined	Ref.
Net income and Synergies						
Net income	**€m**	**A**	**430.1**	**288.9**	**719.0**	**B**
% of Combined Net income	*%*		*60%*	*40%*		
Annual run-rate pre-tax synergies[1]	€m				365.0	
Tax rate	*%*				*31%*	
Annual run-rate post-tax synergies	€m				250.4	C
Net income pro-forma post synergies	**€m**				**969.4**	**D=B+C**
Pre-tax integration costs	€m				(547.5)	
% of Annual run-rate pre-tax synergies[1]					*150%*	
Post-tax integration costs	€m				(375.6)	E
Net income pro-forma post synergies and integration costs	**€m**				**593.8**	**F=D+E**

Figures as of 2015YE	#	Ref.	Banco Popolare	BPM	Combined	Ref.
Shares						
# of Shares pre-capital increase	#m	G	362	4,390		
# of Shares issued – capital increase	#m		466	-		
# of Shares post-capital increase	#m	H	828	4,390		
EPS pre-BP capital increase	€	I=A/G	1.19	0.07		
EPS post-BP capital increase	**€**	**J=A/H**	**0.52**	**0.07**		
Stake in Banco BPM (BBPM) (%)[2]	**%**		**54.63%**	**45.37%**		
No. of shares for 1 BBPM share[3]	x		1.000x	6.386x		
No. of BBPM shares for 1 share	x	K	1.000x	0.157x		
# of Banco BPM Shares	**#m**	**L=H*K**	**828**	**687**	**1,515**	**M**
EPS Accretion / Dilution[4]						
Pre synergies						
Earnings per share (EPS)	€	P	0.47	0.47	0.47	P=B/M
EPS Accretion / Dilution	%	Q=P*M/A-1	(9)%	13%		
Post synergies (incl. integration costs)						
Earnings per share (EPS)	€	S	0.39	0.39	0.39	S=F/M
EPS Accretion / Dilution	%	T=S*M/A-1	(25)%	(7)%		
Post synergies (excl. integ. costs, run rate)						
Earnings per share (EPS)	€	U	0.64	0.64	0.64	U=D/M
EPS Accretion / Dilution	%	W=U*M/A-1	23%	52%		

[1] *Source*: investor presentation dated 24 March 2016.

[2] *Source*: Merger plan (Progetto di fusione) dated 24 May 2016 as supplemented until 12 September 2016.

[3] *Source*: Banco BPM Registration Document.

[4] Illustrative estimate based on publicly available data.

v) Additional information on synergies[3]

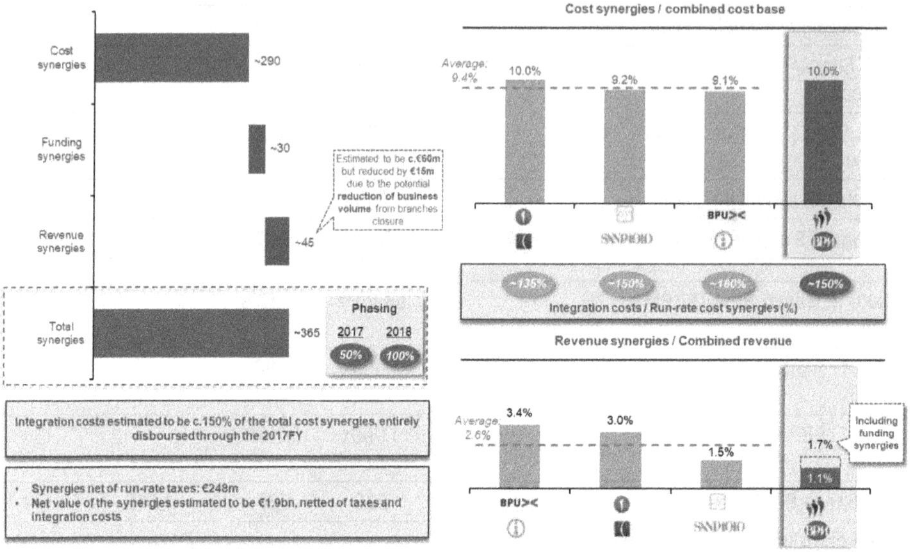

vi) Post-Transaction structure[4]

Banco Popolare shareholders 54.6% → Banco BPM (2015YE) ← BPM shareholders 45.4%

Banco BPM (2015YE)			
Assets			
Financial assets	39,836	Customer deposits	119,743
Loans to customers	112,608	Financial liabilities	9,944
Intangible assets	2,179	Other liabilities	29,026
Goodwill	*1,389*	Equity	11,999
Other assets	16,090	*Combined Entity*	*11,941*
Total assets	**170,713**	**Total liabilities & Equity**	**170,713**

12.1.5 Specific aspects of FIG Deal valuation

The most common methodologies applied for the valuation of a commercial bank include the **dividend discount model** (with the so-called excess capital variant) and the **linear regression method**, both with some specificities *vis-à-vis* non-banking

[3] *Source*: investor presentation dated 24 March 2016.
[4] Illustrative estimates.

firms, in addition to the common market-based methodologies applied for non-financial corporates such as **trading and transaction multiples** (price-to-earnings, price-to book value, and price-to-tangible book value), the **stock market prices method**, and the **target prices provided by research analysts**.

Valuing banks, like insurers, asset managers, and other financial services firms, differs significantly from valuing non-financial corporates, mainly due to the following key factors: i) the nature of their businesses makes it difficult to define both debt and reinvestment, making the estimation of cash flows much more difficult, ii) their accounting treatment can differ substantially from that of non-financial corporates, and iii) they are typically required to maintain pre-defined regulatory capital adequacy ratios based on their equity book value. As a result, book values are often more meaningful measures of value for financial firms than for non-financial ones.

When valuing a non-financial services firm, we tend to talk about debt and equity: a firm raises funds from both equity investors and bondholders (and banks) and uses these funds to make investments. Then the valuation is based on the value of the assets owned by the firm, rather than just the value of its equity. With a financial services firm, **debt has a different connotation** because it is not a source of capital, but a "raw material" to be transformed into other financial products to be sold at a higher price and yield a profit. Consequently, **capital at financial services firms is narrowly defined as including only equity capital**, which is reinforced by the fact that core measures of regulatory capital are built around equity (Damodaran).

These regulatory constraints have an impact on both where and to what extent banks can invest their funds. If we define reinvestment as necessary for future growth, **measuring reinvestment in financial services firms is problematic**: i) with regards to net capital expenditures, financial services invest primarily in intangible assets, and consequently, their investments for future growth are often categorized as operating expenses in accounting statements, and the statement of cash flows to banks shows insignificant capital expenditures and low depreciation, while ii) with reference to working capital, if we define this as the difference between current assets and current liabilities, it should be noted that a large proportion of a bank's balance sheet would fall into one or the other of these categories, and that changes in this number can be both large and volatile and may have no relationship to reinvestment for future growth.

For the reasons above, **dividends or residual income are used as a proxy for free cash flow** and intrinsic valuation of banks is based on a **Dividend Discount Model** rather than a Discount Cash Flow model. Specifically, the so-called "Excess Capital" variant is commonly applied. This valuation methodology is founded on the assumption that the economic value of a company is based on the sum of the net present values of i) the cash flows of the potential future dividends distributable to the shareholders generated over the selected time horizon, without affecting the level of capitalisation required to maintain a predetermined long-term target level of regulatory capital, without consideration of the dividend policy actually planned or adopted by the management, and of ii) the long-term value of the company calculated as the present value of a perpetual annuity estimated on the basis of a normalised distributable cash flow that is economically sustainable and consistent with a long-term growth rate.

Accounting practices are important for bank valuations for two reasons. First, the assets held by banks are typically in the form of financial instruments that have well-defined cash flows (loans, bonds, and other securities as well as derivatives). The majority of bank assets (loans, investments and other assets) are reported at amortised cost. However, for larger banks, many financial instruments are traded in relatively liquid markets, at least under normal conditions, or are substantially similar to traded assets. This is why marking traded, and in some cases non-traded assets to market has long been established practice among banks. With a significant portion of assets on banks' balance sheets treated this way, book values are much closer to market values than is the case for non-financial corporates, where most of the assets are carried at amortised cost. Similarly, depreciation, which can be a key driver of book values for corporates, tends to be much less important for banks, which hold relatively few real assets.

Second, it is natural for bank assets to be subject to credit and other risks that can imply the potential for large, possibly abrupt losses, with loss provisions being made to report estimated credit losses as an allowance reducing the value of the loan portfolio and reported earnings. In practice, **banks have a certain discretion in setting their provisioning policies**, notwithstanding regulatory guidance and requirements. For a given loan portfolio, conservative banks will set aside more for loan losses, implying lower profits during good times than those generated by their more aggressive peers. Indeed, the literature suggests that delayed loss recognition was a significant factor for US banks during the recent financial crisis, especially in the context of their mortgage market exposures. Expected credit loss accounting, implemented through the IFRS 9 accounting standard since 2018, is intended precisely to improve the incorporation of forward-looking credit risks into book asset valuations and earnings. Against this background, depressed price-to-book value ratios would tend to reflect the effect of accounting rules on recognised book values as well as attempts by bank managers to preserve their institutions' (book) capital positions.

Therefore, **for banks and other financial firms, combining book and market-based valuation metrics can provide useful information**. In particular, price-to-book value ratios (P/BV) and price-to-tangible book value ratios (P/TBV, where tangible book value is calculated as the difference between book value and intangible assets including goodwill) that are above one – which have tended to prevail under normal market conditions – will tend to be driven by the market value of assets and liabilities, which in turn may be affected by market developments and the competitive environment in ways that are not reflected in their book values.

Changing economic conditions would thus be expected to affect these multiples largely via their effect on both the asset and liability sides of the balance sheet. For example, if interest rates are low for an extended period, having a stable base of core deposits may be less valuable to banks, to the extent that they are unable to re-price deposit rates in line with rates earned on the asset side of their balance sheets. Similarly, loan relationships may lose value if the economic environment implies a lower ability for banks to benefit from the cross-selling of services.

From this perspective, the above-mentioned **linear regression method** is very relevant given that it assumes that the economic value of a company may be determined on the basis of parameters identified through the **correlation (when statistically significant) between multiples of the stock market price on the book value or tangible book value for a sample of listed companies deemed comparable and the respective prospective earnings levels expressed by the return on (average) book value (Ro(A)BV) or the return on (average) tangible book value for the period (Ro(A)TBV)**. The degree of reliability of the linear regression valuation method and the market multiples method depends on an appropriate adaptation of the method to the specific valuation in question. In this regard, the affinity of the companies included in the reference sample and those subject to valuation, from an operational and financial standpoint, is particularly critical. The significance of the results is in fact dependant on the comparability of the sample.

12.1.6 The process

In May, the **confirmatory due diligence exercise** conducted on Banca Popolare di Milano was concluded, in accordance with that envisaged in the memorandum of understanding. **No elements emerged from said due diligence that required an adjustment to the shareholding percentages**.

Following the completion of Banco Popolare's share capital increase transaction and in application of the above-cited shareholding percentages, the rates of exchange for the merger between Banco Popolare and BPM were established as one share of the new parent company for each Banco Popolare share and one share of the new parent company for every 6.386 shares of BPM in issue at the time the merger took effect.

In July, the transaction received the approval of the Monopolies and Mergers Commission, pursuant to Art. 16, paragraph 4 of Italian Law No. 287 of 10 October 1990.

Following the completion of the preliminary stage, the approval process was concluded in September, and on 8 September, the Bank of Italy authorised the merger in accordance with the provisions of Art. 57 of the Consolidated Banking Law.

On 9 September, the European Central Bank issued the authorisation for the new parent company to practice banking activities.

In October, IVASS (the Italian Supervisory Body for Insurance companies) authorised the new parent company to hold qualified equity investments in the insurance companies AviPop Assicurazioni, AviPop Vita, Popolare Vita, Bipiemme Vita, and Bipiemme Assicurazioni, which currently belong to the companies involved in the merger.

The Extraordinary Shareholders' Meeting of Banco Popolare, held on 15 October, approved the Proposed Merger by a very large majority, as well as the deed of incorporation and the articles of association of the company resulting from the merger, called Banco BPM S.p.A. On the same date, the Extraordinary Shareholders' Meeting of Banca Popolare di Milano took place, which approved the transaction.

Following these resolutions, the next steps of the merger were launched, entailing a request for the newly-issued shares of Banco BPM to be listed on the Electronic Equity Market (MTA), managed by Borsa Italiana.

On 13 December 2016, the merger deed was signed. The merger transaction was finalised following the registration of the merger deed in the relevant Company Registers of Verona and Milan on 1 January 2017. The merger took effect from an accounting and tax perspective on the same date.

The new parent company Banco BPM S.p.A. had a share capital of 7.1 EUR billion, represented by 1,515,182,126 ordinary shares with no nominal value. The shares were listed on the MTA from 2 January 2017, at the same time as trading of the shares of the two banks participating in the merger was revoked. And so a new group was established, the third largest banking group in Italy, characterised by extremely important aggregates (~4 million customers and ~2,500 branches, total assets of over EUR 171 billion, over 25,000 employees, and solid equity and liquidity ratios), which holds a position of excellence in the high value-added business segments of asset management, corporate & investment banking, private banking, bancassurance, and consumer credit. The administration and control system of the new parent company is based on a Board of Directors and a Board of Statutory Auditors. Starting from the effective date of the merger (1 January 2017) the Board of Directors has had 19 members, with Carlo Fratta Pasini as Chairman, Giuseppe Castagna as Chief Executive Officer, and Mauro Paoloni as Acting Deputy Chairman. The Executive Committee, with Pier Francesco Saviotti as Chairman, has six directors, including the Managing Director, the Acting Deputy Chairman, and the two Deputy Chairmen. The General Management team is represented by Maurizio Faroni, as General Manager, and by Joint General Managers Domenico De Angelis and Salvatore Poloni.

The role of Investment Banks was crucial to the success of the transaction, with Mediobanca Banca di Credito Finanziario S.p.A. that acted as advisor to Banco Popolare and Joint Global Coordinator of the Capital Increase.

12.2 Case study: Prysmian's acquisition of General Cable

12.2.1 Introduction

On 4 December 2017, **Prysmian Group** and **General Cable Corporation** ("GC") announced that they would enter into a definitive merger agreement under which Prysmian would acquire General Cable for **$30 per share in cash**, valuing the rival US group at about **$3bn**, including debt (Enterprise Value). Upon the completion of the transaction, Prysmian would acquire all General Cable outstanding shares and the latter would become a privately held company; its shares would no longer be listed on the NYSE or any other public market.

Prysmian said the combination represented an **ideal strategic fit** that would better position the company to meet new opportunities and challenges in the evolving wire and cable worldwide industry.

> "This combination is an ideal strategic fit and ensures we are well-positioned to meet the future opportunities and challenges in the dynamic and evolving wire and cable industry. Together, we will be able to deliver a robust portfolio of products and new product innovation across the full breadth of the wire and cable industry globally. Importantly, Prysmian and General Cable have a shared vision and highly compatible cultures founded on similar values."
> **Michael T. McDonnell, CEO of General Cable**

The operation would notably enhance Prysmian's global footprint and commercial presence, particularly in the Americas Region and in Southern Europe, further enhancing its global leadership role in the telecom and energy cable industry.

> "Through the combination of two of the premier companies in the cable industry, we will be enhancing our position in the sector, by increasing our presence in North America and expanding our footprint in Europe and South America."
> **Valerio Battista, Prysmian Group CEO**

12.2.2 The parties

Prysmian

At the time of the merger, **Prysmian Group** was an Italian public company, a **world leader in the telecom and energy cable industry**. It operated in more than 50 countries, with over 21,000 employees and generated over €7.7bn in annual sales. The group, active in the **international energy and telecom cable market**, had a **very wide range of products and services** ranging from more **standard cables** such as those used for construction and infrastructure in phases of installation and maintenance, to **highly technologically-advanced products** such as submarine cables for high and extra high tension to connect continents; solutions for oil and gas from exploration to production and warehousing; wires and cables for telecommunications and transmission of voice and video data; cable solutions for naval, aerospace, railway, and street transportation and travel. In addition, Prysmian also offered some **more specialized solutions** to support the main global industries, such as defence, commerce, and renewable energy, which underlines the company's willingness to always be up to date with new market opportunities. This desire was enabled by its **decentralized structure**, which allowed for quick reactions that the high-tech markets required to face continuously new challenges and direct contact with local clients and fast/reliable services; reducing the distance from the numerous clients and minimizing distribution costs, therefore mitigating business risks with strong, quick production and delivery capabilities. Moreover, the company's global presence enabled it to avoid being over-dependent on a single market, diversifying the risks associated with countries, raw materials, legislation, and so forth, while exploiting geographical opportunities. The different countries were also important to diversify the source of revenues, generated by four main regions: EMEA (Europe, Middle East and Africa), North America, Latin America, and Asia Pacific, which in FY2017 accounted for 67.3%, 14.9%, 5.5%, and 12.1% of total revenues, respectively.

Nonetheless, before achieving such an international scale, Prysmian Group was a national Italian company whose history is rooted in the origins of Pirelli Group; "Società Cavi Pirelli" that was established in 1879 as the cable division of the company (see **Figure 12.13**). The company first emerged nationally at the end of 19th century when national governments started to make huge investments in the wire and cable industry with the aim of developing their own telecommunications and power grids. Subsequently, government subsidies, the development of the first multinational companies, and the founder's vision combined to allow Pirelli to obtain additional market share not only in Italy, but also on the international landscape (in the Mediterranean countries and then in South America and in the rest of Europe). In the 1950s, Pirelli Cavi e Sistemi was the first company to produce cables for the transmission of high voltage energy higher than 270kW, and in 1982, the first Italian fiber optic producer. However, in 2001, during a re-organization process, Pirelli decided to separate the activities related to wire and cables into two arms: "Cavi e Sistemi Energia" and "Cavi e Sistemi Telecom," which in 2005 were acquired by the private equity fund named Prysmian (Lux) II, owned by the Goldman Sachs Group. Under their leadership, the company was transformed into a public company named Prysmian and listed on the Milan Stock Exchange in 2007 with a price of €15 per share, reaching a market capitalization of €2.7 billion.

Figure 12.13 History of the Prysmian Group

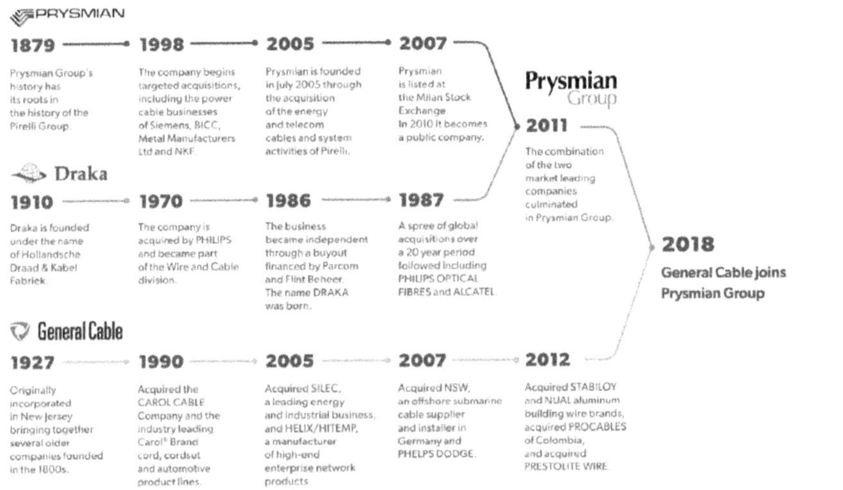

Source: Prysmian Group Website – https://it.prysmiangroup.com/

The role played by Goldman Sachs between 2005 and 2010 was very important to give the company a typically American cultural footprint, that was fundamental for the definition of the ownership model and its multinational strategy, and different from the usual Italian family business ideology. Prysmian became the leading Italian "public company" without a controlling shareholder, and still today, no single Prysmian shareholder owns more than 5% of the company's capital.

Second, as regards its "multinational strategy," it is also notable that Prysmian was able to reach its current global leadership through a 40+ years of M&A activities, of which the General Cable acquisition is the most recent, and remarkable, milestone. As evidence of this, another significant transaction was the successful acquisition of Draka, in 2011 (see **Figure 12.14**).

General Cable

General Cable, headquartered in Highland Heights, Kentucky (USA), was originally incorporated in New Jersey, in 1927. At that time, it brought together the facilities and manufacturing experience of several older companies founded in the 1800s, including Standard Underground Cable, which was founded by American entrepreneur, engineer, and electrical industry pioneer George Westinghouse.

Its first important contract was in 1929 when it produced the first 75,000-volt submarine cable in the US for the Delaware River Crossing, which started **a strong relationship with the US Government** that continued over the years, guaranteeing several projects. Later, during the Second World War, the company deployed 80% of the battlefield telephone wire used by the Allies and the 50% of the Navy's power and communications cables. During the years following the global conflict, the company was acquired by Penn Central Corp. and in turn started to acquire other minor competitors. Subsequently, in 1992, it obtained one of its most important contracts: it **supplied the wire and cable to build the infrastructure used for the Barcelona Olympic Games in 1992**, giving the company experience in the construction of technologies for sporting events. As a consequence, General Cable was also involved by the US Government in the supply of portable power cable for the Winter Olympic Games in Salt Lake City (Utah) in 2002.

Before this date (in 2000), the firm had its first approach with Prysmian when it was still Pirelli Cavi e Sistemi: the two enterprises entered into an agreement for the sale/purchase of underperforming businesses. In the following years, General Cable continued its growth by acquiring other firms and establishing joint ventures aiming at widening its global scope and generating optimal products and internal production processes. The results were evident in 2014 and 2015, when the company was given four Stevie Awards for Sales and Customer Service, and then one of its manufacturing facilities, in Marion (Indiana, US), was named the winner in Industry Week's North America Best Plants Competition.

In 2017, at the time of the acquisition, it was the **fourth largest wire and cable company in the world in terms of sales**, leader in the development, design, manufacture, marketing, and distribution of aluminium, copper, and fiber optic wire and

Figure 12.14 A Landmark Acquisition in Prysmian's Growth Story

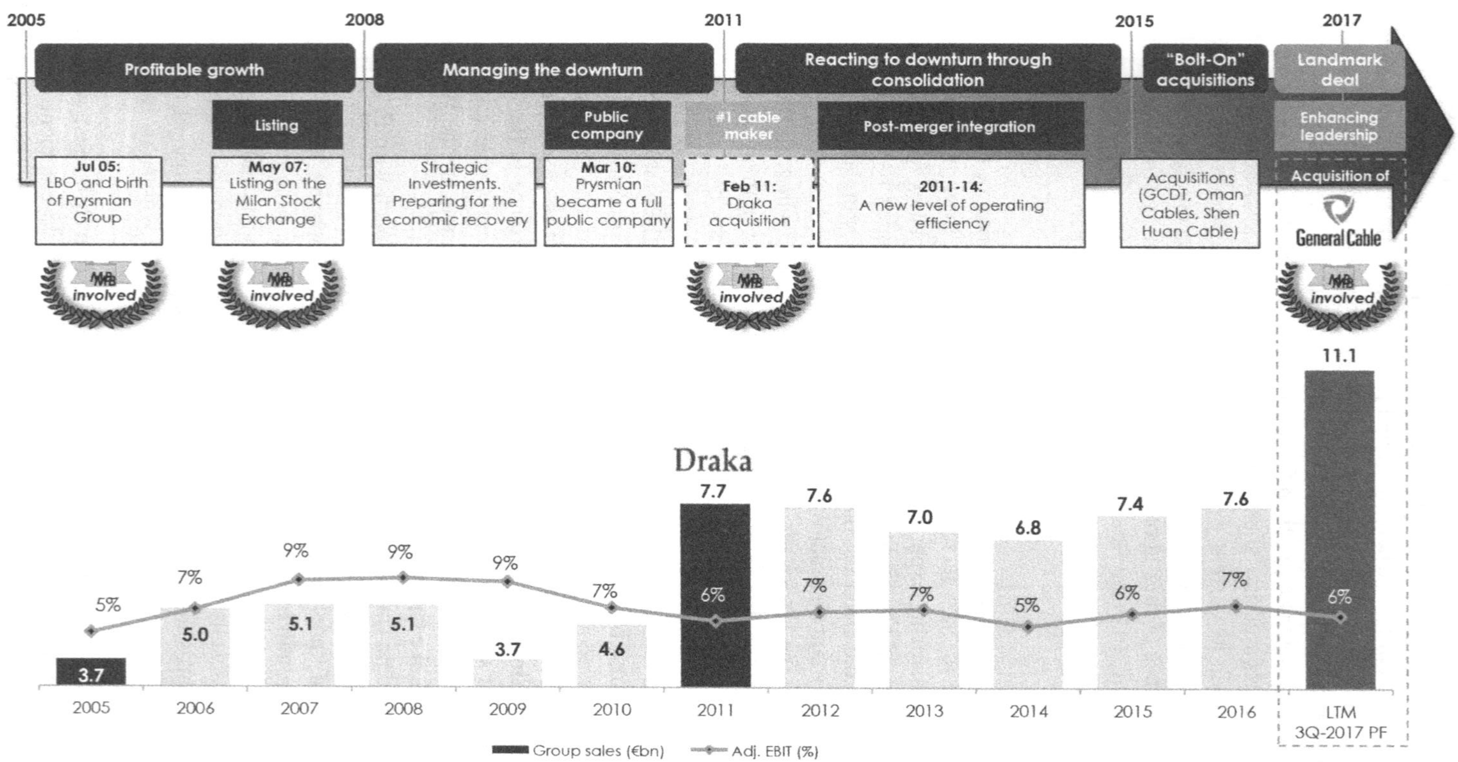

Source: Prysmian Group Presentation – "A Key Milestone in Prysmian's Growth Story – The Acquisition of General Cable." 4 December 2017.

cable products for the energy, communications, automotive, industrial, construction, and specialty segments. It operated in 33 manufacturing facilities in 16 different countries with regional centres around the world. More specifically, General Cable operated through four geographical business segments: North America, consisting of 17 manufacturing facilities, whose revenues accounted for 53% of the total; Europe and Latin America, both consisting of 6 manufacturing facilities with revenues representing 23% and 17% of the total, respectively; Africa/Asia Pacific, consisting of 458 manufacturing plants reporting revenues which represented 7% of the group's total revenues.

Overall, General Cable owned **a strong brand portfolio**, with numerous patents, trademarks, and secret, protected, confidential, and proprietary information. The particular feature of the company was that it was selling its products globally with numerous brands such as Phelps Dodge International Corporation, PDIC global symbols, General Cable, Anaconda, BICC, Carol, GenSpeed, Helix/HiTemp, NextGen, Silec, Polyrad, Prestolite Wire, STABILOY, and NUAL, which have significant recognition within the industry, gaining an intense customer reach. In line with Prysmian, the company had a broad global presence in terms of manufacturing plants and distribution areas, allowing for the reduction of over-dependence on a single market and the establishment of a well-balanced revenue stream formed by different sources of products, reaching different customers and tapping opportunities in new and existing markets.

12.2.3 The rationale behind the transaction

First of all, one of the main drivers that led to this transaction was **General Cable's decision to sell the company**. On 16 July 2017, General Cable publicly announced that it had decided to open itself to the possibility of selling the company, reviewing the strategic alternatives to maximize the shareholder value. This was an important decision after years in which General Cable tried in several ways to continue managing the business on their own. Notwithstanding the numerous difficulties that were faced, in October 2014 the company initiated a **transformation process** to improve its performance: **divestment of all non-core assets in Asia Pacific and Africa**. Nonetheless, the result of this strategy was not so positive, and thus in the fourth quarter of 2015 General Cable committed to a new strategic plan aimed at the optimization of its asset portfolio, developing leading cost and efficiency positions, innovating, and creating an high-performance culture. The plan required significant capital expenditures in new projects, restructuring of facilities in the main regions, hiring of new executive management, and the engagement of external consultants while internally developing a renewed employee culture. **Even if this strategy reached the expected results in terms of cost reduction, as of June 2017, the results had been substantially offset by business and market trends, such as overall weak economic growth in the products and markets in which the firm operated, added to price erosion due to increased competitiveness**. As a consequence, on 21 June

2017, General Cable's Board held a meeting to analyse the recent negative results: the firm obtained flat to declining outcomes in 2016/2017 despite the efforts of the new plans. Consequently, they decided to start considering new initiatives and investments that could lead to performance improvement, with details of each associated cost, risk, time, and payback. Every possibility of continued operations would have led to significant investments with no certain future results in the near-term. Therefore, on 12 July 2017, J.P. Morgan, acting as the financial advisor for General Cable, suggested that the best way to generate the highest value for shareholders would be to initiate **new external strategic alternatives such as a recapitalization with borrowed capital, a sale for cash or for stock or a combination of both**. Each possibility was then presented in terms of costs and benefits and finally the **Board of Directors opted for the sale of the company**, convinced that, in the presence of numerous possible synergies with other parties, the cash obtained would represent the best way to deliver value to shareholders.

Second, the **growing demand** that Prysmian faced also played an important role in the conclusion of the transaction. At the time of the acquisition, the increase of economic activity and urbanization (most of all in developing countries) was expected to increase the number of construction and infrastructure projects, widening operations in the residential, commercial, automotive, energy, power, and telecom industries, which are all related and based on the use of wire and cables. Moreover, as the power, light, and communications sectors increased their importance over time, the "means of transportation" for these products were increasingly essential, further increasing the demand for Prysmian's products and solutions. Therefore, acquiring General Cable enabled the Italian multinational to scale up and improve business efficiency in order to meet the growing demand for cables and wires.

Third, this acquisition was also motivated by Prysmian's willingness to strengthen its already strong competitive position, reducing the number of competitors while fostering its ability to enter and expand into new markets. The transaction involved the first and the fourth largest players in the cable & wire industry, allowing the combined group to reach the top position, outstripping its competitors in terms of total revenues. This astonishing increase was the result of several synergies arising from combining the forces of the two companies:

a) **Complementary geographical footprint**: The two companies, even if both operating globally, had a major focus on different countries. Prysmian had a higher presence in the EMEA and APAC regions, while General Cable was really strong in the American continent, both in North America and LATAM. With the merger of the two firms, the entire group now has the possibility to be actively present all over the world, being the top operator in each market (see **Figure 12.15**).
b) **Complete understanding of the market**: Acting together, the two firms have a complete understanding of the industry, gathering information and possibilities for innovation from every corner of the world. As an example for Prysmian, the entry into the American market represents a real opportunity due to the market's innovative footprint and high level of demand, leading to new ideas and higher

Figure 12.15 **Highly Complementary Geographical Presence with Strong North American Platform**

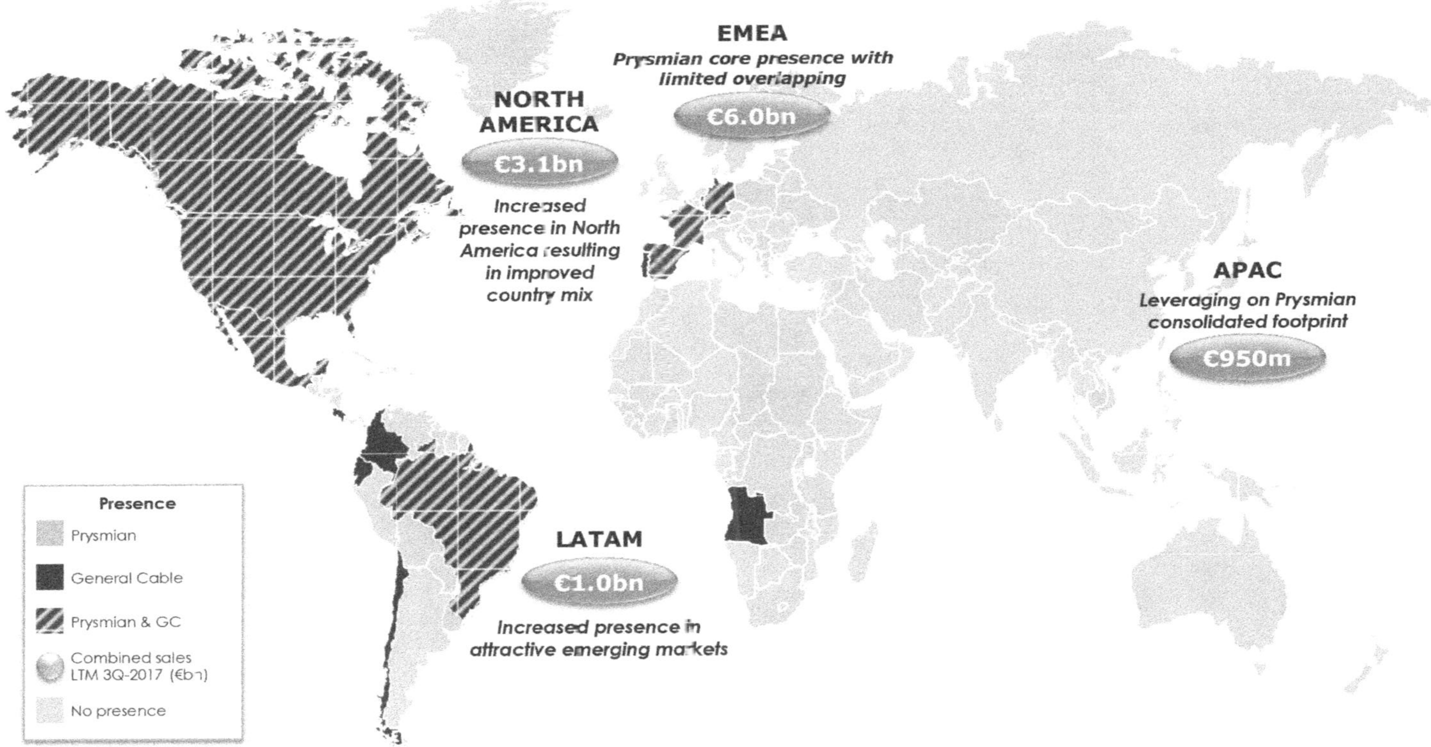

Source: Prysmian Group Presentation – "A Key Milestone in Prysmian's Growth Story – The Acquisition of General Cable." 4 December 2017.

Figure 12.16 Unique and Highly Complementary Combination

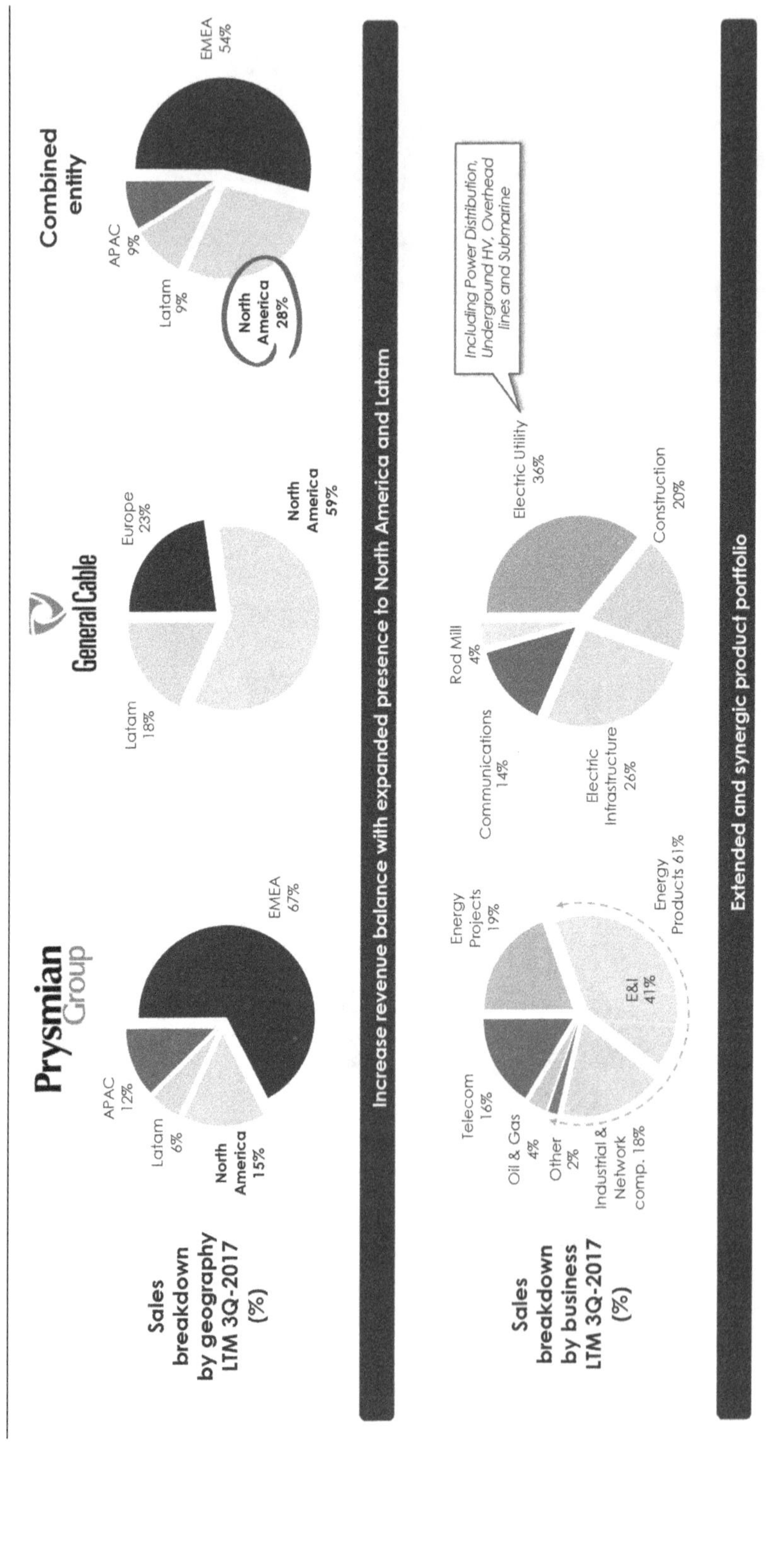

Source: Prysmian Group Presentation – "A Key Milestone in Prysmian's Growth Story – The Acquisition of General Cable." 4 December 2017.

need for further developments in technology. This will be additionally enhanced by the 25 R&D centres, which can now rely on both companies' knowledge and unique patents.

c) **A strong cultural fit**: This is a core element in a merger process, because cultural similarities can facilitate inclusion, teamwork, and accelerate the unification of the two companies. The two entities embrace in the same way values such as efficiency, economic, social, and environmental commitment, and sense of responsibility, placing customers and sustainability at the centre of their strategies. Indeed, the goal of the new entity is to leverage the combined capabilities to serve the customers with cutting-edge technologies, not only satisfying them but also anticipating their needs.
d) **The broadest and most complete product/contract portfolio on the market** (see **Figure 12.16**): Combining the firms' services, products and, present/future contracts with customers located in different parts of the world, the group can now benefit from the largest portfolio of opportunities to increase revenues and gain more experience (see **Figure 12.17**). Prysmian and General Cable are now the world leader in projects such as: deployment of power grids, power transmission, and offshore wind farms; exploration and production of oil and gas, refineries, and petrochemical solutions; construction of the safest power transmission cables for buildings and large-scale infrastructure, cars, trains, airplanes, and ships; optical fiber and telecom networks connecting communities and industries globally; construction of high temperature conductors for overhead powerlines; and provision of advanced systems and solutions to help customers even after the construction of infrastructure, for their management and control.
e) **Procurement, overhead, and manufacturing cost reductions**: Taking into consideration the increasing number of contract possibilities and synergies deriving

Figure 12.17 Top 12 Global Cable & Systems Players by Revenue (€bn)

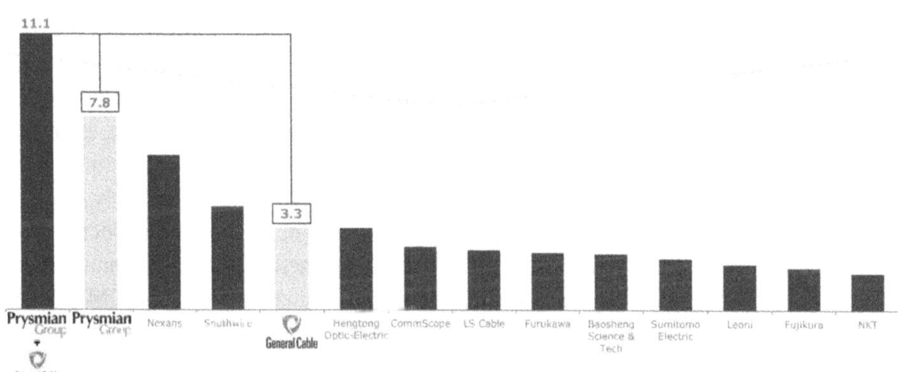

Source: Prysmian Group Presentation – "A Key Milestone in Prysmian's Growth Story – The Acquisition of General Cable." 4 December 2017.

from combined technologies and production facilities, the two companies also estimated a reduction in costs, related to procurement, overhead expenses, and manufacturing. This effect was estimated using the "pre-tax run-rate cost synergies," that is an estimation of the cost savings generated by the synergies with the assumption that all the other conditions will continue as they are in the present year. Therefore, the combined companies were expected to generate pre-tax run-rate cost synergies of around €150 million in the five years after the merger. This represented a fundamental advantage, since the firms competed in markets in which price was a key factor in the clients' decision-making process and in which brand loyalty is very weak. Therefore, the increased size would allow the organization to achieve significant economies of scale, and thus create a more efficient cost structure.

12.2.4 Terms of the transaction

For all the good reasons highlighted previously, on 3 December 2017, Prysmian and General Cable concluded their agreement for the purchase of the latter by the former for a **price of $30 per share in cash**. Prysmian agreed to pay $30 per share, which represented a whopping **81% premium over the undisturbed price** – the price of a General Cable share the last day before the company announced its review of strategic alternatives. This was around $16.55 on 14 July 2017, resulting in a $1.5bn market cap. On top of that, General Cable had around $1.2-1.3bn of net financial debt, increasing the total enterprise value to around **$3bn – 12x the trailing EBITDA**.

Despite the fact that the transaction was expected to be EPS accretive in the range of 10-12% for Prysmian shareholders already within the first year after closing pre-synergies and related implementation costs, the acquisition premium raised a fundamental question:

"Was the premium price too high?"

In order to answer the question, it is important to understand that the value of a company is defined as the **sum of its intrinsic value, minus the risks arising from its integration, plus the benefits from acquiring the company**. In this case, note that €150m of synergies times the EV/EBITDA multiple of Prysmian at the time of the deal (around 8-9x) lead to a total gross value of €1.2/1.4bn, which is fairly close to the premium paid, even though it only takes into account part of the expected synergies (Year 5 but not the previous ones) and does not factor in the additional potential upside from net working capital management flagged by Prysmian. Moreover, from a risk perspective, note also that the announced synergies were "**cost synergies**," hence with lower risk, since they are more dependent on management skills than industry or market fluctuations and dynamics. Therefore, even if we take into account the €220m (cumulative one-off costs) that were expected to be spread over four years, we have no evidence of overpayment (see **Figure 12.18**).

Figure 12.18 Multiple Sources of Synergies All Under Management Control

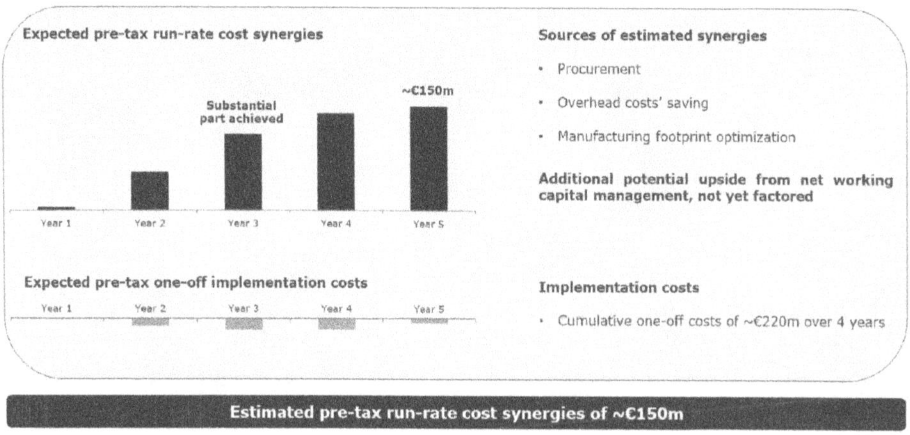

Source: Prysmian Group Presentation – "A Key Milestone in Prysmian's Growth Story – The Acquisition of General Cable." 4 December 2017.

Capital structure

The takeover was fully financed with cash: Prysmian had to put in place a full package for this transaction, which needed to be ready at signing – since it involved a listed company. Before the acquisition, Prysmian had a net financial position close to €600m (0.8x EBITDA), with more than €1bn of available cash on the balance sheet. Nevertheless, the group had to raise an additional €2.4bn: on the one side, this was necessary to finance the cash consideration for the shares ($1.3bn), and on the other, to refinance the current debt of General Cable – reducing its higher cost. The transaction was financed through a mix of new debt, cash, and existing credit lines with a portion of debt (i.e. €500m) which was expected to be refinanced via equity injection as communicated by Prysmian at the time of the deal announcement (see **Figure 12.19**).

Finally, and as planned, after closing Prysmian carried out a capital increase of €500m – which was wholly subscribed and completed by 27 July 2018 – in order to retain a flexible capital structure – reducing its net debt, and consequently improving its net leverage ratio.

Transaction structure

The transaction was carried out through the incorporation of Alisea (a wholly-owned subsidiary of Prysmian) into General Cable Corporation, pursuant to the laws of the State of Delaware (USA).

More specifically, the acquisition agreement was structured in the form of a "**cash**

Figure 12.19 Flexible Capital Structure Coupled with Significant Value Creation

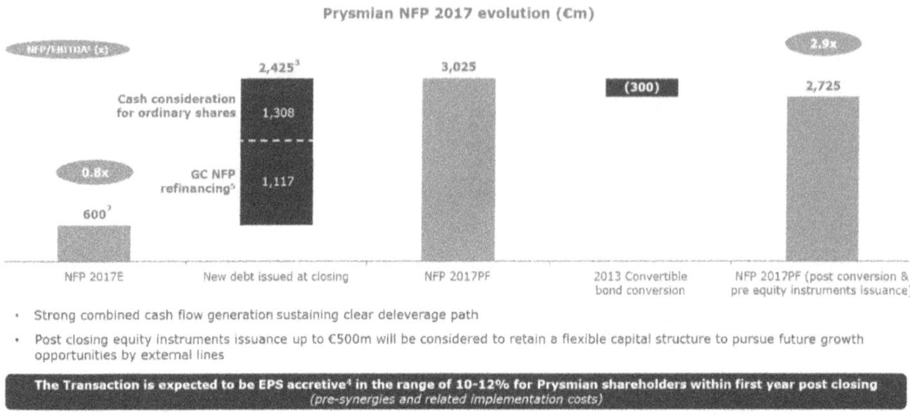

Source: Prysmian Group Presentation – "A Key Milestone in Prysmian's Growth Story – The Acquisition of General Cable." 4 December 2017.

Figure 12.20 Transaction Structure

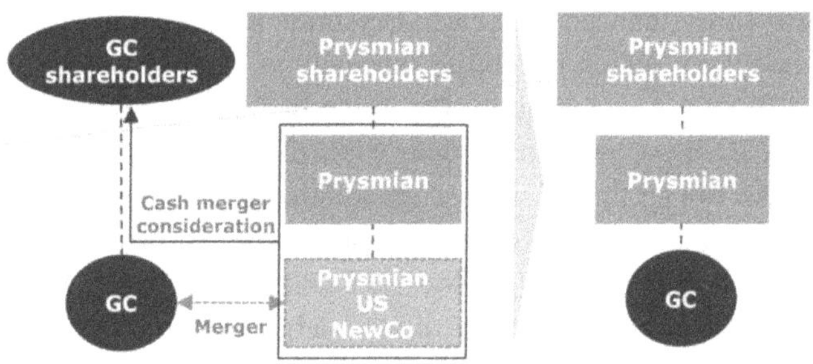

Source: Prysmian Group Presentation – "A Key Milestone in Prysmian's Growth Story – The Acquisition of General Cable." 4 December 2017.

reversed triangular merger" which is typical in acquisitions involving US entities (see **Figure 12.20**). Following the completion of the transaction, General Cable shares were delisted from the NYSE.

Visual Interpretation of the merger

i) Pre-Transaction

The terms of the acquisition envisaged the purchase of 52m shares of General Cable at a price of $30 per share, corresponding to €28 at the prevailing exchange rates, representing a 38% premium over the closing price on the day before the announcement.

Bidder balance sheet (€m)		Target balance sheet (€m)	
Assets	**Liabilities**	**Assets**	**Liabilities**
Net fixed assets 2,610	Equity 1,675	Net fixed assets 593	Equity 124
Goodwill	Net debt 436	Goodwill	Net debt 939
Other net assets (677)		Other net assets (247)	
NWC 178		NWC 717	
2,111	**2,111**	**1,063**	**1,063**

Part of the acquisition, i.e. €500m, was financed by a share capital increase, the remainder by cash obtained through new debt.

ii) Distribution of Synergies

Since this was an acquisition, the synergies were factored into the bid price upfront.

Assets		
EUR/USD @ 04/12/2006		**1.07**
Prysmian share price	€	28.03
General Cable share price	€	19.37
General Cable offer price	**€**	**28.14**
General Cable NoSH pre-combination	**#m**	**52**
Prysmian NoSH pre-combination	**#m**	**217**
Equity consideration	#m	500
Issuance share price	€	28.03
New shared issued	#m	18
NoSH post-transaction	**#m**	**235**

iii) Consolidated Financial Ratios: Accretion/Dilution of EPS

Accretion /Dilution analysis					
		Target	**Bidder**	**Bidder post-transaction**	**Accretion/ (dilution)(%)**
Equity value	€m	1,456	6,088	6,588	
NOSH	#m	52	217	235	
€ p.s.	€	28.14	28.03	28.03	
Net Income 2017E	€m	58	275	333	
EPS 2017E	**€m**	**1.11**	**1.27**	**1.41**	**12%**

Note: net income pre-synergies estimated before the transaction.

iv) Consolidation of the Balance Sheet

The goodwill was calculated as the difference between the target's equity value and its book value of equity (or net value of assets).

Goodwill calculation		
General Cable EqV	**€m**	**1,456**
Book value of BGC equity	€m	124
Goodwill	**€m**	**1,332**

Reclassified balance sheet					
@31/12/2017		**Target**	**Bidder**	**Adj.**	**Bidder post-transaction**
Net fixed assets	€m	593	2,610		3,203
Goodwill	€m			1,332	1,332
Other net assets	€m	(247)	(677)		(924)
Net working capital	€m	717	178		895
Net capital employed	**€m**	**1,063**	**2,111**	**1,332**	**4,505**
Equity	€m	124	1,675	376	2,175
Net debt	€m	939	436	956	2,330
Total equity and funds	**€m**	**1,063**	**2,111**	**1,332**	**4,505**

v) Post-Transaction Structure

Bidder BS post combination (€m)	
Assets	**Liabilities**
Net fixed assets 3,203	Equity 2,175
Goodwill 1,332	Net debt 2,330
Other net assets (924)	
NWC 895	
4,505	**4,505**

12.2.5 The process

The transaction was announced on 3 December 2017 and was closed on 6 June 2018. The announcement was preceded by due diligence – that contributed significantly to enhancing the amount and quality of information available. During the six-month period between signing and closing, three main events took place.

First, on 16 February 2018, General Cable's stockholders approved the acquisition of the company: 38,140,754 shares at a price of $30 per share, representing 75.34% of the total number of shares of common stock outstanding and around 99% of the total votes cast.

Then, on 8 March 2018, just after Prysmian signed a contract with the five syndicating banks to obtain financing, the Group obtained their commitment and the transaction was cleared for antitrust purposes in the US and in six other jurisdictions: Europe, Brazil, Chile, Canada, Mexico, and Colombia.

Finally, the last obstacle and the closing were resolved on 2 June 2018 when the two companies obtained clearance from the CFIUS (Committee on Foreign Investment in the United States), eliminating the last hurdle for the acquisition. Afterwards, on 6 June 2018, Prysmian and General Cable announced the closing of the operation, publicly launching their new organization 5 days later.

A complex transaction such as the Prysmian-General Cable deal can only be successful if carefully designed and executed by a coordinated group of experts. The M&A Advisors, Goldman Sachs and Mediobanca, were primarily involved from the M&A Process launch to the signing, and gave their final contribution at closing.

Bibliography

Agarwal, R. & Helfat, C.E. (2009). "Strategic renewal of organizations." *Organization Science*, 20(2), 281-293. doi:10.1287/orsc.1090.0423

Altman, E.I. (1968). "Financial ratios, discriminant analysis and the prediction of corporate bankruptcy." *The Journal of Finance*, 23(4), 589-609. doi:10.1111/j.1540-6261.1968.tb00843.x

Altman, E.I. (1984). "The success of business failure prediction models." *Journal of Banking and Finance*, 8, 171-198. doi:10.1016/0378-4266(84)90003-7

Altman, E.I. (2002). *Bankruptcy, Credit Risk, and High Yield Bonds*. Oxford: Blackwell Publishers.

Altman, E.I. (2002). "Revisiting Credit Scoring Models in a Basel 2 Environment." Finance Working Papers FIN-02-041. Available at: hdl.handle.net/2451/26485

Altman, E.I. (2013). "Predicting Financial Distress of Companies: Revisiting the Z-Score and Zeta Models." In Bell, A.R., Brooks, C., & Prokopczuk, M. (Ed.), *Handbook of Research Methods and Applications in Empirical Finance*. Cheltenham: Edward Elgar.

Altman, E.I., Resti, A., & Sironi, A. (2003). "Default Recovery Rates in Credit Risk Modeling: A Review of the Literature and Empirical Evidence." Available at: people.stern.nyu.edu/ealtman/Review1.pdf

Ali-Yrkkö, J. (2002). "Mergers and acquisitions: Reason and results (No. 792)." ETLA Discussion Papers, The Research Institute of the Finnish Economy (ETLA). Available at: hdl.handle.net/10419/63797

American Bankruptcy Institute (2005). "Out-of-court Workouts Prepacks and Pre-arranged Cases: A Primer." *American Bankruptcy Institute Journal*.

Amihud, Y., Lev, B., & Travels, N.G. (1990). "Corporate control and the choice of investment financing: The case of corporate acquisitions." *The Journal of Finance*, 45(2), 603-616. doi:10.1111/j.1540-6261.1990.tb03706.x

Andersen, O. (1997). "Internationalization and market entry mode: A review of theories and conceptual frameworks." *MIR: Management International Review*, 27-42. Available at: jstor.org/stable/40228431

Andrade, G., Mitchell, M., & Stafford, E. (2001). "New evidence and perspectives on mergers." *Journal of Economic Perspectives*, 15(2), 103-120.

Andre, P. & Ben-Amar, W. (2009). *Control Threat and Means of Payment: Evidence from Canadian Mergers and Acquisitions*.

Ang, J.S. & Cheng, Y. (2006). "Direct evidence on the market-driven acquisition theory." *Journal of Financial Research*, 29(2), 199-216. doi:10.1111/j.1475-6803.2006.00174.x

Ansoff, H.I. (1965). *Corporate Strategy: An Analytic Approach to Business Policy for Growth and Expansion*. New York: McGraw-Hill.

Ansoff, H.I. (1965). *Corporate Strategy: Business Policy for Growth and Expansion*. New York: McGraw-Hill.

Antoniou, A. & Zhao, H. (2004). "Long-run post takeover stock return: the impact of overlapping return, takeover premium, and method of payment." Centre for Empirical Research in Finance (CERF) Durham Business School University of Durham.

Arrow, K.J. (1971). *Essays in the Theory of Risk*-Bearing (Vol. 2). Amsterdam, London: North- Holland Publishing Company.

Arrow, K.J. (1975). "Vertical integration and communication." *The Bell Journal of Economics*, 6(1), 173-183. doi:10.2307/3003220

Asquith, P., Bruner, R.F., & Mullins, D.W. (1990). "Merger returns and the form of financing." Working Paper #3203-90-EFA. Available at: core.ac.uk/download/pdf/4379978.pdf

Asquith, P., Gertner, R., & Sharfstein, D. (1994). "Anatomy of financial distress: An explanation of junk bond issuers." *The Quarterly Journal of Economics*, 109(3), 625-658. doi:10.2307/2118416

Ayers, B.C., Laplante, S.K., & McGuire, S.T. (2010). "Credit ratings and taxes: The effect of book-tax differences on ratings changes." *Contemporary Accounting Research*, 27(2), 359-402. doi:10.1111/j.1911-3846.2010.01011.x

Babenko I. (2003). "Optimal Capital Structure of the Firm in the Presence of Costs of Financial Distress." EFA 2004 Maastricht Meetings, 5179. doi:10.2139/ssrn.559410

Balakrishnan, S. (1988). "The prognostics of diversifying acquisitions." *Strategic Management Journal*, 9(2), 185-196. doi:10.1002/smj.4250090208

Bank for International Settlements (2018). "Overview of the revised credit risk framework."

Barber, B.M. & Lyon, J.D. (1997). "Detecting long-run abnormal stock returns: The empirical power and specification of test statistics." *Journal of Financial Economics*, 43(3), 341-372. doi:10.1016/S0304-405X(96)00890-2

Barbopoulos, L. & Sudarsanam, S. (2012). "Determinants of earnout as acquisition payment currency and bidder's value gains." *Journal of Banking & Finance*, 36(3), 678-694. doi:10.1016/j.jbankfin.2011.10.007

Barclay, M.J. & Holderness, C.G. (1989). "Private benefits from control of public corporations." *Journal of financial Economics*, 25(2), 371-395. doi:10.1016/0304-405X(89)90088-3

Basel Committee for Banking Supervision (2017). "High-level summary of Basel III reforms." Available at: bis.org

Basel Committee for Banking Supervision (2019). "Definition of capital in Basel III – Executive Summary." Available at: bis.org

Beard, D.R. (2004). "The mitigation of asymmetric information through the use of earnouts." *LSU Doctoral Dissertations*. 2387. Available at: digitalcommons.lsu.edu

Berger, P.G. & Ofek, E. (1995). "Diversification's effect on firm value." *Journal of Financial Economics*, 37(1), 39-65. doi:10.1016/0304-405X(94)00798-6

Berk, J.B. & DeMarzo, P.M. (2014). *Corporate Finance*. New York: Pearson.

Betton, S., Eckbo, B.E., & Thorburn, K. (2008). "Corporate takeovers." In Eckbo, B.E. *Handbook of Empirical Corporate Finance SET* (Vol. 1). Amsterdam: Elsevier, 291-414.

Betton, S., Eckbo, B.E., Thompson, R., & Thorburn, K.S. (2014). "Merger negotiations with stock market feedback." *The Journal of Finance*, 69(4), 1705-1745. doi:10.1111/jofi.12151

Bharadwaj, A. & Shivdasani, A. (2003). "Valuation effects of bank financing in acquisitions." *Journal of Financial Economics*, 67(1), 113-148. doi:10.1016/S0304-405X(02)00233-7

Bhojraj, S. & Lee, C. (2002). "Who is my peer? A valuation-based approach to the selection of comparable firms." *Journal of Accounting Research*, 40(2), 407-439. doi:10.1111/1475-679X.00054

Bibeault, D. (1982). *Corporate Turnaround: How Managers Turn Losers into Winners.* New York: McGraw-Hill.

Bjorvatn, K. (2004). "Economic integration and the profitability of cross-border mergers and acquisitions." *European Economic Review*, 48(6), 1211-1226. doi:10.1016/j.euroecorev.2004.03.007

Black, B.S. (1989). "Bidder overpayment in takeovers." *Stanford Law Review*, 41(3), 597-660. doi:10.2307/1228881

Black, F. & Scholes, M. (1973). "The pricing of options and corporate liabilities." *The Journal of Political Economy*, 81(3), 637-654. Available at: jstor.org/stable/1831029

Bower, J.L. (2001). "Not all M&As are alike—and that matters." *Harvard Business Review*, 79(3), 92-101.

Boyne, G.A. & Meier, K. (2009). "Environmental change, human resources and organizational turnaround." *Journal of Management Studies*, 46(5), 835-863. doi:10.1111/j.1467-6486.2008.00813.x

Brakman, S., Garretsen, H., & Van Marrewijk, C. (2007)." Cross-border mergers and acquisitions: on revealed comparative advantage and merger waves." Tinbergen Institute Discussion Paper No. 08-013/2. Available at: http://www.econstor.eu/bitstream/10419/86870/1/08-013.pdf

Bris, A., Brisley, N., & Cabolis, C. (2008). "Adopting better corporate governance: Evidence from cross-border mergers." *Journal of Corporate Finance*, 14(3), 224-240. doi:10.1016/j.jcorpfin.2008.03.005

Bruner, R.F. (2002). "Does M&A pay? A survey of evidence for the decision-maker." *Journal of Applied Finance*, 12(1), 48-68.

Bruner, R.F. (2004). *Applied Mergers and Acquisitions.* Hoboken, NJ: John Wiley & Sons.

Bruner, R.F. & Eades, K.M. (1992). "The crash of the Revco leveraged buyout: The hypothesis of inadequate capital." *Financial Management*, 35-49. doi:10.2307/3665679

Bruner, R.F. & Stiegler, S. (2001). "Technical note on structuring and valuing incentive payments in M&A: Earnouts and other contingent payments to the seller." Working Paper, Darden Graduate School of Business Administration, University of Virginia.

Cain, M.D., Denis, D.J., & Denis, D.K. (2011). "Earnouts: A study of financial contracting in acquisition agreements." *Journal of Accounting and Economics*, 51(1), 151-170. doi:10.1016/j.jacceco.2010.05.001

Calipha, R., Tarba, S., & Brock, D. (2010). "Mergers and acquisitions: A review of phases, motives, and success factors." In Cooper, C.L. & Finkelstein, S. (Ed.), *Advances in Mergers and Acquisitions.* Bingley: Emerald Group Publishing Limited, 1-24.

Campbell, J.Y., Hilscher, J., & Szilagyi, J. (2008). "In search of distress risk." *Journal of Finance*, 63(6), 2899-2939. doi:10.1111/j.1540-6261.2008.01416.x

Campobasso, G.F. (2017). *Manuale di Diritto Commerciale.* Milan: UTET Giuridica.

Capron, L. (1999). "The long-term performance of horizontal acquisitions." *Strategic Management Journal*, 20(11), 987-1018.

Carow, K., Heron, R., & Saxton, T. (2004). "Do early birds get the returns? An empirical investigation of early-mover advantages in acquisitions." *Strategic Management Journal*, 25(6), 563-585. doi:10.1002/smj.404

Cartwright, S. & Schoenberg, R. (2006). "Thirty years of mergers and acquisitions research: Recent advances and future opportunities." *British Journal of Management*, 17(S1), S1-S5. doi:10.1111/j.1467-8551.2006.00475.x

Caselli, S., Gatti, S., & Visconti, M. (2006). "Managing M&A risk with collars, earnouts and CVRs." *Journal of Applied Corporate Finance*, 18(4), 91-104. doi:10.1111/j.1745-6622.2006.00115.x

Caves, R.E. (1996). *Multinational Enterprise and Economic Analysis.* Cambridge: Cambridge University Press.

Cesario, G. & Gigante, G. (2021). "What drives investment decisions on equity stake in private equity? The Italian case before and after the great financial crisis." *Corporate Ownership & Control*, 18(3), 224-240. doi:10.22495/cocv18i3siart1

Chang, S. & Mais, E. (2000). "Managerial motives and merger financing." *Financial Review*, 35(4), 139-152. doi:10.1111/j.1540-6288.2000.tb01434.x

Chatterjee, S. (1986). "Types of synergy and economic value: The impact of acquisitions on merging and rival firms." *Strategic Management Journal*, 7(2), 119-139. doi:10.1002/smj.4250070203

Chatterjee, S. (2007). "Why is synergy so difficult in mergers of related businesses?" *Strategy & Leadership*, 35(2), 46-52. doi:10.1108/10878570710734534

Chatterjee, R. & Meeks, G. (1996). "The financial effects of takeover: Accounting rates of return and accounting regulation." *Journal of Business Finance & Accounting*, 23(5-6), 851-868. doi:10.1111/j.1468-5957.1996.tb01155.x

Chatterjee, S. & Yan, A. (2008). "Using innovative securities under asymmetric information: Why do some firms pay with contingent value rights?" *Journal of Financial and Quantitative Analysis*, 43(4), 1001-1035. Available at: jstor.org/stable/27647382

Chen, J, Chollete, L., & Ray, R. (2008). "Financial distress and idiosyncratic volatility: An empirical investigation." *Journal of Financial Markets*, 13(2), 249-267. doi:10.1016/j.finmar.2009.10.003

Christofferson, S.A., McNish, R.S. & Sias, D.L. (2004). "Where mergers go wrong." *McKinsey Quarterly.* Available at: mckinsey.com

Clifford Chance (2012). "Cross-border M&A: Perspectives on a changing world." Available at: cliffordchance.com

Corwin, S.A. & Schultz, P. (2005). "The role of IPO underwriting syndicates: Pricing, information production and underwriter competition." *Journal of Finance*, 60(1), 443-486. doi:10.1111/j.1540-6261.2005.00735.x

Cox, J.C., Ross, S.A., & Rubinstein, M. (1979). "Option pricing: A simplified approach." *Journal of Financial Economics*, 7(3), 229-263. doi:10.1016/0304-405X(79)90015-1

Crimmins, P., Gray, B., & Waller, J. (2011). "Earnouts in M&A transactions." *Mayer Brown.* Available at: mayerbrown.com

Dallocchio, M., Taveggia, L., Gremmo, D., Alberti, S., Cotogno, M., & Boellis, A. (2013). "Le ristrutturazioni come strumento per tornare al valore." Working Paper. Milan: Università Bocconi, CReSV.

Dallocchio, M., Le Fur Y., Quiry, P., Salvi, A., & Vernimmen, P. (2017). *Corporate Finance: Theory and Practice, 5th Edition.* Chichester, West Sussex: John Wiley & Sons.

Damodaran, A. (2001). *Corporate Finance: Theory and Practice, 2nd Edition.* New York: Wiley.

Damodaran, A. (2005). "The value of control: Implications for control premia, minority discounts and voting share differentials." New York University - Stern School of Business. doi:10.2139/ssrn.837405

Damodaran, A. (2005). "The value of synergy." New York University - Stern School of Business. doi:10.2139/ssrn.841486

Damodaran, A. (2012). *Investment Valuation: Tools and Techniques for Determining the Value of Any Asset, 3rd Edition.* Hoboken, NJ: John Wiley & Sons.

Danzon, P.M., Epstein, A., & Nicholson, S. (2007). "Mergers and acquisitions in the pharmaceutical and biotech industries." *Managerial and Decision Economics*, 28(4-5), 307-328. doi:10.1002/mde.1343

Datar, S., R. Frankel, M. Wolfson. 2001. "The effects of adverse selection and agency costs on acquisition techniques." *Journal of Law, Economics, & Organization*, 17(1), 201-238. Available at: jstor.org/stable/3555002

Datta, D.K. & Puia, G. (1995). "Cross border acquisitions: An examination of the influence of relatedness and cultural fit on shareholder value creation in US acquiring firms." *MIR: Management International Review*, 337-359. Available at: jstor.org/stable/40228285

Datta, D.K., Pinches, G.E., & Narayanan, V.K. (1992). "Factors influencing wealth creation from mergers and acquisitions: A meta-analysis." *Strategic Management Journal*, 13(1), 67-84. doi:10.1002/smj.4250130106

Davis T. & Higgins J. (2013). "A blockbuster failure: How an outdated business model destroyed a giant." Chapter 11 Bankruptcy Case Studies, The University of Tennessee.

Davydenko, S.A. & Franks, J.R. (2008). "Do bankruptcy codes matter? A study of defaults in France, Germany, and the UK." *The Journal of Finance*, 63(2), 565-608. doi:10.1111/j.1540-6261.2008.01325.x

De La Bruslerie, H. (2013). "Crossing takeover premiums and mix of payment: An empirical test of contractual setting in M&A transactions." *Journal of Banking & Finance*, 37(6), 2106-2123. doi:10.1016/j.jbankfin.2013.01.037

DeLong, G.L. (2001). "Stockholder gains from focusing versus diversifying bank mergers." *Journal of Financial Economics*, 59(2), 221-252. doi:10.1016/S0304-405X(00)00086-6

Demirbag, M., Tatoglu, E., & Glaister, K.W. (2008). "Factors affecting perceptions of the choice between acquisition and greenfield entry: The case of Western FDI in an emerging market." *Management International Review*, 48(1), 5-38. doi:10.1007/s11575-008-0002-3

Denis, D. & Denis, D. (1995). "Causes of financial distress following leveraged recapitalizations." *Journal of Financial Economics*, 37(2), 129-157. doi:10.1016/0304-405X(94)00792-Y

Denis, D.K. & Rodgers, K.J. (2007). "Chapter 11: Duration, outcome, and post-reorganization performance." *The Journal of Financial and Quantitative Analysis*, 42(1), 101-118. Available at: jstor.org/stable/27647287

DePamphilis, D. (2011). *Mergers, Acquisitions, and Other Restructuring Activities, 6th Edition*. London: Academic Press.

DePonte, K. & Warren, N. (2010). "Private equity distressed debt and restructuring market investor survey." Available at: probitaspartners.com

Desai, M.A., Foley, C.F., & Hines, J.R. (2004). "Foreign direct investment in a world of multiple taxes." *Journal of Public Economics*, 88(12), 2727-2744. doi:10.1016/j.jpubeco.2003.08.004

Dichev, I.D. (1998). "Is the risk of bankruptcy a systematic risk?" *Journal of Finance*, 53(3), 1131-1147. doi:10.1111/0022-1082.00046

Dong, M., Hirshleifer, D., Richardson, S., & Teoh, S.H. (2006). "Does investor misvaluation drive the takeover market?" *The Journal of Finance*, 61(2), 725-762. Available at: jstor.org/stable/3699356

Dragich, D.G. (2020). "5 Common Misconceptions About the Chapter 11 Bankruptcy Process." Available at: cfo.com

Dragotă, V. & Ciobanu, R. (2017). "The unusual case of the discount offers for taking the control: Evidence from Romania." *Prague Economic Papers*, 26(1), 36-54. doi:10.18267/j.pep.592

Dragotă, V., Lipară, C., Ciobanu, R. (2013). "Agency problems and synergistic effects in Romania: The determinants of the control premium." *Czech Journal of Economics and Finance*, 63(2), 197-219.

Durand, D. (1959). "The cost of capital, corporation finance, and the theory of investment: Comment." *The American Economic Review*, 49(4), 639-655. Available at: jstor.org/stable/1812918

Dyck, A. & Zingales, L. (2004). "Private benefits of control: An international comparison." *The Journal of Finance*, 59(2), 537-600. doi:10.1111/j.1540-6261.2004.00642.x

Dyer J.H., Kale P., & Singh H. (2004). "When to ally and when to acquire." *Harvard Business Review*, 82(7-8), 108-115.

Eberhart, A., Aggarwal, R., & Altman, E.I. (1999). "The equity performance of firms emerging from bankruptcy." *The Journal of Finance*, 54(5), 1855-1868. doi:10.1111/0022-1082.00169

Erić, D. & Stošić, I. (2013). *Corporate Restructuring*. Belgrade: Čigoja štampa, Institut ekonomskih nauka i Beogradska bankarska akademija.

Eckbo, B.E. (1983). "Horizontal mergers, collusion, and stockholder wealth." *Journal of Financial Economics*, 11(1-4), 241-273. doi:10.1016/0304-405X(83)90013-2

Eckbo, B.E. (2009). "Bidding strategies and takeover premiums: A review." *Journal of Corporate Finance*, 15(1), 149-178. doi:10.1016/j.jcorpfin.2008.09.016

Eckbo, B.E. & Langohr, H. (1989). "Information disclosure, method of payment, and takeover premiums: Public and private tender offers in France." *Journal of Financial Economics*, 24(2), 363-403. doi:10.1016/0304-405X(89)90052-4

Eckbo, B.E., Giammarino, R.M., & Heinkel, R.L. (1990). "Asymmetric information and the medium of exchange in takeovers: Theory and tests." *Review of Financial Studies*, 3(4), 651-675. Available at: jstor.org/stable/2962119

Eichner, T. (2010). *Restructuring and Turnaround of Distressed Manufacturing Firms: An International Empirical Study*. Frankfurt am Main: Peter Lang.

Eisenhardt, K.M. (1989). "Agency theory: An assessment and review." *Academy of Management Review*, 14(1), 57-74. doi:10.2307/258191

Elayan, F.A. & Meyer, T.O. (2001). "The impact of receiving debtor-in-possession financing on the probability of successful emergence and time spent under Chapter 11 bankruptcy." *Journal of Business Finance & Accounting*, 28(7-8), 905-942. doi:10.1111/1468-5957.00398

Erel, I., Liao, R.C., & Weisbach, M.S. (2012). "Determinants of cross-border mergers and acquisitions." *The Journal of Finance*, 67(3), 1045-1082. doi:10.1111/j.1540-6261.2012.01741.x

Ernst & Young. (2012). "Complex deal structures can affect future earnings and other metrics." *Technical Line*, No. 2012-31. Available at: eyjapan.jp

European Banking Authority (2014). "Guidelines for common procedures and methodologies for the supervisory review and evaluation process (SREP) and supervisory stress testing." Available at: eba.europa.eu

European Central Bank (2018). "SSM SREP Methodology Booklet." Available at: bankingsupervision.europa.eu

European Central Bank (2018). "SSM Supervisory Manual" Available at: bankingsupervision.europa.eu

Evanoff, D.D. (2018). *Achieving Financial Stability: Challenges to Prudential Regulation*. New Jersey: World Scientific.

Evenett, S. (2004). "The cross-border mergers and acquisitions wave of the late 1990s." In Baldwin, R.E. & Winters, L.A., *Challenges to Globalization: Analyzing the Economics*. Chicago: University of Chicago Press, 411-470.

Faccio, M. & Masulis, R.W. (2005). "The choice of payment method in European mergers and acquisitions." *The Journal of Finance*, 60(3), 1345-1388. doi:10.1111/j.1540-6261.2005.00764.x

Fama, E.F., and French, K.R. (1996). "Multifactor explanations of asset pricing anomalies." *Journal of Finance*, 51(1), 55-84. doi:10.1111/j.1540-6261.1996.tb05202.x

Fee, C.E. & Thomas, S. (2004). "Sources of gains in horizontal mergers: Evidence from customer, supplier, and rival firms." *Journal of Financial Economics*, 74(3), 423-460. doi:10.1016/j.jfineco.2003.10.002

Fishman, M.J. (1989). "Preemptive bidding and the role of the medium of exchange in acquisitions." *The Journal of Finance*, 44(1), 41-57. doi:10.1111/j.1540-6261.1989.tb02403.x

Forestieri, G. (2009). *Corporate & Investment Banking*. Milan: Egea.

Frankel, M.E.S. (2005). "Save that deal using Earn-outs." *Journal of Corporate Accounting & Finance*, 16(2), 21-25. doi:10.1002/jcaf.20084

Franks, J.R., Harris, R.S., & Mayer, C. (1988). "Means of payment in takeovers: Results for the United Kingdom and the United States." In Auerback, A. *Corporate Takeovers: Causes and Consequences*. Chicago: University of Chicago Press, 221-264.

García-Feijóo, L., Madura, J., & Ngo, T. (2012). "Impact of industry characteristics on the method of payment in mergers." *Journal of Economics and Business*, 64(4), 261-274. doi:10.1016/j.jeconbus.2012.03.003

Garlappi, L. & Yan, H. (2011). "Financial distress and the cross-section of equity returns." *The Journal of Finance*, 66(3), 789-822. doi:10.1111/j.1540-6261.2011.01652.x

Garrido, J.M. (2012). "Out-of-Court Debt Restructuring." World Bank Study. Available at: hdl.handle.net/10986/2230

Gatti, S. (2008). *Project Finance in Theory and Practice*. London: Elsevier.

Geddes, R. (2003). *IPOs & Equity Offerings*. Oxford: Elsevier/Butterworth-Heiemann.

Gehlhar, M. (2005). *The Fashion Designer Survival Guide*. Chicago: Kaplan.

Genentech (2008). "Genentech 2007 Annual Report." Available at: http://www.gene.com/download/pdf/2007_annual-report.pdf

Genentech (2009). "Genentech 2008 Annual Report." Available at: http://www.gene.com/download/pdf/2008_annual-report.pdf

Gertner, R. & Scharfstein, D. (1991). "A theory of workouts and the effects of reorganization law." *The Journal of Finance*, 46(4), 1189-1222. doi:10.1111/j.1540-6261.1991.tb04615.x

Ghosh, A. (2001). "Does operating performance really improve following corporate acquisitions?" *Journal of Corporate Finance*, 7(2), 151-178. doi:10.1016/S0929-1199(01)00018-9

Giddy, I.H. (2003). *Corporate Financial Restructuring*. New York: New York University.

Gigante, G. (2020). *Mergers & Acquisitions*. Roma: Aracne Editrice.

Gigante, G. & Cerri, A. (2021). *Finance Lab*. Milano: Bocconi University Press (BUP), Egea Editore. Available at: hdl.handle.net/11565/4038503

Gigante, G. & Conso, A. (2019). *Le Spac in Italia: Stato di un fenomeno in evoluzione*. Milano: Egea Editore. Available at: hdl.handle.net/11565/4020984

Gilson, S. (1990). "Bankruptcy, boards, and blockholders: Evidence on changes in corporate ownership and control when firms default." *Journal of Financial Economics*, 27(2), 355-387. doi:10.1016/0304-405X(90)90060-D

Gilson, S. (1997). "Transaction costs and capital structure choice." *The Journal of Finance*, 52(1), 161-196. doi:10.1111/j.1540-6261.1997.tb03812.x

Gilson, S.C. (2010). "Valuing Companies in Corporate Restructuring." In *Creating Value through Corporate Restructuring: Case Studies in Bankruptcies, Buyouts, and Breakups*. Hoboken, New Jersey: Wiley. doi:10.1002/9781119204589.app2

Gilson, R.J., Scholes, M.S., & Wolfson, M.A. (1988). "Taxation and the dynamics of corporate control: The uncertain case for tax-motivated acquisitions." In Coffee, J.C. Jr., Lowenstein, L. & Rose-Ackerman, S., *Knights, Raiders and Targets: The Impact of the Hostile Takeover.* New York: Oxford University Press.

Gomes, E., Weber, Y., Brown, C., & Tarba, S.Y. (2011). *Mergers, Acquisitions and Strategic Alliances: Understanding the Process.* New York: Palgrave.

Graham, J.R. & Harvey, C.R. (2001). "The theory and practice of corporate finance: Evidence from the field." *Journal of Financial Economics*, 60(2-3), 187-243. doi:10.1016/S0304-405X(01)00044-7

Graham, J.R., Leary, M.T., & Roberts, M.R. (2015). "A century of capital structure: The leveraging of corporate America." *Journal of Financial Economics*, 118(3), 658-683. doi:10.1016/j.jfineco.2014.08.005

Grant, D. (2011). "Valuing contingent consideration using option pricing." *Business Valuation Review*, 30(4), 121-131. doi:10.5791/BVR-D-11-00016.1

Grant, J. & Neven, D.J. (2005). "The attempted merger between General Electric and Honeywell: A case study of Transatlantic conflict." *Journal of Competition Law and Economics*, 1(3), 595-633. doi:10.1093/joclec/nhi019

Gregory, A. (2000). "Motives underlying the method of payment by UK acquirers: The influence of goodwill." *Accounting and Business Research*, 30(3), 227-240. doi:10.1080/00014788.2000.9728938

Griffin, J.M. & Lemmon, M.L. (2002). "Book-to-market equity, distress risk and stock returns." *The Journal of Finance*, 57(5), 2317-2336. doi:10.1111/1540-6261.00497

Grossman, S.J. & Hart, O.D. (1980). "Takeover bids, the free-rider problem, and the theory of the corporation." *The Bell Journal of Economics*, 11(1), 42-64. Available at: jstor.org/stable/3003400

Grubert, H. & Mutti, J. (1991). "Taxes, tariffs and transfer pricing in multinational corporate decision making." *The Review of Economics and Statistics*, 73(2), 285-93. doi:10.2307/2109519

Hambrick, D.C. & Mason, P.A. (1984). "Upper echelons: The organization as a reflection of its top managers." *Academy of Management Review*, 9(2), 193-206. doi:10.2307/258434

Hansen, R.G. (1987). "A theory for the choice of exchange medium in mergers and acquisitions." *The Journal of Business*, 60(1), 75-95. Available at: jstor.org/stable/2352948

Harford, J. (1999). "Corporate cash reserves and acquisitions." *The Journal of Finance*, 54(6), 1969-1997. doi:10.1111/0022-1082.00179

Harford, J. (2005). "What drives merger waves?" *Journal of Financial Economics*, 77(3), 529-560. doi:10.1016/j.jfineco.2004.05.004

Harmon, M. (2020). "A Primer on Restructuring Your Company's Finances." *Harvard Business Review*, 9 June. Available at: hbr.org

Harris, M. & Raviv, A. (1988). "Corporate control contests and capital structure." *Journal of Financial Economics*, 20, 55-86. doi:10.1016/0304-405X(88)90040-2

Harris, R.S. & Ravenscraft, D. (1991). "The role of acquisitions in foreign direct investment: Evidence from the US stock market." *The Journal of Finance*, 46(3), 825-844. doi:10.2307/2328544

Haunschild, P.R. (1994). "How much is that company worth? Interorganizational relationships, uncertainty, and acquisition premiums." *Administrative Science Quarterly*, 39(3), 391-411. doi:10.2307/2393296

Hayward, M.L. & Hambrick, D.C. (1997). "Explaining the premiums paid for large acquisitions: Evidence of CEO hubris." *Administrative Science Quarterly*, 42(1), 103-127. doi:10.2307/2393810

Healy, P.M., Palepu, K.G., & Ruback, R.S. (1992). "Does corporate performance improve after mergers?" *Journal of Financial Economics*, 31(2), 135-175. doi:10.1016/0304-405X(92)90002-F

Heron, R.A., Lie, E., & Rodgers, K.J. (2009). "Financial restructuring in fresh-start Chapter 11 reorganizations." *Financial Management*, 38(4), 727-745. Available at: jstor.org/stable/40388692

Hertz-Eichenrode, A. (2011) *Private-Equity-Lexikon*. Stuttgart: Schäffer-Pöschel.

Hietala, P., Kaplan, S.N. & Robinson, D.T. (2003). "What is the price of hubris? Using takeover battles to infer overpayments and synergies." *Financial Management*, 32(3), 5-31. doi:10.2307/3666381

Hitt, M.A., Hoskisson, R.E, Johnson, R.A, & Moesel, D.D. (1996). "The market for corporate control and firm innovation." *Academy of Management Journal*, 39(5), 1084-1119. doi:10.5465/256993

Houston, J.F., James, C.M., & Ryngaert, M.D. (2001). "Where do merger gains come from? Bank mergers from the perspective of insiders and outsiders." *Journal of Financial Economics*, 60(2-3), 285-331. doi:10.1016/S0304-405X(01)00046-0

Howells, R. (2020). "Will COVID-19 change global supply chains forever?" *Forbes*, 3 June.

Hsieh, J. & Walkling, R.A. (2005). "Determinants and implications of arbitrage holdings in acquisitions." *Journal of Financial Economics*, 77(3), 605-648. doi:10.1016/j.jfineco.2004.08.003

Hu, H. (2009). "'Empty Creditors' and the Crisis." *Wall Street Journal*, 10 April. Available at: wsj.com

Huang, Y.S. & Walkling, R.A. (1987). "Target abnormal returns associated with acquisition announcements: Payment, acquisition form, and managerial resistance." *Journal of Financial Economics*, 19(2), 329-349. doi:10.1016/0304-405X(87)90008-0

Huizinga, H.P. & Voget, J. (2009). "International taxation and the direction and volume of cross-border M&As." *The Journal of Finance*, 64(3), 1217-1249. doi:10.1111/j.1540-6261.2009.01463.x

Iannotta, G. (2010). *Investment Banking – A Guide to Underwriting and Advisory Service*. Berlin, Heidelberg: Springer.

Ingham, H., Kran, I., & Lovestam, A. (1992). "Mergers and profitability: A managerial success story?" *Journal of Management Studies*, 29(2), 195-208. doi:10.1111/j.1467-6486.1992.tb00660.x

Investopedia. www.investopedia.com

James, C. (1995). "When Do Banks Take Equity in Debt Restructuring." *Review of Financial Studies*, 8(4), 1209-1234. Available at: jstor.org/stable/2962304

Jayadev, M. & Sensarma, R. (2008). "Mergers in Indian Banking: An Analysis." Working Paper. Mumbai: Indian Institute of Banking and Finance.

Jemison, D.B. & Sitkin, S.B. (1986). "Corporate acquisitions: A process perspective." *Academy of Management Review*, 11(1), 145-163. doi:10.2307/258337

Jensen, M.C. (1986). "Agency costs of free cash flow, corporate finance, and takeovers." *The American Economic Review*, 76(2), 323-329. Available at: jstor.org/stable/1818789

Jensen, M.C. & Meckling, W.H. (1976). "Theory of the firm: Managerial behavior, agency costs and ownership structure." *Journal of Financial Economics*, 3(4), 305-360. doi:10.1016/0304-405X(76)90026-X

Jensen, M.C. & Ruback, R.S. (1983). "The market for corporate control: The scientific evidence." *Journal of Financial Economics*, 11(1-4), 5-50. doi:10.1016/0304-405X(83)90004-1

Kapadia, N. (2009). "Tracking down distress risk." *Journal of Financial Economics*, 102(1), 167-182. doi:10.1016/j.jfineco.2011.05.004

Kaplan, S. (1989). "The effects of management buyouts on operating performance and value." *Journal of Financial Economics*, 24(2), 217-254. doi:10.1016/0304-405X(89)90047-0

Kaplan, S.N. (2000). *Mergers and Productivity.* Chicago: University of Chicago Press.

Kaplan, S.N., Mitchell, M.L., & Wruck, K.H. (1997). "A clinical exploration of value creation and destruction in acquisitions: integration, organization design and internal capital markets." NBER Working Paper Series, No. 5999. doi:10.3386/w5999

Kim, E.H. & Singal, V. (1993). "Mergers and Market Power: Evidence from the Airline Industry." *American Economic Review*, 83(3), 549-69. Available at: jstor.org/stable/2117533

Kinnunen J. (2010). "Valuing M&A Synergies as (Fuzzy) Real Options." 14th Annual International Conference on Real Options, Rome, Italy, 16-19 June. Available at: realoptions.org/papers2010/238.pdf

Kirchner, T. (2016). *Merger Arbitrage: How to Profit from Global Event-Driven Arbitrage, 2nd Edition.* Hoboken, NJ: John Wiley & Sons.

Koller, T., Goedhart, M., & Wessels, D. (2010). *Valuation: Measuring and Managing the Value of Companies.* Hoboken, NJ: John Wiley & Sons.

KPMG (1999). "Unlocking shareholder value: The keys to success." Mergers and Acquisitions-Global Research Report.

KPMG (2011). "A new dawn: Good deals in challenging times." Mergers and Acquisitions-Global Research Report.

Krishnamurti, C. & Vishwanath, S.R. (2008). "Real option analysis in mergers and acquisitions." In *Mergers, Acquisitions and Corporate Restructuring.* New Delhi, India: SAGE.

Krishnan, H.A., Hitt, M.A., & Park, D. (2007). "Acquisition premiums, subsequent workforce reductions and post-acquisition performance." *Journal of Management Studies*, 44(5), 709-732. doi:10.1111/j.1467-6486.2006.00672.x

Kummer, C. & Steger, U. (2008). "Why merger and acquisition (M&A) waves reoccur: The vicious circle from pressure to failure." *Strategic Management Review*, 2(1), 44-63.

Kusewitt Jr, J.B. (1985). "An exploratory study of strategic acquisition factors relating to performance." *Strategic Management Journal*, 6(2), 151-169. doi:10.1002/smj.4250060205

Laabs, J.P. (2009). "Study 2: Does Operating Performance Meet Market Expectations?" In *The Long-Term Success of Mergers and Acquisitions in the International Automotive Supply Industry.* Wiesbaden: Gabler, 93-131.

Laamanen, T. (2007). "On the role of acquisition premium in acquisition research." *Strategic Management Journal*, 28(13), 1359-1369. doi:10.1002/smj.639

Lamont, O.A. & Polk, C. (2002). "Does diversification destroy value? Evidence from the industry shocks." *Journal of Financial Economics*, 63(1), 51-77. doi:10.1016/S0304-405X(01)00089-7

Leaman, R., Neissa, J., Pettit, J., Leuca, A., & Kalsekar, A. (2004). "Where M&A pays: Who wins and how?" UBS Investment Bank Research. doi:10.2139/ssrn.641621

Lenz, R. (2008). "The Logic of Merger and Acquisition Pricing." University Library of Munich, Germany. Available at: https://mpra.ub.uni-muenchen.de/26627/

Lins, K. & Servaes, H. (1999). "International evidence on the value of corporate diversification." *The Journal of Finance*, 54(6), 2215-2239. doi:10.1111/0022-1082.00186

Loui, D. & Smith, M. (2006). "Financial distress and corporate turnaround: A review of the literature and agenda for research." Working Paper. Joondalup, Australia: Edith Cowan University.

Louis, P. (1988). *The Economics of Imperfect Information.* Cambridge, UK: Cambridge University Press.

Lubatkin, M. & Rogers, R.C. (1989). "Diversification, systematic risk, and shareholder return: A capital market extension of Rumelt's 1974 study." *Academy of Management Journal*, 32(2), 454-465. doi:10.2307/256370

Lukas, E., Reuer, J.J., & Welling, A. (2012). "Earnouts in mergers and acquisitions: A game-theoretic option pricing approach." *European Journal of Operational Research*, 1(16), 256-263. doi:10.1016/j.ejor.2012.05.017

Lyon, J.D., Barber, B.M., & Tsai, C.L. (1999). "Improved methods for tests of long run abnormal stock returns." *The Journal of Finance*, 54(1), 165-201. doi:10.1111/0022-1082.00101

Makhija, A.K. & Narayanan, R.P. (2007). "Fairness opinions in mergers and acquisitions." Fisher College of Business, Charles A. Dice Center Working Paper No. 2007-11.

Manne, H.G. (1965). "Mergers and the market for corporate control." *Journal of Political Economy*, 73(2), 110-120. Available at: jstor.org/stable/1829527

Marren, J.H. (1993). *Mergers & Acquisitions: A Valuation Handbook.* Homewood, IL: Business One Irwin.

Martin, K.J. (1996). "The method of payment in corporate acquisitions, investment opportunities, and management ownership." *The Journal of Finance*, 51(4), 1227-1246. doi:10.1111/j.1540-6261.1996.tb04068.x

Martynova, M. & Renneboog, L. (2008). "Spillover of corporate governance standards in cross-border mergers and acquisitions." *Journal of Corporate Finance*, 14(3), 200-223. doi:10.1016/j.jcorpfin.2008.03.004

Martynova, M. & Renneboog, L. (2009). "What determines the financing decision in corporate takeovers: cost of capital, agency problems, or the means of payment?" *Journal of Corporate Finance*, 15(3), 290-315.

Massari, M., Gianfrate, G., & Zanetti, L. (2016). *Corporate Valuation: Measuring the Value of Companies in Turbulent Times.* Somerset, NJ: John Wiley & Sons.

Masulis, R.W., Wang, C., & Xie, F. (2007). "Corporate governance and acquirer returns." *The Journal of Finance*, 62(4), 1851-1889. doi:10.1111/j.1540-6261.2007.01259.x

Mathew L.A. Hayward, & Hambrick, D. (1997). "Explaining the premiums paid for large acquisitions: Evidence of CEO hubris." *Administrative Science Quarterly*, 42(1), 103-127. doi:10.2307/2393810.

McKinsey & Company (2010). *Perspectives on Merger Integration.* Available at: mckinsey.com

Meeks, G. (1977). *Disappointing Marriage: A Study of the Gains from Merger.* Cambridge: Cambridge University Press.

Meinshausen, S. & Schiereck, D. (2011). "Dressed to merge – small fits fine: M&A success in the fashion and accessories industry." *International Review of Financial Analysis*, 20(5), 283-291. doi:10.1016/j.irfa.2011.06.007

Miles, D.A. (2011). *Risk Factors and Business Model: Understanding the Five Forces od Entrepreneurial Risk and the Causes of Business Failure.* Boca Raton: Dissertation.Com.

Mitchell, M.L. & Mulherin, J.H. (1996). "The impact of industry shocks on takeover and restructuring activity." *Journal of Financial Economics*, 41(2), 193-229. doi:10.1016/0304-405X(95)00860-H

Modigliani, F. & Miller, M.H. (1958). "The cost of capital, corporation finance and the theory of investment." *American Economic Review*, 48(3), 261-297. Available at: jstor.org/stable/1809766

Modigliani, F. & Miller, M.H. (1963). "Corporate income taxes and the cost of capital: A correction." *American Economic Review*, 53(3), 433-443. Available at: jstor.org/stable/1809167

Moeller, S.B., Schlingemann, F.P., & Stulz, R.M. (2007). "How do diversity of opinion and information asymmetry affect acquirer returns?" *Review of Financial Studies*, 20(6), 2047-2078. doi:10.1093/rfs/hhm040

Mora, N. (2012). "What determines creditor recovery rates?" Economic Review, Federal Reserve Bank of Kansas City, 97(Q II).

Motta, M. & Norman, G. (1996). "Does economic integration cause foreign direct investment?" *International Economic Review*, 37(4), 757-783. doi:10.2307/2527310

Mulherin, J.H. & Boone, A.L. (2000). "Comparing acquisitions and divestitures." *Journal of Corporate Finance*, 6(2), 117-139. doi:10.1016/S0929-1199(00)00010-9

Neisen, M. & Roth, S. (2017). *Basel IV: The Next Generation of Risk Weighted Assets*. Weinheim: Wiley-VCH Verlag GmbH & Co. KGaA.

Nicodano, G. & Sembenelli, A. (2001). "Private benefits, block transaction premiums and ownership structure." *International Review of Financial Analysis*, 13(2), 227-244. doi:10.1016/j.irfa.2004.02.006

Öberg, C. & Holtström, J. (2006). "Are mergers and acquisitions contagious?" *Journal of Business Research*, 59(12), 1267-1275. doi:10.1016/j.jbusres.2006.09.015

Opp, C.C.G. (2013). "Learning, Active Investors, and the Returns of Financially Distressed Firms." Jacobs Levy Equity Management Center for Quantitative Financial Research Paper. doi:10.2139/ssrn.3677227

O'Shaughnessy, K.C. & Flanagan, D.J. (1998). "Determinants of layoff announcements following M&As: An empirical investigation." *Strategic Management Journal*, 19(10), 989-999.

Ozdagli, A.K. (2010). "The Distress Premium Puzzle." Federal Reserve Bank of Boston Working Papers No. 10-13.

Pablo, A.L. (1994). "Determinants of acquisition integration level: A decision-making perspective." *The Academy of Management Journal*, 37(4), 803-836. doi:10.2307/256601

Parrino, J.D. & Harris, R.S. (1999). "Takeovers, management replacement, and post-acquisition operating performance: Some evidence from the 1980s." *Journal of Applied Corporate Finance*, 11(4), 88-96. doi:10.1111/j.1745-6622.1999.tb00518.x

Pisano, G.P. (1991). "The governance of innovation: Vertical integration and collaborative arrangements in the biotechnology industry." *Research Policy*, 20(3), 237-249. doi:10.1016/0048-7333(91)90054-T

Porter, M.E. (1987). "From competitive advantage to corporate strategy." *Harvard Business Review*, 65, 43-59. Available at: hbr.org

Porter, M.E. (2008). "The five competitive forces that shape strategy." *Harvard Business Review*, 86(1), 25-40. Available at: hbr.org

Pratt, S.P. (2009). *Business Valuation Discounts and Premiums*. Hoboken, NJ: John Wiley & Sons.

Preece, D. & Mullineaux, D.J. (1996). "Monitoring, loan renegotiability, and firm value: The role of lending syndicates." *Journal of Banking & Finance*, 20(3), 577-593. doi:10.1016/0378-4266(95)00006-2

PwC (2010). "How synergies drive successful acquisitions: Identifying, realizing, and tracking synergies in the M&A process."

PwC (2012). "Uncovering blind spots in deal valuations."

PwC (2015). "Accounting for contingent consideration: Don't let earnouts lead to earnings surprises."

Quinn, B.J.M. (2013). "Putting your money where your mouth is: The performance of earnouts in corporate acquisitions." Boston College Law School Legal Studies Research Paper No. 251. doi:10.2139/ssrn.1958617

Ragozzino, R. & Reuer, J. (2009). "Contingent earnouts in acquisitions of privately-held targets." *Journal of Management*, 35, 857-879. doi:10.1177/0149206308328503

Rau, P.R. & Vermaelen, T. (1998). "Glamour, value and the post-acquisition performance of acquiring firms." *Journal of Financial Economics*, 49(2), 223-253. doi:10.1016/S0304-405X(98)00023-3

Ravenscraft, D.J. (1987). "The 1980s merger wave: An industrial organization perspective." In *The Merger Boom*. Boston: Federal Reserve Bank of Boston, 17-37.

Ravenscraft, D.J. & Long, W.F. (2000). "Paths to creating value in pharmaceutical mergers." In Kaplan, S.N., *Mergers and Productivity*. Chicago: University of Chicago Press, 287-326.

Ravenscraft, D.J. & Scherer, F.M. (1989). "The profitability of mergers." *International Journal of Industrial Organization*, 7(1), 101-116. doi:10.1016/0167-7187(89)90048-9

Reed, E. (2019). "Leveraged Buyout: Definition, Examples and Uses." *TheStreet*, 14 January. Available at: thestreet.com

Reed, S.F., Lajoux, A.R., & Nesvold, H.P. (1999). *The Art of M&A: A Merger Acquisition Buyout Guide*. New York: McGraw-Hill.

Reuer, J.J., Shenkar, O., & Ragozzino, R. (2004), "Mitigating risk in international mergers and acquisitions: the role of contingent payouts." *Journal of International Business Studies*, 35(1), 19-32. doi:10.1057/palgrave.jibs.8400053

Rhoades, S.A. (1994). "A summary of merger performance studies in banking, 1980-93, and an assessment of the operating performance and event study methodologies." *Federal Reserve Bulletin*, 80(7), 589-590. Available at: federalreserve.gov

Rhodes-Kropf, M. & Robinson, D.T. (2008). "The market for mergers and the boundaries of the firm." *The Journal of Finance*, 63(3), 1169-1211. doi:10.1111/j.1540-6261.2008.01355.x

Roll, R. (1986). "The hubris hypothesis of corporate takeovers." *Journal of Business*, 59(2), 197-216. Available at: jstor.org/stable/2353017

Rosenbaum, J. & Pearl, J. (2009). *Investment Banking: Valuation, Leveraged Buyouts, and Mergers & Acquisitions*. Hoboken, NJ: John Wiley & Sons.

Rouse, T. & Frame, T. (2009). "The 10 steps to successful M&A integration." *Bain & Company*. Available at: bain.com

Salter, M.S. & Weinhold, W.A. (1979). *Diversification Through Acquisition: Strategies for Creating Economic Value*. New York: The Free Press.

Saunders, A. (2019). *Financial Markets and Institutions*. New York: McGraw-Hill Education.

Severson, M.A. (1989). "The merger and acquisition game into the 1990s." *Financial Managers Statement*, 11(5), 6-10.

Shaker, A.T. (2014). "The Equity Performance of U.S. Firms Emerging from Chapter 11 Bankruptcy." *International Journal of Business and Social Research*, 4(1), 19-30. doi:10.18533/ijbsr.v4i1.381

Shimizu, K., Hitt, M.A., Vaidyanath, D., & Pisano, V. (2004). "Theoretical foundations of cross-border mergers and acquisitions: A review of current research and recommendations for the future." *Journal of International Management*, 10(3), 307-353. doi:10.1016/j.intman.2004.05.005

Shleifer, A. & Vishny, R.W. (1986). "Large shareholders and corporate control." *Journal of Political Economy*, 94(3), 461-488. Available at: jstor.org/stable/1833044

Shleifer, A. & Vishny, R.W. (1992). "Liquidation values and debt capacity: A market equilibrium approach." *The Journal of Finance*, 47(4), 1343-1366. doi:10.1111/j.1540-6261.1992.tb04661.x

Shleifer, A. & Vishny, R.W. (1997). "A survey of corporate governance." *The Journal of Finance*, 52(2), 737-783. doi:10.1111/j.1540-6261.1997.tb04820.x

Sironi, A. & Resti, A. (2007). *Risk Management and Shareholders' Value in Banking: From Risk Measurement Models to Capital Allocation Policies.* Chichester: Wiley Finance.

Snow, B. "Steps of the M&A Process." Available at: dummies.com

Turner, A. & Benjamin, I. (2020). "Funding alternatives in difficult times – converting debt to equity." *Farrer&Co*, 18 May. Available at: farrer.co.uk

Tutino, M. & Ranciaro, V. (2020). *Innovation in Financial Restructuring. Focus on Signals, Processes and Tools.* Sumy, Ukraine: Virtus Interpress.

Vazza, D. & Gunter, E.M. (2012). "Default, Transition, and Recovery: Recovery Study (U.S.): Recoveries Come into Focus as the Speculative-Grade Cycle Turns Negative." S&P Global Ratings' Credit Research.

Viarengo, L., Gatti, S., & Prencipe, A. (2016). "The impact of enforcement quality on the use of earnouts in M&A transactions: International evidence." Available at: af.polyu.edu.hk

Walker, M.M. (2000). "Corporate takeovers, strategic objectives, and acquiring-firm shareholder wealth." *Financial Management*, 29(1), 53-66. doi:10.2307/3666361

Walshe, K., Harvey, G., Hyde, P., & Pandit, N. (2004). "Organizational failure and turnaround: Lessons for public services from the for-profit sector." *Public Money and Management*, 24(4), 201-208. doi:10.1111/j.1467-9302.2004.00421.x

Wansley, J.W., Lane, W.R., & Yang, H.C. (1983). "Abnormal returns to acquired firms by type of acquisition and method of payment." *Financial Management*, 12(3), 16-22. doi:10.2307/3665512

Warner, J. (1977). "Bankruptcy costs: Some evidence." *The Journal of Finance*, 32(2), 337-347. doi:10.2307/2326766

Weston, J.F. & Weaver, S.C. (2004). *Mergers & Acquisitions.* New York: McGraw-Hill.

Whitaker, R. (1999). "The Early Stages of Financial Distress." *Journal of Economics and Finance*, 23(2), 123-133. doi:10.1007/BF02745946

Wong, S. (2017). "Retail woes drag takeover premiums to lowest level since 2008." *Bloomberg*, 10 April. Available at: bloomberg.com

Zhang, M. & Guo, S.Y. (2007). "Executive compensation drives merger and acquisition: Evidence from listed companies in China." *Journal of Finance and Economics*, 33(12), 105-115.

Zingales, L. (1994). "The value of the voting right: A study of the Milan stock exchange experience." *The Review of Financial Studies*, 7(1), 125-148. doi:10.1093/rfs/7.1.125

www.ingramcontent.com/pod-product-compliance
Lightning Source LLC
Chambersburg PA
CBHW061150240926
51846CB00006B/967
* 9 7 8 8 8 3 1 3 2 2 1 5 7 *